American History

A Captivating Guide to the History of the United States of America, American Revolution, Civil War, Chicago, Roaring Twenties, Great Depression, Pearl Harbor, and Gulf War

D1694931

Free Bonus from Captivating History (Available for a Limited time)

Hi History Lovers!

Now you have a chance to join our exclusive history list so you can get your first history ebook for free as well as discounts and a potential to get more history books for free! Simply visit the link below to join.

Captivatinghistory.com/ebook

Also, make sure to follow us on Facebook, Twitter and Youtube by searching for Captivating History.

Table of Contents

PART 1: THE HISTORY OF THE UNITED STATES...1

INTRODUCTION..3

CHAPTER 1 – THE PEOPLE WHO WERE THERE FIRST 5

CHAPTER 2 – A TIME OF EXPLORATION 10

CHAPTER 3 – COLONIZING AMERICA 15

CHAPTER 4 – THE FRENCH AND INDIAN WAR....................................20

CHAPTER 5 – THE BOSTON TEA PARTY 25

CHAPTER 6 – THE AMERICAN REVOLUTION 30

CHAPTER 7 – THE FIRST PRESIDENT 34

CHAPTER 8 – RESTLESS TIMES 39

CHAPTER 9 – HORRORS FOR THE NATIVES 43

CHAPTER 10 – AWAKENING 49

CHAPTER 11 – CIVIL WAR 53

CHAPTER 12 – SEEKING FOR PEACE..57

CHAPTER 13 – A RISING POWER 63

CHAPTER 14 – PROGRESS 68

CHAPTER 15 – DISASTER STRIKES 71

CHAPTER 16 – THE BIGGEST BOMB IN THE WORLD 76

CHAPTER 17 – ICY TENSION..81

CHAPTER 18 – FREEDOM ON THE HOME FRONT 85

CHAPTER 19 – TERROR AND ITS WAR...89

CONCLUSION 94

PART 2: THE AMERICAN REVOLUTION...96

    INTRODUCTION...97

    CHAPTER 1 – COLONIAL AMERICA.......................................100

    CHAPTER 2 – THE SEVEN YEARS' WAR AND ITS
    CONSEQUENCES 106

    CHAPTER 3 – TAXATION WITHOUT REPRESENTATION 112

    CHAPTER 4 – THE ROAD TO WAR...119

    CHAPTER 5 – DAVID VERSUS GOLIATH.............................126

    CHAPTER 6 – INDEPENDENCE...132

    CHAPTER 7 – WASHINGTON ON THE ROPES 138

    CHAPTER 8 – THE INTERNATIONAL DIMENSION 144

    CHAPTER 9 – WAR IN THE SOUTH...150

    CHAPTER 10 – SURRENDER AT YORKTOWN.......................156

    CHAPTER 11 – AN IMPERFECT UNION 162

    CHAPTER 12 – A MORE PERFECT UNION.............................167

    CHAPTER 13 – MANIFEST DESTINY.....................................174

    CONCLUSION 180

PART 3: THE CIVIL WAR...183

    INTRODUCTION...184

    CHAPTER 1 – AN UNEASY NATION 186

    CHAPTER 2 – THE FOUNDATION CRACKS.........................192

    CHAPTER 3 – THE FIRST SHOT..205

    CHAPTER 4 – WELCOME TO WAR...209

    CHAPTER 5 – BLOODY DAYS 219

    CHAPTER 6 – PROCLAIMING FREEDOM 228

    CHAPTER 7 – THE WAR LOOKS GRIM.................................234

    CHAPTER 8 – TURNING THE TIDE 238

    CHAPTER 9 – THE FINAL FIGHT 245

    CHAPTER 10 – REUNITED 249

    CHAPTER 11 – POST-WAR AMERICA 257

    CONCLUSION 261

PART 4: HISTORY OF CHICAGO 263

    INTRODUCTION...264

    CHAPTER 1 – THE CHICAGO TRAIL OF TEARS.................265

    CHAPTER 2 – ALL ROADS (AND RAILWAYS) LEAD TO
    CHICAGO..268

    CHAPTER 3 – LABOR AND THE INDUSTRIAL AGE............272

CHAPTER 4 – FILTHIEST CITY IN AMERICA..278

CHAPTER 5 – THE FINANCIAL DISTRICT OF AMERICA 283

CHAPTER 6 – WORKERS' COTTAGE TO SKYSCRAPER; CHICAGO'S ARCHITECTURE AND DESIGN 288

CHAPTER 7 – 1860 REPUBLICAN NATIONAL CONVENTION 293

CHAPTER 8 – WORLD'S COLUMBIAN EXPOSITION IN CHICAGO 297

CHAPTER 9 – THE SPEAKEASY AND AL CAPONE 302

CHAPTER 10 – REAL CHICAGO FLAVOR 306

CHAPTER 11 – THE GREAT DEPRESSION AND LEGISLATED SEGREGATION 310

CHAPTER 12 – CENTURY OF PROGRESS...314

CHAPTER 13 – THE PINKERTON NATIONAL DETECTIVE AGENCY 319

CHAPTER 14 – THE DALEY DYNASTY..323

CHAPTER 15 – OPRAH WINFREY AND HARPO 326

CHAPTER 16 – CHICAGO TODAY 330

PART 5: THE ROARING TWENTIES 333

INTRODUCTION..334

CHAPTER 1 – WORLD WAR ONE AND THE 1920S.............................336

CHAPTER 2 – FEAR OF THE OTHER 344

CHAPTER 3 – OLD CAUSES FINISHING BUSINESS 350

CHAPTER 4 – THE COST OF PROHIBITION...355

CHAPTER 5 – A NEW WORLD 360

CHAPTER 6 – AFRICAN-AMERICANS..368

CHAPTER 7 – POLITICS AND POLICIES 375

CHAPTER 8 – HOW DID IT ALL END? 381

CONCLUSION 386

PART 6: THE GREAT DEPRESSION...388

INTRODUCTION..389

CHAPTER 1: CAUSES OF THE GREAT DEPRESSION 1918-1929..........392

CHAPTER 2: HERBERT HOOVER AND THE EARLY YEARS OF THE DEPRESSION 397

CHAPTER 3: THE ELECTION OF 1932 401

CHAPTER 4: THE 100 DAYS AND FDR'S FIRST TERM, 1933-1937 405

CHAPTER 5: FDR'S SECOND TERM—CHALLENGES AND CRITICS ...411

CHAPTER 6: THE CULTURE OF THE DEPRESSION.............................416

CHAPTER 7: SPORTS AND THE GREAT DEPRESSION........................425

CHAPTER 8: THE OUTLAW CELEBRITY IN THE GREAT DEPRESSION 433

CHAPTER 9: POPULATION SHIFTS AND THE CULTURE OF THE GREAT DEPRESSION 438

CHAPTER 10: INTERNATIONAL ISSUES AND CONCERNS DURING THE DEPRESSION..444

CHAPTER 11: THE COMING STORM AND THE END OF THE DEPRESSION 454

CONCLUSION 461

PART 7: PEARL HARBOR..463

INTRODUCTION...464

CHAPTER 1 – THE PEARL HARBOR NAVAL BASE, PRE-1941..............466

CHAPTER 2 – POST-WORLD WAR I PEARL HARBOR........................470

CHAPTER 3 – POST-WWI JAPAN 474

CHAPTER 4 – THE SECOND SINO-JAPANESE WAR 478

CHAPTER 5 - WAR IN EUROPE 482

CHAPTER 6 – THE OCCUPATION OF ICELAND................................486

CHAPTER 7 – JAPAN CONTEMPLATES WAR 490

CHAPTER 8 – THE PEARL HARBOR ATTACK...................................493

CHAPTER 9 – IMMEDIATE AFTERMATH.......................................497

CHAPTER 10 - THE UNITED STATES GOES TO WAR 501

CHAPTER 11 – AMERICA'S MILITARY PREPARES FOR WAR..............505

CHAPTER 12 – WARTIME IN THE UNITED STATES OF AMERICA...508

CHAPTER 13 – THE TULE LAKE RELOCATION CAMP 511

CHAPTER 14 – ITALY SWITCHES SIDES 515

CHAPTER 15 – D-DAY...518

CHAPTER 16 – PRESIDENT ROOSEVELT DIES 524

CHAPTER 17 – THE B-29 SUPERFORTRESS...................................530

CHAPTER 18 – IWO JIMA AND OKINAWA 534

CHAPTER 19 – THE BOMBARDMENT OF JAPAN 539

CHAPTER 20 – THE MANHATTAN PROJECT...................................543

CHAPTER 21 – THE BOMBING OF HIROSHIMA 548

CHAPTER 22 – THE BOMBING OF NAGASAKI 552

CHAPTER 23 – JAPAN SURRENDERS 555

CHAPTER 24 – POST-WAR OCCUPATION OF JAPAN 560

EPILOGUE..564

PART 8: THE GULF WAR..566

INTRODUCTION..567

CHAPTER 1 – IRAQI-KUWAITI RELATIONS AND THE PRELUDE
TO THE WAR...569

CHAPTER 2 – CIRCUMSTANCES AND CAUSES OF THE GULF
CONFLICT..581

CHAPTER 3 – THE INVASION OF KUWAIT AND THE
BEGINNING OF THE WAR...589

CHAPTER 4 – MILITARY FORCES OF THE GULF WAR......................600

CHAPTER 5 – THE WAR AMONG THE CLOUDS 613

CHAPTER 6 – THE FIRST BATTLES IN THE DESERT 625

CHAPTER 7 – IRAQI DEFEAT AND THE AFTERMATH OF
THE WAR...636

CHAPTER 8 – CASUALTIES, CONSEQUENCES, AND THE
LEGACY OF THE GULF WAR 652

CONCLUSION 666

HERE'S ANOTHER BOOK BY CAPTIVATING HISTORY THAT
YOU MIGHT LIKE...668

FREE BONUS FROM CAPTIVATING HISTORY
(AVAILABLE FOR A LIMITED TIME).............................669

SOURCES..670

Part 1: The History of the United States

A Captivating Guide to American History, Including Events Such as the American Revolution, French and Indian War, Boston Tea Party, Pearl Harbor, and the Gulf War

We here highly resolve that these dead shall not have died in vain—that this nation, under God, shall have a new birth of freedom—and that government of the people, by the people, for the people, shall not perish from the earth.

- Abraham Lincoln, Gettysburg Address, 1863

Introduction

When the first settlers reached the United States of America and started to chip out a living in the wilderness that seemed so fierce and unfamiliar to their European eyes, they could never have dreamed that someday the land upon which they stood would become one of the most powerful countries in the entire world. When Native Americans first witnessed those white sails bringing ships with white sailors into their world for the first time, they could never have dreamed that within a few centuries their population would be all but destroyed, that they would have to endure massacre after massacre, be stripped of their freedom and confined to comparatively tiny reservations, and walk the Trail of Tears within the next few hundred years.

When colonial America clashed with France in the French and Indian War, and Great Britain jumped in to rescue its colonies from the struggle, it could never have dreamed that within a few decades, Americans would revolt against Great Britain itself, throw off its shackles, and declare itself an independent country with its own ideas. When George Washington first carried the message that would precipitate the French and Indian War to its French recipient, a twenty-one-year-old riding through wild territory in falling snow, he could never have dreamed that one day he would become the first president of the United States.

When the preachers of the Great Awakening stood on the backs of wagons or bits of old tree stumps and told the American people a new story of individual freedom and the power of ordinary people, they could never have dreamed that their preaching would trigger a landslide of abolitionism that would end in a civil war that almost tore the entire country apart. When the Civil War was finally won by the Union, and all African Americans' chains were broken at last, the military leaders could never have dreamed that within the next half century, the United States would emerge as one of the world's greatest military powers during the Spanish-American War. And when those soldiers won the struggle against Spain in Cuba, they could never have dreamed that later in the century, Cuba itself would turn against them and become the single greatest threat of nuclear annihilation during the Cold War.

When the Wright Brothers first took to the air and Thomas Edison made the lightbulb, they could never have dreamed that American innovation would produce not only the Ford car, basketball, the telephone, and Facebook, but it would also be instrumental in creating the atomic bombs that killed hundreds of thousands of people and finally brought an end to the Second World War. As for Martin Luther King, Jr., he did dream. He had a dream of equality and brotherhood, and his dream at least partially came true in 2008 when America saw the inauguration of its first black president. Never could the slaves of the great plantations of the South have dreamed that that day would ever come, but it did.

Nobody could have dreamed it, but it all came to pass, and it became the history of the United States of America. And this is how it all happened.

Chapter 1 – The People Who Were There First

Talapas made the world. He created the surface of the earth, building rivers and mountains, trees and hills, rocks and streams. Then he populated the earth with the Totem Spirits—creatures that were partly living and partly spirit.

One of these creatures was the T'soona, or the Thunderbird. It sprang from the back of a fish when the South Wind used his knife to cut the fish the wrong way. Thunderbird leapt forth from the cut and flew up into the air, and the span of its wings was enough to blot out the sun. The sound of its wings was a terrible roar, the flash of its eyes deadly and frightening.

Talapas ordered the Thunderbird to fly to Saddleback Mountain—Kaheese, in the mother tongue. Obediently, the great bird did so. When it reached the mountain, it squatted down and laid five giant, magical eggs before flying away.

It was at this point that a vengeful Giantess arrived. The Giantess had warned the South Wind not to cut the fish sideways instead of down the length of its spine, and she had seen the result of his refusal to heed her warning. Now, she was determined to take and eat the eggs of the Thunderbird. Seizing one, she threw it angrily down the mountain—but she didn't get much further with her quest. With a terrible cry, a great, burning creature swept down out of the sky, its feathers ablaze. It was the Spirit Bird, and it was determined to protect the eggs of the Thunderbird. Swooping down, it set the Giantess alight with its burning wings. Ignited, burning, and screaming, she fell down the side of the mountain, and that was the end of her.

As for the eggs of the Thunderbird, they were safely left on Saddleback Mountain. And when they hatched, the people—the T'sinuk—emerged onto the earth that Talapas made.

- Chinook creation myth

Like the rest of the New World, North America was not unpopulated when the Europeans first arrived. In fact, there were several diverse and complicated cultures residing on the continent by Columbus' arrival in the 15th century, each with their own way of life.

The Origins of the Native Americans

People likely first arrived in North America during the Ice Age. Crossing the Bering Strait, which would have been frozen over at this point, they probably originated in Asia and first set foot in Alaska. Several waves of migrations brought groups of people into North America, taking them through Canada and down into the area that is now the United States. Over time, they expanded into hundreds of different tribes. By 1000 BCE, they had covered the entire continent. The Americas may have been labeled "the New World" by its European discoverers, but in reality, they had been well explored for thousands of years by the time of their arrival.

In fact, by the end of the 15th century, there were millions of native people living all over North America. Some estimates put their population as high as eighteen million—six times the population of England and Wales at that time. By sharp contrast, less than five and a half million Native Americans populate the United States today.

The Earliest Native Americans

Some of the earliest evidence of human activity in North America is actually located on its southern end: New Mexico. Here, the Clovis tribe was one of the first cultures to make their marks on history. During a time when the Columbian mammoth still roamed the earth, this tribe learned how to hunt these behemoths for their hides and meat. A single mammoth could feed an entire village for some time, but bringing it down was not a task for the faint of heart—or for the ill-equipped. In order to be able to hunt these creatures, the Clovis tribe crafted what was probably the first American invention: the Clovis point.

These stone knives were usually carved from jasper, flint, or obsidian, and the workmanship of these points is exquisite. They were designed to be mounted on a shaft to form a deadly and razor-sharp spear that could cut through the mammoth's tough hide. In fact, the Clovis points were so good at what they did that they contributed to the mammoth's untimely demise: these majestic creatures slowly became extinct after the arrival of humans in North America, partially because of habitat loss, but also due to hunting.

Another culture, about three hundred years after the Clovis tribe, emerged in a similar area and with a similar goal. While the mammoth was probably mostly extinct by the time of the Folsom people, they had another large animal to hunt—a species of giant bison. These were faster and more agile than the mammoths, and the spears that the Clovis people had invented were too cumbersome for hunting them. Instead, improving on the Clovis design, the Folsom people developed a device known as an *atlatl*. It could launch a spear much farther and faster than a human arm, allowing its user to bring down the mighty bison.

Migrating into the Great Plains, the native peoples continued to hunt bison, structuring much of their culture around their huge prey; they became nomads who followed the bison herds wherever they went, abandoning their farms and relying on the herds for their prey. This culture would endure for centuries, continuing even after the arrival of the Europeans drove the Native Americans onto small reservations. Millennia before the Europeans arrived, though, the Plano culture was already refining its hunting techniques specifically for the bison. It was this tribe that developed the technique of driving a herd of bison off a cliff in order to kill large amounts of them with less effort.

The Plano culture would also develop new ways of preserving and cooking food. They used stones to grind up grains into a kind of coarse flour, also producing the first "ground beef"—mashed-up bison meat—in this way. The first preserved "beef" was also made by the Plano; while a far cry from modern beef jerky, their dried balls of fat and protein were a nutritious source of long-lasting food in times when hunting was poor.

Along the coast of the Northwest, however, multiple tribes were exploring another way of life: fishing and boating. The ancestors of tribes such as the Haida, Nootka, and Tlingit, these peoples embraced a far more complicated culture. Not only did they build beautiful canoes and hunt sea creatures as big as whales, but they also worked in something that resembled the European feudal system, with chiefs functioning as nobility, presiding over commoners and even slaves. Pride was an integral part of their culture; wealth was seen as a defining symbol of status, and they went to extensive lengths to show off their material gains by throwing elaborate parties for their friends and neighbors. They also built wooden houses and were excellent woodworkers, yet these tribes did not farm or have any concept of agriculture.

Some of the first farmers were the Adena culture, who lived around 1000 BCE. As well as growing many of the crops that American farmers still produce today—such as corn and sunflowers—they also had elaborate burial rituals that involved building huge mounds, possibly including the Great Serpent Mound, in which to bury their dead. The Great Serpent Mound is a mysterious archaeological wonder that has been puzzling historians for centuries. Certainly built by some Native American tribe, this is an effigy mound, built to resemble an animal that possibly had some spiritual significance. Despite being only three feet high, it's almost 1,350 feet long, and its sinuous curves are surprisingly symmetrical. It may have been built either by the Adena or by the Fort Ancients, who lived in the same area over a millennium later.

Native Americans at the Arrival of Columbus

By the late 1400s, when Spanish ships first set sail in the hopes of finding a new route to India, the Native American population was as complicated as it was proliferating. Each tribe had a complete and independent culture whose lives were not that different from those of the Europeans who were about to invade them. Like the Europeans, the Native Americans had cities, trade routes, villages, complicated social structures, rulers, wars among themselves, and hundreds of different languages. They had domesticated several different types of animals, including dogs, turkeys, guinea pigs, and llamas, although the horse was a creature utterly unknown to them—modern horses would only arrive in North America during the sixteenth century.

They also had various belief systems and creation stories which differed from tribe to tribe. Most of these were rooted and aligned in nature. The tribes had been existing closely with plants, animals, and the environment for centuries; they worshiped some creatures as spirits, while others were revered and respected as food sources. Gods were still a part of their religions, usually with multiple gods governed over by a leading creator spirit. Some Native Americans today still practice their ancient cultural beliefs, and the imprint of these beliefs remains in the country in the form of mounds and totem poles.

While there were squabbles among the tribes, and war undoubtedly being a part of their lives, the Native Americans had been existing in relative peace and isolation for thousands of years. All that was about to change. The Europeans were coming, and they would bring with them a level of death, war, and disease that the natives had never had to contend with before.

Chapter 2 – A Time of Exploration

A copy of a John White watercolor, painted in 1590, showing Native Americans building a dugout canoe

https://commons.wikimedia.org/wiki/File:Dugout_canoe_manner_boats_de_bry.jpg

Christopher Columbus did not discover North America.

In fact, the first Europeans to reach North America were probably the Vikings. Leif Erikson, the son of Erik the Red, likely reached Canada in the late 10th century; he spent several months there and may have explored the coast all the way down to the modern-day Bahamas, although there is little evidence to support this claim.

The European Discovery of North America

By the time Christopher Columbus reached Hispaniola in 1492, the Vikings were long gone. Columbus was the first European to actually colonize the Americas; when Columbus returned to Europe, he left a small garrison of men behind on an island known, at the time, as San Salvador. This was the beginnings of the colonization of the New World.

Columbus himself never actually reached what is now the United States. In fact, for the rest of his life, he would remain in denial that he had discovered a new continent at all; he firmly believed that he had succeeded in his goal of finding a new route to Asia, and thus named the natives of the area "Indians," a label that has stuck to this day. While Columbus explored the islands and the mainland of South America, it was a relatively unknown Italian explorer, working for the English, who would land on North America: John Cabot.

We might not celebrate Cabot Day the way we celebrate Columbus Day, but Cabot, in 1497, was the first European since Leif Erikson to reach mainland North America. Commissioned by King Henry VII of England, Cabot's life and voyages are wreathed in mystery. His goal was the same as that of Columbus—to establish a trade route to India—but he believed that sailing farther north would achieve the goal of reaching Asia without having to circumnavigate Africa. When he landed on Newfoundland in June 1497, he, too, believed that he had found a route to India. He named several of the surrounding islands with a distinctly patriotic British flavor, such as the Island of St. John and England's Cape. Returning to the English king to report the happy news, he attempted a second voyage in 1498, and it is thought that he died in a shipwreck.

Spaniards in America

In 1513, the Spanish—who were in the process of subduing Hispaniola, Puerto Rico, Cuba, and other islands of the Caribbean—made their first foray into mainland North America. Led by Juan Ponce de León, who had previously been the governor of Puerto Rico, they landed in modern-day Florida. The swampy, wild marshlands could not have looked that much different from the jungles of South America; in fact, at the time, the explorers likely did not make any distinction between the place they'd just landed in and those they'd already seen. There was no way that they could have known that they were standing on ground that would someday belong to one of the greatest powers in the modern world.

Ponce de León, unlike Cabot and Columbus, was not searching for a way to get to Asia. Material wealth had little appeal to him; instead, according to legend, he himself was searching for something legendary and far more mystical, a concept that had been luring men from all walks of life for centuries: The Fountain of Youth. This fountain was supposed to produce magical water that could reverse the aging process and allow people to live forever.

Searching diligently for the fountain, Ponce de León explored most of Florida's coastline, even naming the peninsula (which he took to be an island) after a Spanish feast known as *Pascua Florida*. The name stuck, and in 1521, Ponce de León returned with a group of men who wanted to colonize the "island." Their efforts were met with strenuous resistance. News of the horrible fates that had been suffered by other natives had reached the Native Americans residing in Florida, and they put up an unexpected fight, wounding Ponce de León so severely that his men had to retreat. He died in Cuba, unable to recover from the injuries he had received in the battle. There would be no Fountain of Youth for this intrepid explorer; instead, he succumbed at the age of 61 to an arrow in the thigh.

French Expeditions

Starting with a voyage in 1524 by Giovanni da Verrazano, the French started to stake their claim in the northern parts of what is now the United States. While the Spanish were controlling Florida and moving ever northward, it was Verrazano—Italian-born, but employed by France—who became one of the first Europeans to lay eyes on the bay that would eventually become New York Harbor.

Jacques Cartier, who is thought to have been with Verrazano on his expedition sailing around modern-day North Carolina and New York, made a second French-funded voyage to North America in 1534. He, too, was seeking passage to Asia; instead, he stumbled upon what has now become Canada, staking the first real French claim in North America, one that would last for centuries.

Verrazano was not the only Italian-born sailor who would leave his mark on the New World and its history. Amerigo Vespucci, a Florentine in the service of Spain, would later claim to have discovered the South American mainland long before Columbus did. History has since proven that Vespucci certainly did not see the mainland before at least 1499, and even this is dubious. Nevertheless, he was believed for long enough that the New World took its name from his own first name: America, after Amerigo.

The Lost Colony

Ultimately, although Spain was actively exploring in the south and France in the north, it would be the English whose grip on the modern-day United States would last the longest of all—and it all started with the Lost Colony.

John White, an English explorer funded by Sir Walter Raleigh (Queen Elizabeth I's favorite adventurer and scoundrel), is thought to have made his first voyage, led by Philip Amadas and Arthur Barlowe, to the New World in 1584, landing near what is now North Carolina. He would return again a year later in a mission that almost killed both him and his men when they made enemies of the natives by murdering one of their leaders. Miraculously, the raiding and marauding Sir Francis Drake—a buccaneer in the service of the queen—stumbled upon the survivors on the shore of Roanoke Island.

Undeterred, White was determined to give his queen a claim to the endless resources of the New World. Legends and stories of mystical treasures and abundant riches filled this era: The Fountain of Youth, a city made entirely of gold, a passage to Asia—the attractions of the New World were both real and legendary. And the British wanted a piece of it. In 1587, White was back, this time to establish a more secure and permanent colony. He brought more than one hundred people to Roanoke Island, including women and children, and they started to build a village. It was here that the first English child was born in North America: Virginia Dare, a little girl named after the surrounding land which Walter Raleigh had named Virginia for England's virgin queen.

This time, White was wise enough not to treat the natives violently. Instead, the Europeans became firm friends with the nearby Croatan tribe; so much so that White himself would paint a series of famous watercolors of these natives. His paintings became the first portrayals of Native Americans that the English back home would ever see.

However, all was still not well with the colony. Supplies started to run low; the English had not yet learned how to survive in America the way the natives did, and before the year was over, White was sailing back to England to gather what was needed to keep the colony healthy. The plan was simply to gather the necessities and sail back as quickly as possible. It was not to be. The Anglo-Spanish War broke out as White arrived back home, turning the waters surrounding the two countries into an open war zone. To sail through it was to invite disaster. Agonizingly, White was stuck in England, utterly unable to contact the settlers he had left behind on Roanoke. And his daughter, Eleanor Dare, and her newborn daughter, little Virginia, were among them.

Three long years dragged past. Three years during which Eleanor could have had no way of knowing what had happened to her father. Did she presume him lost at sea? Killed by pirates? Did she wonder, in the dark moments, if he had simply left her behind to die? It was none of the above, and in 1590, White was finally able to set sail for Roanoke once more. He couldn't wait to see his daughter and to hold his little grandchild in his arms again.

He never would. All that was left of the colony was the word "Croatoan" carved into a wooden post. Whether the word referred to the native tribe living nearby or to a neighboring island, White would never know. Funding for the expedition had run out. He had to return to England, his ships full of supplies and his heart stripped bare, and to this day, no one really knows what happened to the Lost Colony.

Chapter 3 – Colonizing America

Despite the failure that was the Lost Colony, England would still be one of the first countries to establish a permanent colony in North America—and it wasn't far from Roanoke Island itself.

The fervor to colonize the New World sprang not only from a spirit of adventure but also from desperation and necessity. England itself was changing, enduring a time of religious and economic turmoil. To put it simply, England just wasn't big enough for all of its people. The fact that firstborn sons generally inherited the entire estate left many younger sons seeking their fortune; worse, an economic recession had plunged the lower classes into poverty, and the island was struggling to support its ever-growing population. With home no longer welcoming to them, the English started to set their sights further afield. And surrounded by its legends of gold and freedom, the New World seemed like the ideal solution for the adventurers among England's desperate.

It was not only the poverty-stricken, however, that sought wonders and riches in America. King James I himself was watching with trepidation as the Spanish continued to expand their claims in North America. He knew that the entire New World might slip out of his grip if he didn't do something, and so, he granted a charter for Virginia—the area that Walter Raleigh's mission had claimed for England several decades ago—to be thoroughly explored and colonized in 1606.

Jamestown

The Virginia Company of London was a joint-stock company that received the charter to explore Virginia, and it wasted no time in putting together an expedition. Like the fateful journey that Columbus took more than a hundred years earlier when he first stumbled upon the Americas, this voyage would be undertaken in three ships. *Susan Constant, Discovery,* and *Godspeed* arrived in Virginia in 1607. They brought with them 104 English men and boys, led by a council that the Virginia Company had elected. Edward Maria Wingfield was the first president of the colony, but it quickly became apparent that another council member—ex-soldier John Smith—was the real leader of the group. His stern leadership and willingness to bargain and cooperate with the natives went a long way toward keeping the colony alive as they began to build their first settlement. This was named Jamestown, after the king that had sent them there.

The settlers would soon discover why it had taken so long for any colony to be established on the North American mainland. For a start, the continent's human population had been sealed off from the rest of the world for thousands of years, resulting in diseases that were utterly alien to the European immune system. There was no real way of treating these illnesses, and so, they spread like wildfire among the colonists, causing many deaths.

It would also soon become evident that the land the Native Americans found so abundant would prove to be a barren and fruitless wasteland to the English. It had been centuries, and many generations, since the English had had to live off the land; their book knowledge was no good to them now, as they were faced with the reality of needing to hunt and gather in order to survive. Despite assistance from the local Powhatan tribe—who sent food parcels as gifts despite generally keeping their distance from the settlers—the colonists gradually began to starve.

The Starving Time

The situation grew dire in the winter of 1609. For three long years, the colonists had been scraping by, barely able to maintain their settlement, struggling to even stay alive. By the end of the year, about 90% of the original colonists were dead. Only a tiny handful remained, clinging to life and disillusioned as their dreams of gold had been frosted away by the reality of the winter. Worse, they were no longer friendly with the Powhatan. Their only real source of reliable food had dried up; they feared for their lives to go outside, leaving them in a kind of passive, desperate siege inside their settlement. Boot leather and dead bodies had to do for food. The period was known, with simple despair, as the Starving Time.

A new fleet of settlers had been sent to join those already in Jamestown, but a shipwreck had landed them on Bermuda, trapped and unable to reach their fellow colonists. It was only in the spring that they would finally be able to finish building some new boats and sail over to the mainland, where they found the wild-eyed survivors starving and desperate. The decision was made to abandon Jamestown and flee back home—even the turbulent English economy was better than being shot by Indian arrows out in the unknown wilderness. Jamestown was abandoned, but when word arrived of another relief fleet making its way to the shore, the settlers returned.

The Peace-Seeking Powhatan

Once the new governor of Jamestown, Thomas West, Lord De La Warr, had arrived, things began to look up a little for the settlers. John Rolfe—a businessman who had been one of those who survived the shipwreck and made it from Bermuda to Jamestown—came up with the first cash crop that the Virginia Company had been desperately looking for: tobacco. The first crop was planted in 1611, and resources slowly began trickling back into the settlement.

Relations with the Powhatan tribe, however, began to worsen. Raids were launched on the villages, stealing food and supplies. As superior as the Powhatan were in their knowledge of survival in the woods, they could not match the English in terms of warfare. Wielding bows and arrows, they struggled to fight the English and their guns.

Prior to leaving Virginia in 1609, John Smith occasionally led these raids, yet he seemed to be seeking a different solution at one point. Eventually, Powhatan Chief Wahunsenacawh befriended Smith and bestowed upon him the title of werowance, the leader of the colonists as recognized by the Powhatan. He became a liaison between the Powhatan and the English, if an imperfect one, often reverting to raids if the Powhatan did not provide as much food as was demanded.

The situation remained tenuous until 1614 when a strange new union would bring about a kind of peace. Pocahontas, the teenage daughter of Wahunsenacawh, had been kidnapped by English soldiers. Her husband, Kocoum, had been killed during the kidnapping, and her baby stripped out of her arms. However, she would soon meet John Rolfe, the man who had started the tobacco crops. Whether they fell in love or whether Rolfe recognized the importance of an alliance with the Powhatan at this stage is uncertain; either way, he took her out of captivity and married her in 1614. Pocahontas became Rebecca Rolfe, and peace was established between the two nations until her death in 1617.

By that time, Jamestown had been firmly established as an English colony. Women had crossed the Atlantic and either brought their families with them or started new ones when they arrived; Africans were shipped over to work on the tobacco plantations, and the English grip on North America was starting to look permanent.

Other Colonies

With Jamestown starting to flourish, other nations were hot on the British heels to establish permanent colonies on the North American continent. The Dutch, Spanish, and French had already been fishing and exploring the lands and waters of the New World for decades; now, they started to build permanent settlements of their own.

As early as 1608, the French had built their first settlement: Quebec in modern-day Canada. The Spanish, who had started to work in California and Texas as well as New Mexico, were more focused on sending Catholic missionaries to work with the natives, although their settlement of St. Augustine, built in 1565, would grow into the oldest continuously inhabited city in North America.

The Dutch West India Company was also interested in lands and resources in North America. Dutch colonists lived mainly in what was then known as New Netherland, now New York, with their first settlement being founded in 1614.

Many of the first colonists came to the New World fleeing religious persecution. Puritans and French Huguenots arrived in droves. A group of Huguenots who attempted to settle in Florida in 1564 were one of the first European groups to establish a colony; their attempt was ill-fated, however, as the Spaniards who controlled the area quickly discovered and killed them all. The Pilgrims, English Puritans who arrived in 1620 aboard the famous *Mayflower*, were more fortunate. They established Plymouth in modern-day New England.

By 1700, thousands of colonists from all over Europe had arrived in North America and established roots there despite the odds, and the English population of North America numbered a quarter of a million. Some attempted to coexist with the natives, others fought them, and most of them accidentally killed hundreds of them with European diseases for which the natives had no immunity. The colonists battled with disease and a climate that was utterly alien to them, but gradually more and more of them arrived and hung on. The colonists came from all walks of life, all sorts of religious convictions, and many different countries, but they had one thing in common: they were determined to build a life for themselves in the New World, no matter the cost to them.

And no matter the cost to others.

Chapter 4 – The French and Indian War

Wherever people went, war came with them.

The Native American tribes had been skirmishing among one another for generations. When the Europeans arrived, raids and small struggles began almost immediately, and it's not hard to see why. What has now been called "colonization" must have looked, to the Native American eye, like nothing short of an invasion. While some Native American tribes were welcoming, and some Europeans were interested in learning and cooperating with their strange new neighbors, tension was widespread, and fighting became the general rule.

It was the Pilgrims that established Plymouth that signed the first peace treaty between Europeans and Native Americans. These 101 Puritans who arrived from England in 1620 found themselves in what appeared to be a paradise of green fields and clear streams—and introduced to a strange new people whose culture, language, and beliefs were completely different to those of the Pilgrims. The Wampanoags were just as suspicious of the Pilgrims as the Pilgrims were of them, but by March 1621, they were able to put aside their differences long enough to sign a peace treaty whose terms were as simple as they were fair. The treaty vowed that the two nations would do one another no harm, and any who violated the terms of the treaty would be turned over to the opposite nation in order to be punished according to their customs. The terms were strict enough that the treaty held for almost a century.

European War Spills into North America

The first war involving Europeans that took place in North America was not between Europeans and natives but rather a continuation of a great conflict that was consuming the entirety of Europe.

In 1739, near the shores of Cuba, a Spanish soldier boarded the ship of English merchant Robert Jenkins. Simmering tensions between Spain and England led the Spaniard to use his cutlass to cut off the merchant's ear, returning the severed organ to its owner and telling him to take it back to the English king. Jenkins did so, leading to the uniquely-named War of Jenkins' Ear. When the War of the Austrian Succession flared in 1740, it had already assimilated the War of Jenkins' Ear and dragged most of the powers of Europe into a messy fight that eventually spilled over in all directions.

For North Americans, this distant war would come to the colonies with a sharp reality. The French, English, Spanish, and Dutch had been coexisting more or less peacefully for more than a century, being more preoccupied with other problems—such as skirmishing with the natives, surviving alien American diseases, and eking out an existence on the face of a sometimes hostile new continent—but things changed suddenly as King George's War began in 1744. Not as much a separate war as simply the American theater of the War of the Austrian Succession, it pitted the French and English against one another. Its most major action was the capture of Louisbourg, a French fortress located on the Cape Breton Island in Nova Scotia, Canada. The French put great trust in Louisbourg as being their strongest fortress, and when the British captured it in 1745 after a six-week siege in which both sides suffered heavy losses, they were infuriated.

The war ended in 1748 with a treaty that effectively tried to reverse the war—most possessions were returned to their countries according to the way it had been before the war broke out. To the American colonists fighting on the British side, it seemed a cruel and unnecessary thing to strip their hard-won Louisbourg from them and hand it back to the French. They had lost hundreds of good men in the fight to get their hands on the fortress; now, a bunch of men who had likely never even seen battle, sitting in some cozy parlor thousands of miles away, had taken it away from them for no reason that they could understand. It was one of the first blows that would eventually sever Britain and America from one another.

First, though, the animosity between British and French colonies in North America would have to be dealt with – and struggles with the natives were becoming more frequent and violent. The French and Indian War was imminent.

A Warning to the French

The young major had to pull his hat down low over his eyes against the driving snow that howled over the landscape with a vengeful fury, throwing fistfuls of ice against his neck and pushing its cold fingers down the collar of his red coat as he steered his horse down into the Ohio River Valley. He knew that this was some of the most fertile land in North America, greatly valued by British Americans for its good soil and easy access to the Ohio River, which allowed them to transport goods by boat down to the Mississippi for trading. But now, it looked like a barren wasteland of ice and rock. His horse had to tread carefully as it made its way out of British territory and up toward the French-controlled Fort LeBoeuf.

The major was only twenty-one years old, and he was gripped by both fear and excitement as he looked up at the French fortress. It was December 1753, and he had been sixteen years old when King George's War—the latest conflict between the French and English forces—had ended. He remembered it all too well, and despite the signed treaty forming a tenuous barrier between the opposing nations, he still saw the French as the enemy. Especially now that he had been sent here by his commanding officer to deliver a warning. He touched his chest pocket as his horse made its way to the fortress gates, feeling the letter nestled there. Virginia Lt. Governor Robert Dinwiddie had composed the message to warn the French to stay out of British-controlled areas in the valley, and the young major knew that if the French resisted, Dinwiddie would be ready for battle. After all, the British Americans numbered about two million at the time; the French, less than one hundred thousand.

To his surprise, he was warmly received into the fortress. Grooms rushed out to take his horse, and after he had declared his business, he was ushered into a warm room where a blazing fire crackled in the hearth. Warming his blue hands by the flames, the major tried to control his nerves. This would be the first real military mission he had ever been sent on, and he was determined not to let Dinwiddie down.

A Frenchman walked into the room and came over to the major, smiling peacefully and extending a friendly hand. "Captain Jacques Legardeur de Saint-Pierre," he introduced himself.

Fearlessly returning the captain's smile, the major gripped his hand. "Major George Washington."

The War Begins

The delivery of the message from Dinwiddie was one of George Washington's very first missions, and while he succeeded in the delivery, the message did not have its intended effect. Saint-Pierre's response to Dinwiddie was dismissive, claiming that the French king had every right to British lands in the Ohio River Valley. In 1754, Dinwiddie declared war on the French, and a long struggle began.

Despite the fact that the French were hugely outnumbered by the English, they enjoyed early military successes due to their alliances with the natives of the area. This is why the war is known as the French and Indian War, particularly in America. In Britain, the war is viewed as the American theater of the Seven Years' War, a widespread European conflict.

The combination of French and natives was a successful one. For three years, the British side barely stood a chance against their enemy. In fact, it was during this time that George Washington endured his first and final surrender. In 1754, the Battle of Fort Necessity saw 600 French and 100 Native American men attack and defeat Washington's group of 400 soldiers in a ramshackle wooden circle that the British had dubbed "Fort Necessity."

It was the only time Washington would ever surrender. And it was also not the last British defeat during the French and Indian War. Washington and others would fight many heated battles against the French, but in 1757, the new British Prime Minister William Pitt started to invest in the war in America. Increased resources led to increased British successes, and despite Spain allying with France in a bid to undermine the growing British power in the New World, the war officially ended in 1763 with Canada and Florida being surrendered to the British.

A Growing Debt

With the war over, it's easy to think that relations between Great Britain and its colonies in America would have been improved due to Pitt's financial backing during the war. However, the opposite was true. Pitt had invested money that he didn't have into the war, and with decades of war having ravaged the economy, Great Britain found itself up to its neck in national debt. Pitt's solution was to increase taxes on British Americans in a bid to pay off the enormous debt. Themselves crippled by years of war, the British Americans protested against the heavy taxation. Great Britain and British America were more at odds than ever before.

One good thing, however, had come of the French and Indian War: it had provided experience to a young man named George Washington. A young man who was about to change American history.

Chapter 5 – The Boston Tea Party

Rebels disguised as Native Americans throw chests of tea into Boston Harbor
https://commons.wikimedia.org/w/index.php?curid=112653

"No taxation without representation!"

It was the winter of 1770, and this was the cry that filled the streets of Boston and rang across all of the Thirteen Colonies that had been established by the British in America. But it had been 150 years since the Pilgrims had established Plymouth, and now, most British Americans were American-born. They sounded different, they dressed differently, and most of them had never even seen Great Britain itself. Yet there were no British Americans in Parliament, and Parliament made all their choices for them.

Since the French and Indian War, these choices largely consisted of increasing taxes. First, a heavy tax was imposed on all printed paper, from books to newspapers to postage stamps. Then, worse, essentials were being taxed—glass, lead, and even tea. The taxes led to unrest throughout Boston, and this unrest led to thousands of British soldiers pouring into the city to quell the voices of the citizens. Even merchants and shop owners selling British wares came under fire from unhappy citizens and retaliated with violence.

The Boston Massacre

March 5th, 1770, was an icy day. The streets of Boston were coated in snow and ice; where Private Hugh White stood on guard in front of the Custom House, he could see his breath steaming in the air in front of him. The cold was not the only thing that made the atmosphere seem tense. He knew that there had been chaos throughout the city for months. What he didn't know was that he was about to become the unwitting trigger for the worst violence yet.

As Private White stood outside the Custom House, he knew he was guarding money that was almost all destined for Great Britain. With Boston being a port town, its economy depended heavily on trade, and much of the profits from that trade went straight to the coffers of the British king. The colonists saw the Custom House as a blight on their city, a place where stolen money was hoarded before being shipped back to their oppressor. And on this evening, a handful of men decided that they could no longer take it lying down. Appearing in the streets and from the surrounding buildings, the group of colonists started to mock and insult Private White. Shaking their fists at him, they threatened to beat him up and to storm the Custom House and take back what was rightfully theirs.

Private White tried to stand his ground, but eventually, he was overwhelmed. The crowd was pressing thick upon White and his compatriots, and colonists had even begun poking the soldiers to get a rise out of them. And a rise they got when one of the soldiers struck back, hitting one of the colonists in the head with his musket. Blood spilled onto the snow, and as the red droplets splattered on the white ground, something snapped in the atmosphere. The colonists started to throw rocks, sticks, and snowballs at the British soldier; he shouted and gestured wildly with his bayonet, and soon the air was thick with shouting and swearing, cursing and panicking. All over the city, warning bells began to ring, calling more and more colonists out onto the street. Soon, they gathered enough courage to storm White, threatening further violence. He had had enough. He called for reinforcements.

They arrived in the form of Captain Thomas Preston and a group of British soldiers who surged to the defense of their comrade. Usually, the arrival of a mass of angry soldiers was enough to quell a riot, but not today. Incensed, the colonists fell upon the British, knocking one down along with his weapon. It is believed that the fallen soldier fired into the crowd, and after a moment of silence, more soldiers fired as well, despite no order being given to do so. Bullets burst through the air, punching through flesh, splattering blood, as screams of pain and anger filled the crowd. Chaos erupted. The colonists fell upon the soldiers with clubs and sticks; the soldiers fired back, and for a few mad seconds, the streets became a bloodbath.

When it was all over, five colonists were dead. The soldiers escaped with only minor injuries, a fact that was seized upon by propaganda fueled by an angered colony that felt it had been unjustly dealt with. Anti-British sentiment spread like wildfire throughout the city. The Bostonians had had enough.

The Tea Act

One of the heaviest taxes Great Britain had imposed on America involved the Tea Act of 1773. The Boston Massacre, among other things, had eventually persuaded Britain to withdraw some of its heavier taxes, but a heavy tax on tea remained, and in 1773, this was made worse when the British East India Company was effectively given a monopoly on the tea trade since the Tea Act allowed it to sell Chinese tea duty-free. This proved lucrative for the company and for Great Britain but disastrous for independent American merchants hoping to sell their own tea. Since they were subjected to the taxes, their tea was vastly more expensive than the British East India Company's tea, and so, most Americans had no choice but to purchase the British tea even though it was crippling the local economy.

This act was protested by a group of revolutionaries known as the Sons of Liberty. Founded to protest the Stamp Act originally, they continued to push back against British oppression. Led by a man named Samuel Adams, the revolutionaries held rallies and protests throughout the city. And their biggest protest would occur on December 16th, 1773. Three ships—the *Dartmouth*, the *Eleanor*, and the *Beaver*—had arrived in Griffin's Wharf laden with British East India Company tea.

The Boston Tea Party

The vast cargoes of tea provided a tipping point for the enraged citizens of Boston. Gathering in the thousands at the wharf, their protest was vehement enough that a meeting was called at the Old South Meeting House to hear the colonists' opinion on the newly arrived tea. Their vote was almost unanimous: the tea should not be sold or even unloaded in Boston; it should be thrown away or sent back to Great Britain, just as long as it ceased to undermine their local economy.

Their vote was met with almost instant dismissal. Governor Thomas Hutchison brushed them off and ordered the tea to be unloaded. Colonial workers refused to touch it, and soon a plan was made to ensure that none of that tea would ever be drunk in Boston.

As darkness fell over the wharf, a group of men began to gather on a nearby hilltop. Despite the eagle feathers that bristled across the group and the flash of moonlight off tomahawks clutched in desperate hands, none of them were Native Americans. They were colonists from Boston, disguised as Mohawk warriors, and they were determined to wreak havoc on that tea.

The group numbered somewhere between 30 and 130 men; the harbor was surrounded by British warships. The odds were insurmountable, but the colonists' anger was undeterred by danger. When night had enveloped the harbor completely, they stormed the ships. Rushing aboard, spurred on by shouts from their commander, the colonists smashed the padlocks and yanked open the hatches of the ships, plunging into their cargo holds. 342 chests of tea—a cargo that would have been worth more than a million dollars today—lay waiting for them. One by one, the chests were heaved onto the deck, split open with the tomahawks, and then tossed overboard. In the lantern light, tea leaves floated all over the harbor in the millions, each representing lost money for the British East India Company and the British Crown. Each was a triumph for the rebels, who whooped war cries as they flung the chests overboard. Splashes and shouts filled the night, and yet no attempt was made to stop them.

By the end of the night, every last one of the tea chests had been thrown into the harbor. No one was harmed, but the colonists' statement was made perfectly clear: they were done with British taxes.

The Intolerable Acts

Despite the lack of violence, the British would be equally clear in their response to the protest that has gone down in history as the Boston Tea Party. In 1774, only months after the protest, a series of new acts were passed that the British called the Coercive Acts and the Americans called the Intolerable Acts. Either way, they were designed to crush the Americans' spirit, and they blatantly sought to strip power from the colonists. The Quebec Act guaranteed that the colonists of the province of Quebec, just north of Ohio, could freely practice the Catholic faith — something that was deeply offensive to the mainly Puritan colonists. The Boston Port Act closed Boston's harbor to trade, stripping the city of much of its income; the Massachusetts Government Act granted greater power to its British governor; the Quartering Act demanded that colonists freely provide barracks to British troops; and the Administration of Justice Act ordered that trials against government officials would all be held in Great Britain, making it practically impossible for colonists to testify against any officials.

The acts were unfair. But like so many attempts made by tyrants to redouble their grip upon the rising spirit of a revolution, they were also utterly unsuccessful. A new era was coming.

Chapter 6 – The American Revolution

And yet, through the gloom and the light,

The fate of a nation was riding that night;

And the spark struck out by that steed, in his flight,

Kindled the land into flame with its heat.

- Henry Wadsworth Longfellow, "Paul Revere's Ride"

In the dark night of April 18th, 1775, a brown horse flew through the darkness, urged on by a desperate rider who clutched the reins in trembling hands as he mustered the surrounding countryside to battle. The rider was Paul Revere; the horse, a mare named Brown Beauty, a mare whose legs would bear her and her rider an epic distance that night as Revere sought to warn the patriots of Middlesex that a mass of British soldiers had arrived and was marching across the countryside to attack Concord. The British came in determined ranks, their red coats ablaze in the light of every lantern they passed. And ahead of them rode a series of courageous men on horseback, riding like the wind in order to bring the news of the invasion to their fellow rebels.

The Battles of Lexington and Concord

Revere and the other riders achieved their mission, even though some were thrown from their horses and Revere himself was briefly captured and detained at Lexington. Despite the mishaps that befell some of the riders, others got through and brought word to the Middlesex towns about the British attack.

By the time the advance guard of nearly 240 British soldiers arrived in Lexington, the rebels were ready for them. A militia of 77 men had been gathered on the town green in a peaceful show of force, and when the mighty British army appeared on the hilltop, the British commander cried, "Throw down your arms! Ye villains! Ye rebels!"

The rebellious spirit in these men must have given the British army pause, as they stood on the green gazing up at an enemy over three times their size. But they knew that to attack now would be foolhardy. Their commander gave them the order to disperse, but his shouting was half-drowned out by the yelling British. Confused, only some of the militia broke their ranks while others milled around or prepared for battle.

Then, a shot rang out. A terrible crack, followed by the smell of gun smoke. History has not been able to explain who exactly fired that first shot, but fired it was, and it sowed chaos among the assembled soldiers. Spooked, the British fired a volley into the militiamen, their musket balls crashing and ripping through the ranks of the rebels. The colonists returned fire, and with that, the American Revolution had begun.

From Lexington to Concord, to Boston to Cambridge, and finally all the way back to Charlestown Neck, the militiamen harried the British, the initial 77 being joined by more than 3,000 others. While at first the British seemed to have the upper hand, they were soon overwhelmed and put to flight by the colonists, finally ending up hiding in Charlestown Neck under the safety of their naval support. The British were thoroughly shaken by this turn of events, not having expected the colonists to be able to put up that much resistance.

The American Revolution

The first major battle of the revolution (the Battle of Bunker Hill) took place on June 17th, 1775, at Breed's Hill. This British bid to force the Americans away from Boston was a dismal failure, and it further bolstered American morale as they sought to drive the British out of the continent that they had now claimed as their own. George Washington himself, now a general, soon led his troops into the fray; by March 1776, he had forced thousands of British troops out of Boston, keeping the city firmly in America's grasp. And following the signing of the Declaration of Independence on July 4th, 1776, the war began in earnest.

Continued American success drove the British back into Canada and New York. Things had been looking promising for the Americans during the spring of 1776, but this state of affairs didn't last long. Great Britain was sending over more and more troops, determined not to lose its claim on the New World; the British army was growing by the day, and throughout the last half of 1776 and 1777, they launched offensives that proved almost too much for the Americans. Washington himself was defeated in five out of six battles. Things were not looking good for America by the fall of 1777 until the tide finally turned at the two Battles of Saratoga. An American force commanded by General Horatio Gates finally bested the English by using marksmanship from the cover of thick woods to pick off the British where they sat in an open field; the British were forced to surrender.

After this, the British desperately sought alliances from other countries, gaining some help from the Hessians. In a strange twist of events, the French colonies—against whom the Americans had fought so hard in the French and Indian War, incurring the very debt that had ignited the Revolution in the first place—became America's allies, declaring war on Britain in 1778.

For the next three years, the war split more or less into two: a frustrating stalemate in the North and a series of hard struggles in the South. Loyalists to the British administration were more numerous in the South than in the North, and much of the South remained under British control until 1781, when General Nathanael Greene finally scored a few victories early in the year that eventually led to most of the South ending up under American control by the end of the year.

The Battle of Yorktown

By September 1781, Lieutenant-General Charles Cornwallis—the commander of the British forces—had only 9,000 troops under his command, compared with Washington's 17,000. He had been driven back to the Yorktown Peninsula in Virginia, some of the very first lands that the British had ever set foot upon when they first came to North

America. Now, he was holed up in a fortress with his men, watching Washington advance with a strength and sureness that Cornwallis could no longer equal.

Washington laid siege to Yorktown on September 28th, 1781. The fortress held out for three long weeks before finally surrendering on October 19th. The entire army was handed over to Washington, and with that, the fighting on the continent itself was complete. Small naval battles and local skirmishes with loyalists would still occur, but the war was over, and the world knew it. In 1783, Great Britain finally acknowledged the independence of America with the Treaty of Paris. The Declaration of Independence had been recognized by the world at last.

Chapter 7 – The First President

George Washington by John Trumbull
https://commons.wikimedia.org/w/index.php?curid=57115499

With the Revolution over, America found itself a newly independent state that had to find a way to govern itself in peace as well as it had proven itself in war. This was no simple task. At the time, most of the world was governed by some form of monarchy; the New World itself was little more than a collection of colonies presided over by some European superpower, and democracy was a concept that had barely even been introduced throughout the rest of the world. Kings and queens still reigned and made decisions over their countries. But America was a newborn nation, a place where class or birthright had never mattered as much as it did in Great Britain. The brutal struggles of the early days of colonization had birthed a nation of people whose focus had been more on survival than convention. Even the Church, being almost completely Protestant compared to the mostly Catholic or Anglican Europeans, was more liberal in America.

The Articles of Confederation

Starting shortly after the American Revolution, America was governed under the Articles of Confederation. The states were governed by a Congress, consisting of representatives from each state, and all decisions were put to a vote by the states. At least nine of the thirteen states had to agree in order for any changes to be made. This concept attempted to unify the various states, which were based on the original Thirteen Colonies, but failed miserably.

On the surface, this may have seemed like a good idea. No single person had full control over the country; it was hoped that this would prevent the kind of tyranny that had often been seen in Europe under selfish, power-hungry monarchs. Unfortunately, the confederacy quickly disintegrated into a chaos of power-grabbing by the various states, all of which were vying for resources and arguing over their borders.

It quickly became evident that America needed a single, unifying leader who would be able to bring the states together and lead them forward into a new era of peace. America had fought too hard for its independence to lose itself in homeland squabbles. And who better to lead the newly-fledged country than the man who had fought so hard to establish it?

The Unanimous Election

The Constitutional Convention was held in Philadelphia in 1787 where the Constitution of the United States was drawn up. This vital document laid the foundation upon which the government would be built, and while it was amended over the following centuries, it remains the bedrock of American law. At the convention, it was also decided that a president would have to be chosen. Apparently, it was obvious to the Electoral College that there was only one man who would be fit for that role. George Washington had proven himself countless times in battle, and he was an educated man who also happened to come from a fairly aristocratic British family, which would help to gain respect from Great Britain itself. His will for independence and a determination to establish a new and fairer government than the tyrannical monarchies of the Old World was, however, very much American. In early 1789, the Electoral College—consisting of delegates from the different states—cast their votes. Washington was unanimously elected, the only U.S. president ever to receive that honor.

There was just one problem. Washington didn't want to be president. At fifty-seven, having weathered two long wars and seeing more bloodshed than any man was meant to, he wanted nothing but peace. His sole desire was to retire to his beautiful farm at Mount Vernon where he could watch over peaceful fields and gaze upon a country view, enjoying the independence and tranquility that he had fought so hard to bring to his nation. It must have seemed to him that he had done enough. Yet the nation's need for leadership was insatiable, and their voices were adamant: they wanted Washington and nobody else. Reluctantly, he agreed, and he was inaugurated in April 1789 at New York City, which was then the capital of America.

The First Presidency

For this president, there was no precedent. Not only was he the first president of America, but he was also one of the first presidents anywhere; democracy was in its infancy, and there was no model for what Washington was about to do. The concept of the leader being a civil servant as opposed to a ruling monarch was a new one. In Washington's own words, "I walk on untrodden ground."

The politics of the new America were indeed groundbreaking. One defining characteristic of Washington's presidency was his determination to prove that he was an unselfish leader whose purpose was to help and care for the people, not to exploit them; unlike the kings and queens of the Old World, who amassed as much wealth as they could and tended toward filling their own coffers before they thought of filling the stomachs of their people, Washington wouldn't even accept his own presidential salary at first. He wanted to set a standard for other presidents to follow, a standard of unselfishness and dedication. During his first term, he was able to stabilize this new nation, tackling the problem of the national debt it had been left with by the Revolution and succeeding in improving its fledgling finances.

When the presidential elections of 1792 came around again, Washington was once again unanimously elected. Like the first time, Washington did his best to resist, but the people refused to hear him— they needed him, and their decision was final. Eventually, he agreed to serve a second term, and it was a good thing. Britain and France were about to go to war once again, and this left America in a difficult position. Technically it was allied with France, but Washington knew that his little nation was by no means ready to mess with international affairs; they had beaten the British once, but the war had left the nation depleted of resources. The looming giant of the British Empire was also not far away; Canada, right on the border of America, was still a British colony. Wisely, in 1793, Washington decided to maintain a position of neutrality. This broke the terms of his treaty with France, but it proved to be a good decision. America did not get involved in the messy French Revolutionary Wars, which would last for decades.

Despite his best efforts, however, Washington would have to be involved in fighting one last time. When Washington's administration agreed to place a tax on spirits in 1791, it eventually sparked a violent revolt known as the Whiskey Rebellion. The old general himself led a federal militia into Pennsylvania to put down the rebellion; it was quickly and forcefully crushed, and the message was abundantly clear. As much as Washington spoke of peace, the law would be enforced no matter the cost.

A Sad Goodbye

The Congress Hall in Philadelphia was packed with people as George Washington took his place before his people one last time. He gazed out over the assembled multitudes with a mixture of love and relief. For eight years, he had served as their president, and he had done his best to bring them happiness and safety. Now, he was going to address them for the last time.

"Friends and Citizens," he began. "The period for a new election of a citizen to administer the executive government of the United States being not far distant..."

Washington went on to deliver his Farewell Address, a document that has remained famous to this day. It is looked upon as a symbol of what American politics stand for and has long since been used as the standard against which other presidents are measured. The address spent quite some time defending Washington's decision not to serve a third term regardless of how much his people wanted him to—an act of unselfishness and humility that would be intensely rare in the centuries of presidencies to come. In his address, Washington humbly apologized for any mistakes he might unintentionally have made during his presidency. He also pardoned the rebels who had been involved in the Whiskey Rebellion and stepped down from the stand ready to partake in "the benign influence of good laws under a free government, the ever-favorite object of my heart, and the happy reward, as I trust, of our mutual cares, labors, and dangers."

For the next two years, Washington would do just that. He died peacefully on his beloved farm in 1799.

Chapter 8 – Restless Times

After George Washington stepped down in 1797, John Adams was elected president. He had served as Washington's vice president and seemed an able leader, but it wouldn't be long before his presidency was plagued with violence.

The XYZ Affair

Even before Washington's presidency ended, the French had a bone to pick with the United States. Ever since the U.S. had signed Jay's Treaty with Great Britain—which effectively resolved many of the long-standing conflicts that had been plaguing the two nations—the French were bitter and resentful. They had fought on the American side during the Revolution, and they felt that it was extremely unfair that America now sided with Britain, which was France's enemy. The French went as far as seizing American merchant ships.

In a bid to reestablish some kind of diplomatic relations with France, John Adams sent three American diplomats to Paris to meet with the foreign minister of France. At first, the minister refused to see the Americans at all; after much negotiation, he finally agreed to see them but only if they paid him a bribe and agreed to lend money to France. Horrified, the Americans refused. In 1798, Congress rescinded the Treaty of Alliance, and the nations were just a declaration away from open war.

The Quasi-War

While Adams was forced to prepare for war—forming the Department of the Navy and building American warships for the first time—he was wise enough not to declare war openly. Something, however, would have to be done about French attacks on American merchant vessels. American warships were given permission to attack French ships, and several were sent to guard the waters near Long Island.

One of these was the beautiful USS *Constellation.* Named after the then-fifteen stars on the United States flag, the *Constellation* was an elegant frigate, rigged with huge sails and bearing 38 massive guns. She was commanded by Captain Thomas Truxtun and became one of the most successful warships of the Navy during that time, with her first victory being on a wintry day when the French warship *L'Insurgente* came across her patrolling the West Indies on February 9th, 1799. The peaceful waters of the Caribbean boiled and frothed as gunfire exploded above them; splinters crashed into the water, blood curling in the blue ocean, foaming pink on the edges of the tossing waves. *L'Insurgente* managed to get close enough to make an attempt to board the *Constellation,* but Truxtun succeeded in skillfully maneuvering his ship away and returning fire. Outgunned, *L'Insurgente* was forced to surrender.

About a year later, the *Constellation* would also fight one of the last battles of the Quasi-War. On February 1st, 1800, she came across *La Vengeance.* Despite the fact that the French warship had twelve more guns than the *Constellation,* the Americans fired on the French so relentlessly that *La Vengeance* eventually had to flee.

While the United States lost thousands of merchant vessels during the Quasi-War, it was also able to gain 85 French warships. Things were looking good for the U.S. when negotiators finally managed to bring a peaceful resolution to a war that never was declared. The Treaty of Mortefontaine was signed on September 30th, 1800.

Thomas Jefferson as President

Adams served long enough to see the Quasi-War end. Thomas Jefferson, the writer of the Declaration of Independence, was inaugurated in 1801 and served two fairly peaceful terms. He oversaw an era of invention and exploration, as well as the end of America's role in the horrific Middle Passage that had caused so much pain, death, and suffering to African slaves being shipped over the Atlantic. Slavery was still very much a part of American life, but the trade with Africa had ended at last.

During Jefferson's second term, Robert Fulton invented the steamboat. Further advancing a spirit of invention and discovery, Jefferson also commissioned the Lewis and Clark Expedition, which was the first expedition to cross all the way to the western side of the United States. Added to this, he negotiated the Louisiana Purchase, in which the United States paid the equivalent of fifteen million dollars today for the French territory of Louisiana, allowing the U.S. access to the valuable port of New Orleans and the Mississippi River. His successful presidency ended in 1809, and James Madison, the architect of the Constitution, was elected in his place.

The War of 1812

Madison had been president for three years, and America was just getting used to real peace when chaos threatened in Europe once more.

While Adams and Washington—both of the Federalist Party—had worked hard to improve relations with the British, the next two presidents were Democratic-Republicans, who were against working with Britain and wanted to improve an alliance with France instead. With the Democratic-Republicans in office, the relationship with Britain worsened steadily over the years. Trade was injured by struggling relations with both Britain and France, and to make matters worse, the two European powers were squabbling for trading rights with America. American merchants were restless for a resolution so that they could continue to ship their goods to Europe; American farmers were more restless still as they had nowhere to sell their produce. Added to this was the British impressment of sailors, with thousands of American sailors being effectively kidnapped for service in the British navy. Finally, in 1812, Madison signed a declaration of war against Great Britain. The British and Americans were at each other's throats once again.

Much of the war was fought on the Canadian border as the United States made three attempts to invade their British-held neighbor. None of these were successful; instead, the British managed to ally with Native

Americans in the northwestern parts of America, and there were several battles fought and lost between U.S. forces and the Brits with their Indian allies. Chaos reigned for more than two years, costing thousands of lives on both sides before a peace treaty was finally signed in Europe on Christmas Eve, 1814.

The trouble was that nobody in America knew that a treaty had been signed. There was no telephone or Internet in those days; the only way to communicate was by letter or messenger, which took about a month to cross over from Europe to America. Thus, the most decisive battle of the War of 1812 was fought after the war itself had ended. The Battle of New Orleans on January 8th, 1815, saw a fierce American victory when Major General Andrew Jackson, who had been a prisoner of the British during the Revolutionary War, formed an impenetrable line of fire that forced the British back. Despite the fact that the war itself ended in more or less a stalemate, the Battle of New Orleans led the American psyche to consider the war a victory.

Chapter 9 – Horrors for the Natives

The sound of thousands of feet shuffling along the dirt echoed across the landscape. The mass of men, women, and children extended down the trail as far as the eye could see, enveloped in a cloud of dust, disease, and dismay. The barren landscape seemed incapable of yielding so much as a wildflower, let alone any real sustenance, and even if it had, there was no opportunity to stop for hunting or gathering. There was just marching and more marching—day in and day out, for more than a thousand miles, all of it on foot.

The only horses belonged to the white men. They sat upon their steeds with their guns, gesturing angrily with their weapons if any of their unhappy charges dared to do so much as slow down. The wisest thing was simply to lower one's head, stare down at one's feet, and shuffle forward. And with every step, home—a place of lands and farms, with towns and friendships, churches and schools—was left farther and farther behind.

The Cherokee women clutched their children as close as they could as if the strength of their love could somehow shield them from the hardships that lay before them. So many of them had died already. Crammed together in a stifling herd, like so many cattle, the over 16,500 Cherokees were used to hygienic lifestyles. The kids had been in missionary schools. The people had lived in well-built homes, worked all day in fresh air. They had had their own written language. They'd printed newspapers and written songs. The nation had been governed by an organized, elected administration of their own people. All of it had been a bid to fit in, a bid to become like the white men so that they wouldn't be destroyed the way that their neighbors had been. But none of that remained now; all there was now was marching, sometimes in manacles, and trying to survive.

The sounds of coughing filled the defeated ranks as they headed farther away from their ancestral territories in Georgia, Alabama, North Carolina, and Tennessee. Like the Chickasaw, Choctaw, and Creek nations, the Cherokee had been living there for generations upon generations. Ever since the settlers first came, some had been living peacefully among them, while others fought back, often resulting in bloody massacres where both white men and natives committed the most heinous crimes of mass murder and relentless cruelty. But now the greed of the white Americans had won. The Cherokees, like the others, were being forcibly relocated—forced at gunpoint to march to some place called "Indian country." At this point, with children dying all around them from all manner of diseases, diseases that spread like wildfire in their cramped and dirty ranks, many of them had lost any hope of ever seeing this Indian country. Others wondered if it existed at all.

These sad thoughts were not unfounded. By the time they reached Indian country—a part of modern-day Oklahoma—one-quarter of the Cherokee were dead. They had died as a result of disease and starvation as they were driven ruthlessly away from their homes. The 1,200 miles that they had walked became known as the Trail of Tears, a road of anguish and suffering that they would never forget.

Jackson as President

It all began on March 4th, 1829, when Andrew Jackson was inaugurated as president of the United States. This was an understandable move considering that the fledgling democracy limited voting only to white men—no Native Americans, slaves, or women were allowed to vote. If they had any say, Jackson would have been the last man ever allowed to come near the newly-built White House (the old President's House was burned down by the British in 1814).

To those who were allowed to vote, Jackson was a hero. He had been the one to beat the British at the Battle of New Orleans. It was his line of stakes and rifles—the "Jackson Line"—that had held back the mighty force of redcoats and eventually drove them into the wasteland and wilderness. He had proven himself to be tough, tenacious, determined, and ready to do anything needed to protect the interests of those whom he saw as his responsibility.

The trouble was that he had never seen Native Americans as the same kind of human as the other citizens of the United States. Prior to the War of 1812, Jackson's role in the army had mostly consisted of fighting Native Americans. He had spent much time subduing the Creek Nation, eventually seizing 22 million acres of their land and giving them to white farmers instead. This made him hugely popular with the farmers, who expected him to give them even more land once he was president—and they were not disappointed.

The Indian Removal Act

Starting in the early 1830s, Jackson pushed for Native Americans to be forced out of their desirable and fertile lands in the South and driven northwest to barren prairies that nobody really wanted. The discovery of gold in Georgia only made matters worse. Even before any legislation was passed, farmers who had lived peacefully alongside their Native American counterparts started to view their neighbors with suspicion. Some Native Americans made matters worse for themselves by lashing out, often kidnapping white children to be used as pawns in later negotiations with the whites; this only spread the rumors that these "Injuns" were savages, evil, and somehow less than human.

On a more national scale, Jackson was doing everything in his power to seize as much land as possible from the Native Americans. Even before his presidency, he had helped to negotiate a series of treaties that convinced Native Americans to sign over their southern and eastern lands for uncharted territory somewhere in the West. Despite the fact that the natives probably knew the Western lands would be infertile and poor compared to the lands they already owned, many of them agreed, knowing they had little choice. War with the white man would invite disaster; better, then, to go away into the West and hope that they wouldn't be bothered there.

Before he even took the presidency, Jackson had been persecuting Native Americans ruthlessly, being heavily involved in the First Seminole War during the 1810s. In 1830, things got far worse for the Native Americans when Jackson succeeded in passing the Indian Removal Act. This act allowed Jackson to negotiate treaties with the Native Americans that would force them to give up their eastern lands and migrate west of the Mississippi. Arguing that the Native Americans weren't educated enough to make their own decisions, Jackson persuaded Congress that removal would be a good thing for them. The act was supposed to allow only for peaceful and voluntary relocation; those natives that refused to give up their lands were supposed to be granted citizenship of the state where they were currently residing. But with a president so strongly against the natives, this was never going to happen. The Choctaws, signing a treaty in 1830, were the first to leave for their western lands, hoping for a better life there. Some stayed behind but were so badly harassed and mistreated by their white neighbors that they eventually sold their farms and left.

The Cherokee were not so easily fooled. At first, when about 500 Cherokee members, known as the Treaty Party, signed the Treaty of New Echota in 1835, it looked as though they would follow the example of the Choctaws and simply leave. The treaty agreed to hand over the eastern Cherokee lands in exchange for a cash payment, new lands in the West, and some other aid in moving. However, most of the Cherokee, including the tribal leadership, had not agreed to the treaty. This became evident when Chief John Ross put together a petition against the treaty. Signed by 16,000 Cherokee, this petition should have been more than enough to put a stop to the Treaty of New Echota, but it was flatly ignored.

The Trail of Tears

In 1836, the Creek Nation suffered a horrible fate that served as a warning for the Cherokees. The Creeks had been at war with white Americans for decades— in fact, Jackson himself had led 2,500 men to fight against the Creeks in 1813 and 1814. He even ordered General John Coffee to attack a village which ended in the massacre of 186 Creek warriors, including numerous women and children. The butchering had been so terrible that Creek mothers fell to killing their own babies to avoid letting them die brutally at the hands of the Americans.

While the war had ended, the Americans were still not letting the Creeks keep their lands. In 1836, 15,000 Creeks were forcibly marched from their homes in Alabama to Indian country in Oklahoma. Only 11,500 actually made it there.

A similar fate awaited the Cherokees. As much as they kicked back against the treaty, with even the Supreme Court ruling the Cherokee tribe as a sovereign nation, which technically should have given them legal protection against any kind of forced removal, Jackson ignored his own laws and ordered them to be marched to Indian country in 1838. Over 16,500 Cherokees left Georgia; 4,000 of them perished along the way.

The Seminole Wars

The Seminoles, a tribe living in Florida, had long been clashing with white Americans as well. Jackson himself had been sent to subdue them shortly after the War of 1812; he had succeeded in forcing them into a reservation in central Florida, kicked the Spanish out of the state, and claimed it as a United States territory. Despite all this, white settlers continued to clamor for more and more land in their new state.

After the Indian Removal Act was passed, another attempt was made to move the Seminole, this time in a bid to force them out of Florida entirely and relocate them to Oklahoma like the Creeks and Cherokees. A council of Seminole chiefs agreed to journey to the new lands and decide whether or not they were fit for habitation by their tribes. While the chiefs signed the Treaty of Payne's Landing, agreeing to move their tribes, they later told their tribes that they had been forced to sign it. On their return to Florida, they announced that they were not going to move a single family.

Regardless of this, the treaty was ratified, and the Seminole prepared for war. Led by their chief, Osceola, they put up the most strenuous resistance of any Native American tribe at the time. From 1835 to 1842, they fought the white Americans tooth and nail, determined to cling onto the lands where they had been living since their legends could remember. They were eventually defeated, with only a handful left living on their little reservation in Florida, but their defeat came at a high price to the Americans: about 1,600 of their soldiers died in the fighting.

At last, by the early 1840s, the majority of Native Americans had been forced into Indian country. Here they hoped they were going to be left alone in peace and allowed to hold onto their new lands for the rest of their lives. But these hopes were short-lived. The hunger for American expansion knew no limits. The call of the frontier would not be ignored.

Chapter 10 – Awakening

San Francisco Harbor near the height of the Gold Rush
https://commons.wikimedia.org/wiki/California_Gold_Rush#/media/File:SanFranciscoharbor1851c_sharp.jpg

Charles G. Finney's words echoed around the field. An assembly of thousands of faces stared up at him, their expressions rapt, their eyes locked on him as he stood on a stump and rang out the words of one of his most famous sermons.

His eyes shone as he preached. "And in reference to the present, the obvious truth is that if our conscience fully approves of our state, and we are conscious of having acted according to the best light we have, it

contradicts all our just ideas of God to suppose that he condemns us."
He laughed, throwing open his arms, reveling in the wide-eyed wonder of
the people listening. Most of them had grown up learning the Protestant
doctrine; they had always been taught that there was no way to be sure of
salvation. But Finney believed that there was a deeper love in God that
would allow His children to be confident in their eternity. "He is a
father," he went on, "and He cannot but smile on His obedient and
trusting children."

His stirring words raised shouts of "Amen!" from the crowd. All
around him, other preachers' rousing words echoed around the camp
meeting, their clenched fists brandished in the air, their audiences
shouting out, caught up in the joy of the moment. The Second Great
Awakening may have begun in c. 1790, but it was due to preachers like
Finney that the movement gained any traction.

A Religious Revival

Following the Great Awakening of the 1730s through the 1750s in
Great Britain and the Thirteen Colonies, the Second Great Awakening
was another wave of revival that swept through the United States, borne
forward by unlikely preachers. In that era, ministers and church leaders
were usually university educated. Their academics were almost as
rigorous as those of lawyers or doctors; once qualified, they easily fell into
the trap of considering themselves loftier than the people of their flock.
But the Second Great Awakening saw a new idea enter the hearts of the
people: the thought that God could use anyone, no matter how lowly, no
matter how uneducated. That even ordinary people could change the
world.

This awakening followed upon the heels of a nation that was bolstered
by its recent victories in the wars it had been fighting. From the
Revolution through the War of 1812 and the Seminole Wars, the non-
native citizens of the United States had yet to suffer a major defeat. Their
national identity was growing ever stronger; the "Star-Spangled Banner"
was on the lips of every citizen. It was a time of peace and prosperity.
With most of their enemies defeated, the Americans could turn their
thoughts to things other than survival.

The Second Great Awakening would also give birth to two new ideas that would soon shape the history of America: feminism and abolitionism. But first, the nation would be distracted by the discovery of gold.

The Discovery at Sutter's Mill

When James Wilson Marshall first saw the little metallic glimmer in the shallows of the river, he didn't think much of it. His mind was occupied with his work. A carpenter, Marshall was busy building a waterwheel for his client, John Sutter. Turning away from the river, he returned his attention to the wood and nails that he was working with.

But something about that little flash he'd seen in the water was niggling at him. After a few minutes' work, he put down his hammer and went to investigate. Stepping cautiously into the shallows of the American River, he felt the cold water splashing over his feet, freezing his toes with its wintry January bite. He searched the pebbles. Had his eyes deceived him?

Then he saw it. Something bright, wedged between the pebbles. Marshall's heart was pounding. He slowly leaned closer, searching the shallow water, his mouth dry. There it was—a tiny nugget that shone with a warm glow where the sunlight struck it. Marshall reached into the cold water and pinched the lump of metal between his fingertips then drew it out into the air. It lay on his trembling palm, glowing, and Marshall knew at once that it was gold.

The California Gold Rush

Marshall's discovery of gold on January 24th, 1848 in the American River was at first met with suspicion. Other Americans simply couldn't believe that California really held untold wealth. The territory had just been part of the subject of war between America and Mexico; its population numbered just over 6,000 *Californios*—people primarily of Spanish American descent—150,000 Native Americans and only 800 white Americans. There were a few little farms and a few little towns. San Francisco itself was little more than a speck on the map. Surely, of all the places where gold could be, California wasn't it.

Then everything changed a few weeks later when Sam Brannan, a storekeeper in San Francisco, brought a vial of glittering gold into the streets and marched around the town, displaying it for all to see. America was convinced. There was gold in California after all, and suddenly, every American wanted a piece of it.

The California Gold Rush would start in earnest in 1849 and continue into the early 1850s, peaking in 1852. Seized by "gold fever," thousands of American men left their homes, lives, and families behind to make their way to the mines. 75% of San Franciscan men left the city. For the first time, women were forced to become fully independent, running farms and business single-handedly while they raised their kids and cared for their homes. Californians weren't the only ones headed for the frontier—people traveled from as far away as Peru, Hawaii, other parts of the United States, and even China to get their share of the gold.

At first, gold was easy pickings; getting it was as simple as picking it up off the dirt. Later, it had to be panned from the river, and later still, as the supply of gold dwindled in the face of the insatiable thirst for wealth, it had to be obtained by hydraulic mining. Thousands of men had mortgaged their homes or spent everything they had to get to California, and they were desperate to get their investment back. This resulted in thousands of Native Americans being pushed out of their territory.

Lasting Legacy of the Gold Rush

The California Gold Rush's impact on the state and the country remains to this day. Hundreds of small mining towns popped up throughout the state, many of them now large cities. The Gold Rush also expedited California's admittance as the 31st state in 1850. California's economy boomed, as did its population; with over 300,000 Americans moving into the state, the Gold Rush became known as the largest mass migration in American history.

At its peak, the Gold Rush yielded more than $80 million in gold in a single year. After 1852, however, it slowly started to decline until it reached about $45 million in 1857 and remained more or less stable after that. Hydraulic mining, which yielded plenty of gold but wrought havoc on the landscape, was banned in 1884.

Chapter 11 – Civil War

As the Gold Rush brought wealth to thousands and ruin to many more, the United States found itself embroiled in a controversy. California's application to become a state had caused a significant stir in Congress. No one could deny that Californian land was valuable, but the new state brought with it a new question: was it to be a slave or free state?

During that period, the United States was already divided over the issue of slavery. The Second Great Awakening had brought with it a new wave of abolitionism, with many Americans converting to a form of Christianity that renounced the slave trade as being against the will of God. The Northern states, in particular, were mostly free, meaning that slaves could not be kept in them at all. The Southern states, however, relied heavily on the slave trade, both as an economy in itself and for labor to work on lucrative tobacco, cotton, and sugarcane plantations.

Before the admission of California, the states were fairly evenly divided: about half were free states and the other half slave states. The admission of California, Oregon, New Mexico, and Utah, however, was likely to tip the balance in the direction of more free states than slave. This caused widespread anger and even panic among the Southern states, who feared they would lose their power. War came perilously close to breaking out until Henry Clay came up with the Compromise of 1850, which settled the Southern states down but still allowed California to be admitted as a free state.

Chaos on the Frontier

While hundreds of Americans were working their way across the continent, staking their claims in new lands and pushing the border of the country ever outward, the clash between anti- and pro-slavery groups continued to grow. Pioneers moving into the territory of Kansas were particularly violent. The Kansas-Nebraska Act essentially allowed Kansas to decide whether to allow slavery or not, a decision that proved wildly unpopular with strongly convicted Northerners who didn't want their new lands tainted by the slave trade, which they viewed as sinful and criminal. Fights broke out often between anti- and pro-slavery groups, who generally migrated from Missouri, while the anti-slavery parties often came from New England. The violence, known today as "Bleeding Kansas," cost many lives in a variety of bloody massacres.

Bleeding Kansas was just a foreshadow of things to come. The balance of power had undeniably shifted, despite the best efforts of the Southern states; slavery was no longer as fashionable as it had once been, and the suffering of the enslaved blacks was starting to enrage more and more Americans. And in 1861, this disagreement would erupt into full-scale civil war.

The Start of the War

The fate of the nation hinged on the 1860 presidential election. The nation was profoundly divided, with the Democratic party split into a Northern and a Southern faction; the Northern Democrats were fairly neutral on the issue of slavery, while the Southerners were distinctly pro-slavery. The Republican Party, on the other hand, led by Abraham Lincoln, was radically anti-slavery.

When Lincoln won the election, the South felt that this was a terrible injustice. Lincoln had not won any of the Southern states; they had simply been outnumbered and overwhelmed by votes from the more numerous Northern states. Tired of the deep divide between North and South, a group of seven Southern states—Mississippi, Alabama, Texas, Louisiana, Georgia, South Carolina, and Florida—seceded from the United States and renamed themselves the Confederate States of America. They would later be joined by Tennessee, North Carolina, Virginia, and Arkansas.

With the country utterly divided, the Northern states (still known as the United States) refused to recognize the secession. Lincoln and his administration feared that allowing this secession would ultimately divide the United States into a chaotic mass of small countries, not unlike Europe, which had been embroiled in war for centuries. On April 12th, 1861, a Confederate army captured Fort Sumter in Charleston Bay, and the first shots were fired. The Civil War was under way.

Growing Battles

The Civil War would see the largest battles that the United States had ever engaged in. As the Confederate army under Robert E. Lee clashed repeatedly with the Union army commanded by General George G. Meade, the scope of the battles only grew larger and larger. Lincoln's original tactic had been to limit the war as much as possible, simply attempting to subdue what he viewed as a rebellion in the South. However, as the war went on, the cost of the fighting grew, with thousands of human lives being poured into the struggle regarding the freedom of African Americans. Many thousands of these lives belonged to free African Americans from the North, drawn by Lincoln's issue of the Emancipation Proclamation which declared all slaves in the rebel states to be legally free, even though their masters refused to give them up.

The Battle of Gettysburg, taking place on July 1st to July 3rd, 1863, was the turning point of the Civil War. Prior to Gettysburg, Lee had enjoyed multiple victories over the Union. At this fight, however, it was Meade who would win the day—at a horrific cost. There were over 50,000 casualties, including over 7,000 dead, 33,000 wounded, and nearly 11,000 missing. The death toll was so terrible that Lincoln was moved to declare total war on the South, determined to wipe out its entire slave culture for good.

In 1864, Ulysses S. Grant became the leading Union general in the Virginian theater, where the fighting was the most heated. Between Grant, William T. Sherman, and other Union generals, the intense fighting was finally able to push the Confederates back. Grant was the one who was able to corner Lee and force him to surrender on April 9th, 1865.

The Assassination of Abraham Lincoln

Lincoln was only able to enjoy the taste of victory for a sparse five days. On April 14th, 1865, actor and Confederate supporter John Wilkes Booth shot Lincoln in the back of the head while he was peacefully watching a play with his wife and guests. Booth escaped into the night, leading to a nationwide manhunt that ended twelve days later when he was shot and killed.

It was too late for Lincoln, however. He was pronounced dead the next morning on April 15th. Yet his dream was far from dead; the war officially ended a few weeks later on May 9th, 1865, when the last stragglers of the Confederate Army surrendered. Slavery was over, but so were the lives of 620,000 soldiers. To this day, that number is almost half the total amount of American soldiers that have ever died in combat throughout history. Worse, many of these soldiers were fighting against friends and family; no longer were they just fighting a nameless foe but people they knew. The profound rift caused by the war would be as heartbreaking as it was violent.

Freedom had definitely been earned at the dearest cost. Now, it was time to rebuild an entire nation.

Chapter 12 – Seeking for Peace

The task that fell to the next American president would not be an easy one. With Abraham Lincoln dead and the nation in tatters after a decimating civil war, someone was going to have to take the reins and rebuild the country almost from its foundations. Four million African Americans had been freed from slavery; now, they had to be integrated into the rest of society somehow, while the South's economy and infrastructure had to be rebuilt. The task fell to Andrew Johnson, Lincoln's vice president. He had narrowly escaped assassination himself as Booth's co-conspirator, who had been given the task to kill Johnson that night, had elected to drink himself into a stupor instead.

It seemed that Johnson had run out of luck though. Despite the fact that he made numerous achievements in his presidency—including the Alaska Purchase and the 13th Amendment which saw slavery finally abolished in December 1865—Johnson proved unpopular with radical Republicans and many of the former Union states when he effectively allowed the Southern states to govern themselves whichever way they liked, apart from having to adhere to the abolition of slavery. The South responded by passing "black codes" which limited the behavior and freedom of African Americans to such an extent that many Republicans in Congress viewed the codes as little better than slavery.

In 1868, Ulysses S. Grant, the general whose efforts had hugely contributed to the Union victory, was elected president. He and Johnson hated each other so much that Johnson refused to even attend Grant's inauguration, but to most of the U.S., Grant was a hero; it was thought that he would be less likely to cast the hard-won victory of the Union to the winds. He gathered the reins well, placing far more emphasis on the Reconstruction Era than Johnson had.

Opposition to a Rebuilt Nation

In 1870, blacks were given suffrage for the first time in the 15th Amendment. All males, regardless of race, were now allowed to vote. African Americans could now be elected to state governments and even to Congress, and those who had been slaves less than ten years earlier found themselves suddenly possessing the same rights as their white counterparts (although laws were put into place to guarantee these rights would be hard, if impossible, to obtain).

This incensed many white Southerners, some of whom turned to violence against proponents of Reconstruction. White supremacy was not forgotten—instead, it was a cause for which many Southerners were still prepared to fight. The most radical of these formed the strange and severely creepy Ku Klux Klan.

Dressed in robes to disguise their identity so that all that was visible of the wearer was a glimpse of his eyes, members of the Ku Klux Klan existed to sow terror among minorities and those who supported their cause and advance white supremacy in the Southern states once more. Formed almost immediately after the Civil War ended, the Klan committed hundreds of acts of violence against newly-emancipated African Americans and their allies. Their robes provided them with enough anonymity that they felt invincible, and they acted accordingly, murdering and destroying wherever they went. They were very active until the 1870s which is when their activities trailed off, although other iterations of the Klan have taken place throughout the years. Legislation was passed against the Klan which did help suppress the group, but the damage was already done to African Americans, especially when it came to voting and politics.

The interest in Reconstruction began to wane through the mid-1870s as it became evident that the South was functioning once more with African Americans integrated into their new roles, although they still weren't being treated fairly. In 1874, Democrats once again rose to power, gaining control over the House of Representatives. The Civil War seemed to be largely left behind less than ten years after it had ended.

The Wild West

Now that peace had befallen the nation once more, Americans started to turn their focus to expansionism again. The Western frontier was still largely unexplored, and it was here that one of the most dramatic eras of United States history began: that of the legendary Wild West.

The Old West era extended from the Civil War to about 1895—thirty years that would become the American era most immortalized in culture. The names of the famous men and women of that era echo throughout the centuries with irresistible familiarity: Billy the Kid, Jesse James, Calamity Jane, Chief Sitting Bull, Annie Oakley, Wild Bill Hickok. The West was sparsely populated and lawless; while it was mostly inhabited by peaceful cattle ranchers, its open lands provided plenty of space for outlaws to hide, and the little towns held banks for robbing and saloons for entertainment. To tell all of the stories of the Old West would take dozens of books, but the reality of this romanticized era was all too tragic.

America had barely finished its Civil War when it began a long and bloody struggle with the Plains Indians. The Native Americans that had relocated to the West now found themselves surrounded by whites whose hunger for new land had still not been satisfied, and to make matters worse, the West was already inhabited by tribes who had been living there for hundreds of years. The Plains Indians were some of the last tribes left living on their ancestral lands, and they'd seen how attempts at peaceful negotiations with the settlers had ended for other Native American tribes. They were determined to go to war.

To make matters worse, these tribes' livelihoods depended largely on the huge herds of bison that roamed the plains. Unfortunately, bison were a lucrative target for the new settlers; they were killed by the thousands, decimating the population, endangering the species, and stripping the Native Americans of their most important food source.

The Plains Indian tribes—which included the Apache, Sioux, and Cheyenne, among others—were determined not to suffer the same fate that their Southern neighbors had during the Trail of Tears. They fought back, with bloody consequences.

The Wounded Knee Massacre

Chief Spotted Elk knew that he was alone.

Crazy Horse had been dead for over thirteen years. Sitting Bull's blood was still warm on the earth, but he, too, was gone. It was just Spotted Elk now as he led his band of Lakota natives toward the Pine Ridge Reservation. As much as the Native Americans had been struggling against having to go to the reservations, they knew that they had no choice anymore. The very place that they had tried so hard to avoid had become their only safe refuge.

Spotted Elk could only hope that the Ghost Dances would work. Native American religions were as complex as they were dynamic, a moving, growing thing that had assimilated the coming of the white man and produced the Ghost Dance, which they believed would set them free from their oppressors. If they could just perform the Ghost Dance over and over, then their gods would avenge them. A new earth could be recreated—one where the ships never came, where the Native Americans could continue to live with free rein on the continent where their culture had been born.

But the Ghost Dances did nothing except anger and frighten the U.S. Army. Believing that these were war dances, they had kept a close eye on the Ghost Dancers ever since the movement began, and Spotted Elk's little troop would be no exception. On December 28th, as the Lakota were encamped on the banks of Wounded Knee Creek, they found themselves surrounded by the U.S. 7th Cavalry. Its commander, Colonel James Forsyth, told them that they were only there to escort the Lakota to Pine Ridge. But the Hotchkiss guns surrounding the perimeter—machine guns capable of firing up to 500 rounds per minute—told a different story.

Their fears were realized when the U.S. soldiers ordered them to surrender their weapons the next day. Tension filled the camp as some of the Lakota tightened their grips on tomahawks and rifles, wary of the soldiers' motives. Then, the medicine man, Yellow Bird, raised his voice in a thin, droning melody that signaled the start of the Ghost Dance. Seizing the hands of the two people nearest him, he started the shuffling dance. The others hurried to link arms, and before the soldiers knew what was happening, a giant circle of Lakota was moving around and around in the monotony that allowed them to keep their dance going for hours. The Ghost Dance had begun.

The atmosphere was leaden, drawn out with fear on both sides. Nervous shouts to stop echoed from some of the soldiers; however, the dance went on, relentless and unforgiving, the circle only pausing when some of the dancers started to grab handfuls of dirt and flung it into the air, filling the soldiers' vision with turning bodies and flying dust. Amid all this, one of the soldiers spotted Black Coyote, a young warrior, clutching his rifle. The soldier grabbed the rifle, demanding that Black Coyote give it up. He pulled it back, and suddenly, with a deafening crack in the muffled tension, the gun went off.

Panic reigned. Noise filled the camp as the Ghost Dance broke and Native Americans and soldiers alike were in all directions. There was shouting, some of the soldiers firing on Black Coyote, some of the Native Americans trying to stop them—and then the Hotchkiss guns spoke. Bullets poured into the camp, 2,000 a minute. Blood and screams filled the air, soaked into the dirt, and stained the face of U.S. history for all time. When the madness subsided, 300 Lakota were dead. 60 of them were women and children, innocents caught up in the chaos and killed in the crossfire.

The End of the Wars

The Wounded Knee Massacre brought an end to the decades of war between Native Americans and Americans of European descent. Hundreds of thousands of Native Americans had been killed since the Europeans first arrived; the native population dwindled from several million in the 15th century to only a few hundred thousand.

The wars had cost thousands of European American lives, too. The most famous defeat for the settlers, the Battle of the Little Bighorn in 1876, saw an entire regiment of soldiers under Colonel George Armstrong Custer wiped out by a band of Sioux and Cheyenne led by Sitting Bull and Crazy Horse. These were some of the last great Indian chiefs that attempted to rescue their tribes from the oncoming tide of Western expansionism, but after one of his own villages was destroyed by the U.S. Army in retaliation for the Little Bighorn chaos only days after that fateful battle, Crazy Horse surrendered in 1877. He died four months later, stabbed by a bayonet in prison at Fort Robinson.

By 1890, even Sitting Bull had all but given up: while there were still some battles between Plains Indians and the U.S. Army during the 1880s, Sitting Bull would lead no major fights. In fact, he didn't even participate in the Ghost Dances—although the reservation police mistakenly believed he did. In December 1890, they attempted to arrest him, shooting and killing him in the process, and prompting Spotted Elk's flight that eventually led to the last massacre at Wounded Knee. With the last great warrior chiefs gone, the Native Americans no longer put up much of a fight. The wars were over. The West was "won."

Chapter 13 – A Rising Power

By the close of the 19th century, there were 45 U.S. states. Thomas Edison had patented the light bulb, the National Geographic Society had been formed, the Constitution had celebrated its centennial, and Americans were even playing basketball. William McKinley was inaugurated as president in 1897, and, to a large extent, the nation was finally at peace with itself. While Native Americans had been confined to reservations, African Americans at least had been freed, although they still faced simmering racism.

With home affairs mostly under control, the United States began to emerge in foreign affairs as more than just a newly liberated colony. Now, the country was becoming a force to be reckoned with—and it would demonstrate just how powerful it had become with its first engagement in international war since the War of 1812.

The Spanish-American War

In 1898, while Florida had long since become a state, Spain still held several colonies in the Americas. One of these was Cuba, despite the best efforts of the Cubans themselves. Horrendously oppressed by their Spanish masters, Cubans had been fighting a bitter war ever since Carlos Manuel de Céspedes had rung the bell at the door of his sugar mill and told his slaves that they were free. His actions prompted the start of the Ten Years' War from 1868 to 1878, a dark struggle that had ended in hopeless defeat for the Cubans. They attempted to win their freedom again in the Little War of 1879 and were easily crushed by Spain.

For several years, things quietened down in Cuba, but the oppression did not end. Spaniards comprised only 2% of the Cuban population, yet they possessed most of the wealth on the island, leaving Cubans themselves struggling. In 1895, another effort to throw off Spanish shackles began, starting the Cuban War of Independence. The war resulted in nationwide chaos that eventually reached the capital, Havana. American citizens staying in Havana at the time feared for their lives, prompting the United States to send its latest pride and joy, the warship USS *Maine*, to lie at anchor in Havana Harbor as a silent warning to any who dared to drag American citizens into the mess.

The *Maine* was never supposed to go into action unless Americans were threatened. And she never did. Instead, on the evening of February 15th, 1898, she exploded. A fireball ripped out most of her hull, killing hundreds of crew members. The Spanish were widely blamed for the explosion, even though later evidence has strongly suggested that they were innocent and that the sinking of the *Maine* was a tragic accident. Outrage erupted in America, and together with the suffering of the Cuban people (who were, arguably, on their way to victory themselves), yellow journalism and the voice of the people forced President McKinley to declare war on Spain. The declaration was made on April 25th, 1898.

The Spanish-American War was short-lived. Where once America could never have hoped to hold a candle to the might of the Spanish Armada, now the United States had transformed into a military giant, and Spain—unprepared for war with the U.S. and weakened by decades of conflict with Cuba—never really stood a chance. By May 1st, the U.S. had won its first victory at Manila Bay in the Philippines, which was also tired of its status as a Spanish colony. In June, the U.S. Army reached Cuba, dispatching squadrons of men on both sea and land—including Theodore Roosevelt, then Lieutenant Colonel, and his Rough Riders. By July 1st, they were able to take the major city of Santiago de Cuba; in a bid to escape, the Spanish general tried to lead all of his men out of the city in warships on the morning of July 3rd, an attempt that failed dismally when the U.S. Navy was able to capture or sink all of the Spanish ships.

When Santiago de Cuba surrendered in mid-July, the war was practically over. The Spanish had known that they were defeated even before the war started; some fought with a fervor of desperation, but most of them were dragged down by lack of morale before they were defeated in battle. 90% of U.S. losses didn't even result from any form of Spanish resistance but was due to the infectious diseases that thrived in the tropical island of Cuba.

The Treaty of Paris left Spain stripped of several of its colonies. Cuba was granted its independence; Puerto Rico and Guam, on the other hand, were handed over to the United States. The U.S. had firmly established itself as a military juggernaut fully capable of handling itself in wars with Europe. Its new reputation would soon be tested. Within the next two decades, war would break out on a scale that had never been seen before.

Yankees Overseas

The boys were scared, and Ulysses Grant McAlexander knew it. Looking out over his line of white-faced soldiers, the colonel couldn't help but feel his heart go out to them. Just like him, they'd all been largely untested in international warfare—their nation had barely entered the Great War, and this would be the first time that American troops fought on foreign soil since the comparative cakewalk that had been the Spanish-American War twenty years ago.

Now, even McAlexander was starting to wonder if they were up to what they were about to face. He could hear the roar of the guns and voices as the German troops swarmed across the Marne, and he knew that the proximity of the sound meant that they'd already mowed right through the French 6th Army. It was really no surprise; Germany had been gaining ground in their recent offensive across France, despite the best efforts of the combined Allied army standing against them.

McAlexander felt the earth tremble beneath his feet in the trench. The deafening sound of shells was everywhere, sending great sprays of earth and blood flying into the air, scattering shrapnel and human flesh. He could see the Germans coming. They had crushed the French line, and on McAlexander's left and right, he could see his neighboring divisions buckling. Dug in on the riverbank, his 38th Infantry Regiment of the 3rd Division was ready to engage.

Gunfire erupted all around them. McAlexander shouted, cheering his men on as they dared to raise their helmets above the trenches and fire. Machine guns spoke loudly, rifles cracking and popping in the chaos. In the madness, McAlexander looked up to see that the lines on either side of his trench were buckling. The Germans were going to break through—they were going to make it and continue their offensive across France.

Through the smoke and dust of the fighting, McAlexander stared at his men. They were all looking at him, hearing the panicked orders to retreat from officers all around them. Only Colonel McAlexander had not yet told them to flee.

But something in him would not surrender. He took a deep breath. "*Nous resterons la!*" he shouted, loud and clear so that the Frenchmen around him would understand. "*Nous resterons la*! We shall remain here!"

Encouraged by the crystal-clear voice of their colonel, the men buckled down and returned fire courageously as the Germans threatened to overwhelm them. When their flanks became exposed as their allies fell away, left and right, McAlexander dragged them up, forming his division into a U-shape to protect its vulnerable sides. Despite the best that the Germans could throw at them, the 38th Infantry Regiment clung to its place on the edge of the Marne, eventually throwing their foes back when reinforcements rushed up at last to their aid. The Second Battle of the Marne proved instrumental in halting the German offensive, making room for the Allied counteroffensive that would eventually restore the balance of power in favor of the Allies, ultimately leading to their victory. And the heroes of the battle fought on July 15th, 1918, were the American 3rd Infantry Division. They became known as the "Rock of the Marne," and they proved to the rest of the world that the United States could stand shoulder to shoulder with the older nations when it came to military matters.

U.S. Involvement in World War I

American president Woodrow Wilson had never been interested in engaging in the war that was ripping Europe and Asia apart.

When WWI broke out on June 28th, 1914, Wilson had hurried to declare the United States' neutrality. Even though the Spanish-American

War had been such a sweeping victory for the U.S., he knew that a world war was a different matter entirely. America was in its infancy compared to some of the ancient nations that were fighting in the Great War: Britain, Russia, France, and Germany had all been waging war on one another for longer than the United States had even existed. The fighting was mostly centered on Eurasia in any case. Let the war take care of itself.

But President Wilson's hopes that America's neutrality would keep it safe were unfounded. On May 7th, 1915, a British ocean liner became a victim of the deadly German U-boats. These stealthy submarines sent a torpedo spinning into the *Lusitania*'s hull, sinking it and killing more than a thousand people on board, including 128 American citizens. This, alongside an explosion on Black Tom Island in New Jersey orchestrated by German secret agents and a threatening telegram intercepted by British decoders in March 1917 that ordered Mexico to invade the United States, was enough to push Wilson over the edge. The United States declared war on April 6th, 1917.

Led by General John J. "Black Jack" Pershing, the American soldiers proved themselves quickly in battle. Among them was Major George S. Patton, someday to become one of the greatest (and yet most controversial) leaders of the Second World War. While just before WWI the entire American army numbered less than the French losses at the Battle of Verdun alone, by the end of the war, over two million U.S. soldiers had served on the Allied side. They contributed to the final offensive that eventually ended the Great War on November 11th, 1918.

With that, the United States had shown itself to be a formidable opponent in any war. Its military importance was unquestionable; its national pride and identity spurred on by success against its enemies. Yet this was but its baptism through fire. The United States still had a tremendous trial in international warfare to face in the century to come.

Chapter 14 – Progress

With a tenuous and flawed peace established all over the world, America found itself a changed nation.

More than a quarter of the young male population of the United States had served in the military during the First World War. Of that number, about 100,000 never came back. Those that did return to their homes and families when the war was over were not the same people that they had been when they left, fresh-faced and wide-eyed recruits riled up by propaganda and ready for some fighting. Now, they were broken, sometimes physically, often mentally. PTSD didn't have a name then; these men called their ailment shell shock or, often, nothing at all. Sometimes they just tried to carry on as if the death and devastation of the war didn't affect them, forcing them to drink or engage in similarly counterproductive measures in an attempt to cope with what medicine had not yet recognized as a legitimate mental disorder. This may have been part of what prompted Congress to pass the 18th Amendment, prohibiting the widespread consumption of alcohol that was causing social problems across the country. Prohibition eventually proved to be more trouble than it was worth, but it would endure until 1933.

What was more, with two million of their men overseas, the women of the United States had had to step into roles that society had long deemed unsuitable for them. Their newfound independence gave them a sense of power that was the last leg-up they needed to earn the right to vote. And when President Woodrow Wilson was suddenly and unexpectedly incapacitated, the First Lady would secretly do what American women had been doing ever since their men started to leave for the war: she would take over.

Women's Suffrage and Its Secret Leader

October 1st, 1919, was the last day that President Wilson would have full control over his own body. On the morning of October 2nd, he suffered a debilitating stroke that left almost half of his body paralyzed. Confined to his bed, he was constantly attended to by his personal physician, Dr. Cary T. Grayson, whose repeated warnings that Wilson's habit of overworking would lead to some medical disaster eventually, and his wife, First Lady Edith Wilson.

Edith was faced with a weighty responsibility. President Wilson could still speak and had a fair amount of mental clarity, but he was certainly incapable of working at the furious pace that had characterized his much-criticized presidency before the stroke. As much as Wilson's actions had been unpopular with a nation that had begged for war against Germany, he had won the Nobel Peace Prize in 1919 for his efforts in creating the League of Nations and negotiating the Treaty of Versailles—efforts that had contributed to the stroke that had almost killed him. Now, even though America may not have liked him, it needed him to complete the next two years to help navigate the world after the war. Edith's decision was simple: Woodrow would stay president. And she would help.

For the rest of President Wilson's term, Edith would secretly manage most of the affairs of the country. While she described herself as simply a "steward" who put all the important decisions to her husband, and while Woodrow himself likely still made many decisions, Edith was instrumental in running the country until Woodrow's term ended and he could finally be at rest in 1921.

For roughly a century, women had been campaigning for equal rights, demanding to be allowed to own property and to vote, which were only some of the rights that had been denied to them. However, diligent work over the decades by heroines such as Carrie Chapman Catt, Lucy Stone, Helen Blackburn, Susan B. Anthony, and Elizabeth Cady Stanton had secured voting rights for women in many of the states.

And progress was certainly being made. In the throes of the First World War, President Wilson himself had said that allowing women to vote was "vitally essential to the successful prosecution of the great war of humanity in which we are engaged."

The 19th Amendment was finally ratified on August 18th, 1920, allowing all American women the right to have a say in the government of their country. It is an ironic truth that, at the time, the entire country had no idea that a woman was running it. Edith Wilson would never be hailed as a hero, but like the millions of women who had kept businesses, homes, families, farms, and shops going while their men were facing the horrors of the Great War, she was instrumental in keeping America on its feet after the greatest war the world had ever seen.

The Roaring Twenties

Women's suffrage ushered in a decade of burgeoning growth and progress on almost every front. Heroes like Babe Ruth would rise in the sports world; American music would be revolutionized and truly individualized for the very first time, with legends like Louis Armstrong and Bing Crosby taking the stage; and in the industrial world, giants such as Henry Ford would emerge to boost the American economy. However, as successful as the Roaring Twenties were, they would come to an end. The Great War would soon be eclipsed by a breadth of darkness that had never before been dreamed. The Great Depression was coming—and the Second World War was right on its heels.

Chapter 15 – Disaster Strikes

A homeless man stands by an abandoned store in the depths of the Great Depression
https://commons.wikimedia.org/wiki/File:Depression,_Unemployed,destitute_man_leaning_again st_vacant_store-photo_by_Dorothea_Lange_-_NARA_-_195825.tif

Hulda Borowski could barely stand up straight. She swayed, her mind fuzzy, trying to remember which floor she worked on as a clerk in Wall Street. The elevator pinged up through the levels of the brokerage house, and Hulda stared at the numbers on the buttons, trying to make sense of them. She was so, so tired. It was almost two weeks since the Wall Street Crash had sent the economy, the nation, and the globe into a panicking tailspin, but Hulda hadn't even had a chance to be worried. Ever since Black Tuesday, the ticker counters hadn't been able to keep up with how quickly shares were being sold. The clerks, accordingly, were working overtime. More than overtime. Hulda rubbed her eyes, trying to remember the last time she'd slept. Oh, yes—in the wire room. Her boss had found her there and ordered her to go home. She must have napped there. Was it morning already? Hulda wasn't sure, but she knew that she felt utterly exhausted. She was fifty-one years old—too old for this. Too old for all of it, for the economy that she knew was about to disintegrate, for the poverty that she had heard the bankers talking about. The poverty that was coming for hundreds of thousands of Americans just like her.

It was all too much. Hulda had to do something. And at about ten o' clock that morning, she did.

She jumped off the roof, fell forty stories, and died on impact.

The Wall Street Crash of 1929

The Roaring Twenties' wild prosperity had lulled the United States into a false sense of security. As the stock market boomed and consumerism enveloped the culture into a decadent time of credit and careless spending, the entire nation was blind to the disaster that would inevitably come as a result of such excessive living. In fact, most of the world had no idea what was coming. Only a handful of Austrian and British economists dared to sound a warning bell, and they were easily brushed off. The economy had never been better. Failure wasn't even in the cards.

Except that failure, inevitably, would come. There was just too much credit in the United States, credit amassed largely by excessive spending, the new consumerist culture, and millions of dollars' worth of shares being bought on margin. Americans' optimism about the future was leading them deeper and deeper into debt. The economy could no longer support it, and so, the stock market began to decline. At first, it dipped and then rose again, wavering through the month of September. Traders brushed it aside—everyone knew that the market had its bad moments sometimes. But when Black Thursday came on October 24th, 1929, there was no more denying the fact that disaster was about to strike.

And strike it did. Despite the best efforts of investment companies and the like, Black Monday followed, the market plummeting. Black Tuesday, October 29th, was pure chaos. Over sixteen million shares were sold as panicking investors trampled over one another to get rid of their shares before they became a liability. Billions of dollars were effectively flushed down the drain. The economy had collapsed under its own weight, and while the "suicide wave" following the Wall Street Crash was largely a myth when the usual rate of suicides was blown up by the press to fuel sensationalism, there was plenty of cause for dismay. The stock market not only reeled from the punches—it fell flat. Some historians estimate that the United States lost more money in a single day during the Crash than it had spent on the entirety of WWI.

The Wall Street Crash was an unprecedented disaster of the financial world, but an even larger one would follow. Caused in part by the Crash, the Great Depression would plunge the United States into a worse condition than it had been during the throes of the First World War.

The Great Depression

President Herbert Hoover was confronted with an appalling crisis. He had been inaugurated in March 1929, becoming the president of a country whose total wealth had nearly doubled in the last decade, and he anticipated a term of peace, wealth, and luxurious excess just like what his citizens were experiencing. The Wall Street Crash, occurring only a few months after he was elected, was a rude and horrific shock. Perhaps a little in denial, Hoover told others that he expected the crisis to blow over.

It didn't. Two years after the Wall Street Crash, America was plunging deeper and deeper into an economic meltdown that would later become known as the Great Depression. Six million Americans were unemployed. By 1932, that number had risen to fifteen million. Hoover made half-hearted attempts to restore the economy by giving government loans to banks—many of which were liquidating as their clients panicked and demanded all their money back in cash—but this had little effect.

Hoover's term came to an end, and in March 1933, Franklin D.

Roosevelt became president of the United States. His inauguration was a much soberer one than Hoover's; Roosevelt knew that his country was facing a crisis that had 125 million Americans looking to him for help. Things could not have looked much worse. The U.S. Treasury could not even pay its own government employees. Across the country, banks had been ordered to close as neither the banks nor their clients could afford for more banking panics to occur.

FDR himself, however, seemed to be unruffled. His manner held the calmness that Americans needed, providing an anchor in a wild storm. "The only thing we have to fear is fear itself," he told them. His personal touch immediately had a calming effect on a panicking population; addressing the people directly over the radio in his fireside chats, he made them feel a little more at ease, giving them hope that someone cared about them and was trying to help.

For many Americans, that little bit of hope was all they had. The Depression coincided with terrible droughts, which, coupled with decades of over-farming, created tremendous dust storms that enveloped the Western states with such vehemence that those states became known as the Dust Bowl. The storms drove more than half of the West's citizens to seek shelter in other states, leaving thousands of farms abandoned or foreclosed. Food production plummeted, and skyrocketing food prices combined with unemployment contributed to hideous rates of malnutrition and even death by starvation. The juggernaut that had helped to bring down Germany in the First World War was an emaciated giant now, crippled by its own excess.

Yet a new spirit was growing among the American people, one far less exuberant than the chaotic and riotous Roaring Twenties had produced. Now, with little enough to go around, Americans were learning to be more careful and to help each other. Firsthand accounts of the Depression reveal stories of kindness and selflessness even in the midst of intolerable need.

FDR seemed to share this new spirit. He instituted the New Deal, a series of efforts to stabilize the crashing economy and return peace and prosperity beneath the Star-Spangled Banner. Among the programs he put in place were the Social Security Act, providing vulnerable Americans such as children, the unemployed, and the aged with government help, and the Works Progress Administration. This administration employed more than eight million citizens to assist in endeavors that aimed to help the environment, such as planting trees and bringing fish to bodies of water.

Despite another sharp recession in 1937, the New Deal managed to scrape together a little progress, dragging the economy out of the worst of the Great Depression. This economic disaster, however, would not end until a new industry breathed life back into the American economy. Yet this new industry would not so much fix the problems as exchange one tragedy for another.

It was the industry of war. WWII had begun.

Chapter 16 – The Biggest Bomb in the World

The first bombs fell at five minutes before eight. Almost two tons of deadly explosive, it punched through the deck of the USS *Arizona*, ripping through the mighty warship and its human occupants. The sound of it echoed through the entirety of Pearl Harbor, rippling the peaceful waters of the Hawaiian bay. There was a moment of silence as the bomb rested in the ammunition magazine of the ship. Then it blew up. A fireball erupted over the harbor, reflecting in the water and in the shiny metal sides of the surrounding warships of the American Pacific Fleet. With it, over one thousand lives were vaporized, and this was only the beginning.

The sky droned and screamed with a fleet of Japanese planes. It was December 7th, 1941, and Japan had launched a surprise attack that would devastate Pearl Harbor and break millions of American hearts. Despite its reluctance to join the Second World War, the United States was about to get involved, its hand forced by the deadly attack that would be imprinted on the collective psyche of the American people forever.

U.S. Involvement in WWII

The Second World War—a war whose sheer scale of destruction would wildly eclipse the hitherto unheard-of violence of the First World

War—started in 1939 when Nazi Germany first marched into Poland. It was only after the attack on Pearl Harbor in 1941, however, that the United States would enter the war.

President Franklin D. Roosevelt was not as hesitant as Wilson had been to enter the war, but he was certainly cautious. While he felt that joining the war on the Allied side was unavoidable, his administration did its best to stay out of the fight for as long as possible. Unlike the actions of the Wilson administration in WWI, FDR's government didn't sell weapons to the warring nations, nor were Americans permitted to travel with any of the countries involved in the war, preventing a second *Lusitania* from ever occurring.

The Axis, however—comprising of Germany, Italy, and Japan, all at the time fascist nations bent on expanding their empires—was determined to drag the United States into it. Anticipating an eventual conflict, FDR removed the embargo on war provisions in late 1939; by 1940, America was providing Great Britain with large amounts of resources to fuel the war effort.

It was no secret to the Axis that the United States, though officially neutral, was on the side of the Allies. The bombing of Pearl Harbor was Japan's attempt to strike first—and it worked. With a death toll of 2,403, it was a devastating attack. Yet far from crippling the United States, it drove the entire nation into a frenzy, baying for the blood of those who had killed thousands of unprepared people. The very next day, hundreds of thousands of soldiers enlisted in the U.S. Army. Together with those drafted for service overseas, they formed the American armies that would form a staunch portion of the Allied effort. The U. S. had officially sided with the Allies, joining Britain, France, Australia, the Soviet Union, China, Canada, and South Africa, among others.

Over the next four years, more than sixteen million United States soldiers would fight in the Second World War. Efforts at home were also made and became instrumental to the Allied victory; rationing allowed the U.S. government to feed the millions of hungry mouths overseas, and vast numbers of women worked to produce what was necessary to meet the needs of both the country and army.

American heroes brought about moments of tremendous triumph in Europe, Asia, and Africa. Among the most famous was General George S. Patton, the American general who helped to win the Battle of the Bulge and yet proved spectacularly unpopular with his peers and superiors; Second Lieutenant Audie L. Murphy, responsible for 240 German deaths and the most decorated American soldier of the war; General Dwight D. Eisenhower, Supreme Allied Commander and future president of the United States; and perhaps most unusual of all, Corporal Desmond Doss, a hero of the war who never fired a single bullet. Instead, Doss was a combat medic whose faith made him a conscientious objector to any form of violence, yet he rescued more than a hundred wounded soldiers—both American and Japanese—in the face of enemy fire.

Yet none of it was enough. By May 1945, while the European theater finally saw silence as the Allied victory stilled the fighting, the Pacific was still a chaotic mess of death and destruction. Japan just wouldn't give up. Pounded relentlessly by U.S. troops, the Japanese still held firm, pouring their resources into the fighting. The war in the Pacific would cost more than a hundred thousand American lives. President Harry Truman decided in July 1945 that he would have to draw the line somewhere, and he drew it with the Potsdam Declaration, ordering Japan to surrender or face "utter destruction."

The threat was not an empty one. Truman had an ace up his sleeve that had never been seen before, a terrible evil that would end the most terribly evil war of all time at that point and change the face of warfare and the world forever. And he named it Little Boy.

The Detonation of the Atomic Bombs

The first atomic bomb in history was detonated in New Mexico on July 16th, 1945, and killed no people.

Codenamed the Gadget, the bomb was designed and built by a team of scientists and soldiers known as the Manhattan Project. FDR had been behind the formation of the team in 1942 when rumor had it that Germany was working on nuclear weapons. Now, three years later, J. Robert Oppenheimer had succeeded in building the world's first atomic bomb. Its detonation was a success, resulting in a tremendous mushroom cloud that was seen sixty miles away and produced a blast crater five feet deep and thirty feet wide.

After Japan's refusal to surrender, Truman had to make the call. It was time to end the Second World War. The detonation of the atomic bomb would cause hundreds of thousands of deaths, wipe out an entire city, and kill untold multitudes of innocent people. Yet in the face of the atrocity that was WWII, it seemed to be but a small price to pay. The war's total cost in human lives is estimated as high as 85 million. Decimating a few cities in order to end the rising death toll seemed like the only way out.

On August 6th, 1945, that apparent last resort was put into action. The Enola Gay, a B-29 U.S. bomber, soared high over Hiroshima. Did the pilot stare down out of the cockpit at the bustling city far below? Did he know that more than 300,000 people lived there? They were down there cooking, cleaning, playing with their kids, working, fighting. There were soldiers down there and men who had committed unspoken atrocities against fellow Americans. But there were also shopkeepers and accountants and doctors and policemen and paramedics and schoolchildren and housewives and...

And the sound of the Little Boy, the thin whine of it as it plummeted from the belly of the Enola Gay, whistling down toward the city.

The scope of the horrors wrought by the atomic bomb can hardly be explained in words. The cold undeniability truth of numbers serves the purpose better. 9,700 pounds: the weight of the bomb. 15,000 tons of TNT equivalent: its explosive force, fueled by uranium. 5: the number of square miles that the explosion razed to the ground. 80,000: the number of people instantly killed by the explosion, about twice the 2018 population of the country of Monaco. 300,000: the estimated number of deaths caused by Little Boy. 60: the percentage of Hiroshima's population that died from the initial explosion and the devastating radiation poisoning that would follow.

On August 9th, a second atomic bomb was dropped. This one, codename "Fat Man," was plutonium-fueled and killed about 80,000 people in the city where it was dropped—Nagasaki, Japan. The death toll was unfathomable; the landscape, destroyed; the cities, decimated. And

Japan was brought, at last, to its knees. It surrendered five days after the Fat Man was detonated, ending the fighting, and the Second World War was finally and officially over on September 2nd.

The atomic bomb remains one of the most controversial topics in human history. As effective as it was at finally ending WWII, the number of innocent lives claimed in Hiroshima and Nagasaki was—and still is—viewed as an atrocity that cannot be justified. Either way, the detonation of nuclear weapons ushered in a whole new era of warfare. No longer would nations simply wade into war with one another. And in the upcoming decades, two juggernauts of international affairs would find themselves head-to-head yet unable to risk the chance of war. Because with nuclear weapons on both sides, the danger wasn't war—it was an apocalypse.

Chapter 17 – Icy Tension

The streets of Dallas, Texas were lined with an exuberant crowd that waved and cheered as the black Lincoln convertible rolled along. Seated in the open-topped limousine, President John F. Kennedy waved to the crowd, flashing a million-dollar smile. Beside him, his pretty wife Jacqueline smiled shyly; she didn't often attend his political events, but on this day, she'd decided to take a drive with her husband. It would be their last few moments together in this life.

It was November 22nd, 1963. The United States was less than twenty years out of the Second World War, and while the industry of war had revitalized its economy, Americans nonetheless found themselves living in tense times. War with the Soviet Union had been looming for years. Everyone knew that the declaration of war would mean the annihilation of millions, considering that both the Soviet Union and the U.S. possessed nuclear weapons. Already, tens of thousands of U.S. troops had been killed in Vietnam and Korea, proxy wars where the two giants battled it out while trampling upon puny innocents. Many American families had sons, brothers, husbands, or fathers fighting a war abroad even though the Second World War had only recently ended. Cinemas were filled with depictions of imagined consequences of nuclear weaponry, wanton destruction, and mutant villains in hideous costume. The Cuban Missile Crisis of 1962 was still fresh in the minds of the people. But Kennedy had been their champion, the man who had somehow managed to negotiate his way out of nuclear war. Now they cheered him on as he soared through the streets on a tide of applause.

But not everyone was joining in on the celebration. On the sixth floor of the Texas School Book Depository, one angry American lay in wait. Lee Harvey Oswald held a Carcano M91/38 bolt action rifle with a telescopic sight. He squinted through the sight in the noonday sun, a thin trickle of sweat running down his face. A troubled young man at only 24, Oswald's mind was dark and turbulent. He'd been born the same year that the Second World War had started and endured a childhood of lack and abuse that had probably left him with profound mental illnesses. Despite this, he succeeded in becoming a U.S. Marine, but his instability led to multiple court-martials, and he eventually left the Marines in 1959.

Oswald never felt that he tasted the freedom that the United States and capitalism had promised him. So, he looked to another system and found it in the Soviet Union. Moving there directly after his discharge and renouncing his U.S. citizenship, he had worked and even married there before returning to the U.S. in 1962.

Now, he silently thanked the U.S. Marines for the one thing it had given them: training as a sharpshooter. Squinting carefully between the crosshairs, he centered his sights on the handsome face of President John F. Kennedy. Then he pulled the trigger.

The United States and the Cold War

The assassination of JFK, surrounded by controversy as it is with many theories still circulating over whether Oswald really was the lone assassin or not, was an extension of a much larger conflict in which the United States found itself shortly after the Second World War.

The landscape of international affairs had been massively changed by WWII. The mighty giant of Nazi Germany had fallen, Japan was decimated, and the victorious Allies, themselves torn after the epic war, were left to pick up the pieces. Among these Allies, two countries found themselves disagreeing profoundly on every level. While the Soviet Union had stood together with the United States to defeat the Axis, the countries could hardly have been more different. Soviet leader Joseph Stalin was a tyrant. He would exact a reign of terror over his country for more than twenty years, and his communist ways deeply chafed against the United States which had been for democracy ever since its inception. To add to this great difference, the Soviet Union blamed the U.S. for millions of Russian deaths in WWII. The Soviets believed that if the U.S. had opened a second front sooner by attacking Nazi Germany from the west, those deaths could have been prevented. Propaganda fueled both sides of the story, and by 1950, the two countries were embroiled in a silent struggle where hope to avoid conflict clashed with determination to defeat the other.

The Hot Spots of the Cold War

In any other era, the U.S. and the Soviet Union would simply have started shooting at each other. But this was post-WWII, and the stakes had changed dramatically the moment Little Boy devastated Hiroshima. Both countries were equipped with hydrogen bombs, superweapons that dwarfed the scope of the atomic bombs that had ravaged the face of Japan. Each country was equipped with weaponry that could wipe out millions, and eager as the countries were to seize each other by the throat, the memory of the destruction at Nagasaki and Hiroshima was still raw and real.

So, the Cold War was waged for about 45 years. Not a single shot was officially fired, although proxy wars popped up all over the globe as pro-Soviet Union communist nations—most notably Cuba, the U.S.' tiny but mighty neighbor just 90 miles from its Floridian coast—clashed with capitalist nations. The Soviet Union wanted to expand, and the United States did its best to thwart that expansion, engaging with communist leaders, most notably in Vietnam and Korea. Tension soared in October 1962 as the Cuban Missile Crisis revealed that Cuban communist leader, Fidel Castro, was holding Soviet nuclear weapons on his little island right on the doorstep of the U.S. Careful negotiations, however, led to the end of the crisis without nuclear detonation.

For decades, the two opponents were engaged in an arms race, each hurrying to keep up with the other, both nations knowing that if one country was more powerful than the other, then war would become inevitable—and so would defeat.

Even Germany, still reeling from the punch that had been the Allied victory, was profoundly affected by the silent struggle. The Berlin Wall was the physical manifestation of the so-called Iron Curtain, a barrier separating communist Eastern Europe with the capitalist West. It was designed to prevent oppressed citizens of East Berlin from fleeing into a place of freedom, and for decades, it caused despair to hundreds in the city.

The Space Race

Another race that the Soviet Union and the United States ran neck and neck in was the hurry to claim the final frontier of space. The Soviet Union initiated the race by launching Sputnik in 1957, the first man-made projectile to make it into orbit. Americans were both startled by the Soviets' technology and frightened by the implications of it. If they could launch a satellite into space, surely sending a nuclear warhead over to the United States would be nothing. In order to counter the Soviet Union's move, the U.S. rushed to join the race, determined to do one better: not only were American scientists going to send humans into space, but they were also going to put a man on the moon.

Once again, the Soviets beat the United States in sending a man to space for the first time. Yuri Alekseyevich Gagarin's historic flight took place on April 12th, 1961, little more than a year before the Cuban Missile Crisis. America swiftly countered by launching Alan Shepard into orbit about a month later. Attempting to boost his worried nation, JFK rashly promised that America would send a man to the moon. Although he'd been dead for almost six years by the time his promise was fulfilled, JFK wasn't wrong. Neil Armstrong and his crew famously landed on the moon on July 20th, 1969. America won the Space Race—and the Soviet Union would eventually lose the Cold War.

In 1989, Russian Premier Mikhail Gorbachev's efforts resulted in the Berlin Wall crashing down. Communism was rapidly on the decline in Eastern Europe, and the Soviet Union itself crumbled under its own weight in 1991. The Cold War was officially at an end. Today, only five communist nations remain. One of these is Cuba, the little island that almost destroyed the United States, and it remains the only communist country in the Western Hemisphere.

Chapter 18 – Freedom on the Home Front

Illustration VI: Martin Luther King Jr. delivers one of his stirring speeches
https://commons.wikimedia.org/w/index.php?curid=1307066

"We have been repeatedly faced with the cruel irony of watching Negro and white boys on TV screens," Martin Luther King Jr. said, "as they kill and die together for a nation that has been unable to seat them together in the same schools."

King's words proved to be controversial, but they weren't untrue. While the United States was waging the Cold War against powers that it viewed as oppressive and cruel, Uncle Sam himself was not innocent of restricting the freedom of some of its own citizens. Even though the country was fighting communism, it was guilty of profound racism, a fact that smacked of hypocrisy to thousands in the "land of the free" itself.

Thus began the Civil Rights Movement that would finish what the Civil War had started, 90 years after the Civil War ended. It was led by a minister named Martin Luther King Jr., and while it was supported by many whites, this time African Americans would get up and fetch their freedom for themselves, following in the footsteps of the nearly 180,000 African American soldiers that had fought alongside their white fellows in the Union Army during the bloody Civil War.

The Civil Rights Movement

Martin Luther King Jr. stared out over a rippling sea of humanity as he spoke. He had his roots in public speaking in a little Baptist church in Montgomery, Alabama; as a minister, he'd grown comfortable addressing the public. For the past six years, as leader of the Southern Christian Leadership Conference, he'd spoken to larger and larger crowds, but this was something else. The March on Washington in August 1963 had encouraged thousands of African Americans to approach Washington, D. C. in support of new legislation proposed by JFK. It was hoped that Kennedy would pass a new Civil Rights Act, one that would finally grant African Americans the rights that they had been promised as early as the Civil War.

Staring out over the vast assembly, perhaps King felt a flutter of nerves. Perhaps he was gripped, momentarily, by terror. But this minister had been fighting the giant of injustice for years—he wasn't about to let a crowd of 250,000 people scare him. Rising up, he delivered a 17-minute speech that would since be immortalized in history under the iconic title of "I Have a Dream." "I have a dream that one day on the red hills of Georgia sons of former slaves and sons of former slave-owners will be able to sit down together at the table of brotherhood," he told them. "I have a dream that one day even in the state of Mississippi, a state sweltering with the heat of injustice, sweltering with the heat of oppression, will be transformed into an oasis of freedom and justice."

Despite the fact that he himself had grown up in an affluent neighborhood of Atlanta, Georgia, King had been witness to the multitude of injustices still suffered by African Americans. Considered as inferior to whites, they struggled under oppressive laws that allowed for segregation from the white citizens. African Americans had to attend separate schools, ride separate buses, and even go to separate public toilets. They were not permitted to eat with or marry whites. Southern states—the old slave states—still clung to prejudice, embracing the slogan of "separate but equal." Separation in itself would have been enough of an insult, yet when it came to equality, the slogan was nothing but an empty promise. Those facilities designated for African Americans were often of much poorer quality than those given to whites. To make matters worse, African Americans were treated poorly by many whites, often even with violence for no reason other than that their skin color was dark.

Rosa Parks became the accidental catalyst for the Civil Rights Movement. It was an evening in the winter of 1955 when she took her seat on the bus home from work, tired after her long day. She sat in the first row of the "colored" section of the bus, looking forward to a peaceful ride home. As the bus filled up, people were forced to stand. Noticing that white people were standing while black passengers were sitting, the bus driver moved the colored section sign back a row, ordering that Rosa and the others in her row stand up. However, Rosa refused to budge, and in retaliation, the bus driver called the police.

Her arrest sparked the Civil Rights Movement, which would finally abolish segregation for good. In protest against her unfair arrest, King led a group of African American community leaders to boycott the bus system for more than a year. This forced the Supreme Court to put an end to segregated seating in 1956.

The New Civil Rights Acts

President Dwight D. Eisenhower signed a new Civil Rights Act in 1957. This act made it against the law to attempt to prevent anyone from voting; while African Americans were certainly still oppressed by whites, at least now it was a criminal act to stop them from having a say in whom they wanted to govern them. It was the first time that civil rights would be changed in the legislation since the Reconstruction of the 1860s and 1870s.

This was progress, but still, African Americans struggled under many issues, including voting literacy tests, unfair tests that African Americans were forced to take for the right to vote. While many African Americans did pass, often these tests were specifically rigged to be excruciatingly hard to pass, discouraging people from even attempting them. Public facilities were also still segregated. President John F. Kennedy, however, planned to change that. When he announced his intentions to work on new legislation that would reduce segregation, King jumped at the opportunity to demonstrate support for this idea. Knowing that, while King's efforts had all been solely peaceful, civil disobedience and violence had still characterized much of the Civil Rights Movement, and he knew he needed to encourage the people to express their opinions in a peaceful manner. The March on Washington succeeded in this aim.

Undoubtedly influenced by the support shown by African Americans, President Lyndon B. Johnson signed the Civil Rights Act of 1964 after the death of Kennedy. This act leveled the playing field by ordering public facilities to be integrated and making equal employment opportunities a requirement by law. Voting literacy tests, however, would remain until the Voting Rights Act of 1965.

Finally—by law at least—African Americans had equal opportunities. Americans of all races were free now, but Martin Luther King Jr. himself would hardly have any time to enjoy the newfound freedom. He was killed on April 4th, 1968, probably by James Earl Ray who had racial motives for murdering King.

Chapter 19 – Terror and Its War

"I know we're all going to die," Thomas Burnett, Jr., said over the phone. "There's three of us who are going to do something about it." He paused, squeezing his eyes shut, holding his cellphone to his face in a trembling hand. The rumble of jet engines was all around him, a familiar sound that he'd heard many times during his successful career as a business executive. Yet this time he knew it was different. He knew that his words were true, yet there was no real fear in his voice. Ever since his premature birth, Thomas had known in his soul that he was going to die young, even though he was a healthy man. A pious Catholic, he was convinced that God had some spectacular plan for his life—so convinced that he and his wife, Deena, had made plans for the event of his early death.

But now, at this moment, with hijackers controlling the plane and panicking passengers around him, Thomas felt a piercing agony as he thought of Deena and their small children. "I love you, honey," he whispered. Then he put down the phone, grabbed a fire extinguisher that he held like a weapon, and walked toward the cockpit.

Minutes later, United Flight 93 plunged to the earth at more than five hundred miles per hour. The plane smashed into the dirt in a wide-open field near Shanksville, Pennsylvania, disintegrating on impact and killing the 44 people on board. Not a single person on the ground was wounded.

The same could not be said for New York City or Washington, D. C. Both of those cities were burning.

The Tragedy That Shaped a Nation

The September 11th, 2001, terrorist attacks sent a shockwave of horror all over the world. They started early that morning when 19 Islamic terrorists put into action the plan that they'd been painstakingly working on for more than a year. Osama bin Laden, leader of the terrorist group known as Al-Qaeda, was behind it all, but he wasn't actually there. The terrorists who executed the plan all knew that they were going to be killed, but they had been brainwashed thoroughly enough to believe that killing thousands of people would earn them the right to heaven.

The terrorists hijacked four planes that morning. The first crashed into the north tower of the World Trade Center, an American icon standing 110 stories tall in New York City, at 8:46 in the morning. It smashed into the building about two-thirds of the way up, and suddenly, New York was on fire. About twenty minutes later, the second plane was deliberately crashed into the south tower, and the Twin Towers burned together. Sirens filled the streets of NYC as thousands of first responders rushed to the scene.

At 9:37, a third plane was flown directly into the Pentagon in Washington, D. C. The impact ripped a gaping, burning wound in the side of the building. Soon after, Flight 93 fell out of the sky and into the Pennsylvanian field. It was obvious to Americans that this was no tragic accident—this was a deliberate attack by enemies of the United States. The aim was to spread terror and to show the military giant that it was not invincible; that without any weapons, the terrorists could take everyday objects in the life of the average American and use them to sow utter destruction on their home turf.

By the end of the attacks, almost three thousand people were dead. President George W. Bush found himself in the difficult position of having to lend a voice to a nation that was terrified, heartbroken, and shocked what it had just seen. His words, however, would characterize the American response to this terror attack. "These acts shatter steel," he said, referring to the mangled metal guts of the Twin Towers that had been shown spilling gruesomely from the ruined buildings. "But they cannot dent the steel of American resolve."

Osama bin Laden's "Letter to America," written in 2002, did little to advance his aim of terrifying the people of the United States. In it, he revealed his motive for the attacks which have gone down in history simply as "9/11." He pointed to the American culture, which was profoundly different from the extremist Islam religion that bin Laden and his followers strictly adhered to, and to America's involvement in the Middle East. The United States had been involved in the Persian Gulf War and had kept troops stationed in Saudi Arabia ever since. Considering that Mecca and Medina—places of tremendous religious significance in Islam—are located in Saudi Arabia, the presence of American troops was an insult to some of the more radical Muslims.

Bin Laden also saw America's support of the prominently Jewish country, Israel, as an affront to all of his ideologies. This all resulted in his plan to kill thousands of people who had very little to do with the war itself.

The Gulf War

The attacks of September 11th were preceded by the Gulf War, a brief but bloody conflict in which the United States once again proved itself to possess one of the most powerful military forces in the world. It all started on August 2nd, 1990, when Saddam Hussein—the dictatorial leader of Iraq—invaded the neighboring country of Kuwait with the goal of annexing its oil reserves. The United Nations was appalled by this new move by a brutal dictator and decided that the expansion of Iraqi power would have to be stopped at all costs. It banned trade with Iraq worldwide and demanded that Hussein remove his troops from Kuwait, but the Iraqi leader was adamant: he wanted Kuwait, and no amount of threats would stop him. On August 8th, he made his annexation of Kuwait official.

The U.S. and its allies responded by launching a massive operation, known as Operation Desert Shield, bringing hundreds of thousands of troops into Saudi Arabia in order to prevent Iraq from invading there as well—a war that may have had devastating consequences on the world's oil reserves. Alongside new allies from Arabia and Egypt, the U.S. then launched a two-pronged attack on Iraqi troops in Kuwait. The airborne part of the offensive was known as Operation Desert Storm; below the jets and bombers that screamed through the air and pounded the Iraqis with sophisticated explosives and missiles, Operation Desert Sabre, borne forward by American tanks, took on their enemies at ground level. The offensive began in January 1991 and proved to be far too much for Iraq to handle. The U.S. utterly overwhelmed its enemies. By February 28th, a ceasefire was called, with at least 20,000 Iraqi troops dead. The U.S. and its allies lost only about 300.

The Gulf War was another resounding victory for the United States, but the Middle East did not take kindly to this profoundly Western giant flexing its muscles so close to home. American involvement in the Gulf War was likely part of what precipitated the attacks of September 2001, and thus, this war sparked a far larger conflict that still rages today: The War on Terror.

The War on Terror

The United States has been involved in multiple overseas conflicts during the 21st century. The Gulf War was quickly followed by the Iraq War, which began in 2003 when the United States invaded Iraq to overthrow the tyrannical Saddam Hussein. This war ended in 2011 after the Iraqi Special Tribunal found Hussein guilty of crimes against humanity and hanged him in 2006.

Since October 7th, 2001, the U.S. has also been involved in a war in Afghanistan, its original operation codenamed Operation Enduring Freedom—an inspiring moniker in the wake of the September 11th attacks. While that operation has since ended, the war rages on through Operation Freedom's Sentinel. Its purpose is to deny al-Qaeda and the Taliban a safe base of operations. It can be loosely termed the Afghanistan theater of America's "War on Terror," a series of military operations launched against terrorist groups across the globe that have been raging since 9/11.

At least one important victory has already been won in the War on Terror. Almost ten years after orchestrating the attacks that devastated America and the world, Osama bin Laden was finally found hiding out in Pakistan. A group of U.S. Navy Seals was sent in to capture him, and bin Laden was killed during the attempt to arrest him. The War on Terror still goes on, but one of its leading commanders on the side of terrorism is gone for good.

The Election of the First Black President

"Tonight, we give thanks to the countless intelligence and counterterrorism professionals who've worked tirelessly to achieve this outcome," the United States president announced to his people on the evening of bin Laden's death. "The American people do not see their work, nor know their names. But tonight, they feel the satisfaction of their work and the result of their pursuit of justice."

The president who addressed the people on the night of May 2nd, 2011, to announce that Osama bin Laden was killed was President Barack Obama. Not only had he been a Nobel Peace Prize laureate in 2009, but Obama was also the first African American president ever to be elected. In 2008—143 years after slavery was abolished and 44 years after Martin Luther King Jr. at last won his fight for equality—Obama was elected president of the United States. Less than a century and a half before, African Americans had labored beneath the snapping whips and brutal words of overseers; now, an African American was sworn in as president. Despite the chaos in the U.S. and the world, one beacon of progress at least shone through the smoke of 9/11.

Conclusion

Nobody can deny that the United States is a big place. Considering that the United Kingdom can fit into the area of the U.S. about 40 times, the sheer area of the country is impressive, and its diversity even more so. Yet the U.S. is not large only in size but in everything it does: its wars, its successes, its epic blunders, its individuality, its willingness to set a trend, its courageous ability to go against the status quo in the name of freedom, its spirit of entrepreneurship, and its capacity for invention and innovation.

The United States has undeniably been one of the most influential countries in the world. From its books and movies to its multitude of inventions, the U.S. has seeped its way into the collective consciousness of most of the modern world. In fact, despite the fact that the U.S. has vociferously advocated against expansionism for more than a century, it's not unfair to say that its culture has taken over much of the world. The United States hasn't added to its considerable girth since Hawaii's admission in 1959, yet somehow, it's everywhere.

Everyone who has ever turned on an electric light bulb, flown in an airplane, ridden in a Ford car, said the word "OK," been on Facebook, or watched a movie has sipped from the deep well of American innovation. This looming giant has made its share of mistakes, inspiring criticism from many different quarters all over the world, yet everyone knows exactly where they were on 9/11. Anyone old enough to remember can recall the moment when they heard about the first plane that crashed into that north tower on that fateful morning.

There have been centuries of struggle. There have been bloody defeats and tremendous victories. Heroes and villains have risen up and struggled over enormous issues that sometimes the rest of the world has refused to face. Through revolution and civil war, through protest and depression, through colonization and tragedy, all the way from the Lost Colony to the War on Terror, the United States has emerged: a military juggernaut, a cultural trendsetter, and above all, the land of the free. The home of the brave.

Part 2: The American Revolution

A Captivating Guide to the American Revolutionary War and the United States of America's Struggle for Independence from Great Britain

Introduction

The United States has been one of the world's greatest powers for almost a century but began its life as a collection of thirteen colonies in the mighty British Empire. The way in which Americans from the Thirteen Colonies rebelled against British rule and successfully secured independence in war was in many ways miraculous. It marked a turning point in history, not only in terms of the birth of a new state, but because this state was founded on the principles of republicanism, freedoms, and rights, something very distinct from the societies of the old European kingdoms and empires. American independence was by no means inevitable. The tale of the birth of the United States is a story of British colonial mismanagement, of a small and dedicated group of remarkable individuals who found a common interest in defending their livelihoods. It is also a story of Britain's European rivals seeking to exploit British weakness with little eventual gain to show for it. The Thirteen Colonies had been brought closer together by the struggle against the British, but the weakness of the central government threatened the survival of the United States almost from the moment peace was signed with Britain. Although the era of the Founding Fathers may seem remote to most people, they continue to shape contemporary political debate.

This book presents a general outline of the American Revolution, focusing largely on the period between the outbreak of rebellion in 1765 until the ratification of the US Constitution in 1789. In homage to the original thirteen colonies, the book is divided into thirteen chapters. Chapter 1 outlines the context of the Thirteen Colonies as British colonial possessions. Chapters 2-4 deals with American responses to British attempts to raise taxation in the Thirteen Colonies, resulting in a cycle of escalating tensions which finally resulted in the outbreak of military hostilities. Chapter 5 assesses the strengths and weaknesses of the American and British armies at the outbreak of the war, and how these dynamics shifted over the course of the conflict. Chapters 6-10 cover the period of military hostilities from the Declaration of Independence in 1776 to the British surrender at Yorktown in 1781, which would lead to the signing of the Treaty of Paris in 1783. Chapters 11 and 12 cover the uneasy period of peace during which the central government was unable to resolve disputes between individual states, resulting in the adoption of a Constitution which strengthened the powers of central government. Chapter 13 briefly outlines the key debates and themes that would run through American history in the half-century following the adoption of the Constitution.

The United States of America has existed as an independent country for two and a half centuries. In contrast to the Holy Roman Empire, which lasted for one thousand years (800-1806), or the Ottoman Empire which endured for over six hundred (1299-1923), the United States remains relatively young. The United States was conceived as a political experiment and a radical departure from the organizing principles of most European states. It was far from certain that the Union would endure in its early years, and the state once again risked disintegration during the Civil War in the 1860s. In an era where political discourse is becoming increasingly polarized, it is worth reflecting on the circumstances of America's foundation and how states with competing interests and statesmen with competing visions joined together to achieve independence and created a political arena for their new conceptions of government. Some of their compromises, such as those over slavery, were misguided and incompatible with their founding aims, but were made on the basis of political expediency at a time when the American republic was constantly under threat from external enemies, including erstwhile allies. This book seeks to remind readers that the United States was created by a set of founding fathers who had competing visions, but shared a common set of principles dedicated to life, liberty, and the pursuit of happiness.

Chapter 1 – Colonial America

The history of the United States of America begins with European settlement of the New World, or the American continent. Although Viking settlers established a presence in Newfoundland in modern-day Canada, it was not until Christopher Columbus' so-called "Discovery of the Americas" in 1492 when European states began to colonize the Americas. Columbus, serving the Spanish monarchy, paved the path for Spanish colonization of Central America and much of South America. The remaining part—Brazil—was settled by the Portuguese. In the process, the colonizers subjugated the native populations. Through a combination of death by disease and intermarriage with the settlers, the native population declined and was assimilated into the culture of the European colonizers. As the first explorers, Spanish control of the American continent extended as far north as the modern American states of Florida, Texas, and California.

Economic factors served as the primary motivation for colonial activity in the Americas. Each year Spanish galleons laden with gold and silver would sail across the Atlantic to fill the coffers of the king's treasury. In the long run, this would prove to be a mixed blessing, as the import of such large quantities of American gold and silver into Europe devalued the currency. Moreover, these rich treasure ships served as targets for pirates and corsairs. Although in the 16th century the English Royal Navy could not challenge Spain on equal terms, the English sailor Sir Francis

Drake began his career looting Spanish ships in the Caribbean and sending the treasure to Queen Elizabeth I's (1558-1603) Exchequer, or treasury. Over the 17th century, Spanish naval supremacy would come under threat of the so-called Maritime Powers—the Netherlands, which won independence from Spain in 1648 after an eight-year struggle, and England, which became Britain after the Act of Union with Scotland in 1707. Taking advantage of declining Spanish naval control over the Atlantic, the British and Dutch established colonies in the Caribbean and in North America, and they were not the only European powers to do so. France would take control of large parts of modern-day United States and Canada. Sweden, Denmark, and even the tiny Duchy of Courland in the Baltic also established colonies in the Caribbean.

British, French, and Dutch settlements in the Americas was also the result of economic motivations, though the source of wealth was of a different nature than that of Spain's colonial possessions. While North America and the Caribbean did not have the rich deposits of precious metals that Spanish possessions in Mexico and Peru enjoyed, the climate was conducive to growing cash crops such as sugar, coffee, and cotton. While these crops were highly lucrative, their cultivation was highly labor-intensive, and the European colonialists lacked the manpower to fully exploit the wealth of the land. As a result of this demand for labor, a triangular trade developed between Europe, Africa, and the Americas, controlled by the Europeans. The Europeans sent manufactured goods to Africa in exchange for slaves, who were transported to the North American colonies to work the land. The harvested crops and raw materials would then be imported into Europe for consumption and further processing. These goods would be used to buy more slaves from Africa, and so the trade continued, operating until the 19th century.

British settlement in North America was largely restricted to the Eastern seaboard, from Massachusetts in the North to Georgia in the South. In addition to its Canadian possessions, British colonists established thirteen colonies over the course of a century between the 1620s and 1733, when the colony of Georgia was founded. British settlement did not extend much farther west due to the Appalachian Mountains which served as a geographical barrier to further movement. The British also came into conflict with native populations who often emerged victorious in small-scale engagements with the outnumbered colonists. They were also forced to compete with European rivals.; in fact, some British colonies were originally founded by rival European powers. The city of New York was founded by Dutch colonists as New Amsterdam before the British seized control in 1664 and renamed the city after the Duke of York. The surrounding Dutch province, New Netherland, was also renamed New York. While the Dutch were easily defeated, the French settled and lay claim to the Louisiana Territory, comprising of Eastern Canada and much of the Mississippi River Basin on the opposite side of the Appalachians. Meanwhile, the Spanish had a foothold in Florida. As a result, British settlement south of the St. Lawrence River was largely confined to the Thirteen Colonies.

Although the British colonists in America were mostly loyal subjects of the British monarch, they did not share a common "American" identity and instead identified with the colonies in which they lived. A series of interrelated geographical, social, and economic factors contributed to the divergence in the cultural development of the Thirteen Colonies. British possessions in North America could be divided into three distinct groups: New England (New Hampshire, Massachusetts Bay, Providence and Rhode Island, Connecticut); the Middle Colonies (New York, New Jersey, Pennsylvania, Delaware); the Southern Colonies (Virginia, Maryland, North Carolina, South Carolina, Georgia). While most economic activity in the colonies was dominated by agriculture, this was especially true of the Southern Colonies. These large territories supported a plantation economy which depended heavily on slave labor. Slave revolts were frequent but small-scale and easily suppressed. In the smaller colonies in New England, the climate and geography were not conducive to cash crops. The economy was geared toward small-scale industrial activities including the manufacture of rum and shipbuilding. The major ports of New York and Boston, Massachusetts became thriving centers of international trade. Slavery existed in the North, but slaves were employed as domestic servants rather than agricultural laborers.

The economic potential of the New World attracted large numbers of immigrants. Thousands of settlers were enticed by the opportunities offered by colonial companies and made the journey across the Atlantic.

Although the voyage was perilous and settlers were prone to succumbing to disease, survivors could look forward to prosperous and comfortable lifestyles. Unlike in Europe, where land was expensive and owned by aristocrats, land was cheap and plentiful for the European colonists who arrived in the New World. The lower classes enjoyed better living standards than they had in Europe. Through a combination of natural population growth and immigration, the European population in the Thirteen Colonies increased fivefold between 1650 and 1700 from 55,000 to 265,000. The population would reach one million by 1750. In 1751, the Pennsylvanian botanist John Bartram portrayed the Thirteen Colonies as paradise on earth:

> England already has an uninterrupted line of well-peopled provinces on the coast, successively begun within less than 150 years. Every year they are augmented by an accession of subjects, excited by the desire of living under governments and laws formed on the most excellent model upon earth. In vain do we look for an equal prosperity among the plantations of other European nations.

The waves of immigration into the New World was not only motivated by economic factors, but also by religion. Since the Protestant Reformation in 1517, Europe was embroiled in religious conflict between Catholics and Protestants, which reached a climax with the outbreak of the Thirty Years' War (1618-48). Even within Protestant countries, more radical sects came into conflict with established Anglican and Lutheran churches and suffered prosecution. In 1620, the Pilgrim Fathers sailed from Plymouth in southern England to the New World and established Plymouth Colony in Massachusetts Bay, the first permanent colony in New England and the second British colony after Jamestown, Virginia. The pilgrims were Puritans, a radical Protestant sect which sought to remain separate from the Anglican Church. In 1607, they fled the political and religious turmoil of England and settled in the Netherlands, which was relatively tolerant and open to radical Protestant refugees. The difficulties in learning the Dutch language and in finding employment in the Netherlands caused many to return to England by 1617. They then conceived of a plan to sail across the Atlantic and establish a colony in the New World, allowing them to retain their English identity and live in a society governed by their religious principles.

Due to the legacy of the Pilgrim Fathers, the entire region of New England came to be dominated by Puritans. The other colonies were more diverse in terms of religiosity. The Middle Colonies were especially receptive to foreign immigration. A large Irish population—both Protestant and Catholic—settled in New York. German Lutherans migrated in large numbers to Pennsylvania. Anglicans and Baptists dominated the South. Although British immigrants to the Thirteen Colonies were outnumbered by other nationalities during the 18th century, the existing Anglo-Saxon population naturally increased over the course of the 17th century to the extent that a majority of the European population in North America had British ancestry.

The Thirteen Colonies diverged not only in their religious identities and their economic structures, but also in their political structures. While the French and Spanish monarchies exercised direct rule over their territories in the New World, British colonization of the Americas began as private ventures. The earliest colony, Virginia, was owned by the Virginia Company, which was established to finance the colonization. These colonies were known as charter colonies since they were established by companies which had been granted a royal charter. Most colonies were initially established by charter companies. Since the colonization was privately financed, the ventures came at no cost to the British monarchy. The Crown would grant the colonists a charter establishing the rules of government, but charter colonies effectively ruled themselves. All the colonies operated under English common law, and each colony had a bicameral legislature based on the British Parliament in Westminster. The lower house, or assembly, was chosen by electors—largely male property-owning Christians. The upper house, or council, would be appointed by the governor, usually a royal appointee. The powers of the legislatures depended on the extent to which governors played an active role in political life. At the local level, forms of government differed between the regions. The Northern colonies were more urbanized and town councils were the primary form of local government. The rural Southern Colonies relied on rule at the county level. Both town and county rule co-existed in the Middle Colonies.

Over the course of the 17th century, the British state began to take a greater direct interest in North America. Wars against the Dutch and French in Europe spilled over into the New World. The British armed forces were employed against the Dutch and French in North America and seized control of their territories. The Crown granted these territories to trusted individuals and families who would rule the territory as a representative of the British sovereign. Colonies governed by such individuals were known as proprietary colonies. When New York was seized from the Dutch, King Charles II (1660-85) granted the colony to younger brother James, Duke of York, to rule as a proprietary colony. When the Duke of York became King James II (1685-88), New York became a royal colony directly ruled by the king. Another major proprietary colony was Pennsylvania, which was granted by King Charles II to William Penn in 1681 in recompense for a debt he owed to Penn's late father, Admiral William Penn. Over the course of the 17th century, many charter companies were deprived of their charters as the British Crown assumed direct rule. These royal colonies were ruled by governors appointed by the British sovereign. Although most of the colonies would fall under direct rule, during the first half of the 18th century, royal governors continued to allow colonial governments a significant degree of autonomy. In an arrangement which came to be called Salutary Neglect, the governors appointed by the British monarch were happy enough to allow the colonists effective self-government so long as they continued to generate tax revenue for the British state through their economic activities.

Chapter 2 – The Seven Years' War and Its Consequences

The British government's policy of Salutary Neglect was a successful formula until the Thirteen Colonies were threatened by war. Although the colonists were keen to take up arms to defend themselves, the government in London was suspicious of colonial attempts to establish a military force independent from London's command. A previous attempt by the New England Colonies to create an alliance to protect against French and Indian threats contributed to the British government's decision to revoke the charters of the colonies. North America was relatively tranquil during the first half of the 18th century, but conflicts in Europe were starting to spread in the New World. The War of Spanish Succession (1701-14) had already seen British and French armies clash in North America. In 1740, Europe was rocked by a political earthquake in the form of King Frederick II of Prussia (1740-86), who would redraw the map of Europe by seizing Silesia from the Austrian Habsburg Empire. The shock to the Habsburgs was so great that they opted for an alliance with France—the Empire's archenemy for over two centuries—in an effort to regain the territories they lost to Prussia.

In 1756, an alliance consisting of Austria, France, and Russia declared war on Frederick in an effort to restrain Frederick's expansionist aims. In Europe, Prussia could only count on Great Britain as an ally. While the

British Crown had a presence in continental Europe by virtue of the fact that King George II (1727-60) was also Elector of Hanover, the British and Hanoverian armies were of limited value to Frederick and could not make a major difference in land battles. Britain's strength lay primarily in its formidable navy, which could attack French overseas colonies and distract attention from the European theater. The border between British and French territories in North America was disputed by both sides and this influenced decision-making in London. The ensuing Seven Years' War (1756-63) thus acquired international dimensions. While the European theater may be considered a life-or-death struggle for Frederick the Great's Prussia against three much larger enemies, the Seven Years' War was also part of an Anglo-French struggle for global hegemony encompassing the Americas as well as Asia and Africa.

The North American theater of the Seven Years' War was also known as the French and Indian War. Hostilities began in 1754 as the French and British disputed the border between their respective territories. The French constructed a series of forts along the Ohio River Valley. In May, British colonial militia under the command of 22-year-old Colonel George Washington ambushed a French party on its way to Fort Duquesne, a French fort which occupied a major strategic position at the junction of three rivers. Washington ordered the construction of nearby Fort Necessity as a base. However, he was soon forced to surrender the fort to the French when counterattacked. In June 1754, representatives from eleven colonies met in Albany, New York in an effort to establish a confederation which would provide for mutual protection and allow the colonies to present a united front in diplomatic negotiations with Indian tribes. The plan for a union was developed by Benjamin Franklin, a Pennsylvanian polymath who was heavily involved in Pennsylvanian politics. Franklin encouraged support for his plan by producing a cartoon featuring a snake divided into several parts with the caption "Join or Die." Franklin proposed that the new entity would be ruled by a president appointed by the British Crown. While the Albany Congress passed an amended version of Franklin's plan, it was not ratified by the colonial legislatures nor by the British Crown. The dream of union between the Thirteen Colonies would have to wait.

Hostilities in North America intensified once the French and British became embroiled in the war in Europe. The British government began to send regular army units to America commanded by British officers. Although the British authorities demanded that the colonists provide material support for the war effort, they looked down on the colonial militia, causing considerable resentment among men who considered themselves Englishmen. Meanwhile, reinforcements from the French regular army were also sent to American shores. During the initial stages of the war, the French armies enjoyed several successes. Since the French population in North America was a mere five percent of the British population, they decided to form alliances with Indian tribes to bolster their numbers. In August 1757, a French and Indian force under the command of General Louis-Joseph de Montcalm laid siege to Fort William Henry in New York. The commander of the British garrison negotiated a surrender to the besieging army, but Montcalm's Indian allies, deprived of war trophies, broke the agreement and massacred hundreds of British inhabitants, including women and children. The notorious incident strengthened the resolve of the British army and influenced the decisions of the British military command for the remainder of the war.

Military fortunes turned in Britain's favor after the end of 1757. The British successfully held off further assaults from Montcalm. While British reinforcements and supplies were regularly shipped to North America from Britain, the British Royal Navy's naval supremacy hindered French attempts to supply Montcalm. In the summer of 1757, the British government was reorganized following earlier defeats. As secretary of state for the Southern Department in the British government, William Pitt took charge of British foreign policy and the war effort. He proposed a new strategy to tie down French armies in Europe by raising a British army for operations in the European continent, while offering Frederick the Great large subsidies to keep large Prussian armies in the field. In the meantime, the Royal Navy would support expeditions to seize French colonies around the world. Already in 1757 British forces achieved success against the French in India. At the Battle of Plassey in June, Robert Clive led the British East India Company's private army to victory over a French ally in the region. Clive's victory established British rule in Bengal and eventually enabled the British Empire—through the East India Company—to control the entirety of the Indian subcontinent.

In North America, Pitt's strategy called for the conquest of Canada. In 1758, a British force commanded by General Jeffrey Amherst successfully captured the fort of Louisbourg on the mouth of the St. Lawrence River. This enabled the British to proceed to Quebec, the capital of New France and a key strategic target for British forces. Pitt appointed General James Wolfe to lead an army to lay siege to Montcalm's forces in Quebec. Wolfe's army, which was outnumbered by the enemy, lay siege to the city in June 1759. The British maintained the siege for three months, but illness began to spread through the British camp and Wolfe opted for decisive measures. On September 13th, he launched a daring assault at the Plains of Abraham overlooking the city. Wolfe took Montcalm by surprise and the momentum of his men was unstoppable. The British won a famous victory in less than an hour, but Wolfe was killed as he led his men on a charge. Montcalm was mortally wounded and died the following day. Wolfe's victory soon led to the British conquest of New France. French efforts to launch an invasion of Britain failed, and British forces captured Montreal the following year. The war in Europe would last until 1763, but British victory in North America was effectively secured by 1760.

The British may have won the war in North America against the French, but they lost the peace. The war amplified a range of disputes between London and the colonies, and the British government sought to take a more active role in the governance of the Thirteen Colonies. During the 18th century, political power in the United Kingdom gradually transferred from the king (or queen) to Parliament. The British Parliament consisted of an upper house, the House of Lords, and a lower house, the House of Commons. Both chambers sat in opposite wings of the Palace of Westminster. The Lords were unelected landowners who inherited their titles and estates, or were granted them by the king. The Commons was made up of Members of Parliament (MPs) chosen by the electorate—although the vote was limited to a fairly small number of property-owning men. The king would then appoint a government of ministers who could command the support of both Houses of Parliament. The British political system was dominated by two parties, the Tories, who tended to support the king, and the Whigs, who envisaged a greater role for Parliament. However, party affiliations were fluid and governments usually included both Whig and Tory ministers. Since 1721, the British government was led by a prime minister. The first man to assume this role, Robert Walpole (1721-42), proved himself indispensable to King George I (1714-27) in his interactions with Parliament. Walpole remained in this exalted role until 1742 and continues to hold the record for the longest-serving British prime minister.

During the Seven Years' War, the Duke of Newcastle, Thomas Pelham-Holles, served as prime minister (1757-62), although William Pitt effectively shared power as Southern Secretary. Newcastle's Whig government fell in 1762 following the intervention of King George III (1760-1820). The new king believed the Newcastle-Pitt ministry was encroaching on royal privileges and instead championed the cause of the Earl of Bute, who became the first Tory prime minister (1762-63). Although the British were victorious in the Seven Years' War, the conflict was expensive and Britain's national debt doubled as a result. Lord Bute's government believed that the colonies had not contributed enough resources to support the British army in America. Accordingly, the government took steps to establish a greater degree of central control over the colonies. The Westminster government provided for a British regular army of 10,000 men to be stationed in North America to protect colonial interests, which would be paid for by the colonials.

Unsurprisingly, the colonies resisted efforts to be ruled from London and defended their autonomy. The colonials had not been allowed to fight to protect themselves, but were asked to pay for British regular troops. The British army's dismissive attitude toward the colonial militia also led to resentment. During the war, George Washington, the young officer who was involved in the outbreak of hostilities, had been promoted to the rank of brigadier general in the colonial militia. In 1758 he took part in operations which finally led to the conquest of Fort Duquesne, which was replaced by Fort Pitt—now the city of Pittsburgh. Washington hoped to be recognized as an officer in the British regular army, but he was denied the royal commission he dearly sought.

The Seven Years' War had strengthened the bonds between the colonies, despite the failure of the Albany Congress. After seeing off the threat from the French armies, the American colonials recognized the new threat posed by their imperial masters, the British government. Increasing tensions between the two sides became apparent in 1763 following the signing of the Treaty of Paris, which officially ended the Seven Years' War and ceded French territory to Great Britain. Under the terms of the treaty, France ceded its claims east of the Mississippi River to Britain. The population of the existing thirteen British colonies in North America expected to settle in these newly conquered territories. Instead, the colonies once again had cause to feel surrounded and isolated. On October 7th, 1763, King George issued a royal proclamation which confined colonial settlement east of the Appalachian Mountains. Territories west of this line became part of an Indian reserve. During the Seven Years' War, the British had promised the Indians that they would be able to remain on their lands if they abandoned their support for the French. The British decided to honor these promises, rather than the promise of expansion they made with the colonials. Only the British Crown could decide to move this demarcation line farther to the west. Over the subsequent decade, colonial and British land speculators successfully lobbied the British government to open up territories farther west. However, by this time, the Thirteen Colonies were in open rebellion against the British government.

Chapter 3 – Taxation Without Representation

The Treaty of Paris which ended the Seven Years' War was received poorly in London as well as in the colonies. Lord Bute's leniency toward Britain's foes in the war cost him political popularity and he was deprived of King George's favor. In April 1763, the king dismissed Bute and appointed George Grenville (1763-65) in his stead. Although Grenville identified as a Whig, he had been a minister in Bute's government and he retained most of his predecessor's ministers. Accordingly, he pursued a similar policy with regard to Britain's relationship with its North American colonies. In April 1764 Parliament passed the Sugar Act, which aimed to strengthen enforcement of collection of customs duties on sugar. The new legislation damaged the economy of the New England ports which was heavily dependent on the sugar trade. Trade flows were diverted from New England toward the British West Indies, which was unaffected by the tax. A small number of merchants in New England staged protests against the measure by boycotting British goods, though these acts of resistance were of low intensity and were restricted to New England.

The Sugar Act would raise insufficient revenue to finance British military presence in North America. When he introduced the Sugar Act, Grenville announced that "it may be proper to charge certain stamp duties in the said colonies and plantations." Stamp duties were already in the statute books in the United Kingdom, and proved to be an efficient method for the British Exchequer to collect revenue. All documents could only have legal force if stamped, and anything that did not bear a stamp could be rejected as void. The prospect of a new tax made the colonies anxious, and they sought more information on the proposed measures. When colonial agents met with Grenville in May 1764, they insisted that the taxes should be raised by colonial assemblies rather than the British Parliament. Grenville reassured them that he was willing to consider any measure so long as it raised the required revenue, though he provided little insight into how he intended to implement the tax.

Over the following months, it became clear that Grenville was ignoring the colonials' request and planned to impose a direct tax from Parliament. In February 1765, another group of colonial agents met with Grenville to discuss the proposals. The four-man delegation was composed of Benjamin Franklin of Pennsylvania, Jared Ingersoll and Richard Jackson, both representing Connecticut, and South Carolina's Charles Garth. Both Jackson and Garth were also MPs representing English constituencies. The colonial agents repeated their recommendation that the Americans should be allowed to tax themselves. Jackson argued that if Parliament were given the right to directly tax the colonies, royal governors would no longer need to convene the colonial assemblies to raise taxes. Grenville dismissed these concerns. The colonial agents failed to stop Grenville from introducing the tax, which passed through both Houses of Parliament in February and received royal assent in March 1765. Under the terms of the tax, the British government imposed a tax on all commercially printed material in the colonies. The highest taxes applied to court documents and land grants. Taxes also applied to playing cards and dice, a key aspect of 18th-century entertainment and social life. The tax would be enforced by a stamp distributor, a public official appointed by London.

The Stamp Act soon became the most contested item of legislation in the history of British rule in America. The colonials challenged the legislation, not only due to its economic effects, but on grounds of political principles. The debate over the Stamp Act was centered on two opposing interpretations of the British constitution. Grenville and his ministers were adamant believers in the doctrine of parliamentary sovereignty. Under this principle, the British Parliament in Westminster was the supreme lawmaker of the land, and its right to make laws could not be challenged by any other entity or individual. The colonials, on the other hand, who regarded themselves as subjects of the British Crown and entitled to all the rights enjoyed by the imperial center, believed that they had the right to be taxed only if they consented through representative institutions. As early as 1754, Benjamin Franklin raised this issue when he wrote that "it is supposed an undoubted right of Englishmen not to be taxed but by their own consent given through their representatives." The American colonies were not represented in the British Parliament in Westminster and were instead ruled from London by royal governors. The colonies had their own representative legislative assemblies which were more than capable of raising taxes. Consequently, Franklin and others would argue that taxes could only be levied by colonial assemblies rather than directly by the Parliament in Westminster.

A series of protests spread throughout the Thirteen Colonies under the slogan "No taxation without representation." The scale of the protests was unexpected for both the British government and the American representatives stationed in London. Despite their opposition to the Stamp Act, Benjamin Franklin encouraged a friend to seek appointment as a stamp distributor, and Jared Ingersoll successfully secured for himself the office in Connecticut. The common people refused to use the stamps and ended up burning them instead. Protestors took to the streets and targeted stamp distributors, sometimes even before they disembarked from their ships after the journey from Britain. Their effigies were paraded in the streets and mock executions were staged. In August 1765, a radical organization called the Sons of Liberty was formed in Massachusetts. This group aimed to remove Andrew Oliver, who had been chosen as the stamp distributor for Massachusetts. The Sons of Liberty mobilized the mobs in Boston and encouraged them to target Oliver. He eventually resigned after the rioters burned down his office building. Lieutenant Governor Thomas Hutchinson, a known supporter of the Stamp Act, was also targeted and his house ransacked. Radicals from other colonies soon established their own branches of the Sons of

Liberty, using the same methods of intimidation against their stamp distributors. By November, twelve of the thirteen stamp distributors were forced to resign their offices.

The protests and riots in the streets accompanied opposition to the Stamp Act through official political bodies. At the end of May, the Virginia House of Burgesses approved a set of resolutions which stated that Parliament had no authority to tax the colonies. The Virginia Resolves were introduced by a young lawyer named Patrick Henry, who was making his first appearance as a member of the body. In a sense, Henry's position was not revolutionary, since he based his arguments on the basis of rights enjoyed by Englishmen under England's "ancient constitution." Henry's most radical resolve, which was not passed but was printed in newspapers in Rhode Island and Maryland, declared that anyone who defended Parliament's right to tax the colonies would be deemed "an enemy to His Majesty's colony." By the time the Virginia Resolves were passed, most of the colonial legislatures had already dissolved for the summer break. By the time they reconvened in the fall, they followed Virginia's lead. After intense debate, other colonial assemblies passed resolutions denying Parliament the right to tax the colonies. In October, representatives of nine colonies convened the Stamp Act Congress in New York and issued a similar declaration, and petitioned the king and Parliament to repeal the act.

In London, the scale of the protests against the Stamp Act were eventually recognized, and Parliament felt obliged to reexamine the legislation. They were motivated to do so, not only as a result of violence in the colonies, but due to reports from the British merchant community that their revenues suffered as a consequence of a decline in colonial exports. By the end of 1765, Grenville's ministry had already fallen and was replaced by a ministry led by the Marquis of Rockingham. This new ministry believed that the Stamp Act should be repealed, but could not be certain that the repeal measure would win a parliamentary vote. In a series of powerful speeches in the Commons chamber, William Pitt defended the right of the American colonials to protest and argued that they should be taxed by their own institutions. In response, Grenville, who remained an MP, argued that backing down on the Stamp Act would encourage the rebellion to become a revolution. Eventually a compromise was agreed in Parliament. The government moved a bill to repeal the Stamp Act, arguing that further attempts to enforce the Stamp Act would lead to civil war among the Thirteen Colonies. At the same time, the government introduced the Declaratory Act which affirmed Parliament's right to tax the American colonies "in all cases whatsoever." Both pieces of legislation passed on the same day, March 18th, 1766.

The repeal of the Stamp Act was met with jubilation in the colonies. Representatives of twelve colonial legislatures—with the notable exception of Virginia—passed resolutions to give thanks and profess their loyalty to the king. The initial euphoria was curtailed once the colonials began to consider the implications of the Declaratory Act. Meanwhile, London once again experienced a change in government. Rockingham's ministry was unable to command the support of Parliament. The king turned to William Pitt to form a government, despite the mutual antipathy between the two men. Pitt had already refused the king's approaches on three previous occasions, but finally relented. Aged 57, Pitt retained his reputation as a national hero during the Seven Years' War and pursued an ambitious policy to restore order in the colonies and to unite competing factions in the British Parliament. Pitt's decision to accept the title of Earl of Chatham and enter the House of Lords limited his ability to pursue these plans. Pitt, now referred to by his noble title of Lord Chatham, no longer had the right to sit in the House of Commons, the primary arena for political debate. Thus, proceedings in the Commons were led by Charles Townshend, Chancellor of the Exchequer in Chatham's government. Townshend's power increased after Chatham fell ill in March 1767. He proposed a series of measures including the Revenue Act, which imposed customs duties on a number of goods including lead, glass, paper, and tea. The chancellor believed these duties would be more amenable to the colonies, since they were not levied on internal transactions among the colonies, but on external transactions across the seas with British ships.

The Townshend Acts would provoke another set of riots in North America, though Townshend himself would not live to see the consequences, dying suddenly at the age of 42 in September 1767. Debates over the Townshend Acts were more nuanced than those over the Stamp Act. Many colonials accepted that the customs were legal, but that they were nevertheless unjust and improper. New England merchants were encouraged to refuse to import British goods while the colonies attempted to develop industry in New England to replace them. Massachusetts was the first to organize political resistance to Townshend's measures. In February 1768, Samuel Adams, a brewer and influential public figure in Massachusetts, authored the Massachusetts Circular Letter addressed to the other colonies, advising them to join together in opposition to the Townshend Acts. The measure was passed on the second attempt by the Massachusetts House of Representatives, and the Circular Letter was received enthusiastically by Virginia, which submitted a petition to Parliament to revoke the Townshend Acts. Many colonies also passed nonimportation agreements, despite knowing that it would damage the economic interests of the New England ports. The Circular Letter prompted the British to dissolve the House of Representatives and send British army units to maintain order in the city of Boston. Tensions between civilians and British soldiers reached a climax on March 5th, 1770 when a group of eight British soldiers fired on a mob and killed five people. The eight infantrymen were charged with murder, but most were acquitted after a trial thanks to the efforts of their defense lawyer John Adams, a cousin of Samuel Adams. Adams argued that the soldiers acted out of self-defense. Two of the soldiers were charged with manslaughter but received light punishments.

Despite the acquittal of the British soldiers, the incident became known as the Boston Massacre and strengthened colonial opposition to the British authorities. In fact, on the same day as the Boston Massacre, the Revenue Act, the most insidious of the Townshend Acts, was partially repealed by Parliament. The repeal was initiated by Lord North, a Tory who became Prime Minister in January 1770 and would remain in office for another twelve years. While some parliamentarians supported a full repeal, North wished to retain the duties on the import of tea, which was formalized with the Tea Act of 1773. The Tea Act had partially been passed in order to increase the revenues of the East India Company, which was exempt from the taxation applied to colonial merchants. Although these parliamentary measures lessened the burden of taxation on the colonies, the colonials interpreted the Tea Act as yet another attempt by Parliament to assert its right to tax them. Sons of Liberty groups in Pennsylvania and New York were the first to resist the Tea Act and did so by preventing the import of tea into their harbors. In Boston, Samuel Adams was equally keen to ensure that merchant ships carrying tea would be turned away. The arrival of the *Dartmouth* in Boston Harbor with its cargo of tea on November 28th led to a stand-off between the legislature and the consignees for the tea, employees of the East India Company. Neither side was willing to back down, and the ship remained moored while the interested parties attempted to find a solution. On December 16th, Adams sensed that an attempt would be made to unload the tea. In response, a group of fifty men climbed aboard the *Dartmouth* and two other ships moored in Boston Harbor and dumped 90,000 pounds of tea into the harbor. The demonstration was soon celebrated in the press as the Boston Tea Party.

Chapter 4 – The Road to War

The Boston Tea Party shocked observers in Britain. Even parliamentarians sympathetic to the colonies, including Rockingham and Chatham, regarded it as a disgraceful criminal act. Lord North spoke for his parliamentary colleagues when he declared that the events in North America changed the nature of the debate in such a way that it was no longer a dispute about taxation, but about whether the British Crown could command any authority in the Thirteen Colonies. In the spring of 1774, Parliament passed a series of measures designed to punish Boston in order to prevent further demonstrations against British authority. The legislation limited the powers of the Massachusetts legislature, but the greatest restriction came with the Boston Port Act, which stipulated the closure of the port of Boston to commercial trade until the East India Company was compensated by the Bostonians for the destruction of the tea. News of these measures arrived in the colonies in May, and they were soon referred to as the Intolerable Acts. Samuel Adams proposed that Boston suspend trade with Britain and the British West Indies, and encouraged the rest of the colonies to follow suit. While many colonials were sympathetic to Boston's plight and recognized that they might eventually suffer the same treatment, most colonial merchants remained in favor of maintaining a trading relationship with the British.

In September and October 1774, representatives of twelve colonies met in Philadelphia at the first Continental Congress in an effort to determine a united response to the Intolerable Acts. The key grievances remained the same from ten years ago, though the mantra of no taxation without representation had been repeated so often over the previous decade that even though it was heavily contested during the Stamp Act crisis, it was taken for granted in the mid-1770s. Furthermore, by this point colonial opinion was virtually united in denying Parliament's right to make any form of legislation in the colonies. Nevertheless, the delegates found it difficult to agree on the nature of the joint colonial response to the Intolerable Acts. The delegation from Massachusetts took the most radical position, calling for an end to all trade with Britain. The Middle and Southern Colonies were less enthusiastic, being keenly aware of the damage it would do to their agricultural economies. After much negotiation, the delegates consented to an agreement on trade restrictions called the Association, which was signed on October 20th. The final days of the Congress were dedicated to drafting petitions to the king and addresses to the people of Great Britain. The delegates decided not to send a petition to Parliament, believing that it would amount to an admission of parliamentary authority over the colonies. When the delegates closed the Congress on October 26th, they agreed to meet again the following spring.

In Boston, British Governor General Thomas Gage attempted to enforce the Intolerable Acts to the best of his abilities. In October, he dissolved Massachusetts's provincial assembly in order to impose direct rule in the colony. The assembly refused to disband and relocated to Concord, some twenty miles to the west of Boston, calling itself the Provisional Congress. Under the leadership of the wealthy merchant John Hancock, the Provisional Congress assumed the duties of government and took steps to raise a militia. Confined to Boston, Gage found himself facing open rebellion. With only two regiments at his disposal, he did not feel secure in his position and requested reinforcements from London. At the same time, he advised Parliament to repeal the Intolerable Acts to diffuse the rebellion. In order to consolidate his position, Gage gave orders to seize armaments from neighboring towns in Massachusetts. Gage underestimated the determination of the colonials, and in response, militiamen marched to Boston's aid, expecting Gage to initiate hostilities against the port. Over the course of spring 1775, both sides were locked in a spiral of escalation, as each defensive action came to be regarded as an offensive action by the opposing side. On April 14th, Gage received instructions from the Earl of Dartmouth, the colonial secretary in the North ministry, to arrest the members of the Provincial Congress. Both Dartmouth and Gage knew that this would lead to war, but London was of the opinion that it was better to confront the colonials sooner rather than later. Nevertheless, the reinforcements of 20,000 men that Gage requested were not granted. The British believed that victory would come easily.

After receiving authorization from London to act against the Provisional Congress, Gage moved toward Concord. He did not aim to arrest the leaders of the Provisional Congress since most of them were in hiding, but to capture armaments to add to his limited supplies. Although the British general did all he could to conceal his preparations, they were observed by informers sympathetic to the Provisional Congress. The Boston silversmith Paul Revere was engaged as an intelligence officer for the Massachusetts militia. During the night of April 18th, 1775, once the British had finished their preparations and were preparing to march to Concord, Revere rode off to warn the leaders of the Congress, Samuel Adams and John Hancock, who were hiding in the town of Lexington to the east of Concord. Revere never uttered the words "The British are coming!" which were later attributed to him, since Revere and his comrades continued to regard themselves as British citizens. Although Revere was intercepted by British regulars on his way to Concord, others made it to Concord to warn the town of the impending British approach. Militia units from both towns were alerted and awaited orders from their commanders.

The British regulars arrived in Lexington at five o'clock on the morning of April 19th. As the drum sounded, Captain John Parker called upon seventy men drawn up in two ranks on Lexington Green. A column of British light infantrymen approached the town under the command of Major John Pitcairn. Although the militiamen were heavily outnumbered, Captain Parker ordered his men to stand firm. Parker's resolution failed him once Pitcairn urged the militia to disarm and disperse. The militia commander ordered his men to fall out, holding on to their muskets. The British officers were not satisfied by the militia's failure to disarm and repeated his instructions. During this tense standoff, a shot rang out. It is impossible to be certain whether the "shot heard round the world" came from the British regulars or the American militia. Both sides later blamed the other, and it was almost certainly accidental. In response, one of Pitcairn's subordinate officers ordered the men to fire. Pitcairn tried to stop his men from firing, but his orders were lost in the chaos and confusion of the armed confrontation. The British easily overcame the enemy fire, killing eight militiamen and wounding ten in the process. Having removed the obstacle, Pitcairn ordered his men to reform into columns as they resumed their march toward Concord.

The people of Concord had already been alerted to the movements of the British soldiers and made preparations to defend the town. Militiamen from neighboring towns rushed to its defense. The companies of militia showed little resistance against the British regulars who occupied themselves by searching for munitions. Their haphazard manner managed to cause a fire in the courthouse. The militiamen observed the smoke and were under the impression that the British intended to burn down the town. They duly resolved to attack the regulars in the town, in the process inflicting the first casualties the British army would suffer during the war. Over the course of the day, fighting took place along a sixteen-mile front, as militia companies directed their fire at the British regulars on their way back to Boston. The militiamen enjoyed a numerical advantage and had knowledge of the local terrain, but were encumbered by their lack of discipline. Under constant fire, the regulars also found it difficult to maintain their cohesion. Over the course of the entire day, the British received 273 casualties to the Americans' 95. It would become the prelude to much bloodier encounters between the two sides.

News about the battles of Lexington and Concord made its way throughout the colonies over the following days, although accounts of the battle varied in their accuracy. Although the conflict was small in scale and largely triggered by accident, the importance of the day's actions was not lost among political leaders in all thirteen colonies. Men from New England flocked to Boston to reinforce the militiamen who had taken part in the actions at Concord and Lexington. On May 10th, a force of New England militiamen commanded by Benedict Arnold seized Fort

Ticonderoga in New York from the British garrison. Although the fort was dilapidated and poorly garrisoned, it was of great strategic importance due to its position between the St. Lawrence and Hudson Rivers. The New Englanders feared that continued British control of the fort might result in the cutting of communications between states on either side of the Hudson River, allowing the British to defeat the Thirteen Colonies piecemeal. The fort was also home to a large quantity of cannons which were transported to Boston.

The first major battle in the war came in June at Bunker Hill. Dissatisfied by Gage's command in Boston, Dartmouth sent three prominent generals to assist him: William Howe, John Burgoyne, and Henry Clinton. Their arrival caused the British to take more active measures by occupying Dorchester Hill overlooking Boston. In response, the Americans occupied and fortified three hills on the Charlestown Peninsula north of Boston. Howe led the main assault on Bunker Hill and neighboring Breed's Hill. Expecting an easy victory over the colonials, Howe ordered his men to advance slowly and methodically in line formation rather than in columns. This costly tactical error impeded Howe's progress, and his men were met with defiant fire from fortified positions. Although Howe eventually took the hills as the defenders ran out of ammunition, the assault cost the British 1,000 men, including Major Pitcairn who had fought at Lexington. American casualties were far fewer at 300, but the men killed included Joseph Warren, a prominent Massachusetts political leader who had been commissioned as major general in the colonial militia.

While the British and New England forces were engaged in the bloody contest at Bunker Hill, the delegates of the Second Continental Congress were meeting in Philadelphia. The body convened on May 10th, as stipulated by the First Continental Congress seven months earlier. Following the outbreak of hostilities at Concord and Lexington, the delegates agreed that more soldiers were needed to defend the colonies. George Washington, representing Virginia, wore his militia uniform each day to the Congress to remind delegates of the military imperatives. Nevertheless, there was no agreement among the delegates on whether their ultimate objective was reconciliation with the British Empire or independence. Disagreements among the colonies were exacerbated when news of the capture of Fort Ticonderoga arrived on May 17ᵗʰ. The fort was located in New York, but had been captured by Connecticut men under Benedict Arnold and the Green Mountain Boys of Vermont—a militia force headed by Ethan Allen, who was instrumental in establishing Vermont as a separate political entity against the claims of New Hampshire and New York. Arnold and Allen failed to inform the authorities in New York in advance of the attack. Not only did New York feel that its territorial sovereignty had been violated by New Englanders, but the colonial authorities were still reluctant to engage in military action with the British. The Congress did all it could to ignore these conflicts between colonies in order to accelerate preparations for the war. Committees were established to secure military supplies, and on June 14ᵗʰ, the Congress decided to establish a Continental Army and recruit men from across the colonies to support the New Englanders around Boston. The following day they appointed George Washington as commander of the Continental Army.

While the Second Continental Congress was meeting in Philadelphia, political discussions were also taking place in London. Both King George and Parliament appear to have been surprised by the tenacity and resilience of the Americans, whom the British expected to defeat easily. On July 26ᵗʰ, when news of the engagement at Bunker Hill filtered through to London, North's Cabinet authorized sending 2,000 men to reinforce the army in Boston and made provisions for 20,000 men by the following spring. The popular mood was firmly in favor of war, and both the king and his prime minister were at the height of their popularity. When an emissary from the Continental Congress arrived in September to present their Olive Branch Petition to the king, requesting that he mediate between Westminster and the colonies, the king rejected it without hesitation. On October 26ᵗʰ, as the king made his way to Westminster for the state opening of Parliament, large crowds gathered to show their support. In his speech, George declared that America was in rebellion and that his government was determined to put the rebellion down by force. In the parliamentary debates that followed the king's speech, support for North's policy was by no means unanimous. In the Commons, a number of prominent figures including John Wilkes, Edmund Burke and Charles James Fox characterized government policy as unjust and warned that British forces were destined to be defeated by the determined Americans fighting in defense of their natural rights. The debates raged throughout the night until four in the morning, but eventually the Commons voted overwhelmingly in favor of the king's policy.

Chapter 5 – David Versus Goliath

The political decisions made in Philadelphia and London over the course of 1775 transformed the disturbances in New England into a continental war. The American Revolutionary War would also spread to Europe in subsequent years. Before considering the political and military developments in North America over the course of the war, it is important to take a closer look at the opposing forces and their relative strength, not only in terms of numbers but also by considering such factors as organization, logistics, motivation, and leadership. These factors are essential in understanding the trajectory of the war and its eventual outcome. Some of these characteristics were already apparent during the early stages of the war at Lexington, Concord, and Bunker Hill. While both sides would attempt to address their deficiencies over the course of the war to varying degrees of success, most of these factors continued to apply throughout the conflict.

At the beginning of the war, the British military presence in North America numbered little more than a couple of thousand men. By European standards, the British standing army was not a large force. In 1775, it numbered around 36,000 men worldwide. The small size of the British army was both motivated by geography and policy. Since Britain was an island nation, it was a naval power rather than a land power. In times of peace, the Royal Navy would patrol the oceans to protect British colonial interests. In times of war, the navy served as the "wooden walls" which defended Britain, while embarking on aggressive ventures to seize the colonial possessions of rival empires. During wartime, men would be recruited to join the enlarged army, but this was a secondary consideration, and most of these men would be demobilized in peacetime. Over the course of the conflict, the British presence in North America increased to around 50,000 men in total. Recruiting and supplying an army of this size was expensive, so the British also engaged 30,000 German mercenaries, mostly from the state of Hesse. The British army was also supported by locals including 25,000 Loyalists, which were Americans who supported the British cause in the war. At any point in time, the British and their allies might field 70,000 men from Canada in the north to Florida in the South.

While the British government was required to enlarge its small regular army, Washington had to build his Continental Army from scratch. At the start of the war, it amounted to a collection of militia units recruited from New England to defend Boston. British General John Burgoyne dismissed them as a "rabble in arms." When Washington took command of the New Englanders, he could count on around 15,000 men under his disposal. This would be bolstered by the addition of 10,000 men recruited from Pennsylvania, Maryland, and Virginia by the Continental Congress. When the army was established in June 1775, new recruits would serve for one year. Few men decided to stay on in the ranks. Many simply packed their bags and went home, despite their officers' pleas. The Continental Congress raised a new army in 1776, but by 1777, it was faced with the prospect of being heavily outnumbered when the British bolstered their forces in North America with the 30,000 Hessian mercenaries. In response, the Continental Congress decided to extend terms of service of new recruits to three years and to maintain an army of 120 regiments, or around 90,000 men. By the end of the war, 200,000 men saw service in the Continental Army. The army was supported by militias which remained under the control of individual colonies.

The American Revolutionary War is often described as a war between the highly disciplined British regular army and an inexperienced American militia motivated by a glorious cause under the inspired leadership of Washington. This characterization was certainly true at the beginning of the war. Although few in number, British soldiers were highly trained and disciplined. Their predecessors won great victories over King Louis XIV (1643-1715) of France's armies during the War of the Spanish Succession. The British also achieved great success against the French during the Seven Years' War, and many officers were veterans of the conflict who once again found themselves in America. In the rulebook of 18th-century warfare, training and discipline were crucial in enabling armies to execute complicated tactical and strategic maneuvers in order to win victories on the battlefield. A highly trained army could coordinate their fire to achieve maximum impact, before charging en masse with the bayonet against enemy lines with devastating effect. Washington's forces lacked the discipline of the British, and over the course of the war, the American commander labored to impose order on his men. A Virginian aristocrat, he considered the New England soldiers too egalitarian. In Massachusetts, the officers were elected by rank and file, which hindered efforts to impose order. As soon as he arrived in Boston to take up his command, Washington personally ensured that order was maintained among his regiments at camp, a task usually reserved to junior officers in European armies, but the American commander began the war with few capable officers under his command.

Both the British and American armies encountered difficulties supplying their armies. The British government may have had the financial resources to support the war effort through the issuing of government debt, but its army was fighting several thousand miles from home. In order to supply their forces in North America, the Royal Navy had to transport men and munitions over the Atlantic. Since the British enjoyed maritime superiority and the Americans did not have an established naval force, the British were able to supply their armies without much difficulty during the initial years of the war. At the same time, the British Navy could enforce a blockade on American maritime trade. Once France joined the war against Britain, however, the French Navy was in a position to protect American ports and threaten British convoys in the Atlantic, leaving the British land forces more vulnerable. The British could count on the support of Loyalists in America to maintain their armies, but they often operated on hostile territory and dependence on the Loyalists became more difficult over time as public opinion shifted in favor of the revolutionaries.

While the logistical problems facing the British army increased over time, the Continental Army's organization became more effective during the war. When Washington took command, the army lacked basic necessities including money, armaments, clothing, and medicine. The colonial economy remained largely agrarian, so most of the gunpowder had to be smuggled from Europe. Although food was plentiful, the military camps were rife with disease. The ill-discipline in the army was accompanied by poor standards of cleanliness as the soldiers failed to wash their clothes or their cooking utensils, facilitating the spread of disease. Most of the men did not have uniforms and their officers wore few distinguishing marks. The firearms employed by the Continental Army were as varied as their clothes. As the winter of 1775 approached, Washington was well aware that his men lacked the tents and blankets to remain in the field. Without a central government, the colonies lacked the logistical capabilities to supply a field army. While the delegates of the Continental Congress agreed to furnish the Continental Army with supplies, disputes between the colonies over how much each should provide hindered progress. More than anyone else, Washington knew of the difficulties in requesting supplies from the Congress. He knew it was essential for the colonies to set aside their differences to support the war effort. Over time, the colonies managed to cooperate more effectively through the Congress to maintain and support the Continental Army, but during the early stages of the war, Washington was keenly aware that his ill-equipped and undisciplined army could disintegrate at any moment.

One of the key advantages enjoyed by Washington's forces lay in motivation and commitment to a political cause. The British army was like any other European army at the time. Its objectives were not national but dynastic. The British army fought in North America in an effort to maintain King George's rule over the Thirteen Colonies. The army was commanded by an aristocratic officer class with a tradition of service to the king and seeking military glory, but the rank and file hailed from the lowest classes in society and were usually forced into military service. For these men, even if they considered themselves loyal subjects to the king, they were not fighting for their homes but for abstract political objectives. Over the course of the war, some British soldiers realized that there was no sense in fighting and would cross the front line to join the Americans, although there was some traffic in the opposite direction in the initial stages of the war when the Continental Army frequently found itself in desperate situations. In contrast to the British regulars, Washington's army had a clear sense of what it was fighting for. The men under his command were volunteers, usually farmers and tradesmen of various descriptions. They were committed to defending their homes and their ancient rights, and committed to the glorious cause which had brought all the colonies together to fight against British tyranny. Theirs was a war necessitated by self-defense rather than imperialistic ambitions.

Another crucial aspect of the war was military leadership. The British generals were experienced and enjoyed reputations as successful military leaders during the Seven Years' War. Over the course of the war, the British employed four different commanders-in-chief: Thomas Gage was replaced by William Howe in October 1775, who gave way to Sir Henry Clinton in 1778. Clinton was replaced in turn by Guy Carleton in 1782, who was given the task of evacuating men and supplies from North America. The British commanders were reliant on orders from London, which could take more than a month to arrive. All of these commanders, trained in conventional European warfare, underestimated the resolve of the Americans and failed to adapt to the irregular forms of warfare employed by Washington's men. The commanders-in-chief were further encumbered by frosty relationships with both their subordinate generals and admirals in the Royal Navy, and frequent disagreements about strategy hindered the effective prosecution of the war. The British generals tended to move cautiously in order to maintain their lines of communication and supply, even though a decisive blow in the early stages of the war could have destroyed the Continental Army. The British also faced the perennial dilemma encountered by imperial powers seeking to pacify rebellions in their empires. Since they aimed to restore British rule over the Thirteen Colonies, the British army had to ensure that they did not alienate local populations since it would be impossible to reimpose direct rule among a hostile population even if Washington was defeated.

In contrast to the prominent military figures who commanded the British army in America, the only American general of any renown was the commander-in-chief, George Washington. Washington had seen success during the Seven Years' War and proved himself a brave officer. Nevertheless, he had little experience commanding large bodies of men—the largest unit he commanded was a regiment of less than a thousand men. However, his experience commanding the Virginia militia during the war demonstrated the necessity of imposing order in the army and in ensuring that his men were well-supplied. In his fifteen-year absence from military service Washington entered the Virginia House of Burgesses and understood the political issues at stake. He knew that his men needed no encouragement to confront the enemy, and effectively employed irregular units to distract the enemy and help him achieve greater strategic objectives. He recognized that his army was in danger of disintegration at any moment and took all measures to ensure that his army could live to fight another day. He preferred to retreat instead of risking his army against the odds, pursuing a so-called Fabian strategy.

Washington was by no means the only talented general in the Continental Army. Nathanael Greene, 33 years old at the beginning of the war, had only six months' military experience when appointed to the rank of brigadier general. His strategic understanding and commitment to the American cause soon won him promotion to major general in 1776. Henry Knox, aged 25 in 1775, was a skilled artilleryman who managed to bring the guns from Ticonderoga to Boston in the winter of 1775. He would later become the artillery commander in the Continental Army and play a crucial role at the decisive Siege of Yorktown. British generals often advanced through the ranks through seniority and favors to the king. While connections also mattered in the Continental Army, talented American officers were often promoted to senior ranks for the successes they achieved on the battlefield.

Chapter 6 – Independence

When the Second Continental Congress met in the spring of 1775, most of the delegates supported reconciliation with the British. The increasing intensity of the conflict over the course of the year strengthened the desire for independence. The decisions made by Parliament and the North ministry to declare America in rebellion also led many to conclude that reconciliation was impossible. Despite their professed loyalty to the king, the delegates of the Continental Congress and the officers of the Continental Army were identified as traitors to the king, and their prospects in the event of a reconciliation with Britain would have been bleak.

Despite these developments, the Congress refrained from declaring independence at the beginning of 1776. Popular opinion in the Thirteen Colonies was split. When the war began, around a third of the American people were Patriots who supported the revolutionary cause. Another third were Loyalists who identified themselves with their British colonial masters. The remaining third were moderates who did not have strong political opinions and were primarily concerned about their personal interests. At the beginning of the war, this group favored reconciliation with the British and the preservation of the existing order, but over the course of time, they recognized the increasing brutality of British troops and understood that the British were seeking retribution on America.

The cause of independence was effectively advanced in the court of public opinion by the publication of *Common Sense* by Thomas Paine. An Englishman who had only been in America for a little more than a year, Paine was not a natural spokesman for the cause of American independence. After repeated failures in several trades in England, Paine crossed the Atlantic on the recommendation of Benjamin Franklin in late 1774, and soon found himself writing press articles in Pennsylvania newspapers. In *Common Sense*, a political pamphlet published in January 1776, Paine attacked the British constitution for being a vehicle for tyranny. He argued that the institution of monarchy contravened both natural rights and Christian teachings. In a memorable passage criticizing the principle of hereditary succession that governed most European polities of the time, Paine remarked that nature "disapproves of it, otherwise she would not so frequently turn it into ridicule by giving mankind an Ass for a Lion." Based on these precepts, the Americans should not be aiming to restore whatever ancient liberties they enjoyed under the British constitution, but they should declare independence and establish a polity based on natural rights. Some of these arguments had been expressed in earlier debates, but no one expressed it with the eloquence and wit of Thomas Paine. Within a few months, more than 100,000 copies of *Common Sense* appeared across the colonies. Through his writing, Paine promoted the question of independence to the top of the political agenda.

Common Sense emboldened the advocates for independence in the Continental Congress. Independence would not only galvanize the Continental Army behind a great cause, but would also enable Americans to enter alliances with foreign states. By April, colonial legislatures across the Thirteen Colonies authorized their delegates at Congress to seek a confederation which would bring them together and break off relations with the British Crown. The most radical pro-independent delegates included the cousins Samuel and John Adams from Massachusetts, and the brothers Francis Lee and Richard Henry Lee of Virginia. On June 6th,1776, Richard Henry Lee presented a resolution which proposed the dissolution of relations between the united colonies and the British Crown. The resolution also proposed that Congress seek measures to secure foreign assistance and to form a confederation between the colonies. When the proposal was debated by Congress, New England and Virginia were in favor of independence, while the Middle Colonies indicated that the time was not ripe, although they would support independence once the people demanded it. Congress opted to postpone discussions to July 1st and appointed committees to consider the proposals for independence, foreign alliances, and a confederation.

The five-man committee tasked with preparing a declaration of independence included Benjamin Franklin and John Adams, but the document was mainly drafted by the 33-year-old Thomas Jefferson. A Virginia gentleman, Jefferson was related through his mother's side to the Randolph family, one of the most prominent families in Virginia. His mother's cousin Peyton Randolph served as the first president of the Continental Congress before his death in October 1775. As a young man, Jefferson proved to be an excellent student with a particular affinity for Greek and Latin. He graduated from William and Mary College in 1762 before embarking on a career as a lawyer. In 1769, he was elected to the House of Burgesses. In 1774, Jefferson authored *A Summary View of the Rights of British America* in response to the Intolerable Acts. He argued that the people of America had the right to govern themselves and that the Thirteen Colonies were independent from British rule since the foundation of the individual colonies. Jefferson's tract was debated at the First Continental Congress, and he himself was elected to the Second Continental Congress in May 1775.

Jefferson completed his draft of the Declaration of Independence on June 28th, and the document was slightly amended by Adams and Franklin. On July 1st, the Congress voted on the issue of independence. Nine colonies voted in favor, Pennsylvania and South Carolina voted against, Delaware's delegation was split, and New York was not yet authorized by its colonial legislature to vote on the question. The following day, the Congress held another vote in which Pennsylvania, South Carolina, and Delaware voted in favor of independence with only New York remaining uncommitted. Following the landmark vote, John Adams wrote that July 2nd would be recognized by future generations as the day that America broke free from the British Empire. In fact, the Declaration of Independence would not be passed until July 4th, after it was analyzed line by line and approved after many amendments which toned down some of Jefferson's more radical denunciations. It was this day, the Fourth of July, which would be celebrated as Independence Day in the United States of America.

In its introduction, the Declaration of Independence established the Thirteen Colonies as the United States of America. In his famous preamble, Jefferson stated the creed of this new nation: "We hold these truths to be self-evident, that all men are created equal, that they are endowed by their Creator with certain unalienable Rights, that among these are Life, Liberty and the pursuit of Happiness." Although the equality of men was certainly a revolutionary doctrine for the time, both women and slaves were not included in Jefferson's phrasing. The preamble continues to demonstrate that revolution is permissible when a tyrannical government harms the people's natural and God-given rights. Much of the document is dedicated to outlining a list of King George's tyrannical injustices including the suppression of colonial legislative bodies, imposing taxation without consent, and the use of armed force in America. Such injustices made the king "unfit to be the ruler of a free people." This argument was inspired by the liberal philosopher John Locke's concept of a social contract between a monarch and his subjects. A tyrannical monarch was said to have broken the social contract and thus been deprived of political legitimacy. The Declaration continues with a denunciation of the British government in its insistence to impose parliamentary authority in the Thirteen Colonies, before concluding with a statement declaring that the Thirteen Colonies were free and independent states "absolved from all allegiance to the British Crown" and therefore had the authority to make war and peace, and regulate commerce in the fashion of other independent states. The Declaration was signed by 56 men, although some of them were not present on July 4th and added their signatures on later dates, when New York's delegates were finally authorized to vote in favor of independence.

The publication of the Declaration of Independence on July 7th had a galvanizing effect on both the people and the army of the newly-established United States of America. Printing presses worked unceasingly to distribute copies of the document across the country. Spontaneous celebrations broke out on July 6th, when the Continental Army first learned of the decisive vote in favor of independence four days earlier. On July 9th, Washington gave orders for the Declaration to be read aloud to ranks of soldiers gathered on parade grounds. Not only did Jefferson's words stir the hearts of the rank and file who were convinced of the righteousness of their cause, but in declaring independence, the Continental Congress had committed treason against their king. The price of defeat and surrender would be so great that there could be no turning back in their dedication to their cause. Washington's army was no longer fighting for their rights as Englishmen but for a new nation founded on the principles of liberty and equality. After the formal readings on July 9th, soldiers and townspeople expressed their enthusiasm by pulling down an equestrian statue of George III. They then hacked off the head and placed it on a spike. Not all people supported independence, but those who rejected it found themselves in a diminishing minority.

Once the Americans had declared independence from Britain, they had to prove that they could function effectively as an independent entity. The United States of America was a political experiment, and it was by no means certain that the experiment would succeed. The United States was a union of thirteen states, each of which had new governments and political institutions of their own. In order to support the Continental Army and make treaties of alliance against the British Empire, the United States needed a central political authority. As British colonies, relationships between states were defined by a sense of mutual mistrust, especially when territorial claims overlapped. The struggle with Britain enabled the Americans to discover that they had more in common than they initially thought, but differences in the socio-economic character of the states contributed to political differences. Even when delegates in Congress came to agreement on measures such as the boycott of British trade in 1774, these measures would have to be implemented by local and colonial authorities.

The task of drafting a plan of union was entrusted to John Dickinson, who chaired the congressional committee looking into the question. A delegate from Pennsylvania, Dickinson had opposed declaring independence before such a union could be established, believing it would risk conflict between the colonies. The Articles of Confederation and Perpetual Union drafted by Dickinson aimed to balance the interests of individual states with the need for high-level cooperation to support the war against the British. The main part of the document consisted of thirteen articles asserting the sovereignty of the states and detailing their obligations to the union. Each state, depending on population, would choose two to seven delegates for the Congress of the Confederation, but each state would have one vote and therefore each state, big or small, would be given an equal voice. Any decision needed nine votes to agree, and any change in the Articles needed all states to agree. The head of state would be a president, who was limited to serving one year in each three-year congressional term. Most of the powers of Congress were laid out in Article IX of the document. Among the powers accorded to Congress was the right to make war and peace and enter diplomatic agreements, to set weights and measures, and to regulate post and the armed forces. The Congress could not tax or draft people into the military, but would determine how much each state had to send to the common treasury and how many men each state was obliged to send to the Continental Army.

Dickinson's plan was presented to the Continental Congress on July 12th, but the subject of a union between the states was so contentious that Congress would continue to debate the issue for more than a year. These debates revolved around three key issues: division of powers between states and the confederation, representation of states in Congress, and contributions of the states to the union. Moreover, claims of the western lands were made by several states who hoped to expand their own territories and further their economic interests. Maryland was keen to ensure that all states would cede their claims to the western territories to the Union, and resisted ratification even though the twelve other states had done so by February 1779. Maryland eventually ratified the Articles in February 1781, and in March, they were proclaimed as the law of the United States. Even before the ratification of the document by all the states, the Articles of Confederation served as the framework for cooperation between the individual states. The Second Continental Congress continued to meet in order to coordinate the war effort, despite political differences between the states. The support of Congress was necessary for Washington to continue fighting the war since the Continental Army was fighting for its survival.

Chapter 7 – Washington on the Ropes

The military developments during the first half of 1776 were positive for the Continental Army. After an ill-fated attempt to invade Canada at the end of 1775, Washington decided to turn his attention toward the siege of Boston. Although the Americans outnumbered the British, the defenders were behind well-fortified lines and easily supplied by the navy through Boston Harbor. During the winter of 1775, Colonel Henry Knox successfully hauled fifty-six cannons from Fort Ticonderoga to the outskirts of Boston, a journey of almost 300 miles across frozen rivers. Knox personally supervised the mission and did not lose a single gun in transit, bringing the guns to the siege camp outside Boston in late January 1776. For this miraculous operation, Washington immediately appointed Knox to command the artillery in the Continental Army. Strengthened with these extra guns, Washington hoped to immediately launch an assault on British lines but was overruled by his subordinates. Instead, Washington's war council adopted a plan to occupy the Dorchester Heights and entice General Howe's army out of their fortifications. Washington's men successfully occupied the Heights during the night of March 4th-5th. The guns from Ticonderoga could now be trained on the British fleet in Boston Harbor, which provided for Howe's only line of retreat. The heavy bombardment forced Howe to withdraw from Boston and sail to Halifax, Nova Scotia on March 17th.

Although the British had retreated to Canada to reorganize their forces, Washington knew that Howe would eventually move on New York, a city of vital strategic importance. If the British were to occupy New York and control the Hudson River, the United States would be divided into two, and Howe could concentrate his forces to conquer and subdue each portion in turn. With these considerations in mind, after Boston was firmly in American hands, Washington led an army of 18,000 men to New York and arrived at the beginning of April, setting up headquarters at the end of Broadway. He could see that unlike Boston, the Patriots were at a political and strategic disadvantage in New York. While most Bostonians eagerly supported the revolution, not least because their city was specifically targeted by Parliament, New Yorkers were more inclined to remain loyal to the British Crown. Furthermore, with British control of the seas, the Americans would not be able to hold onto the city for long. Nevertheless, there was a political imperative for the Continental Army to make a stand in New York, demonstrating to the Patriots in New York that their city would not be abandoned without a fight. Washington ordered fortifications to be built on Brooklyn Heights overlooking Long Island to the south of the city.

By the end of June, British ships began arriving at Staten Island commanded by Admiral Lord Richard Howe, General Howe's brother. General Howe himself landed on July 2nd, 1776, the same day the Continental Congress voted to declare independence. Although news of the decision invigorated Washington's army, the Americans remained on the back foot. The 120 cannons which Knox had installed on the banks of the Hudson did nothing to prevent Admiral Howe's flagship, the HMS *Eagle*, from entering New York in all its majesty. The Howes had been appointed peace commissioners by Parliament and offered talks with Washington. Their reluctance to address Washington by his title of general led to two refusals, until finally on July 20th, General Washington met with the British. Both sides knew it was unrealistic to expect a peaceful outcome, but both sides believed it was worth trying for political reasons. Washington refused to consider any pardon from the king by insisting that the Americans had done no wrong in defending their liberties. Formalities over, both sides prepared for war. Howe had 32,000 men under his command, including a large contingent of Hessian mercenaries. Washington had no indication of the direction of attack, and despite being outnumbered, decided to divide his forces between Brooklyn and Manhattan, which proved to be a grave tactical error. The assault began on August 23rd and reached its climax on August 27th. The British launched an attack on the Brooklyn Heights while a Hessian force outflanked the American lines and attacked from the rear. In the confusion, some of Washington's men retreated in disorder, while the remaining men valiantly fought on. Washington's attempts to restore order were in vain. The Battle of Brooklyn had been a disastrous defeat for the Continental Army, which sustained casualties of 1,500 men.

Washington knew he had to abandon the Heights, but any attempt to withdraw his men to Manhattan in broad daylight would amount to a suicide mission. Instead, he ordered his men to requisition any boats they could get their hands on to prepare for an evacuation at night. On the night of August 29th, the evacuation began. Although by daybreak not all the Americans had evacuated from Brooklyn, a dense fog continued to shield their retreat. The British camp was filled with a sense of relief that the Americans had evacuated their positions voluntarily, and Howe decided to consolidate his position. Had he carried on the pursuit, he could have brought ruin to Washington's army and the entire American cause. Despite losing many men from desertion in the aftermath of the defeat at Brooklyn, Washington lived to fight another day. The Continentals fought a series of rearguard actions along the Hudson River, retreating at every step while sustaining and inflicting casualties along the way.

The New York campaign had been a disaster, which persuaded Congress to raise 80,000 more men for the Continental Army. The recruiting of men needed time which Washington lacked. His army of 3,500 men retreated to New Jersey in anticipation of an attack on Philadelphia. Thomas Paine, in a series of pamphlets titled *The American Crisis*, described the mood of the Patriots with the famous opening line, "These are the times that try men's souls." By the end of November, Washington crossed the Delaware River to the relative security of Pennsylvania. At this point, Howe decided to halt his pursuit, retaining a 1,500-man garrison of Hessians at Trenton across the

Delaware. After receiving reinforcements, Washington could only count on 6,000 men fit for duty. Nevertheless, Washington resolved to counterattack. Early on the morning of December 26th, just after Christmas, Washington crossed the Delaware and surprised the Hessian garrison, winning an important victory and capturing 1,000 prisoners. The Americans followed up this victory by defeating the British garrison at Princeton before taking up winter quarters at the beginning of 1777. In six months, Washington had relinquished New York, which remained in British hands until the end of the war, but he successfully held onto New Jersey, preserved his army, and could afford to celebrate some successes at the end of the year which restored hope among Patriots that the war could be won.

Despite the successes in late 1776, the Continental Army remained on the defensive. The key objective was the defense of Pennsylvania and Philadelphia, the de facto capital of the United States. In fact, in December 1776, the Continental Congress had already evacuated to Baltimore, Maryland to seek greater security. Once Washington successfully prevented Howe from entering Pennsylvania, the Congress returned to Philadelphia in March 1777. Howe believed the key strategic objective was to destroy Washington's army, and in the spring, he attempted in vain to entice Washington to an open battle in New Jersey. With Washington unwilling to fall into his trap, Howe returned to New York before setting sail in mid-August. Washington guessed that Howe would attempt to land a force on the Delaware River and attack Philadelphia. While Howe was indeed targeting Philadelphia, he landed instead on the Chesapeake in Maryland before marching north. The Continental Army moved to intercept the British march to Philadelphia by establishing headquarters at Wilmington, Delaware. The two armies clashed at Brandywine Creek on September 11th, where Washington's army was once again outflanked by Howe. Although the Continentals fought with greater tenacity than at Brooklyn a year earlier, by the end of the bloody melee, they retreated in disorder.

Once again, the British had won a significant victory over the Americans, but once again Washington managed to prevent his army from disintegrating. There followed weeks of maneuvering during which the Continental Army sought to keep itself between Howe and

Philadelphia. As Washington was shifting his army left and right to cover Howe's movements, part of his army stationed in Paoli, some twenty miles to the northwest of Philadelphia, was surprised by the British during the night and 300 Continentals were killed by British bayonets. The Paoli Massacre prompted Washington to be more careful in his maneuvers, but this allowed Howe to enter Philadelphia on September 26th, forcing the Continental Congress to flee once again, eventually establishing temporary premises at York, a hundred miles to the west of Philadelphia. While this was a significant setback, Washington's army remained intact, and the American commander intended on retaking the city as soon as possible. On October 4th, he attacked Howe's army at Germantown, some five miles to the northwest of Philadelphia. Washington sent four forces along four separate roads which converged on Germantown and an unsuspecting Howe. Although the American plan looked impressive on paper, the separate forces failed to coordinate their attacks effectively. The fact that the battlefield was covered in fog resulted in two of the American columns firing at each other before they discovered their mistake. The British took advantage of the confusion in American ranks and launched a successful counterattack. The Continental Army's defeat at Germantown would prevent the Americans from recapturing Philadelphia until the following year. Washington led his army of 12,000 men to winter quarters at Valley Forge, 20 miles northwest of Philadelphia to reorganize his army.

While Washington's main army suffered defeat in Pennsylvania, American forces in upstate New York enjoyed greater success. With New York City in British hands, the British could seize control of the Hudson River Valley and separate New England from the rest of the United States. This was the plan formulated by General John Burgoyne and adopted by the British government in the spring of 1777. Burgoyne would move south from Canada into upstate New York, while a second force under the command of General Barry St. Leger, would move east from Ontario. Burgoyne also counted on Howe to distract the Continentals in New England. The three forces would meet in Albany— either to destroy Washington's army in tandem or to cut the United States in two. On July 1st, Burgoyne successfully recaptured Fort Ticonderoga with 8,000 men, and continued toward Albany, confronted with increasing numbers of American troops on the way, some of them sent as reinforcements from Washington's army. Burgoyne had expected assistance from Howe, but the senior general turned his attention to Philadelphia, leaving Burgoyne reliant on St. Leger for support. By the beginning of August, St. Leger was besieging Fort Stanwix on the Mohawk River, a hundred miles west of Albany in upstate New York. Two American relief columns hurried to lift the siege, and the arrival of the second under Benedict Arnold resulted in British withdrawal. St. Leger hoped to rejoin with Burgoyne's army via Canada, but Burgoyne was forced to carry on to Albany on his own.

Strategically isolated, Burgoyne staked his army in battle against a force of 9,000 Americans under the command of General Horatio Gates, who served as commander of the Continental Army in the northern sector. Gates' army took up a position on Bemis Heights, some ten miles south of Saratoga. The position was fortified by Tadeusz Kosciuszko, a skilled Polish military engineer. On September 19th, Burgoyne's army attacked Gates' left flank at Freeman's Farm, forcing the enemy to fall back at great cost. . A unit of 500 riflemen under the command of Colonel Daniel Morgan targeted the officers in the British army and inflicted important casualties. Burgoyne would continue his attack on the Heights on October 7th, but by this point the Continental Army was more than twice the size of the British contingent. Once again, Morgan's riflemen inflicted great damage on the British, and Burgoyne himself was almost killed by the sharpshooters. The accurate fire from the Continentals broke the spirit of the British attackers, who retreated back to their lines. Seizing the opportunity, Benedict Arnold led his New England men in an unauthorized attack on the retreating British and secured a famous victory. Burgoyne and his army would surrender on October 17th, leaving the British general to return home disgraced and his army to remain in captivity until the end of the war. Meanwhile, Gates was celebrated as the victor of Saratoga, and some sections of the Continental Army believed he should replace Washington as commander-in-chief.

Chapter 8 – The International Dimension

By late 1777, the American Revolutionary War assumed an international dimension. Britain and France continued to be engaged in their struggle for global hegemony which spanned the 18th century. As hostilities broke out between the British and Americans, France looked to exploit Britain's vulnerability and exact revenge for their defeat during the Seven Years' War. The American revolutionaries were keen to establish an alliance with France following the outbreak of war at Lexington and Concord, and sent several agents to Paris to negotiate a treaty of alliance with France. In March 1776, Silas Deane of Connecticut had been sent by Congress to Paris on a secret mission to negotiate with the French foreign minister, the Comte de Vergennes. In December, he was joined by Benjamin Franklin and Arthur Lee, now in an official capacity as the American diplomatic delegation in France. John Adams would join the trio in the following March. Despite such illustrious personalities representing the American cause, the French were reluctant to formally enter the war. After all, King Louis XVI (1774-91) of France was a crowned monarch who was hesitant to sanction a republican revolution. The French were also concerned about whether the Continental Army could sustain the war. Were Washington to be defeated decisively, France would find itself alone against Britain, allowing the British to concentrate their armed forces against French possessions around the world. News of the American victory in the Saratoga campaign reached Europe in December 1777. Vergennes was sufficiently confident that the Americans were not about to collapse and stood a real chance of winning the war, so he acquiesced to the offer of alliance.

Even before the alliance was formally brokered between France and the nascent United States, army officers from continental Europe were already making their way to North America to enlist in the Continental Army. The Polish military engineer Tadeusz Kosciuszko enlisted in August 1776, and the fortifications he designed enabled the victories at Saratoga against Burgoyne. His compatriot Kazimierz Pulaski, together with the Hungarian hussar (Central European light cavalry) Mihaly Kovats, were instrumental in the creation of cavalry units in the Continental Army. The Prussian General Baron Friedrich Wilhelm von Steuben would arrive in North America at the end of 1777 and was responsible for drilling and training Washington's army in European methods of warfare. By far the most influential foreign officer serving in the Continental Army over the course of the war was Gilbert du Motier, Marquis de Lafayette. Seeking military glory and motivated by the hostility toward Britain, Lafayette traveled to North America at his own expense against the wishes of his family and the French king. After his arrival in July 1777, he was commissioned as a major general in the Continental Army and soon established a close friendship with Washington. He first saw battle at Brandywine, where he received a wound in the leg but continued to issue orders and organize the orderly retreat of the Continental Army. Lafayette served on Washington's staff and shared his privations in the winter of 1777 as the army was encamped in Valley Forge. Once the French formally joined the war in February 1778, Lafayette would prove invaluable as a liaison officer between the Continental Army and the French Navy.

The Treaties of Amity and Commerce and of Alliance between France and the United States were signed in February 1778. The two parties agreed that territorial conquests in North America would be transferred to the United States, while any gains in the Caribbean would pass to France. Most importantly, the two parties agreed not to make a separate peace with Britain. The Franco-American alliance transformed the strategic considerations of the war. The British had previously been able to supply a large army in North America without much difficulty due to its control of the seas. In comparison to the formidable Royal Navy, the naval forces of the American revolutionaries were practically nonexistent. In 1776, the Continental Navy had 27 ships in contrast to the British Navy's 270, and the gap would increase over the course of the war. Nevertheless, British commerce was constantly targeted by American merchant ships, which turned to privateering during the war. Privateering was sanctioned by both the Continental Congress and the individual states, and as many as 70,000 men may have been involved in privateering efforts against British shipping. By the end of 1777, American privateers had taken 560 British merchant vessels conducting trade across the Atlantic. The exploits of John Paul Jones, a naval captain in the Continental Navy, were particularly celebrated. His most famous action came in 1779 at the Battle of Flamborough Head, off the English coast, when he forced the surrender of the British frigate HMS *Serapis* while his own ship, the *Bonhomme Richard*, was already sinking.

While American privateers proved a nuisance for British authorities, French entry in the war brought with it the prospect of the French Navy threatening British supremacy in the American seaboard. The authorities in London therefore switched their attention to the French and proposed to seize the French island of St. Lucia in the West Indies. Not only could the British take control of the lucrative commerce in the Caribbean, but the French Navy would be distracted from their objective of supporting the American forces. Before launching any offensive operations, the British had to decide what to do with the French fleet. The main French fleet was based at Brest on the west coast of France, while a second force under the Comte d'Estaing was being furnished in Toulon on the Mediterranean. The British government and naval command were divided about the best course of action since the navy, poorly maintained since the end of the Seven Years' War, could not maintain an effective blockade of the French ports. Admiral Augustus Keppel, commander of the home fleet, preferred to protect against the prospect of an invasion of the British Isles. This allowed d'Estaing's fleet to sail unopposed to North America, arriving in New York by July 1778 to blockade Admiral Howe's fleet.

D'Estaing's arrival in the North American seaboard was a major setback for the British, although the combined operations between the French Navy and the Continental Army in the second half of 1778 did not achieve much success. Nevertheless, as long as France continued to be part of the war, London would have to protect against invasion of British shores. Although an inconclusive engagement between Admiral Keppel and the Brest fleet under the Comte d'Orvilliers near Ushant in July 1778 ensured that Britain would be safe from invasion for the remainder of the year, the threat of invasion loomed even larger the following year. Spain entered the war in April 1779, not so much as to assist the American revolutionaries, but to recapture Gibraltar from the British. In June, Spanish forces began to lay siege to Gibraltar. Although the British managed to keep Gibraltar well-supplied, an allied Franco-Spanish fleet was threatening to mount an invasion of England. A fleet of 66 ships of the line sailed up the English Channel seeking to distract the Royal Navy, while an army of 40,000 men would be ferried across the channel by 400 transport ships. The appearance of this armada on August 14th alarmed the British, though a fleet of more than thirty ships under the command of Admiral Sir Charles Hardy managed to shadow the enemy fleet. A combination of poor coordination, poor weather, and sickness among the allied crew forced the allied fleet to abandon its venture. Once again, the British shores were secure from invasion, and the French and Spanish did not plan an invasion during the remainder of the war.

Although the British were undoubtedly concerned about French efforts to launch an invasion of Britain, the Royal Navy continued to take part in offensive operations. In accordance with the new strategy adopted in the summer of 1778, a British convoy sailed from New Jersey toward the West Indies with 5,000 men under the command of General James Grant with the task of capturing St. Lucia from the French. On December 14th, the British fleet stationed in the West Indies under the command of Admiral Samuel Barrington defeated d'Estaing's larger fleet, and by December 29th the French surrendered possession of the island to the British. Despite this British success, d'Estaing's fleet continued to enjoy numerical superiority in 1779, and the French successfully seized St. Vincent and Grenada from the British in the summer. A British fleet under Admiral John Byron attacked d'Estaing as the French admiral was sailing away from Grenada, but suffered a heavy defeat in the process. The Battle of Grenada on July 6th was the Royal Navy's worst defeat in almost a century, with Byron losing a thousand men in the engagement. The war in the West Indies would eventually also bring in the Spanish and the Dutch, and the fighting would continue until 1783, after military operations in North America were already concluded.

The distractions caused by the French and Spanish fleets increased the vulnerability of British commerce to American privateers. Between 1777 and 1780, American privateers managed to capture another 1,000 British merchant vessels. Although the Royal Navy managed to maintain control of the American seaboard for much of 1778-80, they continued to experience difficulties supplying their armies. On July 27th, 1780, a large British convoy set sail from Portsmouth destined for North America, escorted by Captain Sir John Moutray's HMS *Ramillies* and two frigates. The convoy of 63 merchant ships carried £1,000,000 of gold, together with 80,000 muskets, 294 artillery pieces, and other equipment intended for the army of 40,000 men in North America. On August 9th, 1780, while the convoy was sailing past the Azores, it was intercepted by a Franco-Spanish fleet commanded by Luis de Cordova. 55 of the British merchant ships mistook the Spanish flagship for the HMS *Ramillies* and were captured by Cordova. The Spanish took more than three thousand British prisoners, and the disaster bankrupted marine insurance underwriters throughout Europe.

Although the British fleet remained the largest in the world, it was unable to patrol the seas effectively against French, Spanish, Dutch, and American hostility. The British authorities had to decide which sectors to prioritize. Unlike in the Seven Years' War, the British could no longer rely on a continental ally to distract its European enemies. Prussia remained neutral as Frederick the Great approached his twilight years. The aging Frederick was well aware that his kingdom had almost been destroyed during the Seven Years' War and did not wish to risk his earlier territorial gains. The British requested an alliance and 20,000 troops from Russia, but Empress Catherine the Great (1762-96) disliked George III and believed the British only had themselves to blame for the revolution in their American colonies. Any hope of winning Catherine's goodwill was lost when the British adopted controversial countermeasures to confiscate neutral shipping which they suspected of carrying contraband to support the American revolutionaries. These measures infuriated Catherine the Great as Russian ships were routinely searched by British naval officers. In March 1780, she issued a Declaration of Armed Neutrality to protect the interests of neutral shipping. The declaration established the rights of neutral vessels in war and provided for their armed protection in case such rights were infringed. Catherine invited other European nations to join a League of Armed Neutrality. By 1781, Denmark, Sweden, Austria, and Prussia joined the League. Although it did not discriminate between American and British interference in neutral shipping, armed neutrality favored the American cause. Faced with armed neutrality, the Royal Navy could do nothing to prevent French and Dutch ships from flying the Russian flag and entering American ports, bringing supplies to the states. By establishing the League, Catherine had effectively recognized the United States as its own independent state on an equal basis with the British, rather than as rebellious provinces of the British Empire.

Chapter 9 – War in the South

The failure of Burgoyne's strategy in Canada, coupled with the French alliance with the American revolutionaries, forced the British to adopt a new plan. In May 1778, Howe relinquished his command to Sir Henry Clinton. Lord George Germain, who had succeeded the Earl of Dartmouth as colonial secretary in 1775, ordered Clinton to evacuate Philadelphia and return to New York. Clinton and his army would then move by sea to attack the Southern states. This new strategy seemed sensible and to play to British advantages. There was no longer any sense in conducting a land campaign in the hostile territory of the Northern states, especially as it became increasingly difficult to supply the army across the Atlantic. Instead, the army would conduct joint operations with the Royal Navy, which continued local superiority in the American seaboard, allowing the army to operate more effectively in the friendlier South. The Southern Colonies of Georgia and South Carolina were dominated by landowners whose commercial interests were limited. They were also younger colonies and had less time to develop a separate identity from their British imperial masters. The British expected to link up with Loyalists in the South and conduct joint operations against the Patriots. This force would gather strength as it moved northward to North Carolina and Virginia. The British expected that American revolutionary sentiment would be dampened by British reconquest of the South, and the war could still be won.

Clinton's army duly evacuated Philadelphia in June 1778, allowing the Continental Congress to return to its former seat by the beginning of July. 3,000 Loyalists were evacuated to New York by Admiral Howe's fleet, but Clinton's army of 10,000 men would march to the city by land. As the British withdrew, Washington and his generals debated what to do next. General Charles Lee, Washington's deputy, argued that the Continentals should allow the British to withdraw and not risk their army in field engagements, while foreign officers, including Steuben and Lafayette, encouraged Washington to assume the offensive and attack Clinton's exposed supply train. Washington eventually decided to seek battle, handing the command of the vanguard to General Lee at the latter's request. Washington's men caught up with the British at Monmouth Court House in New Jersey. Reluctant to go on the offensive, Lee introduced units at a steady pace and allowed the British rearguard under General Charles Cornwallis to seize the initiative and beat back Lee's vanguard. Only the arrival of Washington and Lafayette restored order and discipline, allowing the Continentals to regroup and push Cornwallis backward. The battle ended Lee's military career, but enhanced the reputations of Washington and Lafayette. The British continued to New York without further harassment, arriving in mid-July. Clinton's arrival in New York in mid-July coincided with the appearance of d'Estaing's fleet outside the harbor. The inability of the French ships to pass through the shallow bar of New York Harbor prevented operations against Lord Howe's fleet. A combined amphibious operation against Newport, Rhode Island also came to nothing. The Franco-American alliance at sea had yet to bear fruit.

Unlike in previous years, hostilities continued throughout the winter. Clinton initiated operations against the South at the end of 1778. In November, in addition to the 5,000 men he sent to seize St. Lucia, Clinton dispatched 3,500 men under the command of Lieutenant Colonel Archibald Campbell on an invasion of Georgia, the southernmost state. Campbell landed in Georgia on December 23rd and captured the town of Savannah on the 29th. Over the course of the following month, Campbell joined forces with General Augustine Prevost to take control of Georgia. The success of the British armies mobilized the Loyalist militia who joined the British regulars as they moved north to

South Carolina. Although the British expeditionary force had seen success, Clinton stayed in New York for much of 1779. London was far more concerned about the prospect of Franco-Spanish invasion. Moreover, debates about the conduct of the war dominated political activity in Parliament. The recalled William Howe defended himself and his brother against accusations that he had been lacking in aggression as commander-in-chief of British forces in America. The British military establishment was split between whether the logistical challenges in America were insurmountable, or whether the majority of Americans remained loyal subjects to King George who would provide material support to the British military presence. The debates continued in the public press and demonstrated that support for the war was ebbing away.

Military operations in the American South resumed near the end of the year, when the Continental Army attempted to retake Savannah, assisted by Patriot militia and d'Estaing's fleet, in September. The failure of this operation prompted Clinton to bring his army south. On December 26th, 1779, Clinton left New York with 8,000 men destined for South Carolina. The target was the port of Charleston, the largest city in the southern states with a population of 12,000 citizens. The British began to lay siege on the city in late March. Clinton intended to lay siege to the city with the assistance of the Royal Navy, but disagreements with Admiral Mariot Arbuthnot obligated Clinton to cut off the city without the navy's aid. On April 21st, 1780, the American garrison, under the command of General Benjamin Lincoln, offered to surrender if the Continentals could be allowed to leave the city on their own terms, but this was refused by the British commander. Effective artillery bombardment from the British forced Lincoln to surrender—this time with his men taken into captivity and their arms confiscated. After overseeing the capture of Charleston, Clinton returned to New York and left Cornwallis in command. The latter was given orders to capture the Carolinas before invading Virginia, coordinating an attack with a British force driving south from New York.

The British regulars under Cornwallis, supported by Loyalist militia, successfully overran South Carolina within three months. During this period, a guerrilla war was conducted by militias from both sides, which would characterize the war in the South throughout 1780 and into the following year. Meanwhile, the Continental Army appointed General Horatio Gates, the victor of Saratoga, to command the army in the South. The army Gates was to command consisted of 1,400 Continentals from Delaware and Maryland headed by Johann de Kalb, a Bavarian general who had been in the service of the king of France. This force was reinforced by 2,500 militiamen from North Carolina and Virginia. In August, Gates led this army to Camden, where Cornwallis had established his supply depot in South Carolina. Gates believed that the British force was much smaller than his own, but after receiving reinforcements, Cornwallis could count on 2,000 men. Despite the faulty intelligence, Gates felt compelled to attack and opened battle on August 16th. The encounter was a disaster for the American force. The Virginian and North Carolinian militiamen had been deployed opposite Cornwallis' best troops. The well-disciplined British infantry fired on the advancing Virginia militiamen, who soon panicked and fled the field of battle along with the North Carolinian units, leaving de Kalb's men dangerously exposed. De Kalb himself valiantly fought on until he collapsed from his wounds, dying three days later in British captivity.

The guerilla war between British and American militia continued in the aftermath of Camden. Lieutenant Colonel Banastre Tarleton gained special notoriety for his conduct of this irregular warfare in the South. Tarleton was the commander of the British Legion, a Loyalist force of cavalry and light infantry, and who had played a crucial role in the siege of Charleston. The most notorious act involving Tarleton's men came in the aftermath of the Battle of Waxhaws at the end of May. The Legion defeated a contingent of 400 Continentals under Abraham Buford, whose inexperienced troops fled in the wake of the fearsome Loyalist cavalry. When Buford brought out a white flag with the intention to surrender, Tarleton's men continued their attack and slaughtered over 100 Continentals. Although most contemporary accounts suggest that Tarleton did not give such orders since he had been trapped under his dead horse during the initial stages of the battle, Tarleton and the British Legion gained a reputation for being merciless. The incident at Waxhaws inflamed passions on both sides and contributed to a bloody guerrilla war in which no quarter was given on either side. Cornwallis had handed the task of pacifying South Carolina to Major Patrick Ferguson and a militia force of 1,000 men. Although Ferguson had been largely successful in clearing the area of enemy militia, the Patriots received word of his intention of laying waste to the country and recruited some 1,000 men themselves to confront Ferguson. They surprised and defeated Ferguson at King's Mountain on October 7th. The victorious Patriots refused to accept the surrender of the Loyalist militia and continued to shoot and stab the defeated enemy combatants before their officers managed to restrain them, claiming revenge for the massacre at Waxhaws.

The destruction of Ferguson's militia, whose commander was killed at King's Mountain, forced Cornwallis to abandon his attempt to invade North Carolina. Meanwhile, Nathanael Greene was on his way south to replace the disgraced Gates as commander of the Southern front. On his way, he stopped off in Philadelphia and pleaded to Congress for more men and supplies, citing the precariousness of the military situation. When Greene arrived at Charlotte, North Carolina, he found 1,400 poorly equipped men who could hardly be called an army waiting for him. In order to transform his army into an effective fighting force, Greene relied on the talents of the Continental Army's best foreign officers. Von Steuben worked tirelessly to train troops in Virginia who could reinforce Greene when required. Kosciuszko and other officers scouted the local terrain to ascertain where the army could fight most effectively.

Greene opted to divide his army into two: the main force headed toward Charleston, while General Daniel Morgan would harass the enemy to the west. Although this was a strategic risk, Greene knew that he could not maintain his entire army by marching down a single route. Morgan's contingent, numbering around 1,000 men, was pursued by Tarleton leading a similar number of men. The two armies met at the Battle of Cowpens in northwestern South Carolina on January 17th, 1781. The battle exemplified Tarleton's recklessness and Morgan's tactical resourcefulness. Morgan's infantry induced Tarleton into launching an assault uphill, and engaged in a melee. After firing a couple of volleys, Morgan's second line retreated and maneuvered around the British left. Meanwhile, the reserve cavalry commanded by Colonel William Washington, a cousin of the commander-in-chief, swept down the hill against the British right flank. With his army surrounded on all sides and facing a bayonet charge from the enemy, Tarleton was forced to surrender, affording a crucial victory to the Continentals.

Once Cornwallis learned of Tarleton's defeat at Cowpens, he sought to hunt down Morgan's contingent. Both Morgan and Greene realized that the former's army presented a vulnerable target for Cornwallis and sought to reunite their forces. Meanwhile, Cornwallis' army was encumbered by a lack of intelligence of the enemy's movements, and failed in his effort to cut off Morgan. The reunited Continental troops opted to retreat and managed to cross into Virginia before the British abandoned the pursuit. Cornwallis established headquarters at Hillsboro, North Carolina and issued a proclamation to loyal Americans to join the fight against the Patriots. Motivated by false reports that Cornwallis' proclamation had been a great success, after receiving reinforcements from von Steuben, Greene led his army back into the Carolinas and awaited a British attack on Guilford Court House. The British scored a tactical victory in the ensuing battle but at the cost of a third of their army, while Greene's men had fought well and remained in high spirits. With 1,400 fit men, Cornwallis made the fateful decision to move north into Virginia in an effort to coordinate with Clinton's army in New York. Meanwhile, Greene led his army south to recapture South Carolina and Georgia. Although Greene lost engagements at Hobkirk's Hill and Eutaw Springs, by September the Patriot militia managed to secure most of the Carolinas and Georgia, leaving the British confined to Charleston and Savannah. Over the course of 1781, the war in the South had turned dramatically in the Americans' favor. The widespread loyalist support envisaged by Cornwallis failed to materialize, and any Loyalist militia who operated in conjunction with the British army were confronted by Patriot militia.

Chapter 10 – Surrender at Yorktown

When Cornwallis arrived in Virginia, he was greeted by Benedict Arnold, who had defected to the British army in late 1780. One of the most talented generals in the Continental Army, Arnold had been given command of the garrison in Philadelphia in 1778. Despite his talent on the battlefield, Arnold's relations with his fellow commanders was poor—his insubordination at Saratoga serving as a prime example—and he was aggrieved that he had been passed for more senior commands. Arnold maintained a lavish lifestyle in Philadelphia and was heavily in debt to London creditors. He had also married the young Peggy Shippen, the daughter of a prominent Loyalist family who had supported the British occupation of Philadelphia. Arnold engaged in secret communications with British commander-in-chief Sir Henry Clinton to surrender the fort of West Point in New York, which he had been appointed to command in April 1779. Through Major John André, the head of espionage for the British forces in North America, Arnold agreed on a payment of £20,000 to surrender the fort. Once he established himself at the fort, he took measures to weaken its defenses. After the two men met in late September, André was captured by American militiamen, and the incriminating letters he carried were sent on to Washington. Once he found out evidence of his treason was sent to Washington, Arnold sailed to New York and received a commission as a British officer. West Point remained in American hands while André was executed by hanging on October 2nd.

In December 1780, Clinton dispatched Arnold to Virginia at the head of the American Legion, a force of 1,600 men, most of whom were deserters from the Continental Army. Arnold managed to capture Richmond by surprise, and continued on a devastating rampage through much of the state, destroying houses and farms in the process. He was forced to relinquish Richmond after the arrival of Lafayette. By March, Arnold received reinforcements commanded by William Phillips, who continued the raiding. Phillips died of fever in May, allowing Arnold to reassume command of the 5,000-man army until Cornwallis' arrival on May 20th. Cornwallis took command from Arnold and sent the latter back to New York. Arnold would spend the rest of the war raiding towns in his native Connecticut. Meanwhile, Cornwallis' army defeated Lafayette and recaptured Richmond. He sent Tarleton on a raid against Charlottesville, where Virginia's legislature had been meeting temporarily. Tarleton narrowly failed to capture Thomas Jefferson, who was serving as governor of Virginia. Jefferson escaped barely ten minutes before the arrival of Tarleton at his home in Monticello, and the British officer contented himself by taking several bottles of wine from Jefferson's cellar.

Cornwallis' decision to march to Virginia was taken without the knowledge of General Clinton at headquarters in New York. Once news of Cornwallis' movements reached Clinton, the British commander-in-chief was obliged to reassess the strategic situation. The southern campaign had been a failure, and expected Loyalist support failed to materialize. British anxieties were heightened by the appearance of a French fleet of twenty ships commanded by Admiral Paul de Grasse which sailed from Brest in March and arrived in the West Indies at the end of April. Clinton anticipated a Franco-American attack on New York and requested troops from Cornwallis to bolster the defense of New York. The remainder of Cornwallis' forces were authorized to carry out raids on American positions. Clinton also asked Cornwallis to identify a site to establish a deep-water naval port, since the Royal Navy found it difficult to operate from New York. Cornwallis initially demonstrated a reluctance to remain in Virginia and requested permission to return to

Charleston, but eventually fulfilled Clinton's orders by moving to Yorktown, located on the southern bank of the York River which flows into the Chesapeake Bay. The new base would allow the British to conduct amphibious operations in Virginia, although Cornwallis was concerned that the Chesapeake's network of rivers would be vulnerable to sudden French attack. Cornwallis decided to keep his entire force of 8,000 men with him to fortify the position, and Clinton approved his dispositions. Cornwallis' army in Virginia was shadowed by Lafayette, who commanded an army half the size.

Clinton's anxieties about a joint Franco-American attack on New York were not misguided. Since July 1780, a French force of 5,000 men sent by King Louis XVI had established itself in Newport, Rhode Island. The army was commanded by the Comte de Rochambeau, an experienced officer in European warfare who could not speak English and had no experience of America. Nevertheless, Rochambeau's military abilities and his readiness to subordinate himself to Washington, were appreciated by the American commander. Although the French had made their landing, Rochambeau was reluctant to leave behind his fleet, which was blockaded by the British Navy. In May 1781, Washington and Rochambeau nevertheless agreed to pursue joint operations against New York City, though these plans did not bear much fruit when put into action in July. In August, Washington received news that de Grasse was sailing to the Chesapeake with 29 ships and over 3,000 men, having made an agreement with the Spanish for the Spanish Navy to protect French interests in the Caribbean. Washington immediately informed Rochambeau of his intention to lead the two armies to the Chesapeake as quickly as possible. The march exemplified Washington's genius for organization and logistics, and the army arrived in mid-September.

De Grasse arrived in Virginia at the end of August, and at the beginning of September, he fought the British fleet to a standstill in the Battle of the Chesapeake. De Grasse was reluctant to maintain his fleet in the vulnerable waters of the Chesapeake and was hoping to return to the open seas. Washington and Rochambeau persuaded the admiral to stay for the sake of the Franco-American army, and de Grasse agreed to send 2,000 men to assist an allied siege of Yorktown. At the beginning of September, Cornwallis could have attempted to break out of Yorktown against Lafayette's weak force, but stayed put, expecting reinforcements from Clinton. Once the allied army arrived, Cornwallis' chances to fight his way out were slim. Siege operations began on September 28th as the allied army marched from Williamsburg, setting up camp outside Yorktown by the afternoon. Cornwallis established two lines of defense but soon abandoned the outer line. The combined allied army of 19,000 men seemed destined for victory. At times, the allied army silenced their fire and resorted to beating their drums as a show of force against the defenders. Rochambeau soon put an end to this practice, observing that the drumming attracted enemy fire. During the first week of October, allied engineers strengthened their fortifications and constructed positions to station their artillery. The allies began the bombardment on October 9th, their accuracy of fire taking the besieged British army by surprise.

Cornwallis knew that the fall of Yorktown was inevitable. During the night of October 16th, Cornwallis hoped to evacuate his army across the York River to Gloucester Point on the north bank, but poor weather forced him to abandon the attempt. On October 17th, the British fleet sailed from New York with 6,000 reinforcements, but turned back once it realized it was outnumbered by the French fleet. On the same day, without any knowledge of the attempt to aid his besieged army, Cornwallis sent an officer to Washington to negotiate a surrender. Terms were agreed over the following days, and Washington signed on October 19th. The British garrison laid down their arms and marched out of Yorktown playing the British military tune "The World Turned Upside Down," which seemed to perfectly encapsulate the British experience of the war in America. Cornwallis did not attend the surrender ceremony and sent General Charles O'Hara to deliver his sword in his place. Hoping to avoid the humiliation of surrendering to an American officer, O'Hara first sought to deliver the sword to a French officer. The French refused to receive the surrender, and O'Hara was directed to General Benjamin Lincoln, Washington's second-in-command, at Yorktown. Lincoln took the sword and held it briefly before returning it to O'Hara as convention dictated.

The surrender of Cornwallis' army at Yorktown was a major defeat for the British, but did not necessarily signal British defeat in the war. The British continued to possess a large army in New York, and the British army continued to maintain a presence in Charleston, parts of Georgia, Canada, and the West Indies. However, the disaster at Yorktown finally broke the will of the British authorities in London. Lord North, the architect of the policy which led to the war, resigned from the office of prime minister in March 1782. He was replaced by Rockingham, who once again assumed the supreme office. Rockingham's ministry was given the task of negotiating peace with the Americans. Lord Shelburne became Home Secretary (formerly Southern Secretary) with responsibility for colonial affairs, while Charles James Fox was appointed to serve as Foreign Secretary (formerly Northern Secretary) with responsibility for European affairs. Fox and Shelburne were rivals, but under this arrangement they shared responsibility for diplomatic affairs concerning peace between France and America. Shelburne would later become prime minister himself upon Rockingham's death in July. In April, he appointed Richard Oswald, a Scottish merchant who had spent his youth in Virginia, to serve as the British agent in the negotiations. The American Congress appointed John Adams, Benjamin Franklin, and John Jay to serve as peace commissioners, while the peace talks were held in Paris and hosted by French foreign minister Vergennes.

Although Congress instructed the American negotiators to consult with their French allies and follow their advice while conducting talks with the British, American and French interests diverged on the question of the territorial settlement in North America and the commercial rights of the United States in Canada. The French, although recognizing American independence, cared little for such matters and were keen to protect their interests in the Caribbean. Meanwhile, Spain was primarily concerned about recovering Gibraltar, launching a major last-ditch attack on the British outpost in September 1782. The Americans realized they could get better terms by negotiating directly with London. Talks between the British and American representatives were encumbered by the fact that Oswald had not been given instructions to recognize American independence. Franklin and Jay insisted that the British should recognize American independence before the signing of the peace treaty. A new set of words was drafted which managed to satisfy both sides. Preliminary peace articles were finally agreed on November 30th, and Franklin informed Vergennes of the agreement, which would not come into force until the British and French made their peace. The first article of the treaty was an acknowledgment from the British king that the United States were to be "free and sovereign independent states," while the rest of the document delineated the geographical boundaries and commercial rights of this newly recognized sovereign entity. The terms were highly favorable to the Americans, and Shelburne envisaged that the British and Americans could enjoy profitable trade with each other. Congress also agreed to recommend to state legislatures to restore the property rights of British subjects. Despite this undertaking, the states were reluctant to do so, and many Loyalists opted for British exile. The exiles included Benedict Arnold, who had gone to London in a vain attempt to persuade Parliament to continue the war effort.

On January 20th, 1783, peace was signed between Britain and France. French interests in the Caribbean experienced a setback when de Grasse's fleet was defeated by Admiral George Rodney at the Battle of the Saints in April 1782, with its commander falling into British captivity. The French were keen to put an end to a costly war which was draining the royal treasury. Likewise, after their failed attack on Gibraltar, the Spanish also agreed to peace with Britain. They failed to accomplish their primary objective of recapturing Gibraltar, although the British ceded Menorca and the Floridas to the Spanish. All parties signed the Treaty of Paris on September 3rd, 1783, which was ratified the following May. The British army was evacuated from the United States by Guy Carleton, who replaced Clinton in March 1782 and was given the unenviable task of organizing the transport of men and supplies back to Britain. Meanwhile, the victorious Americans celebrated their victory by toasting General Washington, the Continental Army, and their French allies. The bold new experiment to establish a nation dedicated to life, liberty, and the pursuit of happiness had survived a long and agonizing trial by fire. The United States would now have to learn how to govern itself in times of peace.

Chapter 11 – An Imperfect Union

On December 19th, 1783, George Washington rode to Annapolis, Maryland, the temporary seat of Congress. The victorious American commander was the most famous man in North America and the hero of the revolution. Had he desired to do so, Washington could have become a military dictator with the support of the army, as well as most of the people. Instead, having secured the independence of his country with men under arms, Washington relinquished the commission he had been handed by Congress eight years earlier. He was inspired by the example of the Roman general Cincinnatus, who was appointed dictator in 458 BCE and granted exceptional powers to organize the successful defense of the city against an enemy invasion. Once he secured victory within fifteen days, Cincinnatus relinquished his office and returned to his farm. Washington's gesture was also partly motivated by the Newburgh Conspiracy in March 1783. Throughout the war, the Continental Army received limited assistance from Congress, which was unable to compel the states to provide supplies and money to maintain the army. While encamped in Newburgh, New York, army officers who complained that they had not been paid for several months planned a military coup, encouraged by members of Congress who believed that the remit of Congress should be widened at the expense of the states. When Washington uncovered the conspiracy, he quickly moved to defuse the situation, but the risk of the military subverting the civilian government was clear for everyone to see. Congress eventually agreed to keep the men on half-pay for five years, and most of the army was discharged.

The civilian government of the United States operated under the Articles of Confederation, which came into force on March 1ˢᵗ, 1781 following its ratification by all thirteen states. The chief author John Dickinson had recommended granting extensive powers to Congress, but the text that was eventually passed and ratified limited the power of Congress and left most political power in the hands of the states. Congress itself did not have a permanent seat and moved around the union. The initial sessions were based in the Pennsylvania State House in Philadelphia, where the Continental Congress had met and where the Declaration of Independence was signed. The body later moved to Princeton, New Jersey; Annapolis, Maryland; Trenton, New Jersey; and New York City, New York. During the war, individual states understood the imperative of contributing to the war effort and were more willing to act on the recommendations of Congress. Once the Treaty of Paris had been signed, individual states were keen to retain their liberties. Over the course of the 1780s, Congress was faced with a number of challenges in the fields of economics, foreign affairs, and settlement of new territories. These problems required federal solutions and thus the attention of Congress, but owing to the limited powers accorded to Congress under the Articles of Confederation, it would struggle to persuade the states to implement congressional policies.

The national government had significant expenditures from a number of sources, including soldiers' pay, costs of serving public debt, and day-to-day operating costs, but Congress had no source of revenue to call on. The power of taxation lay with the states. In April 1783, Congress passed a measure to impose a rate of 5 percent on imports to finance the payment of the public debt. Although eleven states approved of the measure by 1786, Pennsylvania and New York opposed the duty, and the required unanimity for the levy to become law was not met. Despite attempts by Congress to persuade the states to contribute financially, in 1785 Congress stopped paying the interest on its debt to France, and in 1787 it defaulted on part of the principal. The drain on the French treasury due to the war partially contributed to the French Revolution in 1789.

In addition to its concerns about public finance, Congress was also concerned about commercial issues. Although trade volumes increased after the war, there remained a sense of unease about falling prices, heavy indebtedness, and inconsistent trade regulation which restricted interstate trade. In 1786, Congressman James Madison of Virginia suggested a convention of states to consider strengthening the powers of Congress to include the regulation of trade and powers of taxation. Only five states attended the convention, and there was little it could do to persuade the other states to cede their powers to Congress.

While Congress was hoping for state approval of the import tax, the national government had to deal with a foreign policy crisis. Although the British had agreed to a generous territorial settlement with the United States, Spain did not recognize the cession of territory east of the Mississippi to American control. Britain and United States had agreed in Paris that the Mississippi River should be open to merchant vessels from both countries, but in 1784, the Spanish closed the lower Mississippi to American navigation. They hoped to persuade settlers in what would become Kentucky and Tennessee to break away from the United States in order to trade through the Spanish port of New Orleans. These settlers seriously considered this as they felt they were neglected by Congress. The United States secretary of foreign affairs at this time was John Jay, a New York lawyer who had previously served as ambassador to Spain and as one of the peace negotiators in Paris. Jay's instructions were drafted by Virginian Congressman James Monroe, which defended the American claim to territories east of the Mississippi and claimed the right of navigation along the whole length of the river. However, as an Easterner, Jay was keen to avoid competition from western states trading via the Mississippi, and was open to accepting Spanish demands. He requested the authority from Congress to provide him with new instructions, but these were not granted as any treaty required the support of nine states for approval. The disputes over Jay's actions hindered further cooperation between the states.

Congress was more successful in regulating the settlement and government of territories to the northwest of the Ohio River. The territory had been claimed by Virginia since the seventeenth century, but it ceded its claim in 1781 as a condition of Maryland's ratification of the

Articles of Confederation. Thomas Jefferson, who served on the congressional committee overseeing the settlement of new territories, envisaged that after a period of territorial government these new lands would join the union with the same status as the original thirteen states. Jefferson also believed that the new territories should be given to settlers for free, but Congress was short of funds and decided to sell land in order to pay off the national debt. In the Land Ordinance of 1785, Congress divided the new territory into townships of 36 square miles with lots of one square miles on sale for at least one dollar per acre. Provisions were also made for land grants to veteran soldiers and public schools. The scheme soon fell victim to speculation, with the Ohio Company buying up the land at low prices. Squatters who settled in the Ohio territory without any right to the land also complicated matters and often found themselves in conflict with local Indian populations. This anarchic process of settlement forced Congress to revise its policy by introducing the Northwest Ordinance of 1787, which gave Congress control of the government. The ordinance was also the first document in American history to prohibit slavery.

Despite the success in the regulation of western settlement, by the late 1780s, there was a general sense that American society and government had failed to realize the idealistic expectations of freedom and progress that fueled the nation during the war against Britain. Thomas Jefferson believed that the principles of liberty and freedom set out in the Declaration of Independence should be translated to American society. As a member of the Virginia House of Delegates, and later as the state's governor, Jefferson hoped to introduce a state constitution that would recognize these principles. He envisaged that the poorest members of society would be granted land for free to develop and cultivate. He believed that slavery was incompatible with liberty and recognized that the institution should somehow come to an end, and advocated enhanced legal rights for slaves. Nevertheless, Jefferson should not be regarded as a racial egalitarian—he was a slaveowner himself, and recent evidence shows that he kept a slave mistress, Sally Hemmings. Jefferson's preferred option to address slavery was colonization, whereby black slaves would be sent to distant territories to keep them apart from the white American population. Jefferson's vision was largely rejected by the state assembly.

The Virginia gentry which controlled state government were keen to maintain the privileges they enjoyed before the revolution. Most Virginians therefore did not encounter much of a change from British rule, with the fabric of society remaining the same. If the United States were to realize its aspirations for freedom and liberty, it had to reduce the power of established state elites who had little to gain and a lot to lose.

The widespread recognition that the Articles of Confederation were not fit for purpose led to calls to amend the document and strengthen the national government. These voices grew louder in the aftermath of Shays' Rebellion in 1786. Daniel Shays was a Massachusetts farmer who had served in the Continental Army at the very beginning of the war at Lexington and Concord. Shays and his supporters, most of whom were farmers from central and western Massachusetts, suffered from the state's financial policy. The state government in Massachusetts was dominated by merchants who imposed high taxes to finance the state debt and its obligations to Congress. These measures eventually provoked a rebellion in August 1786 after the state legislature failed to consider the many petitions for debt relief. Over the ensuing months, the rebellion spread throughout the state, and in January 1787, the rebels threatened to take control of the federal armory at Springfield. Congress was unable to supply an army to suppress the rebellion, so it was up to the authorities at Massachusetts to do so. The state militia, under the command of General William Shepard, seized control of the armory without authorization from Congress, while General Benjamin Lincoln commanded a private militia to confront Shays. By June 1787, the rebellion was successfully suppressed, but it was clear to everyone that radical changes needed to be made if the United States were to survive and fulfill its promise of building a new society.

Chapter 12 – A More Perfect Union

The leading American politicians who recognized that the Articles of Confederation were unsatisfactory met in Philadelphia in May 1787 to discuss proposals to amend the articles. Most of these men, although loyal to their own states, recognized that the authority of the national government had to be increased. James Madison was among the most enthusiastic advocates for increasing the powers of the national government. A member of the Virginia delegation, Madison had been instrumental in convening the Annapolis Convention the previous year, which looked at the question of interstate trade. While there were only five states represented at Annapolis, delegates from twelve states met at Philadelphia—only Rhode Island did not send a delegation. Among Madison's fellow delegates from Virginia was General Washington himself, who had been persuaded to return to politics following his retirement from public life after he relinquished the office of commander-in-chief. Although Washington did not have particularly sophisticated views about how the new government should be structured, his experience with dealing with Congress during the war convinced him that the national government required greater powers. Washington, who continued to enjoy the reputation of a national hero, would also lend further legitimacy to the Philadelphia Convention and any recommendations it would make to the states. Washington was soon elected chairman of the Convention.

The delegates soon decided that the Articles of Confederation could not be amended and a new constitution was required to establish the powers of a new national government. Madison proposed that the government should consist of three separate branches: the legislative, the executive, and the judiciary. The doctrine of separation of powers was inspired by the French philosopher Montesquieu's *The Spirit of the Laws*, which was inspired by the British constitution. The legislature would propose and vote on the laws, the executive would implement them, and the judiciary would ensure that the laws were being followed. While these functions were separated in the British government, they could not be said to be independent. Members of the Houses of Parliament formed both the executive and the judiciary. In the new American constitution, individuals would only serve in one branch of government with very few exceptions. The legislative branch served to ensure that the government would remain accountable to the people. Madison initially proposed that Congress should be bicameral—consisting of two chambers—where the lower house would be directly elected by the people, while the upper house would be chosen by members of the lower house. Proposed legislation would have to meet the approval of both houses before becoming law. The legislative branch would have the power to raise taxation, declare war, and make treaties, the primary functions for any government. The powers of the legislative branch would be laid out in Article I of the new Constitution.

Members of the convention soon split into two camps by the question of state representation in the new legislature. Edmund Randolph of Virginia presented a plan, largely drafted by Madison, which proposed that states should be represented in Congress according to the size of their population. According to this principle, which became known as the Virginia Plan, the more populous states would enjoy greater representation in the national legislature. Virginia's proposal was supported by Pennsylvania and Massachusetts, the second and third most populous states in the union. The smaller states resisted the proposal, recognizing that their representation would be diminished. The three largest states accounted for almost half the American population and would therefore control half the votes in Congress. The smaller states, such as Delaware, Maryland, and even New York, which remained sparsely populated at this stage, supported the plan put forward by New Jersey's William Paterson. The New Jersey Plan proposed that each state's representation would be equal regardless of its population. This was effectively the same principle which governed the Articles of Confederation, where each state could cast one vote in Congress regardless of its size. Eventually Connecticut delegates Oliver Ellsworth and Roger Sherman proposed that a Congress divided into two houses could have proportional representation in the lower house (the House of Representatives) and equal representation in the upper house (the Senate). Although the Pennsylvania and Virginia delegates continued to oppose this, it was eventually approved by the Convention on July 16th, 1787.

A crucial element of the question of representation related to the way in which slaves should be accounted for in determining the representation of the lower house. Slaves were denied the right to vote and therefore would not be represented in the legislature. However, the Southern states, including South Carolina and Georgia, had large slave populations who worked on plantations. These Southern states recognized the predominantly anti-slavery sentiment in the North, and understood that they would need to fight in Congress to preserve the institution of slavery which sustained their economies. If slaves were not counted toward representation, then the Southern states would have a lesser voice in debates. The Convention eventually used the formula by which each slave would account for three-fifths of a freeman in determining the representation for each state. The same formula had been suggested by Madison in 1783 to determine the financial contribution of each state to Congress. Although many Northerners were uncomfortable with making this compromise, the Convention did so in order to ensure that South Carolina and Georgia would remain part of the union. The debate over slavery extended to the Atlantic slave trade. Although many delegates hoped to abolish the import of slaves across the Atlantic, as a compromise the Convention agreed to abolish the external slave trade only by 1808. The question of slavery was one of the most contentious debates during the Philadelphia Convention, but the delegates were careful not to employ the term "slave" in their deliberations. In the eventual document they were referred to as "all other persons."

The deliberations over representation in Congress gave way to the discussions concerning the executive branch. The head of the executive branch would be the president of the United States of America. By virtue of his office, the president would become the commander-in-chief of the United States' armed forces and given the right to appoint army officers. The president was also given the power to appoint ambassadors and federal judges, pending Senate approval. The president's term limits were extended to four years with the right to reelection, though there were disagreements about how the president should be chosen. Madison believed that the president should be elected by the people, but others believed that this could not guarantee that the president would be an individual who was fit for office. The Convention temporarily agreed on July 17th for the president to be elected by the national legislature, but later opted for an electoral college. The states would appoint a number of electors equal to their entire congressional representation who would cast two votes. The individual who received the largest number of votes would serve as president, and the second highest would be vice president. A tie would be determined by the House of Representatives, with each state casting one vote each. In the event that no candidates were to secure a majority of electoral votes, the House of Representatives would choose the president from the five candidates who secured the most votes. The presidency was therefore indirectly elected, though some states opted to allow the electors to be chosen by the people through elections, while others nominated electors through their state legislatures. The powers of the executive were outlined in Article II of the Constitution signed by the Philadelphia Convention. The powers of the judicial branch were outlined in Article III, providing for a Supreme Court of the United States populated by justices appointed by the president for life. On September 17th, 39 of the 55 men who attended the Convention signed the Constitution.

A Constitution had been signed, but there was no guarantee that the states would ratify the new document. Ratification required the approval of nine states, and as soon the Philadelphia Convention had finished its business, the public debate began about the merits of the proposals it produced. The first articles criticizing the proposed Constitution appeared in the press in late September and early October under the pseudonyms of "Cato" and "Brutus," key figures of the Roman Republic. They argued that the new constitution would override the sovereignty of the individual states and make them vulnerable to the tyranny of the central government. They feared that the president would become an effective monarch. In response to these criticisms of the Constitution which would become known as the *Anti-Federalist Papers*, Alexander Hamilton of New York embarked on a project to persuade the states of the merits of the Constitution. A former artillery officer in the Continental Army who served on Washington's staff and later played a key role at the Battle of Yorktown, Hamilton had been a delegate at the Constitutional Convention, though his contribution to the debates was limited. Hamilton published the first of 85 articles, collectively known to history as the *Federalist Papers*, on October 27th, 1787 under the pseudonym "Publius," in honor of Publius Valerius Poplicola, one of the founders of the Roman Republic. In *Federalist Paper* No. 1, Hamilton explained why the union of the states would serve to encourage national prosperity, highlighting the inadequacy of the Articles of Confederation and how the Constitution could serve to protect liberty, property, and the American republic.

Federalist Paper No. 1 outlined the themes that would be covered in the rest of the *Federalist Papers*. Hamilton initially approached his fellow New Yorker John Jay as a collaborator on this project, and Jay duly produced four powerful pieces to follow up Hamilton's first one. After this, Jay fell ill and would only contribute one more article in the series, No. 64. In light of Jay's illness, Hamilton turned to James Madison. The two men worked at a frantic pace, publishing three or four articles a week for several months. Madison's output consisted of at least 29 articles, many of which addressed the concerns of the Anti-Federalists. In response to the fears of tyrannical government, Hamilton and Madison argued that the union was on the verge of collapse, and any dissolution of the union would result in the states coming into conflict with each other, which would make the American republic vulnerable to the designs of European monarchies. They also proposed that any difference in opinion over economic and political interests should be settled in a representative Congress. Madison believed that a clearly defined system and the Constitution's clear delineation of the powers of the federal government would protect the states' rights and individual liberties. Moreover, Madison discussed measures to prevent the tyranny of the majority, and supported the expansion of the United States into a large commercial republic in *Federalist Paper* No. 10. In *Federalist Paper* Nos. 39 and 51, he espoused the principles behind the separation of powers into three branches, as well as the sharing of power between the federal government and the states. The independent branches of government would provide checks and balances on the other and prevent the tyranny of the majority.

Although the *Federalist Papers* were initially published in New York and addressed "To the State and People of New York," they contributed to the national debate concerning ratification and were used by advocates of the Constitution across the union. In the months following the signing of the Constitution, state conventions met to discuss the issue of ratification. Delaware was the first state to ratify, doing so on December 7th. It was soon joined by Pennsylvania, which was destined to be a lynchpin of the new union, and within a month five states had approved the Constitution. In February 1788, Massachusetts approved the Constitution by a narrow margin, with John Hancock and Samuel Adams being persuaded to support the Federalist cause despite some reservations. By June, following New Hampshire's decision to ratify, the Constitution had the support of the nine states that it required to come into force. But two powerful states, Virginia and New York, remained on the sidelines. After intense debate, Virginia ratified it at the end of June. New York was reluctant to ratify the Constitution without a Bill of Rights protecting the rights of the people and the states. Alexander Hamilton had argued against this in *Federalist Paper* No. 84, arguing that the Constitution did not exist to limit the people's rights, but to define the scope of the federal government. Nevertheless, New York only ratified in July on the condition that a Bill of Rights would be introduced. When the new Congress met in the spring of 1789, it prepared a Bill of Rights which was drafted by Madison. Of the twelve articles presented, ten were ratified by 1791. The First Amendment enshrined the freedom of speech among other freedoms, the Second Amendment protected the right to bear arms to protect against tyranny, while the Tenth Amendment stipulated that all powers which were not delegated to the national government were reserved to the states and the people. North Carolina and Rhode Island finally ratified the Constitution in November 1789 and June 1790 respectively and subsequently joined the union.

Chapter 13 – Manifest Destiny

The United States Constitution proved to be a remarkably enduring document. Since the passage of the Bill of Rights, it has been amended only on seventeen further occasions. This was far from guaranteed when the Constitution came into force in July 1788. The federal government began its operations on March 4th, 1789. On that day, members of Congress opened the new congressional session in New York. On April 6th, Congress met to certify the results of the first presidential election. George Washington had been elected unanimously to the presidency. John Adams, who received the second highest number of votes, became vice president. Washington was notified of the results on April 14th and inaugurated at Federal Hall in New York on April 30th. In September, Washington appointed John Jay to serve as the first chief justice of the Supreme Court and chose five other associate justices. The three branches of the federal government were thus in place.

In the summer of 1789, Congress would create three executive departments to assist Washington in the management of government affairs: the state department with responsibility for foreign affairs, the war department for military affairs, and the treasury with responsibility for public finances. Washington appointed Thomas Jefferson as secretary of state. Henry Knox and Alexander Hamilton, two of Washington's former staff officers, were appointed to serve as secretary of war and secretary of the treasury respectively. As a leading advocate for the federal government, Hamilton was the driving force of Washington's administration. Hamilton pursued an agenda to transform the United States into an economic and commercial powerhouse by establishing a system of national credit supported by the First Bank of the United States. While Washington favored Hamilton's stance and approved many of his treasury secretary's proposals, he was keen to appease Jefferson, who was an opponent of Hamilton's attempts to create new federal institutions. Jefferson was concerned that the measures to encourage commerce would favor the Northern states at the expense of the Southern states. As a compromise, in 1790 Hamilton agreed to support proposals to relocate the national capital farther south near Georgetown on the Potomac River. The territory was named District of Columbia and the city named Washington after the president. The federal government temporarily moved to Philadelphia and building work on the new capital began in 1791. Washington had planned to retire from the presidency after a single term, but was persuaded to stay in office for a second term from 1793 to 1797. In 1796, at the end of his second term, Washington decided to relinquish his office, setting a precedent that would not be broken until the 1940s. In his farewell address, published in September 1796, Washington warned the American political classes from engaging in factionalism, which would be injurious to the cause of liberty. Washington's warning fell on deaf ears. The disputes between Hamilton and Jefferson provided the context for the first party system, pitting Hamilton's Federalists against Jeffersonian Republicans. Following Washington's retirement in 1797, John Adams was elected president while Jefferson became vice president. Adams was a Federalist and continued to pursue Hamilton's policies in office. This arrangement meant that the president and vice president were members of opposing parties, and soon the two men, erstwhile friends and leaders of the revolution, were no longer on speaking terms. The first party system would continue until the late 1810s with the Jeffersonian Republicans becoming dominant after the Federalists were considered sympathetic to British interests during the War of 1812 against the British. However, although the fortunes of the parties in question would rise and fall, American politics continue to be dominated by two major parties to the present day.

The uncomfortable situation of president and vice president representing different parties was addressed in the 1800 election when the leading candidates for president selected a running mate as vice president. In order to ensure that the candidates from the same party would not be tied, it was expected that one of the electors would cast a vote for the presidential candidate, and his second vote for a third individual. The Jeffersonians narrowly won the election, with Jefferson winning 73 votes to Adams' 65. However, in the reckoning of the final results, Jefferson and his running mate Aaron Burr both received 73 electoral votes. The tied election was thus thrown to the outgoing House of Representatives, which was controlled by the Federalists. The Federalists saw Jefferson as their leading opponent and sought to deprive him of the presidency by favoring Burr. Hamilton, who no longer held public office, recognized that his fellow New Yorker Burr was the greater threat to the Federalist cause and sought to persuade the Federalist congressmen to support Jefferson. Jefferson was duly elected to the presidency on the 36th ballot in the House vote, with Burr as vice president. Hamilton's intervention to deny Burr the presidency would have long-lasting repercussions. In July 1804, the two men fought a duel, motivated by the 1800 election as well as local New York politics. Hamilton was mortally wounded by Burr, whose political career ended as a result. In order to prevent a recurrence of the crisis of 1800, the 12th Amendment was passed to establish separate elections in the electoral college for president and vice president.

By the early 1800s, the political institutions and processes that would define the United States government had largely been established. Its territorial extent, however, was a fraction of its present size, though new states were already being admitted into the union. The Treaty of Paris had established the western borders of the United States at the Mississippi, though this was disputed by Spain. In 1800, Spain returned the Louisiana Territory to France in exchange for territories in Italy conquered by the French revolutionary armies. Napoleon Bonaparte, who had recently come to power in a military coup, sought to re-establish French commercial interests in North America. The American settlers in the west were concerned about French ambitions in Louisiana, and in 1803, Jefferson's government approached Napoleon, offering to purchase the port of New Orleans from France for $10 million, to ensure that US merchants could trade freely along the whole length of the Mississippi River. Napoleon responded positively to this approach since the French government was in the process of preparing for the resumption of hostilities in Britain. The defeat of the French in the Haitian Revolution of 1803 had presented a setback for Napoleon's North American project. The French therefore offered to sell the whole of Louisiana for $15 million, an offer which was immediately accepted by American agents. The French hoped that American possession of Louisiana would encourage the United States to become a commercial power and a counterweight to British interests.

In 1804, Jefferson sent an expedition of US Army volunteers under the command of Meriwether Lewis and William Clark to survey the new territories he had purchased. The Lewis and Clark expedition set off from St. Louis in May 1804 and traversed the entire Louisiana Territory, encountering many Indian tribes in the process. They then moved farther west through land claimed by the British until they reached the Pacific in November 1805. The expedition team made their return journey the following spring and arrived back in St. Louis in September 1806. Lewis and Clark reported back extensive scientific, geographical, and ethnographical information about the Louisiana Territory, and the expedition also served to lay claim to the Pacific territories. Over the following decades, waves of American settlers would flock westwards in an effort to seek their fortune and escape economic hardship. As increasing numbers of Americans settled these new lands, they came into conflict with indigenous peoples. In the 1800s, five Indian nations in the southeast had been guaranteed the status of autonomous nations by the United States in an effort to encourage their assimilation to American culture, but pressures of American settlement led to land disputes. In 1830, President Andrew Jackson signed the Indian Removal Act which forced the five tribes to relinquish their lands in exchange for less fertile lands to the west in what would become Oklahoma Territory. The measure was violently resisted, and thousands of Indians died as they were forcibly removed on the so-called Trail of Tears during the 1830s.

The purchase of Louisiana more than doubled the size of the United States, but there were still extensive territories to the west controlled by the Spanish Empire. In 1821, these territories became part of Mexico after the latter gained independence from their European colonial masters. American settlers established themselves in the Mexican state of Texas over the 1820s, and soon hostilities broke out against the Mexicans, resulting in Texan independence from Mexico in 1836. The Republic of Texas would later be admitted to the United States in 1846 during the presidency of James K. Polk. Polk believed that it was the manifest destiny of the United States to extend its republican principles across the continent and laid claim to further Mexican territory to the southwest, as well as British lands to the northwest. The Mexican-American War (1846-48) proved to be a catastrophic defeat for the Mexicans. In the ensuing Treaty of Guadalupe Hidalgo, Mexico ceded half its lands to the United States. Polk also brokered a settlement with the British which provided for American control of the southern half of Oregon Country, which would become the states of Washington and Oregon. With these territorial acquisitions, the United States expanded to the Pacific Coast and assumed much of its current territorial extent.

The westward expansion of the United States did not only lead to clashes with Indians, but further fueled the debate over the future of slavery. The United States had been established on a contradictory basis of recognizing the liberties of all men while holding black slaves in bondage. The union was balanced between the Northern anti-slavery states and the Southern slave-owning states. Although the Northern states believed that the federal government did not have the constitutional power to abolish slavery where it already existed, they opposed the further expansion of slavery. With the admission of each new state into the union, each with two senators, this threatened to alter the political balance between the Northern and Southern states. The debate over the admission of Missouri in 1820 threatened the future of the union. Eventually a compromise was brokered by Henry Clay of Kentucky, whereby Missouri would be admitted as a slave state but it would be balanced out by the admission of Maine, formerly part of Massachusetts, as a free state. Territories north of Missouri's southern border would henceforth be restricted to slavery, while those south of the line were open to slavery. This was the first of a set of uneasy compromises over the first half of the nineteenth century. The incorporation of California into the union following the Mexican War resulted in a further compromise over slavery in 1850, once again brokered by Clay at the age of 73.

The disputes over the expansion of slavery continued into the 1850s over the admission of Kansas and Nebraska into the union. The admission of these states was a precondition for the construction of a transcontinental railroad linking Chicago to the Pacific, championed by Senator Stephen Douglas of Illinois. Although both territories were north of the Missouri Compromise Line, Southern senators refused to vote for admission unless slavery was permitted. Douglas suggested that the extension of slavery should depend on the principle of popular sovereignty, allowing the territories themselves to vote on the question. This principle was part of the Kansas-Nebraska Act of 1854, which repealed the Missouri Compromise. The popular sovereignty clause resulted in pro- and anti-slavery factions traveling to Kansas to vote on the issue of slavery, resulting in bloody clashes between the two sides. The violence in Kansas foreshadowed the US Civil War (1861-65), a conflict fundamentally caused by disagreements over slavery. The victory of the US federal government against the Confederate States of America resulted in the abolition of slavery, firstly with the Emancipation Proclamation issued by President Abraham Lincoln in 1863, and officially with the Thirteenth Amendment in 1865. With the abolition of slavery, one of the fundamental contradictions of the American revolutionary years was seemingly resolved.

Conclusion

The success of the American Revolution could be seen as a miracle, by which a colonial militia of farmers and merchants managed to defeat the most professional army in the world. On the other hand, the British defeat could also be seen as an inevitable consequence of attempts to fight a war across an ocean in hostile territory against a people fighting not only for their homes and families, but for a new form of society. Despite the disputes between the states and the relative weakness of the central government, and the often desperate situation of the Continental Army, the Americans avoided defeat in large part due to their commitment to the cause of liberty. Nevertheless, American victory cannot be explained purely in terms of the actions taken by Congress or by Washington and his army. Without French assistance, the war could have been dragged out for much longer. The fact that the war ended when it did, following Cornwallis' defeat at the Siege of Yorktown, was largely the consequence of the changing political environment in London. British policy transformed from attempting to suppress the revolution to encouraging the development of the United States as a close commercial partner.

Compared to the monarchical societies in Europe, the new American republic seemed to represent democratic progress. American political leaders established their state under the inspiration of the liberal political philosophy of Montesquieu and John Locke, and the iconography of Republican Rome. However, as in Rome, the right to life, liberty, and the pursuit of happiness was largely restricted to white men. The rights of the indigenous population were largely ignored as American settlement extended farther west, despite the assistance many Indian peoples provided to the new settlers. Slavery remained legal and constitutional in the United States for ninety years after independence, and necessitated a devastating civil war before the institution was abolished. Even after the abolition of slavery, African-Americans found it difficult to achieve racial equality. The racial prejudices of white Americans continued to define Southern society. African-Americans were barred from voting through intimidation and quasi-discriminatory laws, such as literacy tests. It took until the 1960s, a century after the abolition of slavery, for the civil rights movement to secure greater protections for African-Americans in the United States. It was a similar tale for women, who were only granted the right to vote in 1920 after a century of protest. The election of Barack Obama to the US presidency in 2008 was a major sign of progress, but racial and gender discrimination remains prevalent in American society.

For all its faults, the history of the United States is a tale of progress and success. From a loose confederation of thirteen colonies in the 18th century, in less than two hundred years it had become the most powerful nation in the world. Some of the reasons for American success can be found in the rights enshrined in the Declaration of Independence and the US Constitution. The United States advertised itself as a land of opportunity for Europeans seeking better livelihoods. Andrew Carnegie immigrated to the United States from Scotland as a child in 1848, and built a railroad and steel business empire which made him one of the wealthiest men in the world and a famous philanthropist. Albert Einstein found his home in the United States after Adolf Hitler came to power in his native Germany in 1933. Another Jewish émigré, Henry Kissinger, would become one of the country's most influential statesmen in the 1970s and 80s, a political giant of the age. The ability of the United States to attract talent from all over the world, its spirit of liberalism and constitutional rule in politics and economics, and the idea of American exceptionalism have all contributed to the United States becoming the most powerful nation in the world. American corporations from Microsoft and Apple to McDonalds and Coca-Cola have left their mark throughout the globe.

Although the United States has changed much over the last two and a half centuries, the debates that dominate American political discourse today strongly reflect the same debates during the American Revolution and the early days of the American republic. Issues such as rights and freedoms, the balance of power between federal and state government, and the need to protect liberty in the face of tyranny have been a part of American political discourse since the Massachusetts rebels threw the tea into Boston Harbor. The Founding Fathers of the United States did not share a single political philosophy, and many were initially reluctant to support calls for independence. The United States won its independence through George Washington's army and Thomas Paine's writings, and the early republic was forged through the dynamic tension between the followers of Hamilton and Jefferson, each of whom shaped the United States in their own manner. All of these men believed fundamentally in the rights and liberties of the American people, but had different conceptions about their extent and how best to protect them from tyranny. In order to understand the United States today, it is worth understanding the principles which inspired the founding of the United States, and the circumstances under which it secured its independence.

Part 3: The Civil War

A Captivating Guide to the American Civil War and Its Impact on the History of the United States

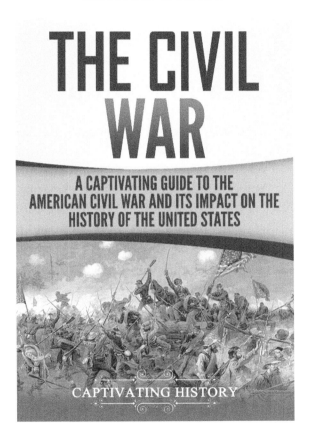

Introduction

No other war in the history of the United States has sparked as much debate and conflict as the American Civil War. For over 150 years, the story of the Civil War has been a source of contention, confusion, and even contempt in American life. Even today, the American public cannot agree on the causes of the Civil War, never mind its lessons or legacy.

More Americans died in the Civil War than in WWI, WWII, and Vietnam combined. The war not only put Americans against Americans but family against family, neighbor against neighbor, friend against friend. The conflict between the Union and the Confederacy still runs deep in some parts of the United States. Indeed, the fundamental questions of the Civil War—questions about racial (in)equality, the rights of citizenship, and the role of government—remain hot debates today. In many ways, the war that claimed over 600,000 American lives a century and a half ago is still the biggest battle being waged on American soil.

By understanding the causes, course, and repercussions of the Civil War, we can better grasp the underlying issues in the current American political climate, and realize the long-lasting scars on the United States population. As we cover the events leading up to the Civil War, we will explore the cracks in the foundation of the Union, the sparks leading to rebellion, and the discord amongst the citizens of the United States. The story of the war itself is one of horrific suffering, as well as jubilant liberation. The period after the war, known as Reconstruction, was a bold experiment in racial equality, and was resisted with equal ferocity by the Old Confederacy as was any Union advance at Gettysburg or Antietam.

Among the American public, if not among historians, the jury is still out on the meaning of the Civil War. Was the Civil War a war fought to keep the Union together? Was it fought to free slaves and end the blight of servitude against the will of the people who were in bondage? Was it a war of Northern aggression, justified through Republican ideals and with disregard to the Southern way of life? Depending on the year, election cycle, and individual perspective, an American might describe the war as one of the greatest achievements, or greatest tragedies, in American history. Through this exploration of the Civil War, we will learn about the origins and impacts of these diverse perspectives. We will also learn how modern historians explain the Civil War, especially when their ideas differ from those held by the general public.

The Civil War is a story full of struggle and despair, and one that is full of hope. It is a story from the American past that has a strong hold on our present. It may even be a story that could change our future.

Chapter 1 – An Uneasy Nation

Tension over slavery and the expansion of slavery into prospective states and territories had become a hot topic of debate. While many believed that the Constitution was clear on the expansion of slavery, there were some who saw their fortunes hanging in the balance as the United States expanded further west, opening new territories and offering new opportunities for citizens of the Union. With many taking a pro- or anti-stance regarding it, the topic of slavery would dominate American politics for the next three decades.

Steps to Secession

The northern and southern states had been at odds about slavery since the formation of the United States. Each state's representation in the United States Congress is determined by its population. When the country was being formed, they took a census of the population of the states to determine the number of representatives that each would be allocated.

The Southern states wanted each slave to be counted as a citizen. The Northern states opposed. They argued that if the slaves did not have the rights of other American citizens, they should not be counted in the population. The first piece of slavery-related legislation ever adopted by America was due to this disagreement.

Coined "The Great Compromise," the legislation required that three of every five slaves be counted toward the total population. This gave southern states more power in terms of the number of their legislators, but not as much power as they would have if all slaves were counted.

While the United States was seeing growth in industry and manufacturing in the North, the South was booming with large-scale agriculture service through slavery. The two largest money-making crops in the South were tobacco and cotton, both of which relied on manual labor in the form of slaves to be profitable. The growing abolitionist movement in the North was pushing for slavery to be banned in new territories. This brought about a deep-seated fear in Southerners that their way of life, and therefore their economy, were at risk. Subsequently, these factors created tensions amongst the North and South.

The South lamented that they were the financial backbone of the North. Southern money paid for necessities and luxuries from the North. Southerners purchased equipment and clothing from the North while simultaneously shipping their cotton North to be processed, and their children North to be educated. The North had a stranglehold on the Southern economy and had the potential to cripple them at will.

In 1819 as westward expansion advanced, a measure was brought to Congress which sought to prohibit slavery in the Missouri Territory. This measure would limit further expansion of cotton farming, as well as tip the balance of Congressional power even further into the hand of the North, since another anti-slavery state entering the union would leave 12 anti-slavery states versus 11 pro-slavery.[1] A compromise was needed.

In 1820 Congress came together and created the Missouri Compromise. The Missouri Compromise would allow Missouri to enter the Union as a slave state and Maine would be entered as a free state, thus allowing 12 states for each side of the slavery issue and keeping power balanced, but the balance was weak.[2]

---

[1] Maus, Louis P. *The Civil War: A Concise History.* New York, Oxford University Press, 2011, 15.

[2] Eicher, David J. *The Longest Night: A Military History of the Civil War.* New York, Simon and Schuster, 2001, 43.

In 1846 the Mexican War threatened to upend the hard work of the Missouri Compromise as a measure was introduced banning "slavery or involuntary servitude" in any territory acquired after the war. The mention of banning slavery riled up the South and threatened an already tense peace.[3]

Uncle Tom's Cabin Published

In 1852, with the dignity of slavery being questioned in the North and feelings of oppression and misunderstanding permeating the south, *Uncle Tom's Cabin* was published. It was met with shock by all United States citizens, but for very different reasons.

In the north, abolitionists clung to the book as their justification for ending slavery in the country. Northerners were astonished by the story of a slave who held great Christian fortitude while being sold like livestock, caring for a sick child with no means to do so, and finally being beaten to death for formulating a plan to free slaves.

Southerners were outraged because they thought the book was an unfair representation of a slave's life on a plantation in the South. Their main argument was that blacks were sub-human and did not have the capacity to feel pain or even love. If slaves were the same class as livestock, they had the right to beat a slave that wouldn't work just as they have the right to whip a mule that doesn't pull a plow. The book added even more tinder to an already huge bonfire that was about to be ignited.

Nebraska-Kansas Act

In 1854 the Nebraska-Kansas Act was passed creating the states of Nebraska and Kansas. With the expansion of the American West came the question of expanding slavery into the new territories. Two factions emerged in Kansas; the "Free-Staters" who wanted Kansas to be a free state without slavery and the "Border Ruffians" who wanted Kansas to enter the Union as a slave state.[4]

---

[3] Maus, Louis P. *The Civil War: A Concise History.* New York, Oxford University Press, 2011, 10-11.

[4] Eicher, David J. *The Longest Night: A Military History of the Civil War.* New York, Simon and Schuster, 2001, 44.

Even the political discourse over whether states would be free or slave-holding became violent. In 1856, Congressman Charles Sumner from Massachusetts was giving an anti-slavery speech on the floor of the House. He began calling Southern slave owners pimps and made derogatory references about the physical handicaps of Mississippi Congressman Preston Brooks' brother.

Brooks became enraged and stormed across the aisle attacking Sumner with his cane. Other pro-slavery congressmen kept people from stopping the beating by waving firearms at would-be interveners. The bludgeoning left Sumner unconscious on the house floor. It took three years for him to recover from the wounds inflicted.

What started as a hotbed political debate quickly turned into more severe actions including ballot rigging, intimidation, and violence. These tactics, practiced by both groups, led to confrontations and an outbreak of violence which culminated in a conflict known as Bleeding Kansas. With this bloodshed already becoming an issue in territories of the United States, many wondered what would happen if the election swung for the abolitionists.

The escalation of conflict between abolitionists and those who were pro-slavery was further strained in 1857 as the Supreme Court ruled against Dred Scott in *Dred Scott v. Sanford*. The ruling stated, "A free negro of the African race, whose ancestors were brought to this country and sold as slaves, is not a "citizen" within the meaning of the Constitution of the United States." And that "The Constitution of the United States recognizes slaves as property and pledges the Federal Government to protect it. And Congress cannot exercise any more authority over property of that description than it may constitutionally exercise over property of any other kind."[5]

The ruling in *Dred Scott* had further ramifications and further emboldened the South to expand slavery since slaves would remain enslaved regardless of which territory they were in. This angered many in the North who had fought hard to abolish slavery by fair and lawful

---

[5] United States Supreme Court, et al. *The Dred Scott decision: opinion of Chief Justice Taney.* New York: Van Evrie, Horton & Co., 1860, 1860. Pdf. Retrieved from the Library of Congress, <www.loc.gov/item/17001543/>.

means. The Southern victory in the Scott case was the final straw for many in the North. The approaching race for President would determine how that ruling would be enforced, and the result of the election would turn out to be the straw to break the back of the uneasy truce.

Lincoln Wins A Close Race

This ruling did more than just embolden the South. In 1859 John Brown planned to raid Virginia to free slaves held there, lead them on to a larger raid, and then bring about a general slave insurrection in that state. Before he could put his plan into action, he needed to obtain more weapons. On October 16, 1859, John Brown led a raid against the Federal armory in Harpers Ferry, Virginia. The raid was considered a success as the twenty-one men (16 whites, four free blacks, and one escaped slave) took the Federal armory without a single shot.[6] This act by abolitionists emboldened both sides towards conflict. The North saw the possibility of securing the freedom of slaves, while the South was focused on states' rights and property rights, the latter of which they believed supported the continued ownership of slaves.

By morning news of the raid had spread and the Virginia Militia exchanged gunfire with Brown and his ragtag band of abolitionists. By the next day, Washington Marines commanded by Robert E. Lee joined the militia and demanded Brown's surrender. His counter-demands led the Marines to assault his position and take Brown into custody. He stood trial ten days later, was found guilty, and sentenced to death by hanging. His action had stirred the hearts of a nation.[7] John Brown had lit a fuse that sparked rebellion in the South and anger in the North.

The raid at Harper's Ferry in 1859 and the upcoming elections lit the fuse on the powder keg of secession. The expansion of slavery into the west was a topic that became the debate among the candidates for President in 1860. In the North the people rallied behind an Illinois politician who spoke about the right of Congress to control the expansion

---

[6] Constable, George, editor. *Brother Against Brother: Time-Life Books History of the Civil War.* New York, Prentice Hall Press, 1990, 32.

[7] Constable, George, editor. *Brother Against Brother: Time-Life Books History of the Civil War.* New York, Prentice Hall Press, 1990, 33.

of slavery into the territories. The South rallied around John C. Breckenridge as their salvation against the ever-growing anti-slavery movement. The election turned into a four-man battle for the Presidency, the viewpoints of which were as varied as the men running for office. This four-man race would be a large part of a change in American politics.

The four-man contest between Abraham Lincoln, John C. Breckinridge, John Bell, and Stephen A. Douglas was a heated and volatile occurrence. In the end Abraham Lincoln won the popular and electoral vote, with 180 electoral votes and almost forty percent of the popular vote.[8] The election result was a catalyst for conflict. An anti-slavery President was to be sworn into the White House and the South was unhappy with the direction of the nation.

A wave of change was ready to sweep the Union. Its effect would be felt for years, decades, and generations to come. The tide was turning against the institution of slavery. With the election reflecting the division of the nation, the eventuality of Abraham Lincoln as President was a prospect that frustrated many and set the union on a course that would forever change the nation.

---

[8] Maus, Louis P. *The Civil War: A Concise History.* New York, Oxford University Press, 2011, 19.

Chapter 2 – The Foundation Cracks

With the changing landscape, and each side of the slavery debate willing to shed blood for their cause, the nation sought to find a middle ground. Many were not open to discussion as each side stood its ground, pushing their beliefs to the west and seeking the government's intervention in the longtime debate. However, some sought to stand their ground and chose to make moves that would have ramifications for years to come.

South Carolina Leads Secession

Following Lincoln's election, the South began to grumble. Lincoln's platform was very much anti-slavery and clearly stated that "Government cannot endure permanently half slave, half free..."[9] This statement by Lincoln prompted South Carolina to secede from the Union on December 20, 1860, a little more than a month after Lincoln had won the Presidency.

With the departure of one state, the fuse was lit for a full secession from the Union. South Carolina looked to be the example for the rest of the South. Slowly the wheels of changed moved in a direction feared by both the North and by the Union as a whole. A change was coming, but

---

[9] Katcher, Philip. *The Civil War Day by Day*. St. Paul, The Brown Reference Group, 2007, 17.

what that change would be was still unclear.

As Lincoln made his way towards Washington, he reiterated his stance and sought to let the people know that he was going to be standing for the Constitution and would uphold the current fugitive slave laws. The goal of the Republicans was to find a peaceful compromise to end slavery. With the secession of South Carolina, there was fear amongst many that there would be a resolution, but that it might not come peacefully.

Fort Moultrie

Following the secession of South Carolina, the Union sought to keep a hold on the defiant state. However, their forces were spread too thin. On December 26, 1860, Major Robert Anderson decided to leave the South Carolina installation at Fort Moultrie, and garrison his troops on an island off the coast of Charleston, South Carolina, named Fort Sumter. By doing this, he hoped to be able to more strongly defend against an attack by the militia of South Carolina. Anderson's abandonment of Fort Moultrie emboldened the South to take and claim the Fort for the Confederacy.[10]

With Anderson's army at Fort Sumter, the South had isolated the Union forces to a single island off the coast of South Carolina. A major change had occurred for the South. With the Union ostensibly on the run in the minds of the South, a clear psychological victory had been achieved. The South had now claimed a Union fort and built a military presence, essentially becoming a foreign power occupying the United States, something not seen in almost a hundred years.

The liberation of Fort Moultrie was not only a huge psychological victory for the South but a big blow to the Union, who wanted to maintain peace and find a way to keep war from coming to the Union. Fort Moultrie's abandonment by the Union epitomized the fear and abandonment felt by the South, sentiments onto which the Confederacy would latch. These strong emotions fueled the South's transformation into the Confederate States of America.

---

[10] Constable, George, editor. *Brother Against Brother: Time-Life Books History of the Civil War.* New York, Prentice Hall Press, 1990, 35.

Confederate Constitution

On February 8, 1861, the delegates of the secession states met in Montgomery, Alabama, to adopt the Provisional Constitution of Confederate States of America. Jefferson Davis was chosen as their President and took the oath of office on February 18, 1861.[11] This drastic separation and formation of an entirely new Republic at the back door of the Union was a slap in the face to Lincoln and the Union.

In his inaugural address Davis warned the North that this was a drastic shift in the state of the Union. He warned the North that the South just wanted to go its separate way and to be left alone. Lincoln also sought to keep peace, but he made it abundantly clear that the Union was more important than the wants of the Southern states. As Lincoln made ready to give his first inaugural address, many held their collective breath hoping that he would preach a peaceful solution rather than bellowing threats of war.

A Nation and a State Divided

In the northwest counties of Virginia, a rebellion was brewing. In this case, it was Unionists rising up against the Confederate powers in Richmond. On May 13, 1861, 425 delegates from northwest Virginia met with the intent of seceding from Virginia and becoming a new state under the laws and protection of the Union. Although fraught with questionable voting practices and other issues, the charter was ratified and the state of West Virginia was created.

Even though West Virginia was under the Union flag, it was teeming with Southern sympathizers. The northern panhandle delegates who developed the state charter wanted to put the capitol in Wheeling where there was more support for the Union. However, Southern loyalists from southern West Virginia didn't want their capitol to be that far north and devised a plan to move it further south.

When the time came to vote on the permanent capitol, legislators from the southern counties of the state started a smear campaign against

---

[11] Maus, Louis P. *The Civil War: A Concise History.* New York, Oxford University Press, 2011, 22.

Wheeling. They argued that the northern constituents didn't support the same values as the majority of the population in the southern portion of the state. Their argument was so convincing that Wheeling didn't even make the ballot and Charleston became the permanent capitol of the state.

The Presidents

The men who led both nations were two of the key players in the Civil War for very different reasons. Even though neither man raised arms on behalf of their nations, their decisions ended the lives of more than 600,000 soldiers. Both men came from somewhat humble backgrounds and yet reached the pinnacle of public service in their respective countries. One man would lead his nation to its demise, while the other would lead his country to its rebirth.

Jefferson Davis

Davis was born in Fairview, Kentucky on June 3, 1808. The youngest of ten children, Davis moved twice in his childhood years ending up in Louisiana via Mississippi. After his father's death at the age of 14, Davis' brother became his surrogate father and pushed him through his education. At the age of 16, Davis' brother got him an appointment at the United States Military Academy. After graduating in the bottom third of his class, and being court-martialed along with 30 percent of his classmates for spiking the Christmas eggnog, he was stationed at Fort Crawford, in the Michigan Territory.

In 1844, he won the election for his first political office representing Mississippi in the United States House of Representatives. When the Mexican-American War broke out, Davis resigned from the House and pulled together a regiment of volunteers from his district to fight in the conflict. Davis fought bravely in multiple battles in the war. He was even dragged off the field of conflict after being shot in the foot during the Battle of Buena Vista.

After the war, Davis returned to Mississippi a hero. He was nominated by the governor to fill a vacancy in one of their senate seats and his appointment was ratified by the state congress in January 1848. He served in that capacity for five years until newly elected President Franklin Pierce picked Davis to be his Secretary of War. During his time in that office, he laid plans for the Transcontinental Railroad and increased the army's size and pay.

After Pierce lost re-election and Davis lost his position of Secretary of War, he won back his seat in the Senate for the state of Mississippi. During this stint as senator, tensions were rising between the North and the South. Heated debates and even violence on the floors of Congress eventually led to the inevitable succession of the state of Mississippi.

Once his home state seceded, Davis contacted the Governor to offer his services to Mississippi. He was made a general in the state's militia but was then nominated for President of the Confederate States of America. On February 19, 1861, Jefferson Davis was sworn in as the first and only holder the office of the fledgling country.

Abraham Lincoln

On February 12, 1809, the sixteenth President of the United States of America was born. In a small one-room log cabin in Hodgenville, Kentucky, Abraham Lincoln breathed air into his lungs for the first time. After many land title disputes in Kentucky, his father moved their family to Indiana due to lack of trust in the land management practices of the Kentucky government.

While living on the Indiana frontier, soon after his ninth birthday, Lincoln's mother died of milk sickness. His father remarried a widow with children of her own a year later. Lincoln became extremely fond of his father's new bride, eventually accepting her as his true mother. Frontier life did not suit young Lincoln. The typical chores bored the self-made scholar. He had more of proficiency in reading, writing, and composing poetry than he did operating a plow.

By the time he reached his teens, Lincoln had become more accustomed to the pioneer lifestyle. He became adept at swinging an ax and won many wrestling matches amongst local ruffians. However, another outbreak of milk sickness along the Ohio River scared the family enough to make them relocate once more. This time they headed further west, near Decatur, Illinois. After another failed attempt at homesteading by his father, Lincoln decided it was time to blaze his own trail.

Getting a job on a flatboat in New Salem, Illinois, his crew was tasked with transporting a load of goods via the Sangamon River to New

Orleans, at the mouth of the Mississippi. As Lincoln unloaded the flatboat in New Orleans, he saw for the first time the brutal reality of slavery. Families being separated at auction, brutal fighting pits for entertainment and the rape of slave women were imprinted on his brain as he headed back home to Illinois, where he would spend the next six years.

During those six years, Lincoln failed in the mercantile business, became an officer in the militia during the Black Hawk Wars, and ran a failed campaign for local office. However, being an avid learner, Lincoln decided to begin studying law. He did not attend any schools; he just read as many law books he could find. He was admitted to the Illinois Bar in 1836, and he practiced law in Springfield, Illinois, until 1844. During his time in Springfield, he was also elected to the Illinois House of Representatives for four straight terms.

Lincoln's advancement to national politics happened in 1846 when he was elected to the United States House of Representatives as a member of the Whig party. After pledging to serve only one term as a representative, Lincoln's hopes of joining the new administration's cabinet were thwarted when they picked his political rival from Illinois. Lincoln was resigned to practicing law again in Illinois after his hopes of staying in Washington were dashed.

Lincoln stayed away from the spotlight for the next few years until giving his opinion on the Bleeding Kansas incident. It was not until late October 1854 that he publicly denounced slavery in a speech in Peoria, Illinois. However, due to the Whig Party split over the slavery issue, Lincoln left in hopes of winning an Illinois senate seat as a Republican from the incumbent Democrat Stephen Douglas.

During the run for the Senate, Lincoln and Douglas partook in a series of seven debates that would become the base argument for not only the legality of slavery, but also the ethical legitimacy of the trade. Most considered Lincoln the winner of the debates and the Republicans won the majority of the popular vote. But, according to the laws at that time, the legislature picked the Senator. Since the majority of the state's legislature were Democrats, Stephen Douglas got the seat in spite of the voters' choice.

Even though Lincoln lost the Senate race, the campaign not only raised his profile in general, but also his popularity in the Republican Party. As 1860 and the next presidential election approached, Lincoln had become a frontrunner for the nomination. On May 18, 1860, Lincoln received the Republican nomination for president and began his rise to fame.

Lincoln's Inauguration

On March 4, 1861, Abraham Lincoln was sworn in as the sixteenth President of the United States.[12] His speech during this swearing in had undercurrents of anger. He was sworn to defend the Union and he would do everything in his power to find a peaceful way to reunite a fractured Union. He used strong and stern language, but never directly threatened the newly-forming Confederacy. He desired peace and sought to find a solution to appease all sides.

When Lincoln stood to make his speech in 1861, he believed that there was still time to rally many in the South to the side of the Union and encourage them to help reach a peaceful resolution, avoiding any further conflict. Through his mastery of words, Lincoln was a natural at the art of persuasion. By way of his many speeches along the campaign, as well as at his inauguration, he had stirred up respect, hope, and even anger. This inaugural address was intended to address all the concerns of both the North and the South as to what he and his administration hoped to accomplish. Although he knew that taking too strong a stance against slavery would provoke the South, he also knew that he had to stand firm regarding the laws of the land and the prevailing view of slavery in the Union.

"Apprehension seems to exist among the people of the Southern States that by the accession of a Republican Administration their property and their peace and personal security are to be endangered. There has never been any reasonable cause for such apprehension. Indeed, the most ample evidence to the contrary has all the while existed and been open to their inspection. It is found in nearly all the published speeches

---

[12] Maus, Louis P. *The Civil War: A Concise History.* New York, Oxford University Press, 2011, 23.

of him who now addresses you. I do but quote from one of those speeches when I declare that-- I have no purpose, directly or indirectly, to interfere with the institution of slavery in the States where it exists."[13]

Lincoln wanted to be clear that he was a supporter of the law the Constitution as well as states' rights. However, many in the South took his comments about the Fugitive Slave law as a statement of his intention to take things further. His goal was to convey his intention to enforce what was already on the law books and not needlessly burden the courts or the South with more laws. Lincoln had every intention of finding a way to abolish slavery. However he did not want that to come at the expense of war or unnecessary bloodshed.

"There is much controversy about the delivering up of fugitives from service or labor. The clause I now read is as plainly written in the Constitution as any other of its provisions: No person held to service or labor in one State, under the laws thereof, escaping into another, shall in consequence of the law or regulation therein be discharged from such service or labor, but shall be delivered up on claim of the party to whom such service or labor may be due."[14]

Lincoln did warn the South sternly that his full intention was to maintain the Union. He knew that in order to maintain peace he would have to warn them that the Constitution was law and that he intended to abide by it. It was meant to be a moment of clarity for the South; for them to see that by keeping the institution of slavery alive they were not abiding by the Constitution. With this statement about the Constitutionality of slavery, he urged the South to rethink their situation, to realize that they were not following the intention of the Constitution, and to amend their laws so they would reflect the supreme law of the land.

---

[13] Lincoln, Abraham. *Abraham Lincoln papers: Series 1. General Correspondence. -1916: Abraham Lincoln, January-February 1861 First Inaugural Address, First Printed Draft.* January, 1861. Manuscript/Mixed Material. Retrieved from the Library of Congress, <www.loc.gov/item/mal0770200/>.

[14] Lincoln, Abraham. *Abraham Lincoln papers: Series 1. General Correspondence. -1916: Abraham Lincoln, January-February 1861 First Inaugural Address, First Printed Draft.* January, 1861. Manuscript/Mixed Material. Retrieved from the Library of Congress, <www.loc.gov/item/mal0770200/>.

"A disruption of the Federal Union, heretofore only menaced, is now formidably attempted. I hold that in contemplation of universal law and of the Constitution the Union of these States is perpetual. Perpetuity is implied, if not expressed, in the fundamental law of all national governments. It is safe to assert that no government proper ever had a provision in its organic law for its own termination. Continue to execute all the express provisions of our National Constitution, and the Union will endure forever, it being impossible to destroy it except by some action not provided for in the instrument itself."[15]

With the intention to enforce the Constitution, Lincoln fiercely warned the South that there would be no use of force unless they struck first. He intended to keep the Union from dissolving and would use all legal and military means to enforce the Constitution, the laws of the land, and the continued peace of the United States. He denounced the legal right of secession and wanted to end the notion before it took root in the South. The firm stance against any action to threaten or disrupt the Union was one that Lincoln did not take lightly. Many in the South saw this part of his speech as a direct threat against their freedom, as well as a condemnation of their desire to secede from the Union in order to maintain their way of life and free themselves from the rule of Lincoln and his perceived tyranny.

"But if destruction of the Union by one or by a part only of the States be lawfully possible, the Union is less perfect than before the Constitution, having lost the vital element of perpetuity. It follows from these views that no State upon its own mere motion can lawfully get out of the Union; that resolves, and ordinances to that effect are legally void, and that acts of violence within any State or States against the authority of the United States are insurrectionary or revolutionary, according to circumstances."[16]

---

[15] Lincoln, Abraham. *Abraham Lincoln papers: Series 1. General Correspondence. -1916: Abraham Lincoln, January-February 1861 First Inaugural Address, First Printed Draft.* January, 1861. Manuscript/Mixed Material. Retrieved from the Library of Congress, <www.loc.gov/item/mal0770200/>.

[16] Lincoln, Abraham. *Abraham Lincoln papers: Series 1. General Correspondence. -1916: Abraham Lincoln, January-February 1861 First Inaugural Address, First Printed Draft.* January, 1861. Manuscript/Mixed Material. Retrieved from the Library of Congress,

Using even stronger words, the speech went on to state that the Union itself was the backbone of liberty, justice, and the supreme law of the land. Any attempt to destroy the Union would be an act of war, and the Union would do everything within its power and scope to keep itself intact and running as it had for all the years since its inception. The Union and the states within it were older than the Constitution, and the South was a necessary part of the Union. Lincoln knew that with division would come a great change to the face of America.

"I trust this will not be regarded as a menace, but only as the declared purpose of the Union that it will constitutionally defend and maintain itself. In doing this there needs to be no bloodshed or violence, and there shall be none unless it be forced upon the national authority. The power confided to me will be used to hold, occupy, and possess the property and places belonging to the Government and to collect the duties and imports; but beyond what may be necessary for these objects, there will be no invasion, no using of force against or among the people anywhere. Where hostility to the United States in any interior locality shall be so great and universal as to prevent competent resident citizens from holding the Federal offices, there will be no attempt to force obnoxious strangers among the people for that object. While the strict legal right may exist in the Government to enforce the exercise of these offices, the attempt to do so would be so irritating and so nearly impracticable withal that I deem it better to forego for the time the uses of such offices."[17]

Lincoln stood firm on his belief in the abolishment of slavery, which hit a nerve in the South since it was their main means of production. He pleaded for moral citizens to step forward and find a way to keep the Union together and to not let slavery be the issue that caused distrust and separation. He intended to use the Constitution to maintain the laws of the Union while also warning the South that he would use all resources at hand to maintain the Union. Again, many in the South felt threatened by

<www.loc.gov/item/mal0770200/>.

[17] Lincoln, Abraham. *Abraham Lincoln papers: Series 1. General Correspondence. -1916: Abraham Lincoln, January-February 1861 First Inaugural Address, First Printed Draft.* January, 1861. Manuscript/Mixed Material. Retrieved from the Library of Congress, <www.loc.gov/item/mal0770200/>.

Lincoln's statements and this further motivated them to try to blaze a trail away from Union and toward the formation of a nation within a nation.

"One section of our country believes slavery is right and ought to be extended, while the other believes it is wrong and ought not to be extended. This is the only substantial dispute. The fugitive- slave clause of the Constitution and the law for the suppression of the foreign slave trade are each as well enforced, perhaps, as any law can ever be in a community where the moral sense of the people imperfectly supports the law itself. The great body of the people abide by the dry legal obligation in both cases, and a few break over in each. This, I think, can not be perfectly cured, and it would be worse in both cases after the separation of the sections than before."[18]

Lincoln explained that secession and violence were not the proper ways to change the government, but that a constitutional amendment was the only acceptable method means of getting what they wanted. However, with a Republican majority, the South did not see that as a promising option. Lincoln knew that each state had the ability to generate such an amendment and bring it forward, but many sensed it would die in Congress, as the abolishment of slavery was in the conscience of the majority.

"This country, with its institutions, belongs to the people who inhabit it. Whenever they shall grow weary of the existing Government, they can exercise their constitutional right of amending it or their revolutionary right to dismember or overthrow it."[19]

As religious as Lincoln was he also knew that Christian ideology was important in the South, and he pleaded with them to take a hard look at their spiritual teachings and see that what they were doing as slave owners would be frowned upon by God. Lincoln understood that the majority

---

[18] Lincoln, Abraham. *Abraham Lincoln papers: Series 1. General Correspondence. -1916: Abraham Lincoln, January-February 1861 First Inaugural Address, First Printed Draft.* January, 1861. Manuscript/Mixed Material. Retrieved from the Library of Congress, <www.loc.gov/item/mal0770200/>.

[19] Lincoln, Abraham. *Abraham Lincoln papers: Series 1. General Correspondence. -1916: Abraham Lincoln, January-February 1861 First Inaugural Address, First Printed Draft.* January, 1861. Manuscript/Mixed Material. Retrieved from the Library of Congress, <www.loc.gov/item/mal0770200/>.

would have the final say and that the momentum against slavery would bring about a fair resolution.

"If the Almighty Ruler of Nations, with His eternal truth and justice, be on your side of the North, or on yours of the South, that truth and that justice will surely prevail by the judgment of this great tribunal of the American people."[20]

With his threats leveled at the South, Lincoln urged them to take time and not be rash. Rushing in into secession or war would lead to irrevocable consequences, which would be detrimental to both the North and the South. The cautionary nature of Lincoln and his belief that anything could be resolved with words, and without bloodshed, gave him hope and was intended to encourage all people of the Union and the South to seek peace before further blood was shed.

"My countrymen, one and all, think calmly and well upon this whole subject. Nothing valuable can be lost by taking time. If there be an object to hurry any of you in hot haste to a step which you would never take deliberately, that object will be frustrated by taking time; but no good object can be frustrated by it."[21]

Lincoln also reiterated his oath to the Constitution as a solemn oath unto God and the Union. With this oath, he knew it would be on his shoulders to maintain the Union and follow the will of the people. The will of the people was strongly against slavery, but he needed to find a way to keep the Union together, hoping that peace could be maintained long enough for the South to see the error of their ways and come to their own conclusion about slavery.

"You have no oath registered in heaven to destroy the Government, while I shall have the most solemn one to "preserve, protect, and defend

---

[20] Lincoln, Abraham. *Abraham Lincoln papers: Series 1. General Correspondence. -1916: Abraham Lincoln, January-February 1861 First Inaugural Address, First Printed Draft.* January, 1861. Manuscript/Mixed Material. Retrieved from the Library of Congress, <www.loc.gov/item/mal0770200/>

[21] Lincoln, Abraham. *Abraham Lincoln papers: Series 1. General Correspondence. -1916: Abraham Lincoln, January-February 1861 First Inaugural Address, First Printed Draft.* January, 1861. Manuscript/Mixed Material. Retrieved from the Library of Congress, <www.loc.gov/item/mal0770200/>.

it. I am loath to close. We are not enemies, but friends. We must not be enemies. Though passion may have strained, it must not break our bonds of affection. The mystic chords of memory, stretching from every battlefield and patriot grave to every living heart and hearthstone all over this broad land, will yet swell the chorus of the Union, when again touched, as surely they will be, by the better angels of our nature."[22]

His words, however, were not taken lightly in the South and a growing tide of disdain for the North surged forth, especially in South Carolina. The following day, Lincoln received an urgent message from a letter from Major Anderson stationed at Fort Sumter, requesting aid and reinforcements for his position in Charleston Harbor. Lincoln, knowing that he was in a precarious situation, ordered a relief mission. He demanded that the navy only land supplies to the troops at Fort Sumter and that no soldiers or further reinforcements be landed at the island.[23] He also demanded that no Confederate troops be engaged unless the Confederates interfered. Fort Sumter had become a prize for both the Union and the Confederacy. With this bold move Lincoln had alerted the Confederacy to the value of the small island, giving them a target on which to set their sights.

The Confederacy had become emboldened and felt that the rash movement by the Union was a sign of weakness. The South sought to assert its independence while hoping that their military victory would drive the Union from the Confederate states and leave them in peace. Lincoln was not so quick to give up. He sought to find a solution to the rebellion, even one that could lead to war: something he had wholeheartedly sought to avoid.

---

[22] Lincoln, Abraham. *Abraham Lincoln papers: Series 1. General Correspondence. -1916: Abraham Lincoln, January-February 1861 First Inaugural Address, First Printed Draft.* January, 1861. Manuscript/Mixed Material. Retrieved from the Library of Congress, <www.loc.gov/item/mal0770200/>.

[23] Stokesbury, James L. *A Short History of the Civil War.* New York, Harper Collins, 1995, 9.

Chapter 3 – The First Shot

Separation through election was the first step towards a divided nation. With the secession of the Southern states and the formation of the Confederate States of America, the next logical step was a movement by either the Union or the Confederacy towards further division. Either the Union would leave the Confederate states alone, or one of them would draw the other into a war, which Lincoln still wanted desperately to avoid. Only time would tell which side would make the first move. Lincoln aspired to resolve the situation diplomatically, but Davis had no problem with conflict. Soon the two would have to come to terms with the reality of the situation.

Fort Sumter

Following Lincoln's Inauguration, the South began to move forward with further secessions. On April 10, 1861, the Confederate Secretary of War Leroy Pope Walker demanded Fort Sumter's immediate evacuation and threated to reduce it to rubble should they refuse. Major Beauregard had been awaiting a response from the Union and in the meantime had encircled Fort Sumter with artillery and had 6,000 men ready for battle.[24]

---

[24] Eicher, David J. *The Longest Night: A Military History of the Civil War.* New York, Simon and Schuster, 2001, 39.

On April 12, 1861, the South again attempted to secure a peaceful surrender from Major Anderson of the Union army. Major Anderson was warned that if he did not comply and surrender within an hour he would be fired upon.[25] The Union would not concede.

Near dawn, Lieutenant Farley of the Confederate army fired the first shot. His shot signaled the beginning of a change as the rest of the Confederate battery opened up on Fort Sumter. Within its walls, Major Anderson braced for a purely defensive battle as his small army of 10 officers, and 68 soldiers could not mount a realistic offense. He was waiting for reinforcements.

It was not until later in the day when the Union fired the first shot at a floating battery anchored near Fort Moultrie, the abandoned Union fortress. The bombardment of Fort Sumter increased as the Confederate army fired oven-heated cannon balls known as "hot shot" into the base burning the walls and setting exposed wood on fire[26].

As the day went on, there was a glimmer of hope as Captain Fox and the steamer *Baltic* sailed into view. The hope was short-lived, as fear of sinking caused the Union ship to turn back to sea and abandon the men at Fort Sumter. As night progressed, rain aided the men in Fort Sumter at putting out fires and the Confederate army took a respite from constant bombardment.[27]

By noon of April 13, 1861, the bombardment had increased, and Fort Sumter was burning. The Fort had ceased returning fire and the Confederacy saw victory approaching. By 7 p.m., Fort Sumter had agreed to surrender. Terms were set and the troops at Fort Sumter departed the base on April 14, marching out to a 100-gun salute put on by the Confederacy for their brave enemies.[28] The Confederacy had fired the first shot of the war and had come away victorious. The Civil War had

[25] Eicher, David J. *The Longest Night: A Military History of the Civil War.* New York, Simon and Schuster, 2001, 40.

[26] Eicher, David J. *The Longest Night: A Military History of the Civil War.* New York, Simon and Schuster, 2001, 40.

[27] Constable, George, editor. *Brother Against Brother: Time-Life Books History of the Civil War.* New York, Prentice Hall Press, 1990, 39.

[28] Stokesbury, James L. *A Short History of the Civil War.* New York, Harper Collins, 1995, 11.

officially begun.

The South Rises

Following the news of the Confederate victory at Fort Sumter, military volunteers started flocking to state militias to aid their brothers in South Carolina. From Virginia to Texas the news of the Southern victory emboldened the previously sullen South. The North was stunned and outraged that the Union had become so divided and reduced to warfare in order to resolve differences. Both sides became concerned that what started as a largely political response could turn into an all-out war.

Both Lincoln and the newly elected Jefferson Davis wanted to avoid bloodshed. Davis understood the advantage the North had in factories, population, and transportation. The South had about a third of the ability of the North. The odds were not in their favor. Davis pleaded with Lincoln to leave the South be and to let bygones be bygones. However, he still asked for 100,000 volunteers to come forward to prepare for war.

Lincoln also acted swiftly and on April 15, 1861, he also issued an order for troops. Lincoln requested 75,000 volunteers for three months' service via executive order.[29] Five days later he ordered a naval blockade on all Southern ports.[30] Lincoln sought to keep peace through military superiority. With Congress on spring recess, Lincoln acted in what he saw as the best way to maintain order until Congress could reconvene and aid Lincoln in either ending the war or declaring it.

Knowing that he needed to rally support and get public opinion on his side he scheduled a special session of Congress on the Fourth of July.[31] The South replied in kind and rallied other states to secession. Some states like Virginia were scheduled to vote on secession, however state militias took matters into their own hands. On April 18, a Virginia militia raided Harpers Ferry. The South bombarded the arsenal. To keep weapons from falling into confederate hands, the Union set fire to 15,000

---

[29] Stokesbury, James L. *A Short History of the Civil War.* New York, Harper Collins, 1995, 11.

[30] Maus, Louis P. *The Civil War: A Concise History.* New York, Oxford University Press, 2011, 25.

[31] Maus, Louis P. *The Civil War: A Concise History.* New York, Oxford University Press, 2011, 27.

weapons and retreated across the Potomac River to Maryland. When the South arrived to claim the fort, they found 5,000 rifles in useable condition and considered the battle a victory.[32]

Riding high on the victory and Harpers Ferry, the Virginia militia raided The Gosport Naval Yard. Upon hearing about the attempted seizure, the commander of the shipyard ordered every ship possible to head to sea, and any that were not seaworthy to be burned and scuttled. Only three vessels made it to sea. The South once again gained a victory, seizing the U.S.S. Merrimack as well as over 1,000 naval guns which could be used to reinforce other fortifications throughout the South.[33]

The U.S.S Merrimack would become known as the C.S.S. Virginia and become a threat to the Union navy. With these small victories the South gained momentum and volunteers. More and more people headed to Virginia to get in on the action and to savor the triumph of what they believed was an already won war. The zeal of victory was so contagious that even Jefferson Davis moved his seat of power to Richmond, Virginia. The tide of change swept through the South as Tennessee, Arkansas, and North Carolina joined the Confederate States of America, making the division of North and South even greater than before. With this taste of victory, the South banded together into a full-fledged nation united against what they saw as a common enemy. While the North licked its wounds and wondered what the fate of this great nation would be Washington D.C. was concerned, as was Lincoln. First blood had been drawn and the Union was worried about its future.

---

[32] Constable, George, editor. *Brother Against Brother: Time-Life Books History of the Civil War.* New York, Prentice Hall Press, 1990, 41-42.

[33] Eicher, David J. *The Longest Night: A Military History of the Civil War.* New York, Simon and Schuster, 2001, 55.

Chapter 4 – Welcome to War

July 4 1861, brought a special session of Congress. President Lincoln took bold action asking for 400,000 men and 400 million dollars to put a stop to the Southern rebellion.[34] He argued that instead of waging war he sought to reunite North and South, bringing an end to the division of the Union. Lincoln also implemented suspension of the writ of habeas corpus on or near military lines, meaning that Southerners could be detained without bringing them before a court.

Strategy moved to the forefront of the Union leadership. The goal of Lincoln and the Union army was to stop the rebellion as quickly as possible. A prolonged war would further divide the nation and pull resources into needless bloodshed. The Union leaders agreed that if Richmond fell the leadership of the South would also fall and the war would end. The sentiment of "On to Richmond" echoed throughout the North.[35]

Lincoln and the Union leadership agreed. The Union army moved into the Shenandoah Valley in early July. A Confederate army responded to this action by moving into a separate position in the same valley. For the first time in almost two hundred years, war would be waged on the American continent. This time it was brother against brother, citizen

---

[34] Stokesbury, James L. *A Short History of the Civil War*. New York, Harper Collins, 1995, 37.

[35] Stokesbury, James L. *A Short History of the Civil War*. New York, Harper Collins, 1995, 44.

against citizen. The stakes of the war were larger than ever before. The Union itself was under threat, and any resulting division could and would have lasting consequences. War was at hand.

An Introduction of the Generals

So much lore surrounds the generals that participated in this war that it is sometimes hard to discern myth from fact when remembering the actions of these men. However, to try to understand where they came from and who they were when they commanded the armies that would determine the future of the United States, for this is essential to understanding the methods they used.

Ulysses S. Grant

Born Hiram Ulysses Grant on April 27, 1822, the future President of the United States of America thrived in the tannery of his strict Methodist father. He not only showed proficiency in the ability to tan animal hides, but also excelled in riding and training the very horses for which his father's leather provided harnesses, bridles, and saddles.

His father used a personal favor from a local politician to get his son admitted to West Point at the age of sixteen. On the entrance form, the politician mistakenly wrote his name as "Ulysses S. Grant" instead of his actual name Hiram. When he tried to change the mistake, he was informed they could not change the records, so the name stayed with him throughout his life.

After a lackluster career at West Point where he finished in the bottom half of his class, he got his first assignment. Even though one of his only accomplishments at the Academy was his horse-riding ability, he was not given cavalry duty. He was assigned to the 4th Infantry Regiment just outside of St. Louis, Missouri. He did not mind his new role, but he had a slight distaste for the military after his subpar performance at the academy. He was looking forward to the end of his four-year tour of duty so he could return to civilian life.

After demonstrating bravery and skill in the Mexican-American War, Grant returned to civilian existence, working in his father's leather shop until the first shots of the Civil War were fired at Fort Sumter. President Lincoln called for 75,000 troops to end the Southern insurrection. Grant had a renewed sense of patriotism and volunteered. Due to his prior military experience, he began training the other volunteers while waiting for his official recommission into the United States Army.

Robert E. Lee

Born to the Governor of Virginia and his wife on January 19, 1807, Lee's life began with the air of aristocracy and privilege that was routinely granted to the owners of large plantations like his father. However, life turned sour quickly for young Lee as his father was forced into debtor's prison. Lee was himself consigned to West Point and a life in the military.

In an almost mirror image of the West Point career of Ulysses S. Grant, Lee excelled at the Army's highest level of education. He finished second in a class of 45 and received no demerits during his entire tenure at the prestigious learning institution. At the time, the two ranking officers at West Point were based in the Army Corps of Engineers, so the curriculum was primarily centered on studies relevant to the engineering field. Therefore, with the majority of his formal education based in engineering, Lee began his military career helping build forts in Georgia and Virginia. He even oversaw the construction of the harbor in St. Louis.

Like Grant, Lee saw his first military action during the Mexican-American War. Working as a reconnaissance officer, he received many citations for his work and bravery during the march to Mexico City. After the war, he reluctantly accepted the position of Superintendent of the Military Academy at West Point. He believed his skills could be put to better use than trying to improve the infrastructure and courses of the institution, but he completed his work with pride and efficiency.

Lee had to take a two-year hiatus from the military beginning in 1857 when his father-in-law passed away. Like his own father, Lee's father-in-law was a large plantation owner in Mississippi. Also like his father, he was horrible with money and his financial dealings were in disarray at the time of his death. After failed efforts to find someone to handle the estate for him, Lee had to go to Mississippi to execute the will himself.

In his late father-in-law's will, he wanted to have his slaves emancipated within five years of his death. The plantation was huge. It had sprawling acres of land that were maintained by the slaves that his father-in-law wanted freed. Along with the sprawling acreage, there were huge amounts of debt that his father-in-law had incurred while mismanaging his plantation. There was no way Lee could allow so much "property" of the plantation to be given away for nothing.

Upon his arrival, Lee was greeted by several slaves that had heard of their former owner's will and did not want to work on the plantation anymore. When confronted, the slaves told him they were as free as Lee was and ran from the plantation. Lee tracked them down and brought them to plantation justice. He ordered the overseer to punish the men with 50 lashes and the women with 20 lashes. The overseer would not whip the women, so Lee had the constable brought to finish the job. Lee returned to service after his hiatus and continued his career.

Lee's first taste of the Civil War was at one of its most pivotal points. During John Brown's raid of the Harpers Ferry arsenal, Lee was ordered to retake the facility. Upon arrival, Lee found that the Harpers Ferry garrison had surrounded Brown and his insurgents inside the building. After a brief battle, Lee captured Brown and put an end to his rebellion.

Lee had been stationed in Texas before that state seceded from the Union. Lee did not initially believe in the secession of the states and returned to Washington D.C. for another command. However, on April 20, 1861, Lee turned in his resignation letter to his commanders because he could not bring up arms against his home state of Virginia; he subsequently joined the Confederate Army.

William Tecumseh Sherman

Born on February 8, 1820, to a state Supreme Court justice and his wife in Lancaster, Ohio, Sherman was given a life of opportunity despite having to hurdle major obstacles early in life. When Sherman was nine years old, his father died suddenly and left no inheritance to his mother for which to raise him and his ten siblings. Luckily, a neighbor who was in the House of Representatives took on the job of raising young Sherman and introduced him to the proper channels in order to succeed in life.

When Sherman was 16, his benefactor was able to pull strings and get Sherman a spot as a cadet at the United States Military Academy at West Point. He excelled academically at West Point, but some of the military acumen that the army required was not to Sherman's liking. He did not see the need to always have a freshly pressed uniform, shoes shined to mirror-like perfection, or why one had to snap to attention and give the proper salute when required. He estimated that he collected at least 150 demerits per semester at the Academy, and he accumulated so many that it cost him his rank as one of the top five graduates in his class.

Upon graduation, Sherman was ordered to report to an artillery regiment in Florida. While there, he battled the Seminole Indian tribe for control of the peninsular state. After the Seminole uprising had been squashed, Sherman began an administrative role in the Army. He boarded a military vessel and sailed around Cape Horn on route to the unsettled western expanse of California.

While most of his class from West Point was busy fighting the Mexican-American War, Sherman began surveying and speculating just ahead of the gold rush that was soon to hit the state of California. He even surveyed and speculated in the area that would become the capitol of the state, Sacramento.

In 1853, the newly-married Sherman resigned his commission and began working with a Missouri-based banking firm in San Francisco. The stress of the business climate in the Bay Area was causing Sherman to have bouts of anxiety, which ultimately impacted his health negatively. Later in life, he would say that it was easier to lead men into battle than to do business in San Francisco.

Sherman returned to the military life by becoming the superintendent of a military school in Louisiana that would later become Louisiana State University. However, as the list of states that left the Union grew, Sherman decided to go to Washington to try to regain his commission in the Army. During inauguration week, Sherman's plea regarding the lack of readiness of the Union Army failed to catch Lincoln's attention. In frustration, he took the job as president of a streetcar company in St. Louis.

That position lasted a few scant months before the first shots were fired over Fort Sumter. After his discussion with the President, Sherman was hesitant to rejoin the Union Army. However, his love of country finally won out and he accepted the commission on June 7, 1861.

Thomas "Stonewall" Jackson

Jackson was born on January 21, 1824, in what is now the state of West Virginia. The exact location is not certain, however. Both Clarksburg and Parkersburg claim to be the birthplace of this Civil War legend. As typhoid fever spread across the area, Jackson's father and sister both contracted and died from the disease. At the age of nine, his mother remarried and gave birth to a half-brother. However, his mother grew ill and died as well, leaving him and his sister orphans.

He and his sister moved to Jackson's Mill where he worked at his uncle's gristmill. He moved to Clarksburg for a time with an abusive Aunt, but that did not suit Jackson. A year later, he trudged back through the wilds to Jackson's Mill where he spent the next six years with his Uncle.

In 1842, Jackson was accepted into the United States Military Academy at West Point. Due to his unstable upbringing, he lacked the formal educational background that the other cadets had received in their childhood. However, the stubbornness and work ethic that he would become famous for began to shine through. Even after starting near the bottom of the class, he graduated 17th out of 59.

After graduation, Jackson joined an artillery regiment fighting in the Mexican-American War. His personality came to the forefront during the battles of the war. He disobeyed direct commands if he felt they were detrimental to his troops. He once refused to retreat when he was caught by a Mexican artillery regiment that had him outgunned. He felt they would be more vulnerable to the shelling if they pulled up and retreated, so he refused the direct order to do so. Jackson's instincts proved to be right. Because he did not retreat, the Mexican artillery focused on him while a brigade of United States infantrymen closed in on the Mexicans and forced their surrender.

In 1852, Jackson took on the role of educator by accepting the position of Artillery Instructor at the Virginia Military Institute. His lack of humor and hypochondria made him very unlikeable to the cadets that he taught. He had a habit of memorizing every lecture that he taught and any time a student had a question he would just repeat what he memorized.

After Virginia seceded in 1861, Jackson began drilling troops for the Army of Virginia. He was given command of a brigade of infantry based in Harpers Ferry. He was in command of this brigade when he received his now-famous nickname, "Stonewall."

During the First Battle of Bull Run, Union soldiers were about to break the ranks of the Rebels. The Confederates reveled when they saw Jackson standing like a stonewall against the northern aggressors.

First Battle of Bull Run

The Union intended to move towards Richmond, Virginia. Their movement was dependent on railroad for more troops and supplies. The route they needed to take was through the Shenandoah Valley, an agriculture hotbed for the South as well as the most natural route to Richmond. The Confederate army knew that if the Union took Manassas Junction they would have an easy way to funnel military power deeper into the South and the war would quickly turn in favor of the North. The valley was a strategic point for both sides moving to take each other's capitals.

Leading the Confederate army was General Beauregard who had become a hero at Fort Sumter for the South. He was outmanned and was low on supplies, but he was determined to stand his ground at Bull Run.

On July 18, 1861, the Union army of 35,000 soldiers moved into the valley. A brigade under the command of Brigadier General Daniel Tyler poured into the valley and was cut down by a waiting Confederate army. He was able to retreat, but not without loss. 19 men died and 64 were wounded or missing.[36]

The Union had to return and figure out a new strategy. Finally, on July 21, 1861, the Union army attacked at Bull Run. They met the South on the battlefield, and for a while, the Confederate army overwhelmed them at Matthew's Hill. As the South advanced, they were met by an overwhelming Union army that eventually used its numbers to crush the Confederates. As the day dragged on Southern reinforcements plugged

---

[36] Constable, George, editor. *Brother Against Brother: Time-Life Books History of the Civil War.* New York, Prentice Hall Press, 1990, 55.

the holes and began to rally back, even though they were still technically in retreat. The turning point came when the 33rd Virginia captured the batteries near Henry House Hill. The batteries became a crucial point, and for the next few hours, the two armies gained control only to lose it again. Late in the afternoon, the Union army fell apart, and troops began to retreat with the Confederate army in pursuit. [37]

The First Battle of Bull Run had become a Confederate victory, strengthening their resolve and rallying more Southerners to what they saw as a winning cause. By the end of the day the battle had taken its toll on both sides as the Union departed with 470 dead, 1,071 wounded, and 1,793 either captured or missing. The Confederate faired only a little better with 387 dead, 1,582 wounded, and 13 missing. [38]

Neither side had achieved an overwhelming victory, but the Confederate states saw it as a major blow to the Union. Each side had taken losses larger than they had envisioned. The South, while still winning, had suffered a heavy toll for holding Bull Run. They had to find a way to weaken the Union. The Union had to find a way to use their superior numbers to push back the South and move to Richmond. The North decided a blockade would weaken the Southern economy. The South saw the blockade as an opportunity. The emboldened Confederacy took their war to the sea.

Monitor vs. Merrimack

War again came to Virginia, this time on the coast. The United States Navy had put a blockade on the Southern ports cutting off over 3,00 miles of coastline from import and export. Knowing that the blockade would severely limit the ability of the South to get resources and export their goods, the Confederates took the scuttled frigate U.S.S Merrimack, which had been captured during the raid on Gosport Naval Yard, armored it, and turned it into the C.S.S. Virginia. [39]

[37] Constable, George, editor. *Brother Against Brother: Time-Life Books History of the Civil War.* New York, Prentice Hall Press, 1990, 59.

[38] Constable, George, editor. *Brother Against Brother: Time-Life Books History of the Civil War.* New York, Prentice Hall Press, 1990, 59.

[39] Katcher, Philip. *The Civil War Day by Day.* St. Paul, The Brown Reference Group, 2007, 29.

The South made use of the supplies they had along the coastline. To defend their ports, the Confederates used mines, which were explosive charges anchored along shipping channels They also devised torpedoes by taking explosives and attaching them to a long pole and attaching the pole to an unarmored vessel. They would then ram the enemy vessel with the torpedo, and the torpedo would explode, causing damage.

The Confederates attempted many raids like this with the C.S.S. Hunley being the most notable. On February 17, 1864, the C.S.S. Hunley a submersible powered by eight men, rammed the U.S.S. Housatonic and sunk it in port. While the blow was important, the entire crew of the Hunley perished in the act.[40]

The Merrimack, now under Confederate control, took to raiding Union ships, destroying the U.S.S Congress and the U.S.S Cumberland before meeting the Union ironclad U.S.S. Monitor. The U.S.S. Monitor was dispatched to protect the frigate U.S.S. Minnesota from falling to the same fate of the other Union ships. The U.S.S Monitor was the Union's ironclad guardian. The meeting of iron giants was underway off the coast of Virginia.

On March 9, 1862, the two ironclads went to battle off the coast of Hampton Roads, Virginia, shooting at each other from as close as a few yards to as far as half a mile. The two ships circled each other for hours firing barrage after barrage of cannon fire trying to stop the other. For four hours the two ships pounded each other, looking for weak spots. Finally, the two ships agreed to call the battle a draw. While the battle of these formidable ironclads was considered a stalemate, the Union army had won a strategic victory, as they lost no other wooden ships to the deadly Merrimack. A psychological victory over the Confederate navy was huge[41]

This battle would change how war at sea was waged. The lessons of the and the lessons of that clash had pushed the Union to turn on Southern coastal towns, shutting down trade and keeping Confederate troops on the defensive, thereby distracting them from moving further

---

[40] Katcher, Philip. *The Civil War Day by Day*. St. Paul, The Brown Reference Group, 2007, 29.

[41] Eicher, David J. *The Longest Night: A Military History of the Civil War*. New York, Simon and Schuster, 2001, 197.

northward. This tactic by the Union allowed them to keep more troops under siege and away from larger battles which, with the Generals of the Confederate army leading them, could turn many future confrontations in the Confederacy's favor. The Union navy's ability to keep things at a standstill and bog down coastal troops was an advantage that cannot be overlooked.

Chapter 5 – Bloody Days

Battle of Shiloh

The worst of the war was soon to come. The armies of the Union, commanded by Ulysses S. Grant, and the armies of the South, commanded by Johnston and Beauregard, the hero of Sumter, met on April 6, 1862, in Shiloh, Tennessee. The two armies were camped only miles apart from each other in the valley with the Shiloh valley measuring 15 miles by 17 miles in the shape of a triangle.[42]

Grant was not confident about his strategy. He and his officers had not come up with a defensive plan and they had failed to put out scouts looking for impending attacks from the Confederate army. Johnston and Beauregard snuck up on the flank of the Union. The Confederates arose during the darkness of the morning, and volleys of artillery flew from the Confederate lines.

As the Union retreated, the Confederates looked to keep the pressure on. The resulting clash confused both Union and Confederate soldiers as they collided in the mid-morning hours. The Confederate army swept into the confused Union lines, and the latter were left attempting to create some sort of defensive measure.

---

[42] Constable, George, editor. *Brother Against Brother: Time-Life Books History of the Civil War.* New York, Prentice Hall Press, 1990, 79.

Grant attempted to rally the troops. He pushed men into the weak spots of the Confederate line and prepared for prolonged action. The Confederates pushed forward, bombarding the Union lines. As they overran Union camps, the Confederate army began to falter. The Confederate troops ceased moving forward and began to scavenge the Union camps. The Union pulled back troops to keep a tight line, inflicting heavy casualties on the attacking Confederate forces.

The Confederate army moved to flank the Union army. As they did so, the Confederate General Johnston was killed in battle. This concerned the Confederate troops, but Beauregard assumed command and moved the Confederate forces forward. By noon the Union army had retreated towards the Savannah River, leaving troops to protect an area called the Hornet's Nest. As the day continued the odds were against the Union soldiers at that position. They were called into retreat and despite attempting to flee, a group of 2,200 men was forced to surrender to the Confederate forces that evening.[43]

Grant fell back and created a line of soldiers known as "Grant's last line". Grant's line of 4,000 men and fifty guns readied themselves for the onslaught of the Confederate army. The Confederate forces pushed towards the Union position with 200 men, only to be cut down as they approached the line. As the sun fell the two armies retreated and set in for a long rainy night.[44]

During the night 25,000 fresh Union troops arrived to reinforce Grant's army[45]. The Union army prepared to push back the Confederate lines, and by 10 a.m., the full force of the Union was upon the Confederacy. The entire Union line erupted with fire from the soldiers' muskets as they marched towards the Confederate forces. By mid-afternoon, Beauregard saw the writing on the wall and called for a retreat of Confederate forces. The Confederate forces' losses were heavy from Shiloh, with 1,728 killed, 8,012 wounded and 955 missing, for a total loss

---

[43] Eicher, David J. *The Longest Night: A Military History of the Civil War.* New York, Simon and Schuster, 2001, 228.

[44] Eicher, David J. *The Longest Night: A Military History of the Civil War.* New York, Simon and Schuster, 2001, 228-229.

[45] Stokesbury, James L. *A Short History of the Civil War.* New York, Harper Collins, 1995, 72.

of 10,694. Shiloh became the largest battle fought on American soil. The Union lost a considerable amount during the battle as well with 1,754 killed, 8,408 wounded, and 2,885 missing, with a total loss of 13,047 soldiers.[46]

Shiloh damaged both sides psychologically, as the Confederates retreated and the Union headed further south. The loss took its mental toll as soldiers saw mounds of dead strewn across the battlefield where they marched. Grant had won a victory, but at a heavy cost.

The Seven Days Campaign

Outside of Richmond Virginia, General Lee of the Confederate army prepared for a Union advance. With an army of over 50,000, he prepared to face an advancing Union army of over 100,000.[47] As he waited for the Union troops to arrive, Lee used his downtime wisely, procuring food and new uniforms for his troops. He stressed discipline and preached sobriety among his army.

Lee sent scouts to check on the approaching army under McClellan. He pulled Stonewall Jackson in and the two planned a full assault to begin on June 26. As he pushed his army forward, Stonewall Jackson and his forces arrived, supposedly to help push against the dug-in Union army. Instead, Jackson had his army set up camp and rest. The momentum gained early had come to a complete halt.[48]

Lee still pushed forward and at Mechanicsville, he suffered heavy casualties. The Confederate army losses totaled 1,484 men killed or wounded while the Union only lost 361 soldiers.[49] During the night McClellan bolstered his flank knowing that Stonewall Jackson's army would be moving in the following morning.

---

[46] Eicher, David J. *The Longest Night: A Military History of the Civil War.* New York, Simon and Schuster, 2001, 230-231.

[47] Constable, George, editor. *Brother Against Brother: Time-Life Books History of the Civil War.* New York, Prentice Hall Press, 1990, 118.

[48] Stokesbury, James L. *A Short History of the Civil War.* New York, Harper Collins, 1995, 91.

[49] Constable, George, editor. *Brother Against Brother: Time-Life Books History of the Civil War.* New York, Prentice Hall Press, 1990, 120.

On June 27, Lee pushed towards the established Union encampments, only to find them emptied during the night. The Confederate forces chased the Union to Gaines' Mill where they proceeded to rush forces at the Union line. The Union line held and kept the advancing Confederate army at bay. Soon Jackson's army arrived and together they pushed into the Union line breaking it apart. The Union line began to crumble and the Confederate Generals could see a glimmer of victory.

In full retreat, the Union army under McClellan abandoned their entrenchments outside Richmond and moved across the river. Lee, sensing something afoot, rallied his own troops and Jackson's to attack the front and rear of the Union army.

On the June 29, the two armies moved to converge on the fleeing Union forces. However, Jackson's army ran into trouble at Grapevine Bridge and spent the day rebuilding it in order to cross. The Union army snaked further away, and the 10-mile line stretched so far apart that they were vulnerable to Confederate attack. Jackson's army could come from the north and Lee's could come from the west, rendering the Union army defenseless. The easy victory was not to be. Instead of Jackson heading to cut off the Union from the North, he finished his bridge building and then proceeded to round up Union stragglers. A huge opportunity was squandered.[50]

Lee continued to move his army forward. He took his troops towards Glendale and sought to take out a Union brigade guarding a supply train. With 18,000 men he attacked the Union brigade, and as he pressed forward, the Union mounted a counterattack, stopping the Confederate advance. As night approached, the fighting between the two armies ceased and the day's losses were counted with Lee and the Confederates losing 3,300 to the Union's 2,853.[51]

The following day Lee pushed south of Glendale towards Malvern Hill. Atop the hill were 250 Union artillery, which Lee bombarded for

[50] Constable, George, editor. *Brother Against Brother: Time-Life Books History of the Civil War.* New York, Prentice Hall Press, 1990, 121.

[51] Constable, George, editor. *Brother Against Brother: Time-Life Books History of the Civil War.* New York, Prentice Hall Press, 1990, 122.

hours. As he wore down the barrage, he pushed his army forward towards the Union troops at Malvern Hill. Confederate troops climbed an 800-yard slope as Union cannons tore holes in the Confederate waves that surged forward. By evening, the Seven Days Battle was over. The Confederates had stopped the Union push to Richmond and the Union had taken what was left of their army to retreat back north.[52]

The campaign cost both sides many more lives and did nothing but invigorate the Confederates' narrative that they could defeat the Union. At the end of the campaign, the Union had suffered 15,849 lost soldiers while the Confederacy had taken a huge blow with the loss of 20,141 soldiers.[53]

Second Battle of Bull Run

In August 1862, The Union commander again decided to take Manassas at Bull Run. With a new Army of Virginia and the Army of The Potomac. With the Confederacy having pushed back the Union during the Seven Days Campaign the Union needed a victory. They had an opportunity as the army of General Lee was surrounded on one side by McClellan's army with the new Union commander John Pope bringing his army to bear.

Lee used strategy to move his army towards Pope's and separate his forces, sending half with Stonewall Jackson and leaving half behind to protect Richmond, the prized capital of the Confederacy. Jackson and his army advanced towards Pope's and pushed them back to Cedar Mountain, slowing their movement and forcing them to wait for McClellan to come to reinforce Pope's army. Knowing that McClellan was on his way, Lee again split his forces and attacked Pope's dwindling army.

By August 26, the Confederate army had cut off Pope's supply line from Washington, seizing and destroying a Union supply depot at Manassas Junction, thereby leaving the Union stuck back at Bull Run. Lee reunited his army with Jackson's and they met Pope on the

---

[52] Stokesbury, James L. *A Short History of the Civil War*. New York, Harper Collins, 1995, 92.

[53] Brash, Sarah, editor. *The American Story: War Between Brothers*. Richmond, Time Life, 1996, 181.

battlefield of Bull Run once again. Jackson and his army dug into the shelter of an unfinished railroad station, and the two lines held because Pope could not coordinate his attacks.[54]

On August 30, 1862, the Union army pushed back against Jackson's troops, but again the Confederate line held. As the day went on, Confederate reinforcements arrived and drove the Union army back to Henry Hill, where the Confederates had made their final stand almost a year earlier. The Union held the hill overnight, and under cover of darkness, Pope sent most of his army in retreat.

In the morning the Union was all but gone, and Jackson pushed them back out of the valley and into Washington, where they retreated behind the defenses of the Union capital. The Second Battle of Bull Run was a success for the Confederates. The Union suffered a loss of 14,462 men while the Confederates lost only 9,474.[55]

With the Union army pushed back into Washington, General Lee had no way to strike. The fortifications around the Union capital were too strong, and the Union had more troops, giving them at least a two-to-one advantage over the Confederacy. Knowing that this could be the push the Confederacy needed to win the war Lee decided to push north into Maryland.[56]

The Push North

As Lee pushed north, he received a reinforcement of 20,000 fresh soldiers. By the time Lee made it to Maryland, his army numbered 50,000.[57] Lee then split his army into four elements and sent them to Harpers Ferry, the Potomac, and the Shenandoah to reinforce the supply lines. The race to the North was on.

The North now had to confront the Confederate threat pushing into Maryland. With Lee moving north, they had no way to know his plans.

[54] Stokesbury, James L. *A Short History of the Civil War*. New York, Harper Collins, 1995, 95.

[55] Constable, George, editor. *Brother Against Brother: Time-Life Books History of the Civil War*. New York, Prentice Hall Press, 1990, 136.

[56] Stokesbury, James L. *A Short History of the Civil War*. New York, Harper Collins, 1995, 96.

[57] Constable, George, editor. *Brother Against Brother: Time-Life Books History of the Civil War*. New York, Prentice Hall Press, 1990, 137.

However, on September 13, 1862, two Union soldiers found three wrapped cigars on the ground.[58] Wrapped around the cigars were the orders Lee had sent to his commanders for the four-way split. The orders were given to McClellan, and the Union now had an ace up their sleeve.

McClellan pushed to overtake Lee's split army and to crush Lee at Sharpsburg, Virginia, meeting him on the grounds near Antietam Creek. The move by McClellan was one that would be a game changer. Rather than being on the defense, the Union sought to push the Confederates back into the South and maintain a barrier between them and Washington. Any incursions above Virginia would put the Union in a risky position.

Antietam

On September 17, the Union army approached Lee's and Jackson's armies at Antietam. As cannons opened up with volleys from both sides, the Union army pushed through the field and into a cornfield filled with the ranks of the Confederacy. Inside the stalks of corn, soldiers met in a blinding and fierce fight that went on throughout the morning.[59]

One brigade of Confederate soldiers suffered a fifty percent casualty rate from the cornfield. The Union and Confederacy fought in the cornfield at point-blank range pushing each other back fifteen times covering the cornstalks in blood.[60]

The Federals pushed through the field and into the pike, which the Confederate army had reinforced. As the Union pushed into the Confederate line, they were greeted by a waiting Georgia unit who fired on them as they approached. The Union kept pushing forward and the Confederates were falling back.

Jackson's army had been eating food and was resting in preparation for a later battle. However the approaching Union army roused them and

---

[58] Eicher, David J. *The Longest Night: A Military History of the Civil War.* New York, Simon and Schuster, 2001, 340.

[59] Constable, George, editor. *Brother Against Brother: Time-Life Books History of the Civil War.* New York, Prentice Hall Press, 1990, 143.

[60] Constable, George, editor. *Brother Against Brother: Time-Life Books History of the Civil War.* New York, Prentice Hall Press, 1990, 142-143.

angered them by interrupting their meal, the first they had gotten in days. The 2,300-man division rushed the Union line and pushed them back to the cornfield, saving the morning for the Confederates.[61]

The Confederate division was met by fresh Union troops who drove them back across the pike and into the woods. They suffered high casualties, and the Union pushed past their previous position and fought across the valley. By 9 a.m. the casualties on both sides had become staggering, with over 8,000 mean dead on both sides.[62]

As the Union army pushed forward, they were squeezed perilously close to one another. The 15th Massachusetts were so crowded that they ended up taking fire from the Union as well as the Confederate army, causing them to lose 344 men from both sides of fire.[63]

The Confederate army fell back to a hill and a trench that they had bolstered with rifles in anticipation of the Union charge. The army lay in wait as the Union soldiers came over a crest only 100 yards away. As they started down the slope, the Confederate rifle trench opened up on them taking out the entire front line of the Union army. More and more Union soldiers poured into the line and were cut down giving the area the nickname Bloody Lane.

The Confederates, who were being pursued by the Union army, retreated into an orchard with the enemy at their heels. The Union chased them down and cut down more of the Confederate troops.

As the day progressed, the Union moved across the bridge at Sharpsburg, pushing the Confederates back. Lee had sent for reinforcements, and they were marching from Harper's Ferry to repel the advancing Union. As the Union army surged forward their lines had become weak.

The army arriving from Harpers Ferry advanced on them and cut into a gap in the Union line, mowing their soldiers quickly. Within minutes of

[61] Eicher, David J. *The Longest Night: A Military History of the Civil War*. New York, Simon and Schuster, 2001, 353.

[62] Constable, George, editor. *Brother Against Brother: Time-Life Books History of the Civil War*. New York, Prentice Hall Press, 1990, 146.

[63] Constable, George, editor. *Brother Against Brother: Time-Life Books History of the Civil War*. New York, Prentice Hall Press, 1990, 147.

the arrival of the Confederates from Harper's Ferry, the Union was pushed back through the cornfield, losing much of the ground they had won earlier in the day. The Union had fallen back, and the battle of Antietam was over. The loss of life on both sides was overwhelming. The union had 2,108 killed, 9,549 wounded, and 753 missing, for a total of 12,410 lost in the battle. The Confederates fared only slightly better with 1,546 dead, 7,752 wounded, and 1,018 missing.[64]

With heavy losses on both sides, each withdrew to lick their wounds. The Union stayed outside Sharpsburg, but they had lost all the ground they had gained. Lee and the Confederates retreated across the river and back into Virginia. The war had arrived at a stalemate.

---

[64] Constable, George, editor. *Brother Against Brother: Time-Life Books History of the Civil War.* New York, Prentice Hall Press, 1990, 150.

Chapter 6 – Proclaiming Freedom

Preliminary Emancipation

On September 12, only five days after Antietam, President Lincoln had a cabinet meeting. He had presented them with the first draft of the Emancipation Proclamation in July of 1862. Before the Battle of Antietam, Lincoln had made a promise to "myself and to my Maker" that should the Confederacy be pushed out of Maryland, he would issue the proclamation.[65] Following Lee's retreat back into Virginia, Lincoln planned to honor his promise.

On September 22, 1862, Lincoln issued the preliminary version of The Emancipation Proclamation. By issuing such a document, even preliminarily, he knew that he could take away some of the South's strength by providing an incentive for slaves to escape. This would provide a distraction and weaken the economic stability of the Confederacy. Without slaves for labor and with its men fighting, the Southern economy would be weakened.

Lincoln united the Republican Party to push for the complete abolishment of slavery and to stave off any military interference on the part of England or France. The Emancipation was a cut at the South just

---

[65] Constable, George, editor. *Brother Against Brother: Time-Life Books History of the Civil War.* New York, Prentice Hall Press, 1990, 150.

as they were gaining the upper hand. As he had stated in his first inaugural address, it was to be the will of the people and the Constitution that guided Lincoln's decision-making. Lincoln had hoped that the Confederates would come to their senses and abandon what he considered a lost cause. With the Emancipation Proclamation, the will of the people of the Union and the Constitution were thrust upon the Confederates. Whether or not they would end the war and return to the Union was entirely their choice.

Fredericksburg

Two months after Antietam, the Union and Confederates were in a different world. The Union had lost McClellan, and General Burnside had picked up leadership of the Union army. Lee and the Confederate army had reorganized and resupplied his army, separated them into two corps, and put them under the command of Jackson and Longstreet. Lee was using his leadership assets as much as his army to push back the Union.

By November, the Union had once again decided they needed to capture Richmond and put an end to the war. Burnside had decided that he would move towards Virginia and trick Lee into thinking he was going to take Gordonsville, and then at the last moment strike at Fredericksburg. Burnside intended for the strike to be fast and unexpected.

The plan to ferry supplies and troops via steamer faltered and Burnside was delayed in setting the attack. The delay allowed Lee to reinforce Fredericksburg and by the end of December, Lee's entire army of 85,000 was defending the Fredericksburg area.[66]

Having delayed long enough, Burnside called upon gunboats to support the attack. However, as they approached, Confederate artillery pushed them back downstream and out of their supporting capacity. On December 11, the Union was set to invade Fredericksburg, and as they crossed the Rappahannock River in the early morning hours, they were met with fire from Confederate sharpshooters on the bank.

---

[66] Eicher, David J. *The Longest Night: A Military History of the Civil War*. New York, Simon and Schuster, 2001, 396.

The Union artillery attempted to reinforce the troops crossing the river and to protect engineers who were trying to form a crossing. After an hour the artillery subsided, and the engineers went back to work again, only to be fired upon once more by Confederate sharpshooters. With the engineers pinned down and the army unable to move, the Union army brought forth 100 guns and fired 5,000 rounds into Fredericksburg.[67] This did not deter the sharpshooters on the bank, and eventually, the Union was forced to launch pontoons of infantry across the river to claim the banks and remove the threat. As they crossed, they too were met with heavy fire. Once they reached the other side they moved out and cleared the bridges and banks, enabling the rest of the army to move forward. With this small victory, the Union army was able to push into Fredericksburg, and the Confederates were forced into retreat.

The Union spent the following day moving across the river without obstruction and looting the town of Fredericksburg. The Confederates under the command of Lee moved into a defensive position, lining up across the railroad tracks outside Fredericksburg. The Confederates had a strong defensive line except for a small wooded area between two bridges the Union army had to cross.

On December 13, under the cover of a morning mist, the Union pushed west and south into the waiting Confederate army. As the fog lifted, the shine of thousands of Confederate bayonets shone across the plains. The Union was shot at as they were crossing the plains and stalled in moving forward. Once the Union regrouped, they moved ahead, only to be bombarded by Confederate artillery ripping apart their ranks.

The Union moved through the unprotected wooded gap and into the Confederate lines. The confusion caused the Confederates to not fire upon the advancing Union soldiers, who then slaughtered the Southerners as they fell upon them. The confusion led the Union to break the Confederate line. Soon the Confederates flanked and attempted to push back the oncoming wave of Union soldiers, only to falter as they ran out of ammunition and other units fell back leaving the front lines unsupported. As both armies retreated to regroup, the

---

[67] Eicher, David J. *The Longest Night: A Military History of the Civil War.* New York, Simon and Schuster, 2001, 399.

casualties of the day mounted. The Union had lost 4,830 men, while the Confederates under the command of Jackson lost 3,415.[68]

On the other side of Fredericksburg, more fighting occurred with Lee's troops holding Marye's Heights outside the city. The Confederates had taken a position behind a four-foot high stone wall enabling them to fire at oncoming Union troops with little to no exposure to return fire. The line was 2,000 strong with reinforcements just beyond the ridge of over 7,000 Confederate troops.[69] Artillery supported the Confederates at Marye's Heights and when the Union was forced to make a march out of the city and into an open plain, they would be assaulted as they trudged up a muddy bluff.

The Union was decimated by artillery as soon as they emerged onto the plains, yet they pushed forward towards the bluff. As they reached the last 125 yards of their march, the Confederates behind the wall opened up with volley after volley of rifle fire killing hundreds of Union soldiers.[70] Still, they pressed on, and some even made it up the bluff, pausing to fire back on the Confederate position and then falling back to reload.

The Union pushed on and was met with gunfire from the ridge. Not one Union soldier made it to the stone wall, and the Union suffered crushing losses. The Union army had 1,284 dead, 9,600 wounded, and 1,769 missing. The Confederates had 595 killed, 4,061 injured, and 1,769 missing.[71] The Union was forced back and lost its momentum towards capturing Richmond.

Emancipation Proclamation

After the issuance of the preliminary Emancipation Proclamation, the Confederacy was offered the opportunity to end the war by the end of

---

[68] Constable, George, editor. *Brother Against Brother: Time-Life Books History of the Civil War.* New York, Prentice Hall Press, 1990, 199.

[69] Constable, George, editor. *Brother Against Brother: Time-Life Books History of the Civil War.* New York, Prentice Hall Press, 1990, 202.

[70] Eicher, David J. *The Longest Night: A Military History of the Civil War.* New York, Simon and Schuster, 2001, 404.

[71] Eicher, David J. *The Longest Night: A Military History of the Civil War.* New York, Simon and Schuster, 2001, 405.

1862. But, the offer was rejected.[72] So, Lincoln moved to make the Emancipation Proclamation official. On January 1, 1863, Lincoln put the Emancipation Proclamation into effect. The proclamation made the war with the South not just a struggle to reunite the Union, but also a civil rights war for black liberation.

With the war at a stalemate and the Union needing a victory, Lincoln knew that by issuing the proclamation the South would have to deal with slave rebellions and insurrections. Abolitionists lauded Lincoln's daring move, and Jefferson Davis of the Confederate States condemned it.

The Union now began to recruit black soldiers and to create black units that would assist in freeing slaves in the Southern states. This push by Lincoln gave the Union a psychological, and eventually military, win as black recruits flocked to the Union army. By the end of 1865, the Union army had more than 180,000 black troops.[73]

While the Emancipation Proclamation did not end slavery, it did lead to freeing and arming slaves who rose up in aid of the Union. Foreign armies who may have once supported the Confederate states backed away, not wanting to be any part of a war that was now intended to stop slavery. The Emancipation Proclamation made the Confederate states reevaluate their position and contemplate the future of the war. With this new threat to their way of life, many wondered how the Confederacy would respond.

Impressment and Military Draft

As the war crept on, the South faced a shortage of supplies. With the Union blockading its ports, and the loss of slaves due to the Emancipation Proclamation, the Confederate states were forced to issue an impressment law which gave army officers the right to take any private property that would aid them in fighting the war. While this was already a common occurrence, this verbalized threat by the Confederate government caused many to worry about the future of the war and to question the legality and implications of such movements.

---

[72] Stokesbury, James L. *A Short History of the Civil War*. New York, Harper Collins, 1995, 134.

[73] Katcher, Philip. *The Civil War Day by Day*. St. Paul, The Brown Reference Group, 2007, 82.

State governors issued officers to seize cattle, clothing, food, horses, iron, slaves, and even free men for the service of the Confederacy. The taking of such goods usually was at a total loss for the property owner. In addition, the Confederacy issued a ten percent "tax in kind" on farm produce, fomenting further Southern anger against the government.[74]

While the Union also had such an act in place it was rarely used, and since the Union had a strong economy, it enabled them to use such acts sparingly. The Confederacy, however, was running ragged. Its currency was rapidly inflating, and the costs of goods and services were being repaid at an outdated rate rather than at a competitive one. The deterioration of the Confederate economy was adding another burden to the already stressed Southern states.

The Union however had bigger issues as they instituted a military draft. The draft required every man to serve in the army unless he could either furnish a substitute or pay the government three hundred dollars. These provisions in the draft law lead to many who were poor or unable to find a surrogate to be thrust into battle. Many of these people were immigrants and working-class folks who in July of 1863, after the names of draftees were published in the newspaper, marched through the streets, resulting in riots, property damage, and lynching. The Union army was sent in with soldiers straight from the front lines of the war. Sadly, when they arrived, they had little sympathy for the protesters and opened fire on the mob. This killed hundreds but ended the riots.[75]

---

[74] Katcher, Philip. *The Civil War Day by Day.* St. Paul, The Brown Reference Group, 2007, 84.

[75] Maus, Louis P. *The Civil War: A Concise History.* New York, Oxford University Press, 2011, 56.

Chapter 7 – The War Looks Grim

The Union and Confederacy were both hurt as the war dragged into yet another year. In Mississippi, the Union led a raid which further upset the balance in the South. For 16 days, Colonel Benjamin Grierson led Union cavalry units from Tennessee to Louisiana, killing over 100 Confederate soldiers, freeing 500 Union troops, and destroying about 60 miles of railroad as well as 3,000 arms stored by the Confederates.[76]

The use of such guerilla tactics was intended to cause the Confederacy to divert its forces in pursuit of the Union cavalry, rather than pushing north. By drawing the forces away from the front and towards a smaller and quicker enemy, many of the resources were also redirected away from the front lines of the Confederate army. Grierson and his cavalry were a strategic move that gave the Union a much-needed edge.

Chancellorsville

Following winter quartering by both the Union and Confederate armies, the war was back on in May of 1863. Outside Fredericksburg, both armies had lingered following their December 1862 clash. The much-needed rest and recuperation experienced by both the Union and the Confederates were apparent.

---

[76] Constable, George, editor. *Brother Against Brother: Time-Life Books History of the Civil War.* New York, Prentice Hall Press, 1990, 237.

The Union decided to move onto Chancellorsville and marched there without resistance. On May 2, Stonewall Jackson surprised the Union army from the west while Lee took his other forces and attacked from the south. Jackson and his 26,000 troops, who had found the Union troops napping and relaxing, caught the Union off guard. The Confederates fell upon the Union army and overran them easily.[77]

While some of the soldiers returned fire, other men scattered and ran from the rush of oncoming Confederate soldiers. The Union attempted to form a defense and stop the rush of Confederate troops. As night fell, Jackson pulled his line back and replaced his exhausted troops so he could attempt a night attack. Jackson rode out to scout the land himself as he returned from his reconnaissance of the Union lines, he was mistaken for a Union troop and shot by his own men. He was taken from the battlefield, his left arm was amputated, and was left to rest in the hope that he would recover.[78]

The Union spent the evening after the raid by Jackson's army reorganizing and preparing for a further assault. The Union troops made a loop around Chancellorsville, building up their fortifications the best they could. More troops poured in to reinforce the beleaguered Union army, swelling their ranks to 76,000 men.[79]

The following day, with Jeb Stuart now in their command, Jackson's troops went to battle with the larger Union army. The Confederate troops came from all sides as the Union repelled wave after wave, pushing them back and forcing them to readjust their approach. By the end of the day both armies were exhausted and could no longer fight.

General Lee took full command on May 4 and hoped to push the army of the Union back both north and east. The two-attack approach of the Union had strained Lee's forces and supplies. Although the Union lost 17,287 soldiers, the Confederates had lost 12,764 as well as the

---

[77] Eicher, David J. *The Longest Night: A Military History of the Civil War*. New York, Simon and Schuster, 2001, 474.

[78] Stokesbury, James L. *A Short History of the Civil War*. New York, Harper Collins, 1995, 158.

[79] Constable, George, editor. *Brother Against Brother: Time-Life Books History of the Civil War*. New York, Prentice Hall Press, 1990, 216.

ability to sustain any further heavy personnel and supply losses.[80] The Confederacy was also about to suffer a misfortune that would be felt all across the South. On May 10 Jackson had succumbed to his wound and died in a field hospital outside Chancellorsville.[81] The Confederacy had suffered a massive blow to its leadership.

Gettysburg

Only months later would the Confederates resume their push north. This time the battlefield would be in Union territory, far north of Washington but within striking distance of it. The battlefield was Gettysburg, Pennsylvania. On July 1, 1863, Lee and his army arrived in Pennsylvania looking for another strategy to make their way into Maryland and neighboring Washington.[82]

In desperation, the Confederates saw Gettysburg as a path they could take to end the war. The first shot at Gettysburg was via a sentry responding to Confederate cavalry. The Union had men on the high ground waiting for an assault on Gettysburg. The Confederates assaulted the ridge and were pushed back. They saw the high ground as a necessary hold to win the battle.

As charge after charge pushed the Union line tighter and caused casualties, the Confederate army also suffered heavy losses, tearing apart their army and making each successive charge weaker and weaker. By July 3rd the Confederacy was at the end of their rope. With little land gained and many lives lost, they need something big to change the tide.

On July 3, Lee knew he needed to do something rash. Lee turned 150 guns and 15,000 men towards Cemetery Ridge, committing a frontal assault. Lead by Pickett's division this event would become known as Pickett's Charge. Beginning at 1 p.m., Lee had 150 guns bombard the Union line for two hours. The Confederate army had to march over open terrain to finish the final assault. As they rushed the Union

---

[80] Brash, Sarah, editor. *The American Story: War Between Brothers*. Richmond, Time Life, 1996, 181.

[81] Stokesbury, James L. *A Short History of the Civil War*. New York, Harper Collins, 1995, 158.

[82] Constable, George, editor. *Brother Against Brother: Time-Life Books History of the Civil War*. New York, Prentice Hall Press, 1990, 258.

positions, 80 guns blasted them apart. While Union soldiers hiding behind a stone wall opened up on the rest of the army, cutting them down where they stand by the end of the charge only 100 men reach the wall only to be called to retreat. The Battle of Gettysburg results in the single biggest defeat for the Confederacy.[83]

Gettysburg saw over 160,000 soldiers engaging in a battle over three days. The Union had mustered 88,000 to the Confederates 75,000.[84] By the end of the battle more than 28,000 Confederate soldiers were killed, injured, or lost while the Union suffered 23,049 losses.[85] Between the two sides, the dead at Gettysburg numbered over 6,000. Lee was forced to retreat to Virginia and out of Union territory.

[83] Eicher, David J. *The Longest Night: A Military History of the Civil War.* New York, Simon and Schuster, 2001, 546-547.

[84] Stokesbury, James L. *A Short History of the Civil War.* New York, Harper Collins, 1995, 170.

[85] Brash, Sarah, editor. *The American Story: War Between Brothers.* Richmond, Time Life, 1996, 181.

Chapter 8 – Turning the Tide

As the fighting continues, each victory meant more than the last. The Union had the ability to keep the war going while every loss the Confederates took was a bigger blow to their cause and their war chest. Both sides had endured a war longer than they could have imagined. Lincoln had thought the rebellion would be crushed within a year and Davis had assumed that the Union would give up and let the Confederate States exist freely. Neither wanted to give up and lose the nations they had sworn to serve.

Vicksburg

Following the loss at Gettysburg, the Confederacy was growing weak. The Union had claimed several other victories securing New Orleans and Memphis from out of Confederate control, leaving Vicksburg as the last link between the two halves of the Confederate states.

General Ulysses S. Grant had the city under siege since May 18 of 1863.[86] Having attempted to take the city two times, the Union had suffered massive casualties at the hands of the reinforced, and heavily fortified, Confederate army in Vicksburg. Grant had attempted frontal assaults, sea batteries, and bombardment. Finally, after learning of Lee's army arriving at Gettysburg, Grant pushed to find a way to take

---

[86] Stokesbury, James L. *A Short History of the Civil War*. New York, Harper Collins, 1995, 99.

Vicksburg.

Having detonated a mine under the fortifications of the city, the Union was trying to force their way under and into the settlement. The city was starving; the people had begun running low on meat, salt, and even water. With Grant knocking at the door, the Confederacy was forced to find a way to end the siege at Vicksburg.

On July 3, 1863, the same day as Lee's defeat at Gettysburg, the leader of the troops at Vicksburg, General John C. Pemberton, sent a message of truce to Grant. The two met to set terms, and Grant asked for an unconditional surrender. Pemberton was willing to capitulate. Grant, however, rethought the situation and offered Pemberton and the Confederate troops parole. All the Confederate soldiers would be released after signing an oath to not fight again until all Union captives were free.[87]

By midnight Pemberton had accepted Grant's terms and the siege of Vicksburg had ended after 48 long days. The siege had taken a huge toll on each army; so much so that they had comforted each other after the siege's end. The humanity of war had become more apparent to both sides. Many wondered how much longer the war could continue, how much longer citizen could fight against citizen.

Following the announcement of the fall of Vicksburg, one final holdout on the Mississippi at Port Hudson surrendered the garrison to the Union navy on July 9, 1863.[88] The South was slowly falling. The mighty Mississippi had fallen to the Union and the Confederates had lost a vital passage for troops and trade.

Battle of Chickamauga

Tennessee was still a contested area or the Confederate army. They had held several areas around Chattanooga and were attempting to repel the Union from the state. On September 18, 1863, General Rosecrans and his army of 62,000 Union soldiers pushed to cut off the Confederate

---

[87]Stokesbury, James L. *A Short History of the Civil War*. New York, Harper Collins, 1995, 148.

[88] Constable, George, editor. *Brother Against Brother: Time-Life Books History of the Civil War*. New York, Prentice Hall Press, 1990, 248.

army and keep them from assaulting the Union army heading to Chattanooga. With 65,000 men the Confederate General Braxton Bragg met at Chickamauga Creek.[89]

The two armies clashed on September 19, with both suffering heavy losses and retiring at the end of the day without either making much advancement. During the night, however, the Union dug trenches and prepared for a Confederate assault. The following day the Confederate army rushed the Union defensive positions and forced them to plug gaps caused by the assault. As they were doing this, a second Confederate assault pushed the Union army back to a wooded ridge where they took a last stand while the bulk of the Union army retreated to Chattanooga. While this was a victory for the South, it did not turn the tide in their favor since they still suffered a loss of 18,454 soldiers versus the Union's somewhat smaller loss of 16,179.[90]

The Union had retreated to the safety of Chattanooga, and the Confederates had only won a small win. Each victory, however, emboldened Davis and the Confederate leadership. Though their resources dwindled and their safety in Richmond was intermittently in peril, they still saw their cause as a just one. Lincoln too sought to state his dedication to the cause and soon used the battlefield at Gettysburg to restate his desire for an end to the war and a reunited Union.

Gettysburg Address

As the Union army picked up steam, pushing Lee and the Confederates out of the North while taking over New Orleans, Mississippi, and Tennessee, Lincoln decided that Gettysburg would be a perfect place to dedicate to a speech to restoring the Union.

On November 19, 1863, upon Lincoln's arrival at Gettysburg, ceremonies began with music, prayers, a two-hour speech by Edward Everett of Massachusetts followed by a hymn, and then a 272-word address known today as the Gettysburg Address.[91]

[89] Katcher, Philip. *The Civil War Day by Day.* St. Paul, The Brown Reference Group, 2007, 113.

[90] Constable, George, editor. *Brother Against Brother: Time-Life Books History of the Civil War.* New York, Prentice Hall Press, 1990, 311.

[91] Cozzens, Peter, editor. *Battles and Leaders of the Civil War, Vol. 5.* University of Illinois, 2002,

Lincoln stood in front of a crowd of 10,00 and spoke slowly and loudly so all could hear. Lincoln proclaimed:

"Fourscore and seven years ago our fathers brought forth, on this continent, a new nation, conceived in liberty, and dedicated to the proposition that all men are created equal. Now we are engaged in a great civil war, testing whether that nation, or any nation so conceived, and so dedicated, can long endure. We are met on a great battle-field of that war. We have come to dedicate a portion of that field, as a final resting-place for those who here gave their lives, that that nation might live. It is altogether fitting and proper that we should do this. But, in a larger sense, we cannot dedicate, we cannot consecrate—we cannot hallow—this ground. The brave men, living and dead, who struggled here, have consecrated it far above our poor power to add or detract. The world will little note, nor long remember what we say here, but it can never forget what they did here. It is for us the living, rather, to be dedicated here to the unfinished work which they who fought here have thus far so nobly advanced. It is rather for us to be here dedicated to the great task remaining before us—that from these honored dead we take increased devotion to that cause for which they here gave the last full measure of devotion—that we here highly resolve that these dead shall not have died in vain—that this nation, under God, shall have a new birth of freedom, and that government of the people, by the people, for the people, shall not perish from the earth."[92]

The speech renewed the call for an end to the war and for the Union and the Confederacy to reunite. In front of a crowd and a free press Lincoln hoped his words would spread to the Confederate states and fall on the ears of Jefferson Davis, awaking in him the realization that the war could not be sustained. With more losses at Gettysburg than either side could handle, Lincoln hoped his speech would be an olive branch to the Confederates. He hoped that things would soon change. 1864 was indeed to be the year that the war changed.

376.

[92] Eicher, David J. *The Longest Night: A Military History of the Civil War*. New York, Simon and Schuster, 2001, 622.

Battle of Wilderness

On May 4, 1864, the Union entered Wilderness, Virginia. The Union army marched to take Wilderness and was cut off by Lee's troops at Orange Turnpike. The two armies clashed, and a battle was fought through dense brush and foliage.

The two armies fought for three days with each pushing the other back. Confederate reinforcements arrived on May 6, and the battle raged on into the night. The battle was so tough that fires started in the brush, causing the armies to take time to stop the fires and remove the injured in order to prevent them from being burned to death.

While the battle was hard-fought, eventually the two armies ended with a draw. However, Grant considered it a victory for the Union as he and his army continued south further into Virginia.

The bloodshed at Wilderness was devastating for both sides; however, the Union took the brunt of the loss. The Union lost 1,766 soldiers compared to the Confederates' 7,500.[93] While Grant claimed victory, he paid a heavy toll at Wilderness.

Siege of Petersburg

In June of 1864, The Union once again pushed to take Richmond, Virginia. They needed to end the war. The strain on both the Union and the Confederacy was becoming unbearable. Hundreds of thousands of men had died for both sides, and the country was torn apart.

The Union pushed into Virginia and to Petersburg. Petersburg was the key to the railroad network that was keeping Lee and the Confederate army alive. Grant decided that if they could cut off supplies, they could shut down the Confederate army and move on to Richmond. Petersburg was heavily defended with artillery covering all the lines of fire and a network of trenches around the city. The Confederates had fortified the city against the oncoming Union army.

On June 18, 1864, Lee and his army met the Union army outside

---

[93] Brash, Sarah, editor. *The American Story: War Between Brothers*. Richmond, Time Life, 1996, 181.

Petersburg and fought for four days, costing the Union 10,000 troops.[94] The small skirmishes continued on and off for the next three weeks with neither gaining ground. Thus began the siege of Petersburg.

Though the two armies sat only hundreds of yards apart, the Union had been given a golden opportunity. Soldiers from Pennsylvania who were former miners were only 130 yards from the Confederate line.[95] The Union formed a plan to dig under the Confederate defenses, blow a hole in it, and breach Petersburg claiming the city.

The miners dug 40 feet a day around the clock to move 510.8 feet to a location beyond the Confederate line. They moved over 18,000 cubic feet of dirt, which they spread across a ravine behind Union lines as to not draw attention.[96] On July 23, 1864, they finished the tunnel and came up with a plan; two brigades would push into Petersburg via this secret hole in the Confederate defenses.

It took them six hours to place 320 kegs of gunpowder and lay in place a 98-foot fuse to light the kegs. Finally, on July 30 at 4:40 in the morning the Union army set off the powder kegs, blasting a hole 200 feet long, 50 feet wide, and 25 to 30 feet deep.[97] The whole was filled with "dust, great blocks of clay, guns, broken carriages, project timbers, and men buried in various ways – some up to their necks, others to their waist, some with only their feet and legs protruding from the earth."[98] At least 256 Confederate soldiers died as a result of the blast.

As the dust cleared, 10,000 black soldiers hurried through the mine and into the crater. Lee and his army stationed near Petersburg attacked troops both in and outside of the crater, causing panic and confusion. The Confederates overwhelmed the Union, and within a matter of hours,

---

[94] Constable, George, editor. *Brother Against Brother: Time-Life Books History of the Civil War.* New York, Prentice Hall Press, 1990, 380.

[95] Constable, George, editor. *Brother Against Brother: Time-Life Books History of the Civil War.* New York, Prentice Hall Press, 1990, 380.

[96] Constable, George, editor. *Brother Against Brother: Time-Life Books History of the Civil War.* New York, Prentice Hall Press, 1990, 382.

[97] Stokesbury, James L. *A Short History of the Civil War.* New York, Harper Collins, 1995, 267.

[98] Constable, George, editor. *Brother Against Brother: Time-Life Books History of the Civil War.* New York, Prentice Hall Press, 1990, 382.

they had lost 3,500 troops to the Confederates' 1,500. The Union lost their chance to take Petersburg.[99]

---

[99] Constable, George, editor. *Brother Against Brother: Time-Life Books History of the Civil War.* New York, Prentice Hall Press, 1990, 384.

Chapter 9 – The Final Fight

The war between the Union and the Confederacy was dragging on into its third year. With no end in sight, the Union went on the offensive in Virginia hoping to force surrender. As the war moved further into the year it was through this push into the heart of the Confederate territory that the Union hoped to end the war and return the Union to unification.

Sherman Burns Atlanta

The Union army in Georgia was gaining ground. General Sherman had been fighting a long land war chasing Hood's army throughout the South. Finally, on August 31, 1864, Sherman had defeated Hood's army and pushed them into Atlanta.[100]

Sherman gave chase and cut the Confederates off north of Jonesborough, destroying the railroad tracks leading into Atlanta and cutting off the last supply line for Hood's army in Atlanta.

The battle at Jonesborough was a massive victory for the Union and a blow to an already weak Confederate army. Sherman pushed the Confederate forces into Atlanta, and with the push, the Confederate army slid closer to defeat. There was no doubt that soon the Confederacy

---

[100] Stokesbury, James L. *A Short History of the Civil War*. New York, Harper Collins, 1995, 284.

would fall.[101]

Sherman's goal was the total and complete destruction of the Confederacy. Every victory over the Confederacy was designed to have the maximum impact so that the Confederacy would lose supplies, soldiers, morale, and the faith of the citizens of the Confederate States of America. The war was coming to an end, and the Union along with Sherman was doing everything possible to shut down the Confederate army and make them want to give up.[102]

Sherman's March to the Sea

After losing the Battle of Atlanta, the Rebel army headed to Tennessee through Alabama. General Sherman decided to split his forces. He gave 60,000 men to Major General George Thomas to meet the Confederates in Nashville. General Sherman took 62,000 men east to take over the major port city of Savannah in order to choke off a major supply line.

As General Thomas headed into Alabama chasing the Confederates, Sherman pushed his troops towards Savannah, instituting a strategy that would become known as "The Scorched Earth Policy." Whatever farm, hamlet, or town Sherman's army encountered on its journey to Savannah; they completely pillaged and destroyed. After taking every item of worth including livestock, food, clothing, and feed, every structure was burned to the ground.

The places Sherman destroyed had already been hit hard. With the majority of men off fighting the war, or in most cases having been killed in the war, the only males left were either extremely old or very young. This lack of resources, both in available goods and available workforce, made it nearly impossible for these communities to rebound. And, this was precisely what General Sherman wanted to happen. If the people had to rebuild just to survive, there wouldn't be time or fervor enough to fight a war.

---

[101] Stokesbury, James L. *A Short History of the Civil War.* New York, Harper Collins, 1995, 280.

[102] Stokesbury, James L. *A Short History of the Civil War.* New York, Harper Collins, 1995, 284=285.

It took nearly three weeks for Sherman to make the 258-mile march to Savannah from Atlanta, breaking the backs and morale of the Southern population along the way. On December 21, 1864, Sherman's army marched through the streets of Savannah, Georgia unopposed. There had been a garrison of 11,000 men stationed there to protect the vital seaport, but upon news of the swath of destruction Sherman had laid down, they fled the city with the news of his imminent arrival. General Sherman found 25,000 unguarded bales of cotton, which he instantly claimed for the Union, proclaiming them an early Christmas present for Abraham Lincoln.

After securing Savannah, Sherman's army turned north for Charleston, South Carolina. He continued his scorched earth policy through South Carolina, declaring, "This Union and its Government must be sustained, at any and every cost," even though the preservation of the Union was paid for with the lives and livelihoods of civilians of the South.

However, the fear of General Sherman and his policy helped end the Siege of Charleston. After nearly two straight years of shelling from the Union armies and their technologically advanced artillery, the besieged Southerners stood resolutely. However, with news of Sherman's ruthless army on route to the embargo-breaking port city, the remaining Southern troops in the city fled. They could endure exploding mortars, countless fires, disease, and starvation, but they withered at the mere mention of an almost mythological figure.

Fall of Richmond

In April of 1865, knowing that the Union was gaining ground and the Confederacy was running low on supplies and troops, they left Petersburg and Richmond, Virginia. The Union had broken the defenses in Petersburg and were about to overrun both Petersburg and Richmond. With little other options, Lee took all he could gather and called a retreat.

The Confederate army under General Lee attempted to fall west, hoping to reorganize with other units in that area. In Danville, on the road out of Virginia near Appomattox, Union cavalry overwhelmed Lee's army, destroying a large part of Lee's supplies. Almost 800 troops were lost along the way as the Union army repeated attacks. Lee's troops were too tired, famished, and unsupplied to mount a proper defense.[103]

Finally, on May 9, 1865, Robert E. Lee surrendered to Ulysses S. Grant at Appomattox Courthouse in Virginia, thereby ending Lee's campaign and the war in Virginia.[104] The agreement signed by both Generals was one intended to reunite the Union. The official surrender of the Confederate army under the command of Lee came on April 12, 1864. Once the soldiers, marching with tears in their eyes, had laid down their arms, the two armies sat together and shared food.[105]

---

[103] Constable, George, editor. *Brother Against Brother: Time-Life Books History of the Civil War.* New York, Prentice Hall Press, 1990, 397.

[104] Stokesbury, James L. *A Short History of the Civil War.* New York, Harper Collins, 1995, 319.

[105] Stokesbury, James L. *A Short History of the Civil War.* New York, Harper Collins, 1995, 320.

Chapter 10 – Reunited

With so many years of war hanging over Lincoln, he sought to find an effective way to strike at the heart of the Confederate states. While the Emancipation Proclamation had helped grant freedom to slaves, it was still far from the total destruction of the institution of slavery that many in the North had called for. Lincoln sought to push forward the 13th Amendment and to, at last, remove the blight of slavery from the face of the United States.

13th Amendment Ends Slavery

On January 31, 1865, the United States Congress passed the 13th which stated, "Neither slavery nor involuntary servitude, except as a punishment for crime whereof the party shall have been duly convicted, shall exist within the United States, or any place subject to their jurisdiction." [106] Finally, on December 6, 1865, the amendment was ratified by the states.

This amendment created a snowball effect, moving many to find ways to grant equal rights to those who were still considered second-class citizens and who were still limited by the words, or lack thereof, within

---

[106] Lincoln, Abraham. *Abraham Lincoln papers: Series 3. General Correspondence. 1837 to 1897: Congress, Wednesday, Joint Resolution Submitting 13th Amendment to the States; signed by Abraham Lincoln and Congress.* February 1, 1865. Manuscript/Mixed Material. Retrieved from the Library of Congress, <www.loc.gov/item/mal4361100/>.

the Constitution.

Second Lincoln Inaugural

With the end of the war looming, Lincoln was elected to a second term. This time he took an opportunity to orate a brief but firm speech, which was to be one of his last. On March 4, 1865, worn and tired from an entire term of war, Lincoln stood before a crowd at the Capitol's East Front and gave the following speech:

"At this second appearing to take the oath of the Presidential office, there is less occasion for an extended address than there was at the first. Then a statement somewhat in detail of a course to be pursued seemed fitting and proper. Now, at the expiration of four years, during which public declarations have been constantly called forth on every point and phase of the great contest which still absorbs the attention and engrosses the energies of the nation, little that is new could be presented. The progress of our arms, upon which all else chiefly depends, is as well known to the public as to myself, and it is, I trust, reasonably satisfactory and encouraging to all. With high hope for the future, no prediction in regard to it is ventured. On the occasion corresponding to this four years ago all thoughts were anxiously directed to an impending civil war. All dreaded it, all sought to avert it. While the inaugural address was being delivered from this place, devoted altogether to saving the Union without war, insurgent agents were in the city seeking to destroy it without war--seeking to dissolve the Union and divide effects by negotiation. Both parties deprecated war, but one of them would make war rather than let the nation survive, and the other would accept war rather than let it perish, and the war came. One-eighth of the whole population were colored slaves, not distributed generally over the Union, but localized in the southern part of it. These slaves constituted a peculiar and powerful interest. All knew that this interest was somehow the cause of the war. To strengthen, perpetuate, and extend this interest was the object for which the insurgents would rend the Union even by war, while the Government claimed no right to do more than to restrict the territorial enlargement of it. Neither party expected for the war the magnitude or the duration which it has already attained. Neither anticipated that the cause of the conflict might cease with or even before the conflict itself should cease.

Each looked for an easier triumph, and a result less fundamental and astounding. Both read the same Bible and pray to the same God, and each invokes His aid against the other. It may seem strange that any men should dare to ask a just God's assistance in wringing their bread from the sweat of other men's faces, but let us judge not, that we be not judged. The prayers of both could not be answered. That of neither has been answered fully. The Almighty has His own purposes. "Woe unto the world because of offenses; for it must needs be that offenses come, but woe to that man by whom the offense cometh." [107]

"If we shall suppose that American slavery is one of those offenses which, in the providence of God, must needs come, but which, having continued through His appointed time, He now wills to remove, and that He gives to both North and South this terrible war as the woe due to those by whom the offense came, shall we discern therein any departure from those divine attributes which the believers in a living God always ascribe to Him? Fondly do we hope, fervently do we pray, that this mighty scourge of war may speedily pass away. Yet, if God wills that it continue until all the wealth piled by the bondsman's two hundred and fifty years of unrequited toil shall be sunk, and until every drop of blood drawn with the lash shall be paid by another drawn with the sword, as was said three thousand years ago, so still it must be said "the judgments of the Lord are true and righteous altogether. With malice toward none, with charity for all, with firmness in the right as God gives us to see the right, let us strive on to finish the work we are in, to bind up the nation's wounds, to care for him who shall have borne the battle and for his widow and his orphan, to do all which may achieve and cherish a just and lasting peace among ourselves and with all nations."[108]

With this speech, Lincoln signaled his desire to end the perpetual war, spelling out his disdain and hatred for the institution of slavery. His words represented the moral high ground that Lincoln had not pushed as hard for before the war, and which he was no longer afraid to express, having

---

[107] Lincoln, Abraham. *Second inaugural address of the late President Lincoln.* James Miller, New York, 1865. Pdf. Retrieved from the Library of Congress, <www.loc.gov/item/scsm000283/>.

[108] Lincoln, Abraham. *Second inaugural address of the late President Lincoln.* James Miller, New York, 1865. Pdf. Retrieved from the Library of Congress, <www.loc.gov/item/scsm000283/>.

experienced through the Civil War the exact opposite of the peace he had sought when he first took office.

Lincoln Shot

John Wilkes Booth was born on May 10, 1838, to English immigrants Junius Brutus Booth, a Shakespearian actor, and his mistress Mary Anne Holmes. More of his youth was spent noticing the rolling Maryland countryside than paying attention to his studies. When Booth was 14, his father died, and he decided to quit his educational endeavors and pursue the path his father and older brother had blazed in the theater.

After making his debut at 17, he realized he would have a hard time breaking free of the shadow of his older brother Edwin's acting career. However, through his good looks and animated performances, his reputation and roles grew larger. He took the leading role in a national touring company, and by the time the 1850s were over, he was making the equivalent of over half a million dollars per year in today's money.

As the Civil War started, Booth's distaste for abolitionists grew. He joined a group of men that formed a militia and marched to Harpers Ferry to revel in the hanging of John Brown. He then spent two weeks in Montreal, a hotbed for Southern sympathizers, while making plans on how to deal with the North, and in particular, the President.

As early as August of 1864, Booth and his conspirators planned to assassinate President Lincoln. He had envisioned many scenarios, including kidnapping Lincoln and holding him hostage in Virginia until the Union released Confederate prisoners of war and let them return to the front lines. Each time Booth planned to eliminate Lincoln, it was somehow prevented.[109]

Finally, on April 14, 1865, Booth and his conspirators had their opportunity to act. President and Mrs. Lincoln, along with Ulysses S. Grant, were set to attend a performance of *Our American Cousin* at Ford's Theater. As he worked out his plan, Booth learned that Grant would not be in attendance and so he switched his second target to

---

[109] Constable, George, editor. *Brother Against Brother: Time-Life Books History of the Civil War.* New York, Prentice Hall Press, 1990, 408.

Secretary of State William Seward. Booth had planned for the assassins to strike at 10:25 p.m., and then ride across the Potomac into the safety of Virginia and the Confederacy.[110]

The Lincolns arrived at 8:30 p.m. and sat in a box overlooking the stage. He and his wife were enjoying the show when Booth entered the theater headed up the stairs and slipped into their private box. As laughter rose from the crowd Booth stepped to the right side of Lincoln, pulled out a derringer, and fired, tearing through Lincoln's left ear and into his brain. Lincoln slumped over as Booth pulled a knife and attacked one of Lincoln's guests at the theater, Major Rathbone. He then leaped from the booth to the stage, reportedly becoming ensnared in a flag as he fell, resulting in a broken leg. Booth still managed to escape from the theater, hop on a waiting horse, and ride away.[111]

With what many viewed as a blow to tyranny, Booth became a hero to those in the South. Some thought that the Union would fold or back away from the Confederates giving them room to breathe, and possibly allow them to live as a separate nation.

Lincoln Dies

After the shooting, Lincoln was tended to immediately by a doctor who was in the crowd. The president was taken from Ford's Theater to a boarding house across the road. He was mortally wounded, but the doctor attempted to do everything he could to save the president. On April 15 at 7:30 a.m., Lincoln was declared dead.[112] A manhunt for John Wiles Booth and his conspirators was in full effect.

Twelve days later, John Wilkes Booth was cornered on a farm near Bowling Green, Virginia. Union troops surrounded the tobacco barn in which he was hiding, and set it ablaze. A gun battle ensued, and Booth was shot through the neck, dying before he could stand trial.[113]

---

[110] Katcher, Philip. *The Civil War Day by Day.* St. Paul, The Brown Reference Group, 2007, 183.

[111] Katcher, Philip. *The Civil War Day by Day.* St. Paul, The Brown Reference Group, 2007, 183.

[112] Katcher, Philip. *The Civil War Day by Day.* St. Paul, The Brown Reference Group, 2007, 183.

[113] Eicher, David J. *The Longest Night: A Military History of the Civil War.* New York, Simon and Schuster, 2001, 829.

Johnston Surrenders

On April 26, 1865, the war moved further toward its close as General Sherman of the Union army and General Johnston of the Confederate army met in Durham, North Carolina. The terms were set according to the agreement reached by General Grant and General Lee at Appomattox just a few weeks before. Their pact allowed troops to deposit their arms and public property then given parole as long as they pledge to not take up arms. All private property is to be retained by officers and soldier and everyone is permitted to return home.[114]

This surrender by the second largest part of the Confederate army numbers 30,000 troops and is a huge blow to the entire Confederacy.[115] As they surrender Confederate President Jefferson Davis meets with his cabinet in Charlotte and they disperse and make their way west of the Mississippi.

The End of The Confederacy

On May 10, 1865, Union troops raided an encampment in Irwinville, Georgia, and arrested President Jefferson Davis.[116] He was taken into custody and not released until May 13, 1867.[117]

On May 23, 1865, the Union army marched down Pennsylvania Avenue, cheered on by crowds of people along with the new President of the United States, Andrew Johnson.[118] The war was officially over. The war that engulfed Lincoln's entire Presidency and cost him his life was won less than a month after his assassination.

On Christmas day in 1868, President Johnson granted amnesty and a pardon to Confederate soldiers and those involved in "rebellion." The

[114]Katcher, Philip. *The Civil War Day by Day.* St. Paul, The Brown Reference Group, 2007, 184.

[115] Katcher, Philip. *The Civil War Day by Day.* St. Paul, The Brown Reference Group, 2007, 184.

[116] Constable, George, editor. *Brother Against Brother: Time-Life Books History of the Civil War.* New York, Prentice Hall Press, 1990, 412.

[117] Constable, George, editor. *Brother Against Brother: Time-Life Books History of the Civil War.* New York, Prentice Hall Press, 1990, 412.

[118] ---. *The Complete Civil War.* London, Wellington House, 1992, 128.

rebels were required to take an oath to the Constitution.[119] Some Confederate Officers fled from justice and hid in Mexico. It is estimated that around 10,000 confederates went into exile in Mexico following the war and Johnson's pardon.[120]

While the actual Confederate States ended with the conclusion of the war and the arrest of Davis, there was still a movement of rebellion in the Southern states. It has permeated the culture of the South since the Civil War and has become a major part of Southern identity, so much so that the Civil War is often referred to as the "War of Northern Aggression" among Southerners. It is this view which has given rise to most of the conflict and race relation issues in the South for more than 150 years.

My Brother, My Prisoner

The Andersonville Prisoner of War Camp was located in southern Georgia. It was 1620 feet long and 779 feet wide, and originally meant to house 10,000 Union prisoners of war. However, within a year, it was holding three times that amount. It was designed to be a modern and efficient facility, but in the end became one of the most shocking displays of inhumanity in modern times.

Walking into the prison after being captured, the Union soldier would be given one rule and one rule only. Stay out of the dead line. The dead line was an 18-foot space from the walls of the stockade towards the center of the camp. Any prisoner that dared cross the line or even touch it would be shot dead by one of the dozens of gun towers on the walls that watched over the camp. You would tend to think that no one would be daring or stupid enough to try to cross that line, but with the conditions in the camp becoming atrocious, many did try and paid with their lives.

Through the middle of the camp ran a small creek originally designed to be used as the prisoner's source of water. However, as the ranks of the Union soldiers swelled in the camp, the small creek could not sustain the needs of the 30,000 men who occupied the camp at any given time. As

---

[119] Eicher, David J. *The Longest Night: A Military History of the Civil War*. New York, Simon and Schuster, 2001, 844.

[120] Katcher, Philip. *The Civil War Day by Day*. St. Paul, The Brown Reference Group, 2007, 188.

the prisoners used the creek, the banks began to erode, causing about a three-acre pond to form in the middle of the already tightly packed camp. The prisoners began using the pond as their latrine. As the waste from tens of thousands of men began to accumulate, so did the number of bodies of prisoners that had died from diseases such as dysentery.

Soldiers began turning on each other inside the camp. A group of desperate men began stealing and intimidating their own in order to just survive. Another group of men with a shred of civility left stood up against the marauders and formed a judicial system inside the camp. They passed down judgments on crimes ranging from theft to murder. Their judgements were swift, and some men even ended up swinging from their neck by a rope.

Upon liberation in May of 1865, a diary was found of a Union soldier. Inside was a painstakingly made list of every inhabitant that arrived at Andersonville during his imprisonment. This list and the story of Andersonville were published after the conclusion of the war in the New York Tribune. The story of the horrific conditions and the inhumane treatment of prisoners shocked the nation, so much so that the list found was used to create a memorial at the site in Georgia to honor the souls who had to endure the darkest natures of man.

Chapter 11 – Post-War America

Union Reunited

The Civil War had served to preserve the Union, which was the main reason Lincoln went into the war. He had stated that he had no other desire than to save the Union. Freeing the slaves and enacting the Emancipation Proclamation represented secondary goals. The Civil War had also closed a chapter on the debate that plagued the United States since its founding as to whether or not states could voluntarily secede from the Union.

The Union was now accepted as permanent; no state may secede from it, and each state is a part of the nation as a whole. The United States would be a single and solitary nation under the same banner, comprised out of the many individual states. This has been important for the future of the country since, while each state has its own laws and regulations, they all subscribe to the law of the land, meaning federal law enacted through the power of the United States government.

Slavery was impacted during the war by the Emancipation Proclamation and the passing of the 13th Amendment. The legacy of the Civil War and its role in the 13th amendment and emancipation was huge, considering that over 180,000 black men served in the Union army, moving forward the need for emancipation in the United States.[121] This change in the perception of African Americans helped them to move northward from the South, transforming the cities of the 20th century and bringing freedom to millions of former slaves who might have otherwise died in the bonds of servitude.

American politics and the ideas of parties were changed after the war. Support of the Republican party rose, and it dominated American politics for decades. The Republicans were perceived to be the party of the North and freedom, while the Democratic party was seen as the party of the South and thus oppressive to minorities.[122]

Reconstruction (1865-1877)

On March 2, 1867, Congress passed the First Reconstruction Act. The Act divided the Confederate states into five military districts and put them under the control of the military, with each district being commanded by a general. The state governments who were rebuilding were only provisional until they drafted new state constitutions and allowed for the enfranchisement of black males and ratification of the Fourteenth Amendment.

Reconstruction was a huge undertaking that changed the face of America. The blacks that were once slaves found themselves free, but without wages or jobs. Many went north to find jobs in the cities.

From 1865 to 1877, there were three monumental changes made to the United States Constitution. These were the thirteenth, fourteenth, and fifteenth amendments, and their inclusion changed the entire nation.

The Thirteenth Amendment permanently abolished slavery everywhere in the United States.

The Fourteenth Amendment provided that the rights of citizenship could not be denied without due process. It states, "All persons born or naturalized in the United States, and subject to the jurisdiction thereof, are citizens of the United States and of the State wherein they reside. No State shall make or enforce any law which shall abridge the privileges or

---

[121] Katcher, Philip. *The Civil War Day by Day*. St. Paul, The Brown Reference Group, 2007, 189.

[122] Katcher, Philip. *The Civil War Day by Day*. St. Paul, The Brown Reference Group, 2007, 189.

immunities of citizens of the United States; nor shall any State deprive any person of life, liberty, or property, without due process of law; nor deny to any person within its jurisdiction the equal protection of the laws."

With this amendment came opposition, not only toward those who supported it but to those that it affected the most, blacks. In the South, there was stern resistance to black equality and Republican politics. In Tennessee, the Ku Klux Klan had been formed in 1866 as a social club, but quickly turned into a rabid anti-Republican and anti-black group with a membership of tens of thousands. The Ku Klux Klan used these numbers to murder black and white Republican leaders, burn buildings, and terrorize freemen.[123]

Following the impeachment of President Andrew Johnson, who had assumed the Presidency at Lincoln's death, a Civil War hero was soon elected President: General Ulysses S. Grant. While political victories were lauded in the higher strata of American society, freemen were being denied their rights. Soon Congress passed several Enforcement Acts intended to prevent election fraud as well as to "enforce the rights of citizens of the United States to vote in the several states of this union."[124]

Still, the rights of the now-free slaves were challenged, and Congress passed the Ku Klux Klan Act which sought to suppress Klan activities and, if necessary, gave the President the ability to suspend habeas corpus in areas in which the Klan operated.[125]

Soon another amendment was passed. The Fifteenth Amendment specifically extended the right to vote to African American men. It states. "The right of citizens of the United States to vote shall not be denied or abridged by the United States or by any State on account of race, color, or previous condition of servitude."[126]

---

[123] Maus, Louis P. *The Civil War: A Concise History.* New York, Oxford University Press, 2011, 85.

[124] Maus, Louis P. *The Civil War: A Concise History.* New York, Oxford University Press, 2011, 87.

[125] Maus, Louis P. *The Civil War: A Concise History.* New York, Oxford University Press, 2011, 87.

[126] https://www.senate.gov/artandhistory/history/common/generic/CivilWarAmendments.htm

While these were important advances, the South still found ways to restrict rights of African Americans and to prevent enforcement of these laws. It would not be for almost another 100 years that the Civil Rights movement would again change the face of America.

In some parts of the country, the Civil War remains a source of pride. Many in the South feel that they weren't given a fair shake and that, had Lincoln left them alone and not threatened them in his initial inauguration, there would have been no war, and eventually, the Union would have reunited.

The cost of the war, however, was devastating, given the total of 620,000 men who had died during the conflict. The Union lost about three soldiers for every two Confederate soldiers, with the Union numbers at 360,000 and the Confederacy at 260,000. Even worse was the effect it had on the number of men in the country since about twenty-five percent of the military-aged males had been lost.[127]

Although the war was intended to unite the Union and the Confederacy and usher in "a new birth of freedom,"[128] the South, no longer their own nation, still had a long, hard road ahead of them. With the amendments that passed, and the Emancipation Proclamation the law of the land, the blacks of the South were for all intents and purposes free. However, they did not enjoy the same freedoms that others enjoyed. In the South blacks were denied rights through legal and political systems designed to keep them from gaining any ground. Although no longer under the conditions of physical slavery, they were kept in economic and political slavery, which left them as second-class citizens at best. The restrictions they faced included segregation, being denied the ability to vote, and even being brought up on charges that only applied to black people.

---

[127] Stokesbury, James L. *A Short History of the Civil War*. New York, Harper Collins, 1995, 324.

[128] Eicher, David J. *The Longest Night: A Military History of the Civil War*. New York, Simon and Schuster, 2001, 622.

Conclusion

The Civil War was about more than North versus South. It was about freedom, rights, and government representation. With the rise of the Republican Party and the movement to abolish slavery, the Southern states felt a great deal of concern over the loss of their way of life. The Democratic Party of the South wanted to maintain its way of life, and when Lincoln delivered his first inaugural address, it was perceived as a threat to their lifestyle.

Secession came soon after, and retaliation against the North for what the South saw as oppression was also swift. The Union responded with political, legal, and eventually military acts to reunite the nation. The Civil War was the result of the actions and reactions of two ideologies that each believed had grown too far apart to exist within the same nation.

President Jefferson Davis and President Lincoln were two sides of the same coin. Both were leaders who wanted what they believed best for the people in their nation and were willing to use every resource available to do what they saw as right. Though the Union had marched into the Confederate states on a mission to reunite the two nations, the war was the worst conflict ever to occur on American soil.

The wounds of those years are still fresh in our collective conscious. Each side has their version of the war, each with its own heroes and villains. While there may always be some tension about the Civil War, it was a war that redefined the United States. The unity of the nation grew stronger as years passed, civil rights became available for more citizens, and eventually, equality under the eyes of the law became the standard.

There is no doubt that the Civil War is a touchy and sensitive subject. Often the Civil War represents slavery, suppression, and violence against African Americans. While those were some of the aspects of the war it was a war of unity. A war that was fought to lift every person, every man, out from under of the oppression of the past and to usher in "a new birth of freedom," which is precisely what resulted from the brutal, bloody, and savage four-year conflict we call the Civil War.

May the lessons enclosed remind us to be vigilant, to learn, to empower ourselves and others so that we may not repeat the sins of the past, but instead move toward a future brighter, bolder, and more magnificent than that which we currently know. Only through history and the gathering of knowledge can we hope to progress towards being as Lincoln said, "...better angels of our nature."[129]

[129] Lincoln, Abraham. *Abraham Lincoln papers: Series 1. General Correspondence. -1916: Abraham Lincoln, January-February 1861 First Inaugural Address, First Printed Draft.* January, 1861. Manuscript/Mixed Material. Retrieved from the Library of Congress, <www.loc.gov/item/mal0770200/>.

Part 4: History of Chicago

A Captivating Guide to the People and Events that Shaped the Windy City's History

Introduction

Chicago burst into life on the banks of Lake Michigan 200 years ago. Founded as a tiny, temporary settlement, the city became a crux of the American fur trade before growing into one of the powerhouses of the Industrial Revolution. From procuring drinking water to implementing racial equality, nothing has ever been simple for the people who have called Chicago home – and yet there is immense pride among Chicagoans for what they and their fellow people have achieved.

The city has been home to some of America's most influential people, be they talk show hosts or U.S. Presidents. Every star on the Chicago flag represents an achievement to be remembered; every building an era that has helped shape the modern city into what it is today.

Before there were deep-dish pizzas and red-hot Chicago-style hot dogs, there were simple people who fished, farmed, and lived among Native Americans who showed them how to survive. Before there were skyscrapers and the Chicago Board of Trade, there were corn, beans, cottages and weavers.

But from the minute African-descended John Baptiste Point du Sable set foot in the plains that would become one of America's greatest cities, Chicago has always been a community of well-meaning, hard-working immigrants looking for a chance to prove themselves.

Chapter 1 – The Chicago Trail of Tears

Modern Chicago is a spectacle of industry and architecture. It's a center for finance, creativity, business, and forward momentum for 10 million people in the Chicago metropolitan area, including 3 million in the city proper. When you behold this iconic American city, you inevitably see the birthplace of the skyscraper, the home of Chicago-style architecture; even the treasured adopted home of Oprah Winfrey. But long before any of these people and structures existed, Chicago was a simple tract of unspoiled prairie land next to a giant freshwater lake.

There were prairie grasses as high as a grown man's waist, spruce and poplar trees that grew thicker and thicker until they formed a vast forest, and crystalline lake waters full of fish. Ten thousand years passed on the American continents without any outside colonial influence, and it was during this time that hundreds of tribes of Bering Land Bridge migrants evolved a new set of cultures. Many Native American people hunted in the tall grass and fished in the lake, including the Sauk, Fox, Algonquin, and Miami. They bonded, fought, made camp, and moved on countless times until one tribe, the Potawatomis, took up semi-permanent residence on the land at the southwest edge of Lake Michigan.

It was the Potawatomi who inhabited the area when French explorers and settlers began to arrive in the seventeenth century. The two groups had a peaceful, or at least neutral, relationship for the first part of that century, but things changed when the New World became Europe's primary source of beaver pelts and furs. Though most European fur traders originally established a working network with members of the Huron nation, the Iroquois started attacking the Huron and any other tribes in the northwest who lay between them and the booming industry.

Unable to withstand the onslaught, the Potawatomis moved west and settled in upper Michigan and the Wisconsin forests, where they could hunt and fish in the way they were accustomed. They left the fertile land to the French, who were happy to build a settlement in the land of wild garlic, called "Chicagoua."

Eventually, the Iroquois' attacks became less frequent and different native bands were once more able to trade with Europeans. Many Potawatomi made their way back to Lake Michigan and became partners with the new residents. The natives traded furs and food items, but also took up the role of middlemen between Europeans and various tribes. They learned French and took up important roles as translators, also settling disputes whenever necessary. This was a huge asset because the Iroquois wars – known as the Beaver Wars – had upset huge numbers of Native Americans who had been forced to move, losing their lands and business prospects.

Despite the changing economy, the Potawatomi natives generally subsisted the way they always had, with hunting, gardening, and fishing. Peaceful, skilled, and willing to assist both native and European people, the tribe's territory grew larger than it had ever been in the past. The era of prosperity and expansion wouldn't last, however.

In 1789, the Potawatomi were subjected to their first land treaty, by which they procured cash and lands further west in exchange for their abandonment of the settlement on Lake Michigan. Wherever they moved, newer land treaties chased them until finally, the remaining bands were forced to become U.S. citizens or face further persecution. Though tribe members had fought with the Americans (and at other times, for the British) in the War of Independence, they were given no favors by either side. In the end, the Potawatomi tribe lost an estimated 89 million acres of pristine hunting and foraging lands, including the settlement by the Great Lake.

The surrender inspired the birth of the Citizen Potawatomi Nation, an attempt by the members of the tribe to conserve their history and culture for future generations. Today, the Citizen Potawatomi Nation is one of 39 federally recognized Native American tribes – but their headquarters are far from Chicago. A Frenchman of African descent, Jean Baptist Point du Sable, is generally credited with the foundation of Chicago as a permanent settlement at some point in the late eighteenth century.

Xasartha, CC BY-SA 3.0 <https://creativecommons.org/licenses/by-sa/3.0>, via Wikimedia Commons
https://commons.wikimedia.org/wiki/File:Flag_of_the_Citizen_Potawatomi_Nation.PNG

When the last group of Potawatomi natives were driven from the area, the tribe members dressed up in full war regalia to perform a war dance. It was the last ever witnessed in Chicago.

Chapter 2 – All Roads (and Railways) Lead to Chicago

French explorers first discovered Chicago by way of the Chicago portage: a strip of land connecting the Mississippi River and the Great Lakes. Here, explorers and nomadic people would carry their canoes from one water's edge to another, thereby connecting the European-established eastern and western sections of the United States. By the mid-eighteenth century, however, things were very different from what Chicago's original inhabitants had experienced. The first step toward modernization was to make transportation as efficient and effective as possible. To that end, in 1848, both the Illinois and Michigan Canal, and the Galena and Chicago Union Railroads were completed.

Teemu008 from Palatine, Illinois, CC BY-SA 2.0 <https://creativecommons.org/licenses/by-sa/2.0>, via Wikimedia Commons
https://commons.wikimedia.org/wiki/File:Illinois_and_Michigan_Canal_(5978670984).jpg

By 1837, the community was not only booming, it was incorporated as a formal city. For a decade after, it was the fastest-growing city in the United States. Originally attractive to settlers and natives as a fur trading center, the city was home to many more growing industries in the nineteenth century. With the support of its two major transportation systems, the population continued to grow as tradespeople and prospective business owners flooded in, looking for opportunities for land, jobs, and money. A few innovative people struck it rich, defining Chicago as a premier American city.

The canal ways allowed ships from the Great Lakes to connect to the Mississippi River and continue inland with cargo and passengers. Shipments of meats, produce, iron, and manufacturing tools provided Victorian Chicagoans with everything they needed to thrive, sustain families and participate in the Industrial Era that had overtaken the entire Western World. From "Annual Review of the Business of Chicago, for the year 1852:"

> The past has been a year of unexampled prosperity, and our city has shared largely in the general progress of the country. In no former year has so much been done to place its business upon a permanent basis and extend its commerce. By the extension of the Galena Railroad to Rockford, we have drawn to this city the trade of portions of Wisconsin, Iowa and Minnesota, that hitherto sought other markets; and when our roads reach the Father of Waters, as two of them will within the present year, we may expect an avalanche of business, for which we fear all our wholesale houses will not be prepared.

It wasn't just supplies and settlers who made their way to Chicago via the canals, roads, and trains; it was seasonal tourists as well. "The opening of the Rock Island Railroad, Oct. 18th to Joliet, Jan. 5th to Morris, Feb. 14th to Ottawa, and to La Salle March 10th, has brought customers during the '*lively winter*' for our businessmen (*ibid.*)"

In colder months, Chicago was visited by its northern connections who came not only to get some relief from harsh weather, but to shop. Almost simultaneous to the construction of the roads and railways, Chicago's streets grew a plethora of storefronts for a variety of products. Jewelry was an early favorite for shoppers, with just one craft house claiming to have dealt in more than $20,000 worth of decorative jewelry and watches by the end of 1852. Of course, visitors with lesser means could also fill their bags while strolling the commercial streets of the city. Chicago's many mid-eighteenth-century shops offered produce, salt, coal, pork, flour, fire-proof bricks, iron, lumber, shingles, books, furniture, dry goods, medicine, chemicals, china, glass, photography services, hardware, cutlery, banking, and insurance.

In 1865, Chicago became home to a young Marshall Field, and the commercial sector of the entire country would never be the same. After working his way through several retail positions at dry goods stores, Cooley, Wadsworth and Co., Field decided to buy into the partnership after the departure of Cooley. The company became Farwell, Field & Co. Field stayed with the general store for three years before buying into a second partnership he was offered by Levi Leiter. There were many more changes in partnership over the years, and by 1881, Marshall Field was at the head of "Marshall Field and Company."

Six years later, "Marshall Field's Wholesale Store" occupied a 4-story brick building that took up an entire city block. Built by Henry Hobson Richardson, the first department store in Chicago was one of the first three of its kind in the whole country at the end of the nineteenth century. Field's wholesale store specialized in selling bulk merchandise to small shops throughout the central and western United States; by the time he died in 1906, Marshall Field was one of the richest people in America.

The district in which the Marshall Field's store was located turned into an important commercial area of Chicago by the turn of the century – one that is still very much in vogue today. Surrounded by an elevated railway and studded with cable car turnarounds, this little piece of the city is nicknamed 'the Loop.'

Marshall Field's store wasn't just a behemoth shopping experience because of its multi-story, sprawling edifice and immense departmentalization; the fact is that Field's was a brand-new shopping experience in part because of how they were treated by staff. Workers at Field's weren't just making change and bagging items; they were there to pamper their customers. The elevator operators had even been through charm school to learn exactly how to play the role of host/hostess. What's more, the attendants at the information desk spoke several languages and happily answered questions about the store and the city. It was a plush experience that perfectly illustrated the world of nineteenth-century American capitalism and entrepreneurship.

The larger Chicago grew, the more its businesses wowed the rest of the country. Just as it had been hundreds of years previously, the settlement on the Great Lake was a hub of economic activity.

Chapter 3 – Labor and the Industrial Age

The Victorian Era was a time of huge change for the entire world, and the young city of Chicago was primed to participate to the fullest. They had a growing population, plentiful natural resources, and a well-formed infrastructure to carry them into the future. Making the move from farming and fur trading to industry seemed almost natural to a young generation of Chicagoans to whom capitalism was the glittering promise of a better future.

As in all industrializing regions, Chicagoan entrepreneurs were quick to build factories and fill them with workers. The first factory jobs were processing pork, milling wheat flour, and sawing lumber – generally making use of the supplies they had available naturally. The processed materials were not only necessary to continue feeding the residents and building more homes, but they were being bought by out-of-towners in need of the same supplies.

In 1852, two train car manufacturers were set up in Chicago. That same year, New Hydraulic Works built more than 9 miles of water pipes and completed a well, all of which were expected to soon supply the entire city with clean fresh water. Other companies in the manufacturing sector blossomed, including Mr. McCormick's reapers, wagon and carriage builders, leather tanneries, stove builders, and watch/jewelry craftsmen.

With an iron-strong infrastructure, Chicago took its next steps toward heavier manufacturing. Business owners wanted to build everything from cooking pots to bicycles, and they needed staff to churn out products in a timely manner. It was a strange time for rural families, who had always relied on farming to support themselves. Many farmers remained faithful to their farms; however, younger generations were subject to the pull of wage labor – money in exchange for hours. So, hopeful young men headed to the growing city in search of a better way of life.

Another kind of job applicant went alongside the rural people: Former slaves, recently independent thanks to the Emancipation Proclamation on January 1, 1863. Suddenly, thousands of people needed to find a place to live and work – and Chicago fit the bill perfectly. In addition to jobs and homes, Chicago offered African-Americans some of the most liberal anti-discrimination laws in the country. School and housing segregation were both outlawed by the 1880s, and though by the 1950s racial tensions had become the norm, the Industrial Revolution was a relatively beneficial time for many black people.

It was also a time of opportunity for Europeans searching for their own piece of the United States to call home. Thousands of immigrants flooded into the U.S., many staying in New York City and many others seeking out Chicago, Philadelphia, and other cities experiencing an economic boom.

This immense influx of willing factory workers was beneficial for Chicago's many capitalists. Factory-processed lumber was again processed into furniture, and milled wheat was turned into bread. Chicago had become entirely self-sufficient, its gears spinning as rapidly as primary supplies and trained workers could maintain them. It seemed like there was nothing a visionary businessperson with enough investment capital couldn't achieve in the "Windy City" (more on that later.) The rest of the country – and the world – couldn't help but notice.

"Chicago," by Carl Sandburg:

"Hog Butcher for the World,

Tool Maker, Stacker of Wheat,

Player with Railroads and the Nation's Freight Handler;

Stormy, husky, brawling,

City of the Big Shoulders."

The "big shoulders" refers to Chicago's strength and importance to the rest of the United States. With money, workers, resources, and manufacturing, the city was storming into the future.

There was just one problem: working conditions – like those in every city of the Industrial Revolution – weren't sustainable. And therefore, neither was the workforce, nor the industry itself.

Tools like the drilling machine, the planer, and the metal press were incredibly dangerous and often the cause of worksite injuries and deaths. In the June 14, 1879, issue of Chicago's The Socialist, it was reported that a boiler at Bryan's Brickworks exploded, killing 5 men and injuring many more. Accidents like this were very common, and at the time, businesses lacked any kind of compensation plans for their employees. On top of that, children as young as 5 years old were regularly employed in factories alongside their family members.

With unsafe conditions, the exploitation of young children, and low wages, factory workers in Chicago were unwilling and literally unable to go on. There were a lot of labor issues to rectify, so they started with an attempt to shorten the workday. They began to talk amongst themselves and organize. After a four-year battle to instill an 8-hour maximum per day for full-time workers, laborers finally planned a strike in 1867. Sponsored by the very first Chicago Trades Assembly, the strike lasted a week and was ultimately successful.

Problems continued, however, and in 1877, a second large-scale strike occurred, this time at the railroad. These marches and protests originated in Martinsburg, West Virginia, before inciting more laborers to walk off their jobs in Philadelphia and Pittsburgh. After weeks of reading the news, Chicagoans had had enough. They took to the streets again, but this time, the protests were violent and deadly.

It wasn't just the workers from the railroad who were out marching; it was workers from the meatpacking plants and employees in the lumber mills. Chicago was incensed by class warfare between rich factory owners and poor, overworked laborers, and eventually the mostly Irish and German working class could take no more. Their grief was fueled by the local socialist group, who used the opportunity to spread its message about the rights of workers and the abuses of the ruling class – which, in this case, was capitalists.

From the 24th to the 28th of July, 1877, Chicago's streets were thick with strikers, police, socialists, and eventually military units. Though Chicagoans had already achieved the 8-hour workday in terms of legislation, employers weren't adhering to the law. Laborers and their colleagues in other cities were insistent on the regulation of their work hours, while strikers from the railways had asked for nationalization between all the stations.

On July 26th, police and the Second Militia Regiment attacked an estimated 5,000 workers at Halsted and 16th Street. Clashes between police and mostly immigrant workers were fierce, and when it was all over, at least 18 people were dead. Hundreds were wounded on all sides of the clash that was dubbed the Battle of the Viaduct.

In another conflict known as the Turner Hall Raid, police broke into a union meeting of German Furniture Workers, killing one man and wounding others. Later, the police officers were found guilty of obstructing the victims' rights to free speech.

Ultimately, the 1877 strike was fruitless for striking workers in all cities. Once order was restored to the streets, Chicago's Mayor Heath asked the factory owners to reopen immediately and "give as much employment to their workmen as possible." For the most part, employees quietly returned to work for the same wages and under the same conditions as before.

Two decades later, Chicago experienced another series of trade strikes, but these were markedly different than the ones that had come before. There were two new factors at work in the city's labor affairs by that point: the governmentally-acknowledged union and politicking. When the Chicago labor force felt it was time for another demonstration in 1894, the strike was led by the American Railway Union. The union's right to protest was recognized by the local government at first, but the immobility of many of America's railways prompted the federal court to allow the company to declare the strike illegal. After the verdict, President Grover Cleveland sent 7,000 Federal Marshals and U.S. troops into Chicago, where violence ensued once again. Even 25,000 unionists could not beat back the powers that be.

After the turn of the century, Illinois established the State Department for Factory Inspection and ceded to a 10-hour workday for women. In 1911, the Occupational Disease Act and the Workmen's Compensation Act both passed. Chicago laborers have continued to strike often in pursuit of ideal working conditions, and in 1971, the Illinois Minimum Wage Law passed.

Chapter 4 – Filthiest City in America

The Industrial Revolution created quite the dichotomy. On one hand, it gave Chicagoans jobs, goods, and connection to the rest of the world. On the other hand, the city was covered in soot, filth, and black smoke from factory chimneys for an entire century before the pollution problem was addressed. The issue came to a head in the 1950s, when workers and families started to demand better conditions for themselves and their children. From the *Chicago Tribune*:

> The smoke and soot were so thick, they blotted out the sun. Residents who hung their clean clothing to dry hauled in dingy white shirts and gritty underwear. Opened windows meant soiled curtains and filthy sills. Brand-new buildings quickly weathered as the caustic pollution ate away the stone. This isn't a dystopian vision of the future. It isn't a description of rapidly industrializing China or India. It's Chicago's past.

In addition to industrial pollution, Chicago faced the same sanitation issues as every populous city in the world: garbage, sewage, and drinking water.

In the beginning, residents drank water from Lake Michigan and put their garbage right back in it. As for wastewater, that went into the

Mississippi River. For a time, these methods proved practical enough, but as Chicago's population exploded, direct solutions for wastewater became necessary.

flickr user mindfrieze, CC BY-SA 2.0 <https://creativecommons.org/licenses/by-sa/2.0>, via Wikimedia Commons
https://commons.wikimedia.org/wiki/File:20090524_Buildings_along_Chicago_River_line_the_so uth_border_of_the_Near_North_Side_and_Streeterville_and_the_north_border_of_Chicago_Lo op,_Lakeshore_East_and_Illinois_Center.jpg

In 1852, the city's first sewer project was undertaken by Chief Engineer Ellis Sylvester Chesbrough. Chesbrough's plan was not particularly complex, but it was incredibly heavy-handed. The first problem he faced was that Chicago was flat and covered in the kind of dirt that turned straight to mud in the rain. Since he wanted the new sewer system to empty into the Chicago River, he'd need to create a gradient by which the water could flow. He did just that by digging earth out of the riverbed and stacking it in the parts of the city that were most congested. Chesbrough piled, installed sewers, then covered them over again. Entirely new streets had to be constructed over the completed sewers.

At the same time, Chesbrough had workers dig an intake tunnel under Lake Michigan that connected to a processing point two miles inland. In a few years' time, the sewer water had reached the mouth of Lake Michigan and begun to pollute the city's water supply. Having seen this problem solve itself during dry seasons when the flow of the river reversed, Chicago planners eventually decided to permanently reverse the Chicago River's flow. To achieve this end, public works staff had to deepen the length of the canal stretching between Bridgeport and Lockport, adding several pumps along the way. Thusly, the canal was transformed into an open sewer that merely watered down the incoming wastewater. Additionally, the intake tunnel under the lake was extended further to keep ahead of the wastewater.

By 1900, the Sanitary District of Chicago was created to deal with ongoing sewage problems. For decades, the public sewage works were entirely canal-based, and soon Chicago came under fire from its neighboring states and Canada for its proposed diversion of water from the Great Lakes. While Chicago awaited legal permission to go ahead with the diversion plan, it dug more canals. Ultimately, despite the concerns of other regions in the U.S. and Canada, Chicago achieved its goal of water diversion for the sewer.

Chicago breathed easier; neighboring St. Louis dealt with the consequences. Almost immediately, the frightening typhoid rate in Chicago plummeted by 80 percent. It was a golden era for Chicagoans, but it would only last a decade.

Ten years after the Great Lakes water diversion began flushing Chicago's sewage due southwest, the canals started to look a bit overwhelmed once more. Short on ideas, it took Chicago's administrative bodies another decade to figure out what to do about it. In the 1920s, the Supreme Court ruled to lessen the Great Lakes water diversion more and more over the course of the next 8 years, which finally motivated the city to focus on proper wastewater management instead of building more canals. In 1922, the Calumet sewage treatment works was built; more plants following in 1928, 1931 and 1939. By 1970, Chicago boasted the largest wastewater sewage system in the entire world – unfortunately, the system has never reached perfection. Even today, some Great Lakes water is still necessary to process canal overflow. Just as it was more than 100 years ago, Chicago's water treatment system is under constant pressure and surveillance.

Garbage sanitation was a whole other job. In Chicago's early days, there were dedicated quarry pits and clay pits for refuse dumping. When the city entered the industrial era, a lot more than biodegradable animal feces, food waste, paper, and natural-fiber clothing started to clog up the streets. In the 1850s, the mouth of the Chicago River started to feature a permanent collection of solid trash. The first solution to hiding all that refuse was shocking. Incredibly innovative Chief Engineer Ellis Sylvester Chesbrough needed substrate to pile on top of his new sewers, so he went ahead and used the trash.

According to the Encyclopedia of Chicago, "Many Chicago buildings and streets now rest on as much as a dozen feet of nineteenth-century refuse. The mouth of the <u>Chicago River</u> was transformed by landfilled refuse, and debris from the Great Fire, along with much ordinary refuse, was used to extend Lake (now <u>Grant) Park</u>."

During the extreme landscaping, countless piles of trash lay in the streets where residents could smell the filth and see the rats. Once the heightened landscape was sealed off with dirt, conditions improved significantly. Unfortunately, garbage collectors no longer had anywhere useful to dump the solid waste of a growing city. Furthermore, the collectors' services were inconsistent, and they tended to leave poorer neighborhoods covered in filth while attending to richer districts of the city.

"Bubbly Creek" is one example of the impact of lax garbage disposal laws. In the 1870s, meatpacking was one of Chicago's most important industries. Due to the economic importance of meat processing plants, government members and sanitation officers tended to look the other way when it came to the disposal of meatpacking waste. As usual, the natural waterways took the brunt of the problem:

> Bubbly Creek, a fork of the <u>Chicago River</u>, was so named because of the bubbles rising from decomposing slaughterhouse wastes. Tanneries, distilleries, and other industries dumped wastes into the North Branch of the Chicago River and the <u>Calumet River</u>. <u>Iron and steel</u> mill wastes were used to extend the lakefront of southeast Chicago and northwestern Indiana.

Thanks to the reversal of Chicago's waterways, the drinking water supply from Lake Michigan remained untouched; however, sections of the city were exposed to waste from the iron, steel, and chemical mills. Even the sewage treatment plants built in the 1920s and 1930s created sludge that wound up in the water and on the land. In the 1940s and 1950s, the advent of nuclear power created even more waste that was astoundingly used as landscape filler. During this time, advances in garbage maintenance had been made in other cities, and it was well-known how to prevent landfills from leaching dangerous toxins into the water table. Chicago, however, chose not to pursue such expensive revamps.

Instead, in the 1950s, Chicago dealt with the constant rise in garbage by choosing to incinerate most of it. Unfortunately, this solution only added to the already big issue of soot and air pollution. The city was forced to burn and bury everything, and by 1962, the city was forced to export nearly 3 million cubic yards of garbage to as many as 72 rural dumps.

The latter half of the twentieth century brought more waste than any part of the world had ever seen thanks to single-use packaging, disposable goods, and widespread commercial plastic use. By the 1980s and 1990s, fortunately, sanitary landfill processes were finally underway and only a few hundred private refuse incinerators were still in use. Illegal dumping continues to plague the city but there are many organizations in place to try to curb it and clean up the worst-polluted parts of the city.

Sanitation is an ongoing battle in what has often been called the Filthiest City in America.

Chapter 5 – The Financial District of America

Public works aside, Chicago worked hard to identify itself as a center for commerce as early as possible. The city became home to the Chicago Board of Trade in 1848, the First Chicago Bank in 1863, and the Federal Reserve Bank in 1914.

The creation of the Chicago Board of Trade was probably inevitable. Chicago's prime location among big industry sectors, coupled with the ever-impressive spider web of railroads, canals (the ones which weren't open sewers) and roads, meant that it was the perfect place for top CEOs and financial experts to gather and plan their futures. As early as the first half of the nineteenth century, that's exactly what they did.

Without a doubt, the founding of the Chicago Board of Trade was one of the most important and formative events for the city and the organization of U.S. finance as a whole. This organization came into being to help buyers and sellers of commodities – two groups who were not in short supply in the hub that was Chicago – protect their investments. It was one of the first futures and options exchanges in the entire world, and it's still an entity under the umbrella brand CME Group today.

The formation of the original Chicago Board of Trade was simple at heart. Producers of commodities like wheat and corn knew that their product was in high enough demand for them to work toward producing more – but in doing so, farmers made it impossible for themselves to grow or produce any other type of commodity. If corn took a dive the next year, they'd lose everything. They wanted security in knowing that their product was guaranteed to sell.

On the other side of the transaction, wholesale consumers of commodities wanted the security of knowing how much stock they would be able to have, and when it was coming.

The answer, as early Chicagoans saw it, was to establish a futures contract between producers and consumers. Therefore, before so much as a bushel of corn was grown, the farmer's expected output was pre-contracted to specific buyers for a predetermined price. In today's market, futures contracts like these are usually referred to as "derivatives."

The formation of the Chicago Board of Trade didn't just affect buyers and sellers in and around Chicago; it attracted American businesspeople from all over the country. Soon, every major industry in America was represented in Chicago: roads, railroads, wagons, horses, cotton, cereals, leather, ship-building, butter, eggs, meat, textiles, and factory machine parts.

With so many different types of commodities and varied buyers, the CBOT had a big responsibility to maintain quality transactions. That's why, in 1864, they created a standardized futures contract to be used in their organization.

In time, some members of the agricultural sector created their own sub-group of the Chicago Board of Trade, calling themselves the Chicago Butter and Egg Board. Founded in 1898, the Butter and Egg Board became the Chicago Mercantile Exchange in the twentieth century, eventually joining back up with the Chicago Board of Trade and forming the CME Group. Before it was taken back into the Chicago Board of Trade fold, the Butter and Egg Board became the primary organization for agricultural sellers and buyers to put together their specialized futures contracts.

In addition to futures, agricultural producers and wholesale buyers started to create "options" contracts amongst themselves. With an option contract between two parties, the buyer or the seller is given the right to buy or sell a commodity at a specific price and by a specific date. An egg producer and the head of a grocery outlet, for example, might agree that if the grocery outlet buys eggs before September, he can buy them for the reduced price of 50 cents per crate.

Trade in Chicago boomed, cementing the direction in which the entire country was headed. Primary commodity production rose; secondary manufacturing continued to evolve in complex ways, and the end-consumer was privy to more products than at any other point in history.

Having consolidated its reputation as a vital cog in the machine that was America, Chicago set up its first banking center 15 years after the Chicago Board of Trade was established. Edmund Aiken and other investors used $100,000 to start the company in 1863. Federally registered as Charter Bank #8, First Chicago Bank played an important role in stabilizing Chicago during and after the American Civil War.

When the Union and the Confederate Armies were at war from 1861 to 1865, Chicago found itself far enough from the front lines to continue manufacturing and shipping goods with little disruption. Unfortunately for other cities like St. Louis and Cincinnati, their adjacent railways and

Mississippi River trade routes were often too close to the fighting to be used. Chicago's factories and laborers picked up the slack, supplying the Union Army with goods, supplies, and transportation to continue Abraham Lincoln's fight for American unity.

Chicago wasn't the only supplier of the Union Army, or even the most important, but it was still a strategic center. The city provided millions of dollars' worth of horses, meat, tents, harnesses, hardtack, and other items to the U.S. Army before the end of the war.

While racial tensions ran high in Chicago as in other cities in the United States, Chicago provided some stability to residents and visitors during the Civil War. The establishment of the First Chicago Bank was so important to area residents who relied on bank transactions to run their businesses and pay their bills that by the end of the Civil War, there were a total of thirteen national banks located there. That was more than any other city in the country.

Following the Civil War, Chicago's factory industry and population had tripled. The city had taken over from St. Louis as the main pork provider for the country, and banking and finance had become just as important to the city as its manufacturing sector.

The original First Chicago Bank chain still operates today under the brand First Chicago. In 1914, the Federal Reserve Bank was built in Chicago. It is still one of America's 12 reserve banks that make up the country's central bank today. Responsible for overseeing the local economy as well as offering regular banking services like payment processing and cash withdrawal, the Federal Reserve Bank employs roughly 1,600 people. It is a staple in the city's banking sector just as it was a century ago.

Today, Chicago's economy ranks about 21st in size when compared to the rest of the world. Its financial sector is ranked the third most competitive in the United States (behind New York City and San Francisco) and the seventh most competitive in the world. Its financial economy is still heavily based on the CME Group, plus the Chicago Stock Exchange, the Chicago Board Options Exchange, NYSE Arca, and many brokerage and insurance companies.

The rest of the city's economy rests on the shoulders of the transportation industry, government services, manufacturing, printing, and food production – all built on the foundation laid by nineteenth-century shopkeepers, farmers, commercial leaders and railway builders.

Chapter 6 – Workers' Cottage to Skyscraper; Chicago's Architecture and Design

While the factory owners were turning Chicago into a capitalist's dream and the banks and trade organizations were stabilizing local industries, the architects got to work transforming the cityscape. From "Annual Review of the Business of Chicago, for the year 1852," "Elegant residences have been built in all parts of the city, splendid blocks of stores have been erected on our principal streets, and the limits of the inhabited part of the city have been greatly extended."

Just like the railroad, the canals and the manufacturing sector had their beginnings in 1852 – so too did Chicago's major architectural themes.

If the lavish commercialism of the mid-nineteenth century wasn't enough to draw the Victorian crowds to Chicago, the beautiful homes did the trick. All the money flowing into the city during the industrial era didn't just bring bulk commodities into Chicago; money was being spent on pristine homes for the city's nouveau-riche. Three-story and four-story houses lined residential streets after the 1850s, replacing the quaint, boxy workers' cottages that had been popular in preceding decades. These were architecturally advanced, highly-detailed, and communicative of a reasonable amount of opulence. They heralded the success and business acumen of the city's business owners.

Before there was wealth, however, there was the worker's cottage. These were what you would have found in Victorian Chicago as the factories were still taking root, while freed slaves and European immigrants found their way to the city in droves.

The humble worker's cottage generally featured a classic A-roof (half-gabled) facing the street, a raised basement and a long, skinny body to fit the classic Chicago land lot. They had two stories, 2-4 bedrooms, a parlor, kitchen, and pantry area. There was a separate outhouse built outside.

The Loop was outfitted with these kinds of houses, usually built by the owners. Cottages tended to be wood before 1871, and brick afterward. Though these simple family homes are a huge part of Chicago's past, today you'll find only a few of them dotting residential streets such as Lincoln Park, the Lower West Side, and West Town. There are two reasons for that. The first is due to fire, and the second is due to modern builders knocking them down.

Unfortunately, the Great Chicago Fire of 1871 wiped out much of the city's Victorian and Civil War-era downtown buildings, but the creative energy with which the city rebuilt itself is something we can see in the post-Great Fire buildings that still exist today. Cottages were still built by middle-class workers, but these were surpassed by townhouses and Chicago's famous Greystone homes.

Greystones were a marvel of beauty, function, and true Chicago ingenuity. The limestones themselves were quarried directly in Illinois, which made the buildings affordable and efficient. The classic Roman style of those first Greystones – built generally between 1890 and 1930 – belied a changing attitude in the contemporary Chicagoan – one of art, intellect, and means. These gorgeous homes possessed recessed windows, columns and arches in a variety of designs.

Though the basic style of Chicago's homes evolved through the decades, the Greystone itself remained popular with builders and home buyers alike. Even now, Greystones with Roman style, Chateau-style, or Queen Anne-style architecture are preserved and presented proudly by owners and preservation organizations.

No retelling of Chicago's love affair with architectural design would be complete without mentioning Frank Lloyd Wright, one of the most famous American building designers to have had a hand in Chicago's ongoing creation.

Wright arrived in Chicago in the late 1880s, not quite two decades after the Great Chicago Fire destroyed most of the downtown section of the city. It was the perfect environment for a man of his talents and drive. Wright came to the city looking for work; it's safe to say he found enough to occupy his time.

When the would-be prodigy from Wisconsin first came to Chicago, he was not impressed by the things he saw around him. He thought the city was dirty and grim, but full of possibilities. After finding employment as a draftsman for Joseph Silbee, Wright learned the foundations of his new career and found himself upwardly mobile in the local industry. As he developed his own design style, the "organic" and "Prairie School" concepts became a part of his signature drawings and concepts, though the latter term was not used by the architect himself.

Wright and his architectural followers (such as Marion Mahoney Griffin, Walter Burley Griffin and Trost & Trost) designed homes with two easy-to-spot features, such as overhanging eaves and bold horizontal lines. Hence the term "prairie" in the stylistic description. Aficionados and historians saw these horizontal expanses as an echo of the original rolling, flat plains that occupied Chicago and other Midwestern cities before urbanization. Wright, though he called the style "organic," was in agreement.

Frank Lloyd Wright's name is pretty much synonymous with twentieth-century American housing, with good reason. He built 500 homes, schools, churches and public spectacles like the Guggenheim Museum, but it is the homes and the overall style that really became part of Chicago for the long haul.

As the man himself said, "Eventually, I think Chicago will be the most beautiful great city left in the world."

While Wright and his colleagues gave the middle-class Chicagoan a new choice in home design, William Le Baron Jenney was making architectural inroads of his own – most significantly, the Home Insurance Building at the corner of LaSalle and Adams Streets.

Le Baron Jenney's most influential innovation wasn't just height; it was the use of metal in place of stone. Since Chicago was already wood-shy in the aftermath of the Great Fire, architects at the end of the nineteenth century generally favored stone building materials. Though stunning and versatile, the immense weight of building stones didn't allow for much height. When metal support beams entered the picture, a squat office building could suddenly be heightened by several stories. So, that's exactly how Le Baron Jenney proceeded. When the Home Insurance building was finished, it stood ten stories tall, framed in steel and covered in stone. It was fire-resistant, gravity-resistant, and at 138 feet, it was the tallest commercial building in the world.

https://commons.wikimedia.org/wiki/File:Chicago_NY_Life_bldg_1912.jpg

Ultimately, the first skyscraper was demolished in 1930 to make way for the brand-new Field Building (also known as the LaSalle National Bank Building.) As it was broken down and carted away, Le Baron Jenney's masterpiece was carefully studied by teams of architects and designers who were keen to cement the building's reputation as the world's first skyscraper. Marshall Field himself appointed a committee to look into the status of the building he was tearing down. According to that committee's report:

We have no hesitation in stating that the Home Insurance building was the first high structure to utilize as its basic principle of its design the method known as skeleton construction and that there is much evidence that William Le Baron Jenney, the architect, in solving the particular problems of height and loads appearing in this building, discovered the true application of skeleton construction in the building of high structures and invented and here utilized for the first time its special forms. We are also of the opinion that owing to its priority and its immediate success and renown the Home Insurance building was in fact the primal influence of skeleton construction, the true father of the modern skyscraper.

Chapter 7 – 1860 Republican National Convention

May 16-18, 1860

Chicago in 1860 was a city of immigrants, second-generation immigrants, capitalists, and laborers. Factory workers were heavily influenced by the local Communist Party because of the latter's support of trade unions and worker strikes. The Whig Party had just disbanded, and the Democratic Party of the United States had become too centrist for a population of Americans who largely supported the abolishment of slavery. Fresh on the scene was the Republican Party – and the electorate was so invested in the outcome of the 1860 convention that Chicago literally couldn't house all the attendees under one roof. Officials built a temporary wooden structure – named the Wigwam – to seat 10,000 Republican delegates and guests. No Southern states sent delegates.

The Wigwam was commissioned by multiple Chicago businesses who specifically wanted to appeal to the Republicans and host them during the convention. It was constructed at Lake and Wacker, and it stood for as long as a decade afterwards. During the impending Civil War, the Wigwam (a Native American word used to refer to a temporary shelter) was used for political and strategy meetings. In 2002, the spot on which the original wigwam stood was designated a Chicago Landmark.

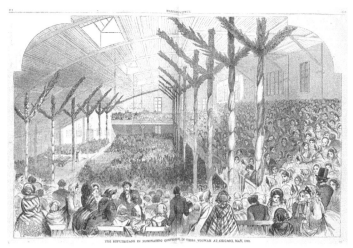

The 1860 Republican Platform was mainly based on the highly-controversial issue of slavery. Though the newly-formed Republican Party was something of a conglomerate of single-issue and fringe parties, each member firmly believed not only in the abolition of Southern slavery, but the establishment of "Free Soil" and gentle fugitive slave legislation throughout the United States.

Free Soilers were focused on keeping slavery out of states in which black people were already free; this was an important issue brought forward by a number of new Republicans who had originally formed their own political party. A number of anti-slavery declarations were listed on the official platform document, but there were unrelated declarations as well. Among these were the stated necessity for including Kansas in the Union, higher wages for workers and farmers, and the provision of free homesteads for pre-screened settlers.

When the platform was read out to delegates and guests at the Republican Convention, it was met with thunderous applause and immediately accepted by unanimous vote.

Afterward, the convention focused on the major task at hand: selecting their candidate for President of the United States. From The Washington Times:

William H. Seward, the Republican front-runner from New York, sent his political team to Chicago to lock up his party's nomination. In the mid-nineteenth century, it was not considered proper for the aspiring candidate to go to the convention himself, so Seward sent his political manager, Thurlow Weed, along with his states' 70 delegates and 13 railroad cars of supporters.

Abraham Lincoln ran his own Presidential campaign regardless of the odds, and according to historian Gordon Leidner, his team performed all kinds of stunts to help their candidate win:

Lincoln's men left no detail unattended in their pursuit of this strategy. They made certain that Seward's New Yorkers were seated far from other critical delegations with whom they might collaborate. They printed hundreds of counterfeit tickets and distributed them to Lincoln supporters with instructions to show up early--in order to displace Seward's supporters. They also assigned two men with noted stentorian voices to lead the cheering. One of these men reportedly had a larynx powerful enough to allow his shout to be heard across Lake Michigan.

When William Seward's delegation belatedly reached the convention on the third and final day, they found that their seats had been taken by the counterfeited Lincoln-supporter tickets. Nevertheless, the frontrunner did well through several rounds of voting, advancing until he and Lincoln were head-to-head.

The Republicans knew that the presidential candidate from the Democratic Party was Stephen A. Douglas, an Illinois-born politician with huge Chicago support. As another son of Illinois, Abraham Lincoln also enjoyed popularity in the convention city. When his campaign gained momentum in leaps and bounds just as planned, the rest of the convened Republicans began to consider the benefits of pitting Lincoln against Douglas directly. The two had previously battled one another for the state governorship two years earlier, with Douglas coming out as the winner.

On the third ballot, Lincoln was just one and one-half votes short of having achieved the nomination. In a shaky, stuttering voice, the delegate from Ohio stood and made an announcement that changed the way in which the future would unfold: four votes were amended and redistributed to Lincoln.

Of course, winning the nomination at the Republican Convention in Chicago was just the first step toward the presidency, but ultimately, Abraham Lincoln won that as well. He appointed William Seward his Secretary of State and saw the Union through a Civil War that eventually led to the nationwide abolishment of slavery – the exact reason for which the Republican Party was formed.

A few months later, after winning the presidential election, Lincoln faced an overwhelming crowd of journalists outside the porch of his home in Springfield, Illinois. Unwilling to give them much of his time, the President-elect spoke for only a brief few minutes. In doing so, he reignited the excitement of the country that had voted for his leadership. "Let us at all times remember that all American citizens are brothers of a common country, and should dwell together in the bonds of fraternal feeling."

Chapter 8 – World's Columbian Exposition in Chicago

It was the 400th anniversary of Christopher Columbus' arrival in the New World, and Americans wanted to celebrate. At least, their government wanted them to.

1893 was a strange year for many people in Chicago. The Great Fire was still present in their memories and the streets; the Civil War was an even closer memory. The Industrial Revolution was in full swing while the Reconstruction of the country petered out into the Gilded Age. People were confused about their place in the world and even in neighboring states. African Americans were crowding into the workplace while many whites still tried to dominate them.

Americans needed a dose of unity, and Congress ultimately decided to give it to them. Though other cities, including New York City, put in strong bids to become hosts, Chicago was the winner for financial and logistical reasons.

Many rich Chicagoans helped to finance the World's Fair, including steel manufacturer Charles H. Schwab, iron magnate Milo Barnum Richardson, and banker Lyman Gage. It was Gage who finally persuaded Congress to award his city with the project thanks to last-minute fundraising that beat out New York City's bid. In addition to the million pledged to the event if Chicago played host, the city was also able to provide the open square-footage necessary to receive hundreds of thousands of people and build immense temporary structures.

Jackson Park was chosen for the exhibition, and the offices for the event were located on Adams Street in the Rand McNally Building. Architect Daniel Burnham was made director; working closely with a small team, he decided to construct an ideal cityscape according to the principles of *Beaux Artes*.

Imported from France, the *Beaux Artes* style was largely neoclassicist. It was featured at the 1889 Paris Universal Exposition, an international event that heavily influenced Burnham's own design for the Chicago Fair. "Make no little plans," Burnham said. "They have no magic to stir men's blood. Make big plans, aim high in hope and work and let your watchword be order and your beacon beauty."

His designs for the Columbian Exposition were impeccable and detailed. In all, the fairgrounds covered over 600 acres of land. There were pavilions to represent 46 nations, a carnival midway, a 264-foot Ferris wheel, reproductions of the Niña, the Pinta, and Santa Maria (built by the U.S. and Spain) and a rudimentary movie theater. A moving platform looped around the grounds, transporting people throughout the fair.

PLATE 105

FERRIS WHEEL —FROM THE WEST

https://commons.wikimedia.org/wiki/File:Ferris_Wheel--From_The_West_%E2%80%94_Official_Views_Of_The_World%27s_Columbian_Exposition_%E2%80%94_105.jpg

The international community had a huge hand in building the spectacle, which was a unique part of Chicago's event. This was the first time other nations had been invited to participate via the national pavilions. Norway sent a classic ship called the Viking, which currently resides in Geneva, Illinois. A German company set up an artillery exhibition that ironically showcased guns which were the precursors to World War I howitzers.

The main structures of the little city were coated in white stucco and the streets were lit brightly with electric lights, giving the entire exhibition a happy glow. It was dubbed the "White City."

https://commons.wikimedia.org/wiki/File:Chicago_World%27s_Fair_1893_by_Boston_Public_Library.jpg

Part of the administrative design of the international pavilions at the fair involved each nation appointing its own delegate. The Haitian pavilion chose Frederick Douglass as its representative. This proved to be a controversial move, given that Douglass was one of the most prominent ex-slaves of the day.

Douglass teamed up with several prominent African-Americans to co-author a pamphlet entitled "The Reason Why the Colored American Is Not in the World's Columbian Exposition." The authors were well-founded in their frustration and anger, given that very few African American people were given jobs or allowed to have their own exhibitions at the event. Zero people of color were allowed to take up the role of exhibition police guard. "Theoretically open to all Americans, the Exposition practically is, literally and figuratively, a 'White City,' in the building of which the Colored American was allowed no helping hand, and in its glorious success he has no share. It remained for the Republic of Hayti [sic] to give the only acceptable representation enjoyed by us in the Fair."

The authors lamented that their people had not been given a chance to celebrate, work with their neighbors and take pride in their achievements.

> The enthusiasm for the work which permeated every phase of our National life, especially inspired the colored people who saw in this great event their first opportunity to show what freedom and citizenship can do for a slave. Less than thirty years have elapsed since 'Grim visaged war smoothed its wrinkled front,' and left as a heritage of its short but eventful existence four millions of freedmen, now the Nation's wards. In its accounting to the world, none felt more keenly than the colored man, that America could not omit from the record the status of the former slave. He hoped that the American people with their never-failing protestation of justice and fair play, would gladly respond to this call, and side by side with the magnificence of its industry, intelligence and wealth give evidence of its broad charity and splendid humane impulses.

> He recognized that during the twenty-five years past the United States in the field of politics and economics has had a work peculiar to itself. He knew that achievements of his country would interest the world, since no event of the century occurred in the life of any nation, of greater importance than the freedom and enfranchisement of the American slaves. He was anxious to respond to this interest by showing to the world, not only what America has done for the Negro, but what the Negro has done for himself.

Though the country's second World's Fair in Philadelphia had been something of a flop, Chicago's Fair was a huge success. An estimated 26 million people came to see the sights between May and October 1893, and some of the structures built for the exhibition remain to this day.

Sadly, the World's Columbian Exhibition came to a close not with celebratory closing ceremonies but with the memorial service of Chicago Mayor Carter Harrison, Sr.

The fair closed for good on October 30, 1893, and the exhibition grounds were once more a public park.

Chapter 9 – The Speakeasy and Al Capone

Like the rest of the United States, Chicago was heavily influenced by the temperance movement of the mid-nineteenth century. Big names like P.T. Barnum and Susan B. Anthony supported the philosophy that alcohol abuse was the root cause of most of the evil in their country. Temperance advocates rallied for prohibition in droves before legislation gave them what they wanted.

Throughout the 1850s, there were a total of 13 U.S. states that voted to ban sales of alcohol. Illinois was not one of them. Unfortunately for those involved in the movement, the American Civil War turned everything on its head. Liquor sales funded both the Union and Confederate Armies, and as long as the country was focused on the war, there was no time to discuss further prohibition in remaining states or as a federal initiative. Temperance, though still a very strong part of American culture in the latter part of the nineteenth and early twentieth century, was not included in reformative planning.

When the United States joined its allies in the First World War, the perfect opportunity presented itself to President Woodrow Wilson. To support the war effort and preserve grain for food production only, the President temporarily banned manufacturing and sales of alcohol throughout the entire country.

As the war wound down to its final conclusion, fewer and fewer American troops were sent overseas into conflict zones. Wilson saw this as evidence that the ban was no longer necessary. From The Literary Digest, May 21, 1919: "The demobilization of the military forces of the country has progressed to such a point that it seems to me entirely safe now to remove the ban upon the manufacture and sale of wines and beers."

Not everyone was happy about the repeal. Despite Woodrow's veto, the nationalization of prohibition was ultimately passed as the Eighteenth Amendment of the United States Constitution in 1918. The law came into effect on January, 17, 1920. The ban lasted for 13 years, ushering in the age of the speakeasy.

Three years later, a New Yorker named Alphonse Gabriel Capone bought a house in Chicago's Park Manor neighborhood. Originally a member of the New York City Five Points gang, Capone sought out a similar position in his new city. He started work with local crime boss Big Jim Colosimo, directly under his recruiter, Johnny Torrio. The same year, Colosimo was murdered. Torrio and Capone worked closely for the next five years until Torrio was shot dead, presumably by a rival gang member.

https://commons.wikimedia.org/wiki/File:AlCaponemugshotCPD.jpg

After 1925, the business of Colosimo/Torrio's gang fell to Capone; it was huge break for the gangster that would eventually earn him millions of dollars a year. The business-focused almost on every perceived vice of the temperance crowd: bootlegged liquor, prostitution, and gambling. Capone's gang covered Chicago's South Side, a section of the city that housed his many brothels, casinos, and speakeasies. His most lucrative property was the Four Deuces, an establishment in which customers could procure both prostitutes and alcoholic beverages. The business stood at 2222 South Wabash Avenue, South Loop.

At first, Al Capone had an excellent reputation among his fellow Chicagoans, particularly those of Italian descent. Born of Italian immigrant parents, Capone was compelled for one reason or another to spearhead a children's milk program and provide free food and drink to Chicago's unemployed and homeless. He opened several soup kitchens, and many people considered him a community leader in the 1920s and 1930s. Some even praised him for providing work to otherwise jobless Chicagoans via the bootleg liquor trade.

In fact, it was the very act of smuggling liquor over the Canadian/American border during Prohibition that gave us the term "bootleg." Smugglers regularly put bottles in their boots to cross into the United States, removing them once safely at home or in the company of friends or colleagues. The industry, also often referred to as "rum running," was heavily supplied from Canadian smuggling, but it was also fed from homemade liquors – so-called bathtub gin and moonshine.

Regardless of his reputation, it's true that Al Capone headed one of America's largest, most successful alcohol businesses under Prohibition. It's also true that he was personally connected to the murders of hundreds of people throughout his gang's territory. The highest numbers of dead come from bombings of Chicago establishments that reportedly refused to sell Capone's products. Though there were plenty of restaurants, coffee shops, and other businesses eager to put liquor back on the menu, Capone and his gang weren't satisfied with them. Every potential client either sold or was bullied into selling Capone's product, or they paid the ultimate price.

The bloodiest chapter of Capone's Prohibition-era occurred on February 14, 1929, known as the Saint Valentine's Day massacre. That day, seven members of Chicago's North Side Gang were rounded up, led down a street in Lincoln Park, and shot dead with Thompson submachine guns. The hit, attributed to Capone's competing gang, was most likely meant to take out the North Side leader, George "Bugs" Moran. Moran wasn't harmed, but a known lookalike, Albert Weinshank, was killed instead.

Leading up to the massacre, Moran had taken over some of Capone's saloons and was purportedly eyeing one of his rival's dog-tracks. On top of the disregard for gang boundaries, the North Side Gang was responsible for numerous kidnappings and murders of people associated with Capone and his Chicago Outfit. No charges could stick to Al Capone, however, since he was in Florida at the time.

The murders shocked Chicago and the rest of the United States. Drinkers who had previously believed bootlegging was a harmless industry were forced to reconsider the true cost of their beer and whiskey. According to the Chicago Tribune, "These murders went out of the comprehension of a civilized city. The butchering of seven men by open daylight raises this question for Chicago: Is it helpless?"

In 1931, Capone was finally arrested after a long-winded tax evasion case. He was sentenced to eleven years in prison, of which he served six and a half, first in Atlanta and then in San Francisco's famous Alcatraz. The crime boss died at home in Palm Island in 1947, his wife by his side.

Chapter 10 – Real Chicago Flavor

The Potawatomis' food culture was complex and well-established. Tribespeople hunted deer and elk, water birds, and freshwater fish like whitefish, bass, and lake trout. They gathered wild rice and farmed corn, squash, and beans, and even tapped maple trees for their sweet sap. When Chicago was still a pristine piece of green prairie land next to the sparkling Great Lakes, people ate extremely well. Their recipes were based on what they called the Three Sisters: corn, squash, and beans.

Friendly natives showed their European counterparts how to make use of all these food sources, but settlers in the area preferred to use the ingredients differently. French immigrants craved butter and cream with their vegetables and fish, as did later generations of Eastern and Western European settlers by the lake. They wanted wheat bread, cheese, and a different variety of meats that included beef and pork. As settlers became more comfortable in their new environment, they learned how to raise and farm these familiar foods, thereby changing the culinary landscape of the Chicago region.

By the time the Native Americans were driven from the area by a succession of treaties, French, English, Irish, German, and other ethnic groups had become reliant on a mixture of local and imported foods. It was the imported foods – particularly pork, beef, and wheat – that would become the most important commodities during the Industrial Revolution.

Another non-local ingredient came into fashion after the 1830s, a time during which many New England Americans came into Chicago for jobs and business opportunities. They brought with them a love of East Coast oysters. The new seafood, imported from New England, became so popular that a brand-new eatery came onto the scene: the oyster saloon. Chicago foodies still remember this unusual part of the city's history, and today you can find modern oyster bars that hearken back to the early nineteenth century-style.

At the same time, Irish immigrants were pouring into Chicago to escape hard times at home, and they were looking for something familiar to eat. They had no problem finding the now-ubiquitous potato, but pickled pork was tough to come by and considerably expensive. Since beef was the preferred meat in Chicago, Irish innovators took a leap and created corned beef. It was a hit, taking off in quick-stop lunch eateries that served it with cabbage, just the way customers liked it.

An interesting component of this story is that, since Irish and Jewish immigrants tended to occupy the same neighborhoods in their adopted city, both developed a strong fondness for corned beef and a range of deli-style meats. Beef was the delicacy of the time, considered by American foodies to be the very best quality. The steakhouse reigned supreme in nineteenth-century Chicago, more so even than the delis and oyster depots that also play an important role in today's regional cuisine. Beef was not just a staple protein in large supply; it was something that rural ranchers surrounding the city raised themselves. It was a meat that thousands of factory workers processed on a daily basis. It was an ingredient that could be cured and prepared in a dozen ways, all of which could satisfy the hunger of the poorest or richest table of diners.

According to the Encyclopedia of Chicago, the classic steakhouse defines – and *still* defines – what Chicago food is at its heart: a collection of hearty staples to fill the belly and relax the soul. Still today, in a city with access to ingredients from anywhere on the planet, the most beloved dinner away from home is the same as it was 170 years ago: "Abundant quantities of red meat, red wine, baked potatoes, creamed vegetables, brandy, and cigars."

In the 1850s, German immigrants introduced their new neighbors to a love of sausages. Pork manufacturing was on the rise, and hot dogs came onto the scene. Vendors with carts suddenly became a constant fixture of the Chicago street corner, something that wouldn't shock a modern Chicagoan. Beer gardens came along with the German beer and bratwursts, adding a relaxed outdoor option for people who were otherwise cooped up in saloons with their drinks.

At the end of the nineteenth century, Chicago became famous for its cafeteria-style dining establishments, particularly because there were no waiters to tip. Waitstaff were usually African American or Irish, two social classes who found themselves occupying the lowest-paid jobs in America. Their reputations were not helped by work in the foodservice industry, unfortunately, since the general belief of the diners was that lower-class waitstaff treated you terribly unless you over-tipped. Contrary to today, women were not often employed as waitresses, as that didn't come to be until several decades later.

Fine dining, though available as early as the 1830s, didn't really take off until the more decadent 1920s. By this point, tables were covered with cloths, menus were printed carefully on cards, and diners took care to dress properly when visiting a restaurant. An evolving palette demanded more exotic flavors, and contemporary commercial kitchens prided themselves on employing Indian or Chinese chefs. French food made a comeback for a few decades, then quickly lost its appeal to a city of modernists who found it stuffy and old-fashioned.

Two specialty foods developed in the twentieth century that Chicago would become internationally known for: the deep-dish pizza and Chicago-style hot dogs.

If you'd asked anyone in the 1850s what food item would last well into the twenty-first century, it's difficult to imagine the answer would have been "the hot dog." Nevertheless, the Chicago-style hot dog is a favorite of Chicagoans and tourists alike. Also known as a red-hot, these beef hot dogs are cradled in a poppy seed bun and piled high with mustard, chopped onions, sweet pickle relish, a dill pickle slice, tomatoes, short peppers, and celery salt. Against every natural instinct possessed by the rest of America, red-hots are ketchup-free!

As for the Chicago deep-dish pizza, it has its origins in the 1940s and 1950s. No one can agree who made the very first, but top contenders are

Ike Sewell and Rudy Malnati. Deep-dish delivers just what it promises, featuring a high edge that gives pizza makers two to three extra inches of space in which to pile cheese, tomato sauce, and other toppings.

It goes against everything an Italian holds sacred, and yet it's a movement that has caught on.

Chapter 11 – The Great Depression and Legislated Segregation

Chicago was a strong city, but it wasn't immune to the stock market crash of 1929. First, the London Stock Market crashed in September following the arrest of several top investors. Wall Street's own crash came no more than a month later, crippling the country and most of the Western world.

Many factors contributed to the economic disaster, including the almost unbridled economic success of the previous decade. America boomed in the Roaring Twenties, and Chicago was no small part of that era. Manufacturing was at an all-time high; goods were plentiful and affordable. Electricity transformed urban centers with light and air conditioning, extending the work day and earning CEOs more money. In the fields, farmers had an almost too-productive season, turning out so much wheat that the price crumbled alongside the Dow Jones.

The NYSE and the Chicago Mercantile Exchange collaborated, implementing a system in which exchange would be stopped for a period of one or two hours if the Dow Jones average fell more than 250 or 400 points. The stoppages were intended to allow traders and brokers time to re-evaluate their strategies and get in contact with clients – though the plan was criticized for inducing panic when the points started to dip.

Despite desperate attempts by America's wealthy to keep the stock prices from plummeting, grand and showy investment designed to demonstrate faith in the market ultimately failed. More Americans than ever had invested their money in the market during the twenties, motivated by soaring stock values that seemed endless. Unfortunately, most of them were borrowing up to two-thirds of the cost to invest. When the crash came, the United States had lent more money than it actually had in circulation. Billions of middle-class dollars were lost, and unemployment swept the nation.

In Chicago, Democrat Edward Kelly became mayor in 1933 by organizing a general coalition that was largely Irish, working-class laborers, and black men. Overjoyed to have one of the country's most powerful cities back in the hands of his own political party, President Franklin D. Roosevelt was liberal with federal funds under an initiative called the New Deal.

The New Deal was designed to redistribute federal money to ailing cities like Chicago with specific programs that provided jobs for residents and funds for civil services. Not only would the money ease Chicago's financial troubles, but it would foster Democratic loyalty in the city's voters. This was especially unprecedented in terms of African American voters, who were virtually all Republican supporters before the stock market crash. Chicago voted Democrat overwhelmingly throughout the 1930s; it also finished construction on Lake Shore Drive, several parks, thirty schools, and a modern public transit system.

Though Roosevelt's administration – and Kelly's, by association – was considered thoroughly modern and liberal at the time, it was responsible for the formation of an era of racial segregation. The Federal Housing Association came into effect in 1934, ostensibly using federal funds to create new housing for the country's many homeless. It did just that, except the fine print of the FHA legislation indicated that the new homes were not to be sold to African Americans. There was even an ownership clause that restricted resale to someone of color. Furthermore, black Americans were denied mortgage insurance.

American historian Richard Rothstein concludes that this housing segregation was completely blatant; it was written plainly in the housing manuals given to developers and salespeople:

> The Federal Housing Administration's justification was that if African-Americans bought homes in these suburbs, or even if they bought homes near these suburbs, the property values of the homes that they were insuring – the white homes that they were insuring – would decline and therefore their loans would be at risk. There was no basis for this claim on the part of the Federal Housing Administration.

There were separate housing projects specifically aimed at black people, strategically located to keep whites and blacks in completely different neighborhoods. White Americans were subsidized by the government to move their families from crowded urban centers to the brand-new outlying suburbs. African Americans were given no such deal; this led to a demographic pattern that persists to this day.

The segregation persisted during the Second World War, when veterans were given special privileges when it came to mortgages and homeownership taxes. Though black veterans were technically able to apply for special housing, the pre-existing whites-only fine print meant they would automatically be turned down. The Fair Housing Act would not be in place until 1968, when most African Americans could no longer afford to buy homes in the affluent suburbs.

Racial profiling aside, the New Deal funds helped Chicago weather the Great Depression in better shape than most industrial cities. What got the city – and the country – out of the economic depression was the Second World War.

Chicago was a hotbed of political debate concerning whether or not the United States should join the Allied Forces in Europe, but before the question could be settled, Japanese forces attacked Pearl Harbor in Hawaii. America joined the war effort and Chicago was one of its primary manufacturers.

Tens of thousands of jobs opened up immediately following the call to war; African Americans, white laborers, and Japanese Americans recently released from wartime detention centers flocked to Chicago in search of employment. In manufacturing aircraft, food rations, parachutes, engines, and dozens of essential military supplies, Chicagoans ensured not only the success of their fellow Americans' forces, but the economic recovery of their country.

Chapter 12 – Century of Progress

"Science Finds, Industry Applies, Man Adapts."

Chicago celebrated its centennial in 1933 and 1934 by hosting another World's Fair. Originally planned to run from May to November of 1933, the event proved so successful that it ran again for six months the following year. The World's Fair: Century of Progress was designed to celebrate how far the city had come since its incorporation and showcase a glimpse into a machine-filled, luxurious future.

At the time, the country was waist-deep in the financial turmoil of the Great Depression. Planned before President Roosevelt's New Deal gave Mayor Edward Kelly and Chicago extra funds for social programs and events, the fair was paid for in part with a $10 million bond purchased the day before the crash. By the time the fair closed for good, the entire debt had been repaid. The bulk of the cost (as much as $100 million) was secured by Rufus Dawes. In exchange, Dawes was given heavy input into the theme of the event, as well as its organization.

Some of the burden was taken on by corporations who were invited to take part in the fair with their very own exhibition buildings. Among other branded features were a General Motors Building and a Sears Pavilion.

A team of local architects, led by Paul Cret and Raymond Hood, was assembled to design the pavilion and exhibits. The team, which included Edward Bennet and Hubert Burnham, is said to have overlooked the obvious choice of Frank Lloyd Wright because he was a terrible team player. All the same, Wright had a hand in concept design.

The Century of Progress exhibition was set up in Chicago's nearby Lakefront Northerly Island peninsula. The strip of land was manmade, but at the time was not technically part of the city of Chicago. As Illinois-owned land, Northerly Island offered architects and designers the unique opportunity to create structures that would not have followed Chicago's building code. These were incredibly inventive for the time, as architects used many new, man-made materials such as prefabricated sheetrock, Masonite, and Maizewood. They also incorporated Douglas fir 5-ply and corrugated metal. In terms of modernist shapes, builders were able to construct the first catenary roof (a dome-like structure) ever used in the U.S. atop the Travel and Transport Building. The Brook Hill Farm Dairy features a multi-vaulted ceiling constructed with thin-shell concrete – another American first.

Where the 1893 Columbian Exposition had incorporated classic architecture into its buildings and spatial design, the Century of Progress pavilions would be constructed from modernist plans that had never been seen before. Not only did the fairgrounds include the Hall of Science, a Travel and Transport Building, Horticultural Building, and the infamous House of Tomorrow, but a Lilliputian City of little people and real babies in incubators.

The Houses of Tomorrow are probably one of the best-remembered exhibitions from the Century of Progress fair. These futuristic model homes captured the imaginations of nearly 40 million ticket-holders in 1933 and 1934 and have since turned up time and again in contemporary art and entertainment. They are synonymous with the 1933 Chicago World's Fair, just as the fair itself is synonymous with a positive, hopeful, and quirky portrayal of the future times in which we live today. The energy and memories of those two years have been carried on in American culture, sometimes in unexpected ways.

Chris Light, CC BY-SA 4.0 <https://creativecommons.org/licenses/by-sa/4.0>, via Wikimedia Commons https://commons.wikimedia.org/wiki/File:Restoration_project_sign_P6090116.JPG

Ray Bradbury wrote a creepy tale called "There Will Come Soft Rains" about a modern home that was entirely computer-controlled. On the lighter side of things, the World's Fair and its popular exhibition have also been memorialized by numerous writers such as Clare Blank, Roy J. Snell, Max Allan Collins, and Jean Shepherd.

There were several model homes exhibited at the fair, one of which bore the superior title "House of Tomorrow." Chicago architect George Fred Keck designed this house. The structure was 12-sided and 3 stories tall. The top two stories were made of glass, while the first floor featured a little personal airplane hangar. A dishwasher was built into the kitchen, and the home featured air conditioning. In an attempt to prove critics of his design wrong, Keck installed a heating system that allowed solar heat to gather within the house during the winter. Unfortunately, the heating system worked too well in the summer, causing the air conditioning unit to fail.

Five of the model homes, including the House of Tomorrow, were bought by Robert Bartlett and shipped over Lake Michigan to their new home in Indiana. In 2013, the House of Tomorrow was declared a national landmark by the National Trust for Historic Preservation, meaning that it could undergo renovations and repairs. It and the other model homes originally moved by Bartlett are available to tour, though the glass walls of the octagonal-home have been replaced for better air flow.

President Roosevelt himself requested that the Century of Progress continue for a second year. In the midst of the Depression, he was impressed by the influence the event had on the average American, who still had an income and a place to live. Roosevelt wanted those people to continue spending so that the gears of the American economy could speed up once again; it was a tactic that worked, and corporations that had declined participation in the 1933 schedule fell over themselves to get a spot in the 1934 run. Among the second-year newcomers was the Ford Motor Company, eager to outshine the popular General Motors' assembly-line exhibition.

Not everything went according to plan at the fair. During the first year, as many as 1,400 people became seriously sick after attending. An investigation was carried out and it was discovered that every case of amoebic dysentery could be traced back to two hotels. The food was tested, but soon it became evident that the hotels shared a contaminated plumbing system in which the sewer lines were leaking into the fresh water pipes. The problem was solved and the fair moved on, but at least 98 people died that year.

The World's Fair Century of Progress made a lasting impression on Chicago and the rest of the United States, and indeed the world. Six years later, New York hosted another World's Fair, dubbed the World of Tomorrow with a clear nod to the earlier Chicago event.

The Chicago city flag, originally designed with two six-pointed red stars between two horizontal blue stripes over a white background, was altered in reverence to the Century of Progress. The first star is for Fort Dearborn, a military outpost that preceded heavy settlement in Chicago. The second star is symbolic of the Great Chicago Fire of 1871. The third and fourth stars represent the 1893 Columbian Exposition and the World's Fair Century of Progress.

Chapter 13 – The Pinkerton National Detective Agency

The Pinkertons have been one of Chicago's most influential and long-lasting organizations, and it all started when a Scottish man named Allan Pinkerton immigrated to an area outside the city in 1842. He found a job-making barrels but within five years had joined the Chicago Police Department. After several years with the police, Pinkerton was made a detective. He opened his own agency in the 1850s, and the Pinkerton National Detective Agency was born. It stood at 80 Washington Street.

Pinkerton's first big case outside of the police department involved protecting dead bodies in Chicago's cemetery. At the time, there was an underground market for cadavers that medical schools could study and research. Very few dead bodies for the medical field were legally provided, but doctors and scientists were just starting to uncover the hidden secrets of the human body and they weren't prepared to stop. People who supplied extra cadavers were known as Resurrectionists.

In the 1850s, Chicago's dead fell prey to the Resurrectionist trade. When four fresh graves were found empty, detectives moved on the area and staked it out for several days. After days of no action, they spotted a buggy pulling away from the cemetery one night, containing two cadavers and Martin Quinlan, the city Sexton. The man was fined $500 after appearing in court.

The grave robbery case made Pinkerton famous in Chicago, but he found national fame when he discovered and prevented a plot to assassinate President-elect Abraham Lincoln on the way to his inauguration. It was called the Baltimore Plot. According to Lincoln's private secretary, John Nicolay, the soon-to-be President had a number of enemies:

> His mail was infested with brutal and vulgar menace, and warnings of all sorts came to him from zealous or nervous friends. But he had himself so sane a mind, and a heart so kindly, even to his enemies, that it was hard for him to believe in political hatred so deadly as to lead to murder.

Nicolay was concerned over the upcoming rail trip to Washington, as was railway executive Samuel Morse Felton. Upon hearing rumors that anti-Union conspirators were planning to besiege his trains, Felton hired the most famous detective he'd heard of: Allen Pinkerton. The detective reportedly set off to meet Felton the moment he read the man's letter.

Though Felton and Pinkerton were equally worried about the upcoming inauguration, it hadn't occurred to either of them that Lincoln's life was in danger. When they discovered an assassination plot awaiting the President-elect in Baltimore, the detective had Lincoln travel through the city secretly, moving on to Washington at the back of the train - in disguise.

Said Pinkerton: "Vice may triumph for a time, crime may flaunt its victories in the face of honest toilers, but in the end the law will follow the wrong-doer to a bitter fate, and dishonor and punishment will be the portion of those who sin."

Following the successful train journey and inauguration, Lincoln hired Pinkerton's agency to look after him during the Civil War. In 1871, Congress' Department of Justice budget ran low, and so internal investigations were outsourced to the Pinkerton Detective Agency. By 1893, this was found to be a conflict of interest that led to the Anti-Pinkerton Act. Nevertheless, the agency played a vital role in the protection of America's business and political interests in the nineteenth century.

One of the agents on the Baltimore Plot case was Kate Warne, the first female detective in the United States. She was a national treasure, described by Pinkerton himself in an 1883 book called The Spy of the Rebellion as:

[A] commanding person, with clear-cut, expressive features...a slender, brown-haired woman, graceful in her movements and self-possessed. Her features, although not what could be called handsome [beautiful], were decidedly of an intellectual cast... her face was honest, which would cause one in distress instinctly [sic] to select her as a confidante.

Pinkerton was surprised when Warne entered his office in Chicago and expressed her interest in becoming a detective. He told her as much, but she argued that a woman would be privy to conversations and situations that men could not so easily access. She won over the boss and was hired, soon proving herself as the star detective in a case against an embezzler with the Adams Express Company. In 1860, Pinkerton created a female detective agency and put Kate Warne in charge.

The Pinkerton detectives cultivated an excellent reputation with businesses and government, but the organization also did its best to stay on good terms with the citizens they were protecting. In the years following the Civil War, America's soldiers, freed slaves, and displaced workers found themselves in troubled times. Thousands of them had no recourse except to walk or ride the rails from city to city, looking for work or a hand-out. Middle-class and wealthy people were afraid to come across such people, and they reached out to the police and local detectives like Pinkerton for protection from the perceived threat. The head of the agency kept his cool when it came to the situation, taking pity instead of making undue arrests:

> What other recourse have these people had save to turn tramp, and beg and pilfer to sustain life? It is a pitiable condition of things, but there is no doubt that the majority of those now upon the road are there from necessity, and not from choice. If thousands are here from abroad who have been compelled to turn tramp, how many of our own people have been forced into the same kind of life as the only way left to live outside of the poor-house?

Today, there are Pinkerton offices all across the United States and the rest of the world; the company specializes in risk management and security. There is still a Pinkerton branch in Chicago, and Kate Warne is buried in the Pinkerton family plot in the city's Graceland Cemetery.

Chapter 14 – The Daley Dynasty

Since the early nineteenth century, Chicago has been home to a robust Irish immigrant population. The city's Irish-Americans have been a driving force in the workplace, as well as some of the most prominent union leaders throughout history. In 1955, Richard J. Daley, an Irish-descended citizen of Chicago, became the city's mayor. He would stay in office until his death in 1975, having served his city for 21 years.

https://commons.wikimedia.org/wiki/File:Mayor Richard J. Daley at the Illinois State Democ ratic Convention in Chicago, Illinois (a).jpg

Under Daley's leadership, Chicago's O'Hare International Airport was constructed to replace the undersized Midway Airport. The features of O'Hare really set it apart from the world's existing airports at the time, including the underground refueling system and direct terminal access from the highway. It was built for the future, and Daley was admittedly very proud of it. O'Hare was the world's busiest airport from 1963 to 1998, and during the Cold War it was an active fighter base.

Daley's time in the mayoral office was not without its turmoil. In fact, several members of his political administration were charged and convicted of corruption. But those two decades were vital in terms of cultural and ethnic evolution. Chicago was home to large ethnic minority groups, including Irish, German, Polish, Italian and African Americans, and yet most of these groups were segregated from middle and upper-class whites in terms of jobs, wages and physical neighborhoods. The New Deal housing policies from the 1930s were still in place. Even Daley himself lived in Bridgeport, a notoriously Irish part of the city.

In 1966, Martin Luther King, Jr. and James Bevel of the Southern Christian Leadership Conference visited Chicago to kick-off civil rights activism in the city. Mayor Daley decided to meet with the two men in a summit conference and signed a pledge promising to work toward fair and open housing. Since the pledge wasn't based in actual legislation, it didn't accomplish much. When King was murdered in 1968, President Lyndon B. Johnson signed the Fair Housing Act into law.

Mayor Daley was harshly criticized for his words following the civil rights activist's murder. When the public found out about King's death, riots broke out across the United States, with Chicago, Baltimore, and Washington D.C. experiencing the worst of it. Discussing a conversation he'd had with police superintendent James B. Conlisk, Daley told the press, "I said to him very emphatically and very definitely that an order be issued by him immediately to shoot to kill any arsonist or anyone with a Molotov cocktail in his hand, because they're potential murderers, and to shoot to maim or cripple anyone looting."

After receiving backlash for his heavy-handed approach to the dissidence, Daley retracted his earlier statement: "It is the established policy of the police department – fully supported by this administration – that only the minimum force necessary be used by policemen in carrying out their duties." Later that month, Daley asserted, "There wasn't any shoot-to-kill order. That was a fabrication."

Things didn't get any easier for Mayor Daley that year. In addition to Martin Luther King, Robert Kennedy had been murdered while running for president. Later, in the midst of the Vietnam War, the United States was also split on whether to stay the course or send troops home. When the Democratic Convention came to Chicago that year, the public took it as an opportunity to voice their concerns. More rioting occurred during the convention, with police stepping in and things turning violent. Daley defended the actions of his police force, and in 1971, he was re-elected for the fifth and final time.

After Daley's death, Michael Anthony Bilandic took over as mayor until 1979. A decade later, Richard M. Daley was elected; he would serve one year more than his famous father had.

The industrial machines of the western world were as strong as ever in the 1950s and 1960s, when the first Daley came to power. By the 1980s, however, the so-called Rust Belt of America had started to form, stretching from New York to Wisconsin. America – and Chicago – was losing industrial and manufacturing jobs to China and Japan, who could produce for less money. Mayor Richard M. Daley could let his city sink into another economic depression, or he could find a way to spark a new economic era. He chose the latter. According to the *Chicago Sun-Times*:

> Daley took over control of the public schools when more timid politicians urged caution. He embraced the Chicago Housing Authority, promising better homes and better lives for residents, knowing there would be political fallout and it was sure to hurt him. He built Millennium Park, brought life and theater back to the Loop at night, created the Museum Campus, made city beautification a top priority and went after O'Hare expansion. He has taken bold action and big risks when he safely could have settled for less, pushing Chicago forward and securing its future.

Chapter 15 – Oprah Winfrey and Harpo

Chicago has been home to many great men and women, but one of those stands out to a generation of African Americans and women: Oprah Winfrey. Not only has her international success story inspired millions, but Winfrey's production company, Harpo, provided jobs, entertainment and a source of pride for Chicago for over two decades. Hers is a story of entrepreneurship and overcoming obstacles that gives hope to many Americans, most of whom will always relate the name Oprah Winfrey to the city of Chicago.

Oprah's story began the way many others in poverty-stricken American did. She was born to a teenage mother in Mississippi, poor and underprivileged due to circumstance and race. The 1950s were still harsh times in America for African Americans, particularly those without a strong family unit and financial stability. After becoming pregnant and losing her unborn son at the age of 14, the young girl went to Tennessee to live with the man who (correctly or not) was named as her father on her 1954 birth certificate.

That's where Oprah's story stops being commonplace because as a young teenager, she began to really focus on making a life for herself. Winfrey picked up a job while still in high school, working at a local all-black radio station. By the time she was nineteen years old, she was co-hosting the local evening news. She moved on to television newscasting in Baltimore and Nashville before finding the job that would land her smack-dab in the middle of the daytime talk show arena in Chicago.

Talk shows were just coming into their own when Oprah was tasked with improving the ratings of a television show called AM Chicago. It was 1984, and Winfrey was breaking all kinds of broadcasting rules in an industry that was largely white and male-centric. That first show didn't go too well - in Oprah's own words, "Everything went wrong. I was cooking, and I don't cook."

Oprah's on-screen personality won the audience over, and within a month, AM Chicago was top-rated in its home city. The next year, she was nominated for an Academy Award for Best Supporting Actress for her role as Sofia in Steven Spielberg's *The Color Purple*, and her skyrocketing popularity inspired the WLS-TV station to rebrand her morning show. Beginning in 1986, the poor girl from Mississippi found herself hosting *The Oprah Winfrey Show*.

The show ran for a total of 25 seasons, broadcasting its final episode in May of 2011. During that time, Oprah started her own production company, Harpo Productions, becoming the producer of her own show. She launched branded magazines and created the Oprah Winfrey Network (OWN). She starred in the movie *Beloved*, in which she played a former slave struggling with her past – and a haunted house. During the show itself, Oprah became known for gifting every single audience member with amazing prizes, including a trip to Disneyland and a brand-new car.

Even after *The Oprah Winfrey Show* was finished, Oprah's various projects and companies employed more than 12,500 people, most of them situated in Chicago. She was – and is – an industry unto herself. In becoming the wealthiest African American woman in history, Oprah was always focused on giving back to the people and the city that had supported her.

Only the Internal Revenue Service truly knows the amount of money Oprah has spent on charities near and far, but even without a full tally it's clear that she'd dedicated millions of dollars to Chicagoans, Americans, and the international community. According to Inside Philanthropy, "The bulk of Winfrey's giving has gone to educational causes, including charter schools, programs that support African-American students, and the Oprah Winfrey Leadership Academy in South Africa."

Hundreds of thousands of Oprah's charitable dollars have been directed at educational facilities, with particular focus on improving educational opportunities for African American students in America and abroad. She founded the Oprah Winfrey Leadership Academy for Girls in South Africa, a school for which she handpicks students who have often been abused multiple times or suffered the loss of family members.

At home in Chicago, Winfrey saw another chance to help underprivileged students at the Providence Saint Mel School on the West Side. With roots going back as far as the Stock Market Crash, St. Mel School was transformed in the 1970s under the leadership of Principal Paul J. Adams. Adams created a strict regime at the school whereby no student was permitted to participate in gang-related behavior, fight on school grounds, or engage in illegal activities like stealing or using drugs. Punishment for any such behavior was expulsion.

Soon after the school's new identity, the Catholic ruling body decided to shut it down. Principal Adams fought to keep it open, which resulted in its independent status as a college preparatory facility. Eventually, it expanded to accept students from pre-kindergarten age to grade 12. Since the 1970s, Saint Mel School boasts that every single graduating student has been accepted to college. The school is considered a cornerstone of Chicago's educational system, but there have been many times it faced financial difficulties. In 1993, Oprah Winfrey gave Providence Saint Mel School $1 million.

The African American female powerhouse of America's "Second City" has also contributed to Habitat for Humanity, Save the Children, the International Brain Research Foundation, Smithsonian's National Museum of African American History and Culture, the National Council of Negro Women, and Green Belt International, and given $1 million to Chicago's Millennium Park.

In 2017, Oprah's visage was painted into a mural on the Chicago Cultural Center alongside other pioneering Chicago personalities like Barbara Gaines (founder and artistic director of Chicago Shakespeare Theater) and Susanne Ghez of the Renaissance Society.

Said Kerry James Marshall, the artist, "Given it's the Cultural Center and its role in the city, it made perfect sense to honor these women who've been important to cultural life in so many institutions."

Winfrey has since relocated to Montecito, California, but her empire continues to employ and inspire people in Chicago and the rest of the United States. She remains a cultural icon and role model for African Americans, Chicagoans, women, and underprivileged black students everywhere.

Chapter 16 – Chicago Today

Modern Chicago is everything the last two hundred years have made it: a skyscraper skyline, repurposed factories housing people, and Generation-Y startups. Mid-century family homes and modernist apartments. A population of immigrant-descendants with pride in their history and hope for their children's children. It's a city that is always on the precipice of the future, whether it likes it or not.

Contemporary Chicago is a city of more than 2 million people, many of whom have genuine beliefs about the correct thickness of a pizza crust, and strict ideas about hot dog toppings. These same people bike through the greenery of Millennium Park or strap on a pair of ice skates to visit the rink at the center of it. They take their kids to the Navy Pier for ice cream and carnival rides. And chances are, they work in the healthcare industry or service sector.

Right now, Chicago's economy is speeding alongside the best of them, adapting to new technology and consumer demands in real-time. It doesn't matter whether beaver pelts, steel beams, or talk shows are the next big thing in the world marketplace, Chicago will find a way to make it and sell it. These days, that innovative spirit is largely at work in medical offices, hospitals, food service, hospitality, and government support offices.

Chicago's multiculturalism is still at the forefront of its identity, though the scars of racial and cultural inequality can still be seen in non-diverse housing areas and ongoing tension between races. Nevertheless, more African American families have begun moving from heavy urban downtown areas and into Chicago's suburbs.

As the struggle for racial equality forges onward, Chicago holds claim to the most popular U.S. President in recent history: Barack Hussein Obama. Born in Hawaii, Obama lived in Seattle, Indonesia, New York, and eventually Chicago. He served in the Illinois Senate from 1997 to 2004 before being elected to the U.S. Senate. He served in the latter until 2008, when he was elected President.

Barack married Michelle in 1992, and the couple lived in Chicago with their growing family until the new President was called to the White House. For African Americans in Chicago, the prestige of sharing their city with an educated, accomplished black person who went on to lead the entire country was unprecedented. Senator and then President Obama represented everything that an African American should be able to accomplish in the modern America. Chicago voted overwhelmingly for the Democrats in both of Obama's presidential campaigns, winning the president 20 electoral votes for Illinois.

After his time in the White House came to an end, Barack Obama gave his hometown an official farewell:

> So I first came to Chicago when I was in my early twenties, and I was still trying to figure out who I was; still searching for a purpose to my life. And it was a neighborhood not far from here where I began working with church groups in the shadows of closed steel mills. It was on these streets where I witnessed the power of faith, and the quiet dignity of working people in the face of struggle and loss.

Later on, amid swarms of supporters *and* protesters – perhaps the hallmark of any major undertaking in Chicago – the city hosted a conference concerning the proposed Obama Presidential Center on the South Side. Ultimately green-lighted by the Chicago City Council, the project is moving forward. The Obama Presidential Center will be a public Presidential library, one that the former President's organization claims will provide 5,000 jobs during construction, and 2,500 jobs for continued administration and maintenance. Obama has made it clear that he wants to give back to Chicago for all the years he spent there raising a family and starting his political career. His foundation has received thousands of letters and postcards asking for the library to be built, and specifically on the classically impoverished South Side.

As it always has, Chicago embraces tomorrow with an expectation of hard work, but the hope of satisfying payoff. It demands the best and strives toward that goal. As Mike Royko, Chicago columnist, once said, "One of the hallmarks of Chicago is that we do so many things in an original manner. What other city has made a river flow backward? What other city makes traffic flow backward?"

Part 5: The Roaring Twenties

A Captivating Guide to a Period of Dramatic Social and Political Change, a False Sense of Prosperity, and Its Impact on the Great Depression

THE ROARING TWENTIES

A CAPTIVATING GUIDE TO A PERIOD OF DRAMATIC SOCIAL AND POLITICAL CHANGE, A FALSE SENSE OF PROSPERITY AND ITS IMPACT ON THE GREAT DEPRESSION

CAPTIVATING HISTORY

Introduction

Few decades capture the imagination like the 1920s. Like so many good stories, it got its start from a time of great turmoil and ended in a dramatic fashion. What happened between 1920 and 1929 has passed beyond history and has become legend.

The event that made the 1920s was the great conflict in the previous decade, World War I. American military involvement was only for a year. However from the beginning of the war in 1914, American eyes were on Europe.

The mass destruction from the fighting, the changes wrought by the shift in the American economy, and the very flawed peace that followed the war all made a profound impact on the decade that followed. Soldiers came back from the war sometimes disturbed, sometimes broken, and almost always disillusioned. The nation experienced a great movement of people, from country to city causing changes in the makeup of cities that would not be recognizable to residents from an earlier era.

As the president looked for a "return to normalcy," the cultural and social landscape did not make any such return journey. Social causes of the early twentieth century were either disregarded or completely rejected. Other social movements took over and revealed a more conservative and isolationist country than the one that had gone to war in 1917.

The effect of the war and the decade on American literature was profound. A modern form of music, uniquely American which some consider the only true American art form, became the soundtrack of the decade. Two new forms of entertainment also altered the decade as well; motion pictures and radio moved from fringe innovations to common entertainments. Some older entertainments, especially baseball, embraced the change of the new decade. After a crippling scandal had rocked the sport in 1919, a new player, Babe Ruth, inspired a new style of baseball which made him a national phenomenon.

Like Babe Ruth and his towering home runs, the economy of the 1920s boomed and people had more money to spend, they brought more into their homes than just radios. The availability of home appliances, coupled with more money and more credit, led people to buy more. The one item that radically changed the United States, however, was the automobile.

Henry Ford took what had been an extravagance for the rich and made it affordable to the masses. With the advent of the Model T, Americans moved further and faster than ever before. In addition, the entire auto industry created or sustained industries that had been small or non-existent before. By the end of the decade, millions of Americans were in cars.

But all was not as it appeared. Certain important segments of the economy, thus the population, were being left behind. Though the boom in manufacturing brought on by the automobile and consumer goods helped many Americans, the decade saw a dramatic decline in farming. As more people than ever before embraced buying on credit, this included speculating on stocks with credit as well. This, along with other causes woven into the fabric of the decade, led to the eventual crash that closed the 1920s.

The lessons of the 1920s are still relevant today. Many of the debates and issues of the era are still part of the national conversation. Economic policies, consumer behaviors and mass culture of the 1920s are reflected in our culture almost 100 years later. By understanding the past, we can better prepare for the future.

Chapter 1 – World War One and the 1920s

In the spring of 1914, Europe was rocked by the assassination of Archduke Ferdinand and his wife in Sarajevo. The Serbian nationalist group, The Black Hand, was responsible for the murder and the Austro-Hungarian Empire demanded justice, not only by punishing the guilty party, but by sending a message to other Serbs and other subjugated people.

This was not easy to carry out. A series of agreements and alliances stretching across the continent made retaliation against the Serbs a dangerous proposition. Russia considered itself the protector of all Slavic people and pledged to defend Serbia. In turn, Germany held a strong alliance with its Germanic neighbor, Austro-Hungary, and pledged to aid them by attacking Russia. By pledging to stand against Russia, an alliance created in 1907 between France, Great Britain, and Russia was activated. Any German action against Russia was an act of war toward the other two powers. By the end of August 1914, World War I had begun.

Within the first six months of the war, the carnage on both the eastern and western fronts was unfathomable. Millions were dead, and after initial progress by the Germans, they were stopped and a stalemate ensued. Some Americans at this time could remember the high casualty counts of Civil War battles, but the news from Europe was even more shocking. New weapons, such as machine guns and chemical warfare, for example mustard gas, made the modern warfare exceptionally devastating.

Seeing this news, Americans wanted no part of the latest European conflict. The president at the time, Woodrow Wilson, made the phrase "He kept us out of the war" a key part of his reelection campaign in 1916. However, events and circumstances made that a hard campaign promise to keep.

The United States tried to remain neutral in the conflict; it was apparent that a Europe controlled by Germany would be less than ideal for American commerce. As the war continued, Germany made two fateful decisions forcing the United States hand. First was the attack on a civilian cruise ship, the Lusitania, in 1915. The cruise liner left New York bound for Great Britain. A German submarine, U-20, fired torpedoes and sank the ship off the coast of Ireland. 1,198 lost their lives, including 128 Americans. The attack was quickly condemned by the United States and much of the international community. The British government insisted that the ship was not carrying any war materiel or munitions. It was largely perceived as an act of naked aggression toward civilians. Many within and outside the US government wanted retribution for such an attack on non-combatants.

The second major condition that moved the United States toward war was a decision by the Germans. In 1917, in order to put a stranglehold on Great Britain, Germany declared open warfare on any nation shipping goods to the British Isles. This included the United States.

The final act that tilted the United States toward a declaration of war on Germany was an intercepted telegram from Germany to Mexico. Referred to as the Zimmerman Telegram, the German government made overtures to Mexico, encouraging Mexico to attack the United States. All that Mexico needed to do was occupy the United States long enough for Germany to defeat Great Britain and France. After the war was over, Germany would help the Mexicans defeat the United States and help restore the US-Mexican border of the 1840s, before the Mexican-American War.

When the Zimmerman Telegram was made public, opinion shifted greatly toward entering the war on the side of the Allies. On April 2, 1917, President Woodrow Wilson asked Congress for an official declaration of war on the German Empire. The Senate voted 82-6 in favor of war and the House of Representatives voted 373-50 in favor.

With the declaration of war, American society and culture changed dramatically. All segments of the nation were geared toward the war effort. Large sections of the economy were controlled by the government as well as consumer activity. The War Industries Board made certain that American manufacturers were doing their part to ensure American victory overseas. This meant changes in production, from consumer goods to military ones. It also meant making sure that factories were running at full capacity.

It also meant a limit on the amount of goods and the availability of goods to consumers. Foodstuffs were especially important to the war effort. Citizens were encouraged to forgo meat and wheat in order to help feed the troops. The victory garden, homegrown vegetables, became a staple of American homes during the war. Herbert Hoover, the head of the Food Administration, was proud of his administration's efforts that led to a fifteen percent reduction in consumption.

One of the commodities that was of particular interest was alcohol. Grain was considered vital to the war effort; therefore, the consumption of alcoholic beverages was greatly curtailed through prohibitionary laws. Part of the push toward the prohibition of alcohol had little to do with war production or supply, but as a means to achieve a long-standing goal of progressive politicians and reformers. In addition to the argument regarding the importance of alcohol to the war effort, groups such as the Anti-Saloon League and Women's Christian Temperance Union stressed the benefits of a sober workforce and army. The success of wartime prohibition paved the way toward a more permanent ban on alcohol at the end of the decade.

In addition to regulating alcohol production and consumption, the federal government formed other agencies directing public life. The Committee on Public Information (CPI) was founded in 1917. This organization was designed for publicity; some would say propaganda. The famed Uncle Sam poster (I Want You!) originates from this period. The office also made the message of the war about a fight for the very soul of civilization, calling the enemy Huns instead of Germans and highlighting that this foreign nation was ruled by a Kaiser, not democracy.

The CPI was also responsible for providing the press with updates about the war overseas and the work of the Wilson Administration. Its goal was to inundate journalists with press releases promoting messages that the government wanted, to control the narrative to use a modern phrase. Many see the efforts of the CPI as the dawning of modern public relations.

The efforts of the CPI perhaps worked too well in some instances. One of the oldest and most established immigrant groups to the United States, German-Americans, were confronted with discrimination that they had rarely encountered since they began arriving in the United States before the Revolutionary War. Other immigrant groups, most notably the Irish, had faced a great deal of resistance from native-born Americans, but the Germans had an easier path of assimilation. That all changed with World War One. German-Americans faced a great deal of harassment in their communities, including threats of violence. The replica statue of Rodin's The Thinker in Chicago needed to be moved indoors because of vandalism.

Also, in Chicago for example, thousands of German-Americans changed their surnames because of the anti-German sentiment throughout the city. More broadly, anti-German sentiment was expressed by changing names of common food items. Sauerkraut was now called liberty cabbage, frankfurters were hot dogs, and hamburgers were referred to as Salisbury steaks. The most disturbing act of anti-German sentiment was the lynching of a German-American man in Collinsville, Illinois because the townspeople were convinced he was a spy for Germany. All who were tried for his murder were acquitted.

Besides citizens willfully changing the names of German-American food items, the US government curtailed free speech with the passage of the Espionage Act of 1917. This made it illegal for anyone to interfere with the war efforts of the United States government. A number of cases were tried under the law and found the defendants guilty of violating the act. Two of the most notable were the convictions of Eugene Debs, a prominent socialist and union organizer, who was found guilty under the

Sedition Act an amendment of the Espionage Act. The other was Charles Schenck, another socialist speaking out against the draft and the war in general. Debs was imprisoned for five years after giving a speech denouncing the war, and the case against Schenck established some of the most well-known limits of the First Amendment.

Both ideas written by Supreme Court Justice Oliver Wendell Holmes likened Schenck's anti-war mailings to imminent dangers, or to use Holmes's phrase, "clear and present danger." In addition, Holmes classified speaking out against the draft as the same misuse of free speech as yelling fire in a crowded room. As the war ended, the mechanisms set up by the court decisions and the wide latitude given to the government through the Espionage Act allowed for the prosecution (and deportation) of other critics of the United States government. Even as the Espionage Act became less relevant, the anti-socialist and anti-communist feelings that it encouraged appeared immediately after the war and into the 1920s.

As industry hummed and reached peak production, the need for workers became more and more crucial. Even before the US entry into the war, labor scarcity was becoming a problem for American manufacturers. When the draft was instituted for the war effort, the situation became dire. In order to meet the demand of industry, a relatively untapped source of labor was recruited and accepted by American companies, African-Americans from the southern states.

After the Civil War and the emancipation of the slaves in the South, there was a brief period of mobility for African-Americans, largely across the South as many former slaves searched for family members. However, as the period of Reconstruction ended in 1877, the ability of African-Americans to move freely was greatly curtailed, by customs, local laws, and intimidation. Further, the post-war economy offered little to the newly freed slaves, so the greatest opportunity for employment for African-Americans was sharecropping on the large plantations. Many former slaves even worked on the same plantations on which they were slaves.

This system remained intact into the twentieth century. It was even bolstered as southern state governments restructured their governments to severely curtail African-American voting rights. Even the federal courts reaffirmed this racial hierarchy with various decisions, most importantly

Plessy v. Ferguson, which established the doctrine of separate but equal.

Events in between 1915-1917 led to a dramatic change in the demographics of the United States and the fortunes of African-Americans. Two events were based in the South and focused on the agrarian economy of the region. First, poor weather made for poor cotton harvests in both 1911 and 1912. Second, and especially detrimental to the cotton crop, was the infestation of the boll weevil. This insect wreaked havoc on southern agriculture, severely hurting sharecroppers. Such poor conditions made it a necessity for African-Americans to look for alternatives.

The event that led to those more lucrative alternatives was World War One. As factories continued to need more and more workers, African-Americans moved north to fill the employment void. In the period from 1914 to 1920, close to one third of all African-Americans moved from the rural world of the South to the urban centers of the North. The African-American population of cities like Chicago, New York, and Pittsburgh exploded, seemingly overnight. Later remembered as the Great Migration, it was one of the largest movements of people across the United States ever.

This was time of cultural exchange, upheaval, and tension. Small African-American communities in northern cities became much larger, and African-Americans who were already settled in the North were wary of their new neighbors and their country ways. Whites living in cities were fearful of the growing number of African-Americans and were determined to keep African-Americans in specific neighborhoods throughout their cities. These neighborhoods would become epicenters of culture in the next decade.

Whites in the North weren't the only people trying to keep African-Americans in their societally assigned place. Throughout the South, white newspapers published articles detailing how African-Americans could not tolerate the cold winters of the North. The newspapers also highlighted any story that showed the racial prejudice of the northern communities. Many southern communities refused to let African-Americans buy tickets for out-of-state destinations or kept them bound to their sharecropping contracts. If all else failed, threatening violence on those that tried to leave was employed. It was all to no avail. Hundreds of thousands of

African-Americans made the move north in hopes of a better life with no intention of returning.

Those that went to war, some 4.7 million American men, 320,000 never returned, had as profound an experience as those on the home front. Like the young European men three years earlier, the young Americans going off to war had visions of a grand adventure and fighting for home and valor, like the Civil War heroes that many of these men knew as grandparents and other older relatives. Also like those Europeans, the Americans were quickly disillusioned about the glory of war. By the time the Americans arrived under the command of John J. Pershing, the Europeans had been fighting in the trenches and doing whatever they could to survive. The fresh-faced "doughboys" were a curiosity more than anything else.

Even if the American soldiers were green, they provided something to the Allies the German Army could not get—fresh bodies. The relationship between the American leadership and that of the French and British was often tense, especially with the Americans refusing the Allied commanders to command any of their troops. Though this would change a bit in the spring of 1918, overall the American troops retained their independence.

The fighting style of the Americans was also novel to the Europeans. As often as they could, the American commanders preferred to engage in strategic mobile warfare. The idea was to get out of the trenches and take the fight to the Germans whenever possible. The energy of the Americans proved pivotal to bringing about the armistice of November 1918. The Americans did not necessarily win the war, but they certainly caused it to end much sooner than it would have otherwise. The fight for survival, however, wasn't over once the bullets stopped flying.

Unfortunately, for many American soldiers, it wasn't the battlefront that killed them, but disease, specifically the Influenza Pandemic of 1918-1919. Estimates vary between 20 to 50 million people worldwide died because of the disease. No area of the globe was spared from the outbreak. The first wave of the epidemic started in January of 1918, but the flu mutated and became far deadlier by the fall of that year, and the death rate soared before finally reducing in the spring of 1919. It is still one of the worst medical disasters to ever occur in the world.

As the troops mustered out and returned home, they were returning as different men. The shared experiences of the soldiers would give so many of the generation a common memory, providing a backdrop for the ensuing decade. The peace process finished in 1919, the world and even the United States didn't quite realize how powerful they had truly become. At the end of the Second World War it was apparent, but at the end of the First World War, America was like a young adult finally realizing that they were stronger and nimbler than their parents. The United States, with all of those that had experienced the war in some fashion, realized over the course of the next decade exactly how far they had progressed.

Chapter 2 – Fear of the Other

Four months after the first US troops arrived in France, an event occurred that had great repercussions for the United States and the world. In October of 1917 (November 1917 Julian Calendar) the Bolsheviks in Russia overthrew the government and declared a new regime. It was a government dedicated to the writings of Karl Marx and Fredrick Engels— in short, communism. Vladimir Lenin and Leon Trotsky along with others established the Politburo and were seen immediately as a threat to most of Western Europe and the United States. Their withdrawal from World War One did little to allay those fears. In 1918, an allied force including US troops landed in Russia with hopes of stopping the spread of the Bolshevik Revolution. It was the first military intervention by the United States to stop the spread of communism.

Closer to home, after the war in 1919, strikes and unrest spread throughout the United States. Massive strikes from Seattle (a general strike) to Boston (police strike) to the steel industry made many fear that a communist revolution was coming to the United States. Further stoking that fear was the eruption of race riots across the country, the largest and most deadly occurring in Chicago. Many believed that outside agitators had a hand in starting the unrest.

After a series of mail bombings, public opinion insisted on some kind of action. The Department of Justice conducted a series of raids on known socialists, communists, and anarchists. Remembered as the Palmer Raids, named after Attorney General Mitchell Palmer, these actions took extralegal measures to round up their targets. Some of those arrested were deported. On January 2, 1920, the very beginning of the new decade, the fears of the prevailing decade were still dictating government action. A massive arrest in over 30 cities rounded up thousands of people suspected of being communists. The next day, even more arrests were made. Such a large action was met with suspicion about its legality. Communism was still seen as a threat, but after it was revealed that the Palmer Raids used unconstitutional and sometimes brutal measures to arrest their subjects, public support of such actions declined.

The Palmer Raids and the failed strikes of 1919 stymied the labor movement in the United States throughout the 1920s. Union membership dropped to its lowest level since the turn of the twentieth century. In addition, the craft unions that were the strength of the labor movement did not have a place in the growing industrial workplace. The large corporations that dominated manufacturing in the 1920s experienced a great deal of growth throughout most of the decade and were able to pay and treat their employees better than in previous generations.

The greatest purveyor of this kinder and gentler workplace was Henry Ford and his automobile manufacturing plants. Inspired by the "disassembly" line of the Chicago Stockyards, Ford perfected the assembly line for the production of the Model T, the automotive symbol of the 1920s. Ford paid his workers better than any of his competitors, gave them better hours, and even gave the entire plant Sunday off. Most memorably, Ford allowed his workers to buy the cars they manufactured, not only on installments, but at a reduced cost. The idea was that the more Ford cars on the road, the better it would be for business. Ford was correct. With the success of mass production, the cost of the car came down and Americans were able to buy the Model T in the millions. In a nod to customer satisfaction, Henry Ford quipped, "They can buy the car in any color, as long as it's black."

This corporate paternalism was prevalent across industries and greatly benefited workers. However, workers still had very little say in the speed of production or in how personnel should be managed. Workers wanted to be more self-determinant, but that was not the thinking of those in charge. Anti-unionism was also a key feature of paternalism. Henry Ford was also a leader in this regard. Even discussing unionization in a Ford plant was grounds for dismissal. Throughout the 1920s, Ford and others like him were determined to make unionism a thing of the past.

Another notion that many in the early years of the 1920s wanted to relegate to the past was open immigration. Over the course of the previous three decades, immigration from southern and eastern Europe exploded. Italians, Greeks, Russian Jews, and various Eastern Europeans flooded into the cities of the United States. They did provide a cheap labor pool, but they were also seen as dramatically altering the culture of the United States. Unlike the previous large group of immigrants, the Irish, they didn't speak English and were largely ignorant of representative government. Though the Irish were Catholic, the more folky and superstitious brand of Catholicism brought by these new groups seemed completely alien, even to the church hierarchy, dominated by the Irish. Add to that a strong belief that ideas such as communism and socialism were born and bred in Eastern Europe and the notion of being the "great melting pot" had lost its appeal to many Americans.

In 1922 the US government passed a bill severely restricting the amount of people immigrating to the United States. The law stipulated that no more than two percent of the 1890 population of an ethnic group could immigrate to the United States. The year 1890 was specifically chosen because it was right before the largest waves of immigration arrived. So, if there were 10,000 Italian-Americans in the United States, no more than 200 were allowed to enter the United States in any given year. What once was a mighty stream of new people arriving on the shore of America was slowed to a trickle during the 1920s.

One group in particular seized on the rejection of radical ideas and the rejection of the other. The Ku Klux Klan experienced a great revival in the 1920s. It did take some of its symbolism and tactics from the first rendition of the Klan, but it was a much larger enterprise in the 1920s. The early Klan was almost completely dedicated to the suppression of African-Americans in the southern states. The new Klan was no friend of African-Americans but was also decidedly nativist. It was anti-immigrant, anti-Jewish and anti-Catholic. Its membership extended well outside of the South with its largest membership in Indiana. The original Klan was much more secretive than its successor. Klansmen publicly ran for office and held various governmental posts. It wasn't the racist and xenophobic rhetoric of the Klan that led to their demise, but the conviction of their leader in Indiana on rape and murder charges. Though the Indiana Klan considered itself independent of the national organization, the terrible crime along with the level of corruption exposed by the trial seriously crippled the influence of the Ku Klux Klan by the end of the decade as participants in local and national elections.

The Ku Klux Klan revival demonstrated that nativist ideas were popular across the country, but one of the most polarizing events that also demonstrated the internal conflict of the United States was the trial of two Italian immigrants, Nicola Sacco and Bartolomeo Vanzetti. In 1920, a clerk and security guard from a shoe company was killed and robbed of the company's payroll, about $15,000, in Braintree, Massachusetts, close to Boston. Witnesses said that two Italian-looking men had perpetrated the crime. Authorities searched for suspects, especially one named Mario Buda. The police were alerted that Buda, along with his friends Sacco and Vanzetti, was in a garage to pick up his car after some repairs. The police arrived after the men had already left but managed to catch up with Sacco and Vanzetti and arrest them for the robbery and murder.

The vague description of Italian men was enough for the Braintree police to suspect the two men, and after questioning, Sacco and Vanzetti were caught in a number of inconsistencies and lies. More alarming and damning was that searches of both of the prisoners' residences revealed anarchist literature, though both claimed not to be anarchists. Coupled with the fact that both had lied about owning weapons, including a pistol similar to the one used to commit the murders, an indictment was issued, and a trial was set.

Much of the trial centered on the material evidence surrounding the case, what guns did Sacco and Vanzetti possess and when did they actually own them, could any witnesses positively identify the men. The prosecution did not actively push the anarchist connection. Sacco and Vanzetti, however, did. The presiding judge charged the jury not to consider the defendants' political leanings, but it is hard to imagine that they didn't come under consideration. The jury only deliberated for three hours before returning a guilty verdict.

The trial of Sacco and Vanzetti could have remained an obscure, local trial. One of the defense attorneys, Fred Moore, however, spoke out about the trial and made the claim that the two men were convicted because of their political beliefs and were only arrested because of the ethnic biases of a corrupt police force. After this storyline gained traction first across the country then around the world, left-leaning citizens and radicals began protesting and raising funds for Sacco's and Vanzetti's appeals.

The legal maneuverings around the Sacco and Vanzetti case took six years to resolve. In all of their appeals, the convictions were upheld. In 1925, another man confessed to the murders, but it was not enough to convince the court to grant a new trial. After all of the possible appeals were exhausted, including a request for a pardon from the governor of Massachusetts, Sacco and Vanzetti were executed on August 22, 1927.

Their deaths were greeted with large protests around the world. Over 10,000 mourners attended their funeral. There were bombings in various cities as acts of protest against their executions. For many, the trial and execution of Sacco and Vanzetti was evidence of a corrupt system that was set against any liberal, let alone radical, thought. The truth of the matter is a little more complicated as the years have passed. There is some evidence that Sacco actually participated in the crimes. In 1961, a forensics test demonstrated that the gun used in the murders was the same gun owned by Sacco. While there is some doubt about the 1961 test, the debate surrounding the case in the 1920s has endured as an example of how divided the nation was concerning both radical politics and immigrants.

Radicalism wasn't only feared in socio-economic circumstances. Concurrent with the trials of Sacco and Vanzetti, a trial in Tennessee also captivated audiences around the nation. John Thomas Scopes substituted in a biology class and proceeded to teach some of the fundamentals of evolutionary theory. In doing so, he violated a state law in Tennessee which prohibited the teaching of evolution in any state-funded school. Scopes was indicted and brought to trial in July of 1925.

It is probably the most covered trial of a crime that carried a fine of only $100. It was more about showcasing the scientific facts against the religious beliefs. Scopes set out to challenge the law and intentionally be brought to trial. As the trial date approached, the story quickly went from a local one to a national one. The local lawyers were all but shoved aside as Clarence Darrow, the most famous lawyer of the era, came in to argue for the defense while William Jennings Bryan presented for the prosecution. Along with the famous lawyers arguing the case, the most famous journalist of the generation, H.L. Menken, covered the proceedings for *The Baltimore Sun*. Menken gave the trial its name, the Monkey Trial. It was also the first trial to be broadcast on radio with WGN from Chicago capturing every moment of the trial.

The trial reached absurd levels when Darrow called his rival, Jennings Bryan, to the stand. It was the showcase of the trial as Darrow questioned and prodded Jennings Bryan about the intricacies of faith and presented how it did not stand up to scientific inquiry. Much of this exchange is dramatically recounted in the award-winning play (and later film), *Inherit the Wind*.

After Bryan's examination, the judge ruled that the entire testimony was irrelevant to the proceedings and the jury shouldn't consider it. Ultimately, Scopes was found guilty, but was cleared on appeal. He did not win his appeal because of the argument between religion and science, but on a legal technicality. Though the trial is often seen as a triumph of reason over tradition, the guilty verdict also highlights that many Americans were not ready for such a radical step in their thinking or education.

Chapter 3 – Old Causes Finishing Business

Many causes and events of the 1920s were a reaction to what many saw as radical changes to what the fabric of America was. The ideas of an earlier era, of the Progressives, seemed far too disruptive after World War One. Radical politics, massive immigration, and new scientific and social ideas were no longer as welcome as they had been in 1913.

Two social movements for the Progressive period reached their apex in 1920, namely women's suffrage and prohibition. Both movements had their modern founding in the middle of the nineteenth century. Both were tied to middle-class women and the mores of evangelical religion. Both were often cast as not only good for society, but as a remedy for some of the worst aspects of society that seemed to be increasing with each passing year. Both grew to massive movements that eventually swelled into millions of supporters. Both movements were committed to their respective causes and worked for decades to finally see their goals achieved in 1920. Only one, however, lasted. The other would become a deadly national farce that quite possibly did more harm than good.

The Seneca Falls Convention of 1848 in the Finger Lakes Region of Upstate New York is considered the beginning of the modern women rights movement. Lucretia Mott and Elizabeth Cady Stanton organized the meeting to discuss the major cause of the day, the abolition of slavery (they even had Frederick Douglass as a speaker), but they also were determined to start the discussion of women's political rights, specifically the right to vote.

After the Civil War and the official end to slavery, many in the abolition movement receded from politics. Stanton and Mott were not among them. The cause of women's suffrage became their prominent focus. With another ally, Susan B. Anthony, they took a page from the abolitionist movement and began publishing a weekly newspaper, The Revolution, to publicize and campaign for women's rights. In addition, various groups dedicated to women's rights were created in the postwar landscape. The National Woman Suffrage Association and the American Woman Suffrage Association were the most prominent. The latter included other prominent women's voices such as Lucy Stone and Julia Ward Howe. Though the groups were often rivals, both of their activities and activism furthered the cause of a woman's right to vote.

Concurrent with the beginnings of the women's suffrage movement, another social movement began, gathering membership from many of the same places. The temperance movement, like the women's movement, sprang from the same halls and churches as the abolition movement did before the Civil War. Like the women's movement, the temperance movement continued after the war was over and became the focal point for many activists. A number of temperance organizations were founded across the country, but the most prominent, the Women's Christian Temperance Union (WTCU), began in 1875. The organization's most prominent leader, Frances Willard, became its president in 1879. While the battle against alcohol was always at the forefront of the WTCU's campaigns, Willard steered the group into such causes as women's suffrage, labor rights, and children's rights.

These two movements grew and matured together and were largely seen as women's causes. Suffrage, naturally, was the main concern, but temperance was as well because it was seen as a means of protecting the family from the ravages of a drunken father and husband. The thinking was that by having women vote and have influence on policy, they could curb some of the most destructive and corrupt tendencies of the male-dominated world of politics.

Both movements borrowed from the tactics of their abolitionist predecessors, namely trying to influence government policy through petitioning state and federal officials. The women's movement engaged in a more piecemeal approach, attempting to affect the suffrage rules of western territories as they became states. In many western territories, women already could vote because the number of women was so sparse in the West that allowing them the right to vote seemed inconsequential to the presiding territory, later state governments. The western region has historically been more liberal regarding social mores. As the recent legalization of the marijuana movement demonstrates, western states are more willing to test new policies.

The women's movement met with success across the West as states allowed women to vote in 1893 through 1896. The temperance movement did not employ the same methods. Instead, the temperance movement of the nineteenth century was identified with large meetings and demonstrations, culminating in the Women's Crusade in 1873-1874, a series of large marches throughout much of the Midwest, made famous by Timothy Shay Arthur's book, Women to the Rescue. In the 1890s, like the suffrage movement, the temperance movement started to look to local politics as a means to change alcohol laws, eventually leading to national prohibition, a concept that wasn't seen as a realistic goal until their first true lobbying group began, the Anti-Saloon League (ASL).

The ASL was founded in 1893 and quickly became the most vocal supporter of national prohibition. It eventually eclipsed the WCTU. By the turn of the century, the ASL was pressuring various politicians from local officials to congressmen and senators to vote for their cause. The Anti-Saloon League publicized its successes through the copious amounts of literature it produced from its publishing house, The American Issue. One of the highlights of their annual report were the county-by-county maps the ASL created showing which counties were dry and touted the gain in dry counties from year to year.

The temperance movement had a flair for the dramatic even into the twentieth century. One of the most flamboyant demonstrators against alcohol was Carrie (Carry A) Nation. Often pictured with a hatchet, the Missouri native became known for entering saloons, famous hatchet in hand. After praying in the barroom, Nation took her ax and destroyed as much of the bar as she could. She toured through much of the Midwest, conducting the same behavior from town to town. Nation was arrested over 30 times but that did not deter her zeal for the prohibition cause. Though not part of the Anti-Saloon League, her destructive theatrics made the measured political approach of the league much more appealing to many supporters.

As the twentieth century progressed, both movements gained momentum. In 1910, the state of Washington granted women the right to vote. More and more industries saw the benefit of a sober workforce and started to support prohibition legislation. Furthermore, the tension between the rural and urban areas was increasing. The nativist stock of the country saw the immigrant-filled cities as the main example of the ill effects of drinking. Combined with the strengthening evangelicalism of the early twentieth century with preachers and the call within progressive politics for reform, prohibition started to look like a real possibility. Also looking like a matter of if and not when was women's suffrage. Between 1911 and 1914, seven states gave women the right to vote. As women marched in the largest suffrage demonstration ever in Washington DC in 1913, there was a confidence in both the suffrage movement and the prohibition movement that wasn't present a generation earlier.

World War One helped both movements reach their zeniths by 1920. When President Wilson authorized the draft to build the nation's army, the labor shortage it created was significant. In record numbers, middle-class women, those same women that were agitating for the right to vote, went to work. Almost all arguments against women being able to cast a vote were discounted. During the war and in the immediate postwar years, women marched in front of the White House urging President Wilson to join their cause. They echoed the same rhetoric that Wilson used regarding the war. If the United States was truly a beacon of democracy to the world, then shouldn't all of its citizens have the right to vote? In October of 1918, the president came out in support of equal suffrage, and the following May, the Susan B. Anthony Amendment was proposed. After making its way through the House and Senate, it was finally ratified by the states in August of 1920.

The route of the prohibition movement was a bit more circuitous, but the end was eventually the same. In order to preserve grain for the domestic and military food supply, prohibition was national policy during World War One. The same year that the wartime prohibition went into effect, Congress proposed the Eighteenth Amendment, banning the manufacture, sale, or transportation of intoxicating liquors. The bill sailed through the House and Senate and was ratified by the states in eleven months on January 29, 1919. One year from that date, the new amendment and corresponding legislation would go into effect. The ASL and WCTU were triumphant and sure that a new age of peace and prosperity was on hand for the United States.

Chapter 4 – The Cost of Prohibition

The passage of two constitutional amendments in one year was practically unheard of in US history. Other than the Bill of Rights and the Reconstruction amendments, changes to the Constitution came slowly, if at all. Two of the great social causes of the latter half of the nineteenth and early twentieth century had reached fruition. The cause of women's suffrage would not be retracted in the ensuing years. The idea of repealing the Nineteenth Amendment seems ludicrous to modern sensibilities. Though the fight for total equality for women continues, taking away the right to vote is preposterous.

Amazingly, it is equally preposterous to modern thinking that there was ever a time where there was a complete ban on alcohol in the United States. People wonder how did lawmakers ever think that prohibition was a good idea? What were they thinking?

That has been the question historians have been trying to answer almost since the Eighteenth Amendment was repealed in 1933. One of the first answers to these questions revolves around the perceived popularity of prohibition. Lawmakers from the federal to the most local level were overwhelmingly in favor of prohibition. Many took this stance out of fear of reprisal from the ASL and their very effective pressure techniques to ensure compliance with their agenda. So as the amendment made its way through Congress then the statehouses across the nation, many policymakers were sure that the enforcement of the amendment wouldn't be a great challenge since, at least according to the number the ASL provided, the people wanted this amendment.

Along these same lines, many people saw prohibition as something for other people to worry about. The strongest support for the amendment came from rural areas of the nation and the amendment was seen as a means to clean up the vices of the city, especially the immigrant and working-class areas of the cities, since these were seen as the worst parts of any given urban area. Similarly, the middle and upper-class people of the cities saw prohibition as a way to clean up the worst part of their cities. Prior to when the law went into effect, many upper-class citizens bought a great deal of alcohol to stock in their cellars. It may be good for the nation as a whole to go dry, but that shouldn't preclude having wine at dinner. Interestingly, when it came to enforcing prohibition, the federal government had much more success in rural areas than it ever did in urban ones.

It was this hubris that contributed to the lack of funding given to the enforcement of prohibition. Up until the Nineteenth Amendment, federal oversight over any single program was more the exception than the rule. To that end, only about $500,000 was spent on prohibition enforcement in 1923. Only 1,500 agents were created within the new Prohibition Bureau (at first housed in the IRS) to enforce the law for the entire nation.

What's more, the Volstead Act, the congressional act that actually created the laws to govern prohibition, was confusing and seemed contradictory at times. There were numerous exceptions to the law. Homebrewing was considered legal, and it was illegal to search private homes for alcohol. There were exceptions made for religious practices and the American Medical Association lobbied for an exception for doctors in order to prescribe alcohol if needed. Considering the small number of agents, the amount of exemptions to the law, and the vast amounts of territory that were expected to be covered, it is amazing that Prohibition agents caught anyone at all.

The exploits of some of the agents became legendary, if not comical. Prohibition agents Isidore "Izzy" Einstein and Moe Smith focused more on the spectacle of an arrest than of bringing about justice. Einstein and Smith would don elaborate costumes to infiltrate illegal drinking establishments and spring on the patrons at the proper moment for dramatic effect. In at least one case, the ruse was so impressive the people at the club applauded Einstein and Smith for their wonderful display. In keeping with the spirit of their approach to enforcing the law, it was common knowledge that after making a significant bust, Einstein and Smith enjoyed a beer or cocktail to unwind.

The whimsy of Einstein and Smith aside, the reality of prohibition had a much darker side. There is a prevailing belief that organized crime didn't start in the United States until the 1920s. One look at the history of the late nineteenth century dispels that notion. The various Tenderloin districts in cities such as Chicago and New York are a testament to the ability of criminals to organize their money-making endeavors. The prohibition of alcohol just gave those same organizations, and some new ones, a great opportunity to make a lot of money. When it comes to substantial money and criminals, violence is sure to follow.

The most famous location of such a vortex of money, corruption, and violence was the city of Chicago. The demand for alcohol was great in the city and many crime organizations were more than happy to oblige. In Chicago, this meant that control of the city's South Side went to the predominantly Italian-American gang, headed by Johnny Torio and Al Capone. The North Side of the city was controlled by the predominantly Irish-American gang, headed by Dean O'Banion. With so much money at stake, a bloody war between the two gangs was inevitable. The murder rate in Chicago spiked. O'Banion was one of the many casualties, shot in his flower shop in 1924. Though the murder victims were almost exclusively gang members, the public perception was that the city was unsafe. In 1929, the most famous murders of all cemented Chicago's reputation as the murder capital of the world.

The St. Valentine's Day Massacre occurred in Chicago's North Side. It was an attempt to kill the current leader of the North Side gang, Bugs Moran. The murderers, disguised as policemen, probably saved Moran's life that day. As he was approaching the place where the murders would occur, Moran noticed a police presence and made a hasty exit. Many of his fellow gangsters weren't so lucky. The members of the North Side

Gang were lined up along a wall and gunned down without prejudice. Even at the time it was largely known that Al Capone had ordered the hit, but there was little proof that he was involved. No matter; with Moran's operation severely hampered, Capone had unprecedented control of the city.

The brutality of the St. Valentine's Day Massacre was the type of crime and violence that prohibition was supposed to stop. Two years before the massacre, in an attempt to bring justice to the Midwestern metropolis, the Bureau of Prohibition (now part of the Treasury Department) sent one of its top agents, Eliot Ness to specifically take on Capone. Ness had some success in hurting Capone's illegal liquor operations, but not enough to put a real dent in Capone's business. As the St. Valentine's Day Massacre revealed, Capone was still able to carry out even the most brutal of actions. At least through the 1920s, Al Capone was truly untouchable.

While many similar events soured public opinion on prohibition, the St. Valentine's Day Massacre convinced many former allies of prohibition that the great social experiment was a failure. A longtime ally to the ASL and the prohibition cause, many Republicans now started to rethink their position. Women, also a stalwart ally to the prohibition movement, began to divide along the issue as well. By the end of the decade, what had seemed like a decided issue in 1920 was an open debate during the presidential election of 1928.

The cultural feelings toward alcohol also shifted during the 1920s. The brutal reality of World War One made many doubt whether drinking or not was a particularly pressing issue anymore. When compared to the world's problems, the concern over people having a drink or two seemed naive and out of date.

This was especially the case when it came to women. With the passage of the Nineteenth Amendment, the idea of the "New Woman" became popular around the country. One of the iconic images of the decade, the flapper, illustrates this new idea of womanhood. A young, energetic woman partaking in a nightlife that had been almost exclusively male was a powerful message. The flapper was often pictured in a short dress, at times smoking a cigarette or holding a cocktail glass. She wore makeup, and while in the company of men was seen as independent. This was in stark contrast to the image of the women who campaigned against alcohol, with their Victorian dresses and stern looks. Ironically, the stuffy, buttoned-up women who worked against alcohol also worked equally hard for the right to vote, which signaled the beginning of this new era.

Chapter 5 – A New World

The flapper wasn't just a symbol for women of the 1920s; it also sums up the idea that the 1920s brought something new to American culture. The postwar world of the United States saw a great deal of innovations and changes that were not even considered before the war. From popular and mass culture to sports and higher culture, the idea of "the new" was at the forefront of American thought and culture.

Along with the flapper, no single invention signified the changing landscape of America more than the automobile. Though invented in the 1890s, it wasn't until Henry Ford and his mass production and distribution of cars made them ubiquitous throughout the country. The car became a symbol of independence and freedom. Railroads were still the preferred method of travel over long distances and airplanes were still exotic, but cars offered a way to travel fast, enclosed, and relatively cheap.

The enclosed feature was especially significant because of the amount of privacy offered, especially in the backseat. The emergence of dating in the 1920s was a significant cultural turning point in the United States. What had before occurred in a more structured and supervised environment became an activity that could escape parental supervision, especially in a car.

Cars didn't just alter personal behavior, but their production created a boom in industries across the economy. Rubber manufacturing transformed the city of Akron and the demand for steel kept the plants in cities like Chicago, Cleveland, and especially Pittsburgh humming right along. Dirt roads were no longer a viable alternative and the brick streets of many cities were not ideal for automobiles. Road construction throughout the United States was a priority for many cities and states.

Though the oil business had been in existence since the late nineteenth century, the advent of the automobile offered a major boost to its revenue. Not only was oil needed as a lubricant for the engines and axles of cars, but after a process of refinement, crude oil could be rendered as gasoline which provided the fuel for cars. The relationship between all of these industries, steel, oil, rubber, along with glass, paint and others, revolved to some degree around the production of automobiles. It was the beginning of an American economy that dominated the world later in the twentieth century.

The ascension of cars wasn't the only culturally significant change of the 1920s. The golden age of radio was also during this decade. News events were broadcast through various stations, but entertainment as well. Music was the most popular format, including Live from the Grand Ole Opry and National Barn Dance featured on WLS in Chicago. Orchestras were broadcast as well. Mysteries and comedies were part of the daily makeup of radio programming. The explosion of radio stations and the amount of money spent on radios between 1921-1927 demonstrates how popular the new technology had become in a relatively short time.

Cultural assimilation was also achieved radio programming. There were many foreign language broadcasts for communities to tune into, but the larger, more commercial stations were also popular among the ethnic neighborhoods of cities. It is telling that the first radio soap opera didn't center on a white middle or upper-class protagonist. Instead, it centered on the stories of an ethnic family living in New York. The Goldbergs was a huge hit and a cultural phenomenon that was later recast as one of the first television shows as well.

Another important part of radio's appeal, especially to immigrant communities, was the playing of music. Much of the classical music played was known by immigrant families, and in cases of German and Italian families, broadcast operas were not only entertainment but points of pride. Ethnic groups heard their language being broadcast to everyone across the nation.

Radio was the main technology to make its way into the American home in the 1920s, but another innovation got people out of their homes—moving pictures. Movies, like automobiles, had been more of a curiosity before World War One. Nickelodeons on boardwalks or perhaps special occasions like the world fairs featured moving pictures, but the movie theater didn't come into its own until after the war. This was due to the fact that the holder of many of the patents on movie-making equipment was Thomas Edison, who was very selective at who could use his materials.

The main solution to this problem was for production companies to get as far away from Edison as they could. Studios started moving out to California in the 1910s, and by the 1920s, all of the major motion picture studios were located in Hollywood. Not only was it financially better for producers to be in Hollywood, the milder climate enabled film producers to make movies year-round. Actors from the silent movies became national stars, another spectacle that had almost exclusively been reserved for politicians and preachers. Douglas Fairbanks Sr., Mary Pickford, Lillian Gish, and Rudolph Valentino all became household names through their popular movies.

In 1927, an experiment by Warner Brothers Studio paid huge dividends for the company. In that year they produced the first film to feature sound, The Jazz Singer, starring Al Jolson. Though much of the dialogue was still rendered on dialogue cards throughout the film, the singing by Jolson was audible. Other studios were skeptical of the new technology until they saw the overwhelming success of The Jazz Singer. The shift from silent pictures to talkies redefined Hollywood.

The story of The Jazz Singer, the son of an immigrant struggling with being true to his heritage versus wanting to be a part of America, was familiar to many first-generation immigrants and ethnic communities. Movies were the most accessible form of American entertainment to the ethnic communities of the American city. Immigrants and their children didn't go to the movies in the large movie palaces of the downtown districts like Times Square in New York or State Street in Chicago, but to the small storefront theaters in their neighborhood. However, with the advent of sound, the expense of retrofitting a theater was prohibitive to ethnic owners. While still not regular patrons, immigrant families went to larger and more commercial theaters to see the latest movies.

The door had been shut on immigrants at the beginning of the decade and there was a fear among ethnic leaders that the lack of new arrivals would lessen the connection to the "old country" for many in their communities. In some ways, this turned out to be the case. An interesting hybrid occurred. More and more immigrants were branching out, like the Jazz Singer, and exploring the new culture of the 1920s, but the ethnic communities that had been established over the course of the early years of the twentieth century were still strong. Distinct enclaves dotted cities all over the United States. Chicago is often called the city of neighborhoods, but those neighborhoods were established by various groups. Bridgeport was Irish, Little Italy was Italian, Maxwell Street was Jewish, and so on. These neighborhood boundaries lasted well past the 1920s, even as many in the communities were experiencing the rest of the city with the other ethnic groups it shared spaces.

Other leisure activities were getting people out of their homes along with movies. Spectator sports saw a dramatic rise in attendance during the 1920s, none more so than the national pastime, baseball. One person brought the most attention to the sport, George Herman Ruth, better known as Babe.

Baseball was in need of a new hero. The 1919 World Series was under suspicion of being fixed. The American League team, the Chicago White Sox, were rumored to have taken money from gamblers in New York in order to sabotage the series. By 1920, a grand jury was called and indictments were being handed down. Though the players were acquitted in the courts, the new commissioner of baseball, Kenesaw Landis, banned the eight players suspected of taking bribes. The large man from Baltimore with the crazy swing was just what baseball needed to get back to the positive light as America's pastime.

Babe Ruth was born in Baltimore, Maryland and began his Major League career in Boston, but it wasn't until his trade to New York for the 1920 season that he become a major draw for the MLB. That first year in New York, Babe Ruth and the New York Yankees drew over a million fans to the ballpark, a number almost unheard of before 1920. The Yankees continued to draw a million plus for almost every year in the decade, routinely topping the Major League in attendance. It wasn't just in New York either; when the Yankees were in town, attendance jumped for the home team.

People also came to see Babe Ruth and the colossal home runs he routinely hit. No one hit home runs the same way as he did, high, far, and soaring over the fence. Until 1920 and Babe Ruth's new approach to hitting by using an uppercut swing and swinging hard, hitters focused more on spraying the ball to all fields, on contact over power. It wasn't just his home runs either; people loved to see him just swing and miss because it was such a violent action. Ruth often spun himself so hard going for a home run that when he missed, he would fall down. It was baseball meeting slapstick comedy.

The 1920s saw, largely because of Babe Ruth, the emergence of the New York Yankees as the preeminent sports franchise in the United States. Before the arrival of Ruth, the Yankees were the third team in the city of New York, behind the Brooklyn Dodgers and the New York Giants, the dominant team of the previous decade. The Yankees were tenants of the Giants in their home ballpark, the Polo Grounds. When Babe Ruth was traded to the Yankees, all of that changed. The Yankees outdrew the Giants to the point where the manager and part owner of the Giants, John McGraw, decided not to renew the lease of the American League upstarts.

It didn't matter to the Yankees and their owner, Jacob Ruppert. He had already made plans to build a modern structure in the Bronx. Yankee Stadium was a massive building, constructed across the river from the Polo Grounds. First used in 1923, it would be home to dozens of championships over the ensuing decades, the first one coming the year it opened.

Three years later, the Yankees, with Ruth as part of the batting order, the famed Murderer's Row dominated the American League for the next three years. Though none of the players rivaled Ruth in playing or celebrity, the team's fame is something that many modern teams are still compared to.

The popularity of Ruth went beyond his playing. He was often seen out and about in New York and other cities. He was, like Hollywood actors, a star. More than any other person though, Ruth embodied the

1920s. He was big, loud, and gregarious. The 1920s are often compared to as a party and Ruth was the life of that party.

Rivaling Ruth for popularity as a sports figure was the heavyweight champion, Jack Dempsey. Like Ruth, Dempsey came from a poor background and used sport as a means to make money and get out from harsh circumstances. It wasn't long into his career that Dempsey took the title and held on to it for seven years. As he defended his crown, Dempsey's fights filled the largest stadiums in the United States, for example, 85,000 in New York's Polo Grounds. Even when he was no longer the champ, his rematch against Gene Tunney drew over 100,000 spectators and over $2 million in gate receipts. Millions more listened to the fight on the radio. The infamous "Long Count Fight" was thought to be the most watched sporting event in history. (Dempsey lost in a decision.)

In addition to baseball and boxing, a relatively new game, largely associated with the upper-class environs of the college and university, started to make its presence known. College football was quite popular with stars like Red Grange playing for the University of Illinois and the Four Horsemen of Notre Dame filling stadiums and headlines across the country. In 1920, a new venture was started in Canton, Ohio. A group of fourteen teams started professional football. In 1922, the league would adopt the name, the National Football League. Playing in small stadiums and usually renting from baseball teams who were not in season, the league was not much of a rival to the big sports of baseball, boxing, and horse racing. It did begin to attract fans, especially when college stars such as Grange decided to play in the league.

As large as any sports celebrity or movie star was a man who symbolized the rugged individualism that was also prominent in the 1920s. Charles Lindbergh made the first solo flight across the Atlantic Ocean in 1927. The daring feat earned him almost instant worldwide fame. Parades and banquets were held in his honor and he received medals from the US and French governments. He was an individual hero for a decade that celebrated personal greatness. Unlike the earlier Progressive Era, which was about social responsibility and about taking care of those who couldn't take care of themselves, the 1920s was about personal accomplishments. Like Babe Ruth and Jack Dempsey,

Lindbergh was a star on his own merits.

Another significant contribution to the culture of the 1920s, one that has endured to help define the era, was writing. Not all of the authors of the time became rich and famous, but many of the most notable did and reflected, like Babe Ruth and Jack Dempsey, the ethos of the age. The most iconic of this generation of writers was F. Scott Fitzgerald.

Fitzgerald, unlike his other famous contemporaries Ruth and Dempsey, came from middle-class means in Minnesota. He attended Princeton and was determined to become a writer. He spent time in the army during World War One, though he never went to Europe on account of the war ending before he could be deployed. His first novel, This Side of Paradise, was an immediate success, and he and his wife, Zelda, began living in Paris and New York.

Fitzgerald published four more novels and numerous short stories, but it was his lifestyle with his wife that made him a celebrity. The couple lived in splendor and spent a great deal of money to keep up appearances. His alcohol consumption became an issue even in a time where drinking was often overlooked. Because of this, Fitzgerald was often struggling to make ends meet.

Other writers who spent time in Paris along with Fitzgerald became known as the "Lost Generation." This moniker encapsulates the idea that much of the culture of the 1920s was a reaction to the First World War. The writings of Fitzgerald's contemporary and friend, Ernest Hemingway, dealt explicitly with the meaning of life after such a horrific experience as a modern war. Sinclair Lewis, perhaps the most commercially successful of the generation, was a fierce social critic through his novels, especially Babbit. William Faulkner is also part of this generation and his work is as profound as his contemporaries, but from a distinctly different point of view. Unlike the writers from New York and Paris, Faulkner completed much of his writing in the South, especially his home state of Mississippi.

Faulkner and his southern inspiration was more of the exception than the rule of the 1920s. According the United States census for 1920, for the first time more people lived in urban areas than in rural ones. The famous song "How Ya Gonna Keep 'Em Down on the Farm?" was a fitting theme for the entire decade. The nightlife of jazz clubs and speakeasies was in the city. The biggest movie houses and all of the sporting venues were in the city. The 1920s are often called a golden age for sports and music, but it was truly the golden age of the American city.

People demanded the modernity that the city promised. Even if they decided not to move, more and more people in rural areas wanted what the city had, especially electricity. Both inside and outside of the city, people wanted items that required electricity. The system that delivered that power was a key component to the infrastructure to the modern city. This new utility became as important to modern life as clean water and drivable streets. Electricity was a symbol of the new mass consumption that came to define the 1920s.

As social movements and new entertainments emerged in the 1920s, the common denominator for them was the city. Whether celebrating the urban lifestyle or reacting against it, the city, unlike previous generations, was at the center of the American consciousness. Frederick Jackson Turner claimed that the American frontier had closed in 1893, but in the decade following World War One, a new frontier was being explored by more people than ever before, the American city.

Chapter 6 – African-Americans

The history of African-Americans is filled with constant hardship and struggle. Emerging from the horrific circumstances of slavery, only to be quickly reduced to second-class citizens through the forces of Jim Crow, African-Americans have endured more than any race in the United States. That began to change as African-Americans moved to the large cities in the North during and after the First World War. Opportunities for personal prosperity and advancement that African-Americans hadn't seen since the Reconstruction era were within reach in their new surroundings. By 1928, the first African-American since the 1870s was elected to Congress from Chicago, Oscar DePriest. By 1930, forty percent of African-Americans had moved to urban areas. African-Americans were earning more money than ever before and casting ballots that had been denied to them throughout the South.

It wasn't easygoing however. White resentment and fear within those same cities sparked riots and random violence that was all too similar to the threats and intimidation that African-Americans experienced in the South. What's more, the African-Americans already settled in northern cities didn't want the less cultured of their race to upset the delicate balance that they had achieved.

Though it was not as established by law in the North as it was in the South, segregation was the reality of the northern cities. Specific neighborhoods were deemed African-American neighborhoods, and it was almost impossible for any African-American to move from those boundaries. The Hill District in Pittsburgh, Bronzeville in Chicago, and Harlem in New York became the centers for black life and culture throughout the 1920s.

It was that culture that blossomed in the 1920s though, especially from the migrants arriving from the South. If one looks at the spread of jazz music from its roots in New Orleans to its popularity in Kansas City, to Chicago and then across the country in places like New York, it practically follows the migration route of thousands of African-Americans. Two of the most prominent jazz musicians followed this familiar route.

Jelly Roll Morton was born in New Orleans and by the age of fourteen was playing piano in brothels around the city. Soon after he began to tour the South and eventually made his way to Chicago where he first recorded some of his music. Morton claimed to have invented a new style of music called jazz and took his new sound to other cities around the country, especially New York.

Morton may or may not have created jazz, but another son of New Orleans made jazz an international phenomenon. Armstrong was a trumpet player by trade and it was as an instrumentalist that he made his first recordings. His Hot Five and Hot Seven groups which began in Chicago were his earliest successes. Armstrong also became known for his distinctive vocal style. When he sang, it sounded unique, sounding in many ways like his baritone-speaking voice. Unlike many singers of the day, Armstrong didn't try to mimic a falsetto or change his voice in any way. His voice was his voice. Armstrong's authenticity influenced later singers like Frank Sinatra and Bob Dylan.

The setting for jazz music was the nightclub, usually in the African-American neighborhood of any given city. The most famous of these, the Cotton Club, hosted live music on a nightly basis, and the city's greatest stars like Babe Ruth and Jack Dempsey frequented the famous nightclub. Everyone came to see the most famous and most influential band leader of the era, Duke Ellington.

Duke Ellington was a musician, composer, manager, and pioneer of jazz. His first residency at the Cotton Club has become something of a legend in the history of jazz. Such performers as Bubber Miley and Lonnie Johnson were part of the orchestra that entertained thousands who made the trip to the club over the course of the orchestra's three-year stay. Ellington and his orchestra played for singers, played their own compositions, and provided dance music for the patrons.

These patrons were also something very new to American culture. The audiences at clubs like the Cotton Club were racially mixed. Clubs that catered to a mixed audience were referred to as "black and tans" clubs. These clubs were in the African-American section of cities and whites who attended saw themselves as "slumming." The voyeuristic attitude and atmosphere contributed little to civil rights, but it did demonstrate that there at least might be some openness on social interaction. It was definitely not a push toward equality. African-Americans entertaining whites had been common since the beginning of the nation. However, in the jazz clubs of the 1920s, whites were actually paying for the privilege to be entertained by black artists. In the clubs that were part of the black community, there was no separate dance floor so interaction had to at the very least be tolerated.

The exception to this divided hierarchy were the white musicians who journeyed to these clubs to see musicians play a type of music that inspired them. The young white musicians were not slumming but learning. Famous musicians, such as Hoagy Carmichael, were rebelling against their rural and suburban upbringings and the racial attitudes expressed there. They were not the typical audience member, but since the music had a profound effect on them, later on when they became bandleaders and recording artists, they supported equal rights to African-American musicians and in some cases wouldn't play in clubs that discriminated against some of their players. It is a small example of social change, but significant. African-Americans and whites sharing a stage was a powerful image that began in the 1920s.

Outside of the United States, another African-American entertainer, Josephine Baker became the one of the most famous Americans in the world. Born in St. Louis, she emigrated to Paris in 1925. She performed throughout Europe, but mostly on the Champs Elysees where the expat community of Americans adored her, especially Ernest Hemingway. Though Baker's debut on Broadway was a failure, over the course of her long career she won over American audiences as well. She was a pioneer in entertainment and used her celebrity to further the cause of civil rights throughout her career.

Dance was also a key import from the South. And as jazz became more and more popular, the dances that were associated with them grew in popularity as well. The Lindy Hop, the Charleston, and the Black Bottom were constantly seen on the dance floors of nightclubs across the nation. The more traditional dances, such as the waltz, were seen as old and out of touch, while the new dances reflected the new times. Young men with slicked back hair held down by pomade and women in short dresses became visible symbols of a generation who were urban, sophisticated, and energetic.

The dance clubs in African-American neighborhoods served a diverse clientele, but many of the businesses in those districts catered to African-Americans. This wasn't because of discrimination on the part of African-American business owners. Since white businesses wouldn't serve black customers, the needs of the community were met by black entrepreneurs. African-Americans started their own insurance companies, funeral parlors, and banks to give other African-Americans the services otherwise denied them. In addition, because white newspapers did not address the issues that concerned the local and national African-American community, black newspapers came to prominence. *The Chicago Defender* and *The Pittsburgh Courier* were two of the largest papers in the black community and had strong circulations outside of their home cities.

Included with these business pioneers were the founders of the first Negro National League, a baseball league made up of players of color which were barred by Major League Baseball. Rube Foster founded the first team, the Chicago Negro Giants, and various cities followed suit with teams of their own. This initial league highlighted some of the best players of the age, including Oscar Charleston and Biz Mackey. Though this first league would not survive the Depression, a new league rose in the 1930s and would last until the late 1950s when integration of baseball was all but complete.

As African-American communities grew and thrived across the United States, one became the epicenter for African-American culture, thought, and political action. Harlem, in New York City, was a symbol to all African-Americans of what their culture was capable of doing. Writers such as Zora Neale Hurston and Langston Hughes were critically acclaimed throughout literary circles.

Harlem is also where African-American political leaders gravitated. A. Philip Randolph, W.E.B. Du Bois, and Marcus Garvey were all active during the 1920s. All three men got their starts in the early part of the twentieth century but met with varying degrees of success in the 1920s. Du Bois was heavily influenced by the experience of African-American soldiers in World War One. After the war, he interviewed many returning African-American soldiers and discovered that those who served were primarily regulated to menial labor. Very few were even issued weapons. Despite this, Du Bois was impressed with the new confidence that many of the returning soldiers had. This new outlook became known as the "New Negro," or the attitude of African-Americans to be more outspoken and vocal for their rights.

As he had been earlier in the century, Du Bois was mostly interested in the integration of African-Americans and whites in US society. After World War One, Du Bois became interested in the concept of Pan-Africanism, the idea that all people descended from the continent of Africa had not only a common background, but a common goal of acceptance and equality around the world. As Du Bois aged, his Pan-Africanism grew into a more socialist, anti-colonial belief system that defined much of his later writings.

At the second Pan-African Congress, Du Bois met another African-American leader who would challenge Du Bois on a number of his goals within United States society. Marcus Garvey, a Jamaican, was influenced by Booker T. Washington. Though Washington believed in the separation of races on an economic level, Garvey went a step further and called for black separatism, with the ultimate goal voiced in Garvey's Back to Africa movement. The idea behind this movement was that all of the peoples of Africa that had been taken from their ancestral home by the force of slavery should return to Africa and build a new society there. Through his Universal Negro Improvement Association (UNIA), Garvey promoted this goal and the philosophy of Pan-Africanism as well.

In order to further this agenda, Garvey instituted two initiatives. First, the UNIA did as much as it could to promote its cause by celebrating African culture. The organization held almost weekly parades through Harlem, filled with pageantry and military dress to demonstrate the diversity and power of Africans from around the world. It was very much in keeping with the idea of the New Negro, of standing up and being recognized. No event did more to further that cause, however, than when the UNIA held a rally at Madison Square Garden. 25,000 people filled the arena in a celebration of Pan-Africanism.

As might be expected, Du Bois was not an admirer of Garvey and his policy of separatism. In a series of articles in *The Crisis* (the magazine of the NAACP), Du Bois referred to Garvey as the "most dangerous enemy to the Negro race in America and the World." Garvey's reputation wasn't helped when he held a meeting with the leader of the Ku Klux Klan in 1922, stating that the KKK was a better friend to Africans than the many hypocritical whites who claimed to help, but in truth had no desire to do so. Though Garvey's thoughts would be echoed in later years, it did little to gain him supporters and made potential allies, like Du Bois, into adversaries.

The return to Africa wasn't just a theory either. In 1919, the UNIA purchased two ocean liners to begin the process of taking goods and eventually people back to Africa. The Black Star Line, the name given to the company, had a number of problems almost from the beginning and eventually ceased operations by 1922. Adding insult to injury, the Bureau of Federal Investigation took an interest in the company almost immediately and later charged Garvey with mail fraud. He was found guilty and served five years in prison. Upon his release in 1927, Garvey was deported back to Jamaica.

Between the two pillars of Du Bois and Garvey stood the figure of Asa Philip Randolph. As a labor organizer, the beginnings of his greatest successes started in the 1920s. He was a strong supporter of socialism and saw it as the main way to achieve equality for African-Americans specifically, but for all workers more generally.

In 1917 Randolph organized the elevator operators in New York City into a union, and in 1919 he was elected president of the National Brotherhood of Workers of America, a union bringing together African-

American dock workers in Virginia. The American Federation of Labor (AFL) pressured the group into disbanding because they felt it was redundant with what they were trying to accomplish with the Longshoremen's union.

Randolph is best known for the union he helped to create, the Brotherhood of Sleeping Car Porters in 1925. There was nothing comparable for the AFL to object to, so the predominantly African-American membership continued to organize. The early years of the union were not particularly successful, as a threatened strike needed to be abandoned because of rumors of strikebreakers being in position to take the union members' jobs. By not following through with the strike, the Brotherhood saw a major decline in its membership. It wouldn't be until the presidency of Franklin Roosevelt and the New Deal that the union would see significant progress in the rights and working conditions of its members.

In spite of the harsh racism that was part of American society in the 1920s, with legal segregation in the South and de facto segregation in the North, African-Americans saw significant gains as a group. A far greater percentage of African-Americans had moved out of the South and were taking better opportunities, even if that meant moving into new cities and creating tensions between them and the whites and established African-American residents For the first time since Reconstruction, African-Americans demonstrated real political and economic power. African-American artists, especially in music, were not just transforming cities, but the national landscape of what American music truly was. Numerous African-American leaders continued to strive for improvements for African-Americans within or perhaps outside of the overall society. This last point continued to be a debate within the ongoing struggle for civil rights.

Chapter 7 – Politics and Policies

The 1920s are remembered as a time of big businesses making substantial profits and the US government supporting those enterprises. As Calvin Coolidge famously said, "The business of America is business." As far as the presidency was concerned in the 1920s, it was the job of the president to promote businesses and stay out of their way as much as possible.

After the First World War and the peace negotiations that followed, a huge shift occurred in the national government. For the first time in a decade, the Republican Party regained the House and the Senate. The midterm elections of 1918 were a bellwether. Voters announced that they were finished with the Progressive agenda that had dominated the first two decades of the twentieth century. Furthermore, it was a clear sign that Americans were finished with Woodrow Wilson's leadership. As the negotiations at Versailles concluded, a backlash against the globalism that Wilson supported was beginning.

The most obvious rejection of American intervention in foreign matters came as the United States Senate rejected the treaty that would have made them members of the League of Nations. The idea of an international body to help govern and solve disputes was one of the signature items of Woodrow Wilson's Fourteen Points, the peace outline he presented at Versailles. By rejecting the League, the Senate was rejecting Wilson's plan for democracy around the globe.

In the fall of 1919, Woodrow Wilson suffered a major stroke and was virtually incapacitated for much of the remainder of his presidency. His wife, Edith, handled much of the day-to-day tasks of the office of the president. She also controlled access to the president. She even doubted members of the president's own party and what they would do if they found out Wilson's condition. He made almost no public appearances or statements. Even so, Wilson needed to be talked out of running for a third term for the presidency.

Warren G. Harding defeated the Democratic nominee, James Cox, with a staggering number of electoral votes, 401 of a possible 531, and an overwhelming percentage of the popular vote, 60.2%. Harding's message which he proclaimed as a "Return to Normalcy" resonated with voters across all demographics and regional areas. The concurrent congressional races added to the Republican majorities in the House and Senate. For the remainder of the decade, all elected branches of the government were dominated by the Republican Party.

Harding was a pretty much a career politician from Ohio, building a strong newspaper until being elected to the Ohio House of Representatives. Though he lost a bid to be governor of the state, he was one of the first senators to be elected under the provisions of the Seventeenth Amendment. As a demonstration of a much different era, Harding barely left Ohio as he campaigned for president, using the "front porch" campaign style also used by past Republican William McKinley.

Harding famously said, "I have no trouble with my enemies. I can take care of my enemies all right. But my damn friends...They're the ones that keep me walking the floor nights!" Harding's administration was riddled with scandals. The most famous of these involved his Secretary of the Interior, Albert Fall. It stemmed from the granting of oil drilling rights in reserves that had been set aside for the US Navy. After the lands were opened for commercial drilling, one parcel in Elk Hills, California and the other in Teapot Dome, Wyoming, two different oil companies that had paid Fall $400,000 were awarded the leases.

Other scandals also involving illicit payments with the office of the Attorney General and the Department of Veteran Affairs dogged Harding's reputation, but not the man himself. On August 2, 1923 Harding, on a trip to the West Coast, died of a heart attack in San

Francisco. Much of the scandal around his administration wasn't revealed until after his death, including his extramarital affairs. At the time of his passing, he was still held in high regard and was still quite popular as president.

Succeeding Harding was his vice president, Calvin Coolidge. When Coolidge died in 1933, noted satirist Dorothy Parker quipped, "How can you tell?" Coolidge may not have been the most expressive of men, but for the better part of the 1920s, he was the President of the United States. His administration shaped policy more than his predecessor and his successor in 1929.

In keeping with the isolationist ideals of the Senate, Coolidge had no plans to enter into any alliance. Though he tried to keep good relations across Europe, his insistence that European nations repay all of their debt did not make for harmony. Germany especially was hard-pressed to repay its reparations costs, but if the United States would not forgive any loan debt—which they did not—other countries had no choice but to continue to insist on keeping Germany's feet to the financial fire.

As noted at the beginning of this chapter, Coolidge was a supporter of big business in the United States. One of the main ways he supported American business, which was conversely detrimental to US relations with other nations, was maintaining high tariffs on imported goods. Five years after the passage of the Fordney-McCumber Tariff, that imposed high tariffs, foreign trading partners began to retaliate and raise their own tariffs on American goods, especially foodstuffs.

Coolidge was dedicated to eliminating the "tyranny of bureaucratic regulation and control." He did little to curb any of the excesses of business that the earlier progressives had tried to control. Overall his policy as far as the federal government was concerned was that the less they did the better. Such policies as child labor and working hour regulations were better left to local and state authorities, not the national government. This was also extended to Wall Street where there was little regulation to begin with; under Coolidge, it was almost nonexistent.

Much in the same vein, Coolidge and his Secretary of the Treasury, Andrew Mellon, believed that lower taxes actually helped the government gain revenue. It was a similar theory as trickle-down economics, wherein the money saved by the wealthy would lead to job creation and growth, thereby making more taxpayers and more revenue for the government. This policy went a considerable way to enriching the already wealthy but did little toward gains of the middle and working class.

Overall though, Americans supported President Coolidge and his policies, especially those that were more protectionist and isolationist. Taxes had been cut and even if the majority of Americans didn't benefit from the cuts, enough did. It all made for a rather predictable 1924 Presidential campaign. It was not quite the landslide of Harding, but it was still a significant win for Coolidge and the Republicans. Coolidge took 382 of a possible 531 electoral votes and received 54% of the popular vote to his Democratic challenger John Davis' total of 28.8%.

Interestingly, one of the constituencies that Coolidge never had a strong relationship with still voted for him. The farmland of the United States, the world's breadbasket, voted solidly for the Republican candidate. The high tariffs especially hurt farmers in the US, especially when other countries raised their tariffs in retaliation. Even if tariffs would have remained low for American goods, American farmers would have still suffered, especially by Coolidge's second term. During and shortly after World War One, American farmers enjoyed a great boom, feeding the warring nations of the world and those devastated after it. By the mid-1920s, however, Europe was starting to recover. American farms were stuck with a surplus that they could only sell at a loss or not at all. The Coolidge Administration proposed the idea of farming cooperatives as a means to stymie overproduction, but it gained little support.

In the Senate, the Mcnary-Haugen Bill was proposed as a means to aid farmers. The main idea was that the government would buy their surplus production and sell it on the world market. In order to recoup their losses, the government could charge the farmers who benefited from the program and also add sale taxes to food to spread the costs more equitably across other citizens. Coolidge and many on his cabinet opposed the bill, seeing it as too much government interference and not allowing farmers to stand on their own two feet. Both houses of Congress passed the bill, and both times President Coolidge vetoed it. Though the 1920s was in an economic boom for much of the economy, especially by the middle of the decade, farming was hurting quite considerably.

Eventually a much more modest bill was proposed and passed in the early days of the Hoover administration.

The election of 1928 saw many of the themes of the previous decade played out. Many assumed that Coolidge would run again, but he declined. Instead the erstwhile Secretary of Commerce, Herbert Hoover, was chosen as the party's candidate. His opposition, Al Smith, split the Democratic Party and brought to bear much of the worst aspects of the 1920s.

Al Smith, Governor of New York, had two issues that caused much dissension between Democrats in urban areas and in the South. First off, Smith was a Roman Catholic, and his religion became a key point throughout the election. Many feared that once elected, the pope would be in control of the United States. Almost solidly Democratic since the Civil War, the South would split when voting in 1928.

Furthermore, an issue that many had thought decided was under debate once again in the campaign of 1928. Smith supported the repeal of prohibition, whereas Herbert Hoover did not. Being from New York and supporting the repeal made those living in rural areas very suspicious of Smith. Adding to that distrust was the fact that many immigrants in urban areas supported Smith.

Supporting an unpopular stance in rural areas, being supported by foreigners, and being a member of a very foreign religion all but doomed Smith's presidential campaign. Hoover, like the two preceding Republican nominees, won handily. He secured 444 electoral votes to Smith's 87, winning all but 7 states. Smith did not even carry his home state of New York. The popular vote wasn't quite as lopsided, with Hoover gaining 58.2% and Smith winning 40.8%. Still, it was a strong support for the policies of the Republican government and a sound rejection of a candidate many believed represented foreign and dangerously anti-American ideas.

In his inaugural address, delivered in March of 1929, Herbert Hoover briefly outlined why he believed he was elected. First, it was because of the preceding years of success, especially the lack of government control in business. Next, by rejecting the anti-prohibitionist, Hoover stated that he felt the nation was demanding that the Eighteenth Amendment be rigorously upheld and enforced. He spoke of improving education and maintaining world peace and concluded on a positive note believing that the best was yet to come.

Chapter 8 – How Did It All End?

Standing before the Capitol Building in the rain during his inauguration on March 4, 1929, Herbert Hoover had full confidence that the future of the country he was about to lead was going to continue on its steady upward trajectory. While there were signs that the economy was slowing, that was acceptable. Hoover was enough of a student of history to realize that there would be setbacks and downturns. Even at the beginning of the decade in the postwar economy there had been struggles. But Hoover believed America and its people would overcome any potential difficulty and come out better than before.

The predicament of farmers was an example of this. A segment of the economy was suffering, but it was not necessarily going to drag the entire economy down along with it. However, there were other industries that were beginning to decline in 1929. Housing construction declined from 1925-1929. Much like farmers, textile manufacturers were hurt by the rebound of Europe after the war, which in turned hurt cotton farmers who had been immune to the difficulties the Midwest was already experiencing.

The conversion economy that of new goods being built and sold to consumers after the war economy had converted to a more domestic focus was also showing signs of slowing down. Many of the goods, like refrigerators and radios, that people had been buying through the course of the early and mid-1920s were no longer selling at the same rate. By the late

1920s, people were buying less even though production remained high or increased. What's more, wages didn't increase much throughout the decade so households were buying more than ever before on credit. Consumer debt, something almost unheard of in the early part of the twentieth century, was at an all-time high by the end of the 1920s.

Debt was becoming a bit of its own national pastime, namely in the buying and selling of stocks. Speculating on the stock market was something that the middle class especially engaged in during the 1920s. People were investing in the chance of making it big on any stock that looked attractive at the time. In order to do this, many people had to borrow money to invest or buy on margin. In some cases, investors only had to put up 25% of the cost while the broker put up the remaining 75%, or the margin. If the stock went up, and through the 1920s it often did, then everybody won. The broker was paid back his margin with interest and the investor reaped the rest of the profits.

In 1929, as Hoover was taking the oath of office, the stock market was still in an overall climb. There was a dip in that month of March, but shortly after that, it looked like the market would continue to rise as it had done for the previous nine years. Throughout the summer months of 1929, the market continued to climb, reaching its highest level ever in September. Economists were so optimistic that they proclaimed the market had reached a new high plateau.

Circumstances did make some investors nervous. In late September, the London Stock Exchange crashed, making Wall Street reluctant to invest in foreign markets. On October 24th, heavy trading caused the market to fall by 11% initially, but the largest financial institutions in the country pooled their resources and bought large amounts of stock at inflated prices to stabilize the market before it closed that Thursday.

The next day and a half (Wall Street was open for half a day on Saturdays), the market showed signs of recovery. However, on Monday, the opening bell saw another rush to sell and the market plunged and closed down 13%. Much of this was anticipated because investors were facing margin calls to open the week. That is, brokers were asking for the money they had lent investors to make stock purchases. This made the situation only worse though. The next day, known as Black Tuesday, saw the largest number of shares ever traded—16 million. The market closed down another 12%.

The heads of the banks couldn't rally the market this time, especially as the one-two punch of Monday and Tuesday made many want to get out of investing altogether. Investors wanted what money they still had, and they wanted it immediately. This demand for cash created a huge problem for many banks, as they took deposits from customers and had invested them in the market. It didn't take more than a rumor that a bank was about to fail for customers to rush to the bank and demand their money. Though the largest bank runs wouldn't occur until 1930 and 1931, banks were already failing because of smaller panics. In 1929, 650 banks failed. In 1930, that number would double and in 1931 still more banks would close, leaving customers without any recourse. Life savings were lost and mistrust in the financial system would last for generations.

For smaller investors who got out of the market entirely or lost a great deal, spending became much more frugal. This not only affected purchases of household items and larger products, but also spending outside the home on entertainment. Even before 1929, people were spending less. After 1929, the ideal of being a free spender was replaced by being a penny pincher.

The stock market crash is often seen as the abrupt beginning of the Great Depression, but it was much more of a slow boil than an explosion. After the shock of the crash had worn off, many thought the worst was over. It was merely a correction after a decade of unprecedented growth. Like a large stone thrown into a pond, however, the ripples from the crash throughout the economy would make a tenuous situation even worse.

Like many Americans, large corporations invested in the stock market, and like everyone involved in the market, those same corporations lost a great deal of money. Additionally, those companies that were traded on the stock market saw the value of their company stock plummet. What had been a decade of expanding wealth for companies to reinvest and expand their business was now all but dried up.

At first, as companies lost money the first strategy was to finally cut production and limit the hours that employees worked. It wasn't enough to hold off further losses. Even though President Hoover elicited a pledge from many of the largest corporations not to cut jobs, eventually they had little recourse but to do so.

Herbert Hoover was not a cold man, nor was he inept as he is sometimes portrayed. He had very strong Christian beliefs, especially in helping one's fellow man. He was a man of compassion who possessed a strong moral compass and deeply held beliefs. Unfortunately, some of those beliefs were at odds with what was needed to combat the worst economic crisis in world history.

Like most Republicans of his era, he believed strongly in a small federal government. More to the point, he believed the power of the federal government should be used sparingly and not be used to compel people or businesses to do anything. Instead, he believed in volunteerism. As the crisis grew, Hoover called on his fellow Americans to aid one another through the tough times. What made that advice almost comical was that most people were in the same condition as their neighbor. Unemployment rose from 3% in 1928 to 30% by the end of Hoover's term. It is tough to care for one's neighbor when it is almost impossible to care for one's self.

Similarly, Hoover called on churches and other charitable organizations to aid those in need of assistance. Unfortunately, those private organizations were already overwhelmed by requests for help. Neighborhood relief agencies, ethnic aid societies, and mutual aid societies all suffered from a shortage of money and supplies to be able to help all those that came looking for help. In the worst circumstances, some of those same relief agencies were forced to close due to the depression.

Another core belief of Hoover's that was detrimental to the health of the nation was his insistence on keeping a balanced budget. It was his belief that creating a deficit was the wrong choice and would be more detrimental to the people and the nation in the long run. Though the idea of keeping a balanced budget did not waiver, Hoover eventually increased government spending to aid the population.

Ultimately, Hoover and his administration were overwhelmed by the enormity of the depression as it grew. It seemed like every step he took to help did little to nothing. His decision to raise tariffs backfired, as other countries immediately retaliated causing American businesses to face more setbacks. Hoover became more melancholy as the years of his term passed. It was no secret that he was held accountable for the collapse. It is not fair that one person should shoulder all of the blame for the depression, but unfortunately that comes with the office of the President of the United States.

The 1930 midterm elections were a portent of things to come in 1932. Republicans barely held on to a majority in the Senate and lost 52 seats in Congress, making the chamber practically even. The Democrats actually held a one-seat advantage in most votes because of an independent member who leaned more their way. By the 1932 elections, the presidency and Congress were in Democratic control for the first time since the end of World War One. Hoover was out as president and Franklin Roosevelt was in.

Conclusion

The tendency in American history to divide eras by decades is hard to resist. It is a convenient way to mark the time and stay organized when thinking about the past. Unlike most eras, however, the 1920s was a fairly self-contained decade. It is probably better understood as the post-World War One era, but overall the ten years between 1920 and 1929 were unique in American history.

The nation was more urban than rural for the first time in its history and the city became the stage for so much of what was innovative and new during that time. Mass culture came into its own as movies and music drew people from the countryside into the city. They drove in automobiles in record numbers and those cars changed the way cities were designed and had a profound effect on society as a whole. Great celebrities also emerged during the decade because of their larger-than-life deeds and personalities.

For the first time since the Reconstruction, African-Americans made inroads into the political, social, and economic life of the greater United States. They too came to the city looking and finding more opportunities than they had experienced in previous generations. Along with the African-Americans of the Great Migration came their distinctive culture, forever changing the cultural landscape of the United States.

Old causes from the Progressive Era were resolved, but one was a logical conclusion that by the end of the decade would never be questioned. The other seemed antiquated even before the first alcohol stores were destroyed. By 1933, the foregone conclusion of prohibition was reversed and the Eighteenth Amendment was repealed. In the years since, people often wondered why the previous generation ever thought it was a good idea.

However, there were still those who opposed such changes. The Ku Klux Klan experienced a revival after the Reconstruction period, expanding well outside of the southern states. The national government responded to people's fears of European influence and more explicitly immigrants by practically closing the door to those that wanted to enter the United States. The radical ideas of the previous era that gained some traction before World War One were now shunned and feared. To be a radical in the 1920s was to court arrest.

It was a time of great economic expansion, with people buying new products, driving businesses to continue to expand. More people than ever before also invested in the stock market, even if they didn't quite have the money to do so. But money was there to be spent, and the people who lived through the 1920s were more than happy to spend it.

And then, as if on cue, it all came to a dramatic, sudden end befitting the roaring decade. What had been an outwardly focused culture for ten years became a much more inwardly focused one. In many eyes, the American way of life was still viable. Unlike the 1920s, the 1930s would be defined by how Americans banded together and tried to define the American way of life. For many, that meant examining traditions of the past that had fallen out of favor during the 1920s.

Many people have come to see the Great Depression as a reckoning, as a correction for the Jazz Age. History doesn't make those judgments. Suffice it to say; the 1920s were a unique moment in time where change and reaction to those changes were more dramatic than any other time in American history.

Part 6: The Great Depression

A Captivating Guide to the Worldwide Economic Depression that Began in the United States, Including the Wall Street Crash, FDR's New deal, Hitler's Rise and More

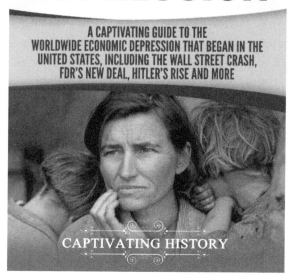

Introduction

The stock market crash of 1929 didn't cause the Great Depression by itself, but it is a powerful symbolic starting point to the greatest economic disaster of the twentieth century. On that dark day in October 1929, fortunes were lost and fear of financial insecurity rose throughout the United States and the world. In 1932, the low point of the Depression, as much as a third of Americans were out of work and even more people were unemployed in other countries. The stock market reached its lowest point ever and wouldn't rise to its pre-Depression levels for almost twenty years.

The scale of the crisis demanded new ways of coping and new ideas about the role of government. The ideas that had dominated American thought about the relationship between the economy and government were now viewed to be outdated at best, dangerous at worst. Notions such as laissez faire and self-made men were eclipsed by ideas of government regulation and community involvement. More than any other person in the United States, Franklin D. Roosevelt and his New Deal changed the United States government in fundamental ways.

That sense of community helped many Americans deal with the harsh realities of the Depression. Citizens joined numerous groups and political parties in an effort to feel useful again. The government also encouraged such organization and many professions received government money to foster such community building.

Citizens not only joined groups looking for a purpose and a connection to their fellow people, but also looked toward cultural traditions and institutions to help identify what it meant to be an American, especially in a time of such uncertainty. Though an extraordinary time of hardship, the era of the Great Depression highlighted a vibrant culture. Jobs and money may have been difficult to come by, but people still watched movies and listened to radio programs. They read books and went to dance halls. In short, people still found ways to entertain themselves even in the most difficult of circumstances.

The culture of the Depression took on multiple characteristics. In some cases, it was a critique of American society, especially of capitalism and the consumer culture of the previous decade. In other cases, there was a drive to discover the real America, an idealized rural, traditional America when life was simpler and less concerned with manufactured material goods. A final aspect of the cultural landscape of the Depression was a drive to escape from the troubles of the present day. Wild fantasies and amazing flights of imagination were some of the most popular pieces produced during the era.

The financial collapse of the United States spread around the globe and deepened crises all over the world, particularly in Western Europe. The continent was still recovering from the First World War when the Great Depression unfolded. Germany was especially hit hard by the economic freefall. That nation's ability to pay off its war debt, difficult in the best of times, was non-existent during the Depression. The new Weimar government was dedicated to democracy, but as circumstances continued to deteriorate, new, darker movements spread throughout Germany. Eventually, Germany was consumed by an evil that plunged the world into its largest war ever.

It was the battle to curb the fascist threat that finally ended the Great Depression. Economic recovery had been slow through much of the 1930s, but as Europe prepared for World War II, American industry met the demand for their allies. When the United States was drawn into the war by the attack on Pearl Harbor, the Great Depression was but a memory.

That memory, however, impacted an entire generation of Americans. After World War II, people still dealt with a scarcity mentality. Public policy was also driven by the fear of another depression starting once all of the wartime boosts to the economy slowed down. Keeping Americans working was the number one domestic policy after the war. When the soldiers came home from Europe, the hope was they would find a job.

If that didn't happen, the government made it possible for thousands of GIs to attend college and defer unemployment. Unfortunately, as the time between the present and the Depression becomes more and more distant, some of the lessons of the era are all but forgotten. While policies and agencies are still in place to prevent another full-blown depression, some of the same practices, or very similar practices, are occurring. Risky business behaviors, challenges to democracy, and shifts in the manufacturing economy all point to a very uncertain future.

Chapter 1: Causes of the Great Depression 1918-1929

The Great Depression didn't occur overnight but was rather a decade in the making. A case can be made for an even longer time frame, focusing on the boom and bust nature of the American economy through the nineteenth and twentieth centuries. That is a discussion better left to economic history. Instead of such a macro examination of the origins of the Great Depression, for brevity's sake, this work focuses on events from the end of the First World War until late in 1929 to shed light on what led to the great global economic crisis of the twentieth century.

The Treaty of Versailles, which ended World War I, had many unintended consequences including the effect on the global economy. One of the key provisions of the treaty was that Germany was not only held entirely responsible for the war, but Germany was the principal nation to make reparations to the allied nations. Germany was already reeling from the military defeat and collapse of their government, but their economy was destroyed from the war. Within Germany, starvation was a real concern. Making a dire situation even worse was that another key provision of the treaty was the confiscation of key German territory. Not only was the nation reduced by a third, but much of the land taken away was the heart of German manufacturing. Asking Germany to repay such a vast sum of money was an impossible condition that was never going to be met.

That didn't stop the allies, especially France and Great Britain, from demanding payment. Part of the reason the French and British were relentless on getting their money from Germany was because of the United States demanding repayment of loans that they had given to the allied powers. The Germans were crippled by the amount of money they needed to pay the allies, and while France and Britain weren't in such dire straits, the debt they carried after the war was a drag on their economies as well.

The solution relied on the United States and their willingness to forgive the war debt. Unfortunately for all European nations, the United States wouldn't budge. The president of the United States, Calvin Coolidge, when asked about forgiving the European debt replied, "They borrowed the money, didn't they? They need to repay it." The long-term effect of this stance was to retard global economic growth. Though much of the United States economy was healthy throughout the 1920s, the limits on foreign markets because of their respective national debt eventually hurt the United States economy.

The first segment of the economy to feel the effects of the global slowdown was farming. The end of the war saw the demand for US farm products plunge, due to European nations focused on reviving their own agriculture and becoming less reliant on foreign aid. The reduction in demand was so severe that farmers were incurring heavy losses throughout much of the 1920s. The US Senate attempted to help farmers by fixing prices on certain agricultural goods, providing funds for farmers to *not* cultivate in certain cases, and for the government to buy surplus goods to sell on the international market. On two occasions, Calvin Coolidge vetoed the measure, arguing that such measures were anti-American.

The rest of the American economy was relatively strong through the 1920s, but key industries were showing signs of slowing down by mid-decade. The coal and steel industries, two of the biggest parts of the economy, were reducing production in large part because the nation's railways were not expanding at the same rate as they had been. In addition, the nation's railways were experiencing a decline in ridership due to the rise of the automobile. New housing construction, a common indicator of economic health, also tapered off between 1925 and 1929. Four industries that employed thousands of workers slowing down was a warning sign that the boom that the American economy was experiencing may have been approaching an end.

However, other industries, especially the nascent auto industry, were booming. The conversion from a wartime economy to a more consumer-centered economy created a great amount of growth. People were buying many new and novel products that American manufacturers were all too happy to keep producing. The aforementioned automobiles were continually setting new records for sales. Other household products like refrigerators, radios, and clothes washers were new to Americans, and many were glad to have these modern conveniences.

In order to get these new products, more people than ever before were buying goods on credit. Unlike in previous generations, carrying personal debt wasn't seen as a particular danger. There was a great deal of confidence that the economy, and most importantly jobs, would continue to be plentiful. As major industries started to slow down, the use of credit also slowed. By the later part of the decade, household spending was reduced significantly, particularly because even while profits were still strong for corporations, wages rose insignificantly. Production of consumer goods didn't slow down at the same rate, and like farming, a surplus was being produced by the end of the decade. However, with less money to spend and less willingness to use credit, the high production was unsustainable in the long run.

The use of credit was also a major factor in the growth of another part of the economy, the stock market. Prior to the 1920s, the market was largely the providence of the upper class. In the 1920s, middle-class Americans began investing. For many, making an investment required more money than was on hand. The practice of buying on margin, where one purchases stock with a certain percentage of the money coming from a loan, was used by smaller investors to get in on the market. An investor could make a purchase with as much as 70 percent borrowed money, or 70 percent on margin. If the investment went up, the margin would be paid back, with the rest of the return going to the buyer. If the investment didn't rise, not only was the personal stake lost, but the borrowed money as well, which still needed to be repaid.

Adding to the spread of participation in the market was the practice of speculating. For many new investors, there was little research being done about the companies where the money was invested. Like real estate speculation in the nineteenth century, where buyers often didn't even know the location of the land they were buying, new investors knew little about the companies they were financing. Such high-risk investments were fine if the market continued to rise, but if the market slowed, or worse plunged, a lot of people would be out of a lot of money.

The volatility of the market in the fall of 1929 was troubling to a greater amount of people than it ever had been. The exclusive domain of brokers and investment bankers had now become the concern of the middle class. The banks that loaned the money for margin buys also were more concerned with the behavior of the market than they had been in previous generations. It would only take one particularly bad downswing to cause a great deal of hardship for a lot of Americans.

When Herbert Hoover was inaugurated in March of 1929, he expressed optimism for the future of the nation. The economy was steadily rising, and there was no need to worry about things going south. By the end of the year, it was apparent that something was seriously wrong with the stock market and with the economy as a whole.

The downturn that was even expected by some economists started on Thursday, October 24. However, as a great sell-off got underway, investors were worried that the market was going to fall too far. In order to pre-empt a sharp decline, JP Morgan infused a great deal of money into the market. The ploy seemed to work. After Morgan's influx of cash, the market stabilized.

However, it was only a temporary fix. The following day the market closed down again, but Morgan was not able to bail it out this time. The weekend offered some respite, but Monday saw another downturn. Tuesday, October 29, 1929, saw the greatest amount of stock traded in the history of the stock market. The loss of volume was staggering. Brokers were selling at massive discounts in hopes of salvaging some money. In the end, it just made the matter worse. The more people were selling at a loss, the more other investors wanted to get out of a bad situation. By the end of the day, known as Black Tuesday, the market was down almost 14,000 points. It was the greatest (and still is by percentage) loss in the history of Wall Street.

Black Tuesday caused great tremors throughout the economy and society, but people and institutions weren't panicking just yet. The ripples needed time to expand. First, those that had been buying on margin were in a tough situation, needing to pay back their loans. Suffering great losses made paying back the loans extremely difficult, if not impossible. Without the return of borrowed money, banks began to feel the pinch and remaining solvent for day-to-day activities became an issue. Some banks were forced to close because of the shortfall. As news and rumors swirled about the health of the banking industry, more and more people lost faith in their respective banks and started to withdraw their money. It was a destructive cycle. The more people that ran to the banks, wanting their money they thought was safe, caused more banks to fail. By 1932, more than 5,000 banks had failed.

The run on the banks accelerated the downward spiral of the economy. Spending had already been slower, but now with entire life savings wiped out, discretionary spending was all but non-existent. Businesses were starting to lay off large amounts of workers to try and reduce the corporate losses they were beginning to see. While businesses were laying people off, they were also cutting wages and hours. What many believed was just a more violent correction to the economy than usual was now seen as a significant downturn. As unemployment began to rise, meeting household expenses became a pressing concern for many families. Under such harsh circumstances, people needed assistance from outside sources. They turned to benevolent societies, churches, neighborhood organizations, and government agencies. As the crisis deepened, citizens called on the government to do more. The response to those calls defined much of the presidency of Herbert Hoover.

Chapter 2: Herbert Hoover and the Early Years of the Depression

Herbert Hoover's name is synonymous with failure. It was during his presidency that the worst economic crisis in American history occurred. Fair or not, Hoover was judged harshly by his contemporaries and by later generations. Even though many of the causes of the Great Depression were years in the making, Hoover was left holding the bag. It didn't help that the solutions he and his administration offered either didn't work or completely backfired. Oftentimes, the treatment by the federal government of those that were in desperate need was seen as cold, uncaring, and even cruel.

It is this description, of being uncaring, that is possibly the most unfair one leveled at Hoover. He came from a humble background, growing up poor in the Midwest. He was also a very religious man who believed strongly in the previous generation's progressive ethos of being helpful to his fellow citizens. His progressivism was of the Republican variety, and, like Roosevelt and Taft, he still saw it as a goal to uplift people. He famously said in 1928 that within a decade poverty could be eliminated from the United States.

After a visit to post-war Germany, Hoover was instrumental in getting an allied blockade around Germany lifted and getting much-needed food to the people of that nation. Hoover believed in aiding others, even former enemies, if the need was great and beyond the ability of those suffering. He also believed just as strongly that offering too much help was morally wrong. Pulling oneself up by the bootstraps was far better than being given a handout. Instilling or reaffirming confidence was far better than simple charity.

Such an ethos had served Hoover well in his rise to the presidency. In his youth, Hoover witnessed when things got difficult, people helping other people, communities taking care of one another. Hoover was certain that such community engagement would buoy people struggling during the current crisis. Unfortunately, when the majority of people are suffering or barely getting by, personal charity isn't realistic. Furthermore, institutions that had often provided a social safety net in the past were completely overwhelmed. Churches, benevolent societies, unions, and other community organizations simply didn't have the resources to meet the demand of people seeking aid.

Like other presidents, Hoover tried to appeal to the consciences of business leaders. Hoover asked many captains of industry to pledge to not reduce wages or lay off any workers during the economic crisis. Many corporations agreed, but as the economic picture continued to darken, they could not (or would not) honor the pledge. Reducing labor costs to cut losses and stay in business was one of the oldest strategies and had been prevalent for 50 years prior. Such ingrained thinking wasn't going to be totally abandoned, pledge or no pledge. By 1932, between 25-30 percent of Americans were out of work. Couple that number with the amount of people who were underemployed or working intermittently and the picture becomes even starker. It is tragic, though not surprising, that in the first years of the Depression the national suicide rate rose by 30 percent.

Another strategy of the past was the implementation of higher tariffs. In 1930, with an eye toward protecting American businesses and American workers, the Harley-Smoot Act was passed. The thinking was that with higher costs on foreign goods, people would buy more American goods, helping to boost the economy. It backfired. People didn't begin to buy in greater numbers, and other nations retaliated with tariffs of their own, hurting American businesses and causing more layoffs.

Along with the self-help ethos and sparingly delivered aid to those in need, another standard that Hoover believed in was maintaining a balanced federal budget. Deficit spending was only permissible in times of war. Domestic strife was not the time to panic and take drastic actions and possibly make things worse overall. As some federal dollars were trickling out to help people deal with the Depression, Hoover proposed a tax increase to maintain the balanced budget. Even though the president's political party was in control of Congress, they did not support Hoover's plan to increase taxes.

Despite his best efforts, Hoover could not stem the tide of the rising economic crisis. Even more, circumstances beyond his control made matters worse for the nation and for the public's perception of the president. Some of the hardest hit states made up the world's breadbasket, and from the Dakotas to Texas, a severe drought in the 1930s made farming there almost impossible. The topsoil across the entire region was so dry that the wind would pick it up and cause near blackout conditions, creating what contemporaries called the Dust Bowl. When the winds stopped blowing, massive drifts of soil covered farming equipment, rose against farm buildings, and made thousands of farms untenable. Though an act of nature, the lack of response by the president added to the perception that he was out of touch or didn't care about average Americans. The slow and perceived lack of response tainted Hoover's legacy.

As the Dust Bowl shifted and moved the soil across the plains, the economic hardships of the Depression caused great displacement among people throughout the United States. Those that were turned out of their homes had little recourse except to create the best shelter that they could. Many families were forced to create makeshift tents or lean-tos in order to provide some shelter. These shanty towns sprang up in every major city in the United States. Though there was little that Hoover could have done, these vagabond settlements became known as Hoovervilles, with the implication being that he was personally at fault.

While the Dust Bowl and Hoovervilles were well beyond Hoover's control, one event that he could have prevented was a public relations nightmare for the president. In 1929, before the Depression started, Congress passed and Hoover signed a bill establishing a monetary bonus for surviving World War I veterans. The payments weren't scheduled to begin until 1945.

When it became apparent that the Depression wasn't a short-term event, the veterans wanted their promised bonuses to come early to help during the present crisis. In order to pressure Congress to act, thousands of veterans camped out on the National Mall in 1932 and expressed their desire to be paid immediately. After a number of days, this "Bonus Army" moved to another section of Washington, DC. At no time were the former soldiers violent, or even threatening violence. However, after a week of protesting simply by their presence, Hoover ordered the active army to clear the veterans from the capital. A cavalry regiment, along with a tank, were sent out to disperse the vets. Under the command of Douglas MacArthur and including other future famous generals such as George Patton and Dwight Eisenhower, the army horsemen rode down the former soldiers. Numerous were injured and two men were killed in the action.

There are very few untouchables in American politics, but military veterans are among them. Since the beginning of the country, former soldiers hold a special place in the national conscience. Even the Bonus Army, made up of those that fought for the nation, was to be respected and honored, not attacked. The public reaction to the event was profoundly negative for Hoover. Even before the Bonus Army episode, Hoover was becoming more and more withdrawn from the public view. After the conflict, Hoover was almost completely out of the public view. He felt that he was being attacked from all sides and remaining out of sight offered him some respite. This was also in keeping with the common attitude of many former presidents. It wasn't the president's job to be present all of the time, to be a public face. Presidents were supposed to be aloof, guarded. As the election of 1932 approached, Hoover was going to run again. Little did he realize that his opponent would change what was expected of a president and define the office for decades to come.

Chapter 3: The Election of 1932

The election of 1928 was one of the most revealing elections for the United States. It demonstrated the power of the urban, ethnic working class and also the deep prejudices that the country still held, especially toward Catholics. Herbert Hoover ran on his past accomplishments in federal government and on the success of his party in the post-war world. The Republican Party also engaged in personal attacks on the Democratic nominee. Al Smith, the Democratic nominee and governor of New York, was a Roman Catholic. The fear of being controlled by the pope and the practice of a very foreign religion for many Americans was capitalized on by Hoover and the Republicans. They claimed that they were fighting to protect the nation from foreign control. In addition, Smith was a "wet," an advocate of repealing prohibition. This combination of a Catholic who supported repeal was too much for the majority of Americans. Even though Prohibition was unpopular, many Americans still saw it as an important way to protect society.

Hoover won the presidency handily in 1928, but he faced a much different electorate in 1932. The economy was approaching the nadir of the Depression. It appeared that Hoover wasn't doing anything to make things better for average Americans. The Republican Party was at the wheel for all of the downfall and was seen as responsible for the current situation. Finally, the great issues that had turned many voters against Al Smith would not be present with the new candidate in 1932.

The new candidate was a part of New York politics and part of one of the most iconic American families. Unlike his elder cousin, Theodore, Franklin Delano made his way for the Democratic Party, not the Republican. He was part of the Wilson administration, and like Al Smith, he was a former governor of New York. Due to late-onset polio when he was in his late thirties, his mobility was limited by the use of a wheelchair.

In many ways, given the backgrounds of the candidates, one might assume Hoover was the Democrat and Roosevelt the Republican. Not only because of the family history with the Grand Old Party, but the Roosevelt family was also one of the first Dutch families to settle in New Amsterdam. By the dawn of Franklin's generation, the family was quite accustomed to wealth and privilege. While both sides of the family believed in the concept of noblesse oblige, Franklin thought it was just as important to use government to better society than to simply serve the people. He harkened back to the activist progressives of the earlier part of the century. Many of his peers considered Roosevelt a traitor to his class.

Two of the main wedge issues that Hoover used against Smith did not work against Roosevelt. Roosevelt was firmly in the American Protestant tradition, so the division by religion was muted. The other issue that was divisive in 1928, prohibition, had almost completely swung toward the position Smith held. By 1932, much of the nation viewed prohibition as a failed experiment. Roosevelt, himself was known to enjoy a cocktail from time to time, even asked during speeches, "Shouldn't a man be able to enjoy a beer after a hard day's labor?" For many Americans, the answer was yes.

Instead of trying to paint their opponent as an outsider harboring a dangerous religion and destructive social behavior, Hoover and the Republicans portrayed Roosevelt as an out of touch dandy who was going to spend the nation's money carelessly. Under Roosevelt, the national debt would rise, businesses would suffer, and the depression would only worsen.

Roosevelt countered by portraying Hoover as a do-nothing president. He wasn't only uncaring, the Democrats insisted, but unwilling to do anything to help the majority of Americans. The Democrats laid the blame for the Great Depression at the feet of Herbert Hoover and the

Republicans in control of Congress. The decision voters faced was between something new or the status quo; at least, it was how the Democrats posed the question.

The candidate Roosevelt wasn't the only new aspect of the Democratic campaign. While he stumped across the country, Roosevelt and many other Democrats promised a "New Deal" for all Americans. The name stuck and was the overarching name for Roosevelt's legislative agenda going forward. It also became a term for those that enacted the agenda, the New Dealers. The term was also the name given to the coalition of voters that Roosevelt was able to knit together for elections for almost twenty years.

The New Deal was more than a catchy name. Roosevelt promised industrial recovery, agricultural recovery, and short-term relief for the jobless. These promises resonated with voters from a broad spectrum of the electorate. The promise of industrial recovery and a reputation for being pro-union attracted the urban, ethnic working class. Promising to focus on agricultural recovery attracted voters from the Midwest and the South. Without the handicap of Catholicism, the Dixiecrats (Democrats for the states that formed the Confederacy in the Civil War) were much more willing to vote for their party's national nominee. Perhaps the most remarkable aspect of the New Deal Coalition was the inclusion of African Americans to the Democratic Party. The election of 1932 saw for the first time that the majority of African Americans voted for a Democratic candidate. Long seen as the party of slavery and racism, the Democrats were able to enhance their appeal to African Americans who were no longer in the South. Instead, African Americans were a much greater part of the urban centers of the United States due to the Great Migration that started during World War I and continued through the 1920s. Once a solid block of voters for the party of Lincoln, African Americans opted for change.

The rest of the nation felt the same way. By a margin of 57 percent to 39 percent, Roosevelt defeated Herbert Hoover. The margin was even greater when looking at the electoral college results. Roosevelt carried 472 electoral votes to Hoover's 59. Hoover was only able to hold 6 states to Roosevelt's 42. It wasn't just the presidential election either. For the first time in over a decade, the Democratic Party gained majorities in the

House of Representatives and the Senate. Americans were ready for a change. They were ready for a new deal.

Chapter 4: The 100 Days and FDR's First Term, 1933-1937

Franklin Delano Roosevelt was sworn in as the thirty-second president of the United States on March 19, 1933. He used the occasion to inspire the nation and projected confidence in the nation that too few actually felt. He said one of the most famous lines ever spoken by a president, "The only thing we have to fear, is fear itself." It is interesting to note that the new president said, we, not you. Roosevelt wanted it to be clear that he was a part of the struggle, and that he was going to work at ending the Depression right along with everyone else. The work started right away. By midsummer, the first 100 days of Roosevelt's first term were complete. Ever since 1933, every first term of a president is judged on that same scale, 100 days.

The flurry of activity that the new administration engaged in was staggering. Roosevelt summed up the philosophy of such an approach by saying, "We are going to try new things. If those don't work, we are going to try something else. No matter we will keep trying until something works." New departments were set up on what seemed like a daily basis. Legislative initiatives from the White House and Congress were constantly being debated and approved. Not all of the proposals worked, as Roosevelt predicted, but he was not going to be considered a do-nothing president from the first day.

Some key policies were enacted in the first 100 days. One of the first was the Emergency Banking Act. A mandatory bank holiday was declared. With all of the banks closed, the federal government assessed which banks were healthy, which could be saved, and which were too far gone and needed to be closed permanently. The banks that could be saved were brought under the management of the government. The eventual goal of the program was to restore faith in the banks and help bolster the economy.

Further reaffirming consumer faith in the banking system was the creation of the Federal Deposit Insurance Corporation. This new government-controlled corporation guaranteed deposits up to $100,000 in the event of the bank's closure. Until the Great Depression, there was no such assurance. Though banks were often seen as safe places to keep money, for that entire generation living through the Depression, even with the FDIC, banks were suspect. Still, the new agency helped to fulfill one of the key campaign promises of Roosevelt and the Democrats, revitalizing the economy.

Another key provision of the New Deal platform was short-term relief for the jobless. To that end, the Roosevelt administration created the Civilian Conservation Corps. The CCC was a program to employ single young men at the onset but later expanded to a greater portion of the population. The enrollees were sent to camps within areas of the United States that needed conservation work, by stopping soil erosion, constructing fire towers, planting trees, and a host of other tasks. By the end of its first year, 1933, the CCC employed over 250,000 men. The program was a success and very popular. It did not solve all of the employment problems facing the United States, but it helped both financially and psychologically. A great number of workers felt useful again. It also further demonstrated that Roosevelt was taking action.

Along those same lines, the Federal Emergency Relief Act established the Federal Emergency Relief Administration. FERA was created in 1933, like the CCC. Instead of being a strictly federal agency, FERA distributed $500 million to state and local agencies to help the unemployed. Many of the jobs created were unskilled labor, but like the jobs at the CCC, they provided a morale boost to those that were out of work.

The most ambitious employment act undertaken was the establishment of the Works Progress Administration. This initiative employed thousands in its first year of existence and reached millions at its peak later in the decade. Many of the buildings and projects constructed under the direction of the WPA are now historically preserved sites. Thousands of schools, post offices, bridges, and hospitals were constructed during the 1930s boom of the WPA. Over 625,000 miles of roads were laid by the organization. It was the greatest expansion of infrastructure ever in the United States.

The construction projects were the greater part of the WPA, but another initiative of the program was specifically directed toward helping unemployed artists. Federal Project Number One was composed of five key parts: the Federal Writers Project, the Federal Theatre Project, the Federal Arts Project, the Federal Music Project, and the Historical Records Project. Thousands of writers, actors, and musicians were employed by the government, creating pamphlets, posters, guides to national parks, and a host of other projects. Many well-known and later successful artists took part in the program including Orson Welles, Burt Lancaster, and Sidney Lumet. One of the most important projects from the WPA was the collection of American slave narratives. The stories of over 2,000 slaves were recorded and preserved, maintaining an important link to one of the most tragic aspects of American history.

Agricultural recovery was another key component of the 1932 platform. To that end, the Roosevelt administration proposed the Agricultural Adjustment Act which, when passed, created the Agricultural Adjustment Administration. The main purpose of this new agency was to help farmers with surpluses and to reduce the amount of food being produced. The government bought and slaughtered surplus livestock and paid farmers not to plant crops that were running surpluses and were not in high demand. For tenant farmers and sharecroppers, the AAA was a bit of a mixed bag. While the landowners were paid not to produce on a portion of their land, those tenants and croppers were all but cut out of the surplus payments. However, many owners allowed the tenants and croppers to stay on the land and plant their own crops. This led to more food for tenants and also allowed them to bring their own crops to market. While the amount of money wasn't large, it helped to raise the standard of living of many tenant farmers and sharecroppers.

Though not strictly a measure for the agricultural sector of the economy, the Tennessee Valley Authority, created in 1933, benefited some of the most remote and underdeveloped areas of the United States. The TVA brought modernization to most of Tennessee, parts of Alabama, Kentucky, Mississippi, Georgia, North Carolina, and Virginia. The Authority built dams, produced fertilizer, and provided electricity throughout the region. In addition to providing such services, the TVA employed thousands in order to deliver those services to the region. The organization is still owned and operated by the federal government.

The most controversial aspect of the first 100 days was the legislation proposed to help industry recover, another key tenant of the campaign trail. The National Industry Recovery Act (NIRA) was eventually passed by the House and Senate but not without a great deal of opposition. The legislation eventually created the National Recovery Administration (NRA) and the Public Works Administration (PWA). The acts' intent was to provide workers with protections they did not currently enjoy, such as allowing collective bargaining and banning the practice of coercing employees to not join a union or engage in a union activity. The act also tried to enforce fair competition and regulated other aspects of various industries. Ultimately, that was where a great deal of criticism for the act was aimed. The NRA produced hundreds of new regulations, seemingly overnight. Many allies of Roosevelt turned against the administration over the NRA, and business leaders especially did not like what they felt to be government overreach.

Though not necessarily a campaign promise, one of the main concerns of many Americans was pulling in the reigns of Wall Street, the entity many blamed for the financial collapse in the first place. The Securities Act of 1933 was the key part of that initiative. The act eventually led to the creation of the Securities and Exchange Commission. It was the first federal legislation to regulate the trade of stocks in the United States. The main thrust of the legislation was to put a curb on speculative buying by requiring tighter disclosures on the terms of a particular sale. In short, all of the risk that an investment might carry needed to be part of any sale that used interstate commerce. The act also provided any investor who was defrauded the avenue to sue the issuer of the sale.

During the first 100 days, Roosevelt also started a regular feature of his presidency that, like the 100-day benchmark, became the standard for future presidents. Each week, Roosevelt did a weekly update on the initiatives that the government was enacting. He also offered words of encouragement to Americans about their current situation and assured them he was doing all he could to turn the country around. These "Fireside Chats" were amazingly successful. Radio was still a relatively new medium for many Americans and such direct contact from the president was unheard of before. Many survivors of the Great Depression remembered listening as a family to the radio to hear what the president, their president, had to say.

The flurry of activity of these 100 days has never been matched by another incoming president. The amount of major legislation reaching various sectors of American life proved to the people of the United States that the new president wasn't all talk. He was good to his campaign word. Not everything worked, but like Roosevelt said, they were willing to try and try again. The financial sector, unemployment, and rural areas all benefited from the first round of legislation within the New Deal. Two other major pieces of legislation came during Roosevelt's first term. Both were cornerstones of the New Deal policy and both are still in effect today. The first dealt with people who were employed and the second for people who have finished working or can no longer work.

The National Labor Relations Act (NLRA), also known as the Wagner Act, established the National Labor Relations Board (NLRB) and provided federal safeguards for collective bargaining, unionizing, and striking. The act defined and tried to stop unfair labor practices, and included protections for employees who testify against their employer in criminal or civil court. The act did not cover workers employed by the railways or working in the federal government. In order to appease Southern lawmakers, domestic workers and agricultural workers were also excluded from the protections of the Wagner Act. These two professions were singled out because the majority of domestic workers and agricultural workers in the South were African Americans.

The other monumental piece of legislation passed in 1935 was the Social Security Act. This act provided former employees a stipend after they had worked, made provisions for unemployment, gave aid to families with dependent children, had provisions for maternal and child welfare, provided for public health, and provided assistance to the blind. It was one of the most ambitious policies ever enacted by the United States government. Until the advent of Social Security, American workers often needed to remain employed well into their advanced age. Often, employees worked until they quite simply couldn't work any longer. If they were lucky, there were savings available, but especially in the Depression with bank closings, that was less likely. In order to pass the legislation, like the NLRA, domestic and agricultural workers were excluded from the legislation.

In both cases, the NLRA and the Social Security Act, the Republican Party and various business groups vehemently opposed the efforts. In the case of the NLRA, employers were especially critical of the Relations Board pro-union bias. While the idea was to be an impartial judge in labor disputes, the NLRB did seem to lean more toward employees than employers. In the case of Social Security, the main criticism was that the program was simply socialism under a different name. Most conservatives in Congress voiced such concerns and voted accordingly, though the bill still passed.

As FDR's first term came to an end, it was hard not to see it as a success, at least as far as enacting an agenda on the national stage. How successful the programs were was a bit more muddled of a picture. Hundreds of thousands were given work, albeit sometimes only temporarily, and people, especially the elderly, were brought back from the brink of great suffering. Programs were enacted to help both urban and rural people, and something resembling confidence was being shown toward the financial sector of the economy. Unemployment, however, remained stubbornly high. Businesses were still not able to bring workers back in large part because people were still unable to buy goods at pre-Depression rates. The situation may have felt better and even looked better, but there was still a long way to go.

Chapter 5: FDR's Second Term— Challenges and Critics

Though no election is a sure thing, in 1936 there was little doubt that Franklin Roosevelt would win a second term. The economy was still struggling, but it was on the upswing. More importantly, the majority of Americans approved of the job Roosevelt was doing. They believed that the aristocrat from New York was the best choice to lead the nation out of the worst economic disaster in the country's history.

The Republican challenger was the governor of Kansas, Alf Landon, who famously remarked during the campaign, "Everywhere I go I see Americans." Obvious observations aside, it is a wonder if Landon actually saw anyone during the campaign. He rarely traveled outside of his home state, while Roosevelt was engaged throughout the campaign season, traveling across the country. Though there was some discussion that it could be a close race, even the most ardent Republican could have predicted the results. Roosevelt won in a landslide, capturing 60 percent of the popular vote, carrying 46 of the 48 states, and capturing 523 of a possible 531 electoral votes. It remains one of the largest margins of victory ever. Along with Roosevelt's crushing victory, the Democrats took even more seats in Congress.

With such a mandate, Roosevelt and Congress were ready to enact further aspects of the New Deal. Unfortunately for FDR, much of his second term was occupied with his dealings with the Supreme Court. According to Roosevelt and his allies, the court was the one stumbling block to keeping the New Deal intact. Starting in 1935, a string of court cases went against Roosevelt and New Deal initiatives. The most notable reverses were against the National Industrial Recovery Act and the Agricultural Adjustment Act. Leading the charge on the court, headed by Chief Justice Charles Evans Hughes, were four conservative justices, later coined the "Four Horsemen." These justices, Pierce Butler, James Clark McReynolds, George Sutherland, and Willis Van Devanter, respectively were seen as the largest opponents of the New Deal. Three of the four were appointed by Republican presidents. The fourth, McReynolds, was appointed by Woodrow Wilson, but was a conservative Southerner. The first case, *Panama Refining Company v. Ryan*, declared that the National Industrial Recovery Act restriction on interstate and international trade of petroleum surpluses was unconstitutional. Chief Justice Hughes wrote the majority opinion and ruled that specific parameters needed to be set in such cases and not at the discretion of the executive branch. In sum, it was a check on Roosevelt's power.

The court went even further against the NIRA in the *Schechter Poultry Corp. v. United States* case. In the unanimous decision, also written by Chief Justice Hughes, the NIRA legislation granted powers to the executive branch that were enumerated for the legislative branch of the government. More damning was the ruling that even the provisions within the law that were within the power of Congress violated the Commerce Clause, which gave Congress the power, albeit limited power, to regulate trade within states.

Another signature piece of the New Deal was declared unconstitutional the following year in 1936. The court ruled in *United States v. Butler* that the Agricultural Adjustment Act violated the Constitution by levying an unfair tax on food producers and went beyond the scope of national government power by regulating how much a farmer could grow. Between 1934 and 1936, of the 16 cases pertaining to New Deal legislation, 10 went against Roosevelt and the New Deal.

In 1937, after his reelection, Roosevelt tried to pass legislation that would tilt the court in his favor. He noted that there was no specific law or requirement that the Supreme Court be made up of nine members.

There were various iterations of the number on the court, but by 1869, nine was the established number. Roosevelt tried to "pack" the court with nominees of his choosing in order to protect New Deal programs. The plan called for the president to nominate a justice for every justice over the age of 70. The president was limited to six such appointments, but could conceivably gain six favorable seats on a court of fifteen potential members. Roosevelt brought his idea to the public during one of his Fireside Chats. He argued that the court was out of touch with reality and with the Constitution. He further argued that his plan was needed to save the New Deal, save the nation, and save the Supreme Court itself.

Reaction was swift and largely negative. Republicans and conservatives saw it as an unprecedented power grab. Many Democrats felt the same way and went public with their feelings. The public was very much against the idea as well. Unlike so many of Roosevelt's proposals and ideas, the plan to pack the court met with only a minority of support from voters. A massive letter writing campaign was launched opposing the bill. It was easily the largest and most costly error of Roosevelt's presidency. It turned many former allies against the administration in Congress, and public opinion of the president suffered as well.

What is ironic in the case of court packing were two events. First the Panama case and Schechter case were unanimous rulings, 9-0. Even with six friendly judges, both still would have been losses for the president. The second event was that Justice Van Devanter, one of the Four Horsemen, retired in 1937. Roosevelt was now presented with appointing a justice, making the "liberal" wing four, the "conservative" three, with two swing voters. As Roosevelt's presidency continued, he would appoint nine justices to the court. More than any other president, Roosevelt shaped the direction of American law for decades by appointing more justices than anyone else. In the end, Roosevelt didn't need a scheme to tilt the court in his favor, just time.

The court-packing controversy saw a great deal of criticism directed at President Roosevelt, but this wasn't the first time he had faced critics. Two, in particular, a demagogue and a Catholic priest, were particularly vocal about the president. They both had considerable followings and considerable platforms to get their anti-Roosevelt message to the public. One hailed from the Deep South, the other from the industrial Midwest, specifically Detroit, Michigan. Huey Long and Father Charles Coughlin weren't the only critics of Roosevelt but were perhaps the most widely known. Both started out as supporters of the New Deal, but soon soured on the program and its architect.

Huey Long was a politician from Louisiana who was known as "The Kingfish" in his native state. Though the name was taken from the famous radio show, "Amos 'n' Andy," there was very little that was humorous about Long and his hold on Louisiana politics. After winning the governorship in 1928, Long consolidated his power by removing any and everyone in the government that stood in opposition to him. He built an enormous patronage system that made practically everyone working in state government loyal to him. Long was not popular with the landed-elite, but in the rest of the state, he was unopposed.

Long was a vehement critic of big business and the financial system of the United States. Much of his policies in Louisiana reflected the same ideals that would define the New Deal in 1933. Long, an elected senator from Louisiana in 1932, was a vocal supporter of Roosevelt and the New Deal. Perhaps he was too vocal. Roosevelt appreciated the help, but also distanced himself from the populist from the South. When the National Industrial Recovery Act was proposed, Long believed that is was too soft on employers and corporations.

Roosevelt all but cut Long out from New Deal strategy and referred to him as "one of the most dangerous men in America." Long continued to be an outspoken critic of American businesses and elites and proposed a new program, "Share Our Wealth," which would limit personal fortunes and redistribute wealth to every American. Not gaining many allies in Congress, Long turned to the people and started the Share Our Wealth Society. By 1935, there were over 7 million members with 27,000 local chapters. Long often reached radio audiences over 25 million strong with his message of wealth distribution.

It is debated whether or not Long was eyeing a presidential run in 1936, but it wasn't out of the realm of possibility. He had a strong base of support, a national platform, and a campaigning ability that was second to none, including Roosevelt. He even had substantial allies both inside and outside of politics. Unfortunately for Huey Long and the Share Our Wealth Society, he had a lot of enemies. One of those enemies, more specifically the son-in-law of one of those enemies, shot and killed Huey Long in September of 1935.

One of Long's allies, and critic of Roosevelt, was Father Charles Coughlin. He was a parish priest in suburban Detroit and began his radio career speaking out against the Ku Klux Klan which was operating in Michigan at the time. His anti-Klan stance and style attracted CBS, and they began to broadcast his show nationally.

With the advent of the Depression, Coughlin spoke more and more about political and economic issues and the need for the national government to do more. With the election of 1932 and the rise of Roosevelt and the New Deal, Coughlin thought his prayers had been answered.

By 1934, like Huey Long, Father Coughlin was disillusioned with Roosevelt and what he considered the slow pace of the New Deal. Coughlin also felt that the president was going beyond the Constitution and was too enamored with capitalism to be truly effective. The priest founded the National Union for Social Justice (NUSJ), which was dedicated to wealth redistribution, nationalizing certain industries, and reforming the entire financial system. The NUSJ and Coughlin were particularly critical of banks and the Federal Reserve System, which he felt was mostly responsible for the Depression.

As the decade continued, Coughlin still had strong support among his listeners. That was about to change, however. As early as 1936, Coughlin started expressing anti-Semitic views and sharing conspiracy theories about Jewish control of the economy. He was continually linked to fascists in Europe, and while Coughlin tried to distance himself from pro-fascist groups in the United States, he sometimes defended Nazi actions. When World War II broke out in Europe, Coughlin was a staunch isolationist. When the United States entered the war in 1941, Coughlin still remained opposed to US involvement. His opposition was seen as sympathetic to the enemy, and steps were started to take him off the air and tried for sedition. The Catholic hierarchy, however, stepped in and ordered Coughlin to end his show and return to being simply a parish priest. In the end, that is what Coughlin did, remaining as a pastor until his retirement in 1966.

Chapter 6: The Culture of the Depression

The Great Depression spawned a number of cultural movements in the United States. Many associate the decade of the Depression with radicalism and political culture. Many artists joined political parties, especially the Communist Party, and expressed their politics in their writings, artwork, films, and plays. Even those that didn't join political movements were influenced by current events.

Though the Communist Party saw its greatest growth during the Great Depression, there was another, less organized aspect of 1930s culture that was equally profound. Many Americans looked to the nation's past for a remedy to the current situation. The idea of discovering what it meant to be an American, what was the American way of life, was a question many tried to answer.

In both approaches, that of radicalism and traditionalism, the overriding theme of the cultural landscape of the Depression was one of coping with hard times. Americans found a way through various media (radio, film, and music to name a few) to find a way of dealing with the harsh realities of the day. Not all of these outlets were just concerned with the New Deal and current events. There were many means of entertainment that were designed to simply help people forget for a while. Escapism was especially helpful to many throughout the era and just as important as other works. Mickey Mouse and Dorothy from *The Wizard of Oz* had just as significant a role in the culture of the 1930s as the Popular Front and the works of John Steinbeck.

Though the medium of radio was already popular in the 1920s, the 1930s was perhaps the golden age of radio. By the 1930s, all of the nation's Major League Baseball teams had broadcasts. There were many cultural and educational programs, including broadcasts of opera and informational programing. The most popular broadcasts, however, were the variety shows and soap operas. The variety hours were reminiscent of vaudeville shows that once traveled across the country. Musical acts, comical skits, and other performances all made their way into family living rooms on a nightly basis.

The soap opera was the programming that dominated the airwaves though. Shows like *The Goldbergs*, which highlighted the lives of an immigrant family living in New York, gained millions of listeners. For many Americans, they could either remember similar circumstances or had family members who lived such events. People identified with the characters and wanted to know what would happen next. Other programs followed a similar formula, all designed to keep people tuned in. Some shows, such as *XXXX*, contained more melodrama and highlighted an almost fantasy life of wealth and fame, but it still kept audiences coming back. A day of hard work, or worse no work, was made better by the familiar rhythms of the serialized drama.

Familiar rhythms were a key to another avenue of entertainment throughout the decade, music. The 1920s saw the advent of jazz as the popular music of the time, but the music of the 1930s expanded on the ideas of jazz and became a bigger sound. Swing music was the music of the 1930s. Big bands played a more dance-friendly style of music, and though money was tight, people still flocked to see, listen, and most importantly dance to new music as often as they could. Dance halls enticed people to come to their places by running contests called dance marathons. Couples would dance until there was only one couple left on the floor. They were the winner and usually won a cash prize. It may not have been the best way to make a living, but it was surely a fun way to earn some extra money on the weekend.

The motion picture industry of the 1930s had aspects of all of these cultural threads, escapism, radicalism, and a search for tradition. In the case of escapism, no company is a better example than Walt Disney Studios. Disney's first success came from the creation of the character that has remained a symbol of the company, Mickey Mouse. First in black and white and then in color, Mickey Mouse short films were extremely popular. But Walt Disney wanted animation to do more, be more. In 1937, the Walt Disney Company produced its first full-length feature, *Snow White and the Seven Dwarves.* It was an instant success. Audiences fell in love with the story, and it was the top grossing movie in 1938. *The Wizard of Oz* from 1939 was also a wonderfully escapist film, with the central idea of recovery, of being safe.

Another genre of film that was enormously popular in the 1930s and was part of the escapist tradition of cinema were monster films. Universal Studios in particular became known for the cast of monster films they produced, including *Frankenstein* (1931), *Dracula* (1931), *The Mummy* (1932), and *The Invisible Man* (1933). All of these movies revolved around similar plots, a great supernatural threat, and the heroes working together to save the world. It was a reassuring message in an otherwise uncertain time. None of these films, however, captured the imagination like *King Kong* (1933), the film some still consider the best horror movie of all time.

Not all of Hollywood's output was strictly of an escapist nature. Many films of the period included social commentary. Obvious messages like in *Robin Hood* (1938) highlighted the concept of wealth redistribution and the upper classes being the enemy of the people. The concept of the power of the everyman was also explored in films like *Mr. Smith Goes to Washington* (1939). Other films, such as *Duck Soup* (1933), contained social commentary about international tensions of the period, and *Modern Times* (1936) starring Charlie Chaplin was a critique of the impersonal nature of the industrial workplace and economy. No series of films or film stars expressed the ethos of the New Deal better than Will Rogers.

Calling himself the "#1 New Dealer," Will Rogers' public persona and popular films had a blend of populism, radical traditionalism, and the redistribution of wealth contained in the stories. The 1930s audience had lost faith in the wealthy and political leaders, but the characters portrayed by Rogers in twenty-four different films reaffirmed the place and power of the community. The lead characters stop putting their faith in Wall Street and corporations and instead put their faith in Americanism. Rogers, the person not the character, brought legitimacy to the message by being deeply rooted in the history of the United States, especially those that were historically marginalized. Rogers was quoted as saying, "My people didn't come over here on the Mayflower," alluding to the fact that he grew up on an Indian reservation in Oklahoma as a part of the Cherokee Nation. His embrace and celebration of what it meant to be an American carried more weight than others. He was more American than the white European upper class that had led the nation to its current predicament. Recent immigrants, African Americans, and lower-class whites all found resonance in the message of Will Rogers.

Will Rogers represented radical traditionalism, but there was also a trend within American culture that focused on finding meaning from the past by looking in the annals of history to see what was good about America and what could be useful for the current state of affairs. *Gone with the Wind* (1936 novel; 1939 film) was a celebration of the Antebellum South. Though the main plot was an epic love story, the theme of rising up after catastrophe was a key element of the appeal of the book and film. If Scarlett (the South) could regain her prominence after devastation, then perhaps the United States could do the same.

Similarly, the works of Laura Ingalls Wilder evoked a similar ethos. Semi-autobiographical in nature, the stories of Wilder tell the tale of a pioneering family as they made their way west in search of a better life. Through a series of adventures, confronting nature, Native Americans, and economic hardship, Wilder and her family were able to persevere and eventually prosper. Written throughout the 1930s, the "Little House" books provided a uniquely American story, one that many middle-class Americans could relate to. They saw in Wilder's story aspects of their own past. If they, like their pioneering forebears, could survive the harsh world of the American West, then perhaps they could similarly weather the storm of the Great Depression.

An overall theme in much of American culture during the Depression was a search for what was the American way of life. To this end, many traditional aspects of American culture were investigated and celebrated. Folk music was of particular interest to cultural curators such as John Lomax and his son Neil. In addition, there was a substantial interest in American folk art, such as nineteenth-century furniture making and quilting. Books, such as *American Humor: A Study in National Character* (1931) by Constance Rourke and *The Flowering of New England* (1936) by Van Wyck Brooks, tried to discover what were the underpinnings of modern America. These books and many other cultural works sought to find out what made America so great, beyond its financial, industrial, and innovative successes of the previous decade. The aspects that still survived after the Depression showed that material success could be very fleeting.

This search for the "real" America was most evident in the resurgence of religion into American life. 1934 is considered a pivotal year in the history of religion in the United States. Evangelical Protestantism saw the greatest strides during the time period. The overall message from many faiths was the establishment of the theological hierarchy that many saw as abandoned in the decade before. Further, it stressed the personal aspects of failure rather than the idea of a systemic failure within the United States. The American way of life was not at fault, but the individual had failed.

Alcoholics Anonymous, founded in 1935, is a strong example of this notion. The individual alcoholic has a problem with drinking, not all of society. In order to recover from alcoholism, the alcoholic needed to "get right with God." The group was founded by a former stockbroker, Bill Wilson, and a proctologist, Dr. Bob Smith. The two met when Wilson was on a business trip to Akron, where Smith practiced medicine. The two met and developed an approach to help the individual alcoholic through personal and group interactions. Their approach was codified in 1939 with the publication of the book, *Alcoholics Anonymous*, where the group got its name. Eventually the group spread across the United States and eventually around the world.

Similarly, the rise of the self-help books, such as *How to Win Friends and Influence People* (1936) by Dale Carnegie, was another example of the individual being at fault, not society. As the New Deal was making wholesale changes to the American economy and other more extreme voices were calling for greater changes, Carnegie emphasized working on one's personal relationships to improve not only one's current situation, but to improve society as a whole, without disruptions to the greater socio-economic structure. Another self-help author like Carnegie, Henry C. Link, published *The Return to Religion* (1936) which bridges the ideas of religion and personality enhancement. In his work, Link even developed a way to discover how effective a person was through their "personality quotient." The message was clear; having a winning personality, not systemic change, was the way out of the Depression.

Just as important to the alcoholic and religious organizations was the idea of working with others. The foundation that many sought as the American way of life was being part of something greater, of joining, of fitting in. In AA's case that was working and meeting with other alcoholics; however, many other groups flourished during the 1930s, if not for completely altruistic or political reasons, but to simply keep busy. However, it was these commitments to others, to organizations, that became the calling card of the decade.

The concept of working with others, of joining together, was also part of a more radical agenda. It would not be fair to say that everyone that joined political organizations in the 1930s was simply doing so to keep busy until employment returned. As the Depression deepened, many intellectuals in the United States openly questioned the viability of capitalism and the western tradition of liberalism. Philosophers such as John Dewey openly questioned traditional modes of thinking about American government and the economy. They looked at the new Soviet Union and saw success. Joseph Stalin seemed to have brought order to a chaotic region of the world while the west was on the brink of collapse. As the Depression worsened under Hoover, many advocated for the abandonment of private enterprise entirely.

When Roosevelt was swept into office and the New Deal became the focal point of government action, more radical thinkers felt that the program did not go far enough. They believed that Roosevelt, himself a scion of wealth and privilege, was too tied to old Republican notions of capitalism. In their view, the New Deal was just as disorganized as capitalism itself. These radical ideas found allies in a number of artists throughout the 1930s. There was a drive to find a true working-class culture within the United States. Authors such as Upton Sinclair, Richard Wright, and James Agee demanded action from the government and society. Perhaps the best-known novel of the period was *The Grapes of Wrath* (1939) by John Steinbeck, which is one of the harshest criticisms of American society that has ever been produced.

According to historian Michael Denning in his work *The Cultural Front* (1996), the 1930s was a second American Renaissance of American culture, largely a product of and influenced by the working class. Or, as he calls it, "the proletarianization of American culture." Much of this working-class culture was an extension of a movement emanating from the Soviet Union, referred to as the Popular Front.

Before discussing in greater detail the Popular Front and its cultural implications, a brief discussion of the Communist Party, specifically the Communist Party USA (CPUSA) is in order. The CPUSA was founded in 1919 as a split of the more left wing of the Socialist Labor Party. It was not the best time to declare a new communist party in the United States. 1919 was a very anti-communist period within the United States, culminating in the Palmer Raids and the First Red Scare. Because of the crackdown on leftist activities from the federal government, especially through the newly formed Federal Bureau of Investigation (FBI) and internecine fighting among party members, CPUSA had only about 6,000 members in 1932.

During the Great Depression, many became disillusioned with capitalism and the structure of the US government. Membership in CPUSA grew by the thousands, reaching a high point later in the decade with 55,000 members. The election of Roosevelt and the New Deal was also a boon for the CPUSA, especially after the party stopped being such a vocal opposition to FDR and Democratic policies. The CPUSA still opposed racial segregation and other racist policies of Southern Democrats, but the upsurge in union membership throughout the decade was seen as a net gain when considering the overall goal of revolution from capitalism. By the election of 1936, the CPUSA didn't openly campaign for the Democrats but did see them as the better alternative.

International developments led to a call for even greater unity among communists, classic liberals, socialists, and centrists. The rise of fascism in Europe in countries like Italy, Spain, and especially Germany made the Communist International (COMINTERN) issue a directive that all communist parties in the world should work together to defeat fascism by creating a Popular Front. Within the United States, the Popular Front was more than just the CPUSA. There was a great deal of activity within the labor movement and also among African Americans living in Harlem.

The political goal of the Popular Front was a united global resistance to fascism. In order to carry out that goal, the Popular Front engaged in various activities, from organizing and protesting to campaigning, and especially cultural outreach. The ideal movement was a combination of proletariats, writers, artists, and intellectuals reaching out to the masses of the US population. One of the main ways to do this was to engage in agitprop, or agitation propaganda. Various artists, such as Woody Guthrie and Paul Robeson, performed various anti-fascist songs and spoke out against fascism and racial injustice.

At various points in the 1930s, the cultural activities of the Popular Front were the proletariat avant-garde, a movement culture, part of the state-sponsored culture and part of the mass culture. Young artists formed clubs and societies to promulgate new directions in leftist art. As part of the movement, many of those same artists performed for union gatherings and at demonstrations. As mentioned in an earlier chapter, many writers, actors, and others were employed in the various artist projects under the WPA.

This combination of art and activism is best exemplified by the unionization of many Hollywood players. The Screen Actors Guild (SAG) was founded in 1933. The Directors Guild of America was founded (as the Screen Directors Guild) in 1936. Throughout the 1930s, screen animators attempted to organize and met with limited success. Their strikes, however, did feature some of the best picket signs ever seen at a strike with favorite cartoon characters saying union slogans.

The Popular Front and the other aspects of the Great Depression era culture make it one of the most vibrant times of American culture. It was not a monolith of leftist propaganda, nor was it simply a time of looking backward, idealizing an American way of life that never really existed. The harsh realities of the time had a great effect on the materials produced in many different genres and art forms. By investigating the culture of the period, we are given a different lens by which we can understand the complexities of the Great Depression and those that experienced it.

Chapter 7: Sports and the Great Depression

Sporting heroes of the 1930s reflected a departure from the glamor of the heroes of the 1920s. Babe Ruth ended his career in 1934, and the baseball player who became the face of baseball couldn't be more different than Ruth. Lou Gehrig was everything that Ruth wasn't. Quiet, reserved, Gehrig went about baseball much more like a workman than a diva. During the 1930s, the number of games that Gehrig played consecutively earned him the nickname, "The Iron Horse." It was that aspect of Gehrig that especially made him so popular during the Depression. His dedication to his job and not taking a day off inspired others to not only appreciate his hard work but to find inspiration from his steady example. When having a job was a victory in and of itself, being steadfast like Gehrig was seen as the ideal.

But Gehrig was more than a simple workman. He was one of the elite players of his era. At first with Babe Ruth, then without the famed slugger, Gehrig led the Yankees to three consecutive World Series championships. He was the league's most valuable player in 1936. He was still playing at a high level in 1937, but there was a considerable drop-off in 1938, and then the unthinkable happened in 1939. Lou Gehrig told his manager to remove him from the starting lineup for the benefit of the team. The Iron Horse couldn't answer the call.

The diagnosis of amyotrophic lateral sclerosis (ALS) shocked the nation. Not only was it a very rare disease, but its debilitating effects were the antithesis of the way Gehrig had approached his craft. A man known for his durability and strength was literally wasting away. Gehrig, however, became perhaps even more of a hero as he faced his future. On July 4th, 1939, Gehrig gave one of the most memorable speeches in American history. The most famous image of the event was of Gehrig, looking frail and standing before the sellout crowd, telling them that he believed he was "the luckiest man on the face of the earth." Gehrig's grace in facing such adversity cemented his legacy as one of the most beloved sports figures of the 1930s and the twentieth century.

Baseball was still the most popular sport in the United States during the 1930s, and Gehrig was one of its biggest stars, representing the everyman with his work ethic. The St. Louis Cardinals and their famed "Gashouse Gang," on the other hand, represented an almost escapist perspective. Unlike the stalwart and businesslike New York Yankees and their leader Gehrig, the Cardinals were a fast and loose outfit, led by a group of brothers that almost sounded like the cast of a Marx Brothers film. Dizzy and Daffy Dean led the team, and as their nicknames suggested, they were more eccentric than the average baseball player. The 1934 team took on the brothers' eccentric persona, and other members of the team were given nicknames by the press as well. The team had a grubby appearance and played the game hard. They outlasted the New York Giants to win the National League and went on to win the World Series over the Detroit Tigers, 4 games to 3.

It was definitely the era of the hard worker. In addition to baseball figures, a horse also captured the imagination of the American people during the 1930s. Seabiscuit was an undersized, slightly below average horse for much of the early part of his career, but in 1936 he became almost unbeatable. Seabiscuit had some success on the eastern part of the racing circuit, but with a move out west, he starting winning handily. In 1937, he won 11 of the 15 races in which he was entered. Seabiscuit was the top money winner for the year as well. The winner of the Triple Crown that year, War Admiral, was named horse of the year.

In 1938, Seabiscuit had another successful year, even though his regular jockey had a series of serious injuries. At the end of the year, in what was called the "Race of the Century," Seabiscuit met War Admiral head-to-head at the Pimlico Race Track. It was a close race, with the lead changing from Seabiscuit to War Admiral on the backstretch. However, on the final 200-yard home stretch, Seabiscuit sped up and took the lead, eventually winning by four lengths. The race was well attended, with spectators jamming the infield, and it was broadcast on radio. It was the crowning achievement of Seabiscuit's career. The horse was retired in 1940 and put to stud for the rest of his life.

Seabiscuit was not the most graceful or beautiful horse, but in him, people saw a racer who worked harder than his competition and were inspired by his feats on the race track. Before his success in 1936, many of the established horse owners and trainers had given up on Seabiscuit, but his owner, Charles Howard, believed in him. Like so many heroes of the era, Seabiscuit was seen as an underdog, a racer who just needed a little faith and an opportunity to become a success.

Similarly, James J. Braddock, the Cinderella Man, was not much of a fighter in the early part of his career but became a hero to many during the decade. Like so many Americans, Braddock struggled during the Depression to find steady work. It appeared his boxing career had ended with a broken right hand. Due to a late cancellation, Braddock was asked to fill in for another boxer. Defying the odds, Braddock won the bout, and over the next year put together a string of victories to earn a shot at the heavyweight title. Coming in as a 10-1 underdog, Braddock upset the champ, Max Baer, and won.

Braddock's appeal came from his rags to riches storyline, but also from the hard work he put in to achieve the title. When out of boxing, Braddock worked intermittently on the docks in New York and had difficulties at times providing food for his family. Braddock was also very frank when discussing his hardships prior to boxing and how lucky he was, inspiring countless fans with his story. Like Gehrig, Braddock was the everyman, the hard worker, and, like Seabiscuit, if given the chance, could do great things. More than anything, this was an ideal that workers in the Depression gravitated toward. Like their larger-than-life heroes, if given the opportunity, they could, on an albeit smaller scale, prove that they were worthy of employment and recognition.

Braddock held the heavyweight title for two years but didn't face any challengers in that time. When a contender did present himself, Braddock lost the title in his first defense. He was knocked out in the eighth round. It was the only time Braddock was knocked out outright, not a technical knockout. The hard-to-put-down Braddock met his match in one of the greatest boxers of all time, Joe Louis. Young and fast with devastating power, Braddock never stood a chance. "The Brown Bomber," as Louis came to be known, was a sensation.

Louis was part of the African American experience of the twentieth century. He was born in rural Alabama. When he was twelve years old, his mother, seeking better opportunities for her and her family, joined the thousands of African Americans moving to the industrial cities of the North as part of the Great Migration. His brother worked for Ford Motor Company and Joe did as well for a short time. Boxing, however, was his true calling. He began his amateur career at 17 and in two years debuted as a professional. Though not officially segregated, professional boxing was not exactly open to African Americans, who were often serious contenders for championships. Many within the white boxing community, promoters, managers, and fans alike, still resented the title reign of Jack Johnson, an African American fighter who challenged Jim Crow laws and social mores by openly defying segregation policies and dating white women. In response, Louis and his management team strictly controlled his public image with the overall goal of gaining access to much more lucrative fights.

The strategy worked. By 1935, Louis was making his way up the rankings in the heavyweight division. He was also becoming the most popular athlete among African Americans. With each victory, African American communities across the country would celebrate "their champion." Louis' appeal, however, crossed racial boundaries. This was especially the case when fighting boxers from other countries, especially those that held decidedly un-American beliefs. The first fight that took on a political dimension was against former champion Italian Primo Carnera. To the public, Carnera represented the fascist government of Mussolini, who was in the process of invading Ethiopia. Louis was seen as the defender of democracy and of the small African country that was being invaded. Louis knocked Carnera out in six rounds, and it was seen as a symbolic victory for oppressed countries and for people of African descent. The greatest rival of Louis' career was also from a fascist country. The bouts between Louis and Max Schmeling became legendary.

Schmeling and Louis fought twice, in 1936 and 1938. Both fights had electric atmospheres with geopolitical implications. In the first fight, both fighters were top contenders for the heavyweight title, but neither held the championship at the time. Louis entered the fight on a 24-bout victory streak and took Schmeling lightly, not training nearly as vigorously as he normally did. Schmeling was ready and defeated Louis by knockout in the 12th of 15 rounds. Schmeling returned to Germany as a national hero and "proof" of the superiority of the Aryan race.

After Louis won the title from Braddock, the fight he needed to prove his legitimacy was a rematch with Schmeling. While the 1936 bout was a large event in its own right, the 1938 rematch is now remembered as one of the most historic sporting events of the twentieth century. Louis trained as hard as he ever had for the fight, wanting to put to rest any doubt that he was the best fighter in the world. In addition, Louis felt an immense amount of pressure to beat the representative of Nazi Germany. Even Franklin Roosevelt pressured Louis, saying that fighters like him were what was needed to beat Germany. For his part, Schmeling was accompanied by a Nazi official who proclaimed that it would be impossible for a black man to defeat the racially superior Schmeling.

Under such popular and political pressure, Louis delivered on all fronts. He defeated Schmeling in the first round, knocking him down three times. Schmeling's trainer saw enough of the beating and threw in the towel, ending the fight. Celebrations erupted across the nation, especially in African American communities. For many, it was vindication of racial equality that they had been striving for their entire lives. In a more general sense, it made Americans believe that despite their differences and hardships of the Depression the nation was strong and if need be able to fight in a war. Interestingly, when the United States entered World War Two, Louis enlisted as a private. Over the course of the war, he traveled over 20,000 miles, participating in countless boxing exhibitions and boosting morale for the United States forces.

Like Joe Louis, another African American athlete symbolically took on Nazism. The 1936 Olympics were held in Berlin, and the competition was intended to be a showcase for Adolf Hitler and his Nazi regime. Not only was the Olympics a chance to show the world how far Germany had come since the First World War, it was also a chance to demonstrate the genetic superiority of the Aryan race. Instead, Jesse Owens dominated the games like few athletes ever did. He won four gold medals, three in individual events and one in the 4 x 100 relay. Like the Louis victory over Schmeling two years later, African Americans saw Owens as an example of their racial equality and of the absurdity of racial segregation. It also exposed to many people around the world to the flawed logic of a superior race.

Some controversy still surrounds what happened after Owens won his medals in Berlin. It was reported at the time that Adolf Hitler snubbed Owens and his fellow African American winners. Owens later maintained that Hitler did not snub the competitors but instead needed to be elsewhere. Robert Vann, the editor for the African American newspaper *The Pittsburgh Courier* wrote that he saw Hitler wave to Owens as he left the stadium. Finally, one of Hitler's ministers wrote that Hitler was annoyed by the victories of non-Aryan people and believed such racers, who had an unfair physical advantage, should be banned from future games. All of these may be true to some degree. Owens didn't believe that Hitler snubbed him, and Hitler left the stadium to avoid further embarrassment of watching the "master race" continue losing.

What brought the hypocrisy of racial injustice to light was when Jesse Owens returned home from the Olympics. As the majority of African Americans were supporting Franklin Roosevelt in his bid for reelection in the fall of 1936, Owens refused, noting that the president didn't send any congratulations to him after his victories, nor did the president extend an invitation to the White House. Instead, Owens campaigned for FDR's Republican opponent, Alf Landon. Furthermore, while in Germany, Owens could move about freely, not segregated from the other Olympians. When he and his wife arrived at the Waldorf-Astoria Hotel in New York, Owens was refused at the front door, even though he was being honored for his Olympic victories. He was forced to enter through the kitchen entrance.

Perhaps the greatest athlete of the 1930s was an Olympic champion, Amateur Athletic Union (AAU) basketball All-American, and one of the greatest golfers of all time. Mildred Ella Didrikson, better known as Babe, seemed to be able to compete in any sport that she entered. She won two gold medals and one silver in track and field during the 1932 Summer Olympics. Capitalizing on her fame as an Olympic champion, Didrikson pitched in a number of major league spring training games in 1934. She also played with the barnstorming team from Michigan, the House of David. It was in 1935, however, that Didrikson found the sport that she was possibly best at, golf. Well before the founding of the Ladies Professional Golf Association (LPGA) in 1950, Didrikson was competing at an elite level on the links. In 1938, she entered the Los Angeles Open and is recognized as the first woman to compete in an event against men. Later in her career, she would enter three more men's tournaments and make the cut in two of them.

Didrikson was a pioneer for women athletics and she inspired future women. It wasn't just her prowess on the course or track oval that was inspiring. Even though she was a popular attraction while out touring, she also faced a great deal of discrimination. She was called unnatural and manly. Reporters often commented on her masculine looks and called her homely. Didrikson not only took it in stride but seemed to thrive on the comments. Like the other famous Babe from sports, Didrikson was bold and brash with a wit that bordered on ribald at times. She changed the way the public viewed female athletes, especially women golfers. She was not some petite society gal. Didrikson was strong, and she was proud to show her strength off to the crowds. It is commonly accepted that she had a lesbian relationship with one of her fellow golfers. Because of the social climate at the time, Didrikson was not able to be open about her sexuality. She was recognized as an LGBTQ pioneer by being inducted on the Legacy Walk in Chicago, Illinois in 2014.

Like other aspects of culture in the Depression, sports played a significant role in the lives of Americans. As a means of escape or inspiration, sports in the 1930s, like other forms of entertainment, provided a valuable means of coping with the realities of the economic crisis. The inspiration went beyond the personal and was inspiration for the nation as it became more and more involved in the currents leading to World War Two. Like other eras, the sporting heroes of the 1930s were a reflection of their time. Hard working and often underdogs, either in their sport (Braddock and Seabiscuit) or in society at large (Louis and Owens), the heroes of the 1930s were relatable to average Americans. People saw hard work paying off and wanted to believe that if they were given a chance, they could prove their worth like their idols.

Chapter 8: The Outlaw Celebrity in the Great Depression

American society and culture have a long history of interest in outlaws and criminals. From the days of the Western frontier until the Prohibition era, there was always an interest in the seedier side of American society. This interest continued and some argue reached a peak during the Great Depression. Especially in the Midwest and Mississippi Valley regions of the country, a fascination with outlaws catapulted some criminals from local celebrities to American legends that still capture our imaginations. Though the real motives of these criminals were far from altruistic, the popular appeal of them stemmed from the perception that they were rebelling against the power structure that many Americans saw as the real criminal. It is no surprise that the favored crime by so many of these lawbreakers was robbing banks. Sometimes operating as a gang and sometimes alone, all of these outlaws still resonate in popular culture.

In one case, it was more than just a criminal gang, but a family affair. After meeting in prison, Fred Barker and Alvin Karpis formed the Barker-Karpis Gang. Shortly after getting a crew together, Fred Barker brought in his brother, Arthur "Doc" Barker. Though there was a rotating cast of associates, the Barkers and Karpis decided which banks to rob. As their reputation grew, they decided that robbing banks had become too risky and decided to try their hand at kidnapping instead. In two high-profile cases, both involving men from the brewing industry, the Barker-Karpis Gang made off with close to $300,000 dollars.

The second kidnapping turned out to be the gang's undoing. The money used to pay the ransom had been sequenced by the FBI, and authorities were able to track down the criminals. It is here that another fascinating aspect of the gang came to light. When federal agents moved on the house where they were hiding, only Fred Barker and his mother were present. An hours-long shootout ensued. In the end, both Fred and Ma Barker were killed. Afterward, the FBI claimed that not only had the mother of the outlaw brothers participated in the fatal shootout but that she was the mastermind behind much of their criminal activity. There is no evidence that Ma Barker had anything to do with the crime spree of the gang, but the idea of it was too much for the public to abandon. Ever since her death in 1934, characterizations of Ma Barker have been a part of films and television. The dominant maternal figure within a crime organization has almost become an archetype.

The picture of a family engaging in a reign of terror was like a sinister version of the Joad family from *The Grapes of Wrath*. Instead of moving west looking for a better life, the Barker family stayed home and seized their own better life by taking it from the banks that had, in the eyes of many, caused the Depression. Even the kidnappings could be viewed as karmic payback. The first victim was William Hamm, son of the owner of Hamm's Brewing. The second victim was Edward Bremer, president of the Commercial State Bank and part of the Schmitt Brewing Company. Especially in the Midwest, brewing companies were some of the largest industries in the region. In Bremer's case, he not only represented big business, but the banking industry as well. While most people would never dream of committing such dastardly crimes, it was a bit of a voyeuristic fantasy to see the well-to-do be taken down a peg.

Another gang that caught the public attention due to the scandalous nature of their relationship was the criminal organization of Bonnie Parker and Clyde Barrow, better known simply as Bonnie and Clyde. Parker met Barrow in 1930 and soon joined up with his gang of outlaws. Over the next four years the Barrow Gang committed robberies and murders from Texas to Minnesota. Their exploits led to a large manhunt throughout the region and multiple gunfights with law enforcement.

It wasn't so much the criminal aspect of their relationship that intrigued the public so much as it was their romantic relationship. The idea of an outlaw couple on the run, engaging in explicit sex while not being married, was something right out of the pulp novels that were popular at the time. In addition, the gruesome details of their death only added to their mystique as criminal star-crossed lovers. Bonnie and Clyde were ambushed by law enforcement on a rural road in Louisiana, and the posse that attacked them fired over 120 rounds into their car.

In death, Bonnie and Clyde may have become even more famous. Over 20,000 people attended Bonnie Parker's funeral. Almost immediately after their deaths, the car they were killed in became a tourist attraction. It is still on display at a restaurant and casino outside of Las Vegas, Nevada. Every year on the anniversary of their deaths, thousands gather at the site of the ambush to celebrate Bonnie and Clyde.

The only criminal that rivals Bonnie and Clyde for enduring popularity is John Dillinger. Like Bonnie and Clyde and the Barkers, Dillinger was a bank robber by trade. It wasn't his robberies, however, that made him famous, but his exploits after he was captured. In the winter of 1934, Dillinger was transported from Arizona to Indiana to face trial for the crimes he committed in that state. On March 3rd, he escaped prison in Crown Point, Indiana. It is still debated how exactly Dillinger managed to do it. According to one account, he had smuggled a gun into his cell. According to the FBI, he carved a fake gun from a potato. Still others believe that he used a razor to carve a gun from the personal effects shelf in his cell. Regardless of the circumstances, Dillinger escaped and led the FBI on a manhunt throughout the upper Midwest.

It was during this time that Dillinger became a national sensation. Like the public feeling toward the robbing of banks as a kind of strike back at the powers that be, Dillinger staying one step ahead of law enforcement made him a kind of hero. The everyman, even if an outlaw, was outsmarting authority. What's more, rumors circulated that he was enjoying his time on the run. Living in Chicago, dating various women, and attending his favorite baseball team's games, The Chicago Cubs, made Dillinger into an almost Robin Hood type figure.

Like Bonnie and Clyde, Dillinger met a violent end and there was a touch of romantic scandal attached. When attending a movie with his girlfriend and a madam who was their mutual friend, the FBI was tipped off by said madam about where Dillinger was going to be. In order to ensure his identity, the madam wore a red dress (some accounts say orange) to point out the group. The infamous "Lady in Red" legend was born. Dillinger, not aware of the betrayal until it was too late, attempted to run down an alley by the theatre and was shot in the back.

Like Bonnie and Clyde, there was a fascination in John Dillinger after his death. People used newspapers and handkerchiefs to soak up his blood from the shooting site. Over 15,000 people came to view the body at the Cook County Morgue, and people still visit his grave in Indianapolis, Indiana.

In addition to the criminals becoming household names, the men who chased and arrested them also gained greater notoriety than law enforcement had previously. There were antecedents to the Federal Bureau of Investigation (FBI), but the agency was officially founded in 1935. The director of the FBI, J. Edgar Hoover, was at the forefront of law and order during the Depression and beyond. Starting during the Prohibition era and carrying on well past repeal of the eighteenth amendment, the FBI publicized their most wanted criminals. Dillinger, Karpis, and a host of other criminals were declared "Public Enemy Number One." With each arrest of the top fugitive, the next person was declared with as much press and fanfare as could be brought to bear.

The agents of the FBI acquired an almost heroic status. Called G-Men (Government Men), those that did the actual field work were revered by the population. One such agent, Melvin Purvis, became almost as well-known as Hoover. Purvis was part of the manhunts that brought in Pretty Boy Floyd, John Dillinger, and Baby-Face Nelson. There is some evidence that Hoover grew jealous of his agent's good press and undermined his career. Purvis resigned from the FBI in 1935 but wasn't finished with civil service. During World War Two, he served as a spy and gathered evidence against the Nazis at the Nuremberg Trials.

In contrast to the appeal of the outlaw, the G-Man was another hero for the time period. Just as there were people who were attracted to the aspect of the crimes attacking the well-to-do, there was also a need within the culture of the Depression for some semblance of order in a chaotic world. So, as people followed the misdeeds of the rogues' gallery of the 1930s, they were also counting on the upright heroes of law enforcement to bring order. Many of the movies of the era reflected this attitude. While the central characters were often criminals, they were always brought to justice in the end.

Chapter 9: Population Shifts and the Culture of the Great Depression

The Great Depression had a significant impact on the culture of the United States. Some of that impact was a result of the movement of large portions of the population across the country. Both movements had profound and lasting effects on American culture, well into the present day. The first, the movement of Southwesterners, largely to California, was largely the result of the devastation of the Dust Bowl. Okie culture, as it became known, made significant changes to California, and the Pacific Coast as a whole. The other movement during the Depression was a continuation of a movement that began during World War One and continued throughout the Depression, the migration of African Americans to the urban centers of the Midwest, Northeast, and later West altered not only the demographics of those cities but the politics and cultures of those cities as well.

The draw of California has been almost a constant pull in American life. The appeal of quick riches was the initial factor in the growth of the state, but people continued to migrate to the Golden State even after the gold rush had worn off. Until the 1930s and the environmental disaster of the Dust Bowl, the migration to California was steady, but not excessive. It also tended to be more of a middle-class phenomenon. As the dust blew across the heartland, however, the economic class was decidedly low. It wasn't necessarily the pull of California, but more of a move of desperation.

Though desperate, the migrants were looking for a better life. The majority of those who set out for California were young and male. Interestingly, though popularly thought of as mostly being rural farm workers, only about 36 percent of those that migrated were farmers. Over 50 percent of those that moved were from urban areas. Like other migratory movements, many of those who traveled did so because they already had relatives or contacts in the area. They moved to two distinct areas within the state, the cities, mostly Los Angeles, and the valleys, where farming was the main industry. Though collectively called Okies, the migrants largely came from four states, Oklahoma (naturally), Arkansas, Missouri, and Texas. California was the main destination for the people because the popular media and the state itself had been advertising the great opportunity that the state provided to the newcomer.

In reality, the idea of greater economic opportunity in California was well outdated by the time many from the Southwest moved. There was no more opportunity in the Golden State than there was anywhere else in the United States thanks to the Depression. Prior to the Depression, the state and local governments, especially that of the city of Los Angeles, were very welcoming of outsiders. After the economic downturn, however, native Californians became much less hospitable and even downright hostile to the Okies, a term used as a pejorative as the migration expanded. The Southwesterners were stereotyped by the native Californians as being strictly rural, backward folk, who were anti-modernism and lesser skilled than natives and other migrants. The Dust Bowl migration gave rise to the belief that there was a "tramp menace" in California, and in the mid-1930s a group was founded, the California Citizens Association, to solve the migrant and transient problem that many perceived.

In the face of such discrimination, the Okies isolated themselves from the greater California population. In both the cities and rural regions, "Little Oklahomas" sprang up. While never the permanent neighborhoods such as a Little Italy or Chinatown, the Little Oklahomas were areas that Southwesterners clustered in. In such isolation, like other ethnic communities, members of the Okie subgroup found ways to conform to the dominant Californian culture. Children and the next generation were able to mix more freely, again much like ethnic children.

Like other enclaves, the Okies brought with them certain attitudes, customs, and cultures to California. The Southwesterners were very influenced by the populism of the early part of the twentieth century, and their anti-elitism and limited equality ethos were keys to their political outlook. It was a limited equality because, like those who remained in the Southwest, the tradition of racism was brought West. While a strong blue-collar sensibility and solidarity was present among the migrants, it only extended as far as their fellow whites.

Also affecting the political behavior of the newcomers was their evangelical religion. Many of the native Californian congregations were not welcoming to the Okies so they were forced to create their own faith communities. Especially influential were the Pentecostal or Holiness congregations. The preaching style and worship services were reminiscent of home for many of the migrants. It is a style of religious behavior that is still practiced across the country and gained a prominence it didn't have prior to finding roots in California.

In addition to the moral flavor of Okie culture, there was also a more secular side. Throughout California where Southwesterners settled, roadhouses and honky-tonks sprang up. For every evangelical spirit, there was also the "good old boy." The most prominent aspect of this is best represented in the music that became popular, namely country music. While the home of country music will always be Nashville, Tennessee, the migrants from the Southwest brought their music with them. The influence of Okie culture could be seen, especially when sound became dominant in motion pictures. As mentioned in the previous chapter, Will Rogers was a native of Oklahoma. Gene Autry became famous as the singing cowboy. The culture of the Southwest was, and still is, a dominant aspect of popular culture.

Like the mass movement of Southwestern whites to California, the movement of African Americans from the rural South to the urban North was a significant demographic trend in twentieth-century US history. Termed the Great Migration, the movement of African

Americans radically altered American cities and the South that they had left.

African Americans began moving during World War One when two key circumstances drove the migration. First, even though the US was not in the war, the industrial cities of the Northeast were desperate for workers because of the demands of the European belligerents. New York, Pittsburgh, Chicago, and many other cities had a labor shortage that needed to be met. Previously, companies often employed African Americans as strikebreakers, so there was some precedent for employing people from the South. In the case of the 1910s, it was just strikebreaking, but the need for more workers to meet demand. Often regulated to the worst jobs and the worst-paying jobs, it was still an opportunity that was often closed to African Americans.

The second key factor prompting African Americans to move to a strange new place was the continuing harsh conditions of the South. With the end of Reconstruction, whites in the South moved quickly to not only disenfranchise African Americans, but to limit them economically and socially. Between 1890 and 1910, all states in the former Confederacy held state constitutional conventions restricting access to the vote. Poll taxes, literacy tests, and comprehension tests, among other methods, were used to deny African Americans the right to vote.

In addition to voter suppression, economic and social restrictions were put in place to keep African Americans out of the power structure of Southern society. Laws were enacted to keep blacks and whites separate in all public areas. These laws were called Jim Crow laws, and they were found to be constitutionally acceptable by the Supreme Court in the 1896 ruling of *Plessy v. Ferguson*. In the court opinion, as long as accommodations were "separate but equal" then it was legal. The era of Jim Crow would last well into the 1960s.

Economically, African Americans found it almost impossible to own any property in the South, partly because they had no wealth post-slavery, but also because they had no means to accrue wealth after Reconstruction. The majority of former slaves either returned to their former plantations or found similar farming enterprises and entered into a very unfair economic practice of sharecropping. Through such a system, African American farmers were kept in a constant cycle of debt.

Those African Americans that were able to buy their own property were often intimidated or forced to give up their land or businesses, sometimes in a very brutal fashion. Over the course of the post-Reconstruction (1877) period through 1950, over 4,000 African Americans were lynched by white mobs. In every case, lynching was an extralegal method to intimidate the African American communities of the South. Mutilated bodies were left on display in order to terrorize African Americans and remind them of the power hierarchy at work in the South. Technically, African Americans were free from slavery, but Southern society looked remarkably like the society before the Civil War.

Added to the severe repression that African Americans dealt with in the postbellum South was an agricultural downturn that the region suffered in the 1910s. A series of poor cotton harvests then an infestation of the boll weevil devastated Southern agriculture. With little work available and many reasons to leave, the labor demand of World War One was a blessing for African Americans. During the war years, 1914-1918, close to half a million African Americans moved North. In the 1920s, over 800,000 African Americans made the move. The Great Depression slowed the migration, but still close to 400,000 people moved during the 1930s. By 1940, almost two million African Americans had moved from the South to the North.

Like the Okies in California, African Americans brought their culture with them to the cities of the North. African American food, religion, and music all had a strong impact on urban culture and the overall culture of the United States. Unlike the Okies, however, African Americans faced a great deal of discrimination and segregation in buying or renting properties in major US cities. In addition, many white institutions denied African Americans services in such areas as insurance, funeral homes, and medical services. These, among other small businesses, became the backbone of African American neighborhoods in cities like New York and Chicago. Serving the black community built a great deal of wealth for many African Americans, and they were able to translate this into financial and political power.

By the Great Depression, like so many other economic communities, the African American enclaves in cities were also hard hit. Upwards of 50 percent of black workers were unemployed in Chicago, Detroit, and

Pittsburgh. However, in the South, African American unemployment reached as high as 70 percent. Many of the New Deal programs, including Social Security, offered little assistance to African Americans, but the neighborhood leaders of the North did their best to bridge the gap for the African American community. For example, Gus Greenlee, a prominent nightclub owner in Pittsburgh, provided turkeys and other groceries throughout the Hill District at Christmastime to families in need.

Though still harshly discriminated against throughout the United States, African Americans believed that Franklin Roosevelt was at least listening to their concerns. Roosevelt tripled the number of African Americans working in the federal government and appointed the first African American judge. A number of African Americans were tapped to act as special advisors to a number of cabinet members and they formed an informal "black cabinet," advising the president on issues affecting the African American community. One of the most famous members of this group was the close friend of Eleanor Roosevelt, Mary McLeod Bethune, a leading voice for African American women's rights. As the Depression was coming to an end because of the conversion to a war economy, Roosevelt issued one of the most significant executive orders of his presidency. Executive Order 8802 prohibited racial discrimination in the hiring practices of companies involved in the national defense industry. Though it was far from perfect and companies found ways to circumvent the order, it still provided a great deal of opportunity for African American workers.

By the end of the 1930s, the demographic picture of the United States had changed considerably. Over a million Americans had relocated in an attempt to find a better opportunity. African Americans continued a movement from the former Confederacy to the cities of the north. When the demand for labor again rose during World War Two, the largest movement of African Americans occurred when over 3 million people moved, including new destinations to the West, especially Los Angeles. During the Great Depression and after, Southern California was transformed by the amount of people moving in, but also by the culture these people brought with them. By the 1950s, California was as diverse as any state in the nation.

Chapter 10: International Issues and Concerns During the Depression

At the beginning of the Depression, the focus of the US government was, understandably, on domestic issues, especially the economy and the various crises facing the nation. Banking instability, unemployment, financial markets in ruins, and many other domestic issues were front and center during the Hoover administration and the first term of Roosevelt's presidency. The Great Depression was more than an American event, however. It was a global disaster that reached every part of the world. Like the United States, governments scrambled to find solutions to dire problems. In some cases, those solutions resembled the activities of the United States, by modifying capitalism, but not abandoning it. Nor did many countries abandon democratic and liberal government.

In Great Britain, the Depression wasn't as far of a fall as the United States experienced. Britain was still recovering from the First World War. When the stock market crashed in 1929, the famed economist John Maynard Keynes predicted that the crash would have little effect on London. As US trade diminished, the situation became more dire. The British government tried to keep trade afloat within the commonwealth countries and empire, by keeping tariffs low, but raising them abroad.

Unfortunately, this had devastating effects. There was almost no demand for British products, and the industrial centers of Britain, especially the northeast of England, Wales and Northern Ireland, were particularly hard hit. In some areas, the unemployment rate reached 70 percent. At its worst, as many as 25 percent of the British population were living on a subsistence diet.

Unlike the United States, however, there were safeguards in place. There was a system of payment to the unemployed, called the dole. The British government also had national health insurance. Both of these programs started in 1911 and during the crisis of the 1930s were expanded to help more of the population. The increase in expenditures did slow any economic recovery, but Great Britain weathered the storm.

Meanwhile, the other western European ally from World War I, France, did not experience many of the problems that assailed Britain and America. Two key factors muted the effect of the Depression on France. First, France and French citizens did not have nearly the amount of capital invested in the world stock exchanges like English and Americans. Second, France did not have the massive industrial companies that dominated the economies of Britain and the United States. The French economy was decidedly smaller in scale, but when the crisis began, it was less open to vulnerabilities. French unemployment never reached the levels of the United States or Britain, and though there were economic hardships later in the decade, ultimately France survived the worst of the Depression with few scars.

The other ally of the war, Russia, was now the greater part of the Soviet Union. For the most part, its communist government was viewed with either outright hostility or at the very least suspicion. After Russia exited World War I, a civil war erupted within the country between the Red Army, led by Vladimir Lenin and Leon Trotsky, and the White Army, led by Russian military officers fresh from fighting Germany. Alexander Kolchak was a former admiral for czarist forces and Nikolai Yudenich a former general. The White Army was backed by the British and Americans. By 1923, the Red forces were victorious, but at great costs to Russia. The combined devastation of World War I and the Russian Civil War all but crippled the region.

After the civil war, leaders of the Red faction worked toward a consolidation of power, especially over numerous, smaller republics in Eastern Europe. As a result, much of Eastern Europe was under the control of Moscow and the communist leadership. Lenin was still the head of the communist regime, but his health was rapidly declining due to a series of strokes. Many had assumed Trotsky would be the new leader, but a younger member of the Communist Central Committee, Joseph Stalin, had been increasing his power within the party. After Lenin's death in 1924, despite a final statement by the former leader to elevate Trotsky and isolate Stalin from the committee, Stalin became the secretary general of the Soviet Union.

Stalin wasted little time in dispatching his enemies and former allies. By 1928, Trotsky was sentenced to eternal exile from the Soviet Union. During much of the 1920s, Stalin focused on restructuring the economy by having the state take complete control of industry and form collectives for agriculture throughout the Soviet Union. The policies weren't particularly popular, especially among the peasant farming class, but there was no denying the rise of Stalinism.

The drive to improve the economy and work toward full employment meant that when the Depression ravaged the Western democracies of the world, the Soviet Union was largely unscathed. In some instances, workers from Germany and the United States traveled to the USSR in search of work. During the 1920s and into the 1930s, workers were educated and given access to health care. Women were accorded the same rights, at least under the letter of the law, as men and were in the workforce at a much greater percentage. Perhaps most significantly, due to a program of immunizations for all children in the USSR, life expectancy rose by almost twenty years by the 1950s.

However, this progress hid a brutality that was truly staggering. Beginning in the 1930s, all organized religion was suppressed. During the Leninist era, the Orthodox Church was subject to persecution, but under Stalin all religions were suppressed. More staggering was the treatment of political enemies under Stalin. A number of trials, only for show purposes were conducted from 1936 through 1938 that purged all members of the party that had been a part of the Bolshevik Revolution in 1917. 1,108 of the 1,966 party officials with ties to the history of the

USSR were arrested, put on a show trial, and either executed or exiled. Because of the ties of the Red Army to Trotsky, thousands of army officers were killed. Even Trotsky, living in exile in Mexico, was found in 1940 and assassinated. The purge extended to anyone who might be considered an enemy of the state—more precisely, an enemy of Stalin. Mass arrests, deportations, and internments were the norm in the Stalinist USSR. In one year alone, 1937-1938, close to 700,000 people were shot by the Soviet Secret Police, the NKVD.

Most of the death toll was kept from the rest of the world, but the trials of senior officials were widely reported. Many governments denounced the treatment of political prisoners and held that the court proceedings were a joke. The Communist Party of the United States (CPUSA), however, was split regarding the trials, with many members supporting Stalin and saying what was happening in the USSR was a necessary evil. Furthermore, the criticism of Stalin by Western democratic leaders was simply a matter of envy. Stalin and his nation were surviving, while the other nations of the world teetered on the brink. The strong support that much of the CPUSA showed Stalin severely hurt the organization, both in their membership and public perception.

Communism was one of three forms of political theory that dominated much of the post-World War One world. The United States, France, and Great Britain, among many other nations, represented liberal democracy and capitalism. Another philosophy, with roots in the nineteenth century, took shape in Italy after the war. Fascism was an authoritarian form of government that was on the far right of the political spectrum. In Italy, in the aftermath of the war, communist insurgents tried to organize left-leaning people, especially workers in the various industries throughout the peninsula. Benito Mussolini and the National Fascist Party he led used the unrest to subdue the strikers and gain favor with the industrialists of the country.

Gaining in popularity, especially among the armed services including local police forces, Mussolini continued to violently oppose workers' unions and socialists of any stripe. Eventually, the fascists didn't just attack party offices and member homes but took over entire cities. By the time Mussolini and his party moved on Rome in 1922, it was all but a fait accompli that he would become the undisputed leader of the country. At the end of October, the figurehead monarch of Italy officially appointed Mussolini prime minister. With the monarchy, industrialists, and even the Catholic Church supporting him, within three years Mussolini did away with the title of prime minister and declared himself Il Duce, or supreme leader.

Underlying fascism were a number of key ideas that, at least initially, were appealing to many, not only across Italy, but throughout the world. The enormity of the devastation from World War One repelled many, but some saw it as the new order of the world. The technological applications that were used to make war inspired some that a state of total war was achievable. In a fascist state, the goal was to be permanently mobilized. Fascism also relied heavily on mass enthusiasm. Large demonstrations, members wearing uniforms, and group activities (usually with violent outcomes) were measured ways to gain followers. In order to sustain such enthusiasm, a strong charismatic leader was needed.

From a more ideological perspective, fascism wasn't a reaction to the outcomes of World War One, where four major monarchies of the world were toppled, but to events prior to the conflict of 1914-1918. At its heart, fascism was a response to the Enlightenment and the French Revolution. Instead of believing in individual rights and the strength of reason, fascist doctrine embraced hierarchy, irrationalism, and emotionalism. The hierarchy extended beyond social order, such as supporting monarchies and other authority figures, but to a racial hierarchy as well. Mussolini was especially adroit at exploiting the fears of Italians about African migration.

Most importantly to fascism was the idea of the state. In a perfect nation, which would constantly be proving itself in war, the state and devotion to it was the pinnacle of being a good citizen. According to Mussolini in his work, *The Doctrine of Fascism* (1932), "The Fascist conception of the State is all-embracing; outside of it no human or spiritual values can exist, much less have value." The goal was to dominate the rest of the inferior world through warfare while the home country continued to produce the machines needed to make total war.

As the Depression overtook other Western European countries, Italy remained strong. Like France, Italy wasn't as dominated by massive corporations nor was the economy very dependent on the financial markets. The worldwide slowdown in trade hurt Italy as much as any country, but unemployment never reached the levels of the United States or Great Britain.

Like the Soviet Union and communism, Italy and fascism had its share of admirers. Many citizens were looking for an alternative to democracy and capitalism, and fascism seemed like a viable choice. Racial and ethnic tensions, along with a call for greater strength, resonated with people all over the world.

Nowhere was the appeal of fascism greater than in Germany. After World War One, the German nation was in an utterly dismal state. The people were near starvation; the economy was in shambles, their structure of government destroyed, and to top it all off, they were defeated by a long-standing enemy. The sense of humiliation and shame was palpable in Germany after the war.

With the Kaiser's abdication of the throne, the structure of the German government needed to be totally overhauled. As part of the Treaty of Versailles, the German delegation agreed to establish a democratic republic in the newly redrawn German state. For the first time, many regions of Germany had an electoral process. The Weimar Republic was tasked with guiding Germany through the painful process of recovery from the war.

Immediately after the war, recovery probably seemed impossible. Conditions were terrible, and an entire generation of men had been taken by the ravages of war. But by the middle of the 1920s, Germany was showing decidedly positive growth. German industry was among the largest in Europe, and cultural life was flowering under the Weimar Republic. Berlin was the place to be in Europe, and though the nation was still recovering, foreign investment was returning.

The Weimar Republic wasn't perfect and it had its fair share of critics from both sides of the political aisle. Communists and socialists tried to work with and undermine the government, depending on the situation. On the opposite side of the political divide was a new party, the National Socialist Party, better known as the Nazi Party.

At first, the Nazis did not gain much traction among the German people. It was made up largely of disgruntled veterans of the war and radicals who believed the Weimar government was forced on them, regardless of the government's current success. Quite influenced by the events in Italy and the message of Mussolini, the Nazis tried to emulate the Italian success of marching on Rome. The Nazis tried to take over the government through an attack on Munich. The Beer Hall Putsch of 1923 was the first attempt by the Nazis to try and take over the government of Germany. It failed miserably. The leader of the party, Adolf Hitler, was imprisoned for 18 months for the attempted coup. While in prison, Hitler wrote *Mein Kampf* which, like Mussolini's *Doctrine*, outlined what Hitler believed. Unlike Mussolini's work, it wasn't a reflection, but a forecast. Hitler was released from prison and decided a full-on paramilitary attack was not the way to advance his agenda. Instead, he and the Nazi Party decided to work through the Weimar system and wait for an opportunity.

The Depression was particularly harsh in Germany. It was the hardest hit nation of Western Europe. Germany had spent the last decade building its industrial strength, and when world trade slowed to a standstill, the German economy ground to a halt as well. The global crisis produced fertile ground for the Nazi Party to campaign and share their ideas. At their heart, the Nazi principles reflected the same notions as Italian fascism. A strong leader was needed to end the current state of affairs. Furthermore, Germany was destined for greatness, if only it hadn't been betrayed by the premature end of the war. Hitler and the Nazis perpetuated the idea that their main political opponents, all liberal democrats within Weimar, were "November criminals" who sold Germany out to France and Great Britain.

The idea of social and racial hierarchy was also a key element of the Nazi message. The fear and prejudice that the Nazis tapped into was against Jews living in Germany. In addition to the ethnic minority of the Jews, the Nazi Party also targeted other political parties that were attempting to disrupt Germany as well. Like the Italian fascists, the Nazis were seen as the better alternative to the socialists and communists. By 1930, the message was working. The Nazi Party gained enough votes to become the second largest political party in Germany.

The Depression worsened in Germany as the number of unemployed workers rose from 4 million to 5.6 million in 1931. The disillusionment that the people had for the Weimar government increased, and by 1932, the Nazi Party was the largest political party in Germany, dominating the German legislature, the Reichstag. Centrist and conservative politicians believed that if they included Hitler in their coalition government, they could perhaps control him, and by extension, the rest of the Nazi Party.

The Nazis, however, proved to be too powerful to control, including Hitler. After being named chancellor in 1933, Hitler and his lieutenants moved swiftly to consolidate their power through all levels of government. After a mysterious fire burned down the Reichstag, Hitler was given emergency, almost absolute, powers to deal with the crisis. Political opponents were arrested, and the Gestapo, the secret police of the Nazi era, was formed. By the end of the year, the Nazi Party was declared the only legal political party in the country.

Political hegemony was almost complete by the end of 1933 for Adolf Hitler. It is often pointed out that Franklin Roosevelt and Hitler came to power in the same year, though by very different means. In 1934, while Roosevelt was working to get the New Deal through Congress, Hitler was finishing his agenda of becoming the supreme leader, the Führer of Germany. Hitler won over the military of Germany by giving the army almost complete autonomy. He also promised to dissolve one of the paramilitary organizations within the Nazi Party, the SA, or brownshirts. What had started as little more than an honor guard in the early days of the Nazi party, the SA had become a powerful organization in its own right, rivaling the army in manpower. In the summer of 1934, the Night of Long Knives occurred. The leader of the SA and many of his most loyal officers were arrested and summarily executed. With the SA taken care of, the German army officer class agreed to back Hitler when the president of the country died and make him chancellor and president of Germany, the head of state and the head of government. This occurred sooner than many thought it would, and by the end of the summer of 1934, Hitler held both offices and took on the title of Führer.

As mentioned earlier, one of the main theories underlying fascism were the ideas of total war and military preparedness. To that end, Hitler outlined an ambitious plan to rearm the German army. Even though such a course of action was prohibited by the Treaty of Versailles, Germany continued to build up their military while the rest of the world simply shrugged. Part of this might well have been because most Western countries saw Nazi Germany as a buffer between Russia and the rest of Western Europe. France and Great Britain were not in any condition either to oppose Germany's military build-up. The next phase of Nazi Germany was to reintegrate lands seized by the allies at the end of World War One back into Germany. The first such case was a small area between France and Germany, Saarland. The British and French agreed that if the residents of the area voted to rejoin Germany, then they would be allowed to do so. With a great assist from the Office of Propaganda in Germany, over 90 percent of the residents voted to rejoin Germany. The next attempts to regain territory were not as easy as a simple vote.

In order to fulfill the fascist vision of the world, the "greater" nations needed to eventually conquer the weaker ones. The first fascist country in Western Europe, Italy, was also the first to invade another country. In 1935, Italy, in an attempt to expand their world influence, invaded Ethiopia. The League of Nations was not able to stop the aggression of Italy, and the Western powers of France, Great Britain, not to mention the United States, did nothing. Taking this inaction as cowardice, Hitler moved German troops into the Rhineland territory of Germany. This was another blatant violation of the Treaty of Versailles. It was apparent that Hitler had little regard for the treaty.

The militarization of the Rhineland was cause for concern, but what gained even more attention, especially among the left in the United States, was the outbreak of the Spanish Civil War. General Francisco Franco led a military coup against the republican government of Spain and was intent on bringing a fascist regime to power on the Iberian Peninsula. Franco had powerful allies, including Germany who sent troops in the form of the Condor Legion, Italy, and Portugal. Opposing the insurgents along with the Spanish republicans were troops from the Soviet Union, France, and the United States, though the US contingent was not officially recognized by the Roosevelt administration. For many in the CPUSA, the fighting in Spain was of vital importance. It was the first real chance to stop the spread of fascism. It also coincided with the principles of the Popular Front. Not everyone fighting for the republic was a communist, but it was a demonstration of a coalition fighting against the greater threat of fascism. The Americans who went to Spain were organized as an international brigade. They took the name the Lincoln Brigade because they were fighting for the survival of the Spanish Republic, similar to Lincoln's fight in the American Civil War. Of the 3,000 volunteers that went overseas, 681 were killed.

It is important to mention that all international tension in the world was not focused on Europe. Throughout the 1930s, tensions between the United States and the Empire of Japan were constantly high. Japanese militarism, much like that of Italy and Germany, went unchecked by the League of Nations. Japan first invaded the Chinese region of Manchuria in 1931. As civil war erupted in China between communist and nationalist forces, Japan exploited the division and gained territory throughout the province. The amount of skirmishing in the region was cause for worldwide concern, but little action came of it. Great Britain, the largest western power in the region, was reluctant to send troops to Asia because of the growing fear of a European conflict. France felt the same, and the United States military was not considered strong enough to be of any real threat. Weighing all of these factors, Japan committed fully to the action in China and a formal declaration of war was issued in July of 1937.

The worldwide tensions of the late thirties touched every nation, including the United States. The growing rivalry between two extreme forms of government, fascism and communism, put the United States squarely in the middle of the global stage. Various factions within the United States supported each side of the overarching conflict. Many on the left supported the Soviet Union, and other organizations demonstrating their support of Germany. Still, others in the United States, especially in the late thirties, wanted to stay completely out of any and all conflicts. Isolation was the watchword for most Americans. How long such a stance could remain tenable was the question that Roosevelt had to consider.

Chapter 11: The Coming Storm and the End of the Depression

On December 7, 1941, the United States was attacked at the naval base at Pearl Harbor in the United States territory of Hawaii. By the end of that week, the United States was at war on two fronts. One was largely based in the Pacific Ocean, fighting the Empire of Japan. The other was on the continent of Europe against the nations of Germany and Italy. The majority of the belligerent nations had been at war since 1939, 1937 in Asia. The United States had remained largely out of the fray, at least when it came to actual troops on the ground. As far as choosing sides and providing aid, the Americans had largely made their intentions known. Even before the US officially entered the war, the war was having an impact on the country. As the second term of Franklin Roosevelt's presidency continued, the greatest conflict of the twentieth century was stirring. It was only a matter of time before it reached across the two oceans and brought the Western Hemisphere into the conflict.

As Roosevelt's second term continued, the American economy was showing great signs of improvement. Unemployment had fallen to under 15 percent, and manufacturing was up, as was per capita earnings. By the fall of 1937 and through most of 1938, unemployment rose again, almost to 20 percent. Manufacturing output fell by over a third. There was great concern that the nation was beginning to slip back into the depth of the

Depression.

Blame was quick to spread between business-oriented conservatives and liberal New Dealers. The business advocates expressed that it was because of the New Deal's inherent prejudice toward corporate interests that recovery would always be retarded. The advocates of the New Deal countered that it was because of FDR abandoning parts of the New Deal, especially when it came to spending. FDR was concerned with balancing the budget and did not want to rely on deficit spending any longer than was necessary. Also, blaming the New Deal and Roosevelt was easy because the president and his administration were quick to take credit for any signs of recovery. Receiving criticism when things went poorly was the second edge to that particular sword.

In reality, the Roosevelt Recession, as it became known, was probably due to the natural business cycle more than any other reason. At the time, however, the two sides blamed one another. Roosevelt himself thought that it was a concerted effort by key Republicans and business leaders trying to create another depression so people would turn against the Democrats in the coming election. He had the FBI investigate numerous business families for collusion. Nothing was ever found. The Roosevelt administration also took more tangible steps to stop the slide. A large spending bill was sent to Congress in 1938 that, like earlier programs, infused the economy with money. While unemployment and production didn't reach the poor levels of early 1937, the recession was all but stopped. Events abroad, especially in Europe, spurred production in the United States.

After Germany reoccupied the Rhineland in the spring of 1936, Hitler moved to improve his image and position on the world stage. First was the great pageant of the 1936 Olympics in Berlin. The German capital never looked better. Though it was more veneer than substance, the Olympics were a showcase for Germany and especially Hitler. Later that year, Germany and Italy signed an alliance, which according to Mussolini would result in the rest of Europe to "rotate on the axis between Berlin and Rome." Later that same year in November, Germany and Japan signed the Anti-Comintern Pact to stop the spread of the Soviet Union and communism around the world. Though it was still years in the future, the Axis Powers were now linked together.

Though both Germany and Japan saw themselves as the true power in their alliance, both were also willing to allow the other their own sphere of influence, Germany in Europe and Japan in Asia. The United States and the Western Hemisphere were not much of a concern. Italy, however, was decidedly a junior partner from the beginning. The goals for Europe were predominantly German goals. Italy and Mussolini were more or less along for the ride.

Even before the annexation of the Rhineland, a key component of the Nazi agenda was the concept of Lebensraum, or living space, for the German people. After World War One, a large portion of Germany was divided up among the victorious nations. As Hitler rose to power and influence in the world, his call for a larger Germany found many sympathetic ears, hence the lack of reaction to the seizure of the Rhineland. The next part of this agenda was to unite Germany with the other former great Germanic nation, Austria. Like Germany, Austria had suffered defeat in World War One. In a demonstration of strength and solidarity, the German army marched into Austria unopposed. It was reminiscent of a Roman triumph, except in the streets of Vienna. The Anschluss, which means joining, was completed in the spring of 1938. In two years, Germany had extended its sphere of influence from the Rhine to the Danube.

German expansion wasn't over. In the fall of 1938, Hitler made his intentions clear about territory boarding Czechoslovakia, referred to as the Sudetenland. In order to protect ethnic Germans living in the territory, Hitler was prepared to invade Czechoslovakia. The rest of Europe opposed such action, but were also opposed to another major war. Great Britain, France, Germany, and Italy met in order to stave off war. On September 30, 1938, the Munich Agreement was signed by the four aforementioned countries. The agreement stipulated that Germany would be allowed to take over the Sudetenland, provided that they would not invade the rest of Czechoslovakia. The Czech people and government were appalled and felt betrayed. A quick look at the map shows that the remaining Czech territory was all but surrounded by a hostile neighbor. The British Prime Minister Neville Chamberlain infamously said that the agreement would result in "peace in our time." In less than a year Great Britain would again be at war with Germany.

The United States was not eager to become engaged in another European war either. In the almost 20 years after the end of World War I, many Americans questioned whether or not the Unites States should have been involved at all. As Germany became more and more belligerent, the US Congress began passing "Neutrality Acts" to ensure that the country would not be pulled into another conflict. The ultimate goal of the acts was to keep United States corporations from selling war materials to hostile nations. Roosevelt was opposed to the acts because he believed it would hurt nations that were friendly toward the United States. As the Spanish Civil War intensified and Germany began its expansion, the 1937 renewal of the Neutrality Acts contained a provision meant to please the president and prevent him from possibly vetoing the act. The "cash and carry" stipulation in the 1937 Neutrality Act allowed countries to trade with the United States, with the exception of munitions, if they took the supplies in their own boats and paid cash up front. Since Britain and to a lesser extent France were the world powers at sea, it meant that the Western democracies and not Germany would most likely be the nations to be a part of the cash and carry program.

Roosevelt was going against the current for much of the late 1930s. Many Republicans and Southern Democrats were staunch isolationists, even as the world slipped further and further into war. In 1937, the same year cash and carry was adopted, Roosevelt gave his "quarantine" speech. He stated that the United States needed to quarantine aggressive nations around the world in order to protect US interests. If he had hoped to inspire a more international concern, Roosevelt failed. It seemed to only intensify the isolationist mood of the country. Even as Germany took the Sudetenland and in 1939 the rest of Czechoslovakia, the US Congress passed another Neutrality Act and refused to extend cash and carry.

As 1939 progressed, the threat of a full-scale war increased with each month. The next target of German expansion was Poland. Much to the disbelief of the world, especially communists living outside of the Soviet Union, the USSR and Germany signed a nonaggression treaty. The agreement pledged both powers not to invade the other for 10 years. Secretly, the Soviet Union and Germany agreed to split up Eastern Europe in the coming years. Hitler was assured that the Soviets would not resist the invasion of Poland. Even without knowledge of the secret agreement, the Communist Party of the United States was divided and lost a great deal of credibility and support among many others on the left in US politics.

In August 1939, the British signed a treaty with Poland promising to fight on their behalf in case of invasion. It did not take long for the agreement to take effect. On September 1, 1939, Germany invaded Poland, starting World War II. Along with the British, the French came to the aid of the Polish. There was little chance to provide aid. Warsaw, the capital of Poland, surrendered on September 27th.

While the British and French had declared war on Germany, they did very little to prevent the quick defeat of Poland. The two Western powers were waiting for Germany to turn its attention toward the west. They did not have to wait for long. The following spring, in 1940, the Germans advanced across the north of Europe, seizing Denmark and Norway in April and moving through Belgium, the Netherlands, and ultimately France by June of 1940.

As Europe fell under German rule, many Americans were still opposed to getting involved. As the British faced a fierce German air assault, remembered as the Blitz, the America First Committee was founded in the United States. The group opposed any intervention by the US government. The group grew to almost 1 million members by 1941. However, the American people were in favor of Britain winning its battle against Germany. There was a great deal of support for aiding Great Britain by all means short of becoming a participant in the war.

To that end, Roosevelt proposed a program for lending nations opposed to Germany and Japan war materials. Roosevelt likened it to lending a neighbor a hose to douse a fire. In theory, the nations that borrowed the materials would return it to the United States. In reality, very little was returned and no one really expected it. The program became known as the Lend-Lease program. Once the US officially entered the war, the United States military was granted no-cost leases among many of its allies as a means of exchange for all of the goods provided.

With the advent of Lend-Lease, the idea of American neutrality was all but dead. As Roosevelt proclaimed about the program, it meant that the United States was the "Arsenal of Democracy." Though the economy wasn't officially a war economy, it practically was. The unemployment rate fell below 15 percent for only the second time since the Depression had started in 1940. By 1941, it would fall below ten percent for the first time since 1930. The United States was out of the Depression, hopefully for good. Just like the Depression, however, the years immediately after the Depression were marked by just as much sacrifice and dedication as the previous decade.

The discussion of isolation and neutrality all but ceased on December 7th, 1941. The Japanese attack on Pearl Harbor was one of the most devastating attacks on a US-held territory. No contemporary of the time could recall a similar event. While there were outliers throughout World War II, the overwhelming majority of Americans were in favor of entering the war. The attack on Pearl Harbor was a surprise to most Americans, but US policies in Asia made such an attack from Japan, not the other Axis Powers, more likely.

As early as 1937, when Japan invaded China, relations between the United States and Japan were strained. The United States almost immediately declared that they supported China in the conflict. The Neutrality Acts of the 1930s limited who the US would and would not trade with; Japan was one of the first nations to be cut out of trade with the US. Important steel, oil, and other materials needed for the war effort of Japan were no longer available from the United States. By 1940, the United States was overt in their support of China against the Japanese, training soldiers and pilots and supplying them war materials through the Lend-Lease program.

For much of 1941, the United States and Japan held negotiations to ease tensions between the two countries and to also bring about a resolution to other conflicts in Asia. It appeared that de-escalation was possible. After Germany invaded Russia in the summer of 1941, the Japanese high command saw their chance to push south toward the Dutch East Indies and sent over 100,000 troops to Indochina. The United States reacted swiftly and harshly. The US froze all Japanese assets in US banks. Roosevelt also ordered all troops on the Philippines be brought under US control. As a final punishment, the US denied the Japanese use of the Panama Canal.

As might be expected, diplomatic relations between the two countries were almost non-existent for the rest of 1941. Military command in the United States was sure there would be an attack on some US holding in the Pacific. Most experts agreed that the attack would be on Midway, Wake Island, Guam, or perhaps even the Philippines. No one thought the Japanese would venture as far away as Hawaii and the home of the US Pacific fleet.

War was declared by the US Congress against the Empire of Japan on December 8th, 1941. Shortly thereafter, Germany and Italy declared war on the United States and the US responded in kind. The United States was already emerging from the Great Depression before the official declaration of war thanks to the industrial needs of the Lend-Lease Program. However, with the US officially in the conflict, unemployment fell below 5 percent for the first time since 1929 and would fall below 2 percent for the remainder of the war. As the need for soldiers rose throughout the war, segments of the population not usually tapped for industrial work were employed, most notably women. After twelve years of economic hardship, the Great Depression was finally over.

Conclusion

When victory was finally declared in September of 1945, the mood of so many Americans was understandably celebratory. The United States defeated two threatening foes and, to paraphrase the departed FDR, preserved the world for democracy. In addition, the United States was the only major combatant that didn't suffer great destruction of its infrastructure and population centers. In many ways, the United States was the last man standing after a terrible, costly war.

However, that position carried with it a set of fundamental concerns, most notably what was going to happen with the war ending. The greatest fear of many in the Truman administration was the return of the depression. Soldiers were returning by the thousands, eager to find employment and begin a new life after surviving the crucible of war. Those that had worked in the factories and fields, the active participants in the "Arsenal of Democracy," weren't ready to vacate those jobs, even if that was the expectation. The vision of hundreds of thousands of unemployed soldiers crowding into cities and across the countryside filled many with a sense of urgency.

The generation that lived through the Depression and fought in the war now needed to sustain the wartime economy in order to ensure that another economic collapse did not occur. Through the Truman and Eisenhower administrations, great federally funded programs bolstered the economy or prepared the returning soldiers to enter the workforce.

Key programs from the New Deal, especially Social Security, were enhanced and expanded. By the 1960s, Medicaid and Medicare would follow in the footsteps of the original Social Security Act. Lyndon Johnson's domestic initiatives to end poverty, called the Great Society was the direct descendant of the New Deal. Those that lived through the Depression were determined to not let it happen again.

In much the same way, working-class Americans, those that felt the brunt of the Depression more severely than anyone else, were determined to ensure their economic stability as well. Instead of demanding a greater voice in management and the means of production, American unions focused on establishing and preserving their members economic and future well-being. Unions demanded strong health insurance and pensions from their employers. Workers were also able to make great gains in wages and, coupled with generous FHA loans or loans through credit unions, were able to buy housing of their own.

The economic lessons of the Great Depression haven't been totally forgotten. The economic recession of 2008 served as a painful reminder. Unlike 1929, the government, another Republican administration ironically, acted swiftly to stave off a total collapse. While the economy slowed down dramatically in 2008, it never approached the dire situation of the 1930s. The Great Depression still looms large in the American consciousness. As debates over tariffs and restructuring Social Security continue to rise, let's hope that the Great Depression still affects thinking and policy in the future.

Part 7: Pearl Harbor

A Captivating Guide to the Surprise Military Strike by the Imperial Japanese Navy Air Service that Caused the United States of America's Formal Entry into World War II

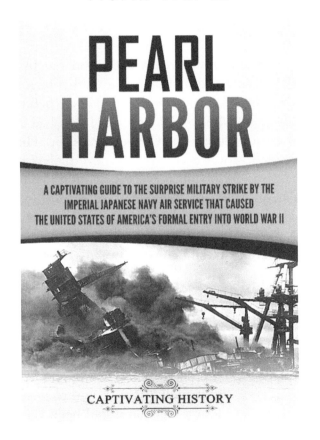

Introduction

World War II is largely considered a European war by spectators and civilians in the Western world, but the reality is that huge portions of the fighting took place in Asia and the Pacific. Even before Adolf Hitler started his march on Czechoslovakia in 1938, Japan had embarked upon a serious military campaign in China. Emperor Hirohito, though personally uninclined to war and violence, nevertheless presided over a government that was hell-bent on Chinese domination. As Japan's military encroached further into China and other neighboring countries, the German army began to occupy Europe. Soon, to avoid the interference of the Western Allied countries, Japan's administration agreed to side with Hitler and therefore proceeded as it wished in Asia.

By 1941, Japan knew that its time on the fringes of the European war was coming to an end. It had already faced fire from Great Britain and feared that the United States of America would very soon enter the conflict against Japan and Germany. To protect itself, Japan made a historic move in striking the United States first, before the nation had so much as made plans to join the Allies. It was a bold and unprecedented move that not only took the United States by complete surprise but also possibly forced the US to join a war that it had been very committed to avoiding altogether.

The attack of the US Pearl Harbor Naval Base changed the entire progress of World War II, and as a result, it was a very formative event both for the United States and Japan. Though the two nations seemed unlikely enemies at the onset of the Second Great War, bloodshed between them would be greater than anyone could have imagined. The future of the world at large was changed on December 7, 1941, when the Empire of Japan chose to make a preemptive strike on its most feared Pacific neighbor, the United States of America.

Chapter 1 – The Pearl Harbor Naval Base, Pre-1941

Pearl Harbor is a natural coastal body of water that connects to the Pearl River on the island of Oahu, Hawaii. The Hawaiians called it "Wai Momi," which translates to "Waters of the Pearl."[130] The legendary Hawaiian High Chief Keaunui is credited with widening the estuary between the bay and the river long ago, making a navigable channel that would eventually be used by trading ships from all over the world. The first real international interest in Pearl Harbor came during the 19th century, when whale oil, sugar, and pineapples caught the attention of Hawaii's potential trading partners.

During the Industrial Era, which started to take off in the mid-19th century, there was a huge worldwide demand for whale oil. Harvested from the blubber of a variety of whales, or from the braincases of sperm whales, whale oil was used for oil lamps, soap-making, and even cooking until the industry faltered in the 20th century. During the peak of the whaling days, an estimated 800 whaling ships made stops in the Kingdom of Hawaii, and for the ships' protection, the United States Navy was tasked with making regular patrols around the Hawaiian Islands. This was

---

[130] "Places - The History of Pearl Harbor." National Park Service, U.S. Department of the Interior. Web.

still a century before Hawaii would join the United States of America as an official state.

Thanks to the marine traffic, Hawaii experienced a local economic boom that saw the creation of shipping repair facilities, eateries, laundromats, blacksmiths, carpentry shops, and hospitality services. There were businesses to cater to ship repair and maintenance, as well as businesses to cater to the maintenance and well-being of the sailors aboard all those ships. Since a majority of the whaling ships in port throughout Hawaii were American, the US Navy posted a permanent warship there to protect the interests of the United States' merchants and investors.

When the United States fell into civil war between 1861 and 1865, the Confederate Army tracked whaling ships belonging to Unionist states and sank them on sight.[131] This, as well as the new petroleum industry, heralded the end of whaling and, therefore, a recession for Hawaii. Nevertheless, negotiations soon began for the establishment of a duty-free trading port at Pearl Harbor, by which the US could buy sugar to import home. After the election of King Kalākaua in March of 1874, the US was granted the sole use of Pearl Harbor, as well as the right to build ship maintenance facilities there.[132]

Despite anti-American sentiment that led to rioting, the arrangement went forward, but by the end of the 19th century, the whaling boom in Hawaii was all but over. For the United States, however, which had come out of its civil war desperate for a new economic boost, that Pearl Harbor foothold in Hawaii was still very important. For the Kingdom of Hawaii, US trade was also highly important, and so, the two nations signed the Reciprocity Treaty of 1875.[133] Even without whale oil, Hawaii had enough sugar and pineapples to make a trade deal worthwhile, particularly since the northern United States had boycotted sugar from the southern states.

Furthermore, the United States Navy was very interested in creating a military base within the Pacific Ocean, where it was otherwise completely

---

[131] "Civil War." *History.com*. Web.

[132] Kuykendall, Ralph S. *The Hawaiian Kingdom*. 1967.

[133] "Reciprocity Treaty of 1875." *Encyclopaedia Britannica*. Web.

lacking in naval intelligence or surveillance. To facilitate the terms of the treaty, US Major General John Schofield and Brevet Brigadier General Alexander traveled to Hawaii aboard the USS *California* in 1873. They spent their time on the islands conducting reconnaissance on the potential of the various Hawaiian Islands to function as defensive or commercial centers. Their report found that the only completely suitable place in which to focus their efforts was the harbor on the Pearl River.

The Reciprocity Treaty was signed two years after the reconnaissance mission, providing duty-free sugar exports to the United States for the Hawaiians in exchange for sole access to the Pearl River inlet. The treaty went into effect in 1876 and was renewed the following year to include permission for the US to establish a naval base at Pearl Harbor.[134]

More than two decades later, the United States and Spain declared war on one another because of their differing ideologies on Cuban freedom. Cuba, under Spanish authority, rebelled and demanded independence; Spain responded by sending in its military and enforcing strict military rule. Practically unprepared for real warfare, the Spanish Caribbean military units were annihilated by the US Navy, and the war lasted just over two months before Spain surrendered. In the subsequent peace treaty between Spain and the US, Spain was forced to grant Cuba its independence and also to hand over Guam and Puerto Rico to the United States. Spain also sold sovereignty of the Philippines to the US for $20 million.[135]

As these political gains were being wrapped up by the US in 1898, the victor of the Spanish-American war decided to go ahead and add Hawaii to the collection as well. The hand-off of Hawaii was enacted via a political coup that began when the leader of Hawaii's American plantation owners, Samuel Dole, deposed reigning Queen Liliuokalani in 1893.[136] The queen had been promoting stricter Hawaiian sovereignty that would have ended the United States' commercial privileges at Pearl Harbor, and US President Benjamin Harrison ordered her palace surrounded by the navy. When she was forced to abdicate in favor of a

---

[134] Ibid.

[135] "Spanish-American War." *History.com*. Web.

[136] "Annexation of Hawaii 1898." *US Department of State*. Web. 2009.

representative government, Dole declared Hawaii an independent republic. President William McKinley processed the formal annexation of the Hawaiian Islands in 1898, and they were officially made a dominion of the United States in 1900. Samuel Dole was the first Hawaiian governor.

Though it would not become an official state of the United States of America until decades later, Hawaii was for all intents and purposes a full-fledged part of the US from that point on.

Chapter 2 – Post-World War I
Pearl Harbor

Upon the outbreak of World War II, popular opinion in the US supported a peaceful stance. The same was true at the beginning of World War I, some two decades earlier—though in both cases, that stance would ultimately be pushed aside for political reasons.

In 1917, the United States of America entered World War I after President Woodrow Wilson received information that threatened an alliance between Germany and Mexico.[137] With much of America already on board to join the war effort due to American casualties in the Atlantic, Wilson knew that he could not ignore the prospect of war on US soil. In addition to sending troops into Britain to join the ranks of the Allies in Europe, the US Army bought a 441-acre Hawaiian island in the middle of Pearl Harbor and began work on an army base there.[138] Construction of the base continued after the European armistice.

The spot was named Ford Island, and in honor of Lieutenant Frank Luke, a US pilot killed during action in WWI, the airfield was named Luke Field. This base was used for air corps training, a new technology

---

[137] "History | Museum History." *Pearl Harbor Aviation Museum.* Web.

[138] Ibid.

within the US military that was obviously going to be of great importance in future conflicts. By 1923, the navy moved its own air service training to Ford Island. With a bevy of new airplane technologies and innovations over the course of the next decade, the island became overcrowded by aircraft and pilots until the army finally moved its own operation to Hickam Field near Honolulu.[139]

Successive US government administrations were aware of the potential of a Japanese-led attack from the opposite side of the Pacific Ocean, as the Japanese Empire was becoming increasingly bothersome to its neighboring countries in Asia, particularly China. Concerned about the functionality of its primary Pacific military base, the United States decided to stage a mock attack on Pearl Harbor in February of 1932.[140]

The nature of the mock attack was specifically to test the resilience of Pearl Harbor Naval Base in the face of a surprise attack. The United States Navy was only able to cover one ocean at a time during that period, and thus its forces were either concentrated in the Pacific via San Diego and San Francisco, or in the Atlantic via timely transfer through the Panama Canal. Should war with Japan erupt, the US Navy's action plan, known as War Plan Orange, focused on readying the warships from Pearl Harbor while leaving Naval Base Subic Bay, in the Philippines, to take the brunt of the first attacks. The latter had already been built by Spain prior to the Spanish-American War and therefore commandeered as part of the subsequent peace treaty.

The US assumed that if Japan attacked unexpectedly, its Filipino base would either be blockaded or overrun outright; the US would then use that time to consolidate its warships and send them up along the country's western coast. Such a move was necessary not only to provide a defensive border around the United States but also to ensure that each warship received its full crew. At that time, US Navy ships generally operated with half their crews, which meant each would need to load up before heading out to face the enemy. Once the ships were fully prepared, they would sail west to Subic Bay and liberate their colleagues before doubling up and heading to Japan. Once there, US Navy ships

---

[139] Ibid.

[140] Micallef, Joseph V. "The First Attack: Pearl Harbor, February 7, 1932." *Military.com*. Web.

planned to blockade the island empire and instigate a decisive battle at sea.

Of course, the US Navy still relied heavily on simulations and had been conducting large-scale mock attacks since 1923, called "Fleet Problems."[141] "Fleet Problem XIII" was code for a mock attack by a fictional Asian island nation against the military base at Pearl Harbor. The US Navy split into two factions, one playing the role of the attacking Asian nation, the other staying on as US defenders. The attackers' force was assigned Rear Admiral Harry Yarnell, one of the navy's few qualified aviators, as its commander.

Yarnell's primary tactic in the mock battle was his assertion that Japan—the nation most likely to play the role of attacker in a real-life situation—tended to attack before making an official declaration of war. To this end, Yarnell's faction used carrier aviation to start the mock war with a surprise attack on Pearl Harbor—and the defenders were accordingly shocked. The fleet in charge of US defense had assumed that they would be attacked with battleships, likely because air strikes had yet to come into common military practice.

Instead of employing common naval battle tactics, however, Yarnell left his battleships behind and launched the company's airplanes from the *Saratoga* and *Lexington* aircraft carriers. Ultimately approaching from a point north-northeast of Hawaii, Yarnell's 152-strong air force attacked at dawn on Sunday, February 7, 1932.[142] Dropping sacks of flour to simulate bombs, Yarnell's fleet took out Pearl Harbor's airfields before taking aim at the battleships. Yarnell's strategy was a complete success, and his fleet achieved total surprise. None of Pearl Harbor's own aircraft managed to get airborne before they were taken out of commission, and the umpires of the mock battle declared Yarnell the clear winner.

The defenders, however, were not impressed by the event and stated that their simulated enemy commander had cheated. There were several reasons why members of both the army and navy administration felt the outcome of the mock battle was null. First, they said dawn was not a

---

[141] Ibid.

[142] Ibid.

reasonable time to expect an attack; furthermore, flying the enemy fleet in from the north-northeast was unrealistic because only aircraft coming in from the United States' mainland were expected to make such an approach. Finally, it was suggested that Asian pilots did not have the necessary hand-eye coordination to pull off the precision bombing of anchored warships.[143]

The War Department agreed that there was nothing realistic about Yarnell's attack on Pearl Harbor and pressured the umpires of the mock battle to reverse their decision. Indeed, the decision was reversed. Although they had not made a single gain during the event, the defending side was documented as the winner. Yarnell was baffled at the outcome, and he remained adamant that not only were his tactics viable but that Pearl Harbor was very vulnerable to an air attack. The navy, however, was mostly populated by admirals who had achieved their high rank via battleship training, and Yarnell was virtually alone in his belief that air attacks would be an important part of the world's military future. No credence was given to the actual outcome of the mock battle, and what's more, the press got ahold of the story and distributed it widely. At the Japanese consulate on Oahu, Japanese naval officers read the details of the report with great interest.

---

[143] Ibid.

Chapter 3 – Post-WWI Japan

On the other side of the Pacific Ocean at that time, Japan was experiencing ongoing political drama. In 1932 alone, there were three prime ministers and two foreign ministers. The acting Emperor of Japan was Hirohito, son of the Emperor Taishō and grandson of the Meiji emperor. Both Hirohito and his government were struggling to stop the spreading of militant chaos that gripped Japan, but the path to serenity was unclear. Furthermore, a great deal of recent history had unfolded in such a way as to put the peace-loving emperor generally at odds with the army and navy.

Born at the Aoyama Palace in Tokyo in 1901, Hirohito was raised in keeping with a custom that required children of the imperial family to be separated from their parents.[144] Cared for first by a former vice-admiral and then a royal servant, Hirohito attended school between the ages of seven and nineteen. Studying at Peer's School and at the Crown Prince's Institute, the future emperor was trained rigorously in military practice as well as the Shinto religion. Hirohito was remarkable in that he did away with the tradition of having concubines when he married Princess Nagako Kuni in 1924.[145] He was also the first crown prince of Japan to travel abroad. He left for Europe in 1921, with more than thirty

---

[144] "Hirohito." *History.* Web. 2019.

[145] "Hirohito, Emperor of Japan." *Encyclopaedia Britannica.* Web.

attendants, and spent six months traveling.[146] Upon his return, his father retired due to mental illness, and he was elected prince regent.

The official emperor, Taishō, died in December of 1926, making Hirohito full Emperor of Japan.[147] It was a seminal time for Japan, as a law had just passed that allowed men to vote for their government representatives. Political parties formed quickly and received overwhelming civilian support, but democracy proved difficult as militant groups also organized and gripped the country. Political assassinations became the norm, and Prime Minister Inukai Tsuyoshi was killed in 1932 by a militant naval group who disliked his decision to limit the number of Japan's warships.[148] The next Prime Minister, Saitō Makoto, was also shot dead a year after his term ended.

Emperor Hirohito personally was not a militant leader, having named his reign "Shōwa," which roughly translates "harmony."[149] As emperor, his role in Japan's affairs was that of a spiritual leader and general of the army, and he is believed to have mostly left politics to the government and acted on the advice of his council. However, the army that fell under the administration of the emperor was in favor of war and national expansion, which meant that Hirohito was forced to consider the best way to meet these expectations.

A major reason for military restlessness in Japan during the 1930s was lingering discord caused by the First Sino-Japanese War. This military campaign, also called the First Chinese-Japanese War, took place in 1894 and 1895 between Japan and China, both of which were pursuing dominance in Korea. Korea was an attractive region to both powerful empires due to its abundance of natural resources, including coal, iron, and gold. Korea already had a long-standing economic relationship with China, but Japan knew the former colonial giant was relatively weak following a population explosion and series of violent political rebellions throughout the 19th century. With military power diverted to keeping the

---

[146] "Hirohito." *History.* Web. 2019.

[147] "Hirohito." *History.* Web. 2019.

[148] Ibid.

[149] "Hirohito, Emperor of Japan." *Encyclopaedia Britannica.* Web.

peace in various regions of China, the nation was not in a strong position in terms of defense. Meanwhile, Japan's military might had only grown during that period.

In 1875, Japan put pressure on Korea to declare itself independent from China so that it could open its market to foreign trade.[150] Of course, that foreign trade would first and foremost benefit Japan. The political pressure was significant and ultimately successful, but China, ruled by Emperor Guangxu, was not willing to step aside and allow Korea to become a full republic. Yuan Shikai, a powerful Chinese military leader, is believed to have arranged a plot in 1894 in which Korea's pro-Japan leader, Kim Ok-Kyun, was lured to Shangai and assassinated.[151] The leader's body was sent back to Korea, where it was mutilated on Chinese orders and displayed as a warning to other anti-Chinese rebels.

The Japanese government was very offended by these acts, and so was the Japanese public. The Tonghak Uprising erupted later the same year in Korea, characterized by peasants and workers demanding social equality and an end to Westernization in their homeland. The Korean government reached out to China for help suppressing the rebellion, while Japan sent its own forces to help with the conflict. Within Korea, Chinese and Japanese troops clashed over how to best deal with the situation. The British ship Kowshing was sent en route to Korea with Chinese reinforcements, which enraged the Japanese administration and caused the latter to sink the ship. The conflict between Japan and China went on for six months before China surrendered and sued for peace.

Tensions remained high between the two nations, however, especially when Japan started its own expansionist campaign in the early 20th century. With the northeastern region of Manchuria in its sights, Japan made efforts to work out an arrangement with China by which to obtain this land, but Russian negotiators won the bid instead. Russia built a railway through the area by means of a 25-year lease of the entire Liaodong Peninsula in which Manchuria was located. The lease,

---

[150] "Introduction to China's Modern History." *Asia for Educators. Columbia University.* 2009. Web.

[151] "Introduction to China's Modern History." *Asia for Educators. Columbia University.* 2009. Web.

procured in 1898, was Russia's way of infringing on land that it knew Japan wanted for itself.[152] War ensued in 1904 and 1905 between Japan and Russia, and upon Japan's victory, Russia gave up its interests in the disputed peninsula.[153]

In 1915, Japan won a 99-year lease of Manchuria in exchange for military support of China during the Chinese Revolution of 1911, and it held on to that tightly during the subsequent Chinese Civil War.[154] The political landscape of Manchuria was extremely unbalanced at the time, as the population was comprised mostly of ethnic Chinese people who were subjugated under a Japanese minority administration. The Chinese were treated like second citizens while Manchuria was in the hands of Japan, but from the viewpoint of Japan's military, its empire was ideally positioned to watch the once-great Chinese Empire fall into chaos. After a series of uprisings that stretched China's military forces to the breaking point, Japan used its control over Manchuria to encroach on the sovereignty of its longtime enemy. In 1931, Japan pushed southward to annex the nearby Chinese city of Shenyang and instill a puppet regime there.[155] The new Nationalist government of China in Nanking did nothing, knowing full well that it did not have the military force to do so.

In 1934, Japan went a great deal further, announcing outright that China was not a sovereign state but a province of Japan, and therefore subject to Japanese rule.[156] Panicked Chinese rebels and communist groups were placed into a tentative alliance with each other and the Nationalist government with the common goal of pushing Japan back out of China. Fighting broke out between both countries on July 7, 1937, at the Marco Polo Bridge outside Beijing, thus beginning the Second Sino-Japanese War.

---

[152] "Manchuria, political region, China." *Encyclopaedia Britannica.* Web.

[153] Ibid.

[154] Ibid.

[155] Ibid.

[156] "Second Sino-Japanese War." *Encylopaedia Britannica.* Web.

Chapter 4 – The Second Sino-Japanese War

Even with all Chinese factions working together, Japan had the superior military and worked quickly to seize most ports, railways, and capital cities within China as far west as Hankow by 1937.[157] Nanking, the Chinese Nationalist capital, was defeated by mid-December of that same year. Known as the Nanking Massacre, the battle for Nanking resulted in the deaths of an estimated 300,000 Chinese civilians and surrendered troops. Japanese Commander Matsui Iwane did not stop there; he ordered his troops to attack tens of thousands of women in the city and surrounding area in a move that would be called the Rape of Nanking.

With Nanking destroyed, Nationalist China established a new capital city at Hankow, in the west. In October 1938, Japanese forces took that city, as well.[158] In a series of Japanese attacks, the Chinese lost Guangzhou, Beijing, Shantung, and three railway systems in the Yangtze valley. Japan had control of the ocean, and its air force was superior above land; it took only months before China's air force was all but wiped out as Japan's air force moved in and bombed urban targets at will.

---

[157] Ibid.

[158] Ibid.

Though China was inundated with Japanese military rule, it refused to concede defeat. The Japanese administration, which had expected to win a quick victory, was forced to continue waging war while generals in occupied cities struggled to set up new governments in which Chinese allies would rule. The Nationalists moved their capital again, this time to Chungking at the west end of the Yangtze gorges in Sichuan, and much of China's Nationalist administration moved north with them. Japan's occupying forces found that their power was limited to the cities and the railways, since Chinese resistance groups, loyal to the Nationalist government, challenged them outside of these areas.

One of the most successful Chinese rebel factions was its Communist group, which proved adept at pushing Japan back with guerrilla tactics. Quickly, Japan's progress through the country slowed to a halt, as Communist troops and activists formed their own militia and pushed behind Japanese lines into large rural areas. Communists organized their own self-defense forces and government administrations in villages and towns, officially forming their own armies: The New Fourth Army and the Eighth Route Army. The Fourth ran operations in the lower Yangtze valley, while the Eighth took a stand in the mountains and plains of northern China.

In 1939, Japan switched tactics and began blockading China to try to force a surrender.[159] Already monitoring China's seaways closely, Japan moved to block its main seaports and cease all trade and commercial movements via water. Meanwhile, in Europe, the Second World War had begun, and German forces led by Adolf Hitler had occupied Czechoslovakia, Poland, and France. Japan quickly saw how this Western conflict could be used to its own advantage and, in 1940, moved into the French Indo-China region to block the coastal railway there.[160] With France completely subdued by Nazi troops on the home front, there was no colonial pushback to fear, and Japan got a military hold on China's eastern region.

In fact, Europe was so preoccupied with fighting the Nazis that Japan succeeded in pressuring France into closing its road from the South

---

[159] Ibid.

[160] Ibid.

China Sea inland. Japan put the same pressure on Great Britain and successfully lobbied to have Britain's Burma Road closed as well, leaving the only open route into China via the Soviet Union. Britain only agreed to this arrangement for three months, however, and reopened the road on schedule thanks to immense displeasure at home and abroad. Members of the British government even opposed caving in to the demands of the Japanese, while American officials protested that their goods were beings turned away from Chinese buyers.

As the Sino-Japanese War raged on, it threatened the rights and earnings of each of China's trading partners, and these events increased political and economic tension between Japan and western nations. Nevertheless, Japan's government set its sights on no less than total control in China, despite the protestations of its emperor. According to Emperor Hirohito's aide, Kuraji Ogura, the leader was disheartened at the will of his country to make war and frustrated that it did not understand the best time to stop.

The emperor is reported to have said:

"Japan underestimated China. It is most wise to end the war quickly and seek to build up our national strength for the next ten years."[161]

The fact was that the emperor was not inclined to impose his will on the country's government, and the true ruler of Japan was Prime Minister Tojo Hideki. Hideki's wishes for Japan matched many of the citizens' wishes in that he wanted nothing more than to expand the Japanese Empire as far across Asia and the Pacific as he could manage. Hideki had no moral conflicts when it came to butting heads with colonial Europe in western Asia.

Hideki held various military roles during the late 1920s and early 1930s, during which he rose through the ranks. He was known as a hardworking, efficient, and decisive officer with the nickname "Razor." Hideki became a member of a hard-line faction of the military that believed it should have a higher degree of control over the Japanese government. The group also believed that expanding into China would have important economic benefits for the empire. As to its impressions

---

[161] "Diary shows Hirohito didn't want war in China: media." *Reuters*. Web. 2007.

of the Western world, Hideki's peer group believed it would be up to them to defend and protect Japan's sovereignty from the United States and its allies.

When the Burma Road reopened, it became China's main supply line for resistance. In a bid for political support and protection against Great Britain and the United States, Japan opted to enter an agreement with Germany and Italy—the Axis powers of World War II—on September 27, 1940.[162] This was the Tripartite Pact, by which each of the signatories promised to come to the aid of the others following an attack by a nation not already participating in the European or Sino-Japanese wars. Simultaneously, each acknowledged that Germany and Italy would be responsible for the establishment of a new political administration in Europe, and Japan would have the same rights in east Asia. Thus, Japan formally entered World War II, if only to bolster its efforts in a Chinese state already overrun with invading forces.

---

[162] "Axis Alliance in WWII." *Holocaust Encyclopedia.* Web.

Chapter 5 - War in Europe

While most of Europe celebrated the end of the First World War, Germany mourned what it believed was a missed opportunity. The German Army had been so confident in its efforts that many decommissioned soldiers were angry that Kaiser Wilhelm surrendered to the Allies. When world leaders gathered at the Palace of Versailles just outside of Paris, France, the following year to sign the Treaty of Versailles, Germany fully realized the implications of losing World War I.

The Allies put the burden of the war squarely on Germany, calling for the disillusioned country to make reparation payments to each of its former enemies. They also forced Germany to surrender war-won lands in Belgium, Czechoslovakia, Poland, and France and give its holdings in Indo-China to the Allies. Allied forces moved into Germany to keep the peace, while the German Army was ordered to minimize operations. Many German veterans, politicians, and other citizens saw this as disgraceful—and they wanted another chance to achieve victory.

One logical reason the Treaty of Versailles was ultimately unsuccessful in legislating peace between the warring nations was that the losers of the war were mostly left out of the drafting process. President Woodrow Wilson of the United States, Prime Minister David Lloyd George of Great Britain, Prime Minister Georges Clemenceau of France, and, to some degree, Italian statesman Vittorio Orlando were responsible for creating the treaty. Not even the less powerful Allied nations were invited to take part in the document's creation.

In the disorder and confusion that followed the armistice, Germans and their allies looked for ways to regain a modicum of national respect and authority. One of those allies was Adolf Hitler, an Austrian-born man who had fought for Germany during the war. Though Hitler was turned away from the Austrian war office due to inadequate physical strength, he was so determined to join the fight that he sent a request straight to Bavarian King Louis III. That request was met, and Hitler joined the Bavarian division of the German Army. During his service in World War I, Hitler was commended many times for his bravery, but when the Axis powers surrendered on November 11, 1918, he was in the hospital recovering from injuries.

Hitler was discharged from the hospital during a time of political uncertainty following Germany's defeat in the First World War. Frustrated at his country's inability to gain sovereignty over a large portion of Europe, and determined not to give up on the prospect of a vast German Empire, Hitler joined the German Workers' Party in 1919.[163] Soon after joining what was ideologically a socialist party, Hitler took over leadership of the group's propaganda, inciting a change of direction and name. Henceforth, the party was the National Socialist German Workers' Party. In German, the party's acronym spelled NAZI (Nazi). In reality, Hitler and many of his supporters had no attachment to the principles of socialism; he merely saw it as a popular theme within Germany upon which to attach his own political desires.

Aligning themselves with entire swathes of the German Army who refused to accept defeat and return to normal civilian life, the Nazi Party grew in numbers and set off a series of violent clashes designed to make it seem powerful. Hitler obtained full leadership of the party in 1921 and used his support base to stage an unsuccessful coup on the republican German government in November of 1923.[164] Violence ensued, and four policemen were killed protecting the government. Hitler was injured and taken into custody, later facing a trial for treason.

---

[163] "Adolf Hitler, Dictator of Germany." *Encyclopaedia Britannica.* Web.

[164] Ibid.

Hitler embraced the trial, using it to firmly call out the government for letting its people down and sweep more Germans into his league of supporters. Nevertheless, the party leader had learned that to orchestrate a coup successfully, one must have some level of legal recourse. Hitler was sentenced to serve five years in prison but only spent nine months in comfortable custody at Landsberg Castle. He spent the time writing down his political treatises in his memoir, *Mein Kampf.*

Adolf Hitler was democratically elected Chancellor of Germany in 1933, but he moved quickly to secure a dictatorship for himself. One of the main points of Hitler's political platform was the belief that all people of German ancestry must be brought together within one nation. To facilitate that goal, Hitler's army occupied Austria and then Sudetenland, the German portion of Czechoslovakia. It was a frightening development for all of Europe, which had only just begun to recover from World War I before facing the worldwide economic depression of the 1930s. Unconcerned, Hitler demanded what he called the emancipation of German people and did not hesitate to use military force.

British Prime Minister Neville Chamberlain believed that quick and effective diplomacy was needed. He went directly to Germany to meet face to face with Adolf Hitler and attempt to come up with a peaceful solution. The leaders met in Munich, along with Prime Minister Daladier of France and Benito Mussolini of Italy. No representative from Czechoslovakia was present, which ultimately implied that the best course of action for Sudetenland was to comply with the decision reached by the international committee. Hitler convinced his visitors that he had every reason to include Sudetenland into Germany and promised that there would be no need for military action if this demand was met. Everyone agreed, and Chamberlain returned to the United Kingdom feeling satisfied with what had been accomplished. Czechoslovakia allowed the affected section of its borderlands to be quietly transferred into German control.

It soon became apparent that the German dictator had no intention of following up on the promise he'd made to his European colleagues. Only six months after the leaders' meeting in Munich, Hitler's armies moved into sovereign Czechoslovakia and established military rule across the entire country. Next, he invaded Poland in September of 1938, brazenly ignoring a treaty he had worked out with the Soviet Union. Two days after Germany marched on Poland, Great Britain and France declared war on Nazi Germany. The Japanese Empire looked on, carefully concocting a plan that would allow it to capitalize on the West's recall to arms.

Chapter 6 – The Occupation of Iceland

German forces quickly plowed through western Europe, occupying Czechoslovakia, Poland, France, Albania, Belgium, Luxembourg, Denmark, Norway, Lithuania, and the Netherlands, all by 1940. With Axis powers present on the western and northern shores of the Atlantic and North Seas, Britain grew very concerned about the ability of Hitler's armies to continue pressing west. Theoretically, Germany could now mount an attack on Great Britain from multiple locations; it could even keep on going west and occupy Iceland, Greenland, and the eastern regions of Canada and the United States. To prevent such an outcome, Britain made the first move on Iceland.

At the time, Iceland was a sovereign nation with its own government, but it was still represented by the Danish monarchy. With Denmark having just been overtaken by the Nazis, Iceland seemed like a logical next move for Hitler. British Prime Minister Winston Churchill planned to beat his enemy there and perform a diplomatic, non-violent occupation that would put a halt to the Axis' westward movement.

The problem was that Iceland was an officially neutral nation during the war, and it outright refused to work with Britain in fear of retribution from Germany. Britain, on the other hand, was convinced that Iceland was at risk despite its neutral status, so the two countries embarked on diplomatic discussions in the spring of 1940. While Iceland's Prime Minister Hermann Jónasson was afraid to put his country's neutrality in jeopardy, Britain worried that prolonged discussions would draw the attention of German intelligence.

Unable to make a formal arrangement to his liking with Iceland, Prime Minister Churchill ordered four Royal Marines ships to leave port in Scotland on May 8[165]. Two days later, the cruisers HMS *Berwick* and HMS *Glasgow* arrived at Iceland, along with destroyers HMS *Fearless* and HMS *Fortune*. The troops on board had just barely finished their formal military training, some of them while actually en route to their destination. Once in place, British aircraft were ordered to scout for enemy submarines and ships in the area. Pilots were warned against flying over any communities to avoid panic. However, a Supermarine Walrus reconnaissance plane from the HMS *Berwick* circled over the Icelandic capital of Reykjavik several times in plain view. The German Consulate in Reykjavik, Werner Gerlach, immediately suspected what was happening.

A faithful member of the German Nazi Party, Gerlich had been specifically stationed in Iceland to try to win the population over to Hitler's side. As a Christian nation with a majority Caucasian population, Iceland was an ideal future ally for a leader whose policy of ethnic cleansing was highly important to him and his followers. The consulate had clearly not managed to succeed in his task because Iceland remained completely unwilling to make a supportive statement in favor of Hitler or his enemies.

There was no time for Germany to intervene, however, as just two hours later, the Royal Marines' ships landed in the port of Reykjavík. People flooded into the docks to see what was happening, and government officials sent a formal message to Britain's Fleet Commander stating that Britain's action had put their neutrality as a nation at risk. The British Consul responded by asking local police to clear the area of civilians so the marines could disembark. Police complied.

---

[165] Guðmundsson, Hjörtur J. "History: British Forces Occupy Iceland." *Iceland Monitor.* 3 May 2016.

British troops secured important locations, and though Iceland's government declared a formal protest, locals obliged the peaceful occupation. Prime Minister Jónasson instructed the police force to keep the peace between civilians and British marines and otherwise to stay out of the way of the occupants. Icelanders continued to protest for several days until their government was promised financial compensation, trade agreements, and the departure of British troops as soon as the war ended. Occupiers also had to promise to step aside in any local disputes. Begrudgingly, the terms were accepted.

For the British, it was of the utmost importance to gain control of Iceland's telecommunication services before news of the invasion could reach the Germans. Accordingly, they quickly seized the local broadcasting service and the Meteorological Office to ensure that all communications were censored or cut off altogether. They also rounded up any German citizens they found and took them into custody, including the German Consul. At the time of his arrest, Werner Gerlich was found busy burning papers in his bathtub. British troops put out the fire and managed to save some of the intelligence documents for their own use.

The Royal Marines suspected they had come just in time, too; there were German crew members in Iceland who had been saved from their sinking ship nearby. As far as the British government was concerned, the ship was probably the intended first wave of a German occupying force. This may well have been true, as intelligence officers reported the Nazis did indeed have plans to occupy Iceland; in British-controlled waters, however, the idea made little sense and was soon given up. Intent on protecting the small country from Hitler, British forces stayed there as long as possible. Unfortunately, as the only military power standing in opposition to the Axis powers throughout 1940, Britain was incredibly strained and in need of help. It reached out to Canada for help in Iceland, and in just a few weeks, the Canadian forces arrived.

Four thousand Canadian troops arrived on March 17th, eventually bringing the occupational forces of Canadian and British troops to 25,000.[166] One year later, US President Roosevelt sent his own troops into

[166] Fairchild, B. "Decision to Land United States Forces in Iceland, 1941." 2000.

Iceland, thereby freeing up British forces that were badly needed on mainland Europe. Prime Minister Churchill accepted the offer most gratefully, and on July 1ˢᵗ, the US Marine Brigade arrived to take Britain's place.[167] Churchill's own troops quickly returned to the home front.

---

[167] "Fact File: Britain Garrisons Iceland." *BBC WWI People's Home*. Web.

Chapter 7 – Japan Contemplates War

Despite its hopes of dissuading the United States and Great Britain from getting involved in its Chinese campaign, Japan's signature on the Tripartite Pact put a target directly on its own back. Between Japan's commitment to the war in Europe and the fact that it refused to stop advancing in China, Western nations had little choice but to come up with a plan to deal with the rogue nation.

First, the United States entered an agreement with the Netherlands and Great Britain to cease all oil exports headed for Japan. This was a major problem for Japan, which imported ninety percent of its oil and could neither continue its military campaign nor meet oil demands on its home territory without imports. Despite restrictions, no nation taking part in the agreement felt it could afford to cut off the Japanese oil market completely, so they decided to cut off other items such as rubber and steel, aircraft engines, and engineering parts.

Early in 1941, Japan negotiated a five-year non-aggression treaty with the Soviet Union, effectively protecting its eastern front and allowing it the chance to expand operations into the western war.[168] For the Soviets,

---

[168] Warfare History Network. "The Forgotten Reason Why Japan Attacked Pearl Harbor." *National Interest.* Web. 2017.

who were already embroiled in World War II, the pact with Japan gave the great relief of not having to also prepare for an attack on their eastern or southern borders. While Europe aligned itself on either side of the German-led war machine, Japan took its opportunity to annex European property throughout Asia. With Europe busy fighting amongst itself, there would surely be little military resistance in such a distance battleground.

Japan marched into French Indochina with additional troops and soon made a move into the Dutch East Indies. Realizing that the Japanese Empire was still active, US President Franklin Roosevelt felt there was nothing left but to cut Japan off from Western resources completely. He therefore placed an embargo on crude oil, and this inspired the Netherlands to quickly do the same. With these restrictions in place, the most logical place for Japan to look for oil remained in the Dutch East Indies, but it was clear that no such attack and seizure would be possible without drawing the US, The Netherlands, and Great Britain into battle. To capture those oilfields would ultimately require beating the British forces in Singapore, the American forces in the Philippines, and ultimately crushing the US Navy at Pearl Harbor to ensure no further American attacks by sea.

Japan and the United States entered negotiations for several months during the embargo but failed to come up with a resolution. The empire had no desire to stop its expansion in Asia and was indeed making plans to push into the Philippines and Malaya, and there was no way to do such a thing without coming face to face with the United States Navy. There was only one way the Japanese Empire wanted to meet the United States in battle, and that was with a surprise attack in its own favor. Therefore, Japan decided to launch a simultaneous attack of all three nations, including a direct hit on America's primary Pacific outpost: Pearl Harbor. Planning for the upcoming attack took months, but within one day of the oil embargo, the empire was ready to strike. The Japanese targeted Pearl Harbor, the Philippines, Singapore, Hong Kong, Northern Malaya, Thailand, Guam, Wake Island, and Midway Atoll, and planned afterward to annex the island of Sumatra and its adjacent airfield and oil refineries. If these attacks were successful, Japan would have much freer reigns with which to conquer Asia, and it would be able to provide its own oil for more military campaigns. Furthermore, if Japan managed to crush the US Navy, it had much less to fear in terms of American retribution since the majority of warships would be destroyed, and the transportation of American soldiers to foreign battlegrounds would be much more difficult.

The only question remaining was whether to formally withdraw from diplomatic negotiations with the United States and declare war. There was controversy within the Japanese war ministry concerning these very issues since The Hague Convention of 1907 had outlined specific protocols for nations about to go to war. It was eventually decided that a message detailing Japan's retreat from the diplomatic process would be sent thirty minutes before the attack was to be carried out—unfortunately, the long, coded message took the Japanese ambassador to the United States a great deal of time longer to transcribe than expected. Hours ticked by, and America did not receive this vital message.

The delay of Japan's message—although its contents would prove to be controversial, anyhow—was of great importance, since it meant that President Roosevelt's administration had no time to prepare against attack. In fact, the United States believed diplomatic negotiations were still underway with Japan and that the two nations were far from war.

While enemy aircraft carriers moved east towards Pearl Harbor overnight, the United States had no reason to be on high alert or to prepare its military defenses.

Chapter 8 – The Pearl Harbor Attack

It was ten years after Harry Yarnell's controversial mock attack on Pearl Harbor that the Japanese Navy orchestrated a startlingly similar campaign, using six aircraft carriers and a fleet of aircraft twice the size of that used in the war games. In addition to the aircraft, the Japanese Navy also carried with it several air-launched torpedoes, the effectiveness of which had been proven a year earlier when the British Royal Navy used similar weapons against the Italians at their Taranto base.

The US Navy had also read reports on those air-launched torpedoes but decided that such weapons weren't relevant to any potential Pearl Harbor attacks because the latter was surrounded by much shallower water than Taranto. Japan's experts made the same assumption but modified their own torpedoes to work effectively for a shallow glide path. Some of those innovations were parked within two miles of Pearl Harbor early in the morning of December 7, 1941.[169]

Five Japanese miniature submarines loomed within torpedo's reach of the opening to Pearl Harbor. At 3:42 a.m., Quartermaster R.C. Uttrick saw something odd in the ocean as he looked through his binoculars

---

[169] Klein, Christopher. "The Midget Subs that Beat the Planes to Pearl Harbor." *History*. Web.

from the deck of the minesweeper USS *Condor*. Less than two miles to the south of the US naval base, Uttrick believed he saw a periscope piercing the surface of the ocean. He reported it to the deck commander, noting that no submarines had been given permission to occupy those waters.

Japan's seventy-eight-foot submarines were an important part of its military attack plan, given that the Americans were unaware of the existence of submarines small enough to function in the shallow waters surrounding Pearl Harbor. Each craft carried two men and two torpedoes and ran on battery power at a speed of nineteen knots in shallow water. Some members of the Japanese military, however, felt that the tiny subs were an unnecessary risk, given that the bulk of their plan centered on an airstrike, just as Harry Yarnell's had.

"Operation Hawaii," as Japan called the attack plan, turned out to be an ideal situation in which to test the new subs. They were ordered to remain submerged until their comrades in the air had appeared and started the attack. Once the air sweep was underway, the subs were to surface and begin targeting their torpedoes, supporting the pilots. As feared by some Japanese, the subs were indeed noticed nearly three hours before the airstrike was scheduled to take place.

Quartermaster R.C. Uttrick's report was passed onto the Condor's colleague, the USS destroyer Ward. Soon afterward, another message reached the Ward, reporting a sighting of the conning tower of an unknown submarine near the mouth of Pearl Harbor. The Ward acted on this information and approached within fifty yards of the mysterious sub.[170] Ward opened fired at 6:45 a.m., sinking the craft into the depths of the Pacific Ocean just as the sun was coming up over the horizon.[171]

Unknown to the crew of the Ward or the Condor, this was the first shot the United States struck in World War II. One hour later, Japan's appointed air force zoomed overhead and launched its attack of Pearl Harbor. There were 353 imperial aircraft involved in the attack, and by the time they retreated, all eight of the US Navy battleships at Pearl

[170] Ibid.

[171] Ibid.

Harbor were damaged. Four of the battleships had sunk, and three cruisers were sunk or damaged, as well. An anti-aircraft training ship and one minelayer ship had also been damaged, and 188 US aircraft were destroyed. In total, 2,403 United States citizens were killed, and 1,178 were wounded.172

The following memorandum was given to US President Franklin Roosevelt after the morning's attack:

The Japs attacked Honolulu time about eight o'clock this morning. The first warning was from a submarine that was outside the harbor which was attacked by a destroyer with depth bombs. Result unknown. Another submarine was sunk by aircraft. They attacked with aircraft, with bombs and torpedoes. At least two aircraft were known to have a swastika sign on them. The attacks were in two divisions; first on the airfields and then on the navy yard. Severe damage. The Oklahoma has capsized in Pearl Harbor. The Tennessee is on fire with a bad list, and the Navy Yard is attempting to dry-dock her.

No. 1 dry-dock was hit by bombs. The Pennsylvania was in dock and apparently undamaged. There were two destroyers hit in dry-dock, one of them blew up. There was one destroyer in a floating dry-dock which is on fire and the deck is being flooded. Two torpedoes hit the sea wall between the Helena, which is 10,000 tons – 6 in. cruiser, and the Oglala. The Oglala is heavily listed and can probably not be saved. She is on fire and is an old mine layer. The power house at Pearl Harbor was hit but is still operating. The Honolulu power house was presumably hit because there is no power on it. The airfields at Ford Island, Hickam, Wheeler and Kanoehe were attacked.

Hangars on fire and Hickam field fire is burning badly. The PBY's outside of hangars are burning. Probably heavy personnel casualties but no figures. So far as Black knows Honolulu was not hit. He does not know how many aircraft were brought down but he knows personally of two. They have both been so busy he has

---

172 Rosenberg, Jennifer. "Facts about the Japanese attack on Pearl Harbor." *ThoughtCo*. Web. 2019.

not contacted Kimmel. There are two task forces at sea, each one of them with a carrier. He knows nothing further on that except that they are at sea. This came over the telephone and we are getting nothing out here whatever. Mr. Vincent called but I have given out nothing, pending further word from you. The Japanese have no details of the damage which they have wrought.[173]

After 2 p.m. that same day, hours after the devastating attack had already taken place, Roosevelt's government finally met with the Japanese Ambassador to receive the delayed message. In a long, fourteen-point document, that message insisted that Japan's faithful search for peace in Asia and the rest of the world had been forestalled by the American government. In closing, the document stated the following:

Thus, the earnest hope of the Japanese Government to adjust Japanese-American relations and to preserve and promote the peace of the Pacific through cooperation with the American Government has finally been lost.

The Japanese Government regrets to have to notify hereby the American Government that in view of the attitude of the American Government it cannot but consider that it is impossible to reach an agreement through further negotiations. 174

The American government did not consider this to be a suitable document to warn against impending attack for two reasons: the decidedly poor timing, and the fact that a declaration of war was never actually made.

---

[173] Yarrington, Gary A. *World War II: personal accounts–Pearl Harbor to V-J Day : a traveling exhibition sponsored by the National Archives and Records Administration, Volume 1, United States.* National Archives and Records Administration Lyndon Baines Johnson Foundation. 1992.

[174] "Japanese Note to the United States United States December 7, 1941." *The Avalon Project.* Yale Law School. Web.

Chapter 9 – Immediate Aftermath

Eleanor Roosevelt wrote the following account of her experiences immediately following the Japanese attack on the United States military base at Pearl Harbor:

> ... As I stepped out of my room, I knew something had happened ... I said nothing because the words I heard over the telephone were quite sufficient to tell me that, finally, the blow had fallen, and we had been attacked.
>
> Attacked in the Philippines, in Hawaii, and on the ocean between San Francisco and Hawaii. Our people had been killed not suspecting there was an enemy, who attacked in the usual ruthless way which Hitler has prepared us to suspect.
>
> Because our nation has lived up to the rules of civilization, it will probably take us a few days to catch up with our enemy, but no one in this country will doubt the ultimate outcome. None of us can help but regret the choice which Japan has made, [but] having made it, she has taken on a coalition of enemies she must underestimate; unless she believes we have sadly deteriorated since our first ships sailed into her harbor.
>
> We must build up the best possible community services, so that all of our people may feel secure because they know we are standing together and that whatever problems have to be met, will

be met by the community and not one lone individual. There is no weakness and insecurity when once this is understood.[173]

Immediately following the attack at Pearl Harbor, the United States was faced with several problems. First, the government needed to launch a full investigation into the event and find out exactly what had happened. They concluded that serious fault lay in the hands of Rear Admiral Husband E. Kimmel and Lieutenant-General Walter Short, who had received multiple reports of unauthorized submarines in the waters surrounding Pearl Harbor and failed to act swiftly. Furthermore, Kimmel and Short were found lacking in their efforts to secure the naval base properly from potential attacks, and, consequently, both were fired from command.

The next issue the United States faced was that of its large population of Japanese Americans. Though not a problem in and of themselves, all people of Japanese heritage living in the United States suddenly found themselves subject to deep distrust by other citizens. Racism against Japanese, German, and Italian people within the United States—even those who were American-born or naturalized citizens—was rampant.

Within a few weeks of the attack on Pearl Harbor, the United States' government began an intensive search for Japanese spies within its own borders. In Hawaii, this was a particularly harsh time, since such a large percentage of Hawaiian citizens had Japanese ancestry—including those who had served and died at the Pearl Harbor Naval Base. Even American-born citizens with Japanese heritage were forbidden from entering the US military, and if they were already enlisted, they were removed from duty. Japanese Americans in Oahu and every other US state were labeled "enemy aliens."[176]

These purported enemies were not only extracted from their positions within the US military but also gathered up forcibly by the police, FBI, and military. The arrests were made without warrants, and the first wave focused on Japanese people who had a record of being investigated by

---

[173] Roosevelt, Eleanor. *Courage in a Dangerous World: The Political Writings of Eleanor Roosevelt.* 1999.

[176] Densho. "At Pearl Harbor, Japanese Americans were victims of the attack — and their own government." *PRI.* 2016.

law enforcement. Deeming them untrustworthy in a time of war, the government mandated locking up these people for the duration of World War II. At the time of most arrests, the individuals' families were told their family members would return in a few hours, but generally, they remained in government facilities for years before being released.

Legally, the Japanese internment camps were legislated into being by President Franklin Roosevelt through his Executive Order 9066 on February 19, 1942.[177] Since the largest Japanese populations in the United States were in California, Oregon, and Washington, the camps were set up in those regions. About 117,000 people of Japanese descent were relocated to the camps, as well as over 2000 people from South America. Mexico and Canada created their own versions of the relocation camps, with more than 21,000 Japanese people being moved from the British Columbia coast in solidarity with President Roosevelt's relocation plan.[178]

Canada, having sought permission from King George VI of Great Britain to declare war, did so in support of the Allies in September of 1939.[179] As a result of all of North and South America's alliance via the United Nations, huge numbers of people with Japanese heritage were completely disenfranchised and sent to camps paid for with the sale of the prisoners' homes and property. Italians and Germans were also interned all throughout the Americas, but at a much lower rate than the Japanese.

The US War Department was in favor of detaining all Japanese Americans, while the US Department of Justice argued that innocent civilians should be left alone. Ultimately, both groups were detained. John J. McCloy, the assistant secretary of war, famously stated that when it came to national security, the American Constitution was "just a scrap of paper," meaning that he didn't care about the civil liberties of those he wanted to arrest. During this fearful time, over 1,200 Japanese community leaders were detained by US authorities. The government also froze all US-based branches of Japanese banks.

---

[177] "Japanese internment camps." *History.* Web. 2019.

[178] Ibid.

[179] Rossignol, Michel. "Parliament, the National Defence Act, and the Decision to Participate." *Public Works and Government Services Canada.* 1992.

Many members of the US government favored an approach that would put all Japanese citizens and residents inland, thereby keeping them far from coastal areas where they might orchestrate further attacks. It was an enormous undertaking since, at the time of the Pearl Harbor attack, there were about 125,000 people of Japanese heritage living in the mainland United States.[180] In Hawaii, which was technically a dominion of the US, there were as many as 200,000 Japanese residents.[181] About 80,000 of these people were second-generation Japanese, born in America and documented as official citizens.[182]

The US government, military, and police insisted that the Japanese detention centers were not centers for punishment, but rather for relocation. Forced evacuations began in the United States on March 24, 1942.[183] Japanese residents were given six days to prepare for their internment and allowed to bring only as many possessions as they were able to carry with them. The terms of internment were strict: Anyone with at least 1/16 Japanese ethnicity was ordered to report to a local relocation center, at which point each would be transferred to a designated military zone. There were an estimated 17,000 children under the age of ten taken to these military zones, as well as many elderly and infirm.[184] In many cases, the residents of the internment camps were housed in facilities not meant for human occupation, including animal stalls or fairground buildings.

There were ten permanent relocation centers in the United States, in which several families were usually housed together with communal dining areas.185 Two of these were erected on Indian reservations, which was authorized by the Bureau of Indian Affairs despite protestations by the native inhabitants. People who were considered a political threat were sent to a camp in Tule Lake, California.

---

[180] "Japanese American internment." *Encyclopaedia Britannica.* Web.

[181] Ibid.

[182] Ibid.

[183] "Japanese internment camps." *History.* Web. 2019.

[184] "Japanese internment camps." *History.* Web. 2019.

[185] Ibid.

Chapter 10 - The United States Goes to War

President Roosevelt had believed from the beginning that, eventually, the United States would have to become involved in the Second World War. Though he was ready to make preparations, the country as a whole was not. Roosevelt's plans were slow-moving, but by November of 1939, he'd managed to convince the US Congress to lift its weapons embargo for France and Great Britain.[186] Sending weapons and military supplies to the Axis powers was the first supporting role America played in World War II. Still, Roosevelt wanted to go further in the summer of 1940, when the Nazis defeated France.[187] To that end, he created the Lend-Lease program.

The Lend-Lease program allowed Roosevelt to assist Great Britain, which was the only Western military power left fighting against Hitler after the fall of France. British Prime Minister Winston Churchill had repeatedly asked the US for help. Still, Roosevelt's hands were tied, given the country's wish to remain out of the war. When the president first explained his idea to the government near the end of 1940, Britain was heavily engaged in the Battle of Britain, which saw intensive aerial

---

[186] "World War II (1939-1945)." *The Eleanor Roosevelt Papers Project.* Web.

[187] Ibid.

bombing campaigns on British soil. The loan scheme Roosevelt proposed would allow the US to send military assistance to any nation whose protection was deemed necessary for the United States' security. He explained that the US could send supplies to help Britain protect itself, and the favor would be repaid in the future. The Lend-Lease bill, however, was not approved by Congress until January 10, 1941.[188]

The Lend-Lease Act was a crucial move that finally allowed American manufacturers to produce and ship hundreds of thousands of tanks, aircraft, and ships to the British Army. Though Britain had managed to push the German Luftwaffe away from its shores, the nation couldn't continue fighting Hitler without weapons, defensive supplies, and more soldiers. In June, Britain's anxiety was considerably lessened when the Soviet Union joined the Allies, following a German attack on their homeland. Despite the fundamental economic and political differences between Western nations and the Soviet Union, neither party could deny the necessity of working together against Hitler.

President Franklin Roosevelt met with the US Congress the day after Japan attacked Pearl Harbor to request that the country formally declare war. Following the events of the previous day, he was well-prepared and emotional, as was the rest of the congregation. The following speech was deeply moving, and it easily achieved its purpose:

Yesterday, December 7, 1941—a date which will live in infamy the United States of America—was suddenly and deliberately attacked by naval and air forces of the Empire of Japan.

The United States was at peace with that Nation and, at the solicitation of Japan, was still in conversation with its Government and its Emperor looking toward the maintenance of peace in the Pacific. Indeed, one hour after Japanese air squadrons had commenced bombing in the American Island of Oahu, the Japanese Ambassador to the United States and his colleague delivered to our Secretary of State a formal reply to a recent American message. And while this reply stated that it seemed useless to continue the existing diplomatic negotiations, it contained no threat or hint of war or of armed attack.

---

[188] Ibid.

It will be recorded that the distance of Hawaii from Japan makes it obvious that the attack was deliberately planned many days or even weeks ago. During the intervening time the Japanese Government has deliberately sought to deceive the United States by false statements and expressions of hope for continued peace.

The attack yesterday on the Hawaiian Islands has caused severe damage to American naval and military forces. I regret to tell you that very many American lives have been lost. In addition, American ships have been reported torpedoed on the high seas between San Francisco and Honolulu.

Yesterday the Japanese Government also launched an attack against Malaya. Last night Japanese forces attacked Hong Kong. Last night Japanese forces attacked Guam. Last night Japanese forces attacked the Philippine Islands. Last night the Japanese attacked Wake Island. And this morning the Japanese attacked Midway Island.

Japan has, therefore, undertaken a surprise offensive extending throughout the Pacific area. The facts of yesterday and today speak for themselves. The people of the United States have already formed their opinions and well understand the implications to the very life and safety of our Nation.

As Commander in Chief of the Army and Navy I have directed that all measures be taken for our defense. But always will our whole Nation remember the character of the onslaught against us. No matter how long it may take us to overcome this premeditated invasion, the American people in their righteous might will win through to absolute victory.[189]

The *Times* reported that the US Army received 2,684 applications in the two days following their nation's declaration of war on Japan.[190] The number of navy staff nearly doubled to over 54,000, and the army accepted more than one million new recruits, expanding its numbers to about 1.5 million.[191] People were scared and angry that they had been so

[189] Retrieved from the Library of Congress. "Franklin D. Roosevelt Speech."

[190] "Attack on Pearl Harbor – 1941." *Atomic Heritage Foundation*. Web.

[191] "Research Starters: US Military by the Numbers." *The National WWII Museum New Orleans*. Web.

shockingly attacked despite having maintained a policy of peace, and many of them wanted to make sure such a thing would not happen again. Finally, the US began shipping out troops instead of just war machines.

With Japan and the Soviet Union pitted against each other in a war with two fronts, Roosevelt recognized the strategic advantage of also lending arms to the Soviet Union to draw the resources of Hitler from western Europe. With the Soviets engaged in the east, ensuring that Japan did not enter Europe, US forces would face less pressure in the west while planning a mass liberation of Europe. American forces soon flooded into the battlegrounds, commanded by military leaders like General Dwight D. Eisenhower, General Douglas MacArthur, and Admiral Chester Nimitz. Eisenhower orchestrated the US approach on the western front of Europe, while MacArthur and Nimitz took control in the Pacific.

Just two days after the US declared war on Japan, Germany delivered its own notice of war against the United States. President Roosevelt reciprocated the same day. The Allies once again stood a chance against Hitler and the Axis powers.

Chapter 11 – America's Military Prepares for War

At the outbreak of war in Europe and Asia, the United States was just starting to pull itself up out of the Great Depression. In an ironic development, it was the presence of war in the rest of the world that helped Americans reinvigorate their own economy. With Europe badly in need of weapons and military vehicles, American factories were kept busy and successful long before Americans overall considered joining the war effort with their political allies. After the Pearl Harbor attack, they had little choice but to get involved to the fullest extent.

Letters were the most significant means of communication between families at home and those serving overseas, much as they had been during the First World War. There were so many letters written during the war that the military supply vessels were flooded with bags of letters to be shipped. Stuffed with letters, ships had precious little room for war materials like ammunition and weapons, and to tackle the problem, a new method of letter-sending called V-mail became popular.

V-mail originated in England, where personal mail between soldiers and their families was photographed and transferred to microfilm before being forwarded to the recipients. Once received, the microfilm images could be blown up and reprinted, thus saving tons of storage space on US and other Allied vessels. V-mail was free for soldiers to use, though family and friends had to pay to use it. As much trouble as it was to ship and handle even the microfilm versions of these letters, correspondence between those at war and those at home was considered hugely beneficial for the morale of the people on the front lines.

The following letter from an American soldier named Frank to his mother was dated September 4, 1942, and sent from an unnamed island in the Pacific:

Dear mother,

I thought I would write you a few lines and tell you some things which we are able too. There are quite a lot of things we cannot mention. I am doing fine and feel all right. We have guard tonight and have had quite a few hikes to keep in condition. I can't say much about the Island outside of that it is not so bad and has plenty of advantages for our protection. I went to church here at camp and enjoyed the outdoor sermon. We train to keep in shape and when they need us to do a job we will be ready. It's good training here as all our fighting will be done in the same kind of islands. I have been going to some school on some valuable subjects. It looks like we are in a good way toward victory after destroying most of the Jap Navy and planes. If everything goes ok we will get leave by Christmas maybe. Musha, I know you will take care of yourself and not worry over anything. I really enjoy the island and as we are kept busy all the time we have quite a few books and movies to keep us happy. The football and baseball games and swimming. Always thinking of you and the boys. I hear the news every evening over radio.[192]

Frank was involved in the Battle of Tulagi that same year, which he also wrote home about:

High bombers overhead dropping eggs all around us. At night a real battle was on. I saw tracers blast from our ships ... heavy fires all around. We can't talk about the losses of the war, so I guess all I can say is we won the battle. It was sure a 4th of July and it happened eight months after the attack on Pearl Harbor.[193]

It was around this time, in November of 1942, that the United States

---

[192] Taken from Dan Lamothe's "Brothers in Arms." *Washington Post.* 2017.

[193] Ibid.

government began using conscription to bring more soldiers into the fold.[194] The draft age was expanded to include men 18 to 37 years old. Previously, due to a bill signed by President Roosevelt in 1940, men between the ages of 21 and 30 were required to register with their local draft boards.[195] In 1943, the draft bill was expanded even further to include black men, who had traditionally been excluded.[196] Though many American men had volunteered to fight following the Pearl Harbor attack, the number of military personnel was not nearly as high as Roosevelt and the military generals required for their large-scale war campaign.

Some men were granted the title of "Conscientious Objector" and allowed to refuse the draft if they could show "sincerity of belief in religious teachings combined with a profound moral aversion to war."[197] For those who did find themselves legally required to join the ranks, their names were chosen at random to serve the military for twelve months. On August 12, 1941, an excruciatingly close vote was held in the House of Representatives, and by a vote of 203 to 202, the House extended the draft beyond twelve months.[198] A further revision was signed after the United States entered the war, which required all men between the age of 18 and 65 to register with the draft office.[199]

Though the United States' full military had begun 1939 with 174,000 soldiers, its combined manpower in 1945 totaled more than 11 million.[200]

[194] "Conscription." *History*. Web.

[195] Glass, Andrew. "FDR Signs Draft Act." *Político*. Web. 2008.

[196] Ibid.

[197] Ibid.

[198] Ibid.

[199] "Training the American GI." *The National WWII Museum New Orleans*. Web.

[200] "Training the American GI." *The National WWII Museum New Orleans*. Web.

Chapter 12 – Wartime in the United States of America

With millions of civilians entering the US military, extensive training needed to start taking place immediately. Most of the people joining the ranks of the army and navy had no military experience whatsoever; they were generally young men who would have been starting families or pursuing post-secondary education had the nation not been at war. Most of them had never left the United States, and their first experience in a foreign land would be at a military training camp.

Volunteers to military service came from many sources, including training programs in high schools and universities such as the Army's Reserve Officer Educational Corps. Many others signed themselves up at local recruitment centers after the Pearl Harbor attack. These volunteers comprised about thirty-nine percent of new military servicemen and women; the majority were called up by conscription, which was officially called the Selective Education and Service Act.[201] From 1940 to 1947, an estimated 10 million people were conscripted into the US military.

All new personnel had a few weeks of basic training designed to transform them from haphazard individuals into members of combatant

---

[201] "Training the American GI." *The National WWII Museum New Orleans*. Web.

groups able to work efficiently together. Immediately upon arrival at one of the many training camps, new recruits handed in their civilian clothing in exchange for uniforms and equipment. Their heads were shaved, and they were each assigned a serial number before being sent to sleep, eat, exercise, and learn alongside their peers. They learned to follow commands promptly and precisely, repeating a set of basic commands over and over. They marched, loaded weapons, unloaded weapons, cleaned their guns, and performed hours of fitness training.

Drill sergeants, in charge of the bulk of this training, zeroed in on the smallest of mistakes made by the recruits and doled out punishments liberally. The payment for not following orders—whether purposeful or otherwise—was usually hard exercise or extra shifts in the kitchen. At the end of boot camp, as this basic training was often called, the recruits who passed were stronger and more confident than ever that they could truly play a crucial role in the coming battles.

Next up came specialized training, pertaining specifically to a recruit's chosen military branch. The US Army, Navy, and Marines needed radio operators, communication experts, specially-trained snipers, and a plethora of other highly-skilled soldiers to fill literally millions of roles. Some of them were sent to as many as seven different training camps to learn each specific skill set before finally being shipped off to their posts in the Atlantic or the Pacific. Paratroopers, antiaircraft teams, desert troops, and other unique units were rigorously trained, and even at their final military bases, US soldiers kept on running drills as long as possible before seeing action.

On the home front, manufacturing was of the greatest concern in an effort to furnish millions of fighting men and women with functional weapons and supplies. The families who stayed behind quickly ran out of items such as nylons, specialty foods, and even housing, and like the British, they soon came under the authority of the rationing board. The government's "Food for Victory" campaign mimicked Prime Minister Churchill's in that it called on citizens to plant vegetable gardens for their own consumption. These "Victory Gardens" took over front and back yards, vacant lots, and public parks, creating an estimated one billion tons of food.

The excess vegetables from America's gardens were canned and stored at home, while heads of household consulted "Victory Cookbooks" for new and innovative ways to prepare what was available. Meanwhile, to keep US soldiers stocked with morale-boosting chocolate, civilians' sugar consumption was closely rationed, as was their meat and coffee. Households were not just asked to make do with less, however; they were also asked to donate in many small ways to the war effort by saving their unusable kitchen fats and scrap metal. The metal could be used in weapons; the fats were used to manufacture glycerine, which was needed for explosives. Even rags, paper, silk, string, rubber, tin, and nylon were badly needed and collected from US homes for the war effort.

To further support the war on a strictly financial level, Roosevelt's government introduced the war bond: a scheme in which the government borrows money from citizens with the promise to pay it back with interest. In addition, federal income taxes were increased, and for the first time, fifty million Americans were required to submit their income tax forms.[202] With so much to do, unemployment plummeted, and America's women became highly-skilled at the manufacturing jobs that kept the country's military supplied with bombs, guns, ships, and even aircraft. Black Americans also had the chance to get involved in better-paying work, though in some areas they still faced discrimination despite the need for workers. To combat this, Roosevelt created the Fair Employment Practices Commission to investigate incidences of black citizens being turned away from jobs usually held by white men.

The home economy was booming, while far away, US soldiers joined their British allies at various strategic military bases. Together, they made plans to win the war against Adolf Hitler and Emperor Hirohito.

---

[202] "Take a closer look: America goes to war." *The National WWII Museum New Orleans*. Web.

Chapter 13 – The Tule Lake
Relocation Camp

In 1943, residents of the Japanese relocation centers were given a questionnaire designed to separate loyal American-born Japanese people from potential troublemakers. Nicknamed the "loyalty questionnaire," it was created with the collaboration of the Office of Naval Intelligence to focus on potential military recruitment of the Nisei cultural group. Nisei was comprised of American-born, second-generation Japanese; first-generation Japanese people called themselves Issei. The loyalty questionnaire provoked some tension between the two cultural groups, and it also forced some interned Japanese to present a negative identity to the US military.

The Office of Naval Intelligence claimed their questionnaire could correctly predict Japanese Americans' allegiance to the United States. Since the War Department needed a standardized method to process Nisei nationality, the tests were administered with a dual purpose. The questionnaires were given to all adult Nisei men in the camps, as well as those who were already serving in the military.

The questions on the loyalty questionnaire mostly related to the identity of the individuals, requiring information about their past residences, education, linguistic skills, ethnicity, group affiliations, family members in Japan, and property in Japan. For each response, the answers were coded into one of two categories: Japanese or American. Each answer that fell into the Japanese category resulted in negative points; each answer in the American category resulted in positive points. Being Christian, for example, added points to one's result, while owning property in Japan resulted in points being taken away.

The questions concerned most responders for several reasons. Men worried that if they admitted they were willing to serve in the US military, that they would be immediately drafted into the war. Women, who eventually received a copy of the same questionnaire, were asked if they would be willing to serve in the Women's Auxiliary. Both were asked if they would pledge unquestioned loyalty to the United States and renounce any such pledge to the Emperor of Japan. Respondents were insulted at the insinuation that they had made any commitment of loyalty to the Emperor of Japan but also worried that renouncing their status as Japanese citizens would leave them without any formal citizenship in the world.

Some of the respondents chose to leave questions blank to avoid undermining their own efforts to protect themselves and their families—but the US military did not take kindly to those unanswered questions. Concerned about the unclear loyalties of some of the respondents, including many who left their questionnaires blank, the authorities chose to move people it considered potentially dangerous to the Tule Lake Relocation Center in California.

The Tule Lake site was located on a dry lake bed that had been drained in 1920 to provide arable land for farming homesteads.[203] The entire area was 4,685 acres in size, with most of that still under cultivation. The living space equated to just over one thousand acres. The camp was also located within the ancestral home of the Modoc tribe, which had suffered its own hardships against the US government a century earlier. The center officially opened on May 27, 1942, with a population of about 11,500 inmates.[204]

---

[203] "Tule Lake." *Densho Encyclopaedia*. Web.

[204] Ibid.

The nearby local communities were extremely unhappy with the nearness of the immense facility and worried about their safety. Locals generally had a very negative perception of the Japanese, especially those locked up at Tule Lake. People living freely in the towns surrounding the relocation center often believed that, while they were suffering under rationing and hard times, the people in the detention camp were being treated to lavish meals and luxurious comforts. That perception was not improved when the residents of Tule Lake protested the enforcement of the loyalty questionnaires, and hundreds of them were sent to country prisons. Lacking formal criminal charges, however, they were moved back to the camp's isolation quarters. Still, thousands refused to answer the questionnaires outright, or would answer but write qualifications beside their answers such as "when my rights are restored."[205] The ambiguity and obviously political nature of the questionnaire resulted in tens of thousands of otherwise lawful Japanese-Americans being transported to Tule Lake, where the issue only grew. The peak population of the camp was 18,789.[206]

On July 15, 1943, the Tule Lake camp was officially rebranded as a Segregation Center.[207] Security was immediately improved around the compound. There was additional barbed wire, and a double fence eight feet high was installed to keep the inmates from escaping. Originally featuring six guard towers, Tule Lake was outfitted with another twenty-two around the site, along with one thousand military policemen.[208] Policeman drove armored cars and tanks, just in case violence broke out. With numbers of inmates swelling, some six thousand detainees who had been identified as loyal to the United States were moved to one of the other relocation centers. Still, the numbers continued to increase as the prisoners labeled "disloyal" in other centers were segregated from their peers.

Inmates at all relocation facilities, Tule Lake included, were given work intended to support the war effort. Detainees were responsible for

---

[205] Ibid.

[206] Ibid.

[207] Ibid

[208] Ibid.

everything from harvesting crops to manufacturing camouflage nets. Some were even hired as teachers and doctors. Whatever the job, detainees were not to be paid any more than an army private. At Tule Lake, agriculture was the main source of inmate employment, given the extensive farmland surrounding the living facilities.

In October of 1943, an accident occurred involving a farm truck, and one prisoner died.[209] Five others were injured. Immediately, the inmate workers went on strike, demanding better working conditions and compensation for any injuries sustained while working at the camp. Raymond Best, Project Director of the Tule Lake Segregation Center, refused to listen to the protests of the workers and simply responded by bringing in replacement workers from one of the "loyal" relocation centers. To further punish the striking harvesters, Best paid the replacement workers an exorbitant $1 an hour, which gave them the same salary in two days as original Tule Lake workers made in a month.[210]

By early November, authorities higher up in the government chain of command visited the camp to oversee negotiations between the prisoners and Best. Still, Best refused to meet any of the inmates' listed demands, including those related to work safety and medical insurance. Tension was high throughout the camp, and as negotiations continued to fail, groups of prisoners began to gather together in solidarity for their representatives. Fearful of violence, Best called in the army. The next morning, Tule Lake prisoners were teargassed and given a show of bravado on the part of the army by way of tanks and gun-mounted Jeeps.

The US Army declared martial law at the Tule Lake site on November 14, beginning a period of intense repression and subjugation. Military police conducted raids on the living quarters and imprisoned more than 200 men in an undersized army stockade. The crimes of those thrown in the stockade were documented for posterity, and they include being "too well educated for his own good," and a "general troublemaker."[211]

---

[209] Ibid.

[210] Ibid.

[211] Ibid.

Chapter 14 – Italy Switches Sides

Italy had already joined the war effort in the summer of 1940 when it became apparent that France had failed to keep the German Army at bay. The country's entry into World War II was announced publicly by the fascist dictator Benito Mussolini, who hoped to capitalize on the war by making land claims. Mussolini allied himself politically with Germany, quickly helping Hitler force France into surrender and then moving onto Greece and North Africa. Italy also sent a quarter of a million soldiers into the Soviet Union to help Germany with the invasion, but an estimated 85,000 of them would never return home.[212]

For Italy, the war was unpopular and unsuccessful. The troops were sent far from home to participate in the fight, and many of them were unsure as to the purpose of their country going to war in the first place. Each step Mussolini took to gain territory for his regime was plagued by Allied resistance so fierce that he was forced to call on Hitler's armies for assistance. On its own, Italy had relatively few tanks and armored guns and no secure transportation for supplies into North Africa and Russia. Getting supplies into Italy proved just as difficult. Heavy bombardment of northern Italian factories between 1942 and 1943 meant that even if they had access to steel, coal, and oil, little work could be done.[213]

---

[212] "Italy, World War II, Military Disaster." *Encyclopaedia Britannica*. Web.

[213] Ibid.

To combat the poor morale of his people and armies, Benito Mussolini promoted careful censorship and propaganda on Italy's radio stations. This was a fairly ineffective move on his part, however, since the people had already realized they could tune into Radio Vatican or Radio London for more truthful news reports. In March of 1943, the main manufacturing centers in Milan and Turin stopped work amid Allied bombing in order to secure safe relocation for their workers' families.[214] With rampant food shortages and the country's manufacturing sectors under heavy fire, hundreds of thousands of Italian civilians fled the cities.

In Sicily, the locals formed their own armed rebel groups to keep out the fascist army, and this helped inspire more anti-fascists on mainland Italy to organize. Throughout 1942 and 1943, the anti-fascist movements slowly gained ground, and with the support of both republican and communist groups, they orchestrated a series of workers' strikes to demand an end to the war. Several political parties were created to support the ideals of the strikers, including the Christian Democratic Party and the New Party of Action. Anti-fascist leaders who had fled Italy altogether at the outbreak of war began to trickle back into their homeland, and these began working together to overthrow Mussolini's regime.

Anti-fascist groups signed a commitment to work together in March of 1943, and by that summer, Italy's fascist dictatorship had all but collapsed. The Allies invaded Sicily and routed out the island's faithful fascists, after which Sicilians largely embraced the Christian Democratic Party. With Mussolini losing the war and the ability to project authority on his people, the Fascist Grand Council met on the 24th and 25th of July to discuss their options. The council met in Rome for the first time since Italy had joined the war and decided on their best course of action. They voted on a motion to invite King Victor Emmanuel III of Italy to accept the reinstatement of his constitutional powers and choose a new prime minister for the country. A large majority of the members voted in favor of the proposal, and that same day King Emmanuel III dismissed Mussolini and gave the Prime Ministership to Marschal Pietro Badoglio. Badoglio was a retired veteran of the First World War and a highly

---

[214] Ibid.

respected person.

Though widespread celebration throughout Italy followed Badoglio's appointment as prime minister, Benito Mussolini had yet to be taken into custody. While anti-fascists raced through the streets, tearing down statues of Mussolini and freeing imprisoned protesters, a faction of local authorities remained loyal to the fascist regime. These attacked and killed eighty-three anti-fascist protesters within a week of the council's decision. Badoglio worked quickly, instructing the army to occupy Rome's important offices, find Mussolini, and take him into custody. Both were done within two days, and Badoglio was formally installed to his office on July 27 by an interim government comprised mostly of ex-fascists.[215]

As for the war, Italy quickly found itself in a sort of tug-of-war between Germany and the Allied forces. As both sides tried desperately to secure the country for their own purposes, Badoglio spoke with Allied representatives in an attempt to end the bombing. He came to an agreement with US General Dwight D. Eisenhower, who oversaw the Allied campaign in the Mediterranean, and declared that Italy would no longer support Adolf Hitler's war. The announcement was made public on September 8, 1943.[216] Essentially, this marked the day when Italy switched sides in the war, denouncing the Nazis and joining the Allies.

Unfortunately, little good came of Badoglio's decision, since Rome was quickly taken by German forces. Unable to beat them back, the government and the king fled south.

---

[215] Ibid.

[216] Ibid.

Chapter 15 – D-Day

American forces joined in the war effort quickly, effectively stabilizing the Atlantic Ocean for safe transportation of Allied troops and supplies. Apart from one, each of the seven US Navy battleships damaged or sunk during the Pearl Harbor attack were raised, repaired, and returned to service in the war. It was General Eisenhower's belief that a detailed, overarching plan was needed to rout the German forces in western Europe effectively; he got to work on the details and named it Operation Overlord. The campaign was to take place in Normandy, an ancient coastal region of France located just across the English Channel from Great Britain.

Preparation was key to Operation Overlord. Not only must the Atlantic be clear of enemy ships and aircraft to facilitate the movement of 800,000 Allied troops eastward, but Normandy itself must be kept as clear as possible.[217] The British Royal Air Force, which had already proven its superiority over the German Luftwaffe during the Battle of Britain, set to work destroying rail lines and bridges connecting inland France with Normandy. Ideally, they wanted to make it impossible for German troops to travel to the coastline, as that was where an immense Allied force would be dropped to kick off the French invasion.

---

[217] Kagan, Neil, and Stephen Hyslop. "History Magazine 'Top Secret' maps reveal the massive Allied effort behind D-Day." *History Magazine*. Web. 2019.

On D-Day, the Allies planned for there to be five divisions set down on the beach at Normandy with the support of three airborne divisions. Each division consisted of about 28,000 soldiers.[218] Since the protection of those divisions was key to a successful French liberation, the plan included a second invasion along the Mediterranean coast. Unfortunately, given the effort needed to land such a huge number of soldiers and equipment at Normandy, the Mediterranean leg of the attack plan had to be delayed by several months. This meant that the Allies risked engagement with Nazis moving in from the south of France.

As for German defense along Normandy beaches, there was only one division stationed there regularly. Knowing it was a weak spot, German commanders buried mines along the beach and filled the coastal water with large debris that made disembarking at high tide almost impossible. The debris would force Allied landing boats to land during low tide, giving the land divisions a longer sprint while vulnerable to German snipers.

German spies in British employ had a great deal to contribute to Operation Overlord as well since they were charged with spreading rumors about the Allied campaign. The goal was to convince Germany that the Normandy invasion was meant as a diversion from a larger attack elsewhere—thereby prompting fewer Germans to be stationed along the beach. Instead of waging a mainland attack, however, Allies planned to set their divisions down along five different sections of the beach: Gold, Juno, Sword, Utah, and Omaha. Omaha beach, the largest of the targets, was subdivided into several more sections.

General Eisenhower was impatient to begin Operation Overlord as soon as all the soldiers and equipment were ready. However, the campaign had to be put off for two weeks due to unfavorable weather. The moon and the tides had to be just right so that paratroopers could move inland before dawn, and the beach-bound soldiers could emerge from the water at sunrise. There was a temporary lull in the storm on June 6th, and the Allies took advantage of it, both to the surprise of the Germans on the coast and the detriment of many Allied fighters.

---

[218] "1st Infantry Division History." *D-Day and Battle of Normandy Encyclopedia.* Web.

In the United States, President Roosevelt addressed the nation on the radio waves, asking for his people to join him in a prayer for the troops on the night of June 6, 1944.

My fellow Americans: Last night, when I spoke with you about the fall of Rome, I knew at that moment that troops of the United States and our allies were crossing the Channel in another and greater operation. It has come to pass with success thus far.

And so, in this poignant hour, I ask you to join with me in prayer:

Almighty God: Our sons, pride of our Nation, this day have set upon a mighty endeavor, a struggle to preserve our Republic, our religion, and our civilization, and to set free a suffering humanity.

Lead them straight and true; give strength to their arms, stoutness to their hearts, steadfastness in their faith.

They will need Thy blessings. Their road will be long and hard. For the enemy is strong. He may hurl back our forces. Success may not come with rushing speed, but we shall return again and again; and we know that by Thy grace, and by the righteousness of our cause, our sons will triumph.

They will be sore tried, by night and by day, without rest —until the victory is won. The darkness will be rent by noise and flame. Men's souls will be shaken with the violences of war.[219]

The ocean had yet to calm from the ongoing storm when the boats set out towards France, and the enormous swells of the water beneath their feet made a great many soldiers sick long before they reached land. Amphibious tanks were sunk on the way, and when the troops landed on the opposite shore, they were met immediately by gunfire. Sick and disoriented, many of the troops were killed before they even made it out of the water. Others were injured or simply terrified, opting to float stiffly and play dead to avoid further shooting. Their comrades floated beside them, dying or dead in the sea.

Omaha Beach was the deadliest of all entry points, with nearly 3,000 Americans killed or wounded there on the first day of the attack.[220]

---

[219] "D-Day 75th." *AJC*. Web. 2019.

[220] Kagan, Neil, and Stephen Hyslop. "History Magazine 'Top Secret' maps reveal the massive

American troops were able to regain a foothold once supporting warships targeted enemy gunners in the cliffs, however, pushing inland towards Colleville-sur-Mer. Another division of American troops landed at Utah Beach with little enemy resistance, and these also managed to push inland. British and Canadian troops on the remaining beaches made it miles inland before facing off with the German 21ˢᵗ Panzer Division.

It was not until that night that Erwin Rommel, in charge of Normandy's German military defense, returned to the coast and realized what had taken place during the day. Believing that the Allies would wait longer before risking the immense attack, Rommel planned to catch them at sea. Instead, he now faced 160,000 Allied troops whose duty was to liberate the country so France could return to the fight alongside them.[221] D-Day was a resounding success, though it was a notoriously hard fight.

On D+1 (one day after the start of the campaign), the Allies needed to secure a port by which to supply their divisions with food, machinery, weapons, and more soldiers. Knowing this would be their next step and expecting the Allies to use an existing nearby port city, German forces gathered at Calais. Operation Overlord was not designed to take a port immediately after landing on the beach, however. Instead, British, American, and Canadian troops used prefabricated parts from Britain to construct their own artificial harbors right in Normandy. Though one of these ports was quickly destroyed by the renewed storm, a second helped the Allies raise their numbers to more than one million by July.[222]

The second campaign, designated Operation Dragoon, took place as planned on August 15 on the French Mediterranean coast. With France now inundated with Allies, the hope of liberation began to reignite among French citizens and resistance groups. Armed French militia began freeing German-occupied Paris even before Allied troops arrived two weeks later. With France in recovery, the Allies moved onto the Netherlands, Belgium, and Luxembourg, while the Soviet Red Army

---

Allied effort behind D-Day." *History Magazine*. Web. 2019.

[221] Kagan, Neil, and Stephen Hyslop. "History Magazine 'Top Secret' maps reveal the massive Allied effort behind D-Day." *History Magazine*. Web. 2019.

[222] Ibid.

invaded East Prussia and moved into Germany from the east. Finally, the Allies had managed to pen Hitler into his own country between two powerful lines. Moving into Germany from the west was no simple feat, however.

The western front soon reached a standstill at the West Wall along Germany's border with France, its contingent having run low on supplies and having reached an impasse with Hitler's forces. Making a desperate counter-offensive against the Americans, French, British, and Commonwealth countries on the west, Hitler mobilized his troops in a move that resulted in the Battle of the Bulge.

The Battle of the Bulge was the major penultimate engagement of the entire war, and it took place in the Ardennes in southern Belgium. For six fierce and bloody weeks, Hitler's army battled the collected forces of the Allied powers in the frozen winter landscape of the Ardennes forest. Conditions were so harsh and unrelenting that even the previously heartened citizens of Allied countries wondered if they had begun to celebrate too soon. To add to the chaos, German troops dressed as American soldiers were parachuted behind the lines, speaking English and spreading misinformation. The German spies changed road signs and used practiced American slang they had learned from American prisoners of war in German camps. Once the American division leaders realized what was happening, they set up frequent identity checks for soldiers on the move. Checks involved various tests, from naming US capital cities to correctly pointing out the line of scrimmage in an American football scene. Finally, on Christmas Day of 1944, the 101st US Airborne Division met with the troops in the Ardennes and turned the tide of the battle in their favor once more.[223] It was exactly the motivation and firepower that the Allies needed to fight their way out of the German trap that had encircled them.

Whenever they had a spare minute, Allied soldiers clamored for their mail and scribbled letters to send back home. Infantryman Burnett Miller got the chance to write his family at Christmastime, 1944, to let them know he was well and thinking of them over the holidays:

---

[223] "Battle of the Bulge." *History*. Web.

December 24, 1944

Dear Mom,

It's the evening before Christmas, but it's quite hard to realize this. I'll just sort of skip this year and we'll all celebrate twice as much next year. We stayed in a fine building last night. And may tonight. It's funny how much a building can mean. This is the first one we've been in since our arrival on the continent. Most of the people here seem to be quite glad to see us. They throw fruit to us. I don't think they're throwing it at us. And we wave quite happily. I hope you and Dad and Grandma all have a happy holiday and that you don't worry too much about me. I'm really quite all right. And even enjoying my little trip up to now very much.

Love,

Burnett[224]

Fighting went on from December 16, 1944, to January 25, 1945, when Allies claimed the victory and moved onward to Berlin.[225]

---

[224] "Communication." *National Archives.* Retrieved from PBS Online. Web.

[225] "Battle of the Bulge." *History.* Web.

Chapter 16 – President Roosevelt Dies

On April 12, 1945, President Franklin Roosevelt died unexpectedly. He had contracted an illness believed to have been polio in the early 1920s and by the end of his life was confined to a wheelchair, but even so, the president had not been ill in the days before his death. It happened while sitting for his portrait painting by the artist Elizabeth Shoumatoff in the living room of his personal home, nicknamed the Little White House, in Warm Springs, Georgia.

While the painting was undertaken, Roosevelt sat comfortably with his dog, Fala, and two of his cousins. Lucy Mercer, his mistress, was also present that day. Early in the afternoon, Roosevelt was suddenly overwhelmed by what he said was a terrible pain in the back of his head. Immediately, he lost consciousness and slumped over in his seat. A doctor was called to him, and, recognizing the symptoms of a brain hemorrhage, he administered a shot of adrenaline to the president's heart. It failed to wake him.

Lucy Mercer left soon after, as did Elizabeth Shoumatoff, both knowing that the president's family would wish to be alone with him and the doctors. Another physician on the scene called the First Lady Eleanor Roosevelt and urged her to come quickly from Washington, D.C. She told the doctor she would plan to travel to Georgia that evening after a scheduled speaking engagement. She would be far too late, however, to see her husband alive again. Doctors in Warm Springs pronounced the president dead at 3:30 p.m., and Eleanor was summoned to the White House to learn the news before she set out for Georgia.[226]

Soon after Eleanor learned what had happened, Eleanor and Franklin's daughter Anna arrived and was informed. Eleanor made calls to her four sons, all of whom were on active military duty at the time. She and Anna changed into black mourning dresses, and early in the evening, Eleanor met with Vice President Harry Truman. Truman, who had no idea what had happened to his colleague, was told quietly by Eleanor herself.

After the president's death, Truman was sworn in as the new president of the United States—but he had a lot to learn about what his predecessor had been doing in secret. So, too, did Eleanor Roosevelt, who was made aware of her husband's extramarital affair after his death. She nevertheless put great effort into the funeral plans and had her husband's body carried on a slow-moving train from Warm Springs to Washington, D.C. Thousands of American citizens came out to see the train and say their goodbyes before Franklin Roosevelt was buried at his family home in Hyde Park, New York City.

The day after Roosevelt's death, *The New York Times* declared, "President Roosevelt is Dead; Truman to Continue Policies." It was the worst possible time for any political changes, as could easily be seen from an accompanying headline in that same newspaper: "U.S. and Red Armies Drive to Meet." The Soviets were closing in on Berlin from the east, the Americans from the west, and the slightest misstep could have prevented the fall of Hitler's capital city.

At the time of Roosevelt's death, Truman had only been vice president for three months, and he was very poorly-informed concerning the Manhattan Project or the meeting between Roosevelt and Churchill. Suddenly, President Truman found himself facing the culmination of the war in Europe and continued war with Japan. As the papers reported, Truman vowed to continue with the plans of his predecessor. The

---

[226] "FDR Dies." *History.* Web.

Cabinet remained the same, and Truman did not see fit to interfere with the current military tactics that had been agreed on between Roosevelt and his generals. For Truman's German enemies, the war was nearly over.

Once the Allies had turned the tides of war and taken control in most occupied countries, the Battle of Berlin raged on in the German capital, where Adolf Hitler himself was positioned to make his last stand. The Soviet's Red Army stood just thirty-seven miles east of the city, regrouping its forces following the capture of Poland.[227] While waiting for the Reds to attack, Berlin readied its defenses and brought in a new army commander, Gotthard Heinrici, to lead the Army Group Vistula, whose ranks were a mix of other army regiments. The sole purpose of Heinrici and the Vistula was to protect Berlin at all costs from falling into Allied control.

The Soviets marched onward towards their target on April 16th, surrounding Berlin on the northern, eastern, and southern sides.[228] By the 20th, which was coincidentally Hitler's 56th birthday, the 1st Belorussian Front had penetrated the city's center.[229] Simultaneously, the 1st Ukrainian Front pressed into Berlin's southern side. Ten days later, with the Allies mostly in control of Berlin, Hitler committed suicide with a gunshot to the head. His wife, Eva Braun, took her own life with cyanide. Still, the Nazis refused to give up their position and continued fighting for two more days before the city's garrison officially surrendered. Even then, many of Berlin's regiments kept on fighting in the western sections of the city.

At that point, most of the Nazi concentration camps had already been liberated, including Bergen-Belsen and Dachau, earlier that April. The sights witnessed by the Allied liberators were unprecedented and haunting: At Auschwitz, the Soviet Army found 14,000 pounds of human hair, one million men's and women's suits, and acres of people dead and dying.[230] As the Germans retreated, they burned many of the camps down

---

[227] "The Allied Push to Berlin." *Lumen Learning*. Web.

[228] Ibid.

[229] Ibid.

[230] "Liberation of Nazi Camps." *Holocaust Encyclopedia*. Web.

behind them and moved thousands of surviving prisoners further and further west. Finally, however, on May 7th, the final camp at Theresienstadt was liberated by the Soviets.[231]

It was probably a great relief when, on May 7, 1945, the US president of twenty-five days received word that Germany had surrendered to American forces in Berlin.[232] The next day was Truman's 61st birthday. He wrote to his family, notifying them of the news, before making his formal announcement to the American people. In interviews later that day with the press, Truman dedicated the victory to Franklin D. Roosevelt, to whom he believed the honor truly belonged.

To the public, Truman said the following:

> This is a solemn but glorious hour. General Eisenhower informs me that the forces of Germany have surrendered to the United Nations. The flags of freedom fly all over Europe. For this victory, we join in offering our thanks to the Providence which has guided and sustained us through the dark days of adversity. Our rejoicing is sobered and subdued by a supreme consciousness of the terrible price we have paid to rid the world of Hitler and his evil band ... I only wish that Franklin D. Roosevelt had lived to witness this day.[233]

The declaration of the end of the war in Europe was transmitted over the radio late in the day to the listeners in Great Britain. The broadcaster interrupted regular programming to make the announcement and to also declare a domestic holiday, Victory in Europe Day, which was to be celebrated the following day. The news spread rapidly around the world, and Victory in Europe Day—or V-E Day—was celebrated in western Europe, the United States, Britain, Australia, and Canada on May 8th, or May 9th in the Soviet Union and New Zealand.[234]

Following the announcements by the British Broadcasting Company (BBC), tens of thousands of joyful people rushed into London's streets,

---

[231] Ibid.

[232] "Germany Surrenders Unconditionally." *History*. Web. 2009.

[233] Grier, Peter. "V-E Day." *The Christian Science Monitor*. Web. 2015

[234] Swick, Gerald D. "V-E Day 1945." *Military Times*. Web.

celebrating until they were pummeled with heavy rains around midnight. On the official V-E Day the next day, parties continued with as much festivity as hosts could manage given the tight food and materials rationing they had been under for the duration of the war. To make the happy occasion more festive, Britain's government declared, "Bonfires will be allowed, but the government trusts that only material with no salvage value will be used."[235] The Board of Trade tried as well, stating, "Until the end of May, you may buy cotton bunting without coupons, as long as it is red, white or blue [to match the Union Jack] and does not cost more than one shilling and three pence a square yard."[236]

In Canada, returning soldiers and their friends and families celebrated an end to the intense hardship of supporting Britain throughout the war. An estimated one million Canadians served in the military between 1939 and 1945, and having succeeded in several significant battles during that time, Canada had earned a good reputation among its Allies. Canada was the fourth-largest provider of wartime supplies to the Allies, and it had sent nearly one-tenth of its population to fight the Nazis. In celebration of their success and the survival of their founding nation, Canadians in Toronto gathered for a massive party, where returning Mosquito bombers dropped ticker tape on the heads of the celebrants.

In Australia, however, celebrations were brief. The *Sydney Morning Herald* asked, "Since when has it been customary to celebrate victory halfway through a contest?"[237] Australia and New Zealand, both Allies and former British colonies remained in direct danger from the Japanese given their location in the south Pacific Ocean. Though these countries had sent troops to assist in Europe, they had also been engaged in defense of their own homelands. It was during World War II that the Australian mainland came under attack for the first time in history, with Japanese aviators bombing Northern Australia and midget submarines launching an attack on Sydney Harbour. By 1945, Australia had lost 39,000 soldiers, with another 30,000 taken prisoner.[238]

---

[235] Ibid.

[236] Ibid.

[237] Ibid.

[238] "Australians in WWII." *AWM London.* Web. 2019.

For those in war-battered Europe, V-E Day felt like an end to five years of fighting; of course, for the United States, Australia, and New Zealand, complete victory had yet to be achieved. When US President Roosevelt agreed to enter the war as an Ally in 1941, his administration agreed to focus on Europe first before moving on to the Asian battlefields. With Europe officially cleared and Hitler dead, it was time for the massive movement of soldiers and supplies into China, Burma, Korea, and Japan. V-E Day was an enormous milestone and motivator for everyone who had fought, but Japan was not yet beaten. The Allies celebrated, some just for the day, and then they were forced to return to the planning stages of another military campaign, this time with Japan in the crosshairs.

In fact, such a campaign had already been underway for some months, beginning in the islands surrounding the Japanese mainland. Backup from the troops who were no longer needed in Europe was greatly appreciated, as Japan turned out to be a particularly vicious enemy.

Chapter 17 – The B-29 Superfortress

President Truman did not let his people forget that the job was still only half done. With Europe under control, the US military turned its attention to the Pacific theater of war, bringing out thousands of its brand-new aircraft: the B-29 Superfortress.

One of the most important contributions the United States made to the Allied war effort, even before it sent millions of soldiers abroad, was aircraft and weapons manufacturing. In 1940, the Boeing company had submitted its design idea for the B-29 bomber to the US Army in anticipation of its necessity in the ongoing World War.[239] Although the new aircraft was originally intended for use against Nazi Germany, design problems and production delays kept Boeing from completing it in time to join the British bombardment of Germany's Luftwaffe. The first B-29s were produced in mid-1943, and these were quickly requested by Allied commanders in each theater of the war.

Boeing's careful planning and design resulted in one of the most advanced airplanes in the world. Though the first of these planes were built before complete testing had taken place, the Army created several

---

[239] "B-29 Superfortress." *Boeing.* Web.

modifications centers to make late changes to aircraft before they were put to work. The B-29 had two crew areas, to the fore and aft, which were pressurized and connected by a long tube so crew members could crawl between them. A third pressurized area housed the tail gunner. The plane's guns could be fired by remote control, and, compared to other warplanes, it boasted increased hit range and higher bomb capacity. Boeing built a total of 2,766 B-29s at plants in Wichita, Kansas, and Renton, Washington. Nearly 700 more were manufactured by the Bell Aircraft Company in Georgia, and 536 were produced by Glenn L. Martin Company in Nebraska.[240]

Most US generals were eager to get their hands on the new bombers, but probably no one more so than Lieutenant General George C. Kenney. Kenney was the air commander in General Douglas MacArthur's Southwest Pacific Area of operations, and he had received little in the way of top-range equipment during the assault on Europe. Now that victory had been achieved against Hitler, Kenney insisted that his regiments receive some of the new B-29s that he himself had a hand in developing. He planned to use them first from a base in Australia before moving on to the Filipino base to assault Japan. Others, such as General Henry H. Arnold, wanted to create a command unit in Washington, D.C.

The decision was ultimately left in the hands of President Roosevelt, whose personal wish was to begin the bombardment of Japan as soon as possible. Roosevelt considered several possible base locations, including Siberia, China, and the Mariana Islands. Siberia, unfortunately, was off-limits despite the Soviet Union's alliance with the US, since Joseph Stalin had pledged to remain neutral towards neighboring Japan. In the end, he chose Tinian, an island near the Marianas. In addition, planes were sent to Marietta, Georgia, for pilot training. Others were shipped to India, where they served as transportation vessels between various bases and supply routes.

The US attempted to fool Japan into thinking that the B-29s were not a direct threat to them. The first B-29 stationed in India stopped in England first, where it was publicly displayed as a new weapon in the war

---

[240] Ibid.

against Germany. When multiple aircraft eventually arrived in India beginning in March of 1944, US intelligence spread misinformation that the bombers had failed in their original design and were only useful as transport vessels.241 Indeed, those planes were tasked with supply runs between Calcutta and Chengtu, but under "Project Matterhorn," the 58th Bomb Wing was stationed there awaiting orders for bombing missions.242

Matterhorn's first missions were intended to begin in June, but several weeks beforehand, plans were changed when Japan started attacking in China again. All B-29s in India were put to work moving supplies to China, their upcoming missions forgotten for the time being. Planned for mid-May, the first B-29 mission was to attack the Makashan railroad yards in Bangkok, Thailand.

With China thoroughly supplied by early June, the mission was back on for June 5th. There were 112 B-29s scheduled to participate, as well as numerous B-24s, but bad weather caused chaos when it came time to take off.243 Low-hanging clouds and poor visibility didn't just threaten aircraft once they were in the air but also meant that some crews were unable to assemble their equipment properly beforehand. Only ninety-eight B-29s managed to take off, and one of those crashed immediately afterward. The entire squadron of B-24s canceled the mission, as did the remaining fourteen B-29 Superfortresses.

Among the aircraft that managed to get off the ground and reach Bangkok, there was a lack of organization and planning. The bombers flew over the city for up to an hour and a half, making independent guesses about where to strike and from what altitude. On the way back to their base, four aircraft were lost in the approaching monsoon, and a fifth crashed upon landing. Dozens of pilots were forced to land in China, and follow-up visuals of the Bangkok railway yard showed relatively little damage to the target. Seventeen crew members were killed during the

---

241 Warfare History Network. "B-29 Superfortress: The plane that bombed Japan into submission." *The National Interest.* Web. 2018.

242 Ibid.

243 Ibid.

mission.244

Despite the rocky start, B-29 Superfortress missions had finally begun, and soon there were fleets of B-29s working the coast of Japan in a campaign to destroy its industrial and manufacturing plants, as well as its infrastructure. The planes had an important role to play in the coming bombardment of mainland Japan, as well as the targeting and occupation of key Japanese islands.

---

[244] Ibid.

Chapter 18 – Iwo Jima and Okinawa

The Japanese military had an important airbase in the Philippine Sea on the island of Iwo Jima, which thereby became the Allies' first major target in the east. US divisions were slated to make the attack, while other Allied nations focused on nearby targets. Unbeknownst to the American and other Allied leaders, however, the Japanese had already prepared the island of Iwo Jima with a series of underground tunnels for higher security. The planned attack was scheduled for February 19, 1945, but no one had counted on the assault lasting for five straight weeks. Japanese troops hid in the tunnels and fortifications they'd constructed underground, making it very difficult for the Americans to rout them. The result was a series of terrifying and bloody close-quarter encounters that the Americans and their comrades feared would be even worse on the enemy mainland.

The tunnels were the brainchild of Japan's General Tadamichi Kuribayashi, the commander on Iwo Jima. Not confident in his ability to fight off an American land invasion, Kuribayashi decided to place most of his army in underground bunkers on the north side of the island linked together by miles of tunnels. Via the tunnels, forces could reach a series of stationery guns and easily retreat if attacked. To keep the gunners safe, other troops were stationed with their guns trained on the beaches upon which the Allies would first step foot. It was the general's hope that such a well-designed and unpredictable defensive system would deter the Allies from launching an assault on Japan's main island.

The Japanese defenses were indeed unprecedented and overwhelming at first, but the US Marines were determined to wreak havoc on the enemy that had caught them so brutally off guard at Pearl Harbor four years earlier. They dug in their heels and pushed onward, never turning back even though thousands were lost in the fray. As the weeks of battle wore on, the invaders noticed less gunfire from the highlands and fewer instances of big gun attacks. Though the bullets were fewer, the terrain grew thicker and more obstinate. Marching through narrow gorges that twisted unexpectedly, Allied forces pushed through landscapes clouded by sulfuric fumes and napalm fuel. The best weapon they had was the flamethrower, several of which had been attached to the division's tanks.

Land forces used 10,000 gallons of napalm-thickened fuel each day, firing their way through the cloudy twists and turns. By using flamethrowers, US troops were able to drive out hidden Japanese soldiers, who were terrified of burning to death inside their caves and tunnels. Despite an eventual lack of large artillery and supplies, the Japanese did not surrender. On February 23, American forces crested Mount Suribachi and placed an American flag at its peak, effectively commemorating their hard-won victory.[245] All told, 6,821 US troops were killed during the siege of Iwo Jima, and 19,217 were wounded.[246] A devastating majority of the 20,000-strong Japanese garrison were also killed, with only a few hundred remaining alive to take into custody.[247]

One of the few left alive, Shuichi Yamaguchi, recounted the battle for Iwo Jima as "a one-sided battle."[248] After weeks of hiding in the tunnels underneath the island's surface, Yamaguchi had seen most of his comrades and friends die—but none of them had gone easily. "Japan had nothing—no ammunition, no supplies—we couldn't strike back effectively.

---

[245] Ibid.

[246] "Iwo Jima and Okinawa." *The National WWII Museum New Orleans.* Web. 2017.

[247] Ibid.

[248] "Iwo Jima: US, Japanese veterans recall horror of pivotal World War II battle, 70 years on." *ABC News.* 2015.

It was a living hell for us. Japanese soldiers were dead all over the place, their bodies were infested with maggots and lice. I don't know whether the Americans disposed their dead or not but I never saw a dead American. I was captured because I left the tunnel to get water for soldiers who were dying."

Iwo Jima was not the end of the road for the US military, however; there was still one more stop on the route to mainland Japan, and that was the island of Okinawa. Just over a month after the US Marines finally took Iwo Jima, another unit made its move on Okinawa, some 1,365 kilometers closer to the main island of Japan. It was April 1ˢᵗ when 60,000 Americans from the US Tenth Army invaded.[249] Once more, they found a strong internal defense system employed there that required the marines to attack via land, sea, and air simultaneously. Fighting was fierce in the southern region of the island, and heavy rainfall and rough terrain made things even worse. Once commenced, the fighting went on for three long months. Just as in Iwo Jima, the intensity of the battle and the unprecedented effectiveness of Okinawa's defensive organization raised the Allies' expectations of what must await them on the mainland.

The US Marines managed to take control of North Okinawa by April 18, but Japanese defenses in the south were insurmountable. The local forces made their base at Shuri Castle, a 15ᵗʰ-century historical palace in the capital city of Naha. Nestled into the ridged landscape of the island, the castle was virtually impenetrable, and this place was also the perfect spot from which to mount counterattacks. One of the most unexpected methods of defense used by Japan's pilots came in the form of *kamikaze*: soldiers who deliberately aimed their aircraft into enemy ships knowing that, in taking out the enemy, they would lose their own lives.[250]

Suicide attacks had begun as soon as the US troops arrived, with as many as 355 kamikaze planes hitting the Allied armada offshore within the first week of engagement. By June, Japan had launched nearly 2,000 suicide attacks, including some carried out by manned rocket-powered Ohka flying bombs. These tactics sank twenty-six ships and damaged

---

[249] Ibid.

[250] "Kamikaze, military tactic." *Encyclopaedia Britannica*. Web.

another 164.[251] During the final offensive campaign in June, the US Army's commander—Lieutenant General Simon Bolivar Buckner Jr.— was killed by a sniper.[252] Nevertheless, his troops won the victory with the seizure of Shuri Castle and the nearby Naha Airfield. On June 22nd, it was all over.[253]

The occupation of Okinawa Island cost over 12,000 American lives, with tens of thousands more injured.[254] As for Japan, the empire lost an estimated 90,000 soldiers and potentially as many as 150,000 civilians.[255] And as for Lieutenant General Mitsuru Ushijima and Lieutenant General Isamu Cho, Japan's commanders on Okinawa, the end of the fighting brought neither escape nor imprisonment. Instead, the two gathered together on a blanket and stabbed themselves in the stomach before an assistant lopped off both of their heads with a sword. General Cho wrote his own epitaph for posterity: "Twenty-second day, sixth month, 20th year of Showa era. I depart without regret, fear, shame or obligation. Age on departure 51 years."[256]

The Japanese suicides became a common sight for the Allies. James Fahey, a member of the US Navy, kept a secret journal of his experiences during the war, and one passage depicts another collection of honor suicides that took place in the Pacific theater:

November 10, 1943

This afternoon, while we were south of Bougainville ... we came across a raft with four live Japs in it ... As the destroyer Spence came close to the raft, the Japs opened with a machine gun at the destroyer. The Jap officer then put the gun in each man's mouth and fired, blowing out the back of each man's skull. One of the Japs did not want to die for the Emperor and put up a struggle. The others held him down. The officer was the last

---

[251] Ibid.

[252] Ibid.

[253] "The Gory Way Japanese Generals Ended Their Battle on Okinawa." *Time*. Web. June 22, 2015.

[254] "Iwo Jima and Okinawa." *The National WWII Museum New Orleans*. Web. 2017.

[255] "Iwo Jima and Okinawa." *The National WWII Museum New Orleans*. Web. 2017.

[256] "The Gory Way Japanese Generals Ended Their Battle on Okinawa." *Time*. Web. June 22, 2015.

to die. He also blew his brains out. The Spence went in to investigate. All the bodies had disappeared into the water. There was nothing left but blood and an empty raft. Swarms of sharks were everywhere. The sharks ate well today ... We went to battle stations ... and at 10 PM we were attacked by enemy planes ... Later darkness descended and the rains came.[257]

As a rule, soldiers were permitted to neither document their time with the military nor tell their families any details about the campaigns and missions they were a part of. Letters were meant to be personal and uplifting, not indicative of the horrors of war. Nevertheless, following the capture of Iwo Jima and Okinawa, tales of the Japanese suicide attacks and honor murders began to trickle home in dribs and drabs.

---

[257] "Communication." *National Archives.* Retrieved from PBS.org. Web.

Chapter 19 – The Bombardment of Japan

With both Okinawa and Iwo Jima in Allied hands, a real invasion plan could truly be put into place. So far, Japanese defenses had proven to be devastatingly difficult to overcome, but not impossible. The Allies knew they had to push on with a mainland attack or risk losing their progress. The British Royal Navy, the US Navy, and the Royal New Zealand Navy came together to target Japan's military and industrial centers. They hoped to lure Japan's air force into battle and reduce its numbers, but the empire's airplanes did not enter the fray.

The main part of the campaign began on July 14th when the United States Third Navy Fleet attacked the city of Kamaishi. The fleet was under the command of Admiral William Halsey, having moved into position from the Leyte Gulf in the Philippines to attack the Japanese home islands. Halsey intended to bombard selected targets with his battleships and cruisers, but first, the fleet sailed near the mainland to search for naval mines. Photo reconnaissance was conducted by the USAAF B-29 Superfortress and B-24 Liberator aircraft, the latter of which collected data on potential targets.

A few days before making its major strike, Task Force 38 began bombing various targets under the command of Vice-Admiral John S. McCain. Aircraft from the fleet's carriers started dropping bombs on

Hokkaido, the northernmost Japanese island, and the northern part of the largest island, Honshu. Though the air force hoped to engage with enemy planes, only a few Japanese aircraft were sent to defend the northern ports. During those early raids, the American forces sank eleven warships and twenty merchant ships, while damaging another twenty-nine ships.[258] An estimated twenty-five Japanese planes were taken down.[259]

The airdrops on northern Japan continued into July 14th when Kamaishi, a coastal city in Honshu, was attacked by the Allied navy. Bombers targeted an iron manufacturing plant there, which was among the largest in Japan despite its working at half capacity due to material shortages. At the time, Allied prisoners of war (POWs) were stationed there as part of the prisoner labor program—information that was unknown to the members of the Third Fleet. At least twenty-seven Allied POWs were killed during the bombardment of Kamaishi.[260] The siege went as planned otherwise, and no Japanese forces were sent to defend the city.

That night, another special task force was sent to attack the city of Muroran on the southeast coast of Hokkaido, where the Japan Steel Company and the Wanishi Iron Works had been targeted. Though cloudy conditions meant that complete destruction was not achieved, enough damage was inflicted on both facilities to cause serious delays in the production of coke and pig iron. On the 15th, Allied aircraft bombed Japan's shipping crews to prevent the movement of coal and other supplies between the islands.

Having dealt with the industrial centers of the north, the US Navy pulled away and joined the British Pacific Fleet to rest and refuel. Two days later, they both headed towards Tokyo. Before reaching the capital, however, a force was sent to target the city of Hitachi, about 80 miles northeast of Tokyo. Allied bombers hit three of nine industrial targets in Hitachi, somewhat disrupting the industrial sector but more heavily damaging the public sector of the city. The effect of the attack was therefore close to what had been intended, except for the civilian

---

[258] Morison, Samuel Eliot. *Victory in the Pacific.* 1960.

[259] Morison, Samuel Eliot. *Victory in the Pacific.* 1960.

[260] Banham, Tony. *We Shall Suffer There: Hong Kong's Defenders Imprisoned, 1942–45.* 2009.

casualties.

On the 18th of July, Allied air forces pelted the Tokyo area while the US Navy focused its efforts on sinking the Japanese ship *Nagato*.[261] Attempts to hit the Japanese radar station on Cape Nojima were unsuccessful, but the Allied attacks were beginning to seriously frighten civilians throughout Japan. The city of Hamamatsu was next, on the south coast of Honshu. The British and Americans each had individual targets, the Japan Musical Instrument Company's Plant No. 1 and No. 2. Normally an odd target for enemy fire, the musical instrument factories were being used to manufacture aircraft propellers. Neither fleet was able to inflict much damage; however, the bombs had the effect of frightening industry workers away from their jobs, which was still quite useful to the Allies. On the way out, Navy forces struck the factories of the Imperial Government Railway. As a result, the factory ceased production for about three months.

Though most of the bombardment was done via airplanes and battleships, Allied submarines also played a role in the attack on Japan. Two submarines, the USS *Barb* and the USS *Trutta*, fired heavily on Japanese targets in June and July of 1945. On the 20th of June, the USS *Barb* moved into the sea adjacent to Japan's northern islands under the command of Commander Gene Fluckey. The ship carried a five-inch rocket launcher that had yet to be properly tested but was intended to be used for bombing the shoreline. After midnight on the 22nd of June, the crew used these on the community of Shari in northeast Hokkaido. The submarine then moved northward and, more than a week later, bombarded the city of Kaiyo in southeast Sakhalin.

A select task force of eight soldiers from the USS *Barb* was sent ashore on the east coast of Sakhalin on July 23rd to sabotage a stretch of rail line.[262] They placed explosives on the track so that, when the train passed by soon afterward, the charges were triggered, and 150 people were killed. Those statistics include civilians. The next day, with its full crew back on board, the USS *Barb* fired thirty-two rockets at Shirutoru

---

[261] *Royal Navy. War with Japan: Volume VI The Advance to Japan. 1995.*

[262] Goldstein, Richard. "Eugene B. Fluckey, Daring Submarine Skipper, Dies at 93". *The New York Times.* 1 July 2007.

and twelve rockets at Kashiho, Motodomari.[263] Chiri was targeted the next day, and dozens of Japanese battleships succumbed to the various attacks.

Though the Allied navy and air campaign did significant damage to the enemy homeland, it failed in bringing out the full Japanese air force. Strategists theorized that the imperial administration was holding back this precious resource and saving it until there were enemy feet on the ground in Japan. An invasion on land, however, was no longer what the Allies had in mind for their next move.

[263] Sturma, Michael. *Surface and Destroy : The Submarine Gun War in the Pacific.* 2011.

Chapter 20 – The Manhattan Project

The United States had begun to fund research into atomic weapons in 1941 following the receipt of an urgent letter by President Roosevelt warning that Germany was likely to develop an atomic bomb.[264] That timely letter had been sent by none other than Germany's own expat nuclear physicists, Albert Einstein and Leo Szilard—then working in the United States—who greatly feared German bomb-makers would learn the secrets of atomic weapons before the Allies.

The following is an excerpt from Einstein's letter to the president:

Sir:

> In the course of the last four months it has been made probable through the work of Joliot in France as well as Fermi and Szilard in America--that it may be possible to set up a nuclear chain reaction in a large mass of uranium, by which vast amounts of power and large quantities of new radium-like elements would be generated. Now it appears almost certain that this could be achieved in the immediate future.

---

[264] "The Manhattan Project." *Atomic Heritage Foundation*. Web. 2017.

This new phenomenon would also lead to the construction of bombs, and it is conceivable—though much less certain—that extremely powerful bombs of this type may thus be constructed. A single bomb of this type, carried by boat and exploded in a port, might very well destroy the whole port together with some of the surrounding territory. However, such bombs might very well prove too heavy for transportation by air.[265]

Einstein went on to advise the president to immediately form a task force to bolster American atomic studies. He also pointed out that, though the United States had no good sources of uranium, there were some in Canada that could be of use—also remarking that Germany had stopped sales of uranium from its annexed mines in Czechoslovakia. The assumption was that Hitler's administration had begun using the uranium for itself, studying and perfecting its own designs for an atomic bomb.

Up until the late 19th century, the only practical use for uranium was in coloring glass and ceramics. Applied to glazes, the mineral lent a greenish-yellow color to decorative glassware and household ceramics. In 1896, French scientist Henri Becquerel realized the uranium in his lab had strange characteristics when he touched it to a photography plate and produced a skewed photograph. One of Becquerel's students, Marie Curie, took great interest in the phenomenon and dedicated herself to better understanding the properties of uranium, which she described as "radioactive."[266] Marie and her husband, Pierre, studied tons of uranium and even discovered another rare radioactive element within some specimens, which they named radium.

Further experimentation with uranium led to the first documented case of nuclear fission, in which a chain reaction of degradation occurs within uranium, causing the nuclei of its molecules to split into multiple pieces. This was achieved by Otto Hahn in Germany in 1939.[267] In the United States, a research team led by Enrico Fermi built the first nuclear reactor at the University of Chicago, though the project was kept secret from the public. Fermi's team achieved the first documented controlled

---

[265] "Einstein's letter to President Roosevelt." 1939. Retrieved from *Atomic Archive*. Web.

[266] "History of Uranium." *Canadian Nuclear Association*. Web.

[267] Ibid.

nuclear reaction in 1942.[268] US research facilities such as this were tasked with catching up to Germany in the nuclear field, and eventually, the quest for military nuclear knowledge was branded as the Manhattan Project.

Named for the location of its original offices, the Manhattan Project was led by General Leslie R. Groves. Groves, tasked with working on the development of a nuclear bomb plan, called that plan the Manhattan Engineer District. The agency received its first substantial government funding in December of 1942 when President Roosevelt allocated $500 million.[269] Generously funded, the Manhattan Project soon moved its headquarters to Washington, D.C., and opened new project sites across the United States. The weapons research laboratory moved to Los Alamos, New Mexico, under the leadership of Dr. Robert Oppenheimer.

Oppenheimer orchestrated the collaboration of thousands of workers, including highly-trained physicists, chemists, metallurgists, bomb experts, and army staff. The US Army provided a tight guard on the town while Oppenheimer worked to physically construct the culmination of their work: the nuclear bombs. The Manhattan Project research also involved alternative bomb blueprints at dozens of other sites across the country. The Monsanto Chemical Company was tasked with separating and purifying radioactive polonium to use as an initiator for the bombs in Dayton, Ohio. Project managers worked across borders with Canadian research groups in Quebec and Ontario, as well as British groups across the Atlantic. An estimated 600,000 people collaborated on the Manhattan Project, and as the Second World War progressed, it became a major focus of the Allied governments.[270]

When it became clear that the project would meet its goal of creating functional nuclear bombs for the US military, the government formed a committee to closely consider the benefits and drawbacks of using them. New President Harry Truman had only just learned of Project Manhattan after the death of Roosevelt and found himself faced with the decision of whether to use weapons he hadn't even dreamed were possible a few

---

[268] Ibid.

[269] Ibid.

[270] Ibid.

months earlier. There was a steep learning curve as US military generals updated their new leader on the existence of the atoms bombs and how they might be employed to put a swift end to the ongoing war in Asia.

Using nuclear weapons would be one of the most important and devastating decisions in history, and President Truman was completely unprepared to make it when he first inherited the job. He delved head-first into the research and secret projects of Roosevelt and ultimately prepared himself as quickly as possible to handle the administration that had been left to him. Truman's Secretary of War was Henry L. Stimson, and it was Stimson who put together the Interim Committee that ultimately recommended using the bombs on Japan. First, however, they had to be properly tested.

The first nuclear bomb test took place on July 16, 1945, at the Trinity Site in New Mexico. The test bomb, codenamed "Gadget," was a plutonium bomb that looked like a giant ball over six feet in height and diameter, covered in electric wires. It exploded as designed with twenty kilotons of force. The subsequent mushroom cloud, the very first of its kind, rose eight miles into the air over a ten-foot deep crater that stretched 1,000 feet in diameter.[271]

That first nuclear explosion was witnessed by many of its collaborative creators, including Enrico Fermi and Robert Oppenheimer. The scientists, engineers, and army authorities clustered together at a base camp roughly ten miles from the explosive device, eager and nervous to see the culmination of all they had been working towards for three years. When everything was ready, they set off the bomb remotely and watched as Gadget exploded just as it was supposed to.

Of the spectacle, Robert Oppenheimer made the following statement:

> And so there was this sense of this ominous cloud hanging over us. It was so brilliant purple, with all the radioactive glowing. And it just seemed to hang there forever. Of course it didn't. It must have been just a very short time until it went up. It was very terrifying. And the thunder from the blast. It bounced on the rocks, and then it went—I don't know where else it bounced. But

---

[271] Ibid.

it never seemed to stop.[272]

Twenty years later, Oppenheimer added to that remark:

> We knew the world would not be the same. A few people laughed, a few people cried, most people were silent. I remembered the line from the Hindu scripture, the Bhagavad-Gita. Vishnu is trying to persuade the Prince that he should do his duty and to impress him takes on his multi-armed form and says, 'Now, I am become Death, the destroyer of worlds.' I suppose we all felt that one way or another.[273]

When Japan refused to surrender per the Allies' plan, Truman conferred with his advisors and decided to act as he believed Roosevelt intended. The first of two nuclear bombs were ordered to be dropped on an appropriate target on mainland Japan in early August of 1945.

---

[272] "Trinity Test Eyewitnesses." *Atomic Heritage Foundation*. Web.

[273] Ibid.

Chapter 21 – The Bombing of Hiroshima

It was by no means an easy decision that the new president of the United States made in sending atomic bombs to the enemy homeland. Many of his own advisors were heavily against it, just as many were in favor. It was the opinion of General Douglas MacArthur that the US should continue its bombardment of Japan's mainland with traditional bombs and torpedoes, followed by a massive land invasion in the style of D-Day in France. They called it "Operation Downfall."[274] This method, the general advised Truman, was likely to personally cost the United States around one million casualties.

President Truman was horrified at this high estimate, and desperate for some way to avoid such a massive death toll of his own people. Despite the fact that General MacArthur, General Eisenhower, Secretary of War Henry Stimson, and even many of the lead scientists in the Manhattan Project preferred not to use the atomic bombs, Truman ultimately chose to deploy them in the belief that they would swiftly end the war and save a million lives. Furthermore, his Secretary of State, James Byrnes, believed that such a powerful move would position the United States as a clear world leader in the months and years following

---

[274] "Bombing of Hiroshima and Nagasaki." *History*. Web.

the war.

Lieutenant Colonel Paul Warfield Tibbets Jr. was chosen to pilot the world's first nuclear mission. He flew one of the specialized B-29 bomber aircraft—which he named Enola Gay after his mother—and worked with a crew he had personally been training since 1944. The Enola Gay was specially equipped to carry the immense plutonium bomb nicknamed "Little Boy."

Two nuclear bombs were prepared by the US military and shipped in parts to the US military base on Tinian, in the Mariana Islands. Tinian had been secured by US forces in August of 1944, and almost immediately, it was transformed into a massive airbase by US Naval Construction Battalions, known as the Navy Seabees.[275] Located 1,500 miles south of Tokyo, B-29 pilots could fly round-trip from Tinian to the Japanese capital in about twelve hours. Within two months of capture, Tinian possessed six runways and the capacity to hold 269 B-29 airplanes.

The Seabees also built docks to receive the USS *Indianapolis*, which had been tasked with transporting the components of the first nuclear bomb. Given the 3,000-mile journey back and forth between Tinian and Tokyo, all B-29s had to be overloaded with fuel to make the trip. Because of this, unbalanced aircraft often suffered crashes at takeoff, which made everyone involved in the nuclear program very nervous. Little Boy, the first bomb, would not explode during a crash, but its successor, "Fat Man," had to be armed before takeoff and therefore posed a very serious threat. Dr. Norman Ramsey, a key scientist in Project Manhattan, suggested that a few changes be made to the B-29s before they were sent to Japan carrying their nuclear payloads. They had to have several parts removed to make space for the atomic bombs, which weighed nearly 10,000 pounds each.

Tibbets' crew consisted of seven aircraft, including the Enola Gay. Three were scheduled to fly ahead of him and check the weather conditions over the targeted city; two were to accompany Tibbets as observational aircraft. One more was stationed in Iwo Jima on standby.

---

[275] "Tinian Island." *Atomic Heritage Foundation.* Web.

The planes got started early on the morning of August 6th, and Little Boy was dropped by parachute over Hiroshima at 9:15 a.m.[276] It exploded 2,000 feet above the city, destroying five square miles.[277] The damage was unlike anything the world had ever seen.

International press quoted pieces of the following news from Radio Tokyo after the event:

> Tokyo said today that the atomic bomb dropped by a B-29 on Hiroshima on Monday literally seared to death "practically all living things, human and animal," and crushed big buildings and small houses alike in an unparalleled holocaust.
>
> Radio Tokyo began broadcasting a detailed account of the horror and ruin left by the bomb soon after an American announcement revealed that four and one-tenth square miles of the once great Honshu industrial city had been destroyed in the raid.
>
> Reconnaissance photographs showed that 60 percent of the built-up area of Hiroshima had vanished almost without trace under the impact of the world's greatest explosion. Five major war plants were levelled, along with scores of lesser factories, office buildings and dwellings.
>
> Only a few skeletons of concrete buildings remained in the obliterated area. Additional damage outside the totally-destroyed section still was being assessed.
>
> Radio Tokyo said both the dead and wounded had been burned beyond recognition and confessed that authorities still were unable to obtain a definite check on civilian casualties.
>
> "Those outdoors burned to death, while those indoors were killed by the indescribable pressure and heat," Tokyo said. It called the city a "disastrous ruin."
>
> Medical relief agencies that were rushed from the neighboring districts were unable to distinguish much less identify the dead from the injured," the enemy broadcast said. They said

---

[276] Ibid.

[277] Ibid.

Hiroshima went up in a mountain of dust, debris, and fire at 9:15 a.m. Monday with an impact like thunder and a flash as brilliant as the sun. Four hours later, smoke and dust swirling up to 40,000 feet still blotted out the city.[278]

The mushroom cloud left behind by the bomb was visible to the B-29 crews for more than 300 miles, and an estimated 80,000 people were instantly killed by its unprecedented force.[279] Another 90,000 to 166,000 died over the course of the next four months, with Japan estimating 237,000 total casualties from the blast, radiation sickness, burns, and cancer.[280]

[278] "Terrifying Results of Hiroshima Blast Told." *Delphos Daily Herald.* 8 August 1945.

[279] "Hiroshima and Nagasaki Bombing Timeline." *Atomic Heritage Foundation.* Web. 2016.

[280] Ibid.

Chapter 22 – The Bombing of Nagasaki

The devastation of Hiroshima still did not persuade the Japanese Council of War to surrender unconditionally. The US had already planned a second nuclear attack—Operation Centerboard II—just in case no agreement could be reached, so the next bomb was set to be dropped on the city of Kokura on August 11th. Poor weather forecasts for that day convinced the US military to deploy the B-29 bomber Bockscar two days early. The plane took off from Tinian Island before dawn under the command of Major Charles W. Sweeney on August 9, 1945.

Sweeney, like many of his colleagues, had been promoted immediately following the Japanese attack on Pearl Harbor. As a lieutenant in the US Army Air Forces, he first participated in aircraft testing of the new four-engine B-29 Superfortress bomber. In late 1944, he moved on to secret training in Utah for aircrews that would eventually handle the nuclear bombs.[281] Having already accompanied Colonel Paul Tibbets to Hiroshima alongside the Enola Gay, Sweeney was as well-prepared as anyone to manage this second nuclear mission.

---

[281] Goldstein, Richard. "Charles Sweeney, 84, Pilot in Bombing of Nagasaki, Dies." *The New York Times.* July 19, 2004.

Bockscar's guns had been removed to fit the five-ton nuclear bomb. At 4:00 a.m., the gunman made his way back to the weapon and pulled out its two green safety plugs, replacing them with red arming plugs. This second bomb was nothing like its predecessor, which had been a rather unremarkable cylinder. The bomb waiting to be deployed over Nagasaki looked like a giant egg, the color of mustard, and nearly six feet tall. There was a stiff fin attached on one side—called the California parachute—designed to keep it from spinning out of control once dropped. The soldiers who had put the bomb together signed their names on the casing and wrote short messages, including "A second kiss for Hirohito."[282]

The sky was dark and stormy for the six-hour journey, and when the airplane arrived near its destination over the island of Yakushima, it circled around to await the arrival of two companions. The companion planes, also B-29s, were designated photographer and technical assistant. The photographer's plane did not appear, so after nearly an hour of waiting, Bockscar and its single companion moved on towards Kokura. Kokura was about half the size of Hiroshima, but per the US military intelligence, it was home to a huge military arsenal. Of several proposed locations for the attack, Kokura was ultimately chosen for this reason.

When the pilots arrived overhead at 10:45 a.m., they found that local fog greatly obscured their view. It had not been there shortly beforehand when the Enola Gay flew over to check conditions, but by the time Bockscar arrived, there was simply too much haze to proceed. The aircrews needed to spot their specific target by eye so as not to risk wasting the attack by dropping the bomb a mile or two off. When waiting proved fruitless, a new destination was chosen: Nagasaki. Nagasaki had never formally been on the list of potential bombing candidates, though it had been the victim of four Allied air attacks. Only one day earlier were the words "and Nagasaki" scribbled on one version of the strike order draft, thereby replacing Niigata on the original copy. When the call was made, however, the pilots shifted course accordingly.

Bockscar arrived at Nagasaki after about eight hours in the air. The mission had very nearly reached the point at which the plane would have

[282] Wellerstein, Alex. "Nagasaki: The Last Bomb." *The New York Times*. 7 August 2015.

to turn back or ditch the bomb in the Pacific Ocean, neither of which options anyone preferred. If the Nagasaki target was not sighted quickly, the mission could be a complete failure. It was difficult to see much of anything since Nagasaki had its own cloud cover to contend with. The bomb was meant to be dropped on the Mitsubishi Steel and Arms Works, which covered an area more than a mile long and a quarter of a mile wide. The factory works lay in the mouth of a valley along a small ocean inlet. It was with minutes to spare that the Mitsubishi factory complex was spotted clearly, and control of the weapon was transferred to Major Sweeney.

Sweeney dropped "Fat Man" at 11:01 a.m. and immediately turned away to avoid the blast. When he looked back, a giant cloud had formed behind the air force crew, which Sweeney later described as colorful and "rising faster than at Hiroshima. It seemed more intense, more angry. It was a mesmerizing sight, at once breathtaking and ominous."[283]

Bockscar nearly didn't make it back to its intended base before running out of fuel; when Sweeney landed on Okinawa, he did so with only enough fuel left to last about a minute. The bomb did its job well, destroying most of the Mitsubishi plant, as well as killing and wounding tens of thousands of workers and civilians. Thousands of homes were also destroyed in the blast, and just as in Hiroshima, tens of thousands of casualties were still to come in the following months.

[283] Goldstein, Richard. "Charles Sweeney, 84, Pilot in Bombing of Nagasaki, Dies." *The New York Times*. July 19, 2004.

Chapter 23 – Japan Surrenders

Emperor Hirohito had the power to end the war via surrender in the months leading up to the nuclear attacks on Japan, but he did not believe that was the best course of action. It was not until twelve hours after the bomb fell on Hiroshima that Emperor Hirohito was actually told about the devastation of the city, but even then, he remained steadfast. It was not because he wanted the war to continue; his refusal to call off the fighting was because he felt the existing surrender negotiations offered by the Allies were inadequate. Personally, Hirohito had been trying to foster a peace treaty between his nation and the Soviet Union; if such an agreement could be made, Japan could continue its military campaigns through China and Asia without backlash from its biggest and most powerful neighbor. Joseph Stalin could not be convinced, however.

The conditions of surrender were laid out by the Allies following the Potsdam Conference, which took place in Berlin from July 17 to August 2nd.[284] The main personalities involved in the conference were Soviet President Joseph Stalin, British Prime Minister Winston Churchill, and his soon-to-be successor, Clement Atlee, and US President Harry S. Truman. The group gathered with other Allied representatives to begin the work of European administration post-war. They were tasked with redrawing the lines of the political map as well as agreeing upon how to

---

[284] "Potsdam Conference, World War Two." *Encyclopaedia Britannica*. Web.

deal with defeated Germany. With the war in Europe over, European nations quickly became colder to the appeals of the Soviet government. Nevertheless, an alliance with Stalin was still necessary to help stamp out the war in Asia.

To Japan, the appeal agreed upon at the Potsdam Conference was simple: The Allies demanded full and unconditional surrender on the part of Japan, or they promised to continue with fiercer air attacks. The ultimatum was issued on July 26th, and when Hirohito and his administration refused, the first nuclear bomb was delivered to Hiroshima. Two days later, on August 7th, Emperor Hirohito found himself with little choice but to surrender, but he was still unprepared to accept the Potsdam Declaration. To stop attacks from the Allies, Japan was required to stop all military campaigns in Asia, which the military leaders believed they could not concede. While Japan struggled to find a solution, the Americans readied their second bomb.

The Allies' military plans did not end with the deployment of those nuclear bombs, however. Though ultimately they would not need to continue the bombardment of their wartime enemy following the dropping of the second bomb, US General Douglas MacArthur was put in charge of the land invasion of Japan. Code-named "Operation Olympic," the campaign was set for November 1945, if Hirohito's military still refused to surrender.[285]

To make the situation worse for Japan, the Soviet Union formally declared war against the nation on August 8, 1945. Until that point, Japan's future in the war had depended on there being no personal fight between them and the USSR. The next day, the Soviets attacked Manchuria and overwhelmed the Japanese stationed there. Hours later, Nagasaki was struck. This time, there was little hesitation from the Japanese emperor. Just before midnight Hirohito met with his Supreme War Council and launched into hours of heated debate. Ultimately, the emperor supported the proposal of Prime Minister Suzuki that they accept the Potsdam Declaration and avoid further devastation on the home front. Hirohito resolved to surrender "with the understanding that said Declaration does not compromise any demand that prejudices the

[285] "Japan Surrenders, bringing an end to WWII." *History*. Web. 2019.

prerogatives of His Majesty as the sovereign ruler."[286] Though his decision was not unanimously supported, it was followed through. On August 10th, the message of surrender was relayed to the United States.

The United States took two days to consider the statement before issuing its own. On August 12, it answered that "the authority of the emperor and the Japanese government to rule the state shall be subject to the Supreme Commander of the Allied Powers."[287] In other words, if Japan upheld its surrender, it would fall under the administration of US President Harry Truman. Another two days passed, during which Emperor Hirohito decided to overlook the obvious threat to his authority. He ordered the Japanese government to send a message back, accepting the terms.

As to notifying the Japanese people of their nation's surrender, Emperor Hirohito recorded a speech intended to be aired on public radio upon his orders. The recording was not immediately broadcasted, but secured within the palace, which gave Hirohito's detractors the chance to retract the surrender and continue the war. If the surrender was not made public, they believed they could keep their military fighting. Led by Major Kenji Hatanaka, the rebels occupied the imperial palace and set fire to Prime Minister Suzuki's home in the very early hours of August 15th.

Major Kenji Hatanaka made the first bold move, killing Lt. Gen. Takeshi Mori of the 1st Imperial Guards Division. He then falsified an order from the dead lieutenant, calling for greatly increased numbers of military guardsmen within the Imperial Palace and Imperial Household Ministry. Hatanaka and the rebels took control of the palace, confusing many guards, whom they instructed to point their guns at government ministers. All entrances and exits were blocked, and telephone wires were cut to prevent communication with the outside world. The rebels searched for the recording for hours but were unsuccessful. The rebellion only lasted until dawn, by which time the government had regained control.

---

[286] "Japan Surrenders, bringing an end to WWII." *History*. Web. 2019.

[287] "Japan Surrenders, bringing an end to WWII." *History*. Web. 2019.

At noon that same day, Emperor Hirohito made the announcement on public radio, which marked the first instance in which an emperor addressed the nation via the airwaves. His isolated royal dialect was strange to hear on the radio, but the message was understood. Emperor Hirohito did not use the word "surrender" during his speech, nor did he decry his country's military aggression leading up to its involvement in the Second World War. In fact, he praised his people and then called for a change in the nation's collective mission, which he described as the following: "To strive for the common prosperity and happiness of all nations as well as the security and well-being of our subjects."[288]

The message was confusing, not just because of Hirohito's strange dialect but because of his indirectness, both of which were part of the Japanese court language. It wasn't long, however, until the purpose of the broadcast was fully understood: Japan was to lay down its arms and await US occupation. Soon after the radio broadcast, Kenji Hatanaka and many of his supporters committed suicide.

As the Supreme Commander of the Allied Powers, General Douglas MacArthur oversaw organizing the formal surrender, which took place on September 2nd. President Truman chose the USS *Missouri*, a battleship that had seen significant action in the Pacific and was named after Truman's native state, as the location of the ceremony. On the allotted day, more than 250 Allied warships pulled in to anchor in Tokyo Bay. On the USS *Missouri*, flags from the United States, Great Britain, the Soviet Union, and China were hung in solidarity.

Japan's Foreign Minister Mamoru Shigemitsu signed the formal surrender document on behalf of the government, and then General Yoshijiro Umezu signed for the Japanese armed forces. Many of the military aides present wept openly as their general signed his name. Supreme Commander MacArthur next signed, stating: "It is my earnest hope and indeed the hope of all mankind that from this solemn occasion a better world shall emerge out of the blood and carnage of the past."[289] Admiral Chester W. Nimitz signed on behalf of the United States of America and was followed by representatives of China, Great Britain, the

---

[288] "Emperor Hirohito." *Atomic Heritage Foundation*. Web.

[289] "Japan Surrenders, bringing an end to WWII." *History*. Web. 2019.

Soviet Union, Australia, Canada, France, the Netherlands, and New Zealand.

Chapter 24 – Post-War Occupation of Japan

Immediately following the ceasefire, Emperor Hirohito signed a new constitution that was written by the United States. The document considerably lessened his authority within Japan, leaving him more of a figurehead than a political leader. He also renounced a core principle of the emperorship, which was that he and his family were divinity incarnate. General Douglas A. MacArthur was given charge of the US occupation of Japan following its surrender in August of 1945. The subject had already been discussed at length with the other Allied leaders, but ultimately the administration of the post-war nation was in the hands of the United States. The most pressing issues were full disarmament, the prevention of future rebellions, stabilizing the economy, and handling the colonies of Korea and Taiwan.

MacArthur, in his role as Supreme Commander of the Allied Forces, first focused on doling out punishment as he saw fit to former military leaders and groups that had committed war crimes. Starting in September of 1945, war crime trials were held in Tokyo, and those found guilty were hanged. Victims of the noose included former Prime Minister and chief of the Kwantung Army Hideki Tojo, as well as Iwane Matsui and Heitaro Kimura. Matsui had organized the Rape of Nanking, while Kimura had tortured prisoners of war.

While the Tokyo trials took place, external trials found an additional 5,000 Japanese citizens guilty of war crimes, for which 900 of these citizens were executed.[290] While the proceedings took place, MacArthur dismantled the Japanese Army and made it illegal for the nation's former military officers to transition into political roles in the new government. To replace Hideki Tojo and his short-term successors, Kuniaki Koiso and Kantarō Suzuki, General Prince Naruhiko Higashikuni served from August to October of 1945.[291] Though he was uncle-in-law to Emperor Hirohito, US intelligence uncovered that the prince had been an opponent to the war against the Allies, and thus he was trusted in the role. Nevertheless, he stepped down shortly after being placed in office.

Following Prince Higashikuni, Japan found a long-term Prime Minister in Shigeru Yoshida, a former ambassador for Japan in the United States and at the Paris Peace Conference. A member of the country's new Liberal Party, Yoshida was hand-picked by the American administration to run not only the party but the country as well, following the general election of 1946. The former head of the party, Ichiro Hatoyama, was purged from political office by US officials, clearing the post explicitly for Yoshida. Yoshida would serve as Japan's Prime Minister for a total of seven years.

As for revamping the economy, MacArthur's administration made land reforms designed to benefit tenant farmers, who held a majority over rich landowners. Though doing so was meant to lessen the burden on tenant farmers, it also took profits away from many of the landowners who had mostly supported the expansion of the Japanese Empire. MacArthur also wanted to establish free-market capitalism throughout the nation, and to facilitate that he did what he could to fragment large business conglomerates.

Despite the efforts of the occupying administration, Japan's economy was in crisis by late 1947 and early 1948. MacArthur's economic ideal of capitalism faltered in the face of the crisis, especially with communism growing in popularity throughout East Asia. The United States knew that the weak Japanese economy would increase the influence of the

---

[290] "Japanese War Criminals Hanged in Tokyo." *History*. Web. 2019.

[291] "Naruhiko Higashikuni." *Encyclopaedia Britannica*. Web.

communist movement within its occupied territory, so further measures were taken to bolster the failing market. Tax reforms were introduced, but these didn't address the primary cause of the problems, which was a lack of raw materials. To bypass this issue, President Truman provided financial grants.

In 1950, American occupation continued as the North Korean Communist Army marched into South Korea. With the Cold War in full swing between the capitalist West and the emerging communist East, the US felt immediately compelled to come to South Korea's aid. In fighting against North Korea, which was supported by the Soviet Union, the United States was essentially embroiled in a proxy war intended both to protect South Korea and prove the superiority of Western ideals. What that meant for Japan was even higher rates of American investment, as Japan was their main base for the war in Korea while it lasted from 1950 to 1953.

Thanks to the increase in suppliers, manufacturers, distributors, and banking facilities during the Korean War, Japan's economy grew every year, in a phase called the Economic Miracle. The Ministry of International Trade and Industry, formed in 1949, also had a lot to do with the economic recovery.[292] The ministry provided a necessary link between the government and the private sector that led to greater industrial productivity and, therefore, to higher profits. Further, it fostered imports of new technology that helped bolster the manufacturing sector.

The Ministry and the government focused on strengthening and growing the cotton, steel, and coal industries. Between 1954 to 1972, Japan experienced unprecedented economic growth thanks in a great part to these sectors.[293] The strong and reliable economy was well-used, with money put into a good education system that turned out highly skilled workers willing to work hard. It was during this period that Japan became one of the most literate countries in the world and one of the most developed in Asia.

---

[292] "What was the Japanese Economic Miracle." *World Atlas.* Web.

[293] Ibid.

Of course, the American occupation did not continue into the final decades of the Cold War; the final agreement between the United States and Japan was signed in September of 1951.[294] The San Francisco Peace Treaty, named for the meeting place, was signed by a total of forty-nine nations that had been involved in World War II. The treaty brought a formal and final end to the post-war occupation in Japan, though it deprived the nation of any territorial claims on Korea or Taiwan. United States troops would stay on and maintain their military bases in Japan, but the nations were no longer in a technical state of war.

In 1952, the treaty came into effect. Four years later, Japan was made a member of the United Nations.

---

[294] "San Francisco Peace Treaty." *University of Pittsburgh.* Web.

Epilogue

The massacres at Hiroshima and Nagasaki stayed with Emperor Hirohito for the rest of his life, and many years later, he expressed personal sorrow for much of what had happened during the war. Once again doing away with the tradition that emperors did not travel outside of their estate, Hirohito visited Hiroshima in 1947 to mourn with his country. In 1975, he visited the United States to meet with President Ford and place a wreath at the Tomb of the Unknown Soldier.[295]

Radiation sickness claimed the lives of thousands of Japanese people after the war, with symptoms including burn scars, deformities, internal bleeding, and hepatitis. The ones who survived the bomb remained acutely ill for long months and years, and when eventually the short-term illness went away, they were left weakened and in poor health for the rest of their lives. For others, especially children who had been exposed to the radiation of the bombs, leukemia was a very real risk. Cancer started to appear about two years after the end of the war, and instances peaked after six years had gone by. After about ten years, non-leukemia-type cancers began to appear with more frequency.

At Tulle Lake, the once vast prisoner village was demolished within a few years from the closing of the camp in the summer of 1946.[296] Several

---

[295] Ibid.

[296] Cart, Julie. "Painful Past, Iffy Future." *Los Angeles Times*. 2006.

structures have been the casualties of time and weather. Much that was left behind has been ransacked, including the iron bars from the prison. The barracks were cut in pieces and given to homesteaders, while the officer's club was turned into a grocery store. Even the headstones remaining there were either taken as souvenirs or plowed over to turn the space into a landfill. Some 300 people were buried at the camp cemetery at its peak; many of these bodies were later moved by families of the deceased, but many remained when the land was prepared to become a garbage collection site.[297]

In recent years, former detainees and their families have petitioned to have what remains of the site preserved and protected, but even now, their memorial ceremonies are interrupted by local residents calling the police. During one Japanese-American tour to the spot, two windows of the tour bus were shot out. The internees of all work camps in the United States were released following the surrender of Japan, but many of the prisoners chose to return to Japan instead of facing further discrimination in the United States.

The US Air Force airplanes that effectively ended the war are now on public display in the United States. The Enola Gay is outside Dulles Airport in Virginia as part of the Smithsonian's National Air and Space Museum exhibitions, and the Bockscar is parked outside the United States Air Force Museum in Dayton, Ohio.

As for the Pearl Harbor Naval Base, it remains an important part of the US Navy, particularly as a home base for the Pacific Fleet. In 2010, the US Navy and Air Force joined their neighboring bases on Oahu, forming the Joint Base Pearl Harbor-Hickam. Japanese Prime Minister Shinzo Abe visited the base in 2016 with President Obama, marking the first time an acting Japanese leader had been present in that place.[298] Memorials have been erected to commemorate the lives of those 2,300 lost during the attack on December 7, 1941.

[297] Kanzaki, Stanley N. "The Desecration of the Tule Lake Cemetery." *Nichi Bei*. 2013.

[298] *Ito, Shingo. "We did our jobs: Japanese participant remembers Pearl Harbor." Atimes. 2016.*

Part 8: The Gulf War

A Captivating Guide to the United States-Led Persian Gulf War against Iraq for Their Invasion and Annexation of Kuwait

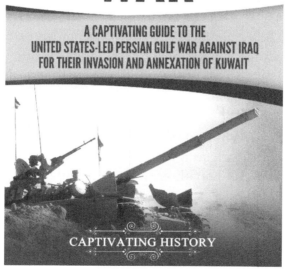

Introduction

The late 1980s and early 1990s were times of significant changes. The Cold War was nearing its end as communism was slowly unraveling, new cyber and communication technologies were becoming more widespread, media was becoming more important and diverse, the economy was steadily growing in most parts of the world, and right-wing political parties and movements were gaining popularity across the globe. Amid all of those changes, a short but impactful war between the United States, aided by several allies, and Iraq occurred. Today it is known by many names, like the First Iraq War, Kuwait War, and, most commonly, the Gulf War or the First Gulf War. It was a rather short conflict, lasting just shy of seven months between late 1990 and early 1991. Yet it was still rather impactful as it showcased several essential innovations and changes in political and technological aspects of warfare, some of which are still part of modern conflicts.

The novelties brought by the Gulf War changed modern warfare in many aspects. It saw the rise of high-tech weapons, which were bolstered by the rising power of computers. No longer were the armaments assessed only by their pure destructive force; they were also judged on their precision and stealth. The sophistication of the US military might left the world in awe. The Gulf War also pioneered a new form of media coverage and control. It was probably the first live broadcasted conflict in history, with the daily video feed from the US bombers shown on cable networks. The combat looked so surreal for the ordinary observer that the audience quickly dubbed it the "Video Game War." These trends continue to this day, as the military industry works on new ways to incorporate the brain of a computer into a weapon. At the same time, the media, especially the internet, makes war and conflict a daily part of our lives.

Another important aspect of the Gulf War was that it was the first conflict after World War II that wasn't fueled by ideological confrontations between communists and capitalists, as the Soviet Union was on its last breath. It demonstrated that the Cold War had more or less ended by this point. Simultaneously, it shattered the beliefs of many who hoped that without the hostility of two blocs world would see fewer wars and conflicts. Thus, although small in size and limited in its immediate outcome and consequences, the Gulf War became a famous landmark in contemporary history. It signaled the break with the old ways of the 20th century and illuminated the path to our world today. For that reason, the Gulf War is still remembered and seen as an essential event in our recent past.

Chapter 1 – Iraqi-Kuwaiti Relations and the Prelude to the War

When talking about the Gulf War, it is not uncommon to start the story with the Iraqi invasion of Kuwait in mid-1990. It was, in fact, the immediate cause of the US-led allied intervention against Iraq. Nonetheless, to begin there would leave the narrative of this war somewhat two-dimensional, focusing solely on the combative aspects of the confrontation. To fully understand all the nuances, deeper causes, political undertones, and other elements of the Gulf War, it is essential to go further back in history. Only by stepping back can one get a better perspective and a fuller picture of the conflict.

Ottoman provinces in 1900, with Kuwait as part of Basra in the lower-right corner.
Julieta39, CC BY-SA 4.0 https://creativecommons.org/licenses/by-sa/4.0 *via Wikimedia Commons* https://commons.wikimedia.org/wiki/File:Map-of-Ottoman-Empire-1900.png

The explanation of why and how the war started must begin with why Iraq decided to invade Kuwait in the first place. The question of Iraq-Kuwait relations can be traced back to the early 20th century to the end of World War I. Before that, both regions were an integral part of the Ottoman Empire. At the time, the city of Kuwait was a district of the Basra province, which was centered around the city of the same name in southern Iraq. However, Kuwait was only under the nominal rule of the Ottomans, as the Turks did not actually rule the city, and it led independent politics throughout most of the 19th century. And since the Ottoman Empire's power was disintegrating, the British tried to take control over the region. At first, they were interested in Kuwait as an important shipping port. In 1899, it became a British protectorate. That meant Kuwait was technically separated from Iraq; however, that bore little immediate consequences since both Kuwait and Iraq remained under the nominal control of the Ottomans. That changed during World War I, though, when the British forces moved into the Mesopotamian region, displacing the Ottoman rule with their own.

Map of the 1920 planned division of the Middle East (Iraq in yellow), without Kuwait.

The factual control of the British was confirmed in 1920 by the League of Nations, the precursor of the modern-day United Nations. At first, Iraq was supposed to become an integral part of the British Empire. Yet after the Iraqi revolt that very same year, the British reconsidered that decision. In 1922, the Anglo-Iraqi Treaty was signed, and Iraq became a semi-independent British-administered kingdom. It was ruled by the Hashemite dynasty, which was an ally of the British. At the time, the British confirmed the separation of Iraq and Kuwait, honoring their promises to their local Kuwaiti allies. Nonetheless, many of the Iraqis felt that Kuwait should be a part of Iraq based on the fact that it was once a part of the Basra province. This idea persisted for a long time, forming the national goals of the Iraqi nationalists. Yet the Kuwaitis, with a brief exception in the 1930s, did not share their sentiment. In 1932, the British mandate ended. Thus, Iraq became an independent state. However, it kept its close ties with Britain both politically and, more importantly, economically. While Iraq was still under British rule, large oil fields were found, and the monopoly on exploration and production of oil in Iraq was given to the Iraq Petroleum Company. Despite its name, it was a British company. Nonetheless, it brought economic improvement to the Kingdom of Iraq. In contrast, Kuwait was going through a rough time, as its economy was left in ruins after World War I, and its status as a trading hub was fading.

Economic disparity, coupled with the fact that the Iraqi government was less oppressive, was enough for the citizens of Kuwait to attempt unification with Iraq in the late 1930s. However, their movement was unsuccessful as the British were opposed to it. Furthermore, the Iraqi government wasn't willing to give full-blown support because of their ties with Britain and because the local Kuwaiti government had imprisoned their leaders. So, the Kuwaitis mostly abandoned the idea of unification, though some remnants of it persisted until the 1950s. Nonetheless, Iraqi nationalists continued to view Kuwait as one of their territorial aspirations. Even so, for a short while, the international political situation stopped them from working on such plans. Still, the Iraqi government continued to negotiate with both Kuwait and Britain as they deemed the Iraq-Kuwait border to be improperly drawn by the British in previous years. These, combined with economic exploitation, pushed Iraq, especially its military circles, toward Nazi Germany. Thus, in 1941, a coup was staged, and a pro-Germany government was formed. Britain didn't wait too long. After a short war, Iraq was firmly under British occupation, and the pro-British government was reinstated. The British Army remained in Iraq until early 1948 when the Anglo-Iraqi Treaty of 1948 was concluded. Under it, Iraq was once again nominally independent but under substantial British control. A joint Anglo-Iraqi defense board oversaw the Iraqi military, while Britain continued to influence the foreign affairs of the Iraqi kingdom.

During the 1950s, the situation changed. By that period, Kuwait once again became quite wealthy, as it had become the largest oil exporter in the Persian Gulf. Oil was found in Kuwait as early as 1938, but it was not until the 1950s that the massive exploitation began, with several more oil fields being discovered during the decade. This meant that the Kuwaitis lost their economic incentive to become a part of Iraq. On the other hand, the Iraqi economy was still in crisis from World War II, as inflation was rising and the quality of life was falling. On top of that, the Iraqis, for most of the decade, were British pawns in the Cold War. Britain used them in an attempt to limit the penetration of communism in the Middle East. For some Iraqis, that was too much, as they felt that the interests of their people were being ignored. The idea of pan-Arabism was also spreading at the time, which was additionally fueled by the unification of Egypt and Syria into the United Arab Republic (UAR) in early 1958. Led by famed Egyptian President Gamal Abdel Nasser, the UAR aimed to unite all the Arabs into a single republic, free of Western interference and influence and under, to a certain degree, socialist economic ideas of equality. For the Kingdom of Iraq, that was a significant threat, and the British were also resentful of the new Arab state. Thus, Iraq and Jordan, both ruled by the same dynasty, united into a single state named the Arab Federation.

The newly formed state was supposed to counter the UAR's rising popularity; however, for at least some of the Iraqis, it was an unpopular move. They saw it as a way for the king and his political leaders to stay in power and maintain their entitled positions while the majority of the population continued to live in poverty. It was also seen as pandering to Western politics as it stood in the way of a united Arab people. In the end, this led to a military coup in mid-1958, where the monarchy was overthrown, and the Iraqi Republic was formed. The leader of the coup, Abd al-Karim Qasim, became the prime minister of the republic. His politics shifted Iraq closer toward the ideas of economic equality and pan-Arabism. Nonetheless, amidst these politics, Qasim still held on to the Iraqi nationalist notion that Kuwait should be a part of Iraq. His pressure on the southern Iraqi neighbor was highest in the summer of 1961 when Kuwait gained its independence from Britain. Qasim threatened with war and occupation, but he never fulfilled his threats. Most historians doubt he ever really planned to attack Kuwait, as it was defended first by the British then by the forces of the Arab League, a regional organization of the Arab states.

Qasim
https://commons.wikimedia.org/wiki/File:Abd_al-Karim_Qasim_5.jpg

Arif
https://commons.wikimedia.org/wiki/File:President_Abd_al-Salam_Arif.jpg

Regardless, Qasim once again kept the Iraqi expansionist idea alive. He continued to use it in his politics until his fall in 1963 when another coup was staged, and he was executed. Colonel Abd ul-Salam Arif, a firm Iraqi nationalist, took his place, proclaiming a more friendly relation with Kuwait. However, it wasn't long before the Kuwaitis realized these were only empty words. The new regime indeed stopped threatening with an invasion, but it wasn't ready to recognize Kuwait as an independent state, and it also pressed hard on the matters of border disputes. Moreover, many members of the Iraqi government still thought that Kuwait should be a part of their country. The negotiations about recognition and borders were started that same year. Those dragged out for several years, with Kuwait even giving loans to Iraq, hoping to soften its position. In the end, these negotiations outlasted the Arif regime, as in 1968, another coup was staged in Iraq. This time, the members of the Arab Socialist Ba'ath Party took power. It was an Iraqi branch of the formerly unitary Ba'ath Party, whose main ideologies were pan-Arab nationalism and progressivism on a social basis. Once again, it seemed that a coup would bring the disputes between the two countries to a close.

Despite the auspicious readiness of Ba'ath Iraq to commence the negotiations, it wasn't long before they hit a dead end. As the new Iraqi regime was more distinctively socialist, with stronger ties to the Soviet Union, its relations with Iran quickly deteriorated. At the time, Iran was a monarchy; it had a shah as its head and was allied with the US and Britain. As such, it saw Ba'ath Iraq as a threat to its security, and the shah even tried to topple the new regime. However, this attempt was unsuccessful, and in 1969, it seemed that an Iranian-Iraqi war was imminent. The Iraqi government used this threat as a pretext to station its troops on parts of Kuwaiti territory. Even though Kuwait accepted this begrudgingly, its minister of defense stated that the Iraqi forces began deploying before an official agreement was made. The war between Iraq and Iran was avoided, but the Iraqi forces still remained in Kuwait, stating that until the Iraqi-Iranian border disputes were settled, the threat remained. In 1973, Iraqi troops tried to reinforce their garrisons in the territory of Kuwait, but the Kuwait Army tried to stop it. This event culminated with an exchange of fire in March of that year. This was enough for the Iraqi government to return to negotiations with Kuwait.

In the 1970s, the main territorial issue between Iraq and Kuwait was, in fact, over the islands of Warbah and Bubiyan. Those were located in the northwestern parts of the Persian Gulf and were quite close to both countries, though slightly closer to Kuwait. None of those islands had any riches on them, but their worth was strategic for both countries. For Iraq, they were essential to ease the control of the western parts of the Persian Gulf while protecting Umm Qasr, a vital Iraqi port near the Kuwait-Iraq border. On the other hand, for Kuwait, the islands were sort of a buffer zone, protecting it from being sucked into a war between Iraq and any other foreign force, mainly Iran. The islands were so close to the mainland, with Warbah being only 325 feet (100 meters) away from the Kuwaiti shore, that Kuwaiti sovereignty would be compromised if any foreign force were to hold it. Not to mention that any fighting there was bound to spill over onto Kuwaiti soil. On top of all that, these islands, though small in relative terms, represented a sizable chunk of Kuwait's entire territory. For this reason, the Kuwaiti government was unable to accept the Ba'ath regime's offers. Kuwait even rejected the Iraqi proposal of leasing the islands from them; in this offer, all other disputed lands would have been recognized as a part of Kuwait.

Map of Kuwait, including the contested islands.
https://commons.wikimedia.org/wiki/File:Kuwait%27s_boundaries_and_other_features.png

By 1975, the Iraqi government had to admit that, at the time, Iran no longer posed a threat to Iraq's security, and so, by 1977, it withdrew its forces from Kuwait. Kuwait continued to confirm its claim over the islands both politically, with a parliament resolution, as well as militarily, by building outposts on them. The status quo was to remain, even though the Iraqis still harbored territorial pretensions toward Kuwait. However, by the late 1970s, Iraq's focus was pointed at Iran. Both countries aimed at hegemony over the Persian Gulf, and despite an agreement signed in 1975, the territorial dispute burdened their relations. Nonetheless, it seemed that both sides were avoiding confrontation. This changed in 1979 with the Iranian Revolution. The monarchy was overthrown, and Iran became an Islamic republic under Ayatollah Ruhollah Khomeini. The revolution spurred a grand revival of both Persian nationalism and Shia Islam fundamentalism. As such, Iran not only retained its aspiration for becoming a hegemon of the Persian Gulf, but now, it also wanted to export its revolution to Iraq as well. Furthermore, in that very same year, Saddam Hussein, an Iraqi politician and general filled with nationalist ideas and dreams, enacted a purge in the Ba'ath Party and became the leader of both the party and the country. This only furthered distrust between the two now rather militant regimes, which led to both countries preparing for war.

Thus, in September of 1980, Iraq attacked Iran, using the Iranian Revolution as a pretext for war. In truth, the fears of Iraq were not unfounded. Shia Muslims were a relative majority in Iraq, and Khomeini saw that as a way to topple the Ba'ath Party from the inside, something he publicly said was his agenda. On the other hand, the Iraqi government wasn't satisfied with the 1975 agreement. It saw this as a chance to expand its territory since Iran was under sanctions and lacked international support. In the end, Iraq's ultimate goal was to become a regional superpower and the de facto leader of the Arab world. However, the Iraqi leaders underestimated the strength of Iran and its people. After some successes in late 1980 and early 1981, the Iraqi invasion was brought to a halt, and in 1982, Iran counterattacked. The war dragged on for years. Both sides had their successes and failures, accompanied by long periods of stagnation and trench warfare. By the mid-1980s, Iraq declared a policy of total war, with a widened military draft and ever-higher defense expenditures. Iran followed a similar path with the emergence of large volunteer armies, which often attacked in large human waves. Because of that, combined with the stalemate, this war reminded international experts of the trench warfare of World War I.

Iranian soldier in a trench during the Iran-Iraq War.
Unknown authorUnknown author (GFDL <http://www.gnu.org/copyleft/fdl.html> or GFDL <http://www.gnu.org/copyleft/fdl.html>), via Wikimedia Commons https://commons.wikimedia.org/wiki/File:Chemical_weapon1.jpg

During this conflict, which lasted much longer than the Iraqi leadership had expected, Iraq quickly ran out of resources. It had to take out loans to cover its financial losses. Its main financiers were its southern neighbors, Saudi Arabia and, more importantly, Kuwait. The Iraqi government asked them for money, representing itself as a defender of the Arab world against the Persian threat. Most of this was just Iraqi propaganda. However, the Iranians did bomb territories of Kuwait in the later stages of the war. Thus, there was a slight possibility that if Iraq was to fall, Kuwait would share its fate. For this reason, Kuwait was willing to lend as much money as Iraq asked for, and it became the main financial backer of its northern neighbor. The war dragged on until 1988. By this time, both sides were exhausted, and Iraq asked for peace, but Iran refused, mostly due to its fanaticism. Iraq then began threatening Iranian civilians with chemical warfare, pushing Iran to agree on a ceasefire in August of that year. The losses on both sides numbered in the hundreds of thousands, including tens of thousands of civilian victims. The war was settled on *status quo ante bellum*, meaning that despite claims from both sides and various observers, the conflict ended without a clear winner. Iraq didn't achieve its territorial expansion, while Iran failed to topple the Ba'ath regime.

President Saddam Hussein speaking by telephone at a frontline command to a field commander at East of Basra sector on Monday. The President personally directed the Iraqi battle against a fresh Iranian attack at the sector which started at midnight on Sunday. After crushing the Iranian attack and pushing the invaders back behind the border, the President returned to Baghdad

Iraqi propaganda during the Iran-Iraq War.
https://commons.wikimedia.org/wiki/File:Saddam_Hussein_on_a_telephone_call,_1988.jpg

Besides the massive losses in human lives, the most tangible result of the Iran-Iraq War was an economic disaster on both sides, with combined spending reaching to about 1.2 trillion dollars. Just prior to the war, Iraq had substantial financial reserves of about 35 billion dollars, with an annual income of about 26 billion dollars from oil exports. Its international debt was at a very low 2.5 billion. In fact, the Iraqi economy before the conflict with Iran was somewhat decent. However, the almost eight-year-long war devastated that relative prosperity. The oil production and exports were lowered, with Iraqi annual exports amounting to only about ten billion dollars. The reserves were spent, and the government accumulated a debt of about 130 billion dollars. The Ba'ath government was put under tremendous pressure as its population, which suffered rather high casualties, were becoming rather unsatisfied with the economic situation. The social upheaval was simmering beneath the surface. The position of the Iraqi government was further destabilized by the dissatisfaction of both the Shia and Kurdish minorities, which suffered significantly during the war. Furthermore, during the Iran-Iraq conflict, the Ba'ath government began shifting toward a more dictatorial regime under the strict rule of its leader, Saddam Hussein.

Faced with such a crisis, the Iraqi government began looking for a way to remedy its economic situation. It hoped to gather funds from revitalized oil exports. However, it ran into a problem that was out of its hands. The oil prices dropped due to the overproduction of certain countries, most notably Kuwait. Iraq turned to the Organization of the Petroleum Exporting Countries (OPEC), which, at that time, consisted mainly of nominally Iraqi-friendly Arab countries. Seeing that the cost of crude oil fell due to the overproduction, Iraq asked the member countries to limit their production and push the prices from about eight dollars per barrel to over twenty dollars. However, most of the OPEC members were reluctant to agree to this proposal as they were also experiencing their own internal problems. They sought to expand their production, not limit it, even though the Iraqi plan had a solid economic foundation. At the same time, the Ba'ath regime also sought financial help from its Arab friends. Iraq asked Saudi Arabia and Kuwait, as well as other Persian Gulf countries, for a moratorium on its wartime credits, as well as an immediate infusion of somewhere between thirty and forty billion dollars for reconstruction. The Iraqi propaganda tried to justify such demands by claiming that Iraq was fighting not only for itself but for all the Arabs, representing itself as a bulwark of the Arab world against the vile Iranians.

These demands, despite being accompanied by somewhat vague threats made by Saddam Hussein, were, of course, rejected by other Arabs. No one wanted to finance Iraqi wars, nor was anyone prepared to lower their oil production quotas. This left the Ba'ath regime in a dangerous position. It had to deal with the crisis or risk being toppled from within. Saddam and his government saw only one possible escape from this problem, which was to deal with Kuwait. It was, in fact, one of the countries that Iraq was most indebted to, and it was also a chief culprit of the oil overproduction. Furthermore, Kuwait had probably the weakest army in the Gulf region. On top of all that, the longstanding border dispute and pretensions of the Iraqi nationalists made it an even "sweeter" target for the Ba'ath government. Thus, by early 1990, Iraq started setting the stage for yet another invasion, one that was to be an even more enormous miscalculation than the war with Iran, causing an even wider economic crisis and more pronounced isolation.

Chapter 2 – Circumstances and Causes of the Gulf Conflict

The economic crisis and the nationalistic ideas were not the only reasons why Iraq decided to invade Kuwait, though they explain a substantial part of the Ba'ath regime's motivation. In the 20th century, no country, conflict, or alliance existed in an isolated bubble. On the contrary, every major event, every nation, and every war were tied together with the much larger, global picture. The Iraqi invasion of Kuwait and the Gulf War are no different, as they were not merely an isolated attack and a justified intervention.

The most crucial aspect of international politics after the end of World War II was undoubtedly the Cold War. Through it, the United States and the Union of Soviet Socialist Republics (USSR) competed for world dominance, usually through remote conflicts in third-world countries. The Middle East was also one of the regions where the influence and agendas of these two superpowers clashed. At the very beginning of the Cold War, the US had close relations with Israel, Iraq, Iran, Kuwait, and Saudi Arabia. These were maintained either directly or through the British, as they had held a strong presence in the region since the 19th century. On the other hand, the USSR began attracting revolutionary regimes of Egypt, Syria, Libya, and Yemen. Through the years, the political constellations changed a bit, with Egypt becoming more pro-Western in the 1970s, while Iraq became more pro-Soviet after the 1958 coup. The most significant change, however, was the position of Iran after 1979. Before the Iranian Revolution, Iran was probably the most important ally of the US in the region. The British even planned to make it the Western "policeman" of the region, tasked with maintaining security from possible pro-Soviet threats. Yet after the revolution, Iran became openly anti-American and anti-Western, which culminated with the Iranian hostage crisis that lasted from 1979 to 1981.

During that event, the US suffered substantial diplomatic humiliation, and US-Iran relations never recovered. Under Ayatollah Khomeini, Iran became one of the fiercest US adversaries in the world. That kind of political rift with one superpower of the Cold War would usually mean that Iran was turning toward the other superpower, the Soviet Union, something the USSR itself hoped for. The USSR was the first country to recognize the new regime of Iran officially, and it tried to create a more tangible relationship with the Islamic Republic of Iran. However, Khomeini saw communism as being in direct opposition to Islam, and so, those relations never expanded to anything concrete. As both superpowers were rebuffed, when the Iran-Iraq War began, both were leaning more toward Iraq. Yet, despite that, both Moscow and Washington continued to sporadically, and rather clandestinely, supply Iran with weapons during the war, most likely trying to win its allegiance in the grander scales of the Cold War. These attempts bore no fruit, however, leaving Iran somewhat isolated in its own aggressive stance toward the world. Yet both the Soviets and the Americans received worldwide backlash for those actions, especially from their Arab allies.

The signing of the Treaty of Friendship and Cooperation between Iraq and the USSR (1972)
https://commons.wikimedia.org/wiki/File:Freundschaftsvertrag_Kossygin_al-Bakr_1972.jpg

Due to this diplomatic failure with Iran, Iraq was left as one of the rare countries of the Cold War era that at one point was allied or at least cordial with both sides. On the one hand, since 1958, Iraq began turning toward the USSR, which began rapidly growing in 1968 and the start of the Ba'ath regime rule. Their close relations were at their peak during the 1970s, especially after 1972, which was when the Treaty of Friendship and Cooperation with the Soviet Union was signed. At the time, Iraq's diplomatic relations with the United States were almost nonexistent. The Ba'ath leadership was rather irritated by the US support of Israel, especially during the Six-Day War (1967) and the Yom Kippur War (1973), but also because they believed Americans were involved in the organization of an anti-Ba'ath coup in 1969, as well as the US somewhat covert helping the Kurdish rebellion in Iraq in the mid-1970s. These factors led the Ba'ath regime to believe that the US government was working on overthrowing them, which pushed them ever closer toward the Soviets. Yet more prominent leaders of the Ba'ath Party, like Saddam Hussein, were also eager not to become simple puppets of the USSR. Because of that, in the late 1970s, Iraq began turning toward other Western countries, mainly France, for armament. Through these efforts, Iraq tried to lower its dependence on the Soviet Union, which was rather high at the time.

For the Iraqi-Soviet relations, 1979 was also an important year. The rise of Saddam Hussein in both the Ba'ath Party and the Republic of Iraq meant that the Ba'ath regime was even more inclined toward moving away from Soviet influence. Saddam didn't want to follow Soviet foreign affairs. He was keen on pursuing a more independent policy based on his own goals of making Iraq at least a local power, if not something more influential. Furthermore, the Soviet invasion of Afghanistan in that same year also put a significant strain on Iraqi-Soviet relations, as it was seen as a communist attack on a fellow Muslim country. After the Iran-Iraq War began, the Soviets attempted to gain diplomatic points by cutting off arms supplies to both Iraq and Iran in the fall of 1980, trying to force them to resolve their issues peacefully. However, the Ba'ath regime interpreted this as a further betrayal. This ban was quickly lifted, but the damage remained. Saddam and his regime began opening up toward the West even more, slowly establishing relations with the US. The United States was eager to form diplomatic ties with Iraq, both because it lost its influence over Iran but also because the Soviets would lose an ally.

As the Iran-Iraq War raged on, US-Iraqi relations began to improve. The United States started to send support, exporting technologies that had dual use in both military and civilian applications, and by 1984, official diplomatic relations were reestablished. By the end of the war, the relations between the US and Iraq were, at the very least, cordial, with the US officially siding with Iraq in an attempt to end the war. At the same time, the US intelligence services shared their intel about Iranian positions, helping the Iraqi generals plan their attacks. Yet despite that rather friendly stance toward the Americans, Saddam didn't cut off all relations with the Soviets. The USSR remained the primary source of armaments of the Iraqi Army, as well as one of their prominent foreign lenders, just behind Kuwait and Saudi Arabia. Thus, in the late 1980s, Iraq found itself to be in a rare position of being in somewhat good graces of both competing superpowers. However, Saddam remained rather suspicious of both the US and the USSR. It is known that despite being mostly pro-Iraqi during the war, both superpowers did also sell arms to the Iranians as well, even though only 23% of total weapons delivered was sent to Iran. The Iraqi government remained under the impression that both powers chose Iraq only because Iran refused to cooperate.

On the other hand, both the US and the USSR realized that the Ba'ath regime was a loose cannon, as it was hard to control and quite volatile. Therefore, their support of the Iraqi government was never fullhearted. Another problematic aspect of the Iraqi government was that, through the years, it became outright dictatorial with a strong leadership cult of Saddam Hussein, who was shown as the savior of Iraq. The war only made it easier for him to transform Iraq into an aggressive militaristic state. Saddam's grip over Iraq tightened, as he was merciless toward any political threat that arose during the 1980s. He showed even less sympathy toward the Kurds, an ethnic minority in northeastern Iraq, who rebelled in 1983. Unsatisfied with the state of things, combined with their long-lasting yearning for independence, they rose up against the Ba'ath regime. Their revolt was drowned in blood, as they were subjected to genocide through the use of chemical warfare, which lasted until mid-1989. At the same time, the Iraqi military also used chemical weapons against the Iranians, against both military and civilian targets. Most of the world, including both the US and the USSR, berated these actions. The UN even issued several resolutions that condemned Iraq for breaking the 1925 Geneva Protocol that banned the use of chemical warfare. Nonetheless, neither superpower acted more tangibly, as both had interests in an Iraqi victory, which would allow them to maintain their influence in the region.

Despite the criticism for its actions and the use of chemical weapons, Iraq remained on the good side of both the US and the USSR. However, by that time, the Cold War was slowly coming to an end, as the Soviet Union was going through its own economic crisis that was followed by political instability. This was followed by the fall of communist regimes across Eastern Europe, perhaps symbolized most vividly by the fall of the Berlin Wall in November 1989. Some historians even claim that with that event, the Cold War was officially over, as it became clear that the USSR had lost its ability to parry the United States. Thus, Saddam was eager to further his cooperation with the US, expressing his opinion in early 1990 that the Soviet Union was finished as a superpower. However, the position of the United States on this alliance was divided. The official Bush Sr. administration was eager to exploit the possibilities of working together with Iraq, as it hoped Iraq would become a pillar of stability and peace in the region, something that US diplomacy needed. On the other hand, public opinion, which could be most clearly seen in the media, was highly critical of Iraq and its regime, especially over the atrocities committed during the war.

Even the US Congress threatened Iraq with sanctions, although President George Bush Sr. spoke up against those kinds of actions. He also said he would use his powers of veto to stop any act of such type. Nonetheless, Saddam and his regime were both confused and annoyed with the dual stance the US held toward them. By mid-1990, he realized that Iraq was not going to receive full American support, especially since the main US ally in the region was Israel, a country with whom the Ba'ath regime had rather bad relations. Yet despite that, it seems that Saddam was confident that even though he wouldn't receive support, the US would not militarily oppose him. On the one hand, he calculated that the American government was too amicable for such work. On the other, he counted on his military prestige in the world, as he had one of the more massive and more experienced armies at the time. Saddam believed that the Vietnam War complex, the fear of high losses, in both lives and money, as well as the war in general, and the fear of prolonged conflict, would prevent the US from actively engaging him in the field of war. Concluding that his position in the worldwide political arena was strong enough, in early 1990, Saddam began planning his actions against Kuwait.

By early summer of that year, Iraq became more vocal against its southern neighbor, which was clearly noticed by the entire world. Some of the governments began fearing a new conflict would arise in the Gulf region. Most concerned was the Arab League, as this war would pose a threat to Arab unity and the entire region. The president of Egypt, Hosni Mubarak, directly intervened, managing to broker a meeting between Iraqi and Kuwaiti representatives in Saudi Arabia, in which he hoped to resolve their grievances peacefully. At the same time, Saddam called the US ambassador in Baghdad, April Glaspie, for a conversation. Together with his minister of foreign affairs, he expressed his dissatisfaction with the American stance toward Iraq, more precisely the critique of the US media, on July 25th, 1990. Glaspie tried to convince him that US President Bush Sr. wanted to better their relations based on the peace and prosperity of the Middle East. Saddam then turned toward Iraqi issues with Kuwait, claiming that low oil prices were devastating his country and that the price of 25 dollars per barrel was not high enough. He proceeded to claim that Kuwait's farms, installations, and border patrols were deployed and built as closely to the border as possible. Combined with the lowering of the oil prices, Saddam saw it as Kuwait placing excessive pressure on Iraq. Saddam then said that if the provocation continued, Iraq would respond to that pressure with force, as it seemed that course of action would be the only way to ensure his people would live decently.

He further added that some of the US citizens who were against Iraq went to Kuwait and other Gulf states to spread fear of his country and persuade them not to help Iraq rebuild. To these statements, Glaspie responded that the US had no opinion on Arab-Arab conflicts, like the one Iraq had with Kuwait. Today, some presume that the Iraqis interpreted this rather indifferent stance offered by the US ambassador as a sign that the US would not intervene in any possible future conflicts. Glaspie did show concern about the Iraqi forces building upon its southern borders, to which Saddam said he just wanted a fair solution to the issue. He further reassured her by saying that the Iraqis were not the aggressors, although they wouldn't accept aggression against them. For the US ambassador, that was enough to calm her, as she was informed about the pending meeting of the two sides in Saudi Arabia. Like most of the Arab League, she believed that the issues between Iraq and Kuwait would be settled there peacefully. Just several days later, on July 31ˢᵗ, the representatives of the two countries met in Jidda (Jeddah) under the patronage of Saudi Arabia, which wanted to act as an "Arab older brother" and ensure peace between them.

The exact details of the direct talks in Jidda are unknown. However, through the later accounts of some of the actors, there is a general idea of what was discussed. Iraqi representatives voiced what their government saw as Kuwaiti transgressions. There was the matter of border disputes, most notably in the case of the Rumaila oil field. The bulk of that oil field lies within Iraqi territory, but its southern tip was in Kuwait. Iraq claimed that its entirety should be de jure Iraqi, while it was de facto partially under Kuwaiti soil. Thus, from the Iraqi perspective, the Kuwaitis were guilty of border transgression and stealing their oil and revenue. Furthermore, Iraqis accused the Kuwaitis of lowering oil prices through overproduction, as well as denying their request for Iraq to fly commercial flights through Kuwaiti airspace. It is also reasonable to assume that the issues of Iraqi debt and the matter of Warbah and Bubiyan were brought up, as they were also an essential part of the Iraqi-Kuwaiti dispute. It seems that the Kuwaiti representatives rebuffed all the accusations and demands of their counterparts without presenting any constructive proposals since the Iraqis left on August 1ˢᵗ. Later, the Kuwaitis claimed that the Kuwaiti side offered to forgive Iraq's debt, or at least part of it, and allow the Iraqi military to construct some facilities on the contested islands. The issue of the Rumaila oil field was offered to be settled through an arbitration of some sort.

It is possible that these offers were only hinted at but not recognized by the Iraqis. It is also not impossible that the Kuwaitis only stated this later to present themselves in a better light in the dispute. Of course, it is not out of the question that by that time, the Iraqis had abandoned the idea of resolving this disagreement through peaceful diplomacy. Regardless, the end result of the Jidda conference was the opposite of what everyone had hoped for. The Iraqi government was left even more unsatisfied and irritated, while the tensions between the two neighboring countries worsened. On August 1ˢᵗ, Saddam held a state meeting where the Iraqi leadership discussed how to proceed. From their point of view, Kuwait had, once again, exhibited no desire to find a compromise while the state of the Iraqi economy and their regime was in dire straits. By that period, several smaller revolts against Saddam's oppression erupted, as the people were feeling the ever-growing pressure of the economic crisis. The Ba'ath leadership either had to act now or see itself fall from power. The only solution for them was a military invasion. Saddam's decision to turn once again to an act of open aggression was eased by his belief that the US would not intervene directly and that the Soviets were too weak to do anything. On top of that, he thought that the Arab League would be more sympathetic toward his position, even hoping that the Arab League would bolster his position as a pan-Arab leader.

Thus, on August 2ⁿᵈ, 1990, Saddam ordered an attack on Kuwait. With that, the Gulf War began. It was a result of a combination of the longstanding Iraqi border issues with Kuwait, the ideology of Iraqi nationalism, the internal economic and political crises of the Ba'ath regime, and the international political atmosphere of the ending of the Cold War, as both superpowers showed little resolution in dealing with the issues of the Persian Gulf region.

Chapter 3 – The Invasion of Kuwait and the Beginning of the War

As the talks between Kuwait and Iraq were slowly falling apart in July 1990, Saddam and his high command met to discuss further steps. It became evident for them that the only way to gain what they wanted was the use of military force. It was something they thought they could get away with due to the international political stage of that time. But the question still remained on how far they should go.

It seems that, at first, the Iraqi leadership wanted to use their military to occupy only the disputed islands of Warbah and Bubiyan, as well as the South Rumaila oil field. But on August 1st, 1990, Saddam Hussein gathered the Revolutionary Command Council (RCC), where he proposed to annex all of Kuwait instead. He opted for that option for two main reasons. One was geopolitical, as Kuwait was seen as a longstanding puppet of Western superpowers whose leaders counted on their support for defense. Thus, Saddam concluded that Kuwaiti rulers would rely on a war of diplomatic attrition in case of partial occupation. In that scenario, the US would eventually put pressure on him to withdraw, leading to his political fall from power in Iraq. In addition to that, Saddam calculated that if the Iraqi Army was to hold all of Kuwait, foreign forces had less chance to intervene militarily. Saddam counted on the fact that by having power over the whole coast of Kuwait and Iraq, Iraq's enemies would have a hard time landing and pushing them back, as he believed that the Saudis would allow foreign troops on their land. Mixed with that was the second reason, the ideological one. He needed a boost of popularity at home, and Kuwait was traditionally seen as a part of Iraq by the nationalists. Saddam hoped this move would help him stabilize his position while at the same time enhancing his image as a true pan-Arab leader.

At this point, it would be easy to simply blame only Saddam Hussein for the beginning of the Gulf War. Yet, even though his advisors may have been surprised, they weren't unsupportive. Both the military and the political leadership were enthusiastic about Saddam's new approach toward the problem of Kuwait. His generals assured him of Iraq's military capabilities, while his advisors told him the Americans were not ready for another war. With the full support of the higher leadership of Iraq, on August 1st, 1990, Saddam ordered his troops to attack. On August 2nd at 1:00 a.m. local time, Iraqi forces invaded Kuwait. Over 100,000 Iraqi soldiers, supported with about 2,000 tanks, poured over the border to the disbelief of almost the entire world. Despite the fact that Iraqi troops had been piling up on the frontier throughout July, many observers saw this move as pure aggressive posturing to force the Kuwaitis to comply. No one thought that after the exhausting war with Iran that Saddam would so eagerly enter a new conflict, least against a fellow Arab country with whom he was actively negotiating to resolve their issues. Not even Kuwait was ready, as its army wasn't fully mobilized and prepared. Thus, within just twelve hours, the Iraqi forces had swiftly overrun the 16,000 strong Kuwait Army, seizing the entire territory of its southern neighbor. The Gulf War had officially begun.

A meeting between Mikhail Gorbachev and George Bush Sr., where they signed an agreement to end the use of chemical weapons (1990).
https://commons.wikimedia.org/wiki/File:President_George_H._W._Bush_and_Mikhail_Gorbachev.jpg

It wasn't long before it became apparent that Saddam had made a mistake in his calculations. In a matter of days, most of the world condemned the invasion of Kuwait, demanding the withdrawal of Iraqi troops. It wasn't surprising that most of the Western allies of Kuwait, like the United States and the United Kingdom, were spearheading this kind of diplomatic pressure, both in the media and in the United Nations. What was surprising to some, if not all, was that the Soviet Union, which had a habit of opposing US actions in the UN, backed American diplomacy. The Soviet president at the time, Mikhail Gorbachev, was willing to support the United States on this matter for several reasons. For one, at the time, the Soviets themselves were going through an economic crisis, and Gorbachev sought to ease it by opening up to the West and counting on their aid. If he was to oppose them, that financial aid would stop. And for that same reason, the Soviet leadership was, at the very least, annoyed that Saddam, their ally on paper, chose to act on his own accord. His actions were damaging both to the Soviet Union's reputation and to their much-needed yet improving relations with the West. Thus, the USSR was ready to issue a joint statement with the US that condemned the Iraqi invasion. In fact, this readiness for the cooperation of the Soviet Union proved to be an important factor in how the Gulf War was to proceed.

Apart from Soviet support, the Arab League also played an essential role in future events. Most of the members, apart from Iraq and Libya, were opposed to Saddam's actions, seeing it as unnecessary Arab on Arab violence. On the 3rd of August, the League passed a resolution calling for the withdrawal of Iraqi troops and to resume peaceful negotiations while at the same time objecting to a possibility of a non-Arab force intervention. This left Saddam without a single considerable ally by the second day of the Iraqi occupation of Kuwait. Yet Saddam's position wasn't ultimately doomed; however, American diplomacy was only gearing up. In the following days, US diplomats were busy on two fronts. One was international, working in the UN for another resolution following the first one issued on August 3rd, which just condemned Iraq's actions. The Americans knew that simply scolding the Iraqi government wouldn't do much to persuade Saddam to retreat. Thus, they began working on a resolution that would enact total economic sanctions on Iraq. For that, the US once again had to attain the Soviet Union's compliance, as its power of veto in the UN Security Council could stop any future resolutions from being passed.

Luckily for the Americans, the economic blockade was acceptable to the Soviets as a peaceful solution. Besides the USSR, it was also crucial that the immediate Iraqi neighbors accepted these sanctions as well. Most of them were ready to comply. The only possible issue was Turkey. Though opposed to the Iraqi invasion, Turkey was worried that those sanctions could damage its economy. This potential problem was resolved by the US sending financial aid to Turkey, with the caveat of questioning Turkey's future in NATO (the North Atlantic Treaty Organization) if it refused to comply. Thus, the diplomacy of the United States secured these economic sanctions, which were first imposed by UN Resolution 661 on August 6th and then enacted by Iraq's neighbors. The economic pressure on Iraq was furthered by the fact that the US and most of the other countries also froze any Iraqi or Kuwaiti assets abroad. However, the American leadership felt that this alone wasn't enough, so simultaneously, it was working on securing its positions if military actions were to become necessary. For that, the US diplomacy team worked firstly with the Saudis and the rest of the Arab League. Their first issue was to secure the permission of Saudi Arabia for the deployment of foreign troops on their territories, which was vital for bypassing Saddam's coastal defenses.

Traditionally, the Saudis were against any non-domestic forces being allowed on their soil, especially non-Muslim ones. Thus, at first, Saudi Arabia, together with other members of the Arab League, tried to mitigate a peaceful solution. It seemed that Saddam was open toward the possibility of an Arab meeting that would resolve the issue. Still, Egypt, which was a longstanding adversary of Iraq, issued a statement condemning Iraq's invasion. After that, Saddam lost his trust in the Arab League. Nonetheless, the Saudi king was still hoping a peaceful solution was possible. At that time, US intelligence showed the Saudi leadership that Iraqi forces were massing on their borders, warning them that they could be next. It is unlikely that Saddam was planning to continue his push into Saudi Arabia as well, but this was enough for the Saudis to be concerned. On top of that, if Kuwait were to remain under Iraqi control, it would become the largest producer of oil in the OPEC countries, dethroning Saudi Arabia from its leadership position in that organization. After much debate among the highest officials of the country, Saudi Arabia decided to allow the deployment of American troops in their territory. They circumvented the traditions by officially inviting them on their soil on August 6th, 1990. By the next day, the first US troops were deployed in Saudi territory. This invitation was also sent to other Arab countries. Egypt and Morocco answered the call rather quickly.

US Defense Secretary Dick Cheney and Saudi Minister of Defense Sultan al-Khair (late 1990).
https://commons.wikimedia.org/wiki/File:Cheney_meeting_with_Prince_Sultan.jpg

By then, Saddam saw that he and his advisors had made a colossal miscalculation. Military intervention by land was now possible. Furthermore, the United States was the first to deploy troops, showing an apparent willingness on their part to enter into a potential armed conflict, while the majority of the Arabs, as well as the Soviet Union, were supportive of the American efforts against Iraq. However, this wasn't enough to make Saddam fall back. Instead, the Iraqi government stubbornly retaliated by first proclaiming Kuwait to be a republic with a provisional government on August 7th and then pronouncing the full annexation of Kuwait on the very next day. It was to become the nineteenth province of Iraq. In that period, Iraqi forces tightened their grip over Kuwait by arresting and executing possible leaders of the opposition. At the same time, the systematic looting of Kuwait was in progress. Iraqis took various everyday and luxurious goods, industrial and electronic equipment, and much more, topping it off with about two billion dollars found in Kuwait's central bank. This helped alleviate the immediate effects of the economic sanctions placed on Iraq. On the foreign diplomacy front, Saddam tried to gain some credibility by attaching Palestine to the invasion of Kuwait. He stated that Iraq was prepared to withdraw from Kuwait if Israel would retreat from the Palestinian lands. Once again, he was presenting himself as a grand pan-Arab leader, fighting not only for the needs of Iraq but for a broader Arab cause as well.

Meeting between Saddam Hussein and the prime minister of the brief Kuwaiti puppet regime (1990).
https://commons.wikimedia.org/wiki/File:Kuwaiti_Prime_Minister_Alaa_Hussein_Ali_1990_with_Iraqi_President_Saddam_Hussein.jpg

This attempt was fruitless. Most of the Arab countries continued to view Iraq as an aggressor and a possible threat, while the US had no intention of acknowledging any connection between the two issues. That, of course, wasn't surprising, as Israel was probably the closest ally the United States had in the Middle East. Thus, the Kuwaiti issue entered into a stalemate. The allied forces were still steadily massing on the Saudi-Iraqi border, while Iraq stubbornly refused to withdraw from Kuwait. From a superficial first glance, Saddam's refusal to end his occupation could be seen as either his hubris and his belief that Iraq could fight against the world or as his nationalistic dictatorial appetite. However, those are, at best, only partially true. Saddam wasn't delusional, and he didn't believe that his armies could attain a straight-up victory against the international forces piling up on Iraqi borders. However, he believed they could bog down their advances in a military stalemate, inflicting high enough casualties to force them to negotiate with him. Also, Saddam's expansionistic appetites weren't as high as most have represented. It seems he would have been satisfied with gaining only the Warbah and Bubiyan Islands and the rights to the South Rumaila oil field. Most likely, he was using the annexation of Kuwait as a bargaining chip.

The problem was that, for most of the world, especially the US, there was nothing to negotiate about. Iraq had to withdraw unconditionally. However, Saddam couldn't accept that. Due to the rising economic crisis caused by the sanctions, which led to rationing and rising dissatisfaction among the common Iraqis, his position was shaky—and not only his but that of the entire Ba'ath leadership. Thus, a withdrawal without any gains would most likely mean their fall from power and possibly something even harsher. The Iraqi government at that time couldn't afford another meaningless war that brought nothing except an economic crisis. The United States was deaf to these facts, but other countries were aware of it. For example, French President François Mitterrand attempted to find a peaceful solution by asking for the withdrawal of all foreign troops in Middle Eastern territories, including Iraqi soldiers in Kuwait, international forces in Saudi Arabia, and Israeli soldiers stationed in the disputed territories. Furthermore, he advocated for allowing the Palestinians to have their own country, as well as the reduction in armaments of the entire region, from Iran to Morocco. Of course, this grandiose plan was rejected by pretty much everyone. Despite that, during the stalemate of the issue, several other nations tried to mediate peace in the region, both for the sake of peace itself but also to gain international prestige of solving such a major problem. In hand with that was the fact that the non-oil-producing countries were also economically suffering from rising oil prices.

Most notable was the Soviet attempt, as Gorbachev wanted to avoid any possible use of international forces against Iraq. In early October, the USSR sent its representative to Baghdad to attempt to persuade the Iraqis to stand down. Gorbachev even sent a letter directly to Saddam through that mission. Yet the Soviets were unable to promise any gains for Iraq. Thus, once again, Saddam had little choice but to continue his occupation, as the US was not prepared to give in the slightest to Iraq's demands. In fact, since the Iraqi invasion, it seemed that the United States was approaching this issue with the policy of "no negotiation"—either Iraq would withdraw or the US would use any force necessary. However, it seemed that the United States was set on going through the United Nations to preserve its international credibility. That choice could be linked with the experience of the Vietnam War, in which much of the world saw the American engagement as unjust. For that reason, the US used the UN Security Council to exert pressure on Iraq. With UN Resolution 660, which was passed on August 2nd and condemned the Iraqi invasion, US diplomacy relied on UN resolutions for legitimacy.

The US Navy ship stationed in the Persian Gulf, enforcing the economic blockade (late 1990/early

https://commons.wikimedia.org/wiki/File:USS_Converse_(DD-509)_in_San_Francisco_Bay,_California_(USA),_on_9_October_1944_(NH_95051).jpg

For example, after UN Resolution 661 was enacted, which was a mere three days after the Iraqi aggression started, most of the world agreed to enact economic sanctions on Iraq. Nonetheless, some countries were either unwilling or incapable of respecting that embargo. For that reason, UN Resolution 665 was adopted on August 25th, 1990, which allowed a naval blockade to impose the economic restrictions on Iraq. This gave the US and its chief ally Great Britain permission to use force if needed to enact the sanctions, something that has been seen as a violation of international law by some. Another issue that arose, which was processed by the UN, was of the foreign nationals (those who were not Iraqis or Kuwaitis) who were left in Kuwait after the occupation. There was a concern about their treatment by the Iraqis, who, through rations, focused their supplies to the military. Seen as hostages since the Iraqi authorities didn't permit them to leave after the occupation, the UN passed Resolution 666 on September 12th, which demanded that the Iraqi government provide them with the necessary supplies. Some countries, like Cuba and Yemen, saw the root of this problem in the economic blockade, which caused famine in Iraq and forced the Ba'ath government to ration their supplies. Yet the UN continued to pass resolutions that became increasingly aggressive in their tone. For example, UN Resolution 674 from late October stated that "the Council will need to take further measures" if Iraq didn't comply with the demands.

The main reason for that was the fact that the US and the British began more actively voicing their opinion that the use of military force was going to be necessary. Thus, the governments of those countries began to gather support for such a move while they tried to persuade other nations that the economic sanctions had failed and that the use of force was the last resort. There have been many critics both at the time and even today who think that there wasn't enough time for the blockade to work and that, given enough time, Saddam would have withdrawn peacefully. However, the governments of both the United States and Great Britain were worried that time was working in favor of the Iraqis. Their main concern was that differences among the permanent members of the UN Security Council would arise, making it rather difficult, if not impossible, for it to adopt any further resolutions about the Iraqi invasion. This fear was fueled by both Soviet and French actions, as those two permanent members of the council were the loudest proponents of a peaceful solution to the Kuwaiti crisis. Thus, by late November, the UN Security Council met and voted on what was to become known as UN Resolution 678. In it, the UN gave a de facto ultimatum to Iraq, stating that the Iraqi forces had until January 15th, 1991, to withdraw from Kuwait. If the Iraqi government failed to comply, the UN granted the Coalition states the right to use "all necessary means" to liberate Kuwait.

The resolution itself was highly criticized, both morally and legally. The main issue that many had against it was the fact that the United States had used somewhat unethical means of persuasion while lobbying for it. For example, the Soviets were quite literally bought off with about seven billion dollars in aid from several countries, including some that were pressured by the US, among them Saudi Arabia, which provided one billion alone. Apart from that, the US itself promised considerable food shipments to the Soviets. On the other hand, the Chinese, who were traditionally against any foreign interventions, were won over by diplomatic favors. The US was to lift economic sanctions imposed after the Tiananmen Square incident in 1989, and a Chinese minister of foreign affairs was to be received by the White House. In return for those favors, China would abstain from voting on the resolution. Other uncertain members of the UN Security Council were also convinced by either economic or diplomatic incentives. This was enough to leave only two countries in the council against it, Cuba and Yemen, which refused to be bribed or intimidated. Yemen, one of the poorest countries at the time, suffered for its "no" in the UN. The US, the International Monetary Fund, and the World Bank immediately stopped their aid program to Yemen, which was worth about seventy million dollars, while Saudi Arabia expelled about 800,000 Yemeni workers.

However, this "stick and carrot" policy used by the United States to secure the votes in the UN Security Council wasn't the only reason why some have questioned the morality of UN Resolution 678. In the eyes of some observers, the very act of awarding the right to use force to the US-led Coalition was, in fact, contrary to the UN's founding charter. Through this action, the UN was avoiding direct responsibility and accountability for the use of this military force, allowing for the unilateral control and orchestration of world policy by the United States.

Furthermore, by doing so, the UN encouraged a departure from the predominantly peaceful and humanitarian values and purpose it was founded on. On the other hand, some jurists have deemed this resolution to be invalid. In their interpretation, the Chinese decision to abstain from voting made the decision void, as the UN Charter states that the decisions of the Security Council need to have concurring votes of at least nine out of fifteen members, including all five of the permanent members. Nonetheless, for the majority of people at the time, including the members of the council, this wasn't an issue. The Chinese themselves were persuaded not to vote against such action. Still, their foreign policy didn't allow them to vote for military intervention in a sovereign state.

In the end, the issues of morality and legality of UN Resolution 678 was of little concern for the Coalition forces, primarily the United States. Those who questioned it were in the minority. Most of the world accepted it since their actions had been officially approved by the United Nations, as it gave the forces the legitimacy it needed for their involvement in a conflict with Iraq. The table had been set for a full-blown war between the Coalition forces and Saddam's army, as most analysts realized that there was little chance for the Iraqis to actually retreat. From November 29th, 1990, to January 15th, 1991, the world was simply waiting for the clash of the two forces to begin.

Chapter 4 – Military Forces of the Gulf War

To fully understand the events of the Gulf War, its course, and its resolution, we first must delve into the states of the opposing forces. On one side was the Iraqi military machine, which had recent combat experience. On the opposing side stood a collation force led by the US military. It had much to prove, both because it still held the cross of the Vietnam War but also because it was the leading power of the emerging post-Cold War world.

On paper, the Iraqi Army was a formidable foe. It had around one million active soldiers, though the estimates vary, with a possibility of doubling that number through the full conscription of men from 18 to 34 years old. Divided into about 60 divisions, it was also supplied with somewhere between 5,500 and 6,000 tanks and about 8,000 armored personnel carriers (APC). It had air support of around 200 helicopters and 900 airplanes, combined with a formidable air defense network that consisted of approximately 10,000 anti-aircraft artillery (AAA). The Iraqi Navy was the only part of Saddam's war machine that seemed unimpressive, which is not surprising due to Iraq's rather short coastline. However, the strength of the Iraqi Army was daunting only when looking at these raw numbers on paper. If one delves deeper into details, it quickly becomes evident that the military power of the Iraqi Army was largely blown out of proportion by the media coverage of the time. Several central issues plagued the Ba'ath forces. Firstly, even though its army was large in number, not all of them were stationed in the south. Some stayed near the Syrian and Iranian borders in case of a surprise attack. On top of that, the majority of the Iraqi soldiers were conscripts that lacked morale and combat training.

Despite how Western media represented them, not all of the operational Iraqi soldiers of that time were active combatants in the Iran-Iraq War. There were substantial numbers of fresh young recruits as well. Even worse for the Iraqi high command was the low morale. The Ba'ath regime was struggling with popularity at the time. This meant that at least some of its soldiers were disillusioned with their leadership, wondering if the new war would bring any better fortunes than the last had. In contrast to those ordinary foot soldiers stood a truly experienced high command, which was, in fact, highly adept at coordinating mass movements, artillery attacks, and complex maneuvers. Their specialty was the strategy of static defense, backed by mobile reserve, which was used against the Iranians. However, the problem that arose was that the Iraqi headquarters had trouble with the common units executing those orders. The notable exception was the Republican Guard, which consisted of better-trained and better-equipped soldiers who were rather loyal to Saddam's regime. In fact, during the Gulf War, it seems that the Republican Guard was the only part of the Iraqi Army that actually exhibited high capability in maneuvering and cooperation. Yet its numbers were rather low (about 150,000), and for most of the conflict, they were used as strategic reserves.

Another issue that plagued the Iraqi Army was how varied its arms and equipment were. In the decade leading to the Gulf War, Iraq was gathering weapons from where it could. As mentioned above, those came from the Soviet Union and their allies, such as France, China, Brazil, etc. That kind of diversity in equipment was a logistic nightmare for the Iraqi high command. It had to concentrate similar types of vehicles and weapon systems into the same units to facilitate both their usage and maintenance. Furthermore, as Iraq faced a substantial economic crisis, most of the arms were not kept in great condition, while the army, in general, lacked the spare parts needed to repair them. The industries in

Iraq were producing some of the extra parts needed, though often not in the quantities needed. Yet more delicate products like microelectronics were above their technological capabilities. In some rare cases, the Iraqi military industry was even able to produce arms improvements based both on indigenous and foreign designs. Nonetheless, the lack of spare parts plagued most of Iraq's armed forces. It was not uncommon for Iraqi engineers to practice "mechanical cannibalization" when the need for them was too dire. This problem also meant that their equipment was often underperforming, further lowering the battle effectiveness of the Ba'ath forces.

Abandoned Iraqi T54/55 main battle tank.
https://commons.wikimedia.org/wiki/File:Abandoned_Iraqi_T-54A,_T-55_or_Type_59_tank.JPEG

However, probably the most crucial problem of the Iraqi Army was the fact that most of the units were equipped with outdated arms. For example, on paper, roughly 6,000 tanks seem like more than a formidable force. Yet, in reality, more than half of those tanks were Soviet T-54/55 tanks or their variations from China (T-59/69-I) and Romania (TR-77), which were originally designed and first produced in the years following World War II. This means that more than half of the Iraqi armored forces were equipped with tanks that were based on 45-year-old technology. The second most used tank in the Iraqi Army, totaling roughly at 1,200 vehicles, was the Soviet T-62. Although it was a feared model when it was first introduced in 1961, the T-62 was a thirty-year-old design by the early 1990s, making it outdated as well. Most of the modern tanks the Iraqis had were the Soviet T-72s, which came in several variations. There were roughly 500 of them in service, and they were mostly attached to the Republican Guard units. These T-72 tanks were sometimes modernized with some modifications, but the basic design was developed by the Soviets in 1971, twenty years prior to the Gulf War. Besides those Soviet-based tanks, the Iraqi Army also had some other tanks, most notably 200 to 300 British Mk. 3/3P and 5/5P Chieftains, which were captured from the Iranians. However, these were also designed and produced in the 1970s, which was when they were sent to the Iranians, who were, at the time, still British allies.

The Iraqi Army had similarly outdated models of the APCs, with most being variations of the Soviet BTR-50 and BTR-60, which were first designed in the 50s and 60s. Unlike the tanks, the types of APCs used by the Iraqis varied more. They used the French AMX 10P and Panhard M3, Italian OTO Melara Type 6614, Brazilian ENGESA EE-9, Yugoslav M60-P, Chinese YW531, and many more. However, most of these were also designed in the 1960s and early 1970s. Probably the only exception was the Soviet BMP-2, which was designed in 1980, but those were attached only to the Republican Guard. Iraqi artillery was similarly varied, mostly consisting of the Yugoslav variation of the 122mm Soviet D-30 howitzer, which was based on a design from the 60s, and the Soviet 100mm D-44 and 130mm M-46 from the 1950s. Along with them, the Iraqi Army used the Austrian GH N-45, South African G5, and the US M114 155mm howitzers. Besides the common types of artillery, Saddam's forces also used self-propelled artillery (SPG) and multiple rocket launchers (MRL), which each made up about 10% of the Iraqi artillery. The Soviet 2S1 and 2S3 SPGs were the most common, but Iraq's military also had the French Mk F3 and GCT, as well as the US M109A1s, which were captured from Iran during the war. The Soviet models were from the 1970s, while the French and the US ones were designed during the 1960s. The MRLs used by the Iraqis were mainly Soviet BM-21s from the 1960s and Brazilian Avibras Astros II from 1983.

In contrast to that, the Iraqi Air Force was much less varied. The bulk of its power consisted of Soviet MiG-21, MiG-23, Mig-25, and MiG-29.

They also used Soviet Su-7, Su-20, Su-22, Su-24, and Su-25. The most modern of these fighter jets were designed during the late 1970s, and they weren't as numerous in the Iraqi arsenal. Along with them, they used French Mirage F1 fighter-bombers from the 1960s and Soviet Tu-16 and Tu-22 bombers from the 50s and 60s. Much more feared among the Coalition forces were the NATO-designated Scud tactical ballistic missiles, most of which originated from the USSR. The most used of these was the so-called Scud-B, originally named by the Soviets as R-17, which were from the late 1960s. The Iraqi military industry also developed its own Al Hussein (al-Husayn) in the late 1980s. These were basically upgrades of the Soviet R-17 to increase their range. Both of these weapons were capable of carrying not only conventional but also chemical, biological, and even nuclear warheads. Their range, which went up to 400 miles (644 kilometers), meant that, on paper, the Iraqi Army could possibly even bomb the Coalition's support units and headquarters. However, neither the tactical missiles nor the conventional artillery ended up posing any real threat to the Coalition forces.

Two Iraqi-modified Al Hussein missiles displayed with their launchers at the 1989 Baghdad arms exhibition.
https://commons.wikimedia.org/wiki/File:IrakScudB1989.jpg

When talking about handheld weaponry, Iraq's military used various types of Soviet AKM and AK-74 assault rifles, which were modifications and modernizations of the famous AK-47. Besides those, the Iraqi Army used the Soviet-made RPD and RPK light machine guns, as well as medium and heavy SGM and PK machine guns. The Iraqis also employed Soviet SPD and Yugoslav M-76 sniper rifles. The most commonly used pistols were the Soviet T-33 and the Iraqi *Tariq*, a design that was based on the Italian Beretta M1951. Another commonly used weapon was the famous RPG-7, an anti-tank handheld rocket launcher. All of these handheld arms were designed during the 60s and 70s but were still rather useful on the battlefield. All in all, when looking at the Iraqi Army, it wasn't a force to be taken lightly, as it had its strengths. However, when looking back on how the world and the news saw Saddam's forces, it becomes clear that most of the media exaggerated its powers to a high degree. At the same time, the Coalition generals were rightfully preparing for the worst possible scenario, which only helped with the overplaying of the Iraqi force. All of this stemmed from the Vietnam experiences of the US Army, which was, at the time, still fresh, both in military circles as well as in the media.

For that reason, the US military was tackling this conflict with the utmost seriousness. The sheer number of American soldiers deployed showcases this. There were roughly 697,000 US soldiers in the Gulf War, which constituted almost three-quarters of the total Coalition forces, which numbered around 955,000 men. In comparison, at the peak of US involvement in the Vietnam War in 1969, there were 543,000 American soldiers deployed. Another essential difference between the US Army during the Vietnam War and the Gulf War was its morale and training. After the failure of the Vietnam War, the US government abandoned the draft system, making the United States military a volunteer-based, professionally trained force. Despite that, some of the media at the time represented the US Army as unprepared for desert warfare, similar to how it was unprepared for the jungles of Vietnam. However, the American forces were regularly training for the harsh conditions of the Middle East in the Mojave Desert, which is located on the border of California and Nevada, as well as in parts of Texas and New Mexico. Some of the troops were even training in Egypt during the 1980s in the form of military exercises with the Egyptian military. Thus, the US soldiers were both well-prepared and high in morale and fighting spirits.

Countries that were members of the Coalition and their approximate contribution in personnel.
https://commons.wikimedia.org/wiki/File:Gulf_War_coalition_map3.png

Besides the US, 34 other countries contributed to the Coalition forces. Among the more numerous were the Saudi forces, with somewhere between 60,000 and 100,000 men, and the British, with about 53,000. Egypt sent 20,000 men, while France deployed 18,000 personnel. Other notable contributors, whose number of soldiers were above 2,000, were Morocco, Syria, Kuwait (those forces that managed to elude the Iraqis during the invasion), Oman, Pakistan, Canada, the United Arab Emirates (UAE), Qatar, and Bangladesh. Others sent a rather insignificant number of men, no more than a few hundred. It is important to note that most of the soldiers from the countries with smaller contributions were actually support staff, like engineers, medics, and base guards, while others participated only in aerial warfare. So not all of the countries were engaged in direct combat. Looking at the raw numbers of the men who were deployed, one thing becomes clear. The Coalition forces were not outnumbered, as some media actually portrayed them. The two sides of this conflict were quite equal in size. It is even debatable that the Iraqis were somewhat outnumbered, as some estimates state only about 650,000- to 750,000 Iraqi soldiers were deployed in the theater of war. Others were stationed in northern regions, though it was possible for them to join the fight if needed.

Egyptian soldiers in the Coalition in prayer.

But the raw numbers and overall training of the US Army, backed with the rest of the Coalition forces, were not the only advantages they held over the Iraqis. The United States military deployed about 2,000 M1A1 Abrams battle tanks, which were 1986 upgraded versions of the 1980s M1 Abrams. These tanks were the most modern and technologically advanced of the time. The M1A1 had a range of fire above 8,200 feet (2,500 meters), while most Iraqi tanks topped at 6,600 feet (2,000 meters). It also had better optics, higher precision, and higher penetration, as well as better armor. Not even the Soviet T-72 was a match to it; it was only comparable to the couple hundreds of M60A1/A3 Patton and M551A1 Sheridan tanks that were used as a backup for the M1A1. Those were older US tanks that were designed and modified during the late 1960s and early 1970s. The United States ground forces were also equipped with about 3,000 APC, most being M2 and M3 Bradleys, which were designed in 1981. Those were equipped not only with a 25mm cannon but also with a TOW missile launcher, making it capable of engaging tanks as well. Besides those, amphibious assault and reconnaissance vehicles, like the LAV-25, which was designed in 1983, and the older AAVP-7A1s from the 1970s, were used. Also present was the M113A2, which was a 1970s modification of the 1960s design.

M1 Abrams tanks in the Iraqi Desert with an M2/M3 Bradley APC in the back.
https://commons.wikimedia.org/wiki/File:Abrams_in_formation.jpg

All in all, the US Army fielded both more advanced and better-equipped ground vehicles than their Iraqi counterparts, which were, of course, also better maintained. Besides the United States, their partners in the Coalition forces also brought their own vehicles. The British brought the FV4030/4 Challenger 1 tank, which, like the Abrams, was a modern tank that entered service in 1983. Besides that, they had the FV 4003 Centurion Mk 5 AVRE 165, a modification from the 1960s. Their APC arsenal had both older vehicles, like the FV432 Trojan that was initially designed in the 1960s, and more modern ones, like the FV 510 Warrior, which entered service in 1988. The French brought their AMX-30B2 tanks, which were modernized versions from 1979 of the original AMX-30 design. Like the British, they brought both older APCs, like the Panhard AML-90, which were used by the Iraqis as well, and the newer AMX-10 RC that was designed in the 1980s. The Saudi Arabian Army brought over 500 tanks, including the French AMX-30S and the US M60A3, which were both older designs from the 60s and 70s. They also had about 1,500 APCs, which were likewise a mixture of older US and French designs, like the M113A1 and the Panhard AML-60/90. The Kuwaiti forces in exile were armed with the British FV4201 Chieftain from the 1960s, as well as with the M84-AB, a Yugoslav 1984 modernization of the T-72, which made them more comparable to the Abrams and Challenger tanks. As for the APCs, the Kuwaiti forces used both the Soviet-made BMP-2 and the US M113A1.

The Egyptians, although they had the Soviet-made vehicles in their arsenal, sent only units equipped by the US M60A3 and M113A2/A3. On the other hand, Syria, a longstanding ally of the Soviets, deployed mostly T-54 and T-62 tanks, along with a few of the T-72 models. Along with them, they used BMP-1 and BTR-60 APCs, which meant they used rather identical vehicles as the Iraqi Army did. In fact, seeing how varied the Iraqi equipment was in general, the Coalition forces were quite wary of possible friendly fire, which proved to be more dangerous than the Iraqi resistance. All in all, when comparing the vehicle firepower of the Iraqi Army and the Coalition forces, it is rather apparent that the latter had the upper hand. Most of their armored transport and tanks were more modern and technologically advanced, while manpower was, at best, minimally better on the Iraqi side, if not equal. This kind of superiority extended even further when it came to aerial warfare. There, the Coalition forces had not only the advantage in technology and modernity but also in numbers. With over 2,000 aircraft, they had more than double the entire Iraqi Air Force.

Most of these planes were the US F-14, F-15, F-16, and F/A-18, which were all designed and built during the 1970s. Alongside them were the French Mirage F1 and Mirage 2000, with the latter being developed in the late 1970s and introduced into service in 1984, as well as the British/French SEPECAT Jaguar and British/German/Italian Tornado, which were both from the 1970s. These were fielded by various members of the Coalition forces, like the French, the British, the Saudis, the Kuwaitis, and the Italians. The US forces also brought some of their older planes, like the B-52 and F-4, but it also employed more unconventional aircraft like the EF-111A Raven, which was introduced in 1983 and used for electronic warfare. More famous than the Raven was the F-117A Nighthawk, a stealth bomber also introduced in 1983 that used advanced technology to remain undetected by enemy radar systems. The Coalition air efficiency was furthered by the use of the Airborne Warning and Control System (AWACS), which were airborne radar systems in the form of the Boeing E-3 Sentry as well as the Boeing KC-135 Stratotanker, a military aerial refueling aircraft, which allowed for attacks deeper into Iraqi territory. Apart from the combat planes, the Coalition forces also used various transport aircraft, like the C-5B Galaxy and the C-130 Hercules.

A US F-117A Nighthawk stealth airplane.
https://commons.wikimedia.org/wiki/File:F-117_Nighthawk_Front.jpg

The aerial superiority of the Coalition forces was furthered by several hundred various helicopters, most of which were deployed by the US military. They ranged from the quite modern attacking helicopters, like the H-64 Apache, which was introduced in the 1980s and armed with the most advanced technologies at the time, to the bit older Vietnam-era AH-1 Cobra. Besides them, an even wider array of transport helicopters was used. The US forces fielded some of the older types, like the iconic HU-1 "Huey," as well as the CH-47 Chinook and the OH-58 Kiowa, all three from the Vietnam War period. But the American forces also used more modern ones, like the UH-60 Black Hawk, which was introduced in 1979, and the highly modified version of that helicopter, the MH-60G/HH-60G Pave Hawk, which entered the service in 1982. Some of the common types used by other members of the Coalition forces were the French SA-342 Gazelle and SA-330 Puma, designed in the late 1960s and early 1970s, and the British WG-13 Lynx, which was introduced in 1978. Thus, when the allied airpower is summarized, it becomes clear that the Iraqis were severely overpowered. Yet, thanks to their air force and anti-aircraft defenses, they could at least try to confront the Coalition forces. That kind of uneven balance of military might was even more apparent when it came to naval warfare.

On the one hand, the Coalition forces brought all kinds of ships, ranging from the impressive aircraft carriers and battleships to mid-size destroyers, frigates, and missile cruisers. The classes of these ships were mostly designed in the 1960s and 1970s, but this meant little, as the Iraqi Navy had only a limited number of small missile boats and common patrol vessels, ships that posed virtually no threat to the Coalition naval forces. What is a more important aspect of the Coalition marine power was its ability to strike with Tomahawk long-range subsonic cruise missiles. It was more than a worthy answer to the threat of the Iraqi Scuds. Introduced in 1983, these missiles used the most advanced technology of that time, combining high precision and high destructive power, as well as carrying 1,000 pounds (450 kilograms) of conventional warheads. As such, they proved to be a valuable addition to the Coalition artillery power. In this field, the main superiority of the Coalition forces once again laid in the fact that their weapons were a generation ahead of the Iraqi Army. The most commonly used SPGs were the US M109A2/A3 and M110A2, which were modernized versions of the original design, as well as the French AMX-30 AuF1, which was introduced into service in 1977. Besides those, there was a wide array of howitzers used, like the US M198 and the French Tr-F1, which were both introduced in 1979 and had 155mm guns, as well as some older models and smaller calibers. The artillery firepower was topped with the most modern MLRs, the US M270 from 1983.

A US ship firing a Tomahawk missile during the Gulf War.
https://commons.wikimedia.org/wiki/File:Missouri_missile_BGM-109_Tomahawk.JPG

The handheld weaponry of the Coalition forces also varied a lot, but the most important ones were the US M16A2 assault rifle, an upgraded and modernized version of the Vietnam War M16. It was made more reliable and precise, entering into wide service in the mid-1980s. Alongside them were the British SA80 L85 from 1985 and the French FAMAS from 1979, as well as some Soviet AKM and AK74 that were used by Egyptian and Syrian soldiers. These were accompanied by numerous types of pistols, snipers, shotguns, submachine guns, and other assault rifles. The Coalition soldiers also used anti-tank weapons, like the older M72 LAW, and, at the time, the most modern US-built AT-4, as well as the British LAW 80, with the latter two both being introduced in 1987. The Egyptians also brought the Soviet RPG-7. In the end, it is also important to note that the superiority of the Coalition forces wasn't only based on weapons but also on other technological innovations, like, for example, the GPS (the Global Positioning System). These innovations, though some were in their infancy like the GPS, provided easer communication, maneuvering, navigation, and cooperation of separate units. That kind of advantage in the logistics capabilities department isn't something to look over, as they largely enhanced the effectiveness and precision of all actions and missions performed by the Coalition forces, even though most of the technology was only available to the US Army.

After comparing the two sides of the Gulf War, one thing becomes clear. This wasn't close to a fair fight as the media sometimes reported it. The Iraqi power was largely blown out of proportion, making it look like a mini superpower, which it wasn't. On the other hand, when talking about the Coalition forces, the focus usually remained on several of their most grabbing pieces of equipment, like the F-117 and Tomahawk missiles, which, though important, weren't the whole story. Behind those stood a massive force armed with the most modern weapons. Iraq stood basically no chance against the allies, even though many thought otherwise.

Chapter 5 – The War among the Clouds

While the diplomats and politicians negotiated and talked, trying to find a peaceful solution to the Iraqi-Kuwaiti problem, the generals were planning their future battles as January 15th, 1991, was closing in. The Iraqis were preparing their ground defenses, hoping that they would be able to cause enough casualties to the Americans to force them to the negotiating table. However, the US generals had other plans. Their first goal was not on the ground but high above, among the clouds.

The Coalition forces, under the overall command of US General Herbert Norman Schwarzkopf Jr., were focused on avoiding the possibility of the Gulf War becoming the "new Vietnam." Thus, instead of merely pushing the entire ground forces toward the Iraqi defenses, the US command opted to soften the target by aerial attacks first. The plan was to use the 2,000 fighting aircraft amassed by the Coalition forces to first establish total air superiority and then proceed with strategic bombings of the Iraqi positions. Of course, the tactic of aerial dominance wasn't something new. It was actually something that the US military had used since World War II. It was even applied during the Vietnam War. The difference was that by the early 1990s, the technology was advanced enough for bombings to be precise enough to transfer the dominance of the air to dominance on the ground. During the Vietnam War, despite the massive bombings, the effects were somewhat limited due to the inability to precisely pick out desired targets. However, in the Gulf War, the Coalition air force was using guided bombs, allowing for almost surgical precision. This meant that a fighter-bomber armed with only two so-called "smart bombs" could achieve the same result as roughly 100 B-17 bombers during the Vietnam War.

Despite that, the US-led Coalition command wasn't about to rely solely on technology. The United States generals devised a plan named "Instant Thunder," conveying a stark contrast to the "Rolling Thunder" from the Vietnam War. Unlike its predecessor, Instant Thunder was to be a short and decisive offensive air campaign, based on careful planning and coordination. The territory in the Kuwaiti theater of operation was divided into 33 square boxes, 30 miles (48 kilometers) in diameter, allowing for the precise allocation of specific areas to a specific group of airplanes. With those "killing boxes," the aerial command, which was located in the Saudi capital of Riyadh, was capable of forming air tasking orders (ATO), a schedule that matched the Coalition assets to their specific targets, all within a coherent timetable. Thus, every aspect of the air operations was tightly managed, from the take-off to the bombing run to the return back to base. With that, the Coalition forces, or, to be more precise, the US forces, as more than 1,800 aircraft were operated by the Americans alone, were ushering in a new aerial strategy by combining cutting-edge technology and careful planning, creating a blueprint that was to be used in all future US-led campaigns.

In contrast to the modern and aggressive approach of the US, the Iraqi Air Force relied on a somewhat outdated, defensive, and quite passive approach. Two factors could explain this tactic. The first was that during the Iran-Iraq War, the Iraqi Air Force suffered substantial losses while carrying out its strategic bombing raids. That shaped the Iraqi aerial tactics toward a more defensive stance. Thus, their planes never left Iraqi airspace or went on attacking missions against the Coalition forces. This strategic complacency was only furthered by the fact that most of the Iraqi airplanes were outdated, even though the Iraqi Air Force had some of the slightly newer MiG-29 fighters. At the same time, they were outnumbered, at least, by three to one. The second factor that contributed toward this defensive and passive stance was Saddam's reliance on his air defenses. Armed with thousands of AAA guns and surface-to-air (SAM) missiles, which were guided by a formidable radar detection system, the Iraqi air defense was supposed to be a much more viable threat to the Coalition air force than the Iraqi Air Force itself. Furthermore, Iraq was also dotted with rather resilient bunkers and shelters made from reinforced concrete, which were key for weathering the Coalition bombings. The key idea behind Iraq's strategy was to endure the aerial attacks until the Iraqi Army could inflict enormous casualties upon the invading ground forces.

An abandoned Iraqi MiG-21 and MiG-25 in the background (after the Gulf War)
https://commons.wikimedia.org/wiki/File:Abandoned_Iraqi_FT-7_in_front_of_the_Al_Asad_ATC_Tower.jpg

Some military experts argued after the war that Saddam would have been in a far better position if he had sent his planes to attack the Coalition forces while they were building up, utilizing the Iraqi Air Force before it lost its aerial superiority. From a purely military point of view, this would have possibly been a better solution. However, the Gulf War was more than just a combat situation. For the entire period between August and January 15th, there was a potential peaceful solution to the Gulf crisis. And despite how the media portrayed Saddam, he wasn't totally disillusioned or craving for war. Thus, during that entire period, the Iraqi Army stayed on its side of the border, with only one incident of a single Iraqi aircraft entering Saudi airspace and leaving before the incident could escalate into something more. Saddam and his high Ba'ath officials were aware that if they pulled the first punch, they would lose all international credibility and possibility to achieve anything through negotiations. Yet, at the same time, they weren't ready to back down and withdraw from the occupation of Kuwait without gaining something tangible. Thus, when January 15th came, the Iraqi troops were still holding their positions. With the passing of the deadline, the Coalition forces were prepared and fully authorized by the UN to act.

The first Coalition attack came on January 17th, around 3 a.m. local time, transforming the original defensive operation, which was codenamed "Desert Shield," into an offensive campaign known as "Desert Storm." The first attack was made under cover of night by eight AH-64 Apache helicopters, which were, in turn, guided by three MH-53 Pave Low helicopters. They flew low, fast, and without lights, attacking two Iraqi early warning radar systems near the Saudi-Iraqi border. Those radars were quickly destroyed with precise firepower, creating a radar-blank corridor through the first lines of the Iraqi air defenses. The helicopter squadron, known as Task Force Normandy, was fired upon but managed to get back to base without any losses. The mission was a success, allowing further attacks by the Coalition airplanes. However, the attack itself was quickly reported to the Iraqi command, alarming it to the upcoming attack. In a matter of minutes after the initial strike, the first of 700 Coalition planes flew toward Iraq. The primary targets of the preliminary air raids were strategic positions connected with Iraqi aerial defenses, like radar stations, airfields, the Nukhayb air defense center, and other government installations. Most of the targets were in southern Iraq, but on the first night, F-117A Nighthawks, as well as Tomahawk missiles fired from US Navy ships, also hit Baghdad.

During the first 24 hours, the Coalition air force flew just shy of 3,000 sorties. Among them was also one of the longest bombing raids in history, as seven B-52Gs flew from a base in Louisiana, located on the mainland of the US, and crossed half the globe to reach Iraq. There, they launched cruise missiles and returned home, covering 14,000 miles (22,500 kilometers) in about 25 hours. Other B-52 bombers were sent from the Indian Ocean, carrying large conventional bombs that killed both with their blast and a concussion shockwave, as their explosions made the ground tremble like in a manmade earthquake. This made those bombing missions reminiscent of the Vietnam War raids, where the US employed similar tactics. The Iraqi Air Force remained mostly inactive, just as Saddam planned, with only a handful of direct confrontations with the attacking aircraft. Those usually ended with the Iraqi planes losing the duels. Thus, the Coalition forces quickly took over the control of the airspace, as the Iraqi air defenses proved to be an inadequate match to the technologically advanced Coalition aircraft. By January 23rd, the US Air Force proclaimed that general air superiority was achieved, though it seemed more like total dominance. In those first six days, over 12,000 sorties were flown, with the US generals claiming only 5 out of 66 Iraqi airfields as still being functional, while an estimated 95 percent of the Iraqi defensive radar system was destroyed. On the other hand, the Coalition losses were minimal to almost nonexistent.

Iraqi MiG-25 destroyed in an aircraft bunker by a US laser-guided bomb.
https://commons.wikimedia.org/wiki/File:Defense.gov_News_Photo_990528-O-9999M-011.jpg

The inactivity of the Iraqi forces when it came to aerial defense took most of the Coalition generals by surprise. They expected a much fiercer opposition by the supposedly fourth strongest army in the world. Yet the Iraqi airplanes were mostly kept on the ground. The only notable exception was an attempted attack on the Saudi Ras Tanura oil production facility. On January 24th, the Iraqi Air Force sent two F1 Mirages, accompanied by two MiG-23s on the only offensive aerial mission during the war. It ended up as a failure, as the two MiGs abandoned the F1 fighter-bombers upon seeing two Saudi F-15s, which proceeded to shoot down the lone Mirages. However, the Iraqis never planned to get involved in a more serious aerial confrontation, a decision that could be dually assessed. From one perspective, it was a huge mistake, as it left the airspace undisputedly in the tight grip of the Coalition forces. This air superiority proved to be an important factor in the later Coalition attacks. At the same time, it could be seen as a conservative decision to save the Iraqi air flotilla. The Iraqi commanders were aware of its inadequacy to stand up to their enemies, which had advantages both in numbers and technology. The Iraqi high command turned to the Scud missiles instead.

By opting to use only ballistic missiles for the offensive actions, the Iraqi Army was capable of targeting rather distant objectives without sacrificing any lives. On top of that, the Scuds had a chance of damaging the Coalition troops' morale, similar to the German World War II V1 and V2 rockets. Yet, like their German predecessors, the Scud missiles were not known for their precision and effectiveness. Nonetheless, after the first Iraqi ballistic weapons were fired on January 18th, the so-called "Scud hunting missions" became one of the top priorities of the Coalition air force. Many feared that Saddam would order the use of chemical or biological warheads, and so, they designated the Scuds as one of their primary targets. However, during the entire Gulf War, none of the 88 ballistic missiles fired by the Iraqis was armed with anything else except conventional warheads. Despite that, the Scud attacks proved to be problematic to the Coalition forces, or, to be more precise, to the US, which led the joint military action. Nearly half of those missiles were fired toward Israel, an officially neutral country that wasn't a part of the Coalition. It was yet another attempt to bind Israel to the Iraqi issue.

Israeli civilian building hit by an Iraqi Scud (January 1991).
Government Press Office (Israel), CC BY-SA 3.0 https://creativecommons.org/licenses/by-sa/3.0 via Wikimedia Commons: https://commons.wikimedia.org/wiki/File:Flickr_-_Government_Press_Office_(GPO)_-_Damage_from_an_Iraqi_Scud_missile.jpg

Saddam Hussein hoped to provoke Israel into retaliating by bombarding cities like Tel Aviv and Haifa. Such action would have almost certainly broken up the allies, as the Arab states would have backed out of the Coalition, which would then lose its international integrity and Saudi territory as its base. In the worst-case scenario for the US, the conflict could turn into another Arab-Israeli War. To prevent that, the Americans installed Patriot SAM systems that were modified to intercept the Iraqi Scuds, offering protection to the Israelis. Despite that, the Patriot system wasn't full-proof, and many of the Iraqi missiles had their warheads intact even after being struck by Patriot projectiles. The Scuds would miss their targets but would still explode and cause damage. Thus, the US, as well as their European allies, offered more than 1.1 billion dollars as compensation for the damages and casualties caused by the Scuds. Their only condition was for Israel to not fire back at Iraq. That stipulation was followed by the Israelis. By the end of the war, 42 missiles had struck their territory, killing roughly 70 civilians and injuring about 250 more, while several thousand houses and buildings were damaged.

The rest of the Iraqi Scuds were fired at Saudi targets, both civilian and military. However, Saudi Arabia suffered lower civilian casualties, most likely because its cities were smaller and less dense. Only one Saudi civilian lost his life, while 78 others were injured. Military losses were much higher, as one Scud missile, which was actually hit by the Patriot defense system, managed to hit the US barracks in eastern Saudi Arabia. It killed 28 soldiers and injured over 100 more. That made it one of the most effective attacks of the Iraqi Army over the entire course of the war, at least in terms of casualties and damages caused. Because of all that, by the second week of the aerial operations, about one-third of the Coalition sorties were aimed at destroying Scud missile launchers. It was an effort that mostly proved ineffective, as it was hard to locate them in the vast Iraqi deserts. At the same time, the allied forces believed they had exhausted their original highly strategic targets, like airfields, radars, and weapons depots. Thus, their missions began shifting toward hitting the Iraqi ground forces, their communications, and their resources. Among them were also so-called "dual-use" targets, such as public highways, bridges, railways, etc.

From a military point of view, those were all valid targets, as they provided Iraqi troops with much-needed supplies and communication lines. However, since those were also used by civilians or were in the vicinity of civilian structures, their bombardment was also threatening the noncombatant population. Of course, civilian casualties were something that public opinion did not tolerate, and the Coalition forces quickly came under pressure from spectators. US President Bush Sr. tried to calm the backlash by claiming that the US Army was doing everything in its powers to avoid and minimize civilian casualties. He further blamed his opponents for relocating Iraqi military and strategic installations, like command and communication centers, into civilian neighborhoods. Those accusations weren't unfounded, as Saddam realized that noncombatant losses could improve his diplomatic position. Because of that, on January 25th, he recalled Western journalists to Baghdad, allowing them to witness firsthand the results of the supposed Coalition precision bombings. Most of them were shocked to realize that despite what the US high command was declaring in press conferences, the accuracy of their attacks was less than ideal. First of all, only about 10% of the total bombs dropped by the Coalition forces were so-called smart bombs. The vast majority were conventional bombs with limited precision, leaving sufficient room for errors.

Yet this was far less surprising for the journalists than the fact that even the precision-guided missiles were less than perfect. For example, in the city of Diwaniya, a telecommunications tower approximately 150 feet (45 meters) tall was entirely missed by four different air raids, but surrounding hotels and market shops were hit and severely damaged or destroyed. They further saw that private houses, schools, and even hospitals were accidentally hit, causing dozens of unnecessary civilian casualties. The issue wasn't always the matter of precision of the laser-guided bombs, as sometimes faulty intel gathered by Coalition surveillance marked the noncombatant public structures as viable targets. An example of that was the bombing of a civilian shelter in the suburbs of Baghdad. It was inaccurately distinguished as an Iraqi command center and was subsequently attacked. The result was somewhere between 500 and 1,000 civilian deaths. Among the victims were about 100 innocent kids. To worsen the situation for the Coalition forces, the estimation of the effects of the aerial raids in the first two weeks of the bombardments proved to be exaggerated. Reevaluation of the original reports showed that about two-thirds of the Iraqi airfields were still at least somewhat operational, while Iraqi defenses had regained about 20% of its radar capabilities. This was most likely caused by the fact that the Coalition bombings only damaged some of the Iraqi equipment, knocking it out only temporarily.

Apart from that, the Iraqi Army managed to preserve most of its tanks, anti-aircraft artillery, and Scud launchers, as well as mobile communication systems. Also, due to the lack of active air defense, the Iraqi Air Force lost less than half of its fighting force. Most of their planes were destroyed on the ground, but over 100 of them flew over to Iran, where they surprisingly found sanctuary. On top of all that, the Iraqi aerial defense began shooting down Coalition aircraft, though not in any significant numbers. Iraq started showing signs of putting up a slightly stiffer resistance. Because of that, the allied air force proved to be less efficient than expected. At the same time, the Scud attacks intensified, causing even more trouble for the Coalition command, as it had to keep resources allocated to finding and destroying Iraqi ballistic missiles, which further lowered the effectiveness of the bombing campaign. For that reason, the US generals leading Operation Desert Storm were forced to prolong the aerial bombing campaign for much longer than what was initially expected, slowing down the four-stage-plan of the attack on Iraq. After two weeks of air raids, the Coalition was still fulfilling the first two stages. The first one was the bombing of strategic command and communication targets, and the other one was attacking strategic reserves and disrupting communications between the Iraqi leadership in Baghdad and the troops stationed in Kuwait.

What was even more troubling for the United States was the fact that the almost universal support to the Coalition mission was slowly winding down beginning in late January. The Soviet Union began expressing concerns that the bombing tactics employed would lead to the destruction of all Iraqi infrastructure, crippling the country for an extended period. Gorbachev himself was also worried that the Gulf War could expand and cause even wider conflicts. Other nations began expressing their disagreement with the direction the Coalition was heading, as well as the conduct of the war, especially concerning civilian casualties. Among them were even the members of the Coalition itself. The French minister of defense claimed that its ultimate goal was not only to expel Iraqi troops from Kuwait but also to overthrow the Ba'ath regime. Because of his disagreements with France's involvement in the war, he even resigned from his office in late January. Coming to a similar conclusion, Egyptian President Mubarak and Saudi King Fahd bin Abdulaziz declared their troops would not fight on Iraqi soil, limiting their actions only to Kuwaiti territory. Even worse, a Pakistani general who was appointed to the Coalition task force accused the West, mainly the US, that the entire war was a conspiracy to weaken the Muslim world by destroying Iraqi power.

Similar sentiments were rising among the ordinary population as well. The anti-war protest began spreading across the world. The most massive ones were held in Muslim countries more sympathetic to the Iraqi cause, like Algeria, Morocco, and Sudan, where the number of protesters went as high as 300,000 to 400,000. On a much lesser scale, protests and strikes also spread among the US allies and Coalition members, including France, Italy, Spain, Turkey, and Germany. Anti-war rallies spread as far as Australia and Japan. Some of these protests were violent, with burning fires in front of the United States embassies and blocking the American military bases. Anti-war rallies appeared in the US as well, most notably in Washington DC, though they represented only a clear minority of the American public. The support of the war there was undeniably still high. However, this made President Bush Sr. and his administration aware that a prolonged war wasn't an option. The US would quickly lose the support of the world, turning the American soldiers into villains once again. Thus, the Coalition pressed on with the bombings, beginning phase three of the plan, which was pressuring Iraqi troops on a tactical level. It was the preparation for the final stage of the war, a ground invasion into both Kuwait and Iraq.

As the bombs continued to fall on Iraq, the Ba'ath regime began to reconsider the benefits of the war. It was becoming clear to Saddam and his high officials that the Gulf War would bring more destruction than anticipated. At the same time, the idea of the "mother of all battles," as Saddam called it, turned out to be wishful thinking. The possibility that the Iraqi troops would fight off the inevitable ground invasion was slim to none, while the aerial bombing began taking its toll. The Coalition losses were minimal, while the Scud attacks proved to be more of a nuisance than a viable threat. Luckily for the Ba'ath regime, even though the Soviets weren't their allies in this war, they were still looking to protect their influence over the country. Thus, in early February, Soviet and Turkish officials called for an end to the devastation of Iraq in a joint statement. At the same time, the Iraqi diplomats started showing interest in negotiations and peace. This prompted President Gorbachev to send an envoy to Baghdad on February 12th to persuade the Ba'ath government that a diplomatic resolution was possible if it accepted requirements set by the UN resolutions. The Soviets hoped to avoid a land war, which would not only be costly in the number of lives lost—it could also mean the fall of the current Iraqi regime.

The crumbling Soviet Union, like many other nations, suspected that the end goal of the US-led Coalition was to topple the Ba'ath regime, replacing it with a more pro-Western government. It seemed that the Soviets managed to convince the Iraqi leadership of that during their contacts in early February. As a result, Saddam's regime declared on

February 15th that it was open to finding a peaceful resolution of the conflict. However, the US was only accepting an immediate and unconditional withdrawal of the Iraqi troops from Kuwait. The USSR instantly became an intermediary between the United States and Iraq, as a direct talk between the two countries was not possible. By mid-February, it looked like a solution without a ground war was possible. Despite that, the Coalition air force continued to bombard Iraqi positions, causing further damage to both military and civilian targets. Not only that, but it was starting to intensify the raids, combining them with probing skirmishes with the Iraqi Army on the ground. The land invasion was undoubtedly drawing near.

Chapter 6 – The First Battles in the Desert

The destruction and casualties caused by the Coalition bombings were enough to convince the Iraqi leadership to seek a peaceful solution to the ongoing crisis. It was clear to everyone that the Iraqi Army, despite the boasting and propaganda on both sides, was no match for the US-led Coalition force. However, no matter how devastating the aerial campaign turned out to be, Saddam and the Ba'ath regime was not ready to accept an unconditional surrender. To achieve that goal, the US had to flex its military muscles even harder and hit the Iraqis on the ground.

However, in a rather surprising turn of events, it was actually the Iraqis who first engaged in land combat. During the last days of January, while the Coalition bombing was reaching its peak, Saddam and his military advisors started forming a plan of attack on Saudi territory. They realized that this prolonged bombardment would only worsen their military positions since the Iraqi air defense wasn't capable of dealing enough casualties to the US forces to turn the Gulf War into a new Vietnam. Thus, they chose to attack the small Saudi city of Khafji. It is located about twelve miles (twenty kilometers) southeast of the Kuwaiti-Saudi border, on the shores of the Persian Gulf. Due to its closeness, it was in the range of Iraqi artillery; thus, its population, at the time roughly numbering about 15,000 people, were evacuated when the war started.

Iraqi generals were likely aware of that fact. For them, it was a rather suitable target void of possible civilian casualties that would further vilify the Iraqis in the eyes of the world. The strategic position of Khafji also made it an alluring target. The city was located on the only junction of the coastal road linking Saudi Arabia with Kuwait to the north and Bahrain, Qatar, the UAE, and Oman to the south. Even more important was the nearby Wafra oil field, which was jointly exploited by the Kuwaitis and the Saudis. Another factor made Khafji viable prey for the Iraqi generals. It was defended mostly by Saudi and Qatar troops, which were undoubtedly a much more desirable opponent for the Iraqi soldiers than the US forces.

After several days of preparation, the plan was set. The Iraqi Army was to attack with mechanized and armored divisions on the land, separated in three columns, while being aided by special forces attacking by the sea. The attack came on the night of January 29th, at about 8 p.m. local time. The Coalition command was surprised by this bold action, even though its reconnaissance teams reported the possibility of an Iraqi movement. The first to attack was the westernmost column, which encountered the lightly armed US troops. This assault was repulsed only when the Coalition air force, most notably the A-10 Tank Killer aircraft and the AC-130 gunships, came in to support. A similar scenario unfolded in the center column as well, where, once again, the aerial support defended the lightly armed US soldiers. However, the easternmost column, which was traveling next to the shoreline, proved to be the most determined. After enduring the bombing of the Coalition air force, it managed to enter the city just after midnight, as the Saudi defenders were ordered to retreat. The Iraqi Army fulfilled its initial goal, essentially achieving victory in the initial stages of the battle.

Nevertheless, it was a pyrrhic victory. The Iraqi troops suffered heavy losses, especially in the number of vehicles lost. The hardest hit was the Iraqi naval force. The fourth column, the commando attack from the sea, was quickly spotted by the Coalition ships. The small Iraqi speedboats were no match for the superior Coalition frigates and cruisers. Some were sunk, while others began to flee. Over the next couple of days, the Coalition vessels and aircraft, led by the British navy, continued to hunt down Iraqi patrol boats and smaller ships. Some tried to escape to the

Iranians, but only one managed to do so. By February 2ⁿᵈ, the Iraqi Navy ceased to exist as a fighting force, as it was almost completely destroyed. Apart from heavy losses, this initial conflict also showcased two aspects of the war that were to become underlying themes in all future ground conflicts between the Coalition and Iraqi forces. One was that aerial superiority was a crucial factor for the Coalition to achieve its ground victories. The second was that the friendly fire was as much of a threat to the Coalition soldiers as the Iraqis were. The US military lost eleven men and two APCs because of misidentification and miscommunication.

A US LAV-AT destroyed by friendly fire in the Battle of Khafji.
https://commons.wikimedia.org/wiki/File:RemnantsofLAV25.jpg

Regardless, the Iraqis were holding the city since the early hours of January 30ᵗʰ. The following day, the effort to recapture Khafji began. The attack was spearheaded by the Saudi troops, which were aided by a Qatari tank division. The US forces provided artillery and aerial support. However, during the first day, the Iraqis managed to hold on to their positions, but they were once again affected by heavy casualties due to the attacks from the air. The Coalition bombers didn't only target the Iraqi troops in the city but also every unit spotted near the Kuwaiti-Saudi border. The plan was to stop any reinforcements and supplies from reaching the troops in Khafji. Thanks to their complete aerial superiority, this task was fulfilled, and the following day, the Saudi forces renewed their attacks. The second attack was more successful, managing to destroy and capture parts of the occupying Iraqi troops, who, by the end of the day, ended up being surrounded. By that time, the morale of the Iraqi soldiers had fallen. When the Coalition attack resumed on February 1ˢᵗ, most of them surrendered without a fight. After only two days of Iraqi occupation, Khafji was back under Saudi control.

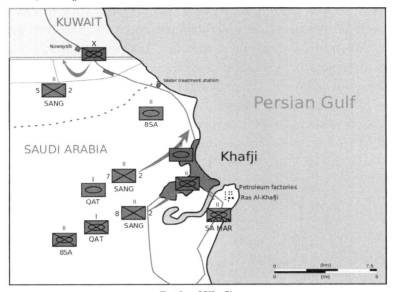

Battle of Khafji.
https://commons.wikimedia.org/wiki/File:Battle_of_Khafji_1991.svg

The result of the Battle of Khafji was a clear military victory for the Coalition. Over the course of just four days, hundreds of Iraqis were killed or captured, the Iraqi Navy was basically obliterated, and the Iraqi Army lost hundreds of tanks and APCs. Most of these losses were caused from enemy aircraft, which severely damaged the morale of the Iraqis. A captured Iraqi soldier said that the Coalition air force caused more damage to his unit in half an hour than the Iranians did during the whole eight years of the Iran-Iraq War. The Iraqi commanders on the ground shared the sentiment, as one of the generals commented that "the mother was killing her children," alluding to Saddam's "mother of all battles" phrase. In contrast to those heavy losses, the combined casualties of the US and the Saudis were about 100 men wounded and killed, with only a handful of vehicles lost. More importantly for them, the Iraqi plan failed, as they didn't manage to lure them into further ground combat. However, the harsh reality didn't stop Saddam from proclaiming victory in this skirmish. He used that notion in both his domestic and international propaganda, trying to gain political points and raise the morale of his soldiers.

The success of the Ba'ath propaganda regarding the Battle of Khafji was at best limited. Internationally, only a few Arab countries welcomed the clash as an Iraqi victory, while most of the world saw nothing good coming from it. More worryingly, the domestic reach of the Khafji story spin was only marginally successful. With daily bombardments and heavy military losses, the citizens of Iraq weren't convinced the war was going in their favor. The Iraqi soldiers seemed even less confident, while the upper Iraqi command started having doubts. Thus, when in the following days the Coalition bombing continued to make Iraqi soil tremble, the Ba'ath leadership was becoming more open to negotiations. Therefore, when the Soviets sent their envoy to Baghdad on February 12th, Saddam's regime was ready to compromise for peace. Only three days later, the Iraqi leadership stepped up with an offer. If the American and other Western forces withdrew from the region, Iraq would be willing to deal with UN Resolution 660, which demanded the immediate and unconditional withdrawal of Iraq, while the future of the country was to be decided by the Arab nations, including Kuwait. Another condition was for the Israeli troops to withdraw from Arab lands. President Bush Sr. dismissed the offer as a hoax and an attempt to divide the Coalition allies. Regardless, the Soviets saw it as a starting offer, something to be explored in the hope of achieving a more peaceful resolution.

In the following days, both President Gorbachev and Tariq Aziz, the Iraqi minister of foreign affairs, came out with their peace proposals. Rather similar in nature, both of their ideas revolved around achieving the ceasefire and withdrawal of Iraqi troops from Kuwait while still linking the peace to the Arab-Israeli conflict. For the US, as well as the Arab Coalition leaders, this was unacceptable. Iraqi withdrawal had to be unconditional. Furthermore, Bush Sr. and his office felt that by allowing the Iraqis to simply retreat would leave the resolution of the conflict rather unclear and ambiguous. In their point of view, that would leave enough room for Saddam to politically exploit the outcome of the war. For some members of Bush's Cabinet, the only successful end of Desert Storm was if Iraq suffered an indisputable military defeat and was penalized for its aggression. For that reason, some more aggressive members of the US government hoped that Iraq wouldn't yield just from the bombing. They wanted the war to expand onto the ground. And while the US held firm on its non-negotiable position, the Soviets talked with the Iraqi representatives to try to find a compromise, hoping to avoid the conflict from broadening even more.

By February 21ˢᵗ, Gorbachev, backed up by Tariq Aziz, proposed a new plan. It called for the unconditional withdrawal of the Iraqi troops, in accordance with Resolution 660, followed by the ceasefire and lifting of all sanctions when two-thirds of the Iraqi soldiers left Kuwait. The war was to be ended with the nullification of all UN resolutions when the withdrawal was complete. However, in contrast to the diplomatic offers, Iraq's behavior on the ground spoke differently. Saddam was giving warmongering speeches, while the soldiers began burning Kuwaiti oil fields and supposedly killing Kuwaiti civilians. Therefore, the latest Soviet plan was once again rejected by the Bush administration, which, on the following day, sent out its own ultimatum. Iraq had 24 hours, until February 23ʳᵈ, 5:00 p.m. GMT, to begin their withdrawal from Kuwait, which was to be finished within seven days. Furthermore, Iraq was to return full control over the territory to the Kuwaiti government, release all prisoners, and give up military control over the Kuwaiti air and land to the Coalition. In return, the Coalition was not to fire upon the retreating Iraqi forces. This ultimatum only sped up the Soviet Union's attempts to avoid a ground war.

A picture of burning Kuwaiti oil fields (March 1991).
https://commons.wikimedia.org/wiki/File:Operation_Desert_Storm_22.jpg

In a matter of hours, Gorbachev came out with a new plan. The Iraqi withdrawal would begin within a day of the ceasefire agreement, and it would be completed in three weeks. The UN resolutions would be annulled after the withdrawal occurred. Early on February 23rd, Tariq Aziz openly accepted this plan. However, Bush Sr. was adamant. The Iraqi Army was to begin pulling out of Kuwait in a matter of hours. The Soviet president tried to convince his US colleague through a phone call to push back the deadline for another 24 hours, as an acceptable compromise was only a day away. These efforts were futile. President Bush wasn't budging, and he had the support of other major members of the Coalition. This left US-USSR relations somewhat strained, as Gorbachev stated that the Americans were more interested in an armed resolution than in a peaceful diplomatic solution, a remark not far from the truth. In the end, the Iraqi leaders didn't fulfill the US ultimatum, and the Coalition wasn't giving them more time to reconsider. Thus, on February 23rd, at 6:00 p.m. GMT, President Bush greenlighted the beginning of the land operations in Iraq. This military operation was codenamed "Desert Sabre."

In the days before the full Coalition ground offensive, while the diplomats and politicians were talking and negotiating, both armies prepared for the inevitable clash. The Coalition forces continued to bombard the Iraqi positions, softening their defenses, knocking out their equipment, and lowering the morale of the Iraqi soldiers. Furthermore, Coalition ground troops began skirmishing with Iraqi soldiers, preventing their reconnaissance teams from observing the Coalition positions. This was only furthered between February 15th and 20th when several US units attacked the Iraqi positions along the Iraq-Kuwait border. However, these attacks were limited feint operations that were designed to make the Iraqis think that the main Coalition invasion would take place near the tripoint of Iraq, Kuwait, and Saudi Arabia. The ploy was helped by the fact that it was a natural invasion route. Thus, after limited clashes, the US troops returned to their original positions, while the Iraqi army focused on defending that sector of the front. The goal was to draw the Iraqi forces from the western portions of the front, where the US VII Army Corps would lead the main Coalition attack. These incursive actions warned the Iraqi high command that an attack was imminent.

Thus, they began preparing their defenses.

Apart from the conventional tactics, like laying down mines and fortifying their positions, the Ba'ath generals also decided to use Kuwaiti oil fields as a part of their natural defenses. They began spilling the oil, burning it in an attempt to create large fire lakes and thick clouds to impede the Coalition advancement and forcing them to enter predetermined "death zones" created by these obstacles. Even if the fires were to run out, the oil residue, mixed with tar and sand, would leave a layer of so-called "tarcrete," which would jam up the tracks of the Coalition tanks. However, it should be noted that not all of the several hundred burning Kuwaiti oil fields should be blamed on the Iraqis. About fifty of them were lit up by Coalition bombings, which were targeting nearby Iraqi units, before mid-February 1991. The Iraqis also dumped large quantities of crude oil just off the shores of Kuwait in the Persian Gulf. They hoped it would cause problems for the expected Coalition naval assault. These tactics were highly controversial worldwide, as many saw them more as an intentional ecological catastrophe than a viable military strategy. From the Iraqi perspective, this tactic made sense because it was also damaging the Kuwaiti oil industry, which was one of the reasons the war even began. Regardless of both the ecological and infrastructural damage, the Iraqi Army was waiting for the imminent attack of the Coalition forces, which finally arrived at 4:00 a.m. local time on February 24th.

The overall plan of the attack was rather simple. The eastern flank, consisting of Saudi, Egyptian, Syrian, and other Arab troops, helped by the US 1st Marine Expeditionary Force, was to push north directly into Kuwait. They were under the command of Saudi Prince Khalid bin Sultan. The reason why the Arab forces were tasked with liberating Kuwait was that they refused to fight on Iraqi territory, limiting the range of their actions to only up to the Kuwait-Iraq border. The main attack on the center of the front was given to the US VII Army Corps, under the command of Lieutenant-General Fred Franks Jr., which was aided by the British troops. Their goal was to flank the Iraqi forces in Kuwait and encircle them. It was expected that the units attacking this sector would encounter the fiercest resistance, as most of the infamous Republican Guard was located on their path. The western flank was left to the US

XVIII Airborne Corps, which was aided by the French troops. Commanded by Lieutenant-General Gary Luck, it was tasked with blocking possible reinforcements the Iraqi Army would send to the south and would have to push the deepest into enemy territory. The success of the plan, which is ascribed to US General Schwarzkopf, hinged on speed. The Coalition forces had to move quickly and relentlessly to avoid being bogged down in prolonged combat, which could lead to higher casualties than needed.

The implementation of Schwarzkopf's plan was more than swift. On the eastern flank, the Arab and US forces moved into Kuwait, first encountering the Iraqi units that attacked Khafji. Unexpectedly, these troops showed little resistance. It seemed their battle morale had dissipated over the weeks of heavy bombardment, combined by the fact that most of the soldiers felt abandoned by Baghdad. Two captured Iraqi officers even stated that they were left without any orders for about two weeks. The extent of how low Iraqi morale was can be illustrated by the US assessment that some 150,000 troops deserted even before the main ground operations had begun. Because of that, the Coalition push into Kuwait proved to be quick and mostly painless, as most of the Iraqis simply surrendered at the first sight of the advancing troops. The fact that they mostly encountered fellow Arabs on the other side possibly made their decision to surrender easier. And as the Arab-US troops advanced on the eastern front, they began forming the anvil for the VII Army Corps hammer, which was breaking through the center of the battlefield. The major attacks on that part of the battlefield were preceded by short artillery barrages, in which more than 10,000 shells were fired to pummel the Iraqi defenses.

The breakthrough in the center of this front was spearheaded by the famous 1st US Infantry Division, the "Big Red One," which wiped out the Iraqi division that opposed it. On the western flank of the "Big Red One," armored and cavalry divisions pushed on, swiveling toward the center. Those were to join the 1st Infantry Division in their primary goal, hunting down the Republican Guard that was stationed in the back of the Iraqi defense lines as a strategic reserve. On the eastern flank of the central front, the British 1st Armored Division, known as the "Desert Rats," pushed through the breach created by the Big Red One. It was racing toward Kuwait in order to protect the VII Army Corps' push toward the Republican Guard. The Iraqi commanders were taken by surprise by the overall actions of the VII Army Corps. First of all, they expected the main attack to happen on the western flank, where the armored and cavalry division poured in. Furthermore, they assumed its main goal was to push toward Kuwait immediately instead of driving deeper into Iraqi territory to face the Republican Guard. When they realized the main intent of the Coalition attack, the Guard began to reposition. Among those units were three elite divisions, the Medina, the Hammurabi, and the Tawakalna. Their main goal was to stop the VII Army Corps from breaching through to the Iraqi rear positions.

In the western sector, the XVIII Airborne Corps proved to be the most successful. In the center, the US 101st Airborne Division pushed about 93 miles (150 kilometers) inside Iraqi territory with a massive airlift involving 400 helicopters. There, they established a forward operating base named Cobra. From there, they pushed 60 miles (96 kilometers) farther north toward the Euphrates River. There, it cut off Highway 8, the main road connecting central and southern Iraq. On their western flank was the French 6th Light Armoured Division, which was aided by the US 82nd Airborne Division. They rushed through the desert to take the Al-Salman Air Base and protect the left flank of the 101st Airborne Division. On the right flank, the US 24th Mechanized Infantry Division, reinforced by the US 3rd Armored Cavalry Regiment, pushed north to meet up with the 101st in the area of the Cobra base before turning eastward to aid the VII Army Corps in its attack on the Republican Guard. The XVIII Airborne Corps managed to fulfill its initial goals ahead of time, prompting General Schwarzkopf to speed up overall operations a few hours ahead of schedule. The unexpected swiftness of the Coalition breakthrough was achieved mostly due to the lack of Iraqi morale. On top of that, the allies had a clear technological advantage, as the Iraqi tanks were no match for the British and US counterparts, while the aerial support further weakened the Iraqi positions.

Saddam Hussein himself further hindered Iraqi resistance. He was more concerned with preserving his regime than holding their positions in the south. Because of that, the Iraqi leader held back some of the more important units and was unwilling to risk losing his most trusted

Republican Guard. Furthermore, if there was ever a time when the Iraqi troops needed at least some air support, it was at the time of this Coalition attack. Unfortunately for them, Saddam kept most of the planes grounded. With such orders, the Iraqi generals were unable to mount a more serious attempt of defense, while the troops on the ground felt as if they were being sacrificed. Even worse, Saddam wanted to withdraw as many soldiers as possible to the north in an attempt to reinforce his own positions. Still, with Highway 8 being cut off, this was not a viable option. However, as the Coalition forces pushed through southern Iraq during February 25th, things began to change slightly. The first Iraqi units started pulling out of Kuwait that night, while, simultaneously, troops on the central front began showing slightly stiffer opposition. Nonetheless, the future of the Iraqi troops looked dim. By the end of that day, the Coalition basically cut off the Iraqi Army in Kuwait and the Basra region from the northern regions of Iraq.

Achieving that in such a short time, within just two days, the allied forces were actually exceeding the goals given to them by the high command. The speed with which they broke through the initial defenses of the Iraqi Army surprised even the most senior officers of the Coalition, let alone the rest of the world. Witnessing just how much the Coalition was overpowered in contrast with the Iraqi Army, it was clear that Saddam lacked the power to resist the Coalition attack. However, it didn't mean that the Iraqis would go down without a fight, at least when it came to the ever-loyal Republican Guard.

Chapter 7 – Iraqi Defeat and the Aftermath of the War

After just about 48 hours, the Coalition forces managed to push deep into Iraqi territory, almost seamlessly. Using their superior technology and air support, the allied units managed to break what little fighting spirit the Iraqi Army had left after weeks of heavy bombardments. Most of the regular troops began piling up around Basra, hoping for a miracle since the reinforcement from the north clearly wasn't coming. It was clear that the liberation of Kuwait was within reach, leaving only the secondary target of the Coalition troops to be achieved. That was to destroy Saddam's loyal elite guards.

Destroyed Iraqi T-62
https://commons.wikimedia.org/wiki/File:Destroyed_Iraqi_T-62.jpg

US artillery firing upon the Iraqi positions – February 1991.

By the early morning of February 26th, the US VII Army Corps finally caught up to the Republican Guard. The first unit they encountered was the Tawakalna Division in a tank battle that lasted for much of the day. The Iraqis dug in, providing a much stiffer resistance than any previous enemy the VII Army Corps had encountered. The Tawakalna proved its elite status, at least when compared to other Iraqi divisions. It held out for much of the day, though it was assisted by poor visibility from the weather conditions. In the end, even the Republican Guard proved to be no match for the US and British forces. Their T-72s were outgunned on the ground and by the Coalition air force, which began picking them off as soon as the weather started to improve. By the end of the 26th, the Tawakalna Division broke and began to withdraw. The Medina Division, another elite unit of the Guard, which was aided by a regular Iraqi Army division, tried to cover their retreat, to no avail. The air raid picked off most of what was left of the Tawakalna. However, parts of the elite Iraqi division survived to fight another day, even though its capabilities were significantly diminished.

During the same day the Tawakalna Division suffered their defeat, Iraqi forces farther south in Kuwait began preparing for an evacuation. The Arab and US troops reached the city itself during the day, while the Iraqis began fleeing. However, remnants of the Iraqi 3rd Armored Division, which were veterans of both the Iran-Iraq War and the 1973

Arab-Israeli Yom Kippur War, decided to hold their ground. It seems they decided to put up a stiff resistance in the hopes of buying some time for their fleeing comrades. Their efforts proved to be futile in more than one way. The Iraqis tried to dig in, relying on what was left of their tanks and APCs (armored personnel carriers), but once again, they proved to be an inadequate match for the more modern equipment heralded by the US troops that were spearheading the attack. Regardless of that, the Iraqi veterans showed stiff resistance, as they were finally defeated only during the next day, making their last stand near the Kuwait International Airport. With that, the liberation of Kuwait was technically finished, and the main objective of the Coalition was achieved. However, this accomplishment was largely tainted by the events that transpired mostly during the night between February 26th and 27th. As the veterans of the Iraqi 3rd Armored Division fought hard in the city to provide at least some time for the other retreating Iraqi troops, their comrades gathered up a large group of mostly civilian vehicles and began their flight north.

They headed up on Highway 80 from Kuwait to Basra. It wasn't long before their flight started resembling traffic congestion. Of course, the Coalition planes spotted them, and on the orders of the high command, they began attacking them. First, they opened fire on the head and the tail of the fleeing column, boxing the rest in between. Then, over the course of more than ten hours in a series of repeated attacks, the Coalition pilots proceeded to basically massacre the Iraqis. By the morning, only charred debris and burnt bodies were left, dotting miles of the road. This caused an uproar among the international public, as many saw it as excessive use of force. The Iraqis were withdrawing, mostly unarmed, prompting some to argue that these attacks violated the Geneva Convention, which bans the killing of soldiers who are out of combat. Others added that there were civilians among the military personnel, which was never completely confirmed. The US command responded by claiming that they were simply destroying the Iraqi military equipment, which could have been used in future combat. Other US officers also added that the killed Iraqis were just "a bunch of rapists, murderers and thugs" who were trying to escape. The number of casualties was also a matter of debate, as some army officials claimed that most of the Iraqis abandoned their vehicles when the attacks started. Regardless, the event on what became known as the "Highway of Death" left a bitter taste to many international observers.

A later picture of the "Highway of Death" with a T-55 in the front (April 1991).
https://commons.wikimedia.org/wiki/File:Destroyed_Iraqi_T-55_on_highway_between_Basra_%26_Kuwait_City_1991-04-18_1.JPEG

However, those events had little effects on the other Coalition troops. On the next day, February 27th, the advancing US forces of the VII Army Corps, led by the US 1st Armored Division, engaged the Medina Division, which was reinforced with minor remnants of the Tawakalna and regular Iraqi Army brigades. Once again, the Iraqi elites justified their reputation. They chose to dig in on the high ground behind a ridge, giving them strong defensive positions with an element of surprise. The advancing American units were unable to see them clearly before passing the ridgeline. Thanks to their tactical choices, as well as their strong will to fight, the Medina Division put up what was most likely the fiercest resistance of the war, even managing to shoot down some of the US aircraft. In the clash that became known as the Battle of Medina Ridge, they held their positions for the entire day. Yet, once again, their equipment proved to be no match for the US artillery and air force. Even the American tanks proved to be too much of a challenge for them simply because they outranged the generation older Soviet T-72s that the Guard used. Thus, by the end of the day, the Medina Division was defeated as well, suffering significant losses, especially in tanks and APCs.

At the same time as the Battle of Medina Ridge, another major clash occurred in the relative vicinity. The US 1ˢᵗ Infantry Division, aided by other American and British armored and artillery divisions, engaged a mishmash of Iraqi armored and infantry divisions that had survived thus far. Even some other remnants of the Tawakalna Division were present. The Iraqis were trying to fortify their positions, as they had no other viable options in their attempts to resist the invading forces. Once again, the Iraqi troops showed some will to resist but to no avail. Their dug-in tanks were easy targets for the Coalition aerial bombardment and artillery. As the day progressed, their resistance was slowly broken, and the Iraqi troops began surrendering. By the end of the day, the Coalition forces marked another important victory. It became known as the Battle of Norfolk, as it was located in a desert area near the Iraq-Kuwait border that the Coalition command called Objective Norfolk. The Iraqi Army lost a large chunk of its fighting force and a substantial number of vehicles and equipment. The exact quantities of both deployed and destroyed Iraqi tanks are still debated, as historians are still arguing which of the two significant battles of the day, the Battle of Medina Ridge or the Battle of Norfolk, hold the title for the largest tank battle of the Gulf War.

A dug-in Iraqi T-72 at the Battle of Norfolk.
https://commons.wikimedia.org/wiki/File:AsadBabil-Dug-in.jpg

Farther north, the US 24th Mechanized Infantry Division followed the Euphrates River eastward, toward the city of Basra. On February 27th, it engaged the Republican Guard forces of the Al-Faw Division, which was aided by smaller detachments from the Nebuchadnezzar and Hammurabi Divisions near the Lake Hammar. The Al-Faw stood valiantly against the 24th Division, giving it the toughest resistance since the division had crossed into Iraq. However, like all the other battles that day, those Iraqi efforts were futile. Most of the Al-Faw Division was rendered combat ineffective, while parts of the Hammurabi and the Nebuchadnezzar Divisions fled back toward Basra. While the US 24th Mechanized Infantry Division was closing down on the city, the US 101st and 82nd Airborne Divisions were locking down the escape routes along the Euphrates River, as well as protecting the back of the Coalition forces. Effectively, by the end of the day, what was left of the Iraqi forces in the south was confined to the area around Basra. The Iraqi Army suffered significant losses and was almost completely surrounded in the so-called "Basra pocket." The only viable escape routes were north of Lake Hammar, which was along the Shatt al-Arab and Tigris Rivers.

At this point, the political and military leadership of the Coalition diverged in opinions. The leading US generals believed their secondary objective, rendering the Republican Guard ineffective, was not yet completely fulfilled. The Iraqi elite units did suffer substantial losses, mostly in terms of equipment, with the Tawakalna and the Al-Faw Divisions supposedly ceasing to exist as fighting forces. However, for the US generals, including General Schwarzkopf, this meant that the job was only partially done. In their eyes, the Guard was still a viable threat in the region. On the other hand, politicians, most notably President Bush Sr. himself, felt the goal of the Coalition was attained. The Iraqi Army was expelled from Kuwait, while the brunt of their fighting force and equipment were destroyed. Combined with horrific images of the Highway of Death and other similar scenes of destruction, it was enough for the international, as well as the US, public to doubt if the Coalition was going for the overkill. This was only furthered by the fact that the UN resolution tasked the Coalition with only liberating Kuwait, not destroying the Iraqi Army or toppling Saddam's regime. This prompted President Bush Sr. to declare a ceasefire at 8:00 a.m. on February 28th, exactly 100 hours since the official ground operations had begun.

This decision of the United States commander-in-chief spurred quite a bit of debate among the American public. One course of thought, more militaristic in nature, saw it as a mistake. Saddam's Ba'ath regime was not only left in charge of Iraq, but it was also allowed to retain too much military power. Others thought it was the right choice since the UN mission was fulfilled, and the Iraqi Army was undoubtedly defeated. This discussion was brought up again after the US invaded Iraq for the second time in 2003. However, in late February 1991, President Bush Sr. had to consider both the diplomatic climate and his own political legacy. By ending the war when he did, the US president prevented unwarranted Iraqi casualties, which would have almost certainly led to international disapproval. It would have tainted both the impressive American victory and his political career. Furthermore, if the US Army decided to continue the war to topple Saddam, the Coalition would have most likely fractured. The Arab members were undoubtedly against the American intervention in what were internal affairs of Iraq. Thus, President Bush Sr. saw only one right choice, leaving both his own and the face of the United States unblemished.

The Iraqi government was eager to accept the ceasefire, and the war was considered to be finished, even though no official document had been signed. It was agreed that the formal peace negotiations were to be held on March 2nd at Safwan Air Base, just a few miles from the Iraq-Kuwait border on the road toward Basra. However, while the talks were ongoing, the Hammurabi Division attempted to withdraw from the Basra pocket toward Baghdad, passing between the Rumaila oil field and Lake Hammar. On its path was the US 24th Mechanized Infantry Division, which had no intention to let them through. Without following any orders from the Iraqi high command, the Hammurabi soldiers opened gunfire on the US troops that tried to block their escape. That provoked a fierce reaction from the American forces. The long column of the retreating Iraqi troops was first enclosed in a killing zone, after which they were subjugated to the systemic destruction from both the US ground forces and their artillery and aircraft support. The Hammurabi Division was devastated. It lost several hundred vehicles, with over 700 soldiers killed and 3,000 captured. The Battle of Rumaila, as this event became known, sparked another round of controversies among the observers of the war.

Charred remains of the Iraqi vehicles after the Battle of Rumaila (March 1991).
https://commons.wikimedia.org/wiki/File:IrakDesertStorm1991.jpg

The question was raised if the 24th Division had justification for unleashing such destruction, even though the Iraqis had fired first. Some even questioned the reason the US unit moved into the way of the retreating Iraqis in the first place, as this took place during the armistice. Especially dubious were the actions of the US soldiers, which were against all rules of civilized combat. Most of the Hammurabi Division wasn't battle-ready, with many of their tanks and other equipment loaded up on transportation vehicles; attacking them was the equivalent of shooting an unarmed man. Even worse, there were reports of US soldiers firing upon wounded, medics, and surrendering Iraqi soldiers. The extent of the violence was shockingly unjustifiable, proving that President Bush Sr. made the right call. If the war continued, it was likely that more similar events would have happened, as American soldiers were more than eager to punish "the evil Iraqis." Of course, this incident caused some friction at the negotiating table, but the Iraqi government had little choice.

The only way both the Ba'ath regime and Iraq as a whole would survive was to agree on the terms given to them by the Coalition command. Thus, on March 3rd, 1991, in Safwan, the hostilities were officially ended as the two sides signed the ceasefire. The Iraqi side agreed on the terms set by the Coalition. Both sides were to exchange prisoners. Iraq had reportedly captured 41 soldiers, some of whom later claimed to have been savagely tortured and beaten in the hopes of extracting information about the Coalition plans. On the other side, the Coalition troops were holding more than 60,000 Iraqis, most of whom seemed to have been dealt with in accordance with the 1949 Geneva Convention. It was a shocking revelation to the Iraqi negotiator, who was unaware of just how extensive the Iraqi defeat was.

Furthermore, the Iraqi Army was to give precise information on the minefields it had laid in the region, most notably in Kuwait. Apart from that, a temporary ceasefire line was drawn to avoid any new unwarranted clashes like the 24th and Hammurabi Divisions had. The Iraqis were also banned from using fixed-wing aircraft, but after their negotiator pleaded, they were permitted the use of helicopters. The Iraqi government argued that with the substantial destruction of the Iraqi infrastructure, helicopters were needed to facilitate movement across the country. Iraq was also ordered to allow the UN representatives on their territory. They were to oversee the removal of chemical and biological weapons, as well as the ballistic missiles with ranges over 93 miles (150 kilometers). The Iraqi government also had to accept and implement all of the UN resolutions concerning the Gulf War and the issue of Kuwait. At the same time, Iraq had to officially recognize the line of the Iraq-Kuwait border as defined under the 1963 agreement.

On top of that, the border between the two countries was demarcated with a demilitarized area, which protruded six miles (ten kilometers) into Iraq, while it was only half as large on the Kuwaiti side. Iraq was further ordered to release all Kuwaiti prisoners and detainees, return all the pillaged property, and pay reparation damages to Kuwait. In return, the UN was to lift its sanctions, which was desperately needed by the Iraqi civilian population. All in all, the Safwan accord was less of a negotiation and more of an Iraqi surrender, a fact that was only confirmed when one looked at the state of the battlefield after the initial ceasefire was proclaimed. As Saddam and his regime accepted the imposed conditions, the Coalition troops slowly began to withdraw from the region. The Coalition victory was celebrated, or at least praised, across most of the world. However, Iraqi propaganda represented it differently. As it was still under the unchallenged control of Saddam Hussein, it informed the Iraqi citizens that the peace was only achieved because their soldiers had fought valiantly, forcing the Coalition to ask for a ceasefire. Thus, the Ba'ath regime proclaimed its triumph in the so-called "mother of all battles."

Demilitarized zone between Iraq and Kuwait
https://commons.wikimedia.org/wiki/File:Kuwait-Iraq_barrier.png

Kuwaiti civilians celebrating with Coalition soldiers over their liberation from the Iraqis
https://commons.wikimedia.org/wiki/File:Gulf_War_Saudi_Flag.JPEG

Of course, most of the Iraqi people were aware that this "news" was mere propaganda ploy. Thousands of disgruntled soldiers were returning home, with full knowledge of just how terrifying their defeat was. Almost all the civilians felt the devastation caused by the Coalition bombardment, and even more of them were affected by the UN economic blockade. The dissatisfaction piled up throughout the Gulf War, but there was nowhere it could be expressed, as the government kept strict control over both the media and the population. Thus, when the war was finished, with even Saddam's most loyal troops and his government apparatus in disarray, local uprisings began rising up. The first flames of revolt lit up during March 1ˢᵗ near the city of Basra before spreading across Iraq. It wasn't a single centralized rebellion, headed by some organization or a leader, and it was not even backed by some broad ideology. It was a simple outburst of frustration among the Iraqi citizens across the country. The rebels were from various ethnic, social, and religious backgrounds. Among them were the long-oppressed Kurds in northern Iraq, the Shia Muslim majority oppressed by the Ba'ath minority, and the far-leftists. Even more worryingly for Saddam's regime was the fact that the rebellion was supported not only by demobilized Iraqi soldiers but also by active ones, making it also partially a military mutiny.

An Iraqi government tank destroyed by the rebels (March 1991).
https://commons.wikimedia.org/wiki/File:Destroyed_tank_1991_uprising_Iraq.jpg

The Ba'ath government had to act quickly if it wanted to reestablish its tight grip over Iraq, as the insurgents achieved some initial minor successes. The central Iraqi government lost control of several cities in southern and northern Iraq. The rebels expressed their frustration by both destroying symbols of the Ba'ath regime, like statues and buildings, but also by killing hundreds of Ba'ath officials, officers, and supporters. Saddam and his high officials didn't respond immediately, as they waited to finish the dealings with the Coalition. Thus, their counteroffensive began on March 7th, with the Republican Guard serving as the tip of the loyalist blade. However, the uprisings proved to be much tougher to extinguish than it would have been before the conflict. The Iraqi Army was not only divided but also severely lacking in equipment and vehicles due to the losses from the war. On the other side, the rebels weren't eager to back down. Their will to fight was only additionally fueled by US messages, which prompted them to liberate themselves from Saddam's dictatorship. President Bush Sr. and his Cabinet believed, or at least hoped, that the Iraqi people could finish off the Ba'ath regime for them, as their hands were tied from interfering directly in Iraqi internal matters.

US pamphlet representing Saddam Hussein as death

Kurdish children playing with abandoned military equipment – March 1991.
https://commons.wikimedia.org/wiki/File:Kurdish_children_play_on_a_Soviet-built_ZPU-4_in_1991.JPEG

To both their and the rebels' shock, the blade of nonintervention cut both sides. While the Coalition forces slowly withdrew from Iraq, the loyalist regime began suppressing the uprising. Their primary tools, to which the insurgents could hardly parry, were the Iraqi Army helicopters. Only a handful of them was destroyed during the war, and they were exempt from the Coalition's no-fly ban. Thus, they began to lead the aerial attacks on the defenseless rebels. They looked to the Americans for support, as they were the ones encouraging their revolt, but the US troops were unable to help them. It would be seen as interfering in Iraqi internal affairs. Therefore, the loyalists were left to massacre their compatriots across the country, while the Coalition could do little more than watch. The Ba'ath regime went on to murder not only the armed combatants of the rebellion but also defenseless civilians that supported them. However, despite their military superiority, the loyalists needed almost a full month to quell all the uprisings. It wasn't until April 5th, 1991, that the rebels were finally defeated, as this was the day that the Ba'ath government declared that it crushed all attempts of sedition, sabotage, and rioting in all Iraqi cities. Ironically, it was on that very same day that the UN adopted Resolution 788, in which it demanded the Ba'ath government stop its repression of the Kurd and Shia population in Iraq. By then, though, tens of thousands were already killed, and the rebel uprising had failed.

Despite the fact that the rebellions had been put down, the United States, Britain, and France established two no-fly zones without seeking an Iraqi agreement. Those zones covered the areas in the north and the south, where most of the uprisings took place. Furthermore, Iraq was forced to replace either allied troops or its own police with UN security in some cities that were part of the rebellion. Iraq objected to many of these decisions, somewhat rightfully claiming they were infringing on its sovereignty. Additionally, after the initial shock of defeat began wearing off and the Coalition troops began to return home, the Ba'ath government began to protest the UN inspectors coming to Iraq to oversee the dismantling of banned weapons and nuclear sites, even though it had agreed on it in the Safwan accord. Not only that, but it began interfering with their work, somewhat obstructing them in their jobs. The Iraqis claimed some of them were Western spies who took photographs and sent sensitive information to the US and Israel. These accusations were usually dismissed without any serious consequences, even though, in some cases, they proved to be partially true. Some of the American members of the UN teams sent the information gathered first to Washington before reporting it to the United Nations.

By early 1992, the last of the Coalition forces left Iraq, even though there were US troops still stationed in the region. Over the next couple of years, those American forces acted unilaterally when it was deemed necessary. Their ships and planes bombarded Iraq whenever the United States estimated the Iraqis were breaking some agreement or possibly jeopardizing others. For example, an Iraqi radar station was destroyed after an American plane detected being scanned by it. At other times, the US bombardment was aimed at Iraqi defenses and ballistic missile sites. The most unique of these punitive actions came in June 1993 when Washington approved 23 Tomahawk cruise missiles to be launched on Baghdad. It was in retaliation for a supposed Iraqi-sponsored assassination attempt on, by that time, former President George Bush Sr., who was visiting Kuwait in May of that year. Washington claimed that the attack was an act of self-defense, which would mean the UN Charter justified it. Nonetheless, for many, it was seen as the US breaching international law, especially since there were signs that the supposed assassination reports seemed to be fabricated. Even worse was the fact that those limited and precision-targeted raids still managed to hit civilian structures and cause further unnecessary casualties. The rest of the world did little more than protest to stop these bombings, while Iraq itself could not do anything significant on its own.

Furthermore, in the months and years following the Gulf War, the United Nations never fully retracted the trade embargo imposed on Iraq. It was claimed that the Iraqi government never fully implemented the terms of the peace, accusations which cannot be disregarded as entirely false. Like the US, Saddam also had his own interpretations of the peace conditions, working in the gray areas that were left. Thus, the UN quite rightfully kept the imposed embargo on military equipment and imports of anything that could be used in war or weaponized. In contrast with that, Iraq was allowed to buy food, medicine, and other similar products it severely lacked. However, a problem arose from the fact that Iraq was still banned from exporting its crude oil. Because of such measures, the Iraqi government was unable to find funds to buy the necessary commodities, while the war and extended sanctions crippled its agriculture and industry. By early 1994, several international organizations warned that Iraq was heading toward famine. This forced the UN to partially lift the embargo on Iraqi oil exports, limiting it to a certain amount, while resources had to be used only for acquiring food and medicine. Despite that, civilian life in Iraq still remained hard and destitute. The reason behind both the prolonged sanctions and the occasional punitive bombardment was the underlying desire of the US to prompt the Iraqis to topple the Ba'ath regime.

The effect was quite the opposite, though. The regime was doing more or less fine, while it was the Iraqi civilians who suffered. It took another war in 2003 to finally depose Saddam and the Ba'ath regime, which was undertaken by the United States without UN approval. Coincidentally, it was only then that the embargo imposed on Iraq was totally lifted. However, Iraq never really recovered from the fate that was brought on by its invasion of Kuwait, as the suffering of the Iraqi civilians continues to this day.

Chapter 8 – Casualties, Consequences, and the Legacy of the Gulf War

To fully understand the story of the Gulf War, it is not enough to talk about the battles and bombings, why it happened, how it got resolved, and when it ended. It is vital to take a closer look at the outcome and ramifications of the conflict, as well as the image of the war that is engraved in our minds today. Only then will the picture of the war be complete, as well as one's comprehension of the event in its fullest.

When it comes to understanding wars, one of the most important questions raised is one of casualties. That portion of the Gulf War remains rather controversial but also very illustrative. The Coalition forces in total had about 380 killed in action, with around 800 more who were wounded. Considering the number of troops involved, these were surprisingly small numbers, making it one of the most successful combat campaigns in history. However, the idealized picture is somewhat tainted by the percentage of friendly fire deaths. Out of the 146 American soldiers killed in action during the war, there were at least 35 confirmed cases of so-called "blue-on-blue" deaths. That is above 20% of the total US losses. The number of wounded American soldiers caused by friendly fire is even higher. The most severe act of "blue-on-blue" fire occurred on

February 26th in the battle between the US VII Army Corps and the Tawakalna Division. No less than 57 American soldiers were injured by friendly fire, even though there were no fatalities. If that wasn't enough, there was a high rate of accidents among the Coalition troops, with a couple of hundred casualties of various nationalities. In the end, it proved that accidents, illness, and friendly fire took more allied lives than the Iraqi Army. Apart from the listed Coalition casualties, it should be noted that during the initial Iraqi invasion and occupation, Kuwait suffered several hundred military deaths and more than 1,000 civilian casualties.

In comparison to that, Iraq paid a much heftier toll. The exact number is unknown, as not even the Iraqi government had precise information. The media and certain experts and army officials of the time estimated that the Iraqi Army suffered about 200,000 killed in action. These numbers were significantly lowered, with most trusted evaluations ranging from about 25,000 to 35,000, with roughly an additional 75,000 wounded. The estimates of the Iraqi civilian deaths range from a rather conservative number of 3,500 upward to 15,000. The number of Iraqi casualties grows significantly higher when the uprisings are added to the final tally. According to various approximations, the number of casualties ranges from about 130,000 to 250,000 casualties when killed, wounded, and missing are all added up. Out of these, about 25,000 to 35,000 were unarmed civilian fatalities. The situation in which Iraq found itself only made its suffering worse. Their infrastructure was devastated, famine was spreading, and their healthcare system was collapsing, causing tens of thousands more deaths in the aftermath of the war. That led to an estimated 205,000 Iraqi deaths from direct and indirect consequences of war. In addition to the casualties, there were up to 1.8 million refugees, mostly Kurds and Shia minorities. They began fleeing the country in high numbers after the uprising was quelled. Running away from Saddam's oppression, they mostly fled to Turkey and Iran.

Seeing how much Iraq suffered from the war, both in casualties and destruction, many Western observers were surprised by Saddam's proclamation of victory. At the very least, they saw it as a propaganda ploy or his own personal delusions. In the grand scheme of things, there is no doubt that Iraq was defeated in the Gulf War, making Saddam's declaration almost laughable. However, for him and his Ba'ath high officials, the war wasn't as disastrous as it could have been. For the regime, which in no small degree went into the war to remain in power, their main goal was achieved. The Ba'ath Party, with Saddam at its head, not only stayed at the helm of Iraq but even tightened their grip. During the uprisings, they dealt with the parts of the Iraqi population who posed the most threat to the regime. Furthermore, the regular Iraqi Army, which had begun losing its faith in the government since the Iran-Iraq War, was decimated. It lost its strength for a possible organized coup. At the same time, the ever-loyal Republican Guard gained in might when compared to the regular Iraqi Army. Yet, the devastating results of the war did change Saddam's rule. The popularity of his regime and the Ba'ath Party was falling, forcing him to turn more toward the countryside tribal groups that were loyal only to him.

Saddam Hussein in 1998
https://commons.wikimedia.org/wiki/File:Saddam_Hussein_in_1998.png

Iraqi flag with added Islamic phrase "The God is great," which was in use from 1991 to 2004
https://commons.wikimedia.org/wiki/File:Flag_of_Syria.svg

From those tribes, Saddam recruited people to serve him in the security services, military, government, and bureaucratic apparatus, making sure that he was surrounded by only loyal Iraqis. Furthermore, the regime began rebuilding and forming new security agencies and intelligence networks, creating a tight and overlapping system to protect it from internal threats. The most vital parts of Saddam's security, those key positions in security and intelligence organizations, were given to his own family members. Apart from the changes in the regime's structure, the ideology of it was changing as well. The pan-Arab nationalism of the Ba'ath Party was largely abandoned. This was partially because Saddam had failed to fulfill his self-proclaimed role as an Arab unifier. Even worse was the fact that most of the Arab world turned against Iraq in its clash with the rest of the world instead of supporting it. Thus, the idea of pan-Arab unity seemed as only wishful thinking for both the common Iraqis as well as the Ba'ath leadership, including Saddam himself. So, the regime instead turned toward Islam as the basis of its ideology. In his speeches, Saddam started to use religious rhetoric, sometimes even depicting himself as a messiah or representative of God. The result of the war on the Iraqi government and society was its shifting from modernity and Arab nationalism toward more traditional and conservative ideas and organizations that were based in Islam and tribalism.

On the other hand, the United States celebrated its victory not only over Iraq but also over its fear of Vietnam. For more than fifteen years after its infamous defeat in Southeast Asia, the American public was very cautious about getting involved in any new wars or interventions. Both the public and the government were afraid of making the same mistakes again. However, after seeing how smoothly they won against the supposedly fourth largest army of the world, their self-confidence grew. Not only was the victory swift and with minimal casualties, but it also wasn't a tremendous burden on the US budget. Unlike the Vietnam War, where the US was both the main fighting force and the main financer, in the Gulf War, Saudi Arabia and Kuwait paid the brunt of the expenses. The cost of the entire war was estimated at around 61 billion dollars (approximately 115 billion in 2019 dollars), with the United States spending only 8 billion (15.1 billion in 2019 dollars). That was roughly 13% of expenses, despite serving as 75% of the fighting force of the Coalition. In contrast, during the Vietnam War, the US spent more than one trillion in 2019 dollars, making the Gulf War one of the "cheapest" conflicts of recent American history, in every sense of the word.

The media coverage only heightened the sense of a tremendous US victory in the war with Iraq. Even before the war began, the US and British media started portraying Saddam Hussein as the ultimate evil, comparing him to Hitler, the devil, or death. With that, the public was not only prepared for the conflict but was in full support of the war efforts. In a public poll conducted in August 1990 in Britain, 42% of those questioned supported not only the bombing of military but civilian targets as well. Furthermore, about 12% was in favor of using nuclear weapons if needed. Demonizing the enemy helped gain support for the war, and the US government intended to keep the support going, in hopes of avoiding "the new Vietnam." The main tactic for achieving this was through the tight control of the media presence and coverage of the war. A so-called "pool system" was organized, where media personnel were given official military news, whose coverage was focused on only successful attacks and events. Moreover, reporters weren't allowed to move as freely on the battlefield as during the Vietnam War, further limiting their perspective of the conflict. Of course, the system wasn't impermeable, as certain reporters found a way to report on civilian casualties and the Coalition blunders. Yet those voices were in the clear minority. It seemed that most of the mainstream media supported the war and was willing to work as instructed by the military.

Media conference held by US Secretary of Defense Dick Chaney with the members of the US military command (February 1991).
https://commons.wikimedia.org/wiki/File:Cheney_Gulf_War_news_conference.jpg

The reason for such media cooperation is twofold. In more straightforward reasoning, the media was dependent on the military for its news and footage. This was especially true when it came to acquiring the videos from high-tech US weapons equipped with cameras. Because of this, the average viewer for the first time was able to see a missile hit its target head-on. That kind of footage was quite popular, and it was great for attracting viewership and raising income for the mainstream media. Without cooperating with the army, these kinds of videos would remain unavailable to the TV networks. Besides this apparent reason, there was also the fact that the behind-the-scenes owners of some of the most prominent networks had connections and business with the US weapons industry, prompting them to support the war effort with their coverage. Hence, most of the US and British media framed the war as an exciting, dramatic, and patriotic event, turning the Gulf War into a spectacle. The networks presented the war as their audience wanted to see it, not as it really was. The exhilaration caused by the US involvement in the fight against Iraq was only furthered by the fact that new technology, such as satellites, allowed for almost 24/7 coverage of the conflict, making the

Gulf War the first "live war" in history.

Additionally, the used footage from the tanks, airplanes, and missiles, combined with the futuristic weapons, made the recordings seem more like a video game than reality. That was enough for the average viewer to be desensitized from the horrors of warfare. In the end, the media produced imagery of the Gulf War that proved to be vital for the Americans to overcome their Vietnam War fears and frustrations. The victory of the US and the Coalition was enhanced by the media-presented image of a clean war through the glorification of the superior military technology of the US and the vilification of Saddam and the Iraqis. Even today, most of the people, at least in the West, see the war as such, despite the evidence of clear misconduct and mistakes of the Coalition forces. Thus, the Gulf War and its media image restored American vigor, ushering in a new era of its worldwide interventionism. However, the Gulf War also left less desirable memories and consequences. Especially controversial among the US citizens was the so-called Gulf War syndrome or illness. It was first described in 1993 with symptoms that vary from soldier to soldier, including headaches, musculoskeletal pain, fatigue, cognitive dysfunction, and insomnia, as well as respiratory and gastrointestinal problems. Over the years, a high number of Gulf War veterans reported such health issues, ranging between 17% and 21% of the US and British forces. Doctors had no explanations for them. The only common point was their service in the war, leading some to conclude it was a new illness related to the war.

Since then, the Gulf War syndrome has become one of the more talked about issues of the conflict. The media leeched on the story, often writing about the problem without any scientific backing. Various veteran deaths and health issues were arbitrarily linked with the syndrome. On the other hand, veteran societies were vocal about helping the suffering soldiers, while the medical community tried to find both a cure and a cause. The treatments ranged from medication to psycho-social cognitive behavioral therapy, though with only limited success. As for the causes, none were confirmed, but several were proposed. One was Iraqi chemical or biological weapons. However, there was no evidence of those being used on the Coalition troops. The other possibilities were either pyridostigmine bromide pills, which were used to protect against exposure to nerve gases, or the organophosphate pesticides and insect repellents. Both were issued by the US and British military to maintain health and hygiene among the troops. Among the less possible explanations were the oil well fires and fumes, posttraumatic stress, or even anti-anthrax vaccines. Another possible culprit was the depleted uranium used for the first time during the Gulf War by the US and British as kinetic energy high-penetrating ammunition for the tanks. Nonetheless, no clear consensus about the cause was ever formed, while in recent years, scientists have begun to negate the existence of the Gulf War syndrome as a single illness altogether. Regardless of that, the syndrome itself became an integral part of the Gulf War legacy.

Major uses of depleted uranium ammunition during the Gulf War
https://commons.wikimedia.org/wiki/File:GWI_DU_map.gif

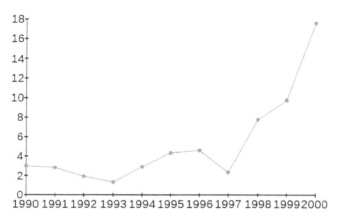
Graph showing the rise in birth defects in the Basra region.
https://commons.wikimedia.org/wiki/File:Basrah_birth_defects.svg

Somewhat connected with the debate of the Gulf War illness, the question of depleted uranium munition was also raised. It had higher penetrating power than regular ammunition, but as it was using radioactive material, many were critical of its use. Its proponents claimed that the low radioactivity of the depleted uranium meant it wasn't much more dangerous than conventional tank shells. They stated that one had to ingest or inhale the uranium to be seriously affected. However, in the years after the war, several medical studies were conducted that showed the Gulf War veterans were two times more prone to have children with birth defects. The veterans were also showing signs of higher rates of immune system disorders and cancers. Furthermore, the Basra region exhibited a sharp increase in genetic deformities and childhood leukemia among babies born in the years after the war. Nonetheless, the depleted uranium ammunition still hasn't been banned, as further experiments were unable to clearly link the depleted uranium as the cause of the birth defects and other diseases. Apart from medical issues, the Gulf War is also remembered for the questions of environmental awareness that were raised during the conflict. The iconic images of Kuwaiti oil wells on fire are still synonymous with the war, but they also caused a great deal of concern for their impact on the climate and ecosystems.

US aircraft flying above the burning oil fields in Kuwait.

Though some scientists at the time predicted the repercussions as catastrophic as a nuclear winter, the smoke from the oil fires was far less destructive. The weather was only affected during the burning of the fires, returning to normal after being put out, although the air quality in the Gulf region was, at the time, significantly worse. In parts of the Arabian Peninsula, there were reports of carbon soot rains and smoke-filled skies. However, these consequences were short-lived, though they did cause an increase in respiratory problems in the Persian Gulf area. More long-lasting was the issue of the oil spill in the Gulf itself, which was done by the Iraqis. The original estimates of a 1993 international study deemed it to be without long-term damage to the ecosystem. However, upon closer examination in later years, it has been concluded that the oil slick, which had a maximum size around 101 miles (160 kilometers) by 42 miles (68 kilometers) and reaching a thickness of about 5 inches (13 centimeters) thick, managed to leave scars on the Gulf marine life. Of about four million US barrels (480,000 meters^3) of oil spilled, only half was recovered. No shoreline cleanup was attempted, leaving more than 500 miles (804 kilometers) of mostly Saudi coastline covered in crude oil, which then permeated deeply into the intertidal sediment. It caused havoc on the living ecosystems of the Saudi Gulf coast, out of which 50% are salt marshes. Plants and living creatures there suffered the most, with some scientists estimating that the full recovery of the salt marshes will take several centuries.

During the Gulf War itself, while both Kuwaiti and Iraqi oil production was virtually stopped and Saudi Arabia's production was potentially endangered, the oil prices spiked shortly. The cost of a barrel spiked at around 46 dollars in October 1990, causing mild economic shocks across the world. However, since the war ended quickly, the longer repercussions on the world economy were averted, as the prices continued to fall during the 90s. The fact that the Kuwaiti oil well fires weren't completely put out until November 1991 didn't cause any further disruptions in the oil prices. As for Kuwait itself, the war left a sizable scar on the population of the country. During the war, no less than 200,000 Palestinians left the country due to coercion and harassment by occupying soldiers or because they were simply fired from their jobs by the short-lived Iraqi authority. A further 200,000 Palestinians left Kuwait after the war ended in March of 1991. Despised by both the Kuwaiti authorities and citizens because the Palestine Liberation Organization publicly supported the Iraqi invasion, the rest of the Palestinian population was forced out of the liberated country. Thus, Kuwait, which before the war had a population of about two million, lost around 20% of the population, as almost all of the total 400,000 Palestinians left Kuwait.

The Iraqi occupation also caused other social and political problems in post-war Kuwait. The Kuwaiti society became divided, as tensions and discord grew between those who fled the country and those who stayed and endured the Iraqi oppression. At the same time, the question of about 600 Kuwaitis who were left missing after the war was never resolved, as the Iraqi government remained silent. This issue kept part of the Kuwaiti society from being unable to move forward after the invasion. Furthermore, liberal political opposition to the undemocratic monarchical rule of the Al-Sabah dynasty gained popularity during the war. Some of the Kuwaitis objected either to the behavior of their emir, who was in exile, or to his somewhat authoritarian regime. The pro-democratic opposition pressured for political liberalization, while a minority hoped that after the war, a total overthrowal of the monarchy would be possible. The most extreme parts of the opposition had hoped that the American presence after the war would help their cause, but the

US had no interest in installing democracy in Kuwait. The monarchical government of the Al-Sabah dynasty at the time was an ally of the United States, while their political oppression was seen as too benign to justify interference. After the war was over and the pre-war government returned to Kuwait, its initial response to the growing opposition was to stage show trials and institute martial law, trying to shut down the pro-democratic movement forcibly.

However, this policy was quickly changed by the wide pressure of the Kuwaiti population, which led to a slight liberation of the system. By the end of 1992, the elections for the Kuwaiti National Assembly were held, and press censorship was lifted. However, the government kept pressuring the journalists and banning public meetings of the opposition. Thus, in the aftermath of Saddam's invasion, Kuwait exhibited both the authoritarian impulses of the monarchist government and the pro-democratic desires among the common population. The struggles between these two opposing forces have marked Kuwaiti politics since then. In other aspects, like in the economy, the recovery was surprisingly quick. The damage to the infrastructure proved to be far less extensive than initially estimated, though repairing and kickstarting the oil industry required some time and hefty investments. After the war, Kuwait kept close ties with the United States, both because of their economic needs but partially due to the fear of renewed aggression by Saddam. For that reason, Kuwait acted as one of the closest US allies on the stage of international politics while at the same time cooperating in the sphere of military affairs. Hence, when the US decided to attack Iraq for the second time in 2003, Kuwait acted as the main base for the invasion.

Unlike the Kuwaitis, who, to this day, remain mostly grateful for the US intervention during the Gulf War, other Arab nations shifted away from the Americans. Some of the Arabs were against the Coalition intervention altogether; however, even those Arab nations that took part in the Gulf War started exhibiting anti-American sentiments. Large parts of Saudi society, regardless of what its government said, were against non-Muslim soldiers being deployed on Saudi soil. Furthermore, the conservative circles began criticizing the US for forcing their decadent lifestyle on the people. Other Arabs started following exhibiting similar ideas, linking the arrival of the American culture with the loss of morality and the righteous path of Islam. As such, despite being active members of the Coalition, many Arab countries began seeing the involvement of the US and other Western nations in the Gulf War as neocolonialism, their attempt to once again dominate the Arab regions, in their hunt for oil. At the same time, the anti-Arab sentiment also grew among the Americans, as throughout the 90s, the Arabs became synonymous with terrorists. That kind of mutual disdain set the stage for the events of September 11th, 2001, and later on US attacks on Iraq and Afghanistan. With that came further changes in the views of the Gulf War itself. The Arabs started linking it more with US imperialism, economic exploitation, and expansionism, while the Americans began linking the Gulf War with the war on terror.

Damaged building in Kuwait after the Gulf War.
https://commons.wikimedia.org/wiki/File:Damaged_building_in_Kuwait_City_1991_DA-ST-92-08901.JPEG

In the rest of the world, the opinions about the war, as well as its legacy, also changed. Many Western countries praised it as a great victory for international law and freedom at the time. However, this view changed a bit during the latter years of the 90s. The prolonged and rather harsh sanctions imposed on Iraq made some of the observers change their views slightly. Over the years, fewer and fewer people saw the US involvement as an act of a paragon of freedom and justice. Instead, they began seeing it as the Americans looking out only for their own interests, as it looked like the main goal of the United States was to depose

Saddam. The imposed sanctions seemed to be just a tool to achieve that goal, no matter the cost. The second war with Iraq only furthered such thoughts, as, to some, it seemed the US only invaded because the previous sanction tactics weren't working out. Other nations, most notably the Russians, kept their generally negative stance toward the Gulf War. In their opinion, the war was avoidable, but the United States was too eager to go to war with the sole aim of thwarting the Ba'ath regime. With that being said, not all nations and people changed their views of the war. Some still celebrate it as a victory for international justice and praise the quickness of the US response.

In the end, when we take a closer look at the consequences and results of the Gulf War, as well as its legacy, it becomes clear that it was neither black nor white. It was, like most of the wars throughout history, a mess of grayness, for which some paid the ultimate price.

Conclusion

At first glance, the Gulf War might seem like a rather simple and straightforward story. An evil oppressor bullies a weaker opponent but ends up getting punished for it. However, as it has been shown in this guide, that wasn't really the case. This conflict had deep roots, reaching back to the early 20th century, as the retreating European colonialism left unsolved matters among two, at the time, young states. It was bred and fed over the decades until a perfect storm pushed it over the edge. The escalation of the war was possible since the Cold War was ending, leaving the landscape of international politics just right to add fuel to the fire. And the combustion was fast and explosive. The war ended quickly, yet it continued to influence future events, and its ripples can still be felt today. Furthermore, it was a conflict that stood on a crossroads between two epochs, exhibiting marks of an age that was ending as well as the new era that was coming.

That bifocal element of the Gulf War is probably the most defining element of it. Smart bombs were being introduced, while conventional grenades were still in use. The news was broadcasted in a new way but used the same words as in previous decades. The casualties were low, but still, too many people died. It was an inevitable war that could have been avoided, and it was a conflict in which all sides triumphed, yet no one really won. Everything was achieved, but nothing was completed. In the end, that may be the most profound legacy of the Gulf War, exhibiting the duality of warfare that has plagued humankind since the dawn of time.

Too often, people focus solely on how astonishing the Coalition victory was, looking at only one aspect of this conflict. It is easy to look back at war, romanticizing how heroic it was and how shiny the shields and swords were. However, the grim reality shows something else. Civilians died, nature was tainted, smart bombs missed, soldiers became sick, and the end result of the fighting was ambiguous. The war itself shouldn't be praised or looked up to. It is never the perfect solution to an issue, and usually, it only leads to more problems than it solved. Thus, when reading about wars, it is vital not only to learn about tactics and strategies but also how to avoid them. The same goes for the Gulf War. Much can be learned from it. It can illuminate the era in which it happened and exhibit how to use technologies and how to unite people behind a cause, among other things. Yet the most significant lesson one can draw from it is that the battlefield is never truly the

Here's another book by Captivating History that you might like

Free Bonus from Captivating History
(Available for a Limited time)

Hi History Lovers!

Now you have a chance to join our exclusive history list so you can get your first history ebook for free as well as discounts and a potential to get more history books for free! Simply visit the link below to join.

Captivatinghistory.com/ebook

Also, make sure to follow us on Facebook, Twitter and Youtube by searching for Captivating History.

Sources

http://www.crystalinks.com/nativeamcreation.html

https://prezi.com/ykvfzcomwc0e/chinook-creation-myth/

https://prezi.com/3kcshnvcqfdt/chinook-creation-myth/

https://www.cleveland.com/expo/life-and-culture/erry-2018/10/71b738640b7079/ohios-serpent-mound-an-archaeo.html

https://www.smithsonianmag.com/history/the-clovis-point-and-the-discovery-of-americas-first-culture-3825828/

https://www.infoplease.com/us/race-population/major-pre-columbian-indian-cultures-united-states

https://www.census.gov/history/pdf/c2010br-10.pdf

https://www.scholastic.com/teachers/articles/teaching-content/history-native-americans/

https://www.historyonthenet.com/native-americans-origins

https://www.history.com/topics/exploration/john-cabot

https://www.history.com/this-day-in-history/ponce-de-leon-discovers-florida

https://fcit.usf.edu/florida/lessons/de_leon/de_leon1.htm

https://www.washingtonpost.com/news/answer-sheet/wp/2013/10/14/christopher-columbus-3-things-you-think-he-did-that-he-didnt/?noredirect=on&utm_term=.e921b34a7cfcme

https://exploration.marinersmuseum.org/subject/jacques-cartier/

https://www.historytoday.com/archive/months-past/birth-amerigo-vespucci

https://www.u-s-history.com/pages/h1138.html

http://mentalfloss.com/article/560395/facts-about-sir-walter-raleigh

https://www.nationalgeographic.com/magazine/2018/06/lost-colony-roanoke-history-theories-croatoan/

https://www.history.com/news/what-happened-to-the-lost-colony-of-roanoke

http://mentalfloss.com/article/69358/8-most-intriguing-disappearances-history

http://www.let.rug.nl/usa/outlines/history-1994/early-america/the-first-europeans.php

https://newsmaven.io/indiancountrytoday/archive/the-true-story-of-pocahontas-historical-myths-versus-sad-reality-WRzmVMu47E6Guz0LudQ3QQ/

http://www.americaslibrary.gov/jb/colonial/jb_colonial_subj.html

https://www.history.com/topics/colonial-america/thirteen-colonies

https://www.texasgateway.org/resource/exploration-and-colonization-america

http://www.loc.gov/teachers/classroommaterials/presentationsandactivities/presentations/timeline/colonial/

https://www.history.com/this-day-in-history/the-pilgrim-wampanoag-peace-treaty

https://www.uswars.net/king-georges-war/

https://www.mountvernon.org/george-washington/french-indian-war/washington-and-the-french-indian-war/

https://www.mountvernon.org/george-washington/french-indian-war/ten-facts-about-george-washington-and-the-french-indian-war/

https://www.history.com/topics/native-american-history/french-and-indian-war

https://www.history.com/topics/american-revolution/boston-massacre

http://www.ushistory.org/declaration/related/massacre.html

https://www.britannica.com/event/Boston-Tea-Party

https://www.history.com/topics/american-revolution/boston-tea-party

http://www.eyewitnesstohistory.com/teaparty.htm

https://www.ducksters.com/history/american_revolution/intolerable_acts.php

http://www.ushistory.org/us/9g.asp

https://www.poets.org/poetsorg/poem/paul-reveres-ride

https://www.history.com/news/11-things-you-may-not-know-about-paul-revere

https://www.history.com/topics/american-revolution/battles-of-lexington-and-concord

https://www.britannica.com/event/Battles-of-Saratoga

https://www.history.com/topics/american-revolution/declaration-of-independence

https://www.britishbattles.com/war-of-the-revolution-1775-to-1783/battle-of-yorktown/

https://www.history.com/this-day-in-history/battle-of-yorktown-begins

https://www.battlefields.org/learn/articles/overview-american-revolutionary-war

https://www.history.com/topics/american-revolution/american-revolution-history

http://sageamericanhistory.net/federalperiod/topics/national1783_89.html

http://avalon.law.yale.edu/18th_century/washing.asp

http://www.ushistory.org/us/17d.asp

https://www.britannica.com/biography/George-Washington/Presidency

https://www.mountvernon.org/george-washington/the-first-president/election/10-facts-about-washingtons-election/

https://www.biography.com/people/george-washington-9524786

https://www.history.com/news/what-was-the-xyz-affair

https://www.americanhistorycentral.com/entries/quasi-war/

https://www.smithsonianmag.com/smart-news/unremembered-us-france-quasi-war-shaped-early-americas-foreign-relations-180963862/

https://2001-2009.state.gov/r/pa/ho/time/nr/16318.htm

http://www.historicships.org/constellation.html

https://www.history.com/topics/war-of-1812/battle-of-new-orleans

https://www.britannica.com/event/War-of-1812

https://www.smithsonianmag.com/history/the-10-things-you-didnt-know-about-the-war-of-1812-102320130/

https://www.history.com/topics/native-american-history/trail-of-tears

https://www.britannica.com/topic/Indian-Removal-Act

https://www.pbs.org/wgbh/aia/part4/4p2959.html

https://www.history.com/news/native-americans-genocide-united-states

http://www.ushistory.org/us/24f.asp

https://cherokee.org/About-The-Nation/History/Trail-of-Tears/A-Brief-History-of-the-Trail-of-Tears

https://www.britannica.com/event/Second-Seminole-War

https://www.thoughtco.com/second-seminole-war-2360813

https://fcit.usf.edu/florida/lessons/sem_war/sem_war1.htm

https://www.sermonsearch.com/sermon-outlines/21975/confidence-in-prayer/

https://www.u-s-history.com/pages/h1091.html

http://www.ushistory.org/us/22c.asp

https://www.pbs.org/wgbh/americanexperience/features/goldrush-california/

https://www.history.com/topics/westward-expansion/gold-rush-of-1849

https://www.historynet.com/california-gold-rush

https://www.britannica.com/event/assassination-of-Abraham-Lincoln

http://www.abrahamlincolnonline.org/lincoln/speeches/gettysburg.htm

https://www.history.com/topics/american-civil-war/battle-of-gettysburg

https://www.battlefields.org/learn/articles/brief-overview-american-civil-war

https://www.history.com/topics/american-civil-war/american-civil-war-history

https://www.history.com/topics/19th-century/bleeding-kansas

https://www.britannica.com/topic/Ku-Klux-Klan

https://www.history.com/topics/american-civil-war/reconstruction

https://www.britannica.com/topic/Civil-Rights-Act-United-States-1875

https://www.britannica.com/topic/Wounded-Knee-Massacre

https://www.thoughtco.com/about-the-native-american-ghost-dance-4125921

https://www.history.com/topics/native-american-history/wounded-knee

https://www.history.com/topics/native-american-history/battle-of-the-little-bighorn

https://www.history.com/news/10-things-you-didnt-know-about-the-old-west

https://www.thevintagenews.com/2017/12/31/wild-west-era-2/

https://www.loc.gov/rr/hispanic/1898/intro.html

https://www.britannica.com/event/Spanish-American-War

https://www.businessinsider.com/major-battles-fought-by-the-us-during-world-war-i-2018-11?IR=T#after-a-decisive-allied-victory-germans-accept-defeat-and-sign-for-peace-10

https://www.nationalgeographic.com/archaeology-and-history/magazine/2017/03-04/world-war-i-united-states-enters/

https://www.thoughtco.com/second-battle-of-the-marne-2361412

https://www.britannica.com/event/Second-Battle-of-the-Marne

https://www.wearethemighty.com/history/this-is-why-the-3rd-infantry-division-is-called-rock-of-the-marne

https://www.history.com/topics/womens-history/19th-amendment-1

https://www.pbs.org/newshour/health/woodrow-wilson-stroke

https://www.archives.gov/publications/prologue/1998/fall/military-service-in-world-war-one.html

https://www.history.com/topics/great-depression/1929-stock-market-crash

http://www.american-historama.org/1929-1945-depression-ww2-era/causes-wall-street-crash.htm

http://www.newworldencyclopedia.org/entry/Wall_Street_Crash_of_1929

https://www.washingtonpost.com/archive/opinions/1987/10/25/the-jumpers-of-29/17dcfff9-f725-43b7-831b-7924ac0a1363/?utm_term=.0d663d5ecc79

http://voices.washingtonpost.com/washingtonpostinvestigations/2009/01/the_wall_street_leap.html

http://professorbuzzkill.com/the-men-who-jumped-during-the-stock-market-crash-of-1929-2/

https://www.history.com/topics/great-depression/great-depression-history

https://www.thebalance.com/the-great-depression-of-1929-3306033

https://www.npr.org/templates/story/story.php?storyId=97468008

https://www.thoughtco.com/great-depression-pictures-1779916

https://www.history.com/topics/world-war-ii/pearl-harbor

https://247wallst.com/special-report/2018/05/25/most-decorated-war-heroes/2/

http://www.pwencycl.kgbudge.com/C/a/Casualties.htm

https://www.atomicheritage.org/history/bombings-hiroshima-and-nagasaki-1945

https://www.atomicheritage.org/history/little-boy-and-fat-man

https://www.history.com/topics/world-war-ii/atomic-bomb-history

https://www2.gwu.edu/~erpapers/teachinger/glossary/world-war-2.cfm

https://www.thoughtco.com/overview-of-world-war-ii-105520

https://www.history.com/topics/cold-war/cold-war-history

https://www.britannica.com/event/Cold-War

https://www.google.com/search?q=assassination+of+jfk+cold+war&ie=utf-8&oe=utf-8

https://www.history.com/this-day-in-history/john-f-kennedy-assassinated

https://www.psychologytoday.com/us/blog/evil-deeds/201311/why-did-lee-harvey-oswald-kill-john-fitzgerald-kennedy

https://www.history.com/topics/cold-war/berlin-wall

https://www.history.com/topics/black-history/martin-luther-king-jr

https://www.history.com/topics/black-history/civil-rights-movement

https://www.inc.com/jeff-haden/two-of-greatest-martin-luther-king-jr-speeches-youve-never-heard.html

https://www.archives.gov/files/press/exhibits/dream-speech.pdf

https://www.nzherald.co.nz/world/news/article.cfm?c_id=2&objectid=12093351

https://www.history.com/topics/21st-century/9-11-attacks

https://patch.com/california/sanramon/were-going-to-do-something-remembering-thomas-burnett-jr

https://www.britannica.com/biography/Barack-Obama/Politics-and-ascent-to-the-presidency

http://edition.cnn.com/2011/WORLD/asiapcf/05/02/bin.laden.announcement/index.html

Brogan, H., *The Penguin History of the United States* (London, 1990).

Chernow, R., *Alexander Hamilton* (New York, 2004).

Chernow, R., *Washington: A Life* (New York, 2010).

Ferling, J., *Almost A Miracle: The American Victory in the War of Independence* (Oxford, 2009).

McCullough, D., *1776: America and Britain at War* (New York, 2005).

Meacham, J., *Thomas Jefferson: The Art of Power* (New York, 2012).

Middlekauff, R., *The Glorious Cause: The American Revolution, 1763-1789* (Oxford, 2005).

Reynolds, D., *America: Empire of Liberty* (London, 2010).

Taylor, A., *American Revolutions: A Continental History, 1750-1804* (New York, 2016).

Van Cleve, G., *We Have Not a Government: The Articles of Confederation and the Road to the Constitution* (Chicago, 2017).

Wood, G. S., *The American Revolution: A History* (New York, 2003).

Avins, Alfred, comp. *The Reconstruction Amendments' Debates: The Legislative History and Contemporary Debates in Congress on the 13th, 14th, and 15th Amendments.* Richmond: Virginia Commission on Constitutional Government, 1967.

Brash, Sarah, editor. *The American Story: War Between Brothers.* Richmond, Time Life, 1996

Constable, George, editor. *Brother Against Brother: Time-Life Books History of the Civil War.* New York, Prentice Hall Press, 1990.

Cozzens, Peter, editor. *Battles and Leaders of the Civil War, Vol. 5*. University of Illinois, 2002.

Eicher, David J. *The Longest Night: A Military History of the Civil War*. New York, Simon and Schuster, 2001.

Katcher, Philip. *The Civil War Day by Day*. St. Paul, The Brown Reference Group, 2007.

---. *The Complete Civil War*. London, Wellington House, 1992.

Maus, Louis P. *The Civil War: A Concise History*. New York, Oxford University Press, 2011.

Stokesbury, James L. *A Short History of the Civil War*. New York, Harper Collins, 1995.

Cohen, Lizbeth. *Making a New Deal: Industrial Workers in Chicago, 1919-1939*. New York: Cambridge University Press, 1990.

Douglas, Ann. *Terrible Honesty: Mongrel Manhattan in the 1920s*. New York: Farrar, Straus and Giroux, 1995.

Gottlieb, Peter. *Making Their Own Way: Southern Black Migration to Pittsburgh, 1916-1930*. Urbana IL: University of Illinois Press, 1987.

Lerner, Michael. *Dry Manhattan: Prohibition in New York City*. Cambridge MA: Harvard University Press, 2007.

Osafsky, Gilbert. *Harlem: The Making of a Ghetto*. New York: Harpers and Row, 1963.

Peretti, Burton W. *The Creation of Jazz: Music, Race and Culture in Urban America*. Chicago: University of Illinois Press, 1994.

Pfeffer, Paula. *A. Philip Randolph, Pioneer of the Civil Rights Movement*. Baton Rouge, LA: Louisiana University Press, 1990.

Platt, Harold. *The Electric City: Energy and Growth of the Chicago Area, 1880-1930*. Chicago: University of Chicago Press, 1991.

Spear, Allen. *Black Chicago*. Chicago: University of Chicago Press: 1967.

Susman, Warren I. *Culture as History: The Transformation of American Society in the Twentieth Century*. Washington: Smithsonian Institution Press, 1984.

Wiebe, Robert. *The Search for Order 1877-1920*. New York: Hill and Wang Publishing, 1967.

Brinkley, Alan. *The End of Reform: New Deal Liberalism in Recession and War*. New York, Vintage Books, 1995.

Cohen, Lizbeth. *Making A New Deal: Workers in Chicago 1919-1939*. Boston, Cambridge Press, 1990.

Denning, Michael. *The Cultural Front: The Laboring of American Culture in the Twentieth Century*. New York, Verso Publishing, 1996.

Douglas, Ann. *Terrible Honesty: Mongrel Manhattan in the 1920s*. New York, Farrar, Straus and Giroux, 1996.

Erenberg, Lewis. *Swingin' In the Dream: Big Band Jazz and the Rebirth of American Culture*. Chicago, University of Chicago Press, 1998.

Kennedy, David. *Freedom From Fear: The American People in Depression and War, 1929-1945*. London, Oxford Press, 2001.

May, Lary. *The Big Tomorrow: Hollywood and the Politics of the American Way*. Chicago, University of Chicago Press, 2000.

Peretti, Burton. *The Creation of Jazz: Music, Race, and Culture in Urban America*. Chicago, University of Illinois Press, 1994.

Pells, Richard. *Radical Visions and American Dreams: Culture and Social Thought in the Great Depression*. Chicago, University of Illinois Press, 1973.

Susman, Warren. *Culture as History: The Transformation of American Society in the Twentieth Century*. Washington DC, Smithsonian Books, 1984.

Adeed Dawisha, *Iraq: A Political History from Independence to Occupation*, New Jersey, Princeton University Press, 2009.

Alastair Finlan, *Essential Histories 55: The Gulf War 1991*, Oxford, Osprey Publishing Ltd., 2003.

Alastair Finlan, *The Royal Navy in the Falklands Conflict and the Gulf War: Culture and Strategy*, London, FRANK CASS PUBLISHERS, 2004.

Al-Marashi I. and Salama S., *Iraq's Armed Forces: An Analytical History*, New York, Routledge, 2008.

Anthony Tucker-Jones, *Modern Warfare – The Gulf War: Operation Desert Storm 1990-1991*, Barnsley, PEN & SWORD MILITARY, 2014.

Bachevich A.J. and Inbar E., *The Gulf War of 1991 Reconsidered*, London, Frank Cass Publishers, 2003.

Charles Tripp, *A History of Iraq—Third Edition*, Cambridge, Cambridge University Press, 2007.

Courtney Hunt, *The History of Iraq*, London, Greenwood Press, 2005.

David R. Willcox, *Propaganda, the Press and Conflict: The Gulf War and Kosovo*, New York, Routledge, 2005.

Desert Shield/Desert Storm: The 20th Anniversary of the Gulf War, Tampa, Defense Media Network, 2010.

Edwin Black, *Banking on Baghdad: Inside Iraq's 7,000-Year History of War, Profit, and Conflict*, New Jersey, John Wiley & Sons, Inc., 2004.

Gary R. Hess, *Presidential Decisions for War: Korea, Vietnam, the Persian Gulf, and Iraq*, Baltimore, The Johns Hopkins University Press, 2009.

Geoff Simons, *The Scourging of Iraq: Sanctions, Law and Natural Justice*, London, MACMILLAN PRESS LTD, 1998.

Hugh McManners, *Gulf War One*, London, Ebury Press, 2010.

Hugh Rockoff, *America's Economic Way of War: War and the US Economy from the Spanish-American War to the Persian Gulf War*, Cambridge, Cambridge University Press, 2012.

Ismael T. Y. and Haddad W. W., *Iraq: The Human Cost of History*, Sterling, Pluto Press, 2004.

Ismael T. Y. and Ismael J. S., *The Gulf War and the New World Order: International Relations of the Middle East*, Gainesville, The University of Florida, 1994.

Jeffords S. and Rabinovitz L., *Seeing through the Media: The Persian Gulf War*, New Jersey, Rutgers University Press, 1994.

John Robertson, *Iraq: A History*, London, Oneworld Publications, 2015.

Kagan F. and Kubik C., *Leaders in War: West Point Remembers the 1991 Gulf War*, New York, Frank Cass, 2005.

Khadduri M. and Ghareeb E., *War in the Gulf, 1990-91: The Iraq-Kuwait Conflict and Its Implications*, New York, Oxford University Press, 1997.

Laurie Collier Hillstrom, *War in the Persian Gulf Biographies: From Operation Desert Storm to Operation Iraqi Freedom*, Detroit, Thomson Gale, 2004.

Laurie Collier Hillstrom, *War in the Persian Gulf Primary Sources: From Operation Desert Storm to Operation Iraqi Freedom*, Detroit, Thomson Gale, 2004.

Lee H. and Jones E., *War and Health: Lessons from the Gulf War*, Chichester, John Wiley & Sons Ltd, 2007.

Marr P. and Al-Marashi I., *The Modern History of Iraq—Fourth Edition*, Boulder, Westview Press, 2017.

Philip Smith, *Why War?: The Cultural Logic of Iraq, the Gulf War, and Suez*, Chicago, The University of Chicago Press, 2005.

Richard Lock-Pullan, *US Intervention Policy and Army Innovation: From Vietnam to Iraq*, New York, Routledge, 2006.

Richard S. Lowry, *The Gulf War Chronicles: A Military History of the First War with Iraq*, Bloomington, iUnivers Star, 2008.

Rodney P. Carlisle, *Iraq War: Updated Edition*, New York, Facts On File, Inc., 2007.

Rottman G. and Hook A., *US Mechanized Infantryman in the First Gulf War*, Oxford, Osprey Publishing, 2009.

Rottman G. and Volstad R., *Armies of the Gulf War*, London, Osprey Military, 1993.

Thabit A. J. Abdullah, *Dictatorship, Imperialism and Chaos: Iraq since 1989*, Black Point, Fernwood Publishing Ltd, 2006.

War in the Persian Gulf: Operations Desert Shield and Desert Storm August 1990 – March 1991, Washington, Center of Military History – United States Army, 2010.

William Rosenau, *Special Operations Forces and Elusive Enemy Ground Targets: Lessons from Vietnam and the Persian Gulf War*, Santa Monica, RAND, 2001.

Williamson M. and Robert H. S. Jr., *The Iraq War: A Military History*, Cambridge, The Belknap Press of Harvard University Press, 2003.

Printed in France by Amazon
Brétigny-sur-Orge, FR

15261188R00397